Leisure Education Program Planning:
A Systematic Approach

Leisure Education Program Planning:
A Systematic Approach

John Dattilo, Ph.D.
The University of Georgia

and

William D. Murphy, Re.D.
The University of Nebraska

Venture Publishing, Inc.
State College, PA

Cover Design: Sandra Sikorski
Cover Illustration: Pam Heidtmann
Production: Bonnie Godbey
Printing and Binding: BookCrafters, Chelsea, MI

Library of Congress Catalogue Card Number 91-66103
ISBN 0-910251-49-5

Acknowledgments

This text was several years in development. As a result, several people have influenced its contents. We wish to thank the many people who provided ideas, suggestions, and encouragement over the years. Specifically, we would like to recognize the following people for their contributions to different sections of the text: Robert Berrian, John Bowman, Julie Converse, Melissa McHugh, Joan Preble, and Renee Tobias for their initial ideas related to the section on Specific Leisure Education Program Components; and Christine Book, Jackie Bradley, Charisse Christiansen, Shawn Flynn, Cheric Glenn, Nancy Rigel, and Marcia Ricketts, for their ideas about the section on Specific Leisure Education Program: Activities. Anne Richard's efforts in the initial organization of the text and Leslie Weltner's contribution during the book's final stages were also appreciated. Our gratitude is extended to Marlee Stewart for her assistance in preparing the figures for the text. We wish to thank Judith A. Kennison, Douglas Kleiber, and Carol A. Peterson for their critical review and helpful suggestions prior to publication. A special thanks is extended to Anne Dattilo for her welcome support and encouragement.

Preface

This text was developed to provide practitioners and students with information on the systematic application of leisure education. The authors hope that readers of the text will develop an appreciation for the dynamic nature of leisure education and an understanding of its relationship to comprehensive leisure services. Recommendations for program development and suggestions for possible areas of concentration were compiled to provide some guidance in developing specific leisure education programs. A systems approach was adopted to assist in the development, planning, implementation, and evaluation of effective leisure education programs. Specific leisure education programs were included that provided examples of the components of leisure education and individual recreation activities. The book contains only a sample of specific programs that are not intended to be comprehensive. Instead, the programs have been developed to provide practitioners and students with a starting place for the development of comprehensive leisure education services. The text was produced in response to requests from practitioners and students for detailed information regarding specific leisure education programs. The programs have been developed following modified guidelines outlined in the text by Carol Ann Peterson and Scout Lee Gunn entitled *Therapeutic Recreation Program Design: Principles and Procedures*. It is our hope that practitioners and students will read and use the book to improve the delivery of leisure services and thus increase the quality of life for all people. We encourage readers to contact us to share their thoughts about the value of the text and suggestions on ways we might improve the book. This feedback will help us make decisions regrading future publications. We view our writing as an evolving process and welcome other individuals' perspectives, ideas, and suggestions.

J.D. & W.D.M.

Table of Contents

Section C   Specific Leisure Education Programs: Activities   255

"Proceed as if all people are capable of learning under instruction. If I proceed in this way, sometimes–perhaps often–I will be right, and that will be good. What will be good is not that I will have been right (much as I enjoy that), but rather that some people, who we otherwise might have thought could not learn, will learn at least something useful to them."

—Baer (1981)

Overview

The text is divided into three distinct sections that contain six chapters each. The following description is presented to provide the reader with an overview of the information contained in each section.

Section A   Introduction to Leisure Education

This section provides readers with an introduction to leisure education as an essential component of leisure services. When formulating an approach to leisure education, practitioners are encouraged to conceptualize leisure as a state of mind rather than as an activity or a segment of time. A sampling of the theoretical and scholarly work that has been conducted in leisure education is included in this section. A model identifying areas of concentration for leisure education as well as the structure used to deliver services is also presented in this section. Section A also contains information on how to conduct leisure education programs. Finally, procedures for adapting the leisure education programs are provided in this section.

Section B   Specific Leisure Education Programs: Components

This section contains six specific programs each focusing on a different component of leisure education including leisure appreciation, awareness of self in leisure, self-determination in leisure, making decisions regarding leisure participation, knowledge and utilization of resources facilitating leisure, and social interaction. Each program provides the reader with an in-depth examination of the application of one particular leisure education component.

Section C   Specific Leisure Education Programs: Activities

Six specific leisure education programs devoted to swimming, walking, gardening, bowling, softball, and volleyball are presented in this section. These programs move beyond basic instruction of the recreation activity skills to the provision of information used to teach components of the leisure education process (e.g., leisure appreciation, decision making) within the context of a recreation activity.

The twelve specific leisure education programs presented in *Sections B and C* contain a program title, purpose statement, program goals, enabling objectives, performance measures, content description, and process description. The programs incorporate visual aids, demonstrations, discussions and debriefing, orientation and learning activities, and conclusions. This was done to create an enjoyable, organized environment that results in development of awareness and appreciation, knowledge acquisition and retention, and skill enhancement. The specific programs provide a starting place for professionals to implement systematic leisure education. We anticipate that practitioners will need to change various aspects of the programs to accommodate the unique talents of the people whom they serve.

Section A

Introduction to Leisure Education

Section A Introduction to Leisure Education

1. Leisure Education as a Component of Comprehensive Leisure Services: Provide a conceptual foundation for understanding leisure education as an integral component of leisure service delivery systems. A brief examination of some commonly accepted definitions of recreation, free time, and leisure is represented. An explanation of the function of therapeutic recreation as a human service is also provided. The remainder of the chapter is focused on information necessary for developing an initial understanding of leisure education.

2. Review of Recommendations and Empirical Considerations for Leisure Education: Provide readers with the opportunity to familiarize themselves with a sampling of the theoretical and scholarly work that has been conducted in leisure education. Understanding the scope of the work that has been accomplished (and what remains to be accomplished) will provide insight into the types of leisure education programs that have been developed and implemented, what their purposes are, the components of the programs, the nature of the participants, and the general strengths and weaknesses of the programs.

3. Suggested Areas of Concentration for Leisure Education: Explain the model that includes the following components: (a) awareness of self in leisure, (b) appreciation of leisure, (c) understanding of self-determination, (d) ability to make decisions regarding leisure participation, (e) knowledge and utilization of leisure resources facilitating leisure participation, (f) knowledge of effective social interaction skills, and (g) recreation activity skills. Education in these areas will assist people in developing leisure attitudes, knowledge, and skills that can be matched with suitably challenging opportunities which facilitate a sense of competence and satisfaction.

4. Systematic Programming for Leisure Education: Describe each specific leisure education program that contains: (a) a program title, (b) a purpose statement, (c) program goals, (d) enabling objectives, (e) performance measures, (f) content description, (g) process description. They begin with an orientation activity that is followed by an introduction of the topic. The programs contain descriptions of presentations that are immediately followed by discussions that actively solicit participant involvement. In addition, learning activities are presented with associated debriefings. Finally, conclusions are provided at the end of each objective.

5. Developing and Conducting Leisure Education Programs: Provide information on preparing and planning of a leisure education session, as well as suggestions for effective service delivery. Concerns related to the appropriateness of leisure education sessions, the environment, and knowledge of the program will be featured in the section devoted to preparation and planning. Suggestions for presentation of sessions will be divided into introduction and explanation, actual implementation of sessions, and bringing closure to session devoted to leisure education.

6. Adaptation of Leisure Education Programs: Encourage practitioners to adapt the information presented in the specific programs as necessary. When needed, these adaptations should permit professional to meet the varying needs and abilities of the people receiving leisure services. The suggestion for adaptations are not intended to be all-inclusive. They are, however, intended to communicate some options available to practitioners to make adjustments intended to facilitate active leisure participation for persons with disabilities.

LEISURE EDUCATION AS
A COMPONENT OF COMPREHENSIVE LEISURE SERVICES

Introduction

This chapter will provide a conceptual foundation for understanding leisure education as an integral component of leisure service delivery systems, specifically therapeutic recreation services. A brief examination of some commonly accepted definitions of recreation, free time, and leisure is presented. An explanation of the function of therapeutic recreation as a human service is also provided. The remainder of the chapter is focused on information necessary for developing an initial understanding of leisure education.

Coming to Terms with Leisure

Leisure may be conceptualized in a variety of ways. Many people agree that leisure can be viewed in terms of (a) specific recreation activities, (b) unobligated or discretionary time, or (c) a state of mind. Although there is continuous debate and discussion about the definitions of leisure and the associated terms of recreation and free time, there appears to be some consensus regarding their meanings among consumers, practitioners, researchers, and theorists.

Typically, *recreation* has been defined as an activity (e.g., swimming, table games, aerobic dance) in which people engage primarily for enjoyment and satisfaction. The notion of recreation is related directly to the activity and is dependent on the feelings and experiences of individual participants. Although the activities in which people engage vary widely, the term recreation generally refers to more organized activity intended for social ends (Kelly, 1990). Recreation is intended to be beneficial for a society and is organized and supported with the expectation of such benefits. People may participate in recreation activities and experience enjoyment and satisfaction; however, it is also possible that people may participate in activities where they encounter failure, rejection, and feelings of helplessness.

Discretionary time is a phrase that is generally used to describe unobligated time, that is, time not spent in daily tasks associated with subsistence or self-maintenance activities. When people are not obligated to perform specified tasks, they then possess free time. Free time is discretionary and can be used according to one's judgment or choice. Many people make choices relative to the use of their free time that result in enjoyable and satisfying experiences. Other people, often including those with disabilities, may be in circumstances where the opportunity for choice is lacking, for a variety of reasons. The circumstances may be such that there is not an array of options from which to choose, or it may be that the ability to make choices is not present. As a result, some individuals' free time may be associated with boredom, anxiety, and despair.

Conceptualizing leisure within a framework of activity or time appears to be too limiting. As Kelly (1990, p. 20) stated, "neither time nor activity provides a clear quantitative definition of leisure." Therefore, many theorists believe the term *leisure* should be reserved for a person's perception that he or she is free to choose to participate in meaningful, enjoyable, and satisfying experiences. According to Mannell, Zuzanek, and Larson (1988), leisure is best understood from the subjective perspective of the participant. This resulted in ideas of perceived freedom and intrinsic motivation becoming the pillars upon which a great deal of leisure theory has been constructed. Roadburg (1983) examined the relationships between perceived freedom and enjoyment of leisure and concluded that freedom is a necessary but not sufficient condition for leisure; enjoyment must also be present in order for people to experience satisfying leisure experiences. As individuals encounter positive emotions (e.g., control, competence, relaxation, excitement) associated with the leisure experience, they will be intrinsically motivated to participate (Dattilo, 1986). People will want to participate in leisure for the feelings inherent in the experience, rather than for some external outcome or reward.

A model developed by Neulinger (1974) described leisure as containing dimensions of freedom, intrinsic motivation, and noninstrumentality. Neulinger explained that individuals engaged in leisure understand they are participating because their actions are the result of a deliberate choice, rather than from being coerced. In addition, participation is chosen for reasons intrinsic to the activity, rather than as a means to an end. Based on this conceptualization, leisure is clearly a mental condition located in the consciousness of the person. Leisure as an experience or state of mind has become a significant theme of scholarship (Mannell, 1984). It is uniquely individual, implying that quality rather than quantity is important.

Unfortunately, some people have not yet developed skills that enable them to participate in traditional recreation activities. In addition, some of those individuals often have extensive amounts of free time that fail to provide them with opportunities for enjoyment, pleasure, and satisfaction. Again, defining leisure in terms of recreation activity or free time appears to be too limiting. Conceptualizing leisure as an individual's state of mind involving the perception of freedom to choose to participate in meaningful, enjoyable, or satisfying experiences is a more appropriate foundation for the provision of therapeutic recreation services.

If the view that leisure is an experience is considered when developing therapeutic recreation programs, the notion of a continuum of services (Peterson and Gunn, 1984) becomes more meaningful. Because some individuals possess limited functional skills, it is extremely important to develop those skills through intensive therapy or treatment. Although these actions are necessary, they are not sufficient when attempting to enhance the leisure lifestyles of individuals. A person may never encounter the freedom of choice that should be associated with the leisure experience when involved only in therapy. Therefore, individuals must receive systematic leisure education that provides them with the skills needed to make choices from an array of options. Based on the previous efforts of Kelly, (1983, 1987) and Kleiber and Kelly (1980), Ashton-Shaeffer and Kleiber (1990) reported that leisure is important to the well-being of people because of the opportunity to interact with others in ways that are not coercive and the emotional value derived from enjoyment.

Typically, when people think of their own leisure, they define the experience as freedom from responsibilities and obligations (e.g., work, school, family, house repairs, car maintenance). Many people feel that if they had more time and money, and fewer responsibilities they could "really" enjoy themselves. Lee and Mobily (1988) identified this type of freedom as "circumstantial," meaning the ability of individuals to act according to their interests, desires, or wishes. Circumstantial freedom, however, not only pertains to the *freedom from* responsibilities but also to the *freedom to* carry out a chosen act. The challenge in providing leisure services for many people is to allow them the freedom to participate in experiences of their own choosing. Leisure education is designed to provide individuals with opportunities to become more aware, knowledgeable, and skillful in those areas that facilitate leisure involvement. Figure 1.1 illustrates the interaction between leisure as experience, recreation as activity, and the notion of discretionary time.

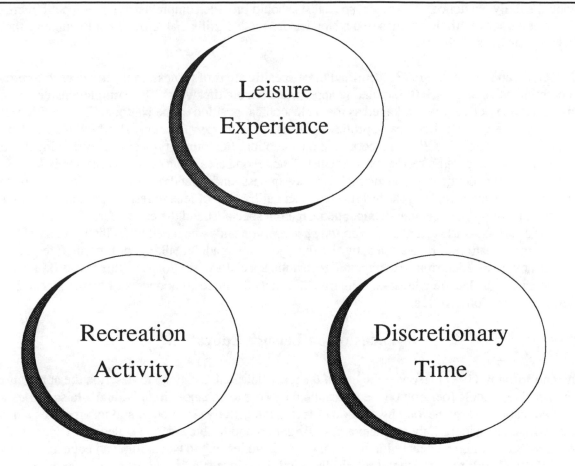

Figure 1.1 Coming to terms with leisure

Understanding Therapeutic Recreation

Leisure education is an important process offered by many leisure service providers. However, the majority of leisure education literature and theory is associated with therapeutic recreation. More generally, this applies to leisure services for people with disabilities. Because of leisure education's close ties with therapeutic recreation, it is appropriate to present a model of therapeutic recreation to illustrate the application of leisure education within this specific service delivery model.

Peterson and Gunn (1984) have identified the purpose of *therapeutic recreation* as facilitating the development, maintenance, and expression of an appropriate leisure lifestyle for individuals with physical, mental, emotional, or social limitations. The phrase *leisure lifestyle* refers to the day-to-day behavioral expression of one's leisure-related attitudes, awareness, and activities as a part of the total life experience (Peterson, 1981). Therapeutic recreation places special emphasis on the development of an appropriate leisure lifestyle as an integral part of independent functioning (American Therapeutic Recreation Association, 1984). According to Peterson and Gunn (1984), the most essential aspect is the focus on day-to-day behavioral expression, implying that leisure lifestyle is a routine part of an individual's daily existence. Therefore, specialists should provide comprehensive therapeutic recreation services for persons with disabilities to develop leisure-related skills that allow them to enhance the quality of their lives each day.

Gunn and Peterson (1978) identified three specific areas of professional service used to provide this comprehensive approach to facilitating appropriate leisure lifestyles. This comprehensive approach to leisure service delivery was adopted as the philosophical position of the National Therapeutic Recreation Society (1982). The first area of professional service is *therapy (treatment),* which is intended to enhance basic functional skills (e.g., coordination, attention, flexibility) typically requiring intensive supervision by a therapeutic recreation specialist. The second area of professional service is *leisure education,* which is devoted to enhancing leisure awareness, understanding, and skills (e.g., awareness of self in leisure, decision-making skills, knowledge and utilization of leisure resources) and requires a shared responsibility between the therapeutic recreation specialist and the consumer. The third area of professional service is identified as *recreation participation* and is intended to facilitate freely chosen, independent participation in recreation activities (e.g., jogging, reading, talking with friends) requiring limited, if any, assistance from a therapeutic recreation specialist. The focus of this text is on the area of service identified as leisure education. Figure 1.2 depicts the three components of comprehensive therapeutic recreation services.

Focusing on Leisure Education

Chinn and Joswiak (1981) reserved the use of the term "leisure education" to describe the application of comprehensive models focusing on the educational process to enhance an individual's leisure lifestyle. Leisure education moves beyond instruction of recreation activity skills only, and incorporates a dynamic process with clearly identifiable content areas. Brightbill and Mobley (1977) stated that leisure and education are closely and irrevocably intertwined, with leisure leading to education, and education back to leisure. Kelly (1990) reported that through education, individuals learn and prepare for expressions of leisure and in leisure, they use education to teach themselves further about leisure's relative freedom and self-determination.

According to Kleiber (1981), the premise for leisure education may include a recognition that free time is often misused and that leisure may be the best context for self-actualization. If leisure service providers are specifically interested in developing the leisure literacy of persons and promoting their self-actualization, Howe (1989) suggested that they assume the role of leisure educator. In this role they can encourage the development of self-directed, freely chosen, healthy, intrinsically motivated, and pleasurable leisure participation patterns. "The concept of education for leisure aims at exposing all people to the possibilities that leisure may hold for them to live creatively and give expression to the wide assortment of their capabilities" (Bucher, Shivers, & Bucher, 1984, p. 290).

Leisure Education as a Human Right

An important consideration for human beings is that the individual have a full measure of freedom, autonomy, choice, and self-determination (Murphy, 1975). Within the context of Lee and Mobily's (1988) assertion that natural freedom involves the irrevocable power that humans have for self-determination, and Bregha's (1985) position that leisure is the most precious expression of our freedom, a convincing case can be made that leisure is an inherent right of all humans. Therefore, every attempt must be made to assist persons with disabilities in being involved in active leisure participation.

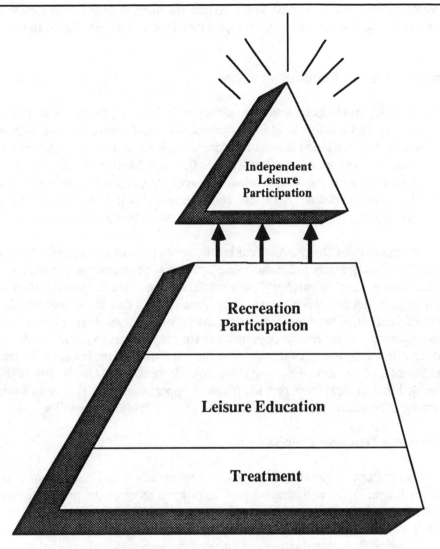

Figure 1.2 The therapeutic recreation process

According to Kelly (1990, p. 385), "the main issue is that of opportunity: If leisure is the element of life in which unique opportunities for expression, development and relationships are found, then should not a full range of opportunities be available for everyone?" The underlying assumption is that all persons, including people with disabilities, should have opportunities for leisure experiences (Austin, 1989). According to Halberg (1989) all people have the right to a desired leisure lifestyle and optimal leisure independence through the highest quality of coordinated services possible. Therefore, leisure education is based on the premise that all individuals, regardless of race, socioeconomic status, gender, color, religion, or ability, possess the human right to experience leisure.

Wade and Hoover (1985) identified a lack of education and training as a major constraint to developing a sense of control during leisure participation. To overcome this practitioners are encouraged to explore participants' leisure attitudes, increase their understanding of leisure, and enhance their awareness of available opportunities. The challenge in providing leisure services for many people is first in helping them overcome barriers. The next step is to provide them with opportunities to develop the skills, awareness, and understanding needed to experience freedom to participate in individually chosen experiences.

Leisure Education as Option Building

The intent of leisure education is to facilitate the ability of individuals to choose to participate independently in meaningful experiences resulting in enjoyment and satisfaction. Practitioners wanting to facilitate participants' ability to experience natural freedom associated with leisure participation should develop programs that develop options for participants (Lee and Mobily, 1988). Through leisure education, people should gain the awareness, appreciation, knowledge, and skills necessary for them to responsibly choose to be involved in leisure. Schleien, Tuckner, and Heyne (1985) identified self-initiated, independent leisure functioning in ordinary environments as the ultimate goal of leisure education.

A critical component of the provision of leisure services is incorporation of choice. Unfortunately, choice-making among many individuals (e.g., people with disabilities) continues to receive little attention from practitioners and researchers. As a result, activities are frequently offered as passive stimulation, with limited thought given to providing opportunities that allow individuals to express their preferences for participation. These preferences should be of major concern when developing leisure programs. If practitioners are to provide opportunities for participants to demonstrate leisure preferences, it is critical that they develop strategies to recognize the exhibition of preferences for people unable to indicate choices through conventional means (Houghton, Bronicki, and Guess, 1987). Nietupski et al. (1986) recommended that practitioners provide frequent opportunities for choice in a structured fashion, rather than assuming individuals with severe disabilities lack self-initiation skills.

Leisure Education as a Dynamic Process

Leisure education is far from stagnant; it is a dynamic process involving continuous enhancement of leisure-related knowledge, skills, and awareness. The process requires the presentation of unique content intended to help individuals identify and clarify their leisure participation patterns. The intention of leisure education is to instill a leisure ethic within people, so that they may freely and willingly take part in activities that can bring them satisfaction and enjoyment, with the ultimate goal of enriching and enhancing their lives.

A focus of leisure education is helping individuals develop an increased sense of awareness (Peterson and Gunn, 1984). Development of an awareness of self in relation to leisure and of methods to facilitate involvement enhances the possibility that people will experience leisure. Similar to the critical step in conquering chemical dependency, an important element in leisure education involves participants accepting responsibility for their leisure. Ultimately, they must feel that their ability to be happy and have fun is up to them.

Leisure education also implies that individuals accept the idea that they can change and improve their current leisure participation patterns. Beliefs associated with phrases such as "I cannot do this," must change to "I do not do this now, but I will try," and further evolve into "I will be able to do this!" To become self-determining, individuals must be able to make choices, demonstrate preferences, and ultimately make decisions related to their leisure participation. Therefore, individuals with disabilities must learn to examine and increase their options relative to leisure involvement. Leisure education is provided to teach individuals that they have the power to improve their lives through leisure participation that is rewarding and fulfilling.

Leisure Education as Balance and Core

Among the major challenges facing practitioners is determining what to teach their consumers. Many people with disabilities who seek therapeutic recreation do so to overcome barriers that obstruct satisfying, enjoyable, and meaningful leisure participation. As a result, professionals must work with their constituents to enhance those skills and abilities which have the most potential for increasing the quality of lives for people with disabilities. Ideally, one of the major outcomes of a leisure education program will be skills and abilities that last a lifetime. Information developed by Kelly (1990, 1987) may help therapeutic recreation specialists develop the most effective and efficient leisure education programs.

Kelly advocated a balanced approach to leisure by encouraging the development of a broad leisure repertoire. This recommendation was made in response to the observation that people pursue a variety of leisure experiences, resulting in a multiplicity of meanings. Most individuals tend to select recreation activities that result in a balance between social and solitary, active and restful, high and low intensity, and engagement and escape environments. They also seek different combinations of environments, investments, and outcomes. Therefore, leisure education programs should include diversity. This diversity may result in a leisure education program that contains multiple goals. These include:

(a) increase social skills required to develop new friends, deepen ongoing intimacies, gain interpersonal acceptance, and strengthen role relationships,
(b) attain a sense of awareness and appreciation useful in self-development,
(c) express individuality, and
(d) develop philosophical positions.

Some people, especially those who have disabilities and are older, lack a broadness and balance in their leisure involvement creating a serious obstacle to participation in community-based leisure programs (Boyd, 1990). Boyd encourages professionals to develop effective leisure education programs to alleviate this obstacle to active community participation.

Although it is very important for individuals to develop a repertoire of leisure skills to provide them with the flexibility to experience leisure in a variety of contexts and circumstances, another consideration is of equal importance. Frequently, the time practitioners have available to spend with individual participants is extremely limited (e.g., some psychiatric facilities may provide services for people that have less than a 30-day stay). In addition, some people (e.g., persons with mental retardation or individuals who recently experienced a stroke) learn at a slower rate than their same-age peers. As a result, professionals may be able to teach only a few skills to any given person. The skills must then be selected with extreme care and in collaboration with consumers.

Professionals may need of guidelines to assist them in selecting skills to be included in leisure education programs. Perhaps the best guidelines available can be found by identifying those common day-to-day skills most significantly impacting the quality of an individual's life. Kelly (1983) identified a significant set of activities consisting of typically low-cost and accessible engagements that are common to most adults and do not vary greatly across the life span. A leisure education program incorporating this model of core leisure may include such things as teaching individuals how to:

(a) interact informally with other household members,
(b) converse in a variety of settings,
(c) develop relationships and experience intimacy,
(d) enhance living environments, and
(e) maintain fitness through activities such as walking.

This core of experiences occupies a great deal of time, especially those periods between scheduled events.

It appears that a combination of a balance and core approach to leisure education may be useful. Consideration of core experiences allows professionals to provide extremely relevant services that can be used immediately and consistently by consumers. Inclusion of a balance of experiences in a leisure education program expands opportunities that permit diversity and variety in their leisure lifestyles. Refer to Figure 1.3 for identification of the aforementioned characteristics of leisure education.

Conclusion

Leisure education is an essential component of leisure services. It is a multifaceted process that requires a clear understanding of the purpose of leisure services and how it contributes to that purpose. Conceptualizing leisure as a state of mind rather than as an activity or a segment of time is useful when formulating an approach to leisure education. Activity and time may comprise the context in which participation occurs, but they are the means to the end, not the end itself.

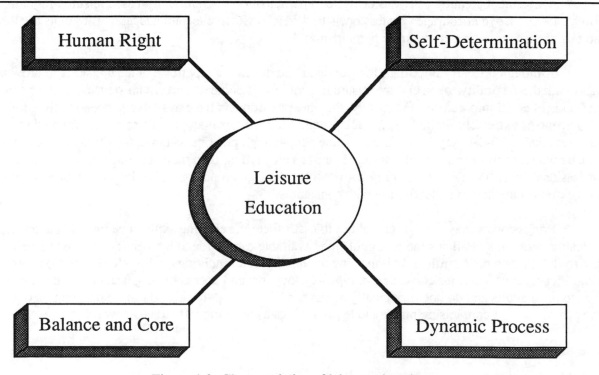

Figure 1.3 Characteristics of leisure education

REVIEW OF RECOMMENDATIONS AND EMPIRICAL CONSIDERATIONS FOR LEISURE EDUCATION

Introduction

This chapter will allow readers to familiarize themselves with a sampling of the theoretical and scholarly work that has been conducted in leisure education. Understanding the scope of the work that has been accomplished (and what remains to be accomplished) will provide insight into the types of leisure education programs that have been developed and implemented. It will give insight into what their purposes were, the components of the programs, the nature of the participants, and the general strengths and weaknesses of the programs. Knowledge based on this insight should assist practitioners in developing defensible rationales for the leisure education programs they might devise and enable them to justify leisure education to administrators, supervisors, staff, program participants, and other interested parties. The focus of the following recommendations and considerations is on the application of leisure education services to people who happen to possess a disability. Although the concepts presented below are primarily based on the works of people providing services for individuals with disabilities, the information has relevance to all recipients of leisure services.

Recommendations

Although the topics of leisure and education have been debated for centuries, it was not until the late 1970s that the literature began to contain descriptions of how to systematically provide leisure education. The following description of texts and articles devoted to leisure education is not intended to be exhaustive. However, it is hoped that the reader will gain an appreciation for the body of knowledge associated with leisure education. In addition, professionals are encouraged to pursue these additional resources to increase their understanding of leisure education and to facilitate systematic attempts at leisure education. Many useful articles and texts have been developed that are devoted specifically to leisure counseling (e.g., Compton and Goldstein, 1977; Dowd, 1984; Epperson, Witt, and Hitzhusen, 1977; McDowell, 1976); however, since the focus of this text is on leisure education, detailed analysis of this body of literature will not occur.

Based on his observations that many people with disabilities fail to adjust to community living because of inappropriate use of their leisure, Hayes (1977a, 1977b) recommended implementation of a program combining leisure education and recreation counseling intended to help individuals select and participate in recreation activities and develop necessary skills for meaningful leisure involvement. Hayes proposed a leisure education model designed to involve participants in meaningful recreation activities within the community, resulting in the development of positive feelings. He suggested that procedures must be developed to adequately prepare individuals to cope with free time and facilitate their reintegration into total community living.

In their text on leisure education, Mundy and Odum (1979) suggested that leisure education provides a vehicle for developing an awareness of activities and resources and for acquiring skills necessary for participation in leisure throughout the life span. As a result of leisure education, individuals will be able to enhance their experiences in leisure and understand the opportunities, potentials, and challenges that are available through leisure. The impact of leisure education can be seen in the development of individuals' ability to understand the influence of leisure on the day-to-day pattern of their existence. As individuals with disabilities acquire the knowledge, skills, and appreciations that enable them to participate in broad leisure experiences, they will improve the overall quality of their lives. To implement leisure education services, Mundy and Odum developed a systematic process intended to stimulate leisure and self-awareness, decision-making, social interaction, and leisure skill application.

Joswiak (1979) proposed a leisure education program emphasizing development of an awareness of leisure resources within the home and community. Implementing a systems approach to program design, Joswiak presented a program intended for participants with developmental disabilities to increase awareness of three important aspects of leisure involvement: (a) the meaning of play and leisure, (b) leisure resources in the home, and (c) leisure resources in the community. The author recommended the application of systematic assessment and evaluation procedures to determine participant and practitioner success, as well as identifying strategies for enhancing future programmatic effectiveness.

Based on observations that public schools have done little to develop social-leisure skills and attitudes for individuals with disabilities, Collard (1981) identified ways to support interdisciplinary cooperation for leisure education in the schools. After presenting an organized rationale for inclusion of leisure education in the public schools, the author proposed potential roles for the therapeutic recreation specialist and the classroom teacher designed to facilitate the introduction of leisure education in the schools. Specific guidelines on becoming an advocate for leisure education were presented. These identifying the right people to approach (e.g., parent groups, educators, administrators, nonprofit organizations, governmental agencies) and what to say to these people once their attention is obtained.

As an alternative to the provision of diversional recreation activities, Dunn (1981) encouraged practitioners to employ leisure education strategies that facilitate increased leisure independence of persons residing in psychiatric transitional facilities. Possible leisure education goals, objectives, and program processes were outlined. The author suggested various implementation ideas intended to promote community adjustment.

In a text written by Wuerch and Voeltz (1982) and described in the article by Voeltz and Wuerch (1981) the authors outlined a process for leisure education designed to encourage extensive involvement by persons with severe disabilities and their families. The structure for an initial assessment to determine leisure activity selection, appropriateness of activities, preferences, and skill performance levels was described. Based on results of the initial assessment, the authors strongly encouraged practitioners to provide "choice training" designed to permit individuals to exert control over their environment.

Voeltz, Wuerch, and Wilcox (1982) stated that a rationale for leisure education can be provided by examining its effects, not only in the area of leisure but also in the participant's entire life patterns. The effects of leisure education can be enhanced by the acquisition of skills that prepare individuals for community adjustment in least restrictive environments. According to the authors, it is important to involve parents, other family members, treatment team members, and integrated service personnel, as well as the person with disabilities when developing a leisure education plan.

McDowell (1983) published a set of ten booklets designed to assist readers in gaining an understanding of the concepts and helping strategies associated with developing "leisure wellness." The author leads readers through an exploration of self and leisure wellness by having them:

(a) learn about the concept of leisure wellness,
(b) understand the concepts and principles associated with wellness,
(c) develop intimate relationships,
(d) explore self-identify and social roles,
(e) develop strategies for fitness,
(f) assess leisure lifestyle and formulate strategies,
(g) develop coping strategies and manage stress,
(h) manage attitudes, affirmation and assertion,
(i) manage economics, time, and cultural forces, and
(j) establish a new model for leisure.

The information is presented in booklet format in an attempt to increase readability and practical use by professionals.

Beck-Ford and Brown (1984) developed a systematic leisure education model that provided a logical sequence of learning experiences for young adults with severe disabilities. The project that was reported in a text incorporated opportunities available in the community and provided guidelines for the development of individual step-by-step programs. Based on the early work of Mundy (1976), the authors explained that the leisure education process includes awareness of self and leisure, decision making, social interaction, and leisure and related skills.

Peterson and Gunn (1984) identified leisure education as a critical component of therapeutic recreation services that is focused on the development and acquisition of leisure-related skills, attitudes, and knowledge. The authors emphasized the need for professionals to do more than merely offer activity skills. Practitioners must also facilitate satisfying leisure involvement for participants by providing opportunities for developing an understanding of leisure. They must also develop positive attitudes toward leisure experiences, participatory and decision-making skills, and knowledge and utilization of leisure resources. Peterson and Gunn described the importance of individuals' developing leisure awareness that included knowledge of leisure, self-awareness, leisure and play attitudes, and decision-making skills. A major component of their leisure education model was identified as leisure resources. It included activity opportunities, as well as personal, family, home, community, state, and national resources. The authors also highlighted the importance of developing social interaction and leisure activity skills.

Witt, Ellis, and Niles (1984) developed a model of leisure education based on the belief that freedom is a critical element in leisure involvement and, therefore, efforts to reduce deficiencies in functioning require careful examination of individuals' perceptions of personal freedom. The authors recommended that practitioners work to increase participants' control and enhance their perceived competence in leisure experiences. They should also encourage development of intrinsic motivation, and stimulate depth of involvement and playfulness. Throughout their presentation of leisure education, Witt and colleagues emphasized optimizing leisure functioning in the appropriate environmental circumstances through a shared responsibility between people with disabilities and leisure service providers. Leisure education, as conceptualized by Witt, Ellis, and Niles, is reflected in the Leisure Diagnostic Battery (LDB). The LDB (Ellis and Witt, 1986), identified by Dunn (1984) as one of the most comprehensive measures in therapeutic recreation, contains the following components: leisure preferences, playfulness, knowledge of leisure opportunities, leisure barriers, depth of involvement, leisure needs, perceived competence, and perceived control. Dunn reported that conceptualization of the LDB is well established and provides a basis for construct validity, absent in most other assessment procedures used in therapeutic recreation.

Development of age-appropriate, community-based leisure skill repertoires that facilitate successful integration into the community is extremely important for individuals with disabilities. Ford et al. (1984) suggested the development of the same leisure skills that are utilized by individuals without disabilities in a wide variety of integrated community environments. Therefore, practitioners should encourage persons with disabilities to acquire leisure skills that are age-appropriate and comparable to their peers. Practitioners should ensure the teaching of those leisure skills that have the potential of being performed in the presence of, or in interaction with, peers without disabilities (Schleien & Ray, 1988).

Wehman and Moon (1985) recommended inclusion of fun and enjoyment when designing and implementing leisure programs for individuals with severe disabilities. They stated that leisure education programs should stimulate constructive or purposeful behavior, accompanied by participation in activities. The programs should encourage self-initiated behavior and choice. More specifically, the authors emphasized the importance of considering chronological age-appropriateness when selecting leisure skills for instruction. Practitioners should consider the attitudes of family members when developing programs intended to reduce barriers to leisure participation. Consideration should also be given to the availability of leisure materials in the home and the types of community resources that are available. Consulting with consumers is critical to any leisure program designed to allow practitioners the opportunity to respond to the attitudes, aptitudes, and skills of the participants.

Putnam, Werder, and Schleien (1985) made suggestions for developing leisure services for persons with disabilities based on qualitative aspects of leisure involvement and participants' individual preferences. Practitioners should give attention to the implications of participation on people's quality of life. Incorporation of the principle of normalization is extremely useful in the development of any educational program devoted to enhancing leisure participation for persons with disabilities. Each individual's least restrictive environment should be considered when developing a comprehensive leisure education program. The authors identified several recent trends to be addressed when developing a leisure curriculum. Community-referenced instruction that incorporates environmental inventories is an important step in validating leisure instruction and preparing persons with disabilities for active leisure participation within the community. All leisure programs should be appropriate for the age of the participants, regardless of skill level. Therapeutic recreation programs incorporating leisure education should attempt to individualize the programs to respond to individual participant preferences. In addition, Putnam, Werder, and Schleien strongly advocated leisure participation in community settings and provided useful guidelines to facilitate this participation. Practitioners should investigate all community leisure services and identify inhibitors and facilitators of leisure participation. Development and support of leisure programs fostering community involvement should utilize all community programs that provide leisure services for persons with disabilities.

Fine, Welch-Burke, and Fondario (1985) proposed a model as a framework for development of a leisure skills curriculum for persons with severe disabilities. The model accentuated the importance of systematic observation and assessment of the individual, followed by formulation of goals designed to develop appropriate leisure behaviors. The authors suggested implementation of instructional methods to facilitate achievement of goals and encouraged utilization and generalization of leisure skills. Bringing about an awareness of leisure resources encouraging self-initiated involvement was identified as a critical component of leisure education. Compton and Touchstone (1977) proposed a similar model emphasizing individualized therapeutic recreation services for persons with severe disabilities.

Bregha (1985) suggested that leisure understanding, awareness, and control can be accomplished through leisure education. The goal of leisure education is to encourage people to make effective leisure choices. A comprehensive leisure education program can help participants develop skills and behaviors and allow them to realize that their behaviors can have an effect on the environment.

Gushikin, Treftz, Porter, and Snowberg (1986) described a leisure education program to help cardiac patients safely achieve meaningful leisure on their own. The authors stressed the importance of identification of leisure interests and deficiencies, which should then be matched with existing leisure opportunities. The value of teaching individuals new skills and conducting sessions identifying barriers that inhibit leisure involvement was highlighted. An important thrust of the program developed by Gushkin and colleagues was inclusion of follow-up appointments to ensure that program participants were receiving the assistance necessary to engage in leisure activities.

Falvey (1986) identified many activity dimensions to consider when designing, developing, and implementing leisure programs for persons with severe disabilities. She, too, suggested that leisure opportunities be chronologically age-appropriate. Professionals are encouraged to provide opportunities for interaction with all peers for individuals with disabilities. A variety of skills and knowledge should be presented to individuals and efforts should be made to increase accessibility to leisure services. Preferences of participants and their families should be considered, as well as relevance of specific leisure skills to a variety of environments. When specific skills are targeted for instruction, the potential for adaptation should be examined. To facilitate implementation of an effective leisure curriculum, Falvey recommended inclusion of components originally identified by Williams, Brown, and Certo (1975). They suggested the components for instructional programs should be focused on the following questions:

(a) What activity should be taught?
(b) Why should an activity be taught?
(c) Where should an activity be taught?
(d) How should an activity be taught?
(e) What performance criteria should be sought?
(f) What materials should be used? and
(g) What measurement strategies should be used?

Stumbo and Thompson (1986) compiled a manual of activities and resources associated with leisure education. The leisure education activities were categorized as mixers, social interaction skills, and leisure awareness activity skills and resources. The authors included specific information relevant to implementing these activities, such as space requirements, equipment and materials, type of group, program goals, description and procedure, leadership considerations, and variations. Stumbo and Thompson included a variety of activities associated with leisure education, with the intent that the activities would be used to initiate or expand leisure services.

Aguilar (1986) presented a four-phase framework for development and evaluation of leisure education programs for individuals residing in institutions. The first phase requires specialists to define leisure and identify education needs, identify desired outcomes of the leisure education program, design a feasible program and consider unique characteristics of participants. During the second phase, educational content should be identified in the areas of leisure resources, knowledge of recreation opportunities, recreation skills, and leisure skills and appreciation. The third phase involves identification of educational approaches requiring specification of intervention techniques, learning tools, conducive environment, and appropriate modeling behavior. Finally, Aguilar strongly recommended systematic evaluation of the leisure education program, characterized by thorough examination of program design, employment of practical procedures, provision of outcomes, application of triangulation approach, and useful information resulting in program enhancement.

Howe-Murphy and Charboneau (1987) supported application of integration and normalization principles in all aspects of leisure education programs. Perceived competence, self-awareness, decision-making, leisure skill development, resource awareness and utilization, and social skill development were identified as important areas of focus. According to Howe-Murphy and Charboneau, a major emphasis of leisure education programs should be facilitating social integration and interaction.

Hultsman, Black, Seehafer, and Hovell (1987) described the development of an implementation strategy for leisure counseling based on the Purdue Stepped Approach Model. This model increases the intensity of intervention presented in a five step series and is based on Neulinger's (1981a, 1981b) paradigm of leisure and its criteria of perceived freedom and intrinsic motivation. The initial step involves minimal assistance involving the simplest and least costly intervention that works for the individual. Next, the media-assisted instruction step incorporates the implementation of a self-help treatment program that requires participants to read and complete assignments independently. The third step involves minimal contact resulting in brief and infrequent, but regularly scheduled, counseling contacts that are not necessarily face-to-face. Regularly scheduled group counseling sessions are contained in the fourth step of the model. Finally, the fifth step employs regularly scheduled individual counseling sessions. The authors' intention was to encourage the application of the Purdue Stepped Approach Model to leisure counseling to produce a potentially cost-effective alternative to traditional resource-intensive counseling approaches.

Witman, Kurtz, and Nichols (1987) developed a booklet, intended to be a frame of reference for leisure education, that contained activities, techniques, and resources. The authors used a sequential approach to organize the booklet into sections containing activities associated with reflection, recognition, and reaffirmation. Initially, readers are provided with activities encouraging them to consider leisure as something unique to them. Following this portion of the booklet, activities are presented that allow readers to clarify the role of leisure in their lives. In the final section, activities are provided to help readers determine the directions in which to proceed following instruction. The authors' approach to leisure education is founded on the principles of quality education for adults that include such aspects as collaborative planning, respect for "learned experience" of participants, and emphasis on processing and support.

The Rehabilitation Research and Training Center in Mental Illness (1987) in cooperation with a number of organizations developed a training module on recreation and leisure designed to help a wide range of people in all age groups become more self-reliant and resourceful in the use of their free time. Although the module was developed primarily for adults with mental disorders, the authors contend that the module can be helpful for a variety of people of different ages and with different skills and abilities. The recreation and leisure module contains a trainer's manual, a videotape, and a workbook. In each of these learning materials the following four skill areas are presented:

(a) identifying benefits of recreational activities,
(b) getting information about recreation activities,
(c) finding out what is needed for a recreation activity, and
(d) evaluating and maintaining a recreational activity.

Each of these four skill areas is divided into seven learning activities:

    (a) introduction,
    (b) videotape and questions-answers,
    (c) role playing,
    (d) resource management,
    (e) outcome problems,
    (f) in vivo exercises, and
    (g) homework assignments.

The general concept of problem solving is addressed throughout every aspect of the module.

Keller, McCombs, Pilgrim, and Booth (1987) developing a booklet designed to help practitioners encourage older adults to develop active leisure lifestyles. The authors presented a step-by-step process that was designed to assist professionals in helping their clientele develop leisure habits and lifestyles which promote wellness. The six step process includes information on:

    (a) discovering leisure time activities and interests,
    (b) exploring leisure interests,
    (c) selecting a leisure activity,
    (d) beginning the activity,
    (e) checking on participant's progress, and
    (f) investigating additional leisure pursuits.

The process was designed to enable professionals to help their clients achieve their potential in a relaxed and nonthreatening environment with a minimum of time commitment.

Dattilo and Murphy (1987a) presented five guidelines designed to assist practitioners with the task of developing effective leisure education programs on adventure recreation. The first guideline involved participants learning about safety measures designed to protect them without detracting from the sense of challenge and adventure. The authors also suggested that participants learn about available opportunities and resources for further participation. Mastering the skills required to successfully engage in specific adventure activities was identified as another important aspect of a leisure education program. An additional component required participants to develop the ability to make appropriate decisions based on their skill level, requirements of the activity, and possible consequences of participation. Finally, practitioners were encouraged help people participate in the actual adventure experiences. The process described by Dattilo and Murphy can be applied to all individuals, including people who possess disabilities.

Schlcien and Ray (1988) identified the importance of working to integrate people with disabilities into their communities through instruction in leisure skills that are naturally occurring, frequently demanded, and have a specific purpose. In addition, the authors encouraged instruction of leisure skills that are typically performed by the same-age peers of participants in the leisure education program. Involvement of people with disabilities in functional recreation activities that are age-appropriate should be an ultimate goal of leisure education programs in therapeutic recreation.

Bedini and Bullock (1988) presented a model of leisure education that was taught within the school system and through cooperative community-based programs. The model was based on the premise that the leisure education program would contribute to successful transition and maintenance into the community of youth and young adults with disabilities. Bedini and Bullock included the following three phases in their model:

(a) establishing a foundation by reviewing records, conducting leisure classes, meeting with families,

(b) testing and modification of leisure knowledge and skills within the classroom and community, and

(c) follow-up to get families to support integration by emphasizing areas such as motivation, transportation, interaction with peers, and personal choice.

The authors concluded that leisure education is an effective process to aid in the successful integration of persons with mental disabilities into their communities. Specifically, Bedini and Bullock emphasized the importance of cooperative programming among personnel associated with recreation, special education, and community resources.

Kimeldorf (1989) developed a workbook intended to help create a spirit of playfulness within its readers. To achieve this state of playfulness, the author compiled games, exercises, daydreams, and scripts to facilitate people's search for leisure. Kimeldorf organized the workbook into five sections. The first portion of the booklet is devoted to having readers examine leisure by answering questions. Second, the booklet contains activities that encourage readers to explore what they have done in the past, examine their current patterns, and project into the future relative to leisure participation. Activities that provide readers with assistance in making decisions about specific leisure participation choices are provided in the third section. The fourth section describes a seven step process to assist people in researching new leisure possibilities. Finally, the booklet concludes with a section connecting participants with leisure opportunities by having them phone or visit with people to get information. The book is arranged in a logical progression to assist readers in developing a more meaningful leisure lifestyle.

After interviewing 19 adults with mental retardation who resided in group homes, Malik (1990) noted participants limited understanding of the terms "recreation" and "leisure." In response to this observation, she recommended that service providers offer leisure education programs that focus on knowledge and awareness of leisure and recreation. In addition, the author reported that respondents indicated that friendships and social interaction were extremely important to them. This result prompted Malik to suggest the provision of leisure education programs that also include social interaction training and facilitation of friendships. Finally, the author noted that respondents were very interested in learning skills that were "adult skills." Therefore professionals need to teach age-appropriate skills consistent with the principle of normalization.

In the process of describing the emerging challenge of serving older adults with mental retardation, Boyd and James (1990) reported that leisure education is usually a prerequisite for independent recreation participation. The authors warned that professionals should not interpret this as implying that a once-in-a-lifetime program would be sufficient to eradicate learned helplessness in many of the lives of people receiving therapeutic recreation services. The authors strongly advocated the provision of leisure education in order to empower individuals with disabilities to voice preferences and make decisions. These recommendations are especially true for older adults with disabilities who may have spent many years in protective and highly structured environments that resulted in repeated circumstances that denied most opportunities for choice and control.

Dattilo and St. Peter (1991) proposed a model for systematic and comprehensive leisure education services designed to overcome the barrier of limited leisure awareness, knowledge, and skills of young adults with mental retardation that prevents them from making successful transitions into active community living. The authors suggested development and implementation of a leisure education course. This course should be supplemented with community support by a leisure coach and active participation of individuals' family and friends. The leisure instruction was designed to instill self-determination, leisure appreciation, self awareness, decision making, social interaction, knowledge and utilization of leisure resources, and recreation participation into the lives of young adults with mental retardation, thus assisting them in making the transition to community living as an adult.

Empirical Considerations

This text has been written from a leisure-oriented perspective on leisure education. According to Peterson (1989), a leisure-oriented perspective implies that the ultimate outcome of leisure services is related to leisure behavior and the orientation draws on existing knowledge relevant to leisure. The remainder of this chapter is a summary of selected studies drawn from the literature on leisure behavior and provides insight into the effects of leisure education.

Some investigations have focused on the impact of extremely brief leisure education programs on individuals with disabilities (primarily adolescents identified as delinquents). Munson, Baker, and Lundegren (1985) implemented a program comprising 30-minute leisure education sessions in conjunction with 60-minute strength training sessions, three times per week over a seven week period (totaling 10.5 hours of leisure education). They then examined the effects of the program on the self-esteem, leisure attitudes, and leisure behaviors of 30 males who had been identified as juvenile delinquents. Aguilar (1987) investigated the effects of a five-week leisure education program involving a two-hour session per week (totaling 10 instructional hours) on expressed attitudes toward recreation and delinquency by 38 adolescents labeled as delinquent. Zoerink (1988) analyzed the effects of a leisure education program involving six sequential 90-minute sessions (totaling nine hours of instruction) using value clarification strategies on the leisure functioning of four young people with spina bifida. He concluded that the leisure education program affected participants differently and, as a result, demonstrated no systematic changes in perceived competence, perceived control, leisure needs, depth of involvement, playfulness, and personal and motivational barriers (as measured by the Leisure Diagnostic Battery). Munson (1988) compared the effects of a leisure education program meeting one hour per week for 10 weeks (totaling 10 hours of instruction) on the self-esteem, leisure functioning, attitudes, leisure participation and satisfaction of 39 youths with behavioral disorders. In all four investigations, the impact of the leisure education programs was not deemed to be significant. Each investigator acknowledged that the brevity of the programs might seriously limit the ability of trainers to positively influence leisure-related behaviors. Aguilar reported that amount of time for a leisure education program will require considerable attention in the future. Munson identified several factors influencing program length (e.g., staff availability, facility scheduling, client attendance, administrative support) and stated that the issue of duration of leisure education programs has not been addressed in the literature.

Anderson and Allen (1985) conducted an investigation incorporating Joswiak's (1979) leisure education program, using two 80-minute sessions per week for nine weeks (totaling 24 hours of instruction) for 40 individuals with mental retardation. Unlike the design of the aforementioned studies, Anderson and Allen used the dependent measure of activity involvement. They found that participation in a leisure education program that emphasized knowledge of leisure resources increased the frequency of activity involvement. The program, however, did not appear to affect duration of activity involvement, frequency of social interaction, or duration of social interaction. The investigators recommended that social skill development become a priority in leisure education and that training should continue beyond the brief program they used. Although the results of their investigation were mixed, they strongly supported the inclusion of planned intervention following activity involvement.

Backman and Mannell (1986) compared the effectiveness of using a traditional approach to teaching recreation activities and exposing people to new activities with a leisure education approach focused on changing the attitudes and awareness of leisure of 40 residents of a senior citizens' facility. The residents involved in the program were encouraged to explore their feelings about work, leisure, and free time and to plan for themselves. These residents changed their attitudes to become more positive about leisure. However, the residents provided with the traditional approach exhibited no change in their attitudes. The investigators observed that the development of more positive attitudes toward leisure appeared to allow higher levels of satisfaction to be derived from participation.

Sheffield, Waigandt, and Miller (1986) investigated the post-rape leisure behavior of sexual assault victims by analyzing data relative to leisure and social activity. Leisure behavior in the areas of physical and social activity appeared to be a factor in the successful recovery of participants. The authors suggested that leisure education programs intended to assist the adjustment of sexual assault victims should include counseling for appropriate lskills in the areas of social interaction, self-control, and relaxation.

According to Iso-Ahola and Weissinger (1987), individuals lack of awareness of the psychological value of leisure seems to be a major factor leading to perceptions of boredom. Results indicated a need for leisure education programs that build positive attitudes toward leisure. Weissinger and Caldwell (1990) replicated the previous work by Iso-Ahola and Weissinger and concluded that there is an obvious need for the provision of leisure education services designed to address the psychological and sociological barriers that inhibit functional behaviors. According to the authors, the factors most significant in the development of boredom perceptions are potentially amenable to remediation. Iso-Ahola and Weissinger (1990) provided support for the reliability and validity of the Leisure Boredom Scale that could be used in clinical and practical situations involving examination of leisure dysfunctions. The authors reported that professionals can use the scale to conduct individual participant assessments that may result in the prescription of various leisure education programs.

Caldwell, Adolph, and Gilbert (1989) presented an interesting study providing some useful recommendations for practitioners implementing leisure education programs. The researchers found that when 155 individuals discharged from a rehabilitation hospital were interviewed over the telephone, the people who received leisure counseling reported being more bored, and less satisfied with their leisure. They perceived more internal barriers to recreation participation than those respondents who did not receive leisure education. There are many possible explanations for the differences between groups other than the intervention effects (e.g., the sample receiving leisure education was different from the onset than those who did not receive the training). Or perhaps raised expectations and enhanced skills that were not realized upon discharge into the community contributed to the results. Based on this possibility, the authors recommended that professionals conducting leisure education programs should not only raise expectations about abilities and opportunities, but also should educate participants as to what might prevent them from experiencing leisure after discharge. Caldwell and colleagues agreed that leisure education should be an important component of the ongoing rehabilitation process but cautioned professionals to be aware of short- and long-term effects of such programs.

McDonald and Howe (1989) developed a challenge/initiative program using a leisure education approach for 38 child abuse victims. They supplemented a 40 minute activity period with a required 20 minute debriefing discussion that emphasized group dynamics and self-awareness. The program ran for 28 consecutive days. Results indicated the educational program significantly enhanced self-concepts of participants and supported the model for leisure education in adventure recreation proposed by Dattilo and Murphy (1987a). McDonald and Howe suggested further examination of the use of debriefing sessions in association with recreation activities focused on self-concept and other leisure-related factors.

Lanagan and Dattilo (1989) demonstrated that a leisure education program for adults with mental retardation can produce a higher incidence of involvement than a recreation participation program and shows potential for knowledge retention. They reported favorable results for a leisure education program for 39 adults with mental retardation, consisting of 30 minute periods for 55 sessions across a two-month time span. The results may indicate that a little leisure education goes a long way. Therefore, professionals should consider the inclusion of leisure education programs when attempting to provide comprehensive therapeutic recreation services.

Searle and Mahon (1990) examined the effects of a leisure education program for older adults whose mean age was 77 years. The participants resided in a day hospital where 26 of the adults were assigned to an experimental group and 27 to a control group. The experimental group participated in one hour leisure education sessions once a week for eight weeks. Results of the analysis of covariance for the dependent variables (locus of control, perceived competence, and self-esteem) were all statistically significant. The authors concluded that the study provided further evidence of the effectiveness of leisure education, specifically as a technique to enhance older adults' ability to sustain themselves in an independent living environment.

Bedini (1990) provided an update of the status of leisure education in higher education and in therapeutic recreation by reporting the results of a questionnaire mailed to 133 chairs of recreation and leisure departments and 52 facilities with therapeutic recreation departments identified in the American Hospital Association's Directory of Hospitals. Results indicated that leisure education instruction has increased in recreation and leisure curricula and the existence of leisure education programs in therapeutic recreation is high. The author concluded that leisure education is an area of intervention that can have a positive impact on the quality of life of individuals with disabilities and specifically addresses their needs as they leave a treatment facility and attempt to integrate into their communities.

Conclusion

Although some empirical investigations demonstrating the effects of leisure education have been conducted, more are needed to improve leisure services for people with disabilities. Ellis (1989) suggested that professionals in therapeutic recreation continue to search for answers to fundamental questions about leisure in the lives of people with disabilities. He strongly urged practitioners to continue their search for applications of this knowledge and to develop assessment and intervention techniques that create positive changes in the lives of people with disabilities. Austin (1989) stated that systematic investigation of effective leisure services for people with disabilities needs to occur among all professionals associated with the field of therapeutic recreation.

This review of leisure education programs that have been implemented, and the suggestions emanating from them, will provide professionals and other professionals with a grasp of the current level of knowledge related to leisure education. Such knowledge can be incorporated into a cohesive foundation supporting the provision of quality leisure education. Leisure education programs may vary in content, frequency, duration, format, participants, and other factors. They may also vary in the resources required to implement them. The thread that does connect all leisure education programs is their goal of providing assistance to participants to enable them to add meaning to their lives through leisure.

SUGGESTED AREAS OF CONCENTRATION FOR LEISURE EDUCATION

Introduction

Leisure education has the potential to exert a positive influence on the lives of all people who engage in the process. It provides a vehicle for developing an awareness of leisure activities and resources and for acquiring skills for participation throughout life (Howe-Murphy and Charboneau, 1987). It is a process through which individuals can develop and enhance their knowledge, interests, skills, abilities, and behaviors to a level where leisure can make a significant contribution to the quality of their lives. It can enable individuals to determine for themselves the importance of leisure in their lives, establish their own leisure goals, plan the steps needed to achieve those goals, choose the activities in which they wish to be involved, and participate in those activities. As a result of leisure education, individuals are able to understand the opportunities, potentials, and challenges in leisure, understand the impact of leisure on the quality of their lives, and develop skills that enable broad leisure participation (Mundy and Odum, 1979).

Although leisure education is important to everyone, it assumes an added significance in the lives of individuals with various physical, mental, emotional, and social limitations. In spite of the very real progress that has been made in recent years regarding leisure involvement for people, much remains to be done. Many individuals not only have to cope with the barriers that are a direct result of their specific limitation, but they are also faced with constraints of various kinds imposed by our society. These constraints include physical, attitudinal, and programmatic barriers that work against the achievement of a full and satisfying involvement in many aspects of life, including leisure.

Some individuals within our society are likely to be confronted with larger amounts of unobligated time than other people because of the scarcity of education and employment opportunities available to them. These large blocks of time can be both unfilled and unfulfilling. They may be unfulfilling because the lack of leisure knowledge, skill, ability, awareness, and opportunity for participation conspires to prevent or inhibit a meaningful level of involvement in leisure. An effective leisure education program lessens these problems. It also has the potential to result in skills, competencies, and attitudes (e.g., problem-solving, responsibility for self, increased awareness) that can be useful in other aspects of life.

To achieve benefits previously identified by Howe-Murphy and Charboneau, as well as Mundy and Odum, a model of leisure education is proposed in this chapter. The model is based on previous suggestions identified in articles and texts reported throughout this book (e.g., Mundy and Odum, 1979; Peterson and Gunn, 1984; Witt, Ellis, and Niles, 1984; Wuerch and Voeltz, 1982). The writings of many previous authors allowed us to learn about leisure education and provided the impetus for conceptualizing this model. The following components are included in the model:

  (a) awareness of self in leisure,
  (b) appreciation of leisure,
  (c) understanding of self-determination in leisure,
  (d) ability to make decisions regarding leisure participation,
  (e) knowledge and utilization of resources facilitating leisure participation,
  (f) knowledge of effective social interaction skills, and
  (g) recreation activity skills.

Education in these areas will assist people in developing leisure attitudes, knowledge, and skills that can be matched with suitably challenging opportunities which facilitate a sense of competence and satisfaction (Ewart and Hollenhorst, 1989). Figure 3.1 depicts the characteristics of an individual who has a comprehensive awareness, appreciation, understanding, and skills associated with a given leisure pursuit.

Awareness of Self in Leisure

An important ingredient of any effective leisure education program is the focus on assisting participants to explore, discover, and develop knowledge about themselves in a leisure context. Part of self-awareness is having *knowledge of one's own preferences* relative to leisure activity and involvement. This knowledge is necessary in order to make appropriate choices regarding leisure participation and is a

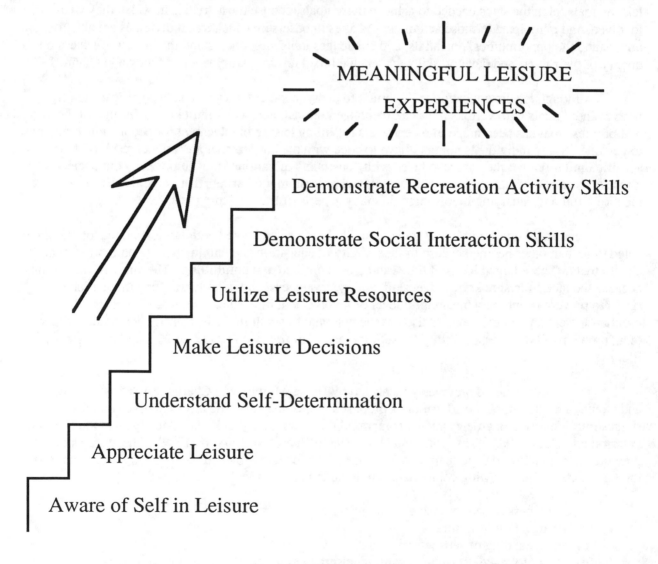

Figure 3.1 Characteristics of a person prepared through leisure education

preliminary step toward independent functioning. Knowing about preferences enables individuals to think about what is required to fulfill their needs and to begin formulating steps to work toward reaching fulfillment.

For many individuals, another part of developing self-awareness is *reflecting on past and current leisure involvement.* Such reflection can bring into focus the activities that provide enjoyment, as well as the skills that individuals possess that enable them to participate. It can also help to identify barriers of various kinds that deter participation and it assists one in thinking about the attributes one has that aid in coping with those barriers. Individuals can also be encouraged to use their reflections of past and current involvement to help them consider what they would like to do in the future regarding leisure participation.

Another facet of self-awareness is working toward the achievement of a *realistic perception of one's skills and abilities* and how they match with the requirements of specific activities. It is essential that a view of one's competencies recognizes the existence of limitations and constraints, as well as those assets that aid participation. As individuals gain an understanding of their preferences and abilities, they should be encouraged to take a realistic view of their abilities in terms of what they want to achieve in their leisure participation. Unrealistic perceptions of competency can lead to disappointment and failure if the demands of an activity greatly exceed the skills that are actually possessed by an individual. Conversely, they can also discourage individuals from participating in activities that they could, in fact, master and in which they could experience success.

Examination of skills and abilities is an important part of gaining knowledge of oneself. An equally important aspect of developing self-awareness is *examining one's values and attitudes toward leisure* and participation in leisure activities. The degree of interest and involvement in activities may be closely related to the degree to which leisure is valued by an individual. In a leisure education program, examination of attitudes might appropriately precede an examination of skills and abilities. Whatever its place in the sequence of a leisure education program, the influence of attitudes on skills, abilities, and participation must be recognized. Johnson and Zoerink (1977), as well as Connolly (1977), recommended the use of values clarification techniques to help individuals learn about themselves. Once people become aware of their values and the implications these values have on choice of activities, people can make leisure choices thus retaining the power and responsibility for making their own decisions (Tinsley and Tinsley, 1984)

Additional facets of self-awareness include *motivation, behavior while participating,* and *the context in which leisure participation occurs.* Attention can be given to identifying the factors that impel one to participate in an activity, or conversely, to decline to participate. Recollection of one's behavior while participating in activities, and consideration of its appropriateness, can also contribute to an increase in self-awareness. Thinking about the context of one's leisure participation can also be of value. For example, is participation with family or friends more valued than participating alone? Is participation in programs offered by others more desirable than in activities devised by oneself?

Satisfaction should be strongly linked with the leisure participation patterns of individuals. People with disabilities should be encouraged to *determine if they are currently satisfied* with the scope of their leisure participation. Perhaps identification of quality leisure by each individual will assist in developing a sense of satisfaction for persons with disabilities. In addition, people should be encouraged to examine their leisure choices to determine if those choices are compatible with their values.

Arriving at an adequate level of self-awareness is a task that requires thoughtful, purposeful action. Different people may require different degrees of assistance in this task. Leisure education programs can be designed to provide participants the opportunities needed to achieve greater knowledge of self.

Leisure Appreciation

Another significant component of leisure education is the development of a sense of appreciation relative to leisure and its potential contribution to the quality of life for individuals. *Understanding the concepts of leisure and leisure lifestyle* is an important part of developing a sense of appreciation. This sense of appreciation for leisure lends itself to an openness to issues related to cross cultural communication (Cappel, 1990). Cappel encouraged professionals to facilitate nonjudgmental exploration and discussion of the origin and impact of cultural, societal, and personal attitudes via leisure education sessions emphasizing leisure awareness.

Iso-Ahola and Weissinger (1990) observed that people who do not have the awareness that leisure can be psychologically rewarding are those who are most likely to perceive leisure as boredom. Therefore, an essential facet of leisure appreciation is the *realization that leisure is a legitimate source of pleasure and satisfaction* and should be available to everyone. Development of a sense of appreciation may require the concomitant elimination of the notion that leisure can be enjoyed only after it has been earned by gainful employment, an idea of considerable import to people with disabilities who may be unemployed. Leisure education can assist in the removal of feelings of guilt associated with vestiges of the work ethic. Appreciation of leisure can be based on understanding the central position leisure occupies in contemporary society.

Another aspect of leisure appreciation is *acceptance of the idea that leisure does not require a special time-frame* in which to occur but that it can, and should, be experienced whenever the opportunity presents itself during the normal course of the day. This is the embodiment of the concept of leisure lifestyle. If people begin to understand and embrace the concepts of leisure and leisure lifestyle, their ability to participate in recreation activities resulting in satisfaction and enjoyment will be enhanced. By having leisure appreciation as a focus, leisure education can assist individuals in the development of a sensitivity for the uniqueness of leisure.

Leisure appreciation means more than liking or approving of leisure as a social or personal experience; it also means understanding of the experience. People may require help in becoming aware of different possibilities that can promote leisure experiences. Leisure education should help individuals identify a variety of *possible circumstances, environments, and activities likely to provide a context in which to experience leisure*. Understanding the way our society views leisure and its impact on total life experiences will also assist individuals in enhancing their leisure patterns.

Self-Determination in Leisure

A third essential component of a comprehensive leisure education program is developing the perception of leisure competence in the program participants. Witt, Ellis, and Niles (1984) emphasized the need for practitioners to provide leisure education services that promote perception of leisure control, leisure competence, and intrinsic motivation to enhance an individual's sense of freedom of choice. Self-determination in leisure is based on perceptions arising from the related phenomena of:

- a *sense of freedom of choice* regarding activity and involvement,
- *intrinsic motivation,*
- *control over one's actions,* and
- the *ability to influence* one's immediate environment.

Many contemporary theorists, including Iso-Ahola (1980), and Neulinger (1982), have argued for the inclusion of freedom of choice in any conceptualization of leisure. Practitioners should incorporate the notion of choice into their leisure education programs.

Some individuals have been sheltered and over-protected from decision-making. As a result, their ability to take personal responsibility for their own leisure involvement may be drastically reduced. If the essence of leisure is freedom of choice, then it follows naturally that it must be accompanied by the *responsibility to make appropriate choices*. Therefore, leisure education should include an emphasis that leisure participation requires taking responsibility for one's enjoyment and satisfaction (Scheltens, 1990). To aid in the development of a sense of responsibility, individuals may need assistance in understanding the potential outcomes of their decisions regarding leisure participation.

An example of a leisure curriculum focusing on choice was developed by Wuerch and Voeltz (1982). Their leisure training project was dedicated to providing people with opportunities to *learn to make choices* during their free time, with the ultimate goal of encouraging development of self-initiated leisure skills. Dattilo and Barnett (1985) demonstrated that when recipients of therapeutic recreation services are provided opportunities and the means to freely select activities, spontaneous initiation of activity, engagement with elements of the environment, and assertion of a degree of control over one's surroundings are often the result. Development of a sense of self-determination in leisure facilitates the ability of individuals to make choices and sets the stage for acquisition of more complex decision-making strategies. Teaching individuals to make choices has several benefits, including (a) increasing interactions with materials that can encourage leisure, especially during times when other people are unavailable, (b) improving the quality of life for individuals by allowing them to participate in the services they receive, and (c) increasing quality of programming by having participants indicate their likes and dislikes (Realon, Favell, and Lowerre, 1990).

Among the goals of leisure education programs is the promotion of self-initiated, *independent use of free time with chronologically age-appropriate recreation activities*. Adherence to this goal has fostered leisure education projects that focus on providing participants with opportunities to learn to make choices during their free time. Among the specific aims of these projects are: (a) the acquisition of leisure skills that are both developmentally and age-appropriate and which also may be generalized to integrated community settings; (b) encouragement of the development of self-initiated leisure skills that are enjoyable; and (c) facilitation of cooperative leisure planning. Such projects nurture the perception of leisure competence in their participants.

Reid (1975) observed that professionals working with individuals who possess disabilities often choose the activity in which the person with the disability participates, rather than allowing the individual to decide. It is likely that the omission of choice in the participation process prevents the individual from experiencing leisure and obtaining the maximum benefit that is potentially available. It is also likely that continuous involvement in situations failing to provide opportunities for choice will result in feelings of helplessness (Seligman, 1975). People who experience helplessness have difficulty in learning that their actions produce outcomes. This tends to reduce voluntary participation and exploration on their part. Further, it is likely that a high incidence of learned helplessness among individuals with disabilities occurs because they are not afforded opportunities to learn and exhibit self-determined behaviors. To prevent learned helplessness, it is recommended that individuals *be afforded early exposure to controllable situations* (DeVellis, 1977); they should be taught to *initiate and terminate their leisure experiences* (Nietupski and Svoboda, 1982). Leisure services that include elements of choice may be critical in the prevention and treatment of learned helplessness and the encouragement of future recreation participation (Iso-Ahola, MacNeil, and Szymanski, 1980). Incorporation of the concept of choice in leisure education programs is not only justifiable, it is necessary. If the perception of self-determination in leisure is to be achieved, it must be built on a foundation that includes a sense of freedom of choice.

Establishment of a sense of self-determination in leisure can be assisted by the development of *assertive behaviors*. People must understand their rights and needs, as well as to respect the rights and needs of others. Understanding that personal preferences relate to what one would like to have, not what one must have, is important for individuals to feel satisfied on a regular basis.

Reducing interpersonal comparisons and focusing on incremental improvement is also useful in developing a sense of leisure competence. Fait and Billing (1978) suggested a redirection of an emphasis on direct competition (requiring a rivalry between opposing forces in which the interests of both are not mutually obtainable) to learning and development fostered by indirect competition (improving previous personal achievement or attaining a goal).

Leisure Decision Making

Encouraging the acquisition and development of decision-making skills should be a major component of leisure education. If it is accepted that one of the goals of leisure services is to foster independence in individuals, then it is imperative that the ability to make appropriate decisions regarding specific tasks be encouraged during recreation participation (Dattilo and Murphy, 1987a). According to Dattilo and Murphy, an intended benefit of recreation participation is an increase in personal effectiveness that can result from the making of timely and correct decisions. Persons who do not possess the *appropriate appraisal and judgment skills* needed for activity involvement will be more likely to acquire these skills if they participate in actual recreation activities. Practitioners should encourage participants to evaluate their decisions, determine the effectiveness of their decisions, and, given similar circumstances, decide whether they would act in a similar fashion or change their behavior in some manner.

Some individuals encounter difficulty in making decisions related to many aspects of their lives. This problem is often evident in relation to their leisure lifestyle. Hayes (1977b) recommended that practitioners teach the decision-making process to individuals and encourage them to select and engage in appropriate recreation activities. Making a decision related to leisure participation is facilitated by an individual's awareness of self in relation to leisure and an appreciation of the value of leisure, as well as the development of a sense of self-determination related to leisure involvement. A person's leisure participation decisions should be *compatible with one's values and desires*. Decision making in leisure is aided by self-awareness, an appreciation of leisure, and an understanding of self-determination, all of which are essential components of leisure education.

McDowell (1976) identified the importance of using rational problem-solving and decision-making techniques to promote the independent responsibility of individuals for making wise decisions about their leisure involvement. According to McDowell, successful decision making can be enhanced by an assessment of leisure interests and attitudes, identified as leisure appreciation and self-determination. Identification of realistic leisure goals and *determination of needs met through goal attainment* are also important aspects of the decision-making process. Murphy (1975) identified removal of barriers that impede or prohibit participation because of discrimination as a primary goal of leisure services. Many people with disabilities experience numerous intrinsic and environmental barriers to leisure involvement. Therefore, decision-making training should also focus on the identification of barriers preventing leisure involvement and the development of strategies for overcoming these barriers. To effectively make decisions, people should be able to identify alternatives for their leisure goals and reasonably predict participation outcomes. McDowell concluded his description of decision making with the recommendation that individuals establish a plan for leisure participation.

A potential plan for leisure participation for individuals may involve the development of *problem-solving skills*. To solve a problem, it is first necessary to clarify and define the problem. An analysis of possible forces influencing the circumstances may be useful in placing the problem in the correct perspective. After the problem and its associated forces are identified, the generation of possible solutions should occur in a free and accepting environment (i.e., brainstorming). Solutions generated during the brainstorming process should then be analyzed and evaluated, using predetermined criteria to assess the feasibility and ramifications of different solutions. After a solution is agreed upon, roles and responsibilities of relevant parties, as well as procedures to implement actions to solve the problem, should be clearly delineated. Following this logical preparation for solving a problem, participants should be encouraged to take the actions necessary to implement their decision. Implementation of a decision, however, does not mean the process is completed. As a final step, individuals must evaluate the success of their actions. Information obtained from the evaluation should strongly influence their future leisure participation patterns. Further information on problem solving is reported by Bouffard (1990), Bransford, Sherwood, Vye, and Rieser (1986), and Spitz (1987).

Knowledge and Utilization of Leisure Resources

Luckey and Shapiro (1974) observed that a major contributor to the failure of many persons with disabilities to adjust to community living may be a result of a lack of awareness of recreation resources and the inability to use them. Therefore, *knowing about the existence of leisure resources and how to use them* should be an important element of leisure education programs. There are instances when recreation programs assist individuals in acquiring and developing the skills necessary to participate in specific activities and, as a culminating experience, provide opportunities for actual participation in those activities. Participation in the activities is the pinnacle of the program. After the individuals have participated in the program, frequently, the program is terminated or their involvement in it is terminated. It is unfortunate, but true, that when the program is ended, the participants may not possess sufficient knowledge regarding potential leisure resources to continue their involvement in the activities they have just been taught. Therefore, a critically important consideration in a comprehensive approach to leisure education is the provision of information relative to leisure resources. According to Overs, Taylor and Adkins (1974a, 1974b), problems associated with making leisure choices may stem from individuals' lack of knowledge about self, leisure, or community resources. If people are to independently experience active leisure participation, they must possess knowledge of available leisure opportunities and the ability to access resources that will enable them to capitalize on those opportunities.

To enhance their ability to experience leisure, individuals must develop an understanding that other *people can be valuable resources* for leisure participation. Personnel associated with community enterprises (e.g., fitness clubs, bowling alleys, movies theaters) that provide recreation activities can provide useful information about the recreation activities they sponsor. People associated with agencies or organizations that serve as clearing houses identifying community leisure opportunities (e.g., travel agencies, chambers of commerce, park and recreation departments) can also provide helpful information. Knowledge of organizations promoting a membership of active participants (e.g., bridge clubs, outing associations, track clubs) can greatly enhance the ability of individuals to continue or expand their leisure participation. Identification of experts in a particular area of interest (e.g., naturalists, artists, musicians) may allow for increased education, mentoring, and skill development permitting more active and, perhaps, more meaningful leisure participation.

If individuals are interested in a particular recreation activity, they should be able to independently identify and locate *facilities or environments* providing opportunities to participate in that activity. Accurate identification of relevant locations should be accompanied by the ability to reach those sites. Reaching destinations requires people to identify their current location and to understand directions to a desired location. If people know where a desired facility or environment is located, they are in a position to walk there or arrange alternative methods of transportation. Alternative forms of transportation may also require specific skill development (e.g., learning to drive, using public transportation, asking family or friends).

Prior to arriving at a destination, participants should possess knowledge of the *requirements associated with participation* in a desired activity. One requirement may be a specific cost for participation. Knowledge of entry fees and funds required for continued participation is important to planning for leisure involvement (e.g., fitness clubs). An understanding of the schedule of events is also needed to plan for active participation (e.g., movie theaters). Participation in a particular recreation activity may be contingent on specific eligibility requirements that should be known prior to attempting entry to programs (e.g., advanced swimming lessons). Individuals with mobility impairments should identify the degree of accessibility associated with a given environment (e.g., entrance ramps, accessible rest rooms).

Participation in recreation activities may require a minimum level of proficiency that should be identified prior to attendance. Knowledge of activity requirements will allow individuals the opportunity to prepare for their participation and develop realistic expectations regarding their ability (e.g., ballet). Understanding the rules associated with a particular event may encourage people to actively participate or enhance their ability to become interested spectators (e.g., basketball). If people become knowledgeable about the equipment and apparel associated with different activities, they will then be better able to prepare for participation in those activities. Some equipment (e.g., skateboard) may be required for participation while other equipment (e.g., hiking boots) may simply enhance performance. Use of appropriate apparel may prevent injuries (e.g., helmet) while other apparel may prevent embarrassment (e.g., swimming suit). Although these factors may not be central to the development of the specific recreation activity skill, they may be the determining factor between successful, enjoyable participation and failure.

Knowledge of leisure resources and the ability to utilize those resources appears to be an important element in the establishment of an independent leisure lifestyle (Peterson and Gunn, 1984). Therefore, Dattilo and Murphy (1987a) recommended that practitioners teach participants not only how to participate in an activity but *how they can find answers to questions* associated with the activity. For example:

(a) Where can one participate?
(b) Are there others who participate?
(c) How much will participation cost?
(d) What type of transportation is available? and
(e) Where can a person learn more about a particular recreation activity?

In addition to the need for people to acquire knowledge of community leisure resources, it is crucial that they be given opportunities to access those resources. If feasible, they should be given assistance until they can independently utilize the resources to become active participants in community life (Richler, 1984).

Social Interaction Skills

Leisure education programs should also include a focus on assisting participants in the development of skills and abilities that will facilitate their integration into social groups and the larger community. Although some people experience many problems that prevent them from developing a satisfying leisure lifestyle, a somewhat prevalent problem is the lack of social interaction skills. Absence of social skills is particularly noticeable during leisure participation and frequently leads to isolation and an inability to function successfully. Many researchers such as Faught and colleagues (1983) as well as McEvoy and associates (1990) have observed that improvements in social interaction skills for persons with disabilities will not reliably occur without implementation of specific interventions. Development of social skills used in leisure situations appears to be important for individuals with disabilities because acquisition of these skills facilitates integration. Therefore, social interaction skills should be a focus of leisure education programs.

An absence of meaningful friendships is a frequent barrier experienced by persons and leads to isolation and withdrawal from community life (Reiter and Levi, 1980). According to Ashton-Schaeffer and Kleiber (1990), social leisure skills appear to be essential for individuals to form and maintain *friendships*. Development of meaningful friendships and effective social interaction skills can be taught through systematic leisure education programs. Schleien and Ray (1988) reported that successful social integration of persons with disabilities into recreation activities may be determined by many factors. The number and quality of social interactions strongly influence the ability of individuals to develop meaningful relationships. People need to develop the ability to maintain an appropriate amount of eye contact, judge adequate physical proximity, and handle physical contact. Each of these skills varies according to the activity, environment, and the people involved, which makes the development of these skills all the more difficult. When a particular situation requires people to play together, the people need to be able to share equipment and materials, engage in cooperative tasks, and develop friendships.

Communication is a key element in social interactions. Both verbal and nonverbal behaviors play an important role in communication. Attempts at mastery of basic verbal communication skills will enhance the likelihood of success in a given leisure environment. The ability of individuals to greet other people, ask questions, wait their turn to speak, and contribute to a discussion are a few examples of verbal skills that are helpful in developing friendships. Nonverbal behaviors also influence perceptions of social competence. Mastery of basic skills such as gesturing, facial expressions, posture, and voice volume and pitch all affect an individual's ability to communicate and consequently develop social relationships.

A *problem-solving* approach to help individuals with disabilities learn and generalize social interaction skills holds some promise. Based on the earlier writings of McFall (1982) and Trower (1984), who proposed a process approach to social skills training that relied on the person's understanding and acting upon the rules of a social situation, Park and Gaylord-Ross (1989) developed and tested a four-step training process. In their successful attempt at teaching social interaction skills to three youth with mental retardation, the authors taught participants to first interpret or decode the meaning of social situations. Next, participants learned to describe possible alternative ways and then select one of these choices to cope successfully with the social situation. Last, they evaluated their performance. Park and Gaylord-Ross reported that if individuals learn general rules of social conduct, their ability to transfer learning across different settings may be enhanced.

Meyer, Cole, McQuarter, and Reichle (1990) reported on the development and validation of an assessment of *social competence* for children and young adults with developmental disabilities. The authors identified a series of functions that appear to be crucial in determining social competence. In addition, Meyer and colleagues presented definitions of these functions, analysis of levels of the functions, and specific items associated with each function. The following eleven functions indicative of social competence were identified:

    (a) joins an ongoing interaction or starts a new one,
    (b) manages own behavior without instruction from others,
    (c) follows rules, guidelines, and routines of activities,
    (d) provides positive feedback and reinforcement to others,
    (e) provides negative feedback and consequences for others,
    (f) obtains and responds to relevant situational cues,
    (g) provides information and offers assistance to others,
    (h) requests and accepts assistance from others,
    (i) makes choices from among available and possible alternatives,
    (j) exhibits alternative strategies to cope with negative situations, and
    (k) terminates or withdraws from an interaction and/or activity.

Mastery of these social interaction skills can lead to development of positive social relationships that produce enjoyment and satisfaction.

Along similar lines to Meyer and her colleagues, Chadsey-Rusch (1990) examined the social interactions of youth with severe disabilities and discussed her findings in reference to facilitating individuals' transition from school to work. Chadsey-Rusch identified the following eleven critical behaviors representing social interaction:

    (a) direct others,
    (b) question,
    (c) criticize,
    (d) praise,
    (e) request assistance,
    (f) offer assistance,
    (g) be polite and demonstrate social amenities,
    (h) greet/depart,
    (i) tease or joke,
    (j) converse/comment/share information, and
    (k) get attention.

Identification of these behaviors provides practitioners with possible areas that could lead to development of individualized social interaction objectives for their constituents. Chadsey-Rusch provided specific delineation of these behaviors that would facilitate both the development of behavioral objectives and associated performance measures.

Recreation Activity Skills

The core of many leisure education programs is the development of the participant's ability to choose and successfully engage in recreation activities of sufficient scope and variety to experience satisfaction and enjoyment. If it is believed that choice is a critical aspect of leisure participation and choice involves options, then it appears logical that an array of recreation activities and opportunities should exist from which individuals could choose to experience meaningful leisure (Peterson and Gunn, 1984). Participants in recreation programs should be encouraged to *select and develop recreation skills having the most potential for providing them with enjoyment and satisfaction*. Selection of recreation activity skills should be contingent on the needs, interests, motivations, and aspirations of the person (Howe-Murphy and Charboneau, 1987), and it is important to remember the role the participant should play in the choice of activities. Howe-Murphy and Charboneau reported that recreation activity skill development can provide physical and emotional support assisting participants in overcoming fear of the unknown and failure. Reduction of fear associated with leisure participation should lessen the hesitancy of people with disabilities to become active participants in community life.

Conclusion

The quality and success of leisure education programs is dependent on many factors, not the least of which is program content. The program components that have been presented in this chapter meet the test of logic and have a research foundation that merits their inclusion in leisure education efforts. Practitioners preparing people to live successfully within their communities are encouraged to consider the incorporation of these components in their programs aimed at educating individuals for active leisure participation. The intent of this text is to present comprehensive and feasible leisure education procedures to practitioners dedicated to enhancing leisure opportunities for all persons, including people with disabilities. We hope that professionals will not only include leisure instruction in their services but also provide educational opportunities that move beyond skill development to a more comprehensive strategy. This strategy should attempt to instill awareness of self, appreciation of leisure, self-determination and decision-making relative to leisure, knowledge and utilization of leisure resources, and development of skills in the areas of social interaction and recreation activities.

SYSTEMATIC PROGRAMMING FOR LEISURE EDUCATION

Introduction

Agencies providing leisure services should have a clearly delineated purpose statement to guide their service delivery. Based on this purpose statement, goals should be generated that further specify the intent of the department or agency. After a statement of purpose and goals has been generated, the practitioner must then develop specific programs that make the department's goals operational (Peterson and Gunn, 1984). According to the authors, a *specific program* is defined as a set of activities and their corresponding interactions that are designed to achieve predetermined objectives selected for a given group of clients, implemented and evaluated independent of all other specific programs. Peterson and Gunn suggested that some major aspect of treatment, leisure education or recreation participation should be addressed in each specific program. The specific programs contained in this text will be devoted to the service area of leisure education.

The Specific Programs

Specific leisure education programs have been included in this text lend assistance to practitioners who provide programs to develop satisfying leisure lifestyles. The development of appropriate leisure lifestyles should be an integral training component of all individuals. Programs that increase the rates of leisure involvement for participants provide opportunities that enhance the quality of their lives (Hopper and Wambold, 1978). Therefore, individuals must be taught a comprehensive range of leisure skills (Nietupski and Svoboda, 1982). To assist practitioners in achieving this goal, the authors have compiled twelve leisure education programs that have been divided into two major sections. The specific programs were developed based on experiences of the authors with input from practitioners and students. The newly developed specific programs reported in the text have yet to be implemented in their current form. The first section will contain one specific program for each of the six leisure education components identified in the first chapter of the text. As a result, there will be a specific program for each of the following six areas included in the section *"Specific Leisure Education Programs: Components"* : (a) leisure appreciation, (b) awareness of self in leisure, (c) self-determination in leisure (d) making decisions regarding leisure participation, (e) knowledge and utilization of resources facilitating leisure, and (f) social interaction. The second section will contain six specific leisure education programs that concentrate on recreation activity skills. The following leisure education programs have been included in *"Specific Leisure Education Programs: Activities"* : (a) swimming, (b) walking, (c) gardening, (d) bowling, (e) volleyball, and (f) softball.

Format for the Specific Programs

The format for the specific leisure education programs in this text is a revised version of an approach developed by Peterson and Gunn (1984). Each specific leisure education program contains:

(a) a program title,
(b) a purpose statement,
(c) program goals,
(d) enabling objectives,
(e) performance measures,
(f) content description, and
(g) process description.

To accommodate the varying acquisition rates of different participants, sequencing of the individual sessions is not included in this text. Practitioners are encouraged to sequence the material according to the needs of the specific people they serve. Practitioners should view each aspect of the specific program as a starting place for implementation of their leisure education program. Therefore, practitioners are encouraged to make changes to the programs to meet the individual needs and interests of the people they serve. This text will provide practitioners with information required for developing a leisure education program. The components of the format for each specific program have been clearly described by Peterson and Gunn.

Each specific leisure education program is identified by a title that reflects the program purpose. The twelve specific programs contain a concise, one-sentence *statement of purpose* describing the intent of the leisure education program from the point of view of the recreation department. The purpose statements are comprehensive, yet concise and clear to the reader (see Figure 4.1).

Program goals (identified by Peterson and Gunn as Terminal Program Objectives) are included in each program to further delineate the purpose of the program. The program goals are written as general participant outcome statements that specify what participants should gain from participating in the program. The goals specify whether the intent is to increase awareness and sensitivity of a particular concept, develop an understanding of knowledge associated with a specific area, or acquire specific skills related to successful leisure participation.

The program goals for each specific leisure education program have been divided into a number of behavioral units identified as enabling *objectives*. According to Busser (1990), objectives are the specific intended measurable outcomes of the program that serve as the anchor for the design of the program. The objectives are written using behavioral terms that describe the outcome that is desired from the participant.

Performance measures have been developed that correspond with each enabling objective. "The performance measure is a statement of the exact behavior that will be taken as evidence that the intent of the enabling objective has been achieved." (Peterson and Gunn, 1984, p. 101). Therefore, the performance measure must specify the exact criteria and conditions under which the behavior identified in the objective must be achieved. The performance measure specifies the measurement procedure that will be employed to determine if participants completed the objective. Therefore, the performance measure must permit examination of a sufficient amount of the desired behavior, a representative sample, to increase practitioners' confidence that the person achieved the objective.

Specific Program

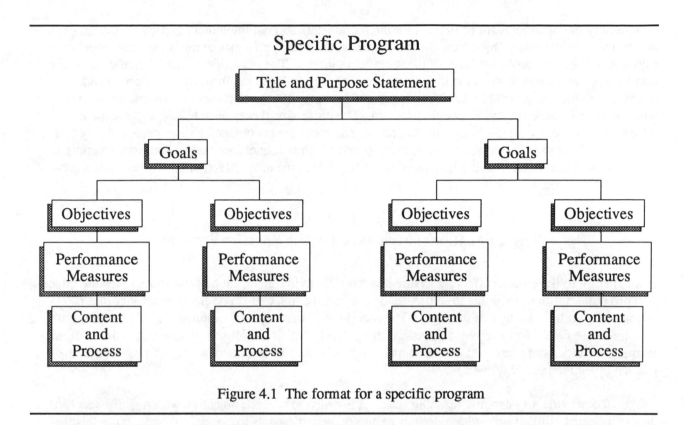

Figure 4.1 The format for a specific program

The majority of information contained in the specific programs describes the content and process required to conduct the program. The *content* contained in the specific program "is what is to be done in the program to achieve the intent of the enabling objectives." (Peterson and Gunn, 1984, p. 113). An attempt has been made to specify a sufficient amount of material to act as a starting place for program delivery. Frequently, tasks associated with the objectives were analyzed and the components presented in a step-by-step fashion.

Although identification of the material for the content is extremely important, it is not sufficient when planning a leisure education session. Many of us have experienced a teacher who obviously had command of the material (the content) but was an ineffective educator. The failure of some educational experiences to maintain participants' attention and result in knowledge and skill acquisition, as well as retention is highly dependent on the way in which the material is presented. The "*process* refers to the way the content is presented to the clients." (Peterson and Gunn, 1984, p. 118). Therefore, the way in which each element of the content will be presented is delineated in the specific programs in the process section. The programs incorporated visual aids, demonstrations, discussions and debriefings, orientation and learning activities, and conclusions. This was done as an attempt to create an enjoyable, organized environment that results in development of awareness and appreciation, knowledge acquisition and retention, and skill enhancement.

The information contained in the format for the twelve specific programs is designed to encourage practitioners to provide systematic leisure education for the people whom they serve. As stated at the beginning of this chapter, it is anticipated that practitioners will need to change some aspects of the programs provided in Section B and C to accommodate the unique talents of their clientele. For example, the number of objectives established in a specific program may be too many to complete during the amount of time participants will be available to attend the program. Therefore, the professional may choose only the most relevant objectives for the participants and not implement aspects of the program associated with the other objectives. In another situation, some performance measures may appear too rigorous for people enrolled in one of the specific programs. The practitioner should then modify the performance measures to meet the individual needs of the participants. In addition, when considering the needs of a particular group of individuals a professional may choose to present more detail associated with the content described in a specific program. The professional may wish to add to the existing information presented in this book. In general, practitioners are encouraged to use whatever they feel is useful from the examples presented in Sections B and C. Practitioners are also encouraged to apply their professional judgment in making modifications that produce the most effective leisure education program for the people they serve.

The Educational Structure for the Specific Programs

In an attempt to develop an effective leisure educational environment, each of the specific leisure education programs follows a similar structure. Each program begins with an orientation activity that is followed by an introduction of the topic. The specific programs contain descriptions of presentations that are immediately followed by discussions that actively solicit participant involvement. In addition, learning activities are presented with associated debriefings. Finally, conclusions are provided at the end of each objective (see Figure 4.2).

To provide a systematic teaching strategy, instruction on each objective within every specific program begins with an *orientation activity* to introduce participants to one another and to the leisure education material. The orientation activity is included to create an atmosphere of fun and enjoyment, as well as one that will stimulate learning and development. As a result, the orientation activities not only introduce the individual participants to each other but these activities provide a preview to the participants of what is to come in the program. These orientation activities are designed to set the learning climate. Since the first few minutes of an educational session are the most crucial, they should be interesting, relevant, and pleasant (Davis, 1974).

The orientation activity is followed by an *introduction* of the leisure education program. The introduction will briefly acquaint the participants with the topic and the objective to be covered in the session. The intent of the introduction is to provide participants with a preview of what is to come in the next minutes. According to McKeachie (1986), if people know what they are expected to learn from an educational session, they learn more of the material.

Once an introduction is provided, each objective contains a series of *presentations* and associated *discussions*. The combination of these two procedures allows the rapid dissemination of material during the presentation, complemented by discussions requiring participants to actively contribute to the learning process. McKeachie (1986) recommended the use of lecture to communicate information and model problem solving as well as the use of discussion to allow participants to practice problem-solving skills.

Enjoyable *learning activities* are incorporated into the educational program associated with each leisure education objective. The learning activities were developed to allow participants to practice the information they acquired during the presentations. The activities were designed to be fun and yet require participants to assimilate the relevant material. Immediate communication of their understanding of the material was required via the learning activities. Participants were put in situations where they were actively involved in an experience encouraging them to use the skills presented in the presentation.

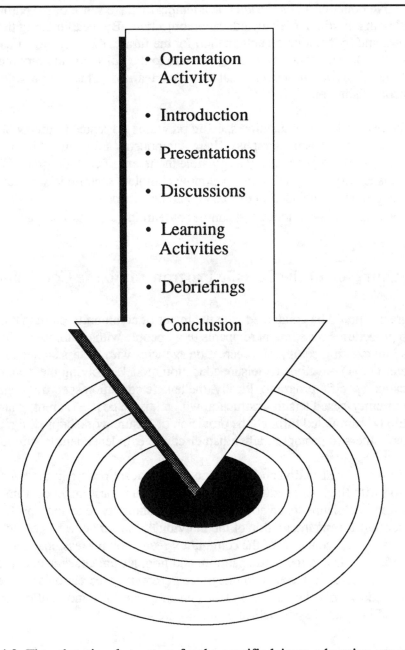

- Orientation Activity

- Introduction

- Presentations

- Discussions

- Learning Activities

- Debriefings

- Conclusion

Figure 4.2 The educational structure for the specific leisure education programs

The learning activities are immediately followed by *debriefings*. The debriefing consists of a series of questions that require participants to reflect on the learning activity. The debriefings encourage the participants to consider the relevance of the learning activity and identify accomplishments and barriers experienced in the learning activity. Results of an investigation by McDonald and Howe (1989) illustrated the value of debriefing in enabling self-expression, enlightenment, and empathy. The involvement of a facilitator who is an expert in the area and can establish a caring relationship with participants is also of value.

Each objective contains a *conclusion* that attempts to make sense of the entire educational process associated with a particular leisure education objective. By recapitulating the major points, proposing questions, and by creating an anticipation for the future, the practitioner can help participants learn (McKeachie, 1986). The conclusion brings closure to the objective and provides an opportunity for participants to ask questions and reflect on what they have learned. This can provide the participants with a sense of accomplishment.

Each of the twelve leisure education specific programs presented in this book contains the components described in the previous paragraphs. These components are included in an attempt to communicate as clearly, completely, and concisely as possible the intent of each program. The information in the specific programs is only a beginning in developing complete specific leisure education programs. Many aspects of the programs included in this text could be enhanced with the addition of more presentations and discussions, as well as an increased number of learning activities and debriefings.

Outreach of the Specific Programs Into the Community

The specific programs should be conducted with the intent of community participation. Therefore, systematic follow-up procedures for some participants (e.g., people with disabilities) should be developed to place participants into existing community recreation agencies with the assistance of leisure coaches. Dattilo and St. Peter (1991) developed a leisure education model involving the development of a structured leisure education specific program. Ideally, the leisure education specific program is accompanied by systematic community-based leisure instruction with a leisure coach. Parent, guardian and/or sibling participation should be stimulated through the provision of leisure workshops designed to increase the ability of significant others to promote, rather than discourage, independent leisure functioning.

Community-based instruction and education of significant people in the lives of individuals can occur in conjunction with the leisure education specific programs or it may occur immediately following formalized instruction. A leisure coach could meet with community recreation professionals and provide consultation and support for the integration of the individual. Leisure coaches could be available to respond to the questions and concerns of the community recreation professional and act as advocates for both recreation professionals and the participant. In addition, leisure coaches may provide assistance to participants as needed, while they engage in integrated community recreation activities. As the environment begins to respond to individual needs and the person gains skills and confidence, the presence of the leisure coach could be faded systematically (see Figure 4.3).

Possible Specific Program Areas

Leisure service providers are concerned with increasing the leisure repertoires of their consumers. As individuals' repertoires of skill expand as a result of participation in a leisure education program, there should be a corresponding increase in their abilities to make effective choices related to leisure and to make progress in gaining mastery over a significant portion of their lives. The determination of which activities to include in leisure education programs becomes a complex task requiring assessment of individual needs and preferences. It is important to remember that the activities selected for inclusion in a program are the conduits through which the provision of opportunities to develop skills and abilities occurs.

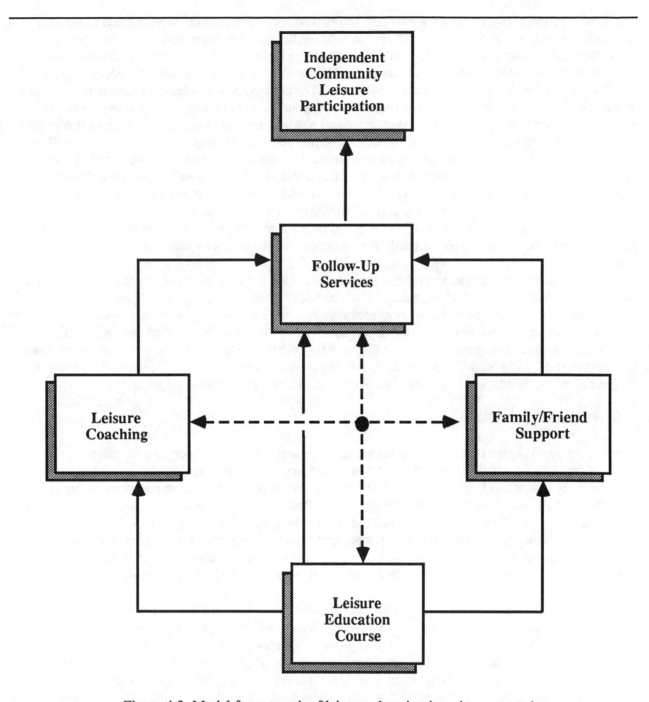

Figure 4.3 Model for outreach of leisure education into the community

After practitioners have completed a thorough assessment of needs and preferences, appropriate decisions are made which to seek to "match" the skills and desires of the program participants with the demands and opportunities present in the activities selected for inclusion in the program. Although it is universally recognized that needs and interests vary greatly across individuals and groups, many people do share some common needs. Three typical needs of people today are: (a) fitness, (b) lifetime interests, and (c) social interaction. Therefore, the authors have included two specific leisure education programs that focus on fitness, two on lifetime interests, and two on social interaction. Walking and swimming programs are included in this text to address the need for fitness. Although there are many benefits associated with swimming and walking, a major advantage is that people often achieve fitness goals when they engage in these activities consistently. Frequently, the primary reason for people engaging in swimming and walking is to increase their fitness. The development of lifetime interests is possible by participation in the leisure education programs on gardening and bowling. Many activities can be performed throughout a person's life. Gardening and bowling are two examples of activities that people can continue to engage in across the life span. These two activities are enjoyed by children, as well as adults. The specific leisure education programs devoted to softball and volleyball were included because these activities often require and promote social interaction between and among participants. Although many activities can involve social interaction, such as swimming, walking, gardening, and bowling, the activities of volleyball and softball were chosen because they require team participation. Inherent in team play is the need to engage in social interaction with fellow team members. Many people participate in these two activities primarily for the opportunity to interact with others.

The authors are not suggesting that these activities are the best suited, or the only activities that can be used as vehicles to achieve the stated goals and objectives of the programs. These activities are included because they are available in most communities, participation requirements are within the reach of most people, and leadership requirements are not difficult to obtain. In addition, depending on the circumstances, they each generally possess the potential to lend themselves to the development of fitness, lifetime interests, and social interaction skills (see Figure 4.4). The model that is provided for these activities can be easily adapted to any number of other activities a professional might choose.

Leisure Education for Fitness

Most professionals agree that all people, including those with disabilities, need to maintain adequate levels of physical fitness (Dattilo, 1986). Despite this agreement on the need for fitness and the commitment of many practitioners to promote it, many participants in leisure education programs are substantially below the fitness levels of their same-age peers. Possible reasons for lower fitness levels of some individuals (e.g., people with disabilities) include delayed physical development, lack of opportunity to participate in those activities that promote fitness, and decreased expectancy to perform motor skills (Wade and Hoover, 1985). According to Wade and Hoover, the problem of appropriate physical fitness is a result of the lack of opportunity for individuals with disabilities to participate in fitness activities.

In recognition of the need to provide opportunities for individuals to achieve and maintain a desired level of fitness, this text contains two specific leisure education programs that were developed primarily to accomplish this purpose. The first program focuses on the development of *swimming* skills, while the second is a *walking* program. Both of these programs were developed because they are readily available to many individuals. In addition, people can generally control the frequency, length, and rigor of their participation in these programs. Typically, swimming and walking are relatively inexpensive pursuits and do not require a large number of people for participants to enjoy engaging in them. In many communities, participation in swimming is possible on a year-round basis. Walking is also an activity that can be accomplished throughout the year. The accessibility of these two programs, together with their potential for enhancing the physical fitness of participants, has resulted in people of all ages actively engaging in these pursuits. Therefore, the acquisition of those skills needed to participate in swimming and walking may result in a lifetime of age-appropriate leisure participation, as well as the achievement and maintenance of an appropriate level of physical fitness.

Figure 4.4 Possible areas for concentration for leisure education

Leisure Education for Lifetime Interests

Discovering and maintaining interest in activities that can be sustained over long periods of time is an important component of many individuals' leisure lifestyle. Activities that allow participation at different levels of involvement and throughout various life stages are especially appealing as long-term interests. Those activities that demand high levels of physical exertion offered in formats that emphasize competition do not easily lend themselves to becoming lifelong interests. Instead, they often discourage former participants, and reduce their level of involvement to that of being a spectator. Leisure education programs should provide opportunities for the acquisition and development of skills, abilities, and interests in activities that can be engaged in for a lifetime, with the individual participants controlling the frequency and intensity of their involvement. To illustrate the opportunities for people to develop interests and acquire skills needed for lifetime pursuits, the specific leisure education programs of gardening and bowling are included in this text.

Gardening is an activity that is appropriate for people of all ages and is especially popular with adults. It provides individuals with opportunities to gain a sense of competence in a context that promotes an understanding and appreciation for the environment. Gardening also provides opportunities for people to enjoy the outdoors while they participate in an activity of their choosing. Although gardening primarily occurs in the outdoors, there are numerous opportunities to reap the benefits of gardening in an indoor environment. Many people believe the major benefits that come from gardening are focused on the observation of the miracle of life in plant form and the acceptance of the responsibility of nurturing that life. Often, tangible results are produced through gardening such as food and flowers. Gardening can be an activity in which young people easily engage, as well as a source of enjoyment and satisfaction well into the late years of life. It is also an activity in which the participants can regulate the scope and depth of their involvement.

In addition to gardening, *bowling* has been included in this text. Bowling is another activity that can be enjoyed by people of all ages. It is an activity that is readily adaptable for people with various disabilities. Bowling provides numerous opportunities for individuals to make choices and express themselves. Participants can determine the level of competition with which they are comfortable. Bowling is very appropriate as a lifelong interest.

Both gardening and bowling provide opportunities to develop skills and interests that can be used for a lifetime. In addition, people often enjoy these activities as an active participant rather than focusing on the product. For instance, the responsibility associated with caring for a living plant can bring joy into the lives of people, while bowling with a group of friends provides excellent opportunities for fellowship and fun.

Leisure Education for Active Socialization

As previously discussed in the text, inadequate social behavior is a major problem for some individuals (e.g., people with disabilities). If integration into the community is recognized as one of the legitimate purposes of leisure education programs, the provision of opportunities for the acquisition and refinement of social interaction skills is necessary. Social interaction skills are the basis of meaningful friendships. They are also the foundation upon which social integration and the ability to function effectively with small and large groups is based. Social interaction skills can be acquired only if there are purposeful plans designed to teach participants about these skills, coupled with opportunities for participants to apply them in practical, real-life situations. Such opportunities are available in leisure education program activities where participation is both required and enhanced by interaction with others.

Two specific leisure education programs have been included in the text that provide numerous opportunities for social interaction. *Softball* is presented because of its popularity with people of all ages and economic backgrounds. Typically, softball is inexpensive and provides an opportunity for active participation in the outdoors with a large group of individuals. Another activity often available in many contexts is *volleyball*. Volleyball can be enjoyed in many different environments, ranging from structured league play to pick-up games in the backyard, with any number of people playing. The contexts for softball and volleyball provide numerous opportunities for people to interact. The higher the quality of interaction, the greater the benefits derived from participation. Social interaction skills derived from participation in these activities can be successfully applied in many other life situations.

Conclusion

This chapter provided an overview of the format, structure, outreach capability, and areas of concentration related to the specific programs contained in this text. The suggested format for the specific programs provides a systems approach to the provision of leisure education services. To provide an organized educational structure to the specific programs, each objective for every program included an orientation activity, introduction, presentations, discussions, learning activities, debriefing, and a conclusion. A model was presented to encourage practitioners to stimulate integration through leisure education within the community that incorporates a leisure education course, leisure coaching, family and friend participation and systematic follow-up. Finally, leisure education programming that addresses fitness, lifetime interests, and socialization was recommended.

DEVELOPING AND CONDUCTING LEISURE EDUCATION PROGRAMS

Introduction

This text will provide the reader with information about the conceptualization of leisure education and some examples of specific leisure education programs. The specific programs contained in this text are not intended to be depictions of complete programs. Rather, they will provide a starting point for practitioners and students to begin systematic instruction of leisure education. Therefore, practitioners and students are encouraged to develop additional leisure education goals, objectives, content, process and any strategies that increase their ability to educate the people they serve. While this additional information is being developed, careful consideration relative to conducting leisure education sessions should occur. This chapter will provide some suggestions for students and practitioners to consider when developing and conducting leisure education programs.

This chapter is based on the work of Dattilo and Sneegas (1987), who presented suggestions to practitioners attempting to lead recreation activities. The material has been adapted and revised to address the concerns of conducting effective leisure education sessions. It will provide information on preparation and planning of a leisure education session, as well as suggestions for effective service delivery. Concerns related to the appropriateness of leisure education sessions, the environment, and knowledge of the program will be featured in the section devoted to preparation and planning. Suggestions for presentation of sessions will be divided into introduction and explanation, actual implementation of sessions, and bringing closure to sessions devoted to leisure education.

Preparation

Session Appropriateness

When preparing and planning to lead a session on leisure education, it is important for the recreation professional to determine the appropriateness of the session, both for the participants and for achieving preestablished goals and *objectives*. If, for example, the professional wished to select a leisure education session for a group of teenagers with mental retardation, the session would need to have appropriate leisure education content and be of an appropriate level for the cognitive functioning of the group. After establishing the goals and objectives associated with a specific leisure education program, practitioners should determine the degree of *rigor associated with the content*. In conjunction with a thorough examination of the program content, the professional must conduct an accurate *assessment of the participant* to determine the appropriateness of the content. Assessment data should be compiled relative to the participants' skills, interests, and needs. After analysis of the session has been conducted, the assessment of the client has been performed, and the goals of the program have been determined, the appropriate *match* of an session with the participant can occur. The ability of the practitioner to match the session content with the skills of the participants is strongly influenced by the manner in which the practitioner plans to present the content. The intended presentation strategy, *the process,* requires the specialist to determine how the material will be presented (e.g., the level of material to be communicated, the rate of information dissemination, the amount of practice, the use of audio visual aids, the number and type of learning activities, the amount of participant involvement).

In addition to these procedures for determining appropriateness of a leisure education session, the professional should also consider issues of time and safety. One of the more difficult aspects of conducting leisure education programs is determining the *amount of time* required for presentations, discussions and learning activities. It is very important to choose those activities that can be properly initiated and completed. The practitioner should examine the time allotted for the session and then determine the approximate length of time needed to successfully conduct the session. *Safety* must be considered continuously by the professional. A proactive posture should be assumed to anticipate and prevent problems. Figure 5.1 identifies considerations in determining the appropriateness of leisure education sessions.

Environmental Concerns

As practitioners plan to conduct a session devoted to leisure education, they should consider characteristics of the existing environment. Thoughtful consideration of the arrangement of the environment can aid in creating an enjoyable atmosphere for learning and active participation. Arrangement of *furniture*

Figure 5.1 Considerations in determining appropriateness of leisure education sessions

and recreational and educational *equipment* and the establishment of *boundaries* prior to the arrival of participants may alleviate confusion and boredom for them. Another approach is for practitioners to engage participants in these preparatory tasks. This may increase their sense of involvement in the overall experience.

Examination of equipment to be used during the session in advance of actual implementation can prevent practitioners' confusion and embarrassment. Electrical devices such as cassette tape players and record players should be tested, as well as the tapes and records to be used. *Examination of resources* at the session site, such as electrical outlets, should also be made to increase the likelihood of the equipment working when needed. Alternative plans should be developed in the event of equipment failure (see Figure 5.2).

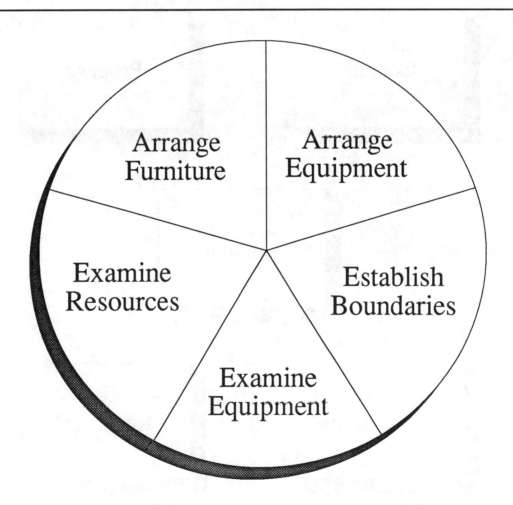

Figure 5.2 Actions to take to resolve environmental concerns
when preparing for a leisure education session

Knowledge of Session

Another important step in planning and preparing to conduct a leisure education session is for the practitioner to have a thorough *understanding of the content and process* employed in that session. The professional should review the content and process associated with the particular leisure education objective and practice communicating the information to other people (see Figure 5.3).

An understanding of the *sequence of events* will encourage the practitioner to conduct a cohesive session rather than one that involves interruptions and appears disjointed. The use of transitions from one portion of the session to another will allow participants to better understand how components of the leisure education session relate to each other. Practitioners should apply a sequence that initially uses introductory activities, if the participants do not know each other, and then alternate between presentations, discussions, learning activities, and debriefings.

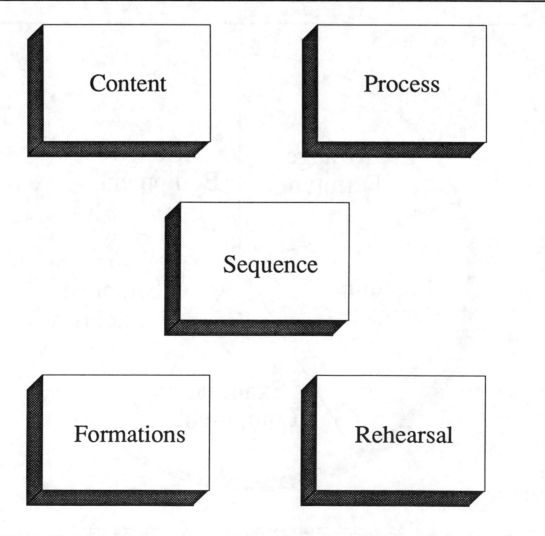

Figure 5.3 Information to acquire to gain knowledge about the leisure education system

When preparing for a session on leisure education, the professional should consider the most appropriate *formation* for the participants. A circle may be a more appropriate formation when discussion is desired, while rows may be used when observation is important. The nature of the content and the proposed process, along with the intended outcomes, should determine the chosen formation.

Many practitioners have shared the experience of believing they have a thorough understanding of an session until they actually attempt to engage the participants. Communication of the intent of the session and specific directions provided during the session may not be as clear to participants as they are to the practitioner. Therefore, once the professional has considered all of the aforementioned steps, it is extremely useful to *rehearse* the session.

Presentation

Introduction and Explanation

A leisure education session should begin with an effective introduction and explanation. Regardless of the skills practitioners may possess, if they do not gain the attention of the participants, the session will not be successful (see Figure 5.4, next page). Practitioners can *develop a consistent signal* allowing participants to know when the session is ready to begin. A signal may involve the playing of background music prior to a session and then stopping the music when the session is to begin. Another signal that can be used is the flickering of lights.

Once a signal is given, it is useful for the professional to *recite the title* of the leisure education program, the goals and objectives to be addressed, and the name of any learning activities employed during the session. The naming of the leisure education program, possibly accompanied by some instruction related to the name, will allow participants to refer to the program more accurately in the future.

Sometimes practitioners may feel they must raise their *voices* to gain participants' attention. However, at times, practitioners can attract the participants' attention by lowering their voices instead.

If some participants are not yet paying attention to the practitioner, the *proximity* of the participant to the practitioner may be considered. The professional can often gain participants' attention by moving closer to these individuals. This action allows the recreation professional to gain participants' attention without disrupting introduction of the session. Moving closer to a participant also allows practitioners to avoid accidentally reinforcing the behavior an inattentive participant.

One of the most exciting aspects of an session can occur during the *grouping* of participants. This critical component of leadership is often not adequately considered and may result in some participants being bored, embarrassed, or rejected. Alternatives to the traditional method of "number call" and "choosing sides" should be employed to stimulate interest and eliminate cliques.

Grouping is an excellent time to provide opportunities for leisure education by having participants group and regroup according to how they perceive themselves relative to leisure. For instance, the professional might ask all participants who consider themselves to be more like "leaders" during their leisure to form one group and those who consider themselves "followers" to form another. Once they are arranged in these groups, participants may be encouraged to discuss why they chose that group. This technique may not be feasible when it is important to develop groups of equal number.

Providing participants with a playing card is another possible way to group people. Participants will then be asked to form a group with those people with the same card color (two groups), the same suit (four groups), or the same number (groups of four). By providing them with a concrete cue (the playing card), this approach reduces the likelihood of participants forgetting which group they belong to. It also allows the specialist to regulate the size of the group. The number of ways specialists group participants is limited only by the specialists' imagination.

When explaining an session, practitioners should consider how they are positioned relative to the participants. Proper *positioning* should allow each participant to adequately observe the specialist and hear what is being said.

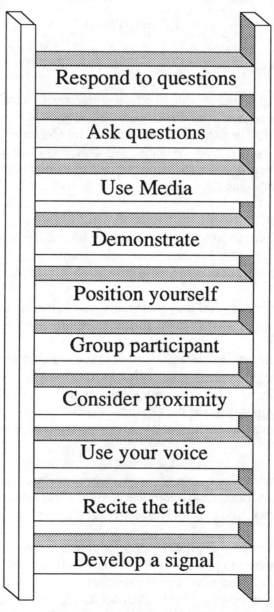

Figure 5.4 Steps to follow when introducing and explaining a leisure education topic

The practitioner should use the four "C"s when providing *directions* for a session. The directions for a session (a) should be clear to the participants, (b) should be concise by stating only information critical to comprehension, (c) should be complete so as to give participants all information needed to successfully complete identified tasks, and (d) should compare the identified activity and learning tasks to activities and tasks familiar to participants.

Practitioners often discover that some participants have difficulty understanding verbal directions. Therefore, it is helpful to use *demonstrations* in the introduction or explanation of a topic. Inclusion of additional prompts, such as the use of *media,* may also allow the professional to better introduce the session.

One of the most difficult skills to master when conducting a leisure education session is the ability to provide opportunities for *questions* and then effectively respond to the questions. The act of frequently pausing during instructions can provide a greater opportunity for participants to raise concerns. Professionals should also evaluate participants' understanding of the directions. To evaluate their understanding, the professional can either ask specific questions or provide the participants with the opportunity to ask questions. During a question and answer exchange, the practitioner must make every attempt to accurately respond to a question posed by a participant. If practitioners are unable to answer relevant questions, they should acknowledge the fact that they do not know and describe to participants what actions can be taken by the profesional or the participants to answer the question.

Implementation

After a session on leisure education has been explained and introduced, it is time to implement the session (see Figure 5.5, next page). Throughout the implementation process, the practitioner should provide adequate *encouragement* to participants. More encouragement is typically given when individuals are first learning a skill, as opposed to practicing a skill that has previously been mastered. The professional should attend to those individuals demonstrating understanding, as well as those participants who may require additional instruction. The type of acknowledgments should be systematically altered to maintain the interest of the participants.

Practitioners should provide participants with *assistance* when needed. It is important that they maintain a balance between providing participants with assistance and encouraging independent behavior. If participants are encountering difficulty completing a task, the practitioner may need to provide feedback to the participants about their performance. It is often less embarrassing if group corrections are made, rather than singling out individuals. For instance, during a practice period you may notice one of the participants performing a skill incorrectly. You can obtain the entire groups attention and demonstrate the correct skill with all participants modeling your behavior, rather than identifying the person performing the skill incorrectly. Group corrections allow practitioners to maintain participants' attention without focusing their concentration on a participant who is encountering difficulties.

Practitioners should continuously monitor their *verbal delivery* style. The professional's voice should be loud enough to be heard and of an appropriate pitch. People with auditory impairments often have difficulty hearing higher tones, and many people find a very high-pitched voice to be distracting. In addition, the pitch and volume of the practitioner's voice should vary to avoid a monotone quality of speech. The delivery speed of speech should be closely monitored by the professional. The participants' attention will often be lost if the speech is too slow, resulting in boredom, or too fast, resulting in confusion.

Practitioners can make the participants feel as if they are being spoken to directly by establishing *eye contact.* A sense of concern and interest can be communicated by directing one's gaze at an intended audience. The directions of practitioners' bodies and their stance can also communicate interest. Their movements can either accentuate their presentation by providing helpful embellishments and visual representations of speech, or detract from their presentation if their actions are idiosyncrasies irrelevant to the presentation.

Closure

Just as it is important for the recreation professional to introduce a concept effectively, it is important to thoughtfully terminate a session (see Figure 5.6). Adequate closure provides participants with a sense of accomplishment, as well as encouraging participation for future involvement. It is generally helpful to *end a session while interest is high,* rather than allowing participation to gradually fade.

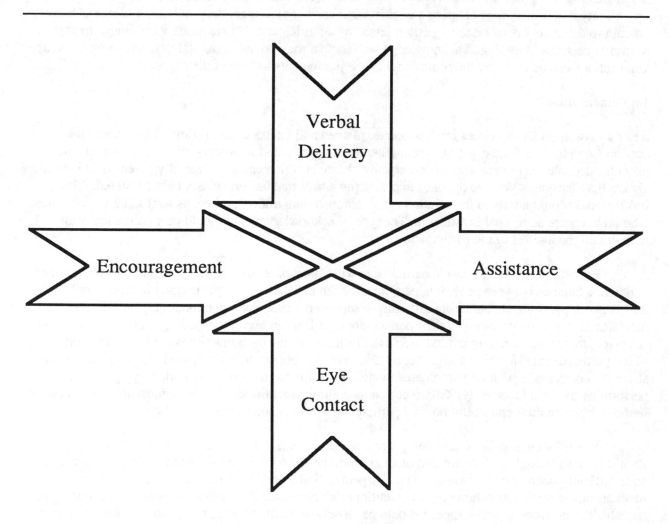

Figure 5.5 Consideration when implementing a leisure education program

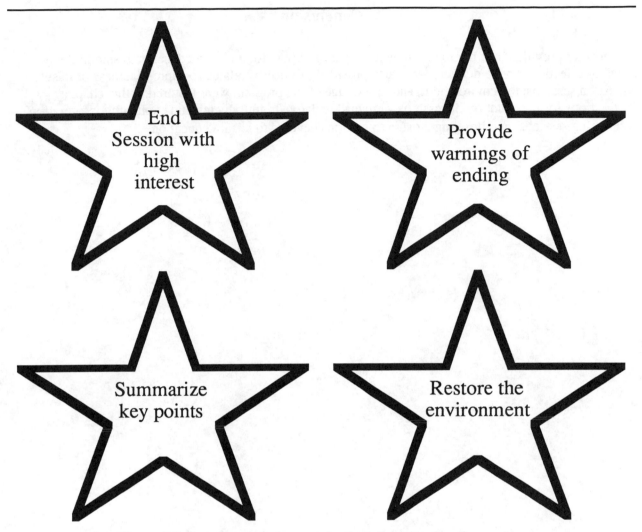

Figure 5.6 Steps to take when conducting a leisure education system

Rather than ending a session abruptly, the practitioner may *provide warnings* to participants that the session is coming to a close. For example, the professional might say that a few minutes remain in the session and encourage participants to begin completing their assigned tasks. In another situation, the professional may announce that there is only time for two more questions, again notifying the participants that the session is winding down.

A useful technique for providing adequate closure is to *summarize* the preceding events. Helping the group to reconstruct what was done and the purpose therein allows for continued participant involvement to the end of the session.

A final consideration in ending a session is *environmental restoration*. Practitioners and participants should leave the area where a leisure education program was completed in better condition than when they arrived. Participants should be encouraged to become actively involved in restoration and cleaning activities. With a little creativity, cleaning tasks can be effectively incorporated into a lcisure education session.

Conclusion

The chapter provided information on how to prepare and plan for a leisure education session. Suggestions for effective service delivery were also provided. Concerns related to appropriateness of leisure education sessions, the environment, and knowledge of the program were featured in this chapter. Suggestions for presentation of sessions were made relative to introducing and explaining information, conducting sessions, and bringing closure to sessions devoted to leisure education.

ADAPTATION OF LEISURE EDUCATION PROGRAMS

Introduction

The specific leisure education programs presented in this text have been designed generically; that is, the programs were not developed with a particular population in mind. Instead, they were designed for people experiencing barriers to a satisfying, enjoyable and meaningful leisure lifestyle. The programs were designed in this fashion to facilitate greater application by practitioners working in a variety of settings attempting to provide leisure education for people possessing different abilities. We must admit, however, that the absence of the identification of a particular group of individuals associated with each specific program does have its shortcomings. Some practitioners may need to adapt the programs to meet various individual's needs. We do not suggest that the programs in this text can be used as is by all practitioners. What we do believe is that the programs provide a significant starting point from which practitioners can adapt and expand their leisure education services.

This chapter, devoted to adaptations, is designed to encourage practitioners to adapt the information presented in the specific programs as necessary. When needed, these adaptations should permit professionals to meet the varying needs and abilities of the people receiving leisure services. The suggestions for adaptations are not intended to be all inclusive. They are, however, intended to describe some options available to practitioners to make adjustments intended to facilitate active leisure participation for all people.

General Considerations

Emphasis on The Person First

Individualize Adaptations. A key to adapting leisure education programs is to consider the individual needs of each participant. Because many people possess differing levels of skills and experience a variety of consequences as a result of different disabling conditions, practitioners are encouraged to individualize their adaptations.

Focus on Abilities. A person first philosophy also requires practitioners to focus on participants' abilities rather than on their disabilities. Too often, assessments associated with leisure education content areas are such that they initially identify what participants cannot do. Next, practitioners design adaptations to accommodate this limitation. Perhaps a more useful procedure may be to initially focus on the skills and abilities of participants and then make adaptations building upon these skills. When people's abilities become the focus of attention, practitioners are more likely to allow participants to be as independent as possible; therefore, they will tend to avoid stifling these individuals by making unnecessary adaptations that fail to capitalize on skills they possess.

Match Challenge and Skills. Each leisure education program contains learning experiences that possess a certain degree of challenge. In addition, prior to conducting a leisure education program, practitioners should systematically assess the skills and interests of the people for whom the leisure education program is designed. Then, when conducting leisure education programs, professionals will be in a position to better achieve the delicate balance between the challenge of specific activities and the skills of the participants. If an imbalance exists between the degree of challenge of a program and the participants' skills, barriers may be created to leisure participation. For instance, if a specific leisure education learning activity is too easy for participants, boredom often results. However, if a learning activity is too difficult, frustration can occur. One way to reduce these barriers is through adaptation. Adaptations can permit modification of the challenge associated with a leisure education program to meet the abilities of the participants. Once adaptations are made, they must continually be adjusted to meet the changing skills of the participants. Figure 6.1 illustrates the need for considering the person first when making adaptations.

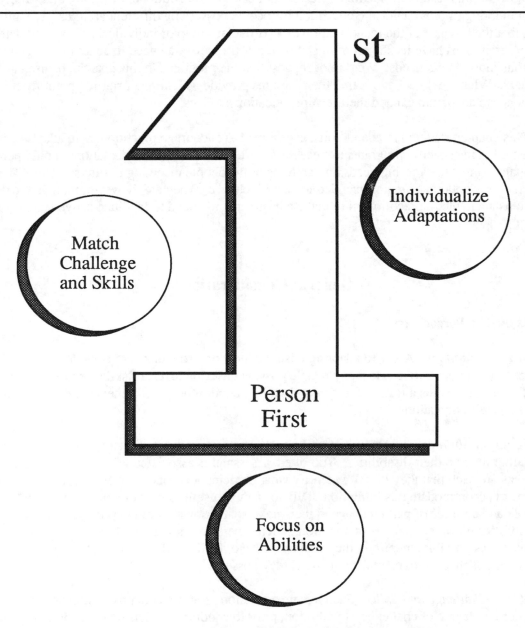

Figure 6.1 Emphasizing the person first when making adaptations

Encouragement of Participant Autonomy

Facilitate Independence. When practitioners adapt a leisure education program to permit participation, they should design the adaptation to encourage the individual to participate as independently as possible. Therefore, modifications should decrease the ability of participants to rely on others for assistance and provide people with disabilities with increased opportunities to actively participate in leisure as independently as possible. Since leisure education is designed to increase independence, practitioners should adopt the goal of independence when adapting leisure education programs.

Determine Necessity of Adaptation. Because many people with disabilities experience barriers to leisure participation, some practitioners may be quick to change a leisure education program. In addition, changes may be readily made to a given program because recreation practitioners are often highly skilled at modifications. Sometimes these changes are made with the knowledge of the general characteristics of a group rather than with explicit information about the specific participants. Although this practice may be practical in some situations, it may also create a problem. Some aspects of leisure education programs may be changed when they need not be. Therefore, it is important for practitioners to examine each adaptation and decide if it is actually necessary.

View Adaptations as Transitional. Adaptations to leisure education programs can permit active participation for persons with a wide range of knowledge and skills. The very nature of leisure education implies that individuals will learn and change. As this takes place, skills and knowledge fluctuate. Many individuals receiving therapeutic recreation services will develop skills and knowledge associated with leisure participation. Therefore, if an adaptation was made at one time, it may no longer be appropriate because the individual has now acquired the abilities to participate without any adaptations. At that point, the adaptations may impair, rather than encourage, leisure participation. Other people participating in leisure education programs may possess degenerative or progressive conditions that require continual modifications. A previous slight adaptation to a particular learning activity may be insufficient later to provide the person with the opportunity to participate. In any case, practitioners must be willing to adopt the view that any adaptations they make to a given situation may need to be altered in the future. Figure 6.2 (see page 60) illustrates the need for encouraging participant autonomy when making adaptations.

Participant Involvement in Adaptation Process

Discuss adaptations with consumers. In almost every aspect of recreation planning, practitioners are encouraged to consult with consumers regarding their opinions and desires. A critical task in motivating people to take part in leisure education programs is to encourage them to perceive that they have input into their program. Active involvement in shaping a leisure education program can provide individuals with a sense of investment that may increase their motivation to initiate and maintain participation. This principle applies as well to adapting aspects of the leisure education program. Discussions with participants may provide practitioners with valuable information on methods to adapt the activity and instill feelings of control and commitment by the participants. When participants do not currently possess the skills to effectively communicate their feelings and ideas toward an adaptation, then observations can be used to obtain input from these consumers.

Determine feasibility of adaptation. Involving participants in the process of adapting leisure education programs can provide practitioners with a means to determine the feasibility and usability of the adaptation. If participants feel that the adaptation detracts from the program, their motivation may be

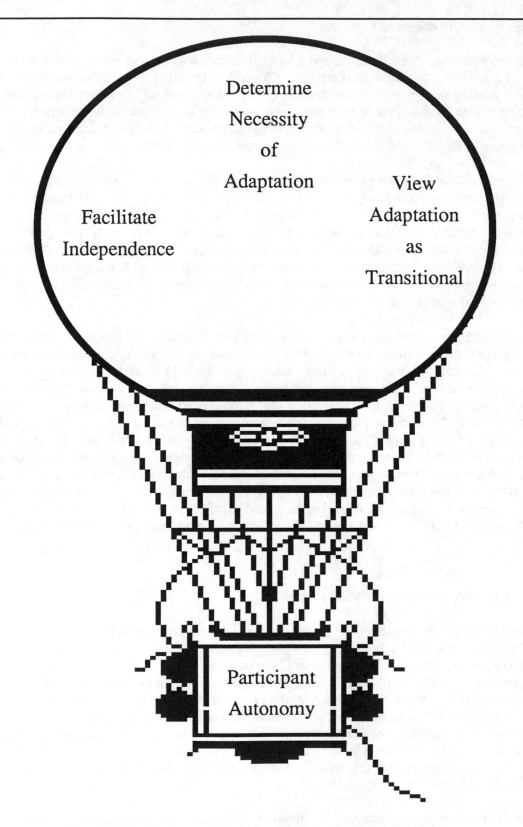

Figure 6.2 Facilitating participant autononomy when making adaptations

reduced. Therefore, asking participants their opinions of adaptations and encouraging them to make suggestions for different adaptations can enhance the ability of recreation professionals to make feasible adaptations. Sometimes, practitioners may go to great lengths to adapt a specific learning activity, only to find that as a result of the adaptation people are no longer interested in participation. Discussion with consumers prior to and during adaptations can help encourage active leisure participation following adaptations.

Ensure safety of adaptations. The most critical element to remember when making changes to any recreation program is safety. Commercially available equipment, materials, games and many other aspects of a leisure education program typically have been tested and retested to determine their safety for potential participants. Anytime an adaptation is made, the previous research conducted by the manufacturers is compromised and associated safety claims change. Therefore, practitioners must examine and evaluate any program they adapt and consider the safety of participants. One strategy to help practitioners evaluate the safety of an adaptation is to actively seek participants' input regarding ways to ensure and increase the safety associated with a given aspect of a leisure education program. Figure 6.3 illustrates the need for soliciting participant involvement when making adaptations.

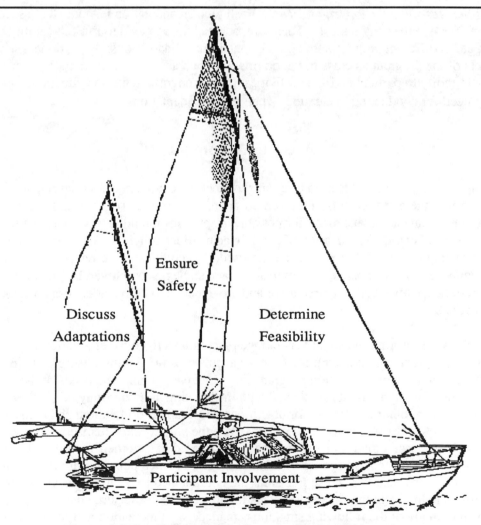

Figure 6.3 Involving participants when making adaptations

Evaluation as a Critical Element

Conduct Systematic Observations. When adaptations are made to specific aspects of a leisure education program, practitioners should continuously observe individuals participating in the program. Observations of individual participation should allow practitioners to determine if the adaptations are achieving their intended goals. These observations provide practitioners with the ability to examine unanticipated difficulties participants may be experiencing relative to the adaptations. Continuous observations put practitioners in a position to be able to understand the effectiveness of the adaptations.

Make Necessary Adjustments. Observations provide practitioners with the opportunity to discover problems with adaptations. When problems are identified, practitioners must then be willing to respond to any difficulties associated with adaptations. This willingness to change an adaptation must stem from the belief that even if a great deal of time and energy is put into a given task, it may need to be altered to permit active leisure participation for persons with disabilities. A slight adjustment to an aspect of a leisure education program may make the difference between active and meaningful participation or failure.

Consider Resemblance to Original Task. Each time an adaptation is made, that aspect of the program becomes less like the original task. Therefore, adaptations can tend to limit the ability of individuals to participate in different programs that do not contain such adaptations. Practitioners should attempt to keep aspects of the program as close to the original program as possible to encourage participants to generalize their ability to participate in the activities in other environments and situations. Figure 6.4 illustrates the need for conducting evaluations when making adaptations.

Areas of Adaptation

When adapting existing leisure education programs to meet the unique needs of participants, practitioners should consider the many aspects of a given program. A multitude of facets associated with leisure education programs that can be examined for possible adaptations intended to increase participation. For the purposes of this text, identification of possible adaptations of leisure education programs will be divided into five major areas: (a) materials that are used, (b) activities, (c) environment in which the activity is conducted, (d) participants, and (e) instructional strategies employed by practitioners. These five areas are not necessarily mutually exclusive and are intended to help readers organize the suggestions on adaptations.

The following information should encourage practitioners to consider a variety of aspects of the leisure education programs when attempting to make adaptations facilitating leisure participation. The *materials* used during a leisure education program can be adapted to meet the needs of the participants. In addition, the specific requirements associated with the learning *activities* may be changed. The *environment* provides another alternative for practitioners to adapt to bring about active involvement for participants. Efforts toward adaptation can be focused on the *participants* themselves to increase the likelihood of their success. Finally, practitioners are encouraged to turn their focus of adaptations inward and examine possible ways to modify *instructional strategies* to teach persons with disabilities about leisure. The descriptions related to these five areas are not intended to be all inclusive but are designed to assist practitioners in beginning to develop plans for adaptations for leisure education programs. Examples given in many of the following situations are made with recreation activities, rather than leisure education activities, to provide instances that readers are familiar with and to enable visualization of the suggested adaptation. Figure 6.5. (see page 64) illustrates five areas to consider when making adaptations.

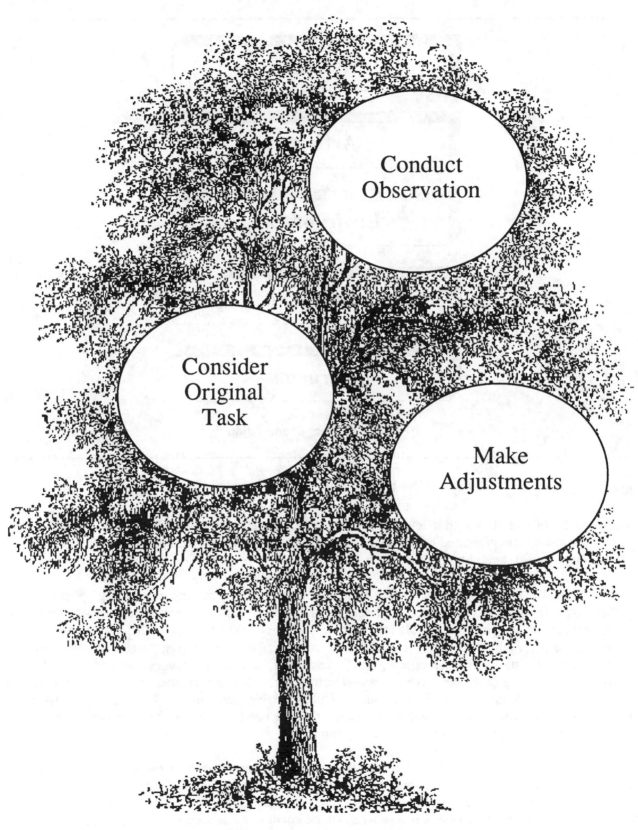

Figure 6.4 Collecting evaluations when making adaptations

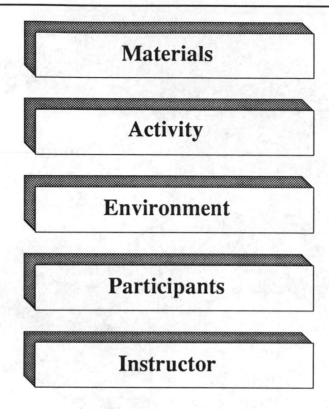

Figure 6.5 Areas of adaptation

Materials

Many aspects of materials used in leisure education programs can be adapted. Examples of methods for adapting materials are presented below relative to the following areas: (a) size, (b) speed, (c) weight, (d) stabilization, (e) durability, and (f) safety.

Size. The size of materials can be adjusted for participants by making objects (e.g., puzzle pieces) larger for those having difficulty grasping small objects. Tape can be wrapped around handles to increase their size and permit manipulation. Conversely, other people may have difficulty grasping larger objects (e.g., felt tip markers) so smaller ones could be used. Decreasing the size of objects that are intended to be inserted into an opening (e.g., a basketball) can increase success, while making the opening larger (e.g., a basketball hoop) may also lessen the requirements of an activity. Large colorful cards can assist individuals with visual problems in playing table games designed to teach about leisure. If individuals are participating in racquet sports, the racquets can be shortened for more control or lengthened to allow participants to cover more ground.

Speed. Some individuals with disabilities may experience problems associated with gross motor coordination. A coordination problem can be quickly observed as individuals respond to moving objects. One way to increase the success of persons responding to objects is to reduce the speed of the moving object. Air can be removed from a ball so when struck it will move at a slower speed. Wedges can be placed under any angled surface to reduce the incline on which a ball may be placed to slow the ball (e.g., pinball) or increase the angle of a ramp (e.g., bowling) to increase the speed of the ball.

Weight. The weight of objects can be adjusted to meet the strength of the participants. Wooden and metal materials can be exchanged for those that are made from plastic or rubber. For instance, plastic balls, Nerf™ balls and balloons can be substituted for heavier balls in some situations, while lighter plastic or Nerf™ bats can be used in lieu of heavier metal or wooden bats.

Stabilization. Sometimes people who have unsteady movements may be prevented from using some expensive technology because they are likely to break the equipment. Suction cups and clamps can be used to stabilize the material (e.g., a tape recorder). In this way the person can use the material without fear of accidently damaging it. People participating in craft projects that possess grasping skills with only one portion of their bodies can be assisted by securing the project to a board or table (e.g., tape paper to a desk for drawing or painting).

Durability. Material for leisure education programs should be made durable. Duct tape is often helpful in reinforcing many different pieces of equipment. Game boards and playing cards should be laminated to increase the ability of the objects to withstand regular use. Velcro™ can also be used to secure objects that need to be removed at different times.

Safety. When making any adaptations to objects it is critical to continuously evaluate each adaptation in reference to safety. No toxic substances should be added. If changes to objects occur, they should be examined and any sharp edges removed. The dangers of ingestion of objects and suffocation should be anticipated. In all cases, problems should be anticipated and steps taken toward prevention of any injuries. Figure 6.6 (see page 66) illustrates considerations when adapting materials.

Activities

Many traditional recreation activities can be adapted to encourage more active participation by individuals with disabilities. Some examples of methods for adapting activities are presented below relative to the following areas: (a) physical aspects, (b) cognitive requirements, and (c) social conditions.

Physical aspects. Individuals receiving recreation services vary a great deal in terms of physical strength, speed at which they move, endurance, energy level, gross motor coordination, eye-hand coordination, flexibility, agility and many other physical skills. To adapt a physical requirement of a program, the typical *number of people* associated with a game can be changed. For instance, the number of people participating in volleyball can be changed from six to ten people for persons with limited speed and agility. People with limited endurance and strength may benefit from making the requirements to complete an activity not as strenuous by reducing either the *number of points* needed (e.g., 8 points to win a Ping-Pong™ game rather than 21) or the *length of time* a game lasts (e.g., reduce the time to complete an activity from 30 to 15 minutes). While learning some activities, the *physical movements* can be changed by requiring participants to walk instead of run (e.g., basketball). For those individuals who have impaired mobility, changing the required *body position* from standing to sitting may provide opportunities for participation (e.g., throwing a Frisbee™). Some people receiving leisure services may have limited physical endurance; therefore, practitioners should provide more *opportunities to rest* during certain events, such as hiking.

Cognitive requirements. Some people may encounter problems associated with cognitive requirements as a result of a disabling condition. For example, people may have impaired cognitive functioning because of a trauma due to a head injury, neurological disorders such as cerebral vascular accident, the developmental disability of mental retardation, learning disability due to dyslexia, mental

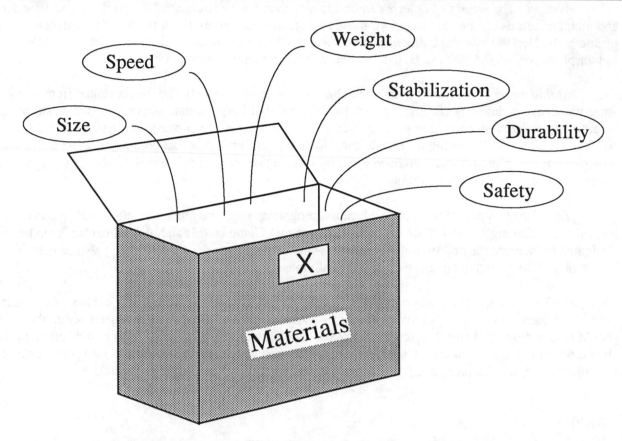

Figure 6.6 Considerations when adapting materials

health problems such as depression, or from the side effects of medications taken for physical illness. To accommodate these individuals' reduced cognitive functioning, the *rules* associated with different games can be changed. For instance, if short term memory appears to be a problem for persons with head injuries, the number of cards used in a card game can be reduced (e.g., rather than using all cards in a deck in a game of concentration, only the face cards can be used). People who do not yet possess counting skills may be able to play a game by substituting matching of colors, instead of requiring the recognition of numbers or words to move game pieces. If the requirements for *scoring* during an activity are too difficult for participants, changes can be made such as having people with mental retardation initially keep track only of the number of pins they knock down, rather than using scoring procedures associated with calculating spares and strikes. Some individuals with learning difficulties may require some minimal assistance with reading cards used for a table game. Practitioners may wish to change the game from requiring individuals to play alone to participation with *partners*. Often, teams of participants can be developed that allow the individual team members to complement each others' skills and abilities. In addition, friendships may be developed from the team interaction.

Social conditions. Many people participating in leisure recreation programs are doing so because they may be experiencing barriers to their leisure involvement. Frequently, these barriers are related to problems encountered in a social context. Some individuals may be intimidated by activities requiring larger groups. A reluctance to participate in larger groups may be a result of previous experiences associated with failure and perhaps ridicule. To assist people in gaining the confidence needed to participate in large group activities, practitioners may initially choose to *reduce the number of people* required to participate in an activity and begin instruction and practice of an activity in small groups or, if resources are available, on a one-to-one basis. For instance, social skills instruction related to learning how to make friends may be conducted initially with a few individuals. As participants acquire the social skills, the context could be expanded to include more participants. The pressure involved in some activities involving direct competition against another team may be extremely threatening for some people with disabilities. A person's failure to perform may result in the entire team losing to an opponent. This failure can decrease confidence and self-esteem and contribute to a reduced motivation to participate. One approach to adapting an activity could be changing the activity so *cooperation is emphasized* and direct competition against another team is eliminated. To accomplish this cooperative atmosphere, practitioners may decide to eliminate the opposing team. The opposing team would be replaced by a series of established goals to be achieved by the team. For instance, in lieu of the traditional game of basketball, one team could participate by establishing goals related to making a basket (e.g., begin at the opposite end of the court, require all five team members to dribble the ball as it is brought down the court, attempt to make a basket in the least amount of time). Figure 6.7 illustrates considerations when adapting activities.

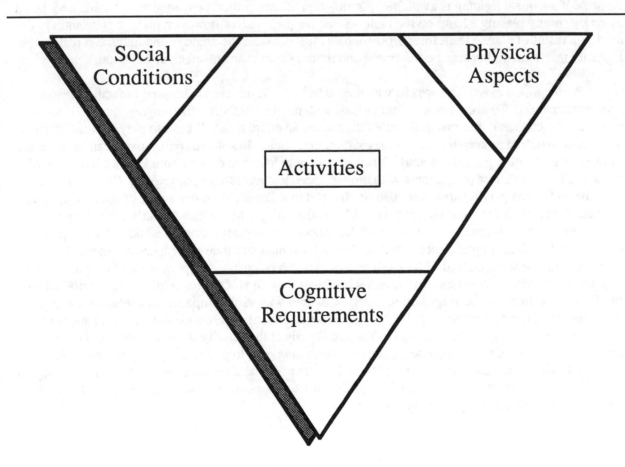

Figure 6.7 Considerations when adapting activities

Environment

The environment can play an important role in the ability of individuals to actively pursue leisure involvement. Practitioners may be in a position to adapt the environment in which leisure participation is intended to occur or to make recommendations for changing the environment. Because practitioners are attempting to provide leisure education in a variety of contexts, possible adaptations to the environment that relate directly to (a) sensory factors and the (b) participation area are suggested in this section.

Sensory factors. Participation can be enhanced for some individuals by simply manipulating the *sounds* occurring within the environment during participation. For instance, when playing a leisure education game, some people who are easily distracted may have difficulty concentrating when the game is being played in a multi-purpose room with other people present talking to one another as they engage in other activities. Moving the leisure education game to a small, quiet room where only people participating in the game are present may facilitate more active participation for some individuals. In addition, some people using hearing aids can experience difficulty when participating in a gymnasium because of the echoing effect that can occur. Placement of drapes and sound absorbing tiles near the ceiling may muffle some distracting sounds and allow persons with hearing impairments to hear and follow directions more easily. Providing an environment that permits people to see as much as possible is important when attempting to teach people. Therefore, practitioners should examine the context of an activity and determine if adequate *lighting* is available. Completion of craft projects engaged in at a table may be enhanced by simply placing a lamp on the table. Some people's vision, however, may be substantially impaired as a result of glare. Therefore, professionals must consider the angle of the lights and realize the possibility that some lights may be too bright and inhibit rather than enhance participation.

Participation area. The area in which an activity is played can be adapted to facilitate more active participation. To accommodate individuals with reduced mobility, the *playing area* used for an activity can be changed. For instance, rather than using an entire baseball field to play kick ball, participants can be required to keep the ball in play within the infield. In softball, participants can be required to hit to one side of the pitchers mound allowing more individuals to cover a small area. Reduction of the playing area can allow participants with limited speed to successfully participate. *Boundaries* designating the end of the playing areas can also be changed to make people more aware of these designations. Wider chalk marks can be used on a soccer fields to allow people to see more clearly when they are approaching an area designated as out-of-bounds. Ropes can be placed along a walking trail to permit individuals with visual impairments to follow the trail and maintain their awareness of boundaries associated with the walking trail. The *surface area* can also be changed to permit some people to more easily access activities. A person who uses a wheelchair may be able to join a hiking expedition when some firm foundation has been applied to a trail. Children with visual impairments, who are using playground equipment, may be signalled that they are moving toward different equipment by changes in textures on the ground and adjacent walls. The *facility* where the activity is conducted may be also changed. For instance, ramps may be placed in a swimming pool to permit access by persons with limited mobility. In addition, the water in the swimming pool could be lowered to only two or three feet to initially accommodate those people with significant fears associated with water. Figure 6.8 illustrates considerations when adapting the environment.

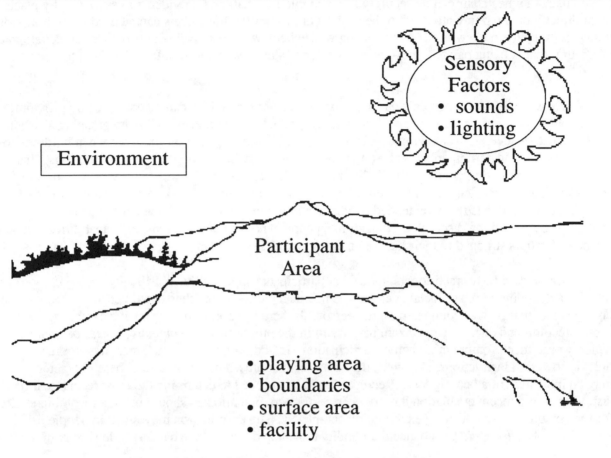

Figure 6.8 Considerations when adapting the environment

Participants

When considering adaptations, the changes which were previously mentioned in this chapter associated with materials, activities and the environment often come to mind. If, however, adaptations are viewed as changes that are made to facilitate active leisure participation, then another category for making adaptations may be established. The participants themselves may actually be changed to encourage active participation in those experiences that bring them joy and satisfaction. Modifying the way individuals are (a) positioned, (b) aided with prostheses and sensory aids, (c) provided with opportunities for increased mobility, (d) are able to communicate, and (e) the skills they possess can dramatically influence their level of participation. This section of the chapter provides suggestions on how to make some of these adaptations to the participants.

Positioning. The optimal condition for individuals to learn and actively participate is for them to be in a "ready state." That is, participants should be sitting or standing as erect as possible, not in discomfort, able to reach materials and objects associated with an activity, and facing in the direction of the activity. Pillows, foam wedges and support belts can be used to help individuals prepare for activity involvement. If individuals who have limited muscle control wish to read a book, a triangle wedge can be placed under their chest with the larger side close to their neck and the smaller side near their stomach. The book can be placed on the floor and can be controlled with their hands. In another situation, a person using a wheelchair can be securely fastened into the chair and provided access to toys by placing them directly on a lap tray attached to the chair. For swimming, life jackets can be used to support individuals as they learn to swim. If people using wheelchairs wish to actively contribute to the development of a mural that is being painted, they can be positioned sideways to the wall to allow them to reach the mural.

Prosthesis. Many people's participation in recreation activities can be enhanced by providing prosthetic support for the individuals. For instance, people may encounter difficulty grasping a fishing pole because of severely weak wrists. A brace may be used to help support the wrist when holding the fishing pole. Some participants involved in a nature walk may have a limited range of motion. This reduced range of motion would typically limit their ability to bend at the waist and collect samples of leaves, bark and other items used for debriefing sessions following the walk. Providing them with a scooping device attached to an extended handle would permit them to participate more actively in the walk and accompanying discussion. In addition, people who have limited grasping capabilities can paint, if a paint brush is strapped to their hand by using Velcro™.

Sensory aids. If practitioners notice that participants appear to have difficulty seeing demonstrations or responding to other visual cues used to facilitate participation, they should check to see when the last eye examination was completed on the person. If there has not been a recent eye exam, the specialist should recommend one. The eye exam may result in the prescription of *corrective lenses or contacts* which would then promote more active participation. In addition, some participants may not respond quickly to verbal instructions. At times, they may seem confused or inattentive. These characteristics may be indicative of a hearing loss. Records should be checked to determine the most recent hearing test. Again, if a recent evaluation has not been performed, practitioners should make a recommendation for the person to have a hearing examination completed. The examination may result in people using some form of *hearing aid* to enhance their ability to hear and thus reduce barriers to leisure participation.

Method of mobility. Individuals receiving recreation services may have reduced mobility as a result of many different conditions. For instance, mobility may be limited because of a degenerative disease, such as multiple sclerosis, a traumatic accident resulting in injury to the central nervous system, such as a spinal cord injury, or from an orthopedic disorder resulting in reduced range of motion, such as arthritis. In response to this reduced mobility, people may be helped to move by using a variety of aids (e.g., wheelchairs, crutches, walkers, braces). Although their primary means of getting around may be effective most of the time, they may be able to participate more actively in some leisure education activities with a different variation of the mobility aid. For children who use wheelchairs and are participating in activities in a gymnasium, a *scooter board* can inject fun and increased speed into the activity. For instance, when playing kick ball, children could use scooter boards to move about. This adaptation could be made in conjunction with an activity modification by establishing the rule that participants use their hands to hit the ball and then move to the bases quickly on the scooter boards. Some people's personal wheelchair may be the most appropriate for their daily experiences. There are, however, many commercially available *sport wheelchairs* designed specifically for the requirements associated with particular types of sports. For instance, there are chairs designed for activities that require a great deal of rapid turning. These types of chairs may be used when participating in activities such as tennis, basketball, and racquetball. Other people may wish to participate in races on or off the track. These individuals frequently use chairs designed for speed and movement in a forward direction. Practitioners should examine the participation patterns of persons with reduced mobility and consider variations to their typical mode of transportation that may enhance leisure involvement.

Mode of communication. Some individuals cannot meet their communication needs through standard forms of speech (Vanderheiden and Yoder, 1986). Therefore, practitioners must be willing to modify the required response mode for a particular activity. These individuals may require augmentative and alternative communication systems (AAC) to fulfill their needs. AAC systems include those that are unaided (e.g., gestures, sign language, finger spelling), nonelectronic aided systems (e.g., communication boards or books containing symbols, words or pictures) and computer-based assistive technology producing speech synthesis and/or word printouts. AAC systems vary considerably according to message storage and retrieval systems, communication speed, and communication aid output capabilities (Vanderheiden and Loyd, 1986). Persons using AAC systems typically acquire their disabilities from congenital physical disabilities (e.g., cerebral palsy, mental retardation), acquired neurogenic disorders (e.g., closed head injury, cerebral vascular accident), progressive neurological diseases (e.g., multiple sclerosis, muscular dystrophy) and temporary conditions such as those resulting from shock, trauma, or surgery. There is a large range of competencies and abilities across individuals using AAC systems (Kraat, 1985) resulting in an extremely heterogeneous population (Light, 1988). Practitioners must be open to these alternative forms of communication and be willing to change the required mode of communication for a specific activity to permit active participation by persons using communication systems other than speech.

Skills. As stated previously in the chapter, if an imbalance exists between the degree of challenge of a program and the participants' skills, barriers may be created to leisure participation. The majority of this chapter has focused on adaptations that can permit modification of the challenge associated with a leisure education program to meet the abilities of the participants. Practitioners, however, possess another option when attempting to assist individuals in matching the requirements of an activity. Leisure education is designed to *teach people skills and knowledge* that facilitate their ability to meet the challenges encountered when attempting to experience leisure. For instance, if people do not possess the skills to access public transportation to go to a fitness club, instruction related to use of public transportation will increase the ability of individuals to meet the challenges associated with enhancing their physical fitness. In addition, *systematic instruction* may need to occur within the facility with professionals and persons with disabilities to provide the opportunity for independent participation in community recreation programs. Through systematic instruction, practitioners can encourage individuals with disabilities to increase their skills and knowledge. In the most general sense, a change has been made in the individuals. The people have adapted themselves to meet the demands and challenges associated with a particular experience. Figure 6.9 illustrates considerations when adapting aspects of the participants.

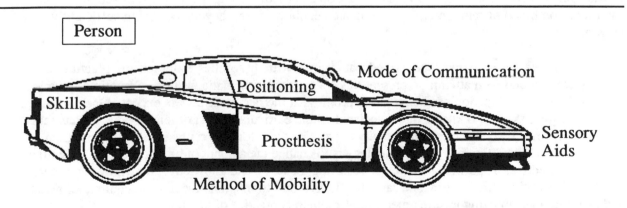

Figure 6.9 Considerations when adapting the person

Instructional Strategies

The four areas for making previously mentioned adaptations have required practitioners to focus their attention away from themselves and onto the participants, activity, materials and environment. The fifth and final area of consideration presented should encourage professionals to examine their practice of leisure service delivery. If people receiving leisure services are not developing leisure skills and knowledge at a rate consistent with their potential, there may be ways to improve the instructional strategies employed by the professionals to allow individuals to more effectively and efficiently meet their needs. The next section will address the following considerations related to instructional strategies: (a) establishment of objectives, (b) development of instructional steps, (c) implementation of practice, (d) inclusion of instructional prompts, (e) application of reinforcement, and (f) consideration of personnel.

Establishment of objectives. At times, consumers of recreation services may find it difficult to achieve preestablished objectives. Practitioners may continue to focus on the inability of individuals to achieve their objectives and thus create further difficulty. A possible problem may have occurred during the establishment of objectives, resulting in tasks that may be too difficult to master. If this occurs, practitioners should reassess the objectives and change them to meet the needs of participants. This is not to say that practitioners should develop objectives that are not challenging. In fact, they should be monitored closely for the possibility of having objectives that are too easily completed by participants. Rather than create frustration for both participants and practitioners as with overly rigorous objectives, the development of objectives demanding too little of the individuals can create an environment conducive to boredom and apathy.

Development of instructional steps. An extremely useful tool in providing leisure services is task analysis. Task analysis involves the segmenting of a task into components that can be taught separately. The instructional components can then be sequenced together to allow individuals to complete an identified task. The procedure of task analysis is used when attempting to teach a multifaceted task that may appear complex for participants. Although task analysis requires identification of components that, when accomplished in sequence, permit completion of the task, the number of components identified for any given task may vary considerably. For instance, in one situation the act of swinging a Ping-Pong™ paddle to hit a Ping-Pong™ ball may be divided into four steps, while in another circumstance the task may be divided into 10 components. The skills of individual participants should determine the level of specificity associated with a task analysis. Therefore, if people are encountering difficulty learning a skill, practitioners should examine the components being taught. They should determine if further delineation is needed for those individuals stuck on a particular component or if some components should be combined or removed to accommodate people who feel they are not being sufficiently challenged.

Implementation of practice. To educate people with disabilities about leisure, practitioners develop content and then attempt to present this content in a systematic fashion. Sometimes people enrolled in leisure education programs fail to progress at the rate practitioners expect. One reason people may not acquire skills and knowledge associated with a particular aspect of leisure education is that they may not have received sufficient opportunity to practice the information presented in the program. Another way to adapt the instructional strategy is to change the amount of practice associated with a particular objective. If participants are not acquiring the skills and knowledge, they may need more practice. Repetition through practice can allow individuals to integrate the newly acquired knowledge and skill into their existing leisure repertoire. Continuous practice of previously learned skills can increase the likelihood that individuals will maintain the skills over time. When planning practice sessions, practitioners should be creative and make these opportunities as interesting and fun as possible. Frequently, people do not acquire an understanding of a concept the first time they are presented with the idea. Practice provides experiences that permit repetition of concepts and ideas that enable people to retain that information more easily.

Inclusion of instructional prompts. As practitioners provide instruction, they may observe that participants are not responding to their directions. Therefore, they may wish to use prompts to assist participants. Prompts can provide auditory cues for individuals, typically through verbal instructions. There are, however, other forms of prompts that can be used. Environmental prompts can encourage participants involvement by simply manipulating the context in which an activity is provided. For instance, one way to encourage use of leisure education table games in a recreation lounge may be for the practitioner to place the games on tables in the room or open the closets where they are stored so that participants entering the area will see the games. Additional visual cues may be provided to stimulate participation. Modeling appropriate behaviors and providing systematic demonstrations may allow participants to see more clearly the desired leisure behavior. In addition, hand-over-hand physical guidance may permit individuals to feel the specific movements associated with participation and thus increase their ability to perform the skill correctly. Because, people may respond differently to various prompts, practitioners must examine their procedures and be willing to modify the way they are prompting participants to learn and apply new leisure skills.

Application of reinforcement. Sometimes practitioners mistakenly assume that the object or event they provide individuals to encourage the acquisition of leisure skills and knowledge is a positive reinforcer. The object or event, however, may not be perceived by the participant to be a reinforcer. Dattilo and Murphy (1987b) reported that reinforcers differ from one person to another. According to the authors, "selection of an object or event to serve as a positive reinforcer must be person specific; that is, it must be something that will effectively influence that individual's behavior" (p. 54). Therefore, practitioners must monitor the response of participants to a consequence in order to determine if it is truly a powerful enough reinforcer to influence behavior. If, over time, behaviors do not improve in response to administration of a specific item or activity, practitioners should be willing to make adaptations. Testing various items and activities until reinforcers are identified may provide practitioners with a systematic procedure for identification of reinforcers.

Consideration of personnel. Interaction between participants and practitioners is a highly complex process. Some participants may respond to some practitioners more enthusiastically than to others. Failure of some program participants to progress at an anticipated rate may be significantly influenced by the professionals who are delivering the services. Practitioners should closely monitor their interactions with participants as well as other personnel delivering leisure services. In-service training can be provided in an attempt to improve skills of practitioners. In addition, adapting schedules to accommodate both staff and participant needs may also encourage more effective implementation of leisure education programs. Figure 6.10 (see next page) illustrates considerations when adapting instructional strategies.

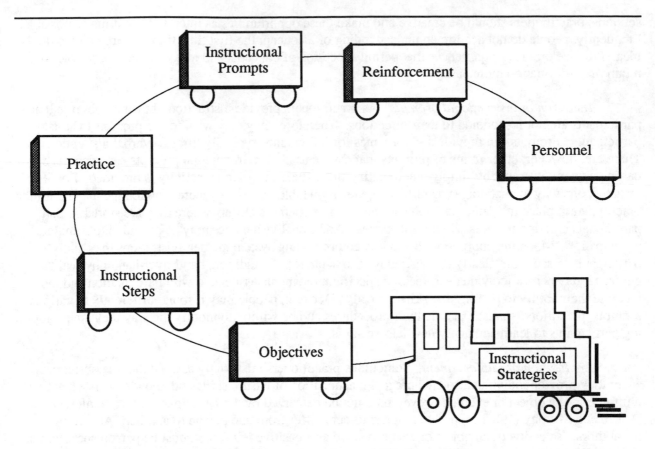

Figure 6.10 Considerations when adapting the instructional strategies

Conclusion

This chapter focused on ways to make adaptations. These adaptations should permit practitioners to meet the varying needs and abilities of the people attending leisure education programs. The suggestions communicate some options available to practitioners to make adjustments needed to facilitate active leisure participation for persons with disabilities. General considerations were initially presented in the chapter to provide guidelines when making any adaptation intended to promote leisure involvement. The remaining portion of the chapter was devoted to providing suggestions on adaptations related to materials that are used, the activity, the environment in which the activity is conducted, the participants, and instructional strategies employed by practitioners.

Section B

Specific Leisure Education Programs:
Components

Section B   Specific Leisure Education Programs: Components

1. Leisure Appreciation: Provide opportunities for participants to learn the definitions of leisure and leisure lifestyle, understand the role leisure plays in our society, become familiar with outcomes of leisure participation, identify barriers to leisure participation, and determine ways to overcome barriers to their leisure.

2. Awareness of Self in Leisure: Provide opportunities for participants to become aware of their attitudes toward leisure, understand factors that may affect their leisure participation, examine their past recreation involvement, consider their current recreation involvement, and identify possible preferred future recreation activities.

3. Self-Determination in Leisure: Provide opportunities for participants to learn about their personal successes in leisure, understand the importance of personal growth and responsibility for leisure participation, learn to express preferences, and understand how to be assertive.

4. Making Decisions Regarding Leisure Participation: Provide opportunities for participants to learn about the decision-making process needed for leisure participation, identify personal leisure participation goals and activities to achieve these goals, determine requirements of these activities and available personal resources needed for participation, and choose activities intended to achieve leisure goals.

5. Knowledge and Utilization of Resources Facilitating Leisure: Provide opportunities for participants to learn how to identify sources of information about leisure opportunities, identify specifics to solicit from information sources about leisure, and use printed/human/agency resources that facilitate leisure participation.

6. Social Interaction: Provide opportunities for participants to learn the dynamics of social interaction, gain knowledge about the appropriateness of social interaction behaviors, demonstrate verbal and non-verbal behaviors encouraging attention to speakers and exhibit verbal behaviors required of an effective speaker.

LEISURE EDUCATION: LEISURE APPRECIATION

Purpose, Goal, and Objectives

Purpose: Provide opportunities for participants to learn the definitions of leisure and leisure lifestyle, understand the role leisure plays in our society, become familiar with outcomes of leisure participation, identify barriers to leisure participation, and determine ways to overcome barriers to their leisure.

Goal 1: Demonstrate an appreciation of leisure.

Objective 1.1.   Demonstrate knowledge of the definitions of leisure and leisure lifestyle.
Objective 1.2.   Demonstrate knowledge of the role leisure plays in our society.
Objective 1.3.   Demonstrate knowledge of the outcomes of leisure participation.
Objective 1.4.   Demonstrate knowledge of barriers to leisure participation.
Objective 1.5.   Demonstrate knowledge of strategies to overcome barriers to leisure.

Goal, Objectives, and Performance Measures

Goal 1: Demonstrate an appreciation of leisure.

Objective 1.1: Demonstrate knowledge of the definitions of leisure and leisure lifestyle.

Performance Measure: Given paper and pencil, in five minutes participant will:
  (a) write a description of leisure that includes at least five of the nine following elements: freedom, choice, control, enjoyment, satisfaction, growth, responsibility, preferences, and self-determination, and
  (b) write a description of leisure lifestyle that includes four of the five following components: day-to-day, expression of leisure appreciation, leisure awareness, leisure skills, and in context of entire life,
with 100% accuracy on three consecutive occasions.

Objective 1.2: Demonstrate knowledge of the role leisure plays in our society.

Performance Measure: Given paper and pencil, in 15 minutes participant will:
  (a) describe four ways our society has changed during the past two decades that demonstrates an increased interest in leisure (e.g., increase in number of fitness centers, increase in sales of recreation equipment and apparel, creation of recreation programs at work sites, increase in number of community recreation programs for people with disabilities), and
  (b) give specific examples of two of these trends in the local community (e.g., community recreation programs for people with disabilities: "Programs are now accessible for everyone;" increase in sales of recreation equipment and apparel: "Everyone seems to be wearing jogging suits now."),
with 100% accuracy on two consecutive occasions.

Objective 1.3: Demonstrate knowledge of the outcomes of leisure participation.

Performance Measure: Given paper and pencil, in 15 minutes participant will:
- (a)   identify five possible outcomes of leisure participation (e.g., fun, self-esteem, relaxation, release of tension, acquisition of skills, increase in fitness, sense of freedom, perception of mastery), and
- (b)   for each of the five outcomes, identify one recreation activity that could facilitate that outcome (e.g., increase in fitness: jogging; fun: telling jokes; self-esteem: helping others in need; relaxation: yoga; release of tension: participating in martial arts),

with 100% accuracy on two consecutive occasions.

Objective 1.4: Demonstrate knowledge of barriers to leisure participation.

Performance Measure: Given a list of six factors affecting leisure participation (e.g., existing funds, free time, availability, societal role expectations, health, and skills), paper and pencil, in 10 minutes participant will:
- (a)   describe how these factors can be barriers to leisure involvement (e.g., existing funds: "not enough money,"; free time: "not enough time."), and
- (b)   identify one example of how each of the six factors may be a barrier in an individual's life (e.g., existing funds: "I only have $1.00, so I cannot go bowling."; free time: "It takes me so long to get dressed that I do not have enough time to go bowling."),

with 100% accuracy on two consecutive occasions.

Objective 1.5: Demonstrate knowledge of strategies to overcome barriers to leisure.

Performance Measure: Given a list of six barriers to leisure participation (e.g., existing funds, free time, availability, societal role expectations, health, and skills), paper and pencil, in 15 minutes participant will:
- (a)   identify two ways that each barrier could be reduced (e.g., lack of skills: "attend a class to learn the skill" or "adapt the materials associated with an activity"), and
- (b)   provide an example for each way identified to reduce barriers (e.g., attend class to learn the skill: "I do not know how to paint, but I am going to enroll in a painting class."; adapt the materials associated with an activity: "I do not have the strength to make a basket in basketball, so I am going to use a smaller, lighter ball and lower the hoop."),

with 100% accuracy on two consecutive occasions.

Goal, Objectives, Content, and Process

Goal 1: Demonstrate an appreciation of leisure.

Objective 1.1: Demonstrate knowledge of the definitions of leisure and leisure lifestyle.

1. Orientation Activity

Content: "We are going to participate in an activity that will help us to meet one another and get us started thinking about leisure. Please arrange your chairs in a circle. When it is your turn to participate, state your first name and a recreation activity that begins with the first letter of your first name. For example, if your name is John you could say jogging; if your name is Anne, you could say angling. Each person will repeat the preceding name and activity that was stated and then give his or her name and activity. I will select a person to start the activity and we will proceed clockwise until everyone has had his or her turn."

Process: Use this activity as an ice-breaker. When participants enter the room, have them arrange chairs in a circle. Explain activity. Activity continues until everyone in the group has had opportunity to introduce himself of herself.

2. Debriefing

Content:
   a.   Was it difficult to think of recreation activities when it was your turn? If so, why?
   b.   How do you think recreation activities relate to your leisure?
   c.   What did you learn about other group members?

Process: Conduct debriefing using above questions. Provide opportunity for each person to respond. Encourage those who did not contribute.

3. Introduction

Content: "Leisure and leisure lifestyle can be difficult ideas to understand. But if we can develop an understanding and appreciation of these ideas and act on the new knowledge that they will bring us, it can result in additional opportunities for us to get satisfaction and joy from our lives. The place for us to start is to examine the meaning of leisure and lifestyle."

Process: Introduce topic of defining leisure and leisure lifestyle.

4. Presentation

Content: "One of the reasons that leisure is difficult to understand is because it can be thought of in several different contexts and there is a lack of agreement about which context is correct. The absence of a precise definition will not stand in the way of us understanding leisure. In fact, the flexibility that is associated with leisure, the room for different interpretations of its meaning, may be one of its most appealing features. Leisure may be regarded as (a) activity, (b) as unobligated time, (c) as a state of mind or being, or as (d) a combination of activity, time, and state of mind.

"When leisure is regarded as activity, it is the activity that is the determining factor as to whether or not it is thought to be leisure. For example, washing the dishes, dusting, mowing the lawn, and doing laundry are activities that must be accomplished but they are not regarded as leisure. On the other hand, playing cards, swimming, going to the movies, and bowling are things that do not have to be accomplished and are usually thought to be leisure activities. The first examples are associated with a sense of obligation. They are things that must be done; they are like work. The second set of examples is not associated with any sense of compulsion; they are generally thought to be fun.

"The difficulty associated with thinking of leisure as activity is that sometimes activities that are thought to be fun do not turn out that way and activities that are thought to be compulsory (like work) can turn out to be fun. It appears that it is not the activity that is leisure; it is how we feel about the activity that helps determine whether or not it is leisure."

Process: Present information. Use board to list four ways of thinking about leisure. Underline the word "leisure" on the chalkboard as it is being discussed and list the following:

LEISURE

• activity
• unobligated time
• state of mind or being
• combinations of all three

5. Discussion

Content:
   a   What determines whether or not an activity is leisure?
   b.   Can an activity be leisure for some people but not for others? How so?
   c.   Can an activity be leisure at one time for a person but not at another time for the same person? How so?
   d.   Who determines whether or not an activity is leisure?

Process: Conduct discussion using above questions. Encourage all participants to contribute to the discussion.

6. Learning Activity

Content: "Each of you has pencil and paper. Think about recreation activities in which you like to participate and which you regard to be leisure. List five such activities on your paper. When you are finished, we will put the activities on the board and ask some questions about them."

Process: Explain activity. Provide pencil and paper. Allow sufficient time for thinking and writing. When participants are finished, ask them to take turns and read their activities aloud. List activities on board. Move to debriefing.

7. Debriefing

Content:
   a.   Are there activities on the board that you do not consider to be leisure for you? If so, which ones? Why?
   b.   What influence should your opinion have on someone who feels those activities are leisure?
   c.   How should other people's opinions influence your choice of activities?
   d.   What is your opinion of the diversity of activities that are listed?

Process: Conduct debriefing using above questions. Encourage all participants to contribute to the debriefing.

8. Presentation

Content: "Leisure can be thought of as unobligated time, the time an individual has remaining after work and self-maintenance requirements have been met. That is, when you are finished with work, school, family, hygiene, house and car maintenance and other similar responsibilities. This unobligated time is sometimes referred to as discretionary time. It is the time when an individual is free to choose what to do. The notion of choice is important. Choosing to participate in an activity that brings enjoyment and satisfaction is fundamental to this and other concepts of leisure."

Process: Present information on leisure as unobligated time. Circle the word "time" on the chalkboard as the content is being presented.

9. Discussion

Content:
    a. Is any time really free from obligation? How so?
    b. How often do we have the chance of making choices to please ourselves?
    c. Did you have a choice of whether or not to come to this session?
    d. What would have been the consequences if you had chosen not to come to here?
    e. Does this have any application in making choices for leisure? How so?
    f. How much time do you choose to take for leisure?

Process: Conduct discussion using above questions. Encourage all participants to contribute to the discussion.

10. Learning Activity

Content: "We have an activity period now but some of you are needed to help us get some work done. I am going to divide you into two groups, which we will call Group A and Group B. I need Group A to help me pull some weeds. Group B may remain inside and play with any of the games or equipment that is here."

Process: Explain activity. At beginning, do not reveal the purpose of the activity is to emphasize the difference between being required to do something and having a choice of what to do. Do not reveal that the groups will reverse roles midway through the period. Provide staff supervision for each group. Choose a task that has the connotation of work (e.g., pull weeds, wash dishes, sweep floors, shovel snow from sidewalk).

11. Debriefing

Content:
    a. How did you feel when you were told you were required to do a task?
    b. How did you feel when you were free to choose what you wanted to do?
    c. Can you compare the two feelings?
    d. How important is choice to the concept of leisure?

Process: Conduct debriefing using above questions. Encourage all participants to contribute to the debriefing.

12. Presentation

Content: "Leisure can be thought of as a state of mind or a state of being. It is characterized by feelings of freedom, of independence, of choice, of being in control, of creativity, reward and self-fulfillment, and of being competent. People enjoy participating in activities that result in these feelings. Experiencing these feelings is the reason why people choose to participate in certain activities. This concept is referred to as intrinsic motivation.

"The perception of freedom of choice and intrinsic motivation are the two supports on which rests the concept of leisure as a state of mind. This concept is broader than the concepts of leisure as activity or as unobligated time. It focuses on the feelings one experiences (the state of mind) rather than the activity or when participation takes place. This concept provides the flexibility needed to allow individuals to vary widely in their choice of activities and the time-frame in which those activities occur. It is the perception of the individual that is the basis of leisure."

Process: Present information on leisure as a state of mind. Make sure that each participant understands what is meant by the words "freedom," "independence," "creativity," "self-fulfillment," "competence," "intrinsic motivation," and "unobligated." Take time to assess their knowledge of these important concepts. Perhaps reviewing the definitions of these words may be useful for some participants.

13. Discussion

Content:
   a.   What is the meaning of intrinsic motivation?
   b.   What are some of the feelings that are the basis for intrinsic motivation?
   c.   Are you intrinsically motivated by any activities? If so, which ones?
   d.   How does leisure as a state of mind differ from leisure as activity or unobligated time?

Process: Conduct discussion using above questions. Encourage all participants to contribute to the discussion. Be sensitive to the terminology used. Review definitions of key terms, checking to see if participants understand the words associated with leisure as a state of mind.

14. Learning Activity

Content: "Chances for leisure are all around us. We are going to divide into groups of three or four and each group will go for a 15-20 minute walk in the area. Each group will be supplied with pencil and paper and one person in each group will be the recorder. As you walk, take note of the potential leisure opportunities you see. Each group should make a list of at least 10 opportunities. When you return, we will share the lists."

Process: Explain activity. Provide pencil and paper, designate one person in each group as recorder. If necessary, assign staff supervision for each group's walk. When groups return, ask them to read their lists. Put activities on board. Proceed to debriefing.

15. Debriefing

Content:
    a.   In which of the listed activities have you participated?
    b.   Which new ones would you like to try?
    c.   Are any of your favorite activities listed? If so, which ones?
    d.   What is your opinion of the diversity of activities listed?

Process: Conduct debriefing by using above questions. Encourage each participant to respond to at least one of the questions.

16. Presentation

Content: "If leisure is regarded as a state of mind, then leisure is more than special activities or events or free time. It can be the little things we enjoy in our day, such as talking to a friend, reading a newspaper, listening to a bird, or enjoying a sunset or a starry night. Leisure can be all the enjoyable things that we experience from day to day. This is referred to as a leisure lifestyle. Leisure lifestyle can be regarded as the way you approach daily living to get satisfaction from it. A leisure lifestyle can grow and develop or it can wither away. Your leisure lifestyle requires attention. A positive leisure lifestyle can provide additional opportunities for you to enhance the quality of your life."

Process: Present information on leisure lifestyle.

17. Discussion

Content:
    a.   What is meant by leisure lifestyle?
    b.   How would you describe your leisure lifestyle?
    c.   Would you like to change your leisure lifestyle? If so, how?
    d.   What would you need to do to change your leisure lifestyle?

Process: Conduct discussion using above questions. Encourage all participants to contribute to the discussion.

18. Learning Activity

Content: "We are going to do an activity entitled 10 Things I Enjoy. This activity should help you become more aware of your leisure lifestyle. Each of you will receive a pencil and a handout that has spaces for 10 activities. List as many activities as you enjoy that you can think of. After you have completed this, return to each activity and check the appropriate columns to its right. When you are finished, we will have a discussion focused on the activities you chose and any leisure patterns you may have noticed."

Process: Explain activity. Develop a handout containing 10 lines, with each line numbered in succession. To the right of the space for the activities, 14 columns should intersect the lines, forming a grid pattern. The columns should be headed as follows: (1) Something I Enjoy Doing, (2) Have Been Doing For Less Than Two Years, (3) Will Probably Do Two Years From Now,(4) Will Probably Be Doing After I'm 65, (5) Expensive, (6) Inexpensive, (7) Requires Risk, (8) Requires No Risk, (9) Group Activity, (10) Individual Activity, (11) Advanced Planning, (12) Spontaneous, (13) Requires Equipment, and (14) Requires No Equipment. Participants remain seated for this activity. Distribute pencil and handouts. Instruct participants to list their activities on these lines and check the columns that are appropriate for each activity. When participants are finished, proceed to debriefing.

19. Debriefing

Content:
    a. Did you notice any patterns after you checked the columns? If so, what were they?
    b. Does this give you any insight into your leisure lifestyle? How so?
    c. How will you make use of this information?

Process: Conduct debriefing using above questions. Encourage each participants to respond to at least one question.

20. Conclusion

Content: "Leisure and leisure lifestyle are important concepts. Although leisure can be thought of in several different ways, the two essential ingredients are freedom of choice and intrinsic motivation. If an individual can develop an appreciation for leisure and the potential benefits that can be derived from it, the possibility exists for an increase in the quality of that person's life. This could be a very significant accomplishment."

Process: Make concluding statements. Provide opportunities for questions.

Objective 1.2: Demonstrate knowledge of the role leisure plays in our society.

1. Orientation Activity

Content: "We are going to have a round-table discussion about society's attitude about leisure. Societal attitudes are often reflected in common sayings or expressions. These expressions are thought to represent knowledge or wisdom that has been present for several generations and has become part of our folklore. I want each of you to think about common expressions that reflect a social attitude about leisure or work. Each of you will be asked to share the saying which you thought of with the group and we will discuss its meaning. For example, someone might remember that 'All work and no play makes Jack a dull boy' is a common saying. This would lead to a discussion about the necessity for leisure in a balanced life. When it is your turn, introduce yourself to the group and share the saying which came to mind, even if you are not sure it relates to leisure."

Process: Explain activity. Write expressions on board. Encourage participation from all participants. If participants have difficulty in thinking of expressions, provide hints or give expressions yourself. For example:

> • Idle hands are the devil's workshop.
> • An honest day's work for an honest day's pay.
> • Families that play together stay together.
> • Play after your work is done.
> • Anything worth doing is worth doing well.
> • Winning is the only thing.
> • Play is the work of children.

2. Debriefing

Content:
    a. Do these expressions reflect society's attitude toward leisure or work? If so, how?
    b. Do any expressions have particular meaning to you? If so, which ones and why?
    c. Do more expressions seem to be supportive of leisure as a positive experience or do more of them seem to regard leisure as less significant than other parts of our lives?

Process: Conduct debriefing using above questions. Encourage each participant to respond to at least one question.

3. Introduction

Content: "An individual's attitude toward aspects of life is often influenced heavily by the attitudes of others. This is as true of attitudes toward leisure as it is of anything else. Many in our society believe that leisure is a waste of time; others model their leisure behavior after their work behavior. These attitudes have their roots deep in America's past. Developing an understanding of our past will help us better understand the present."

Process: Introduce topic of the role leisure plays in our society.

4. Presentation

Content: "Although several factors have played a role in shaping current societal attitudes toward lcisure, we are going to focus on two of the most significant historical ones from our past: (a) the Puritan Ethic and (b) industrialization. We are also going to identify and examine some current events and their potential effects on current attitudes toward leisure.

"Americans have long been influenced by a concept that is often referred to as the Puritan Ethic or the work ethic. It is a legacy that comes to us from the time of the early American colonists, specifically the Puritans who settled in the New England area. The Puritans were religious dissenters. As such, they were opposed to many of the beliefs and practices of the Church of England. Among the things to which they were opposed were the activities in which many English engaged in their free time. This included such things as cards, bowling, dice, dancing, and many other activities. The Puritans were opposed to these activities because the Church of England tolerated them. The Puritans brought this opposition with them to the American colonies.

"When the Puritans arrived in the New England region, they were faced with a harsh environment. Constant effort was required to make the countryside habitable and to produce food and other materials necessary for survival. There was no time for recreation and leisure; all efforts had to be focused on work. In the New England colonies, if people were not working, they were expected to be engaged in some type of religious activity. In this way, work and religion became closely associated with each other and anything that detracted from them was considered to be harmful or evil. This became the essence of the Puritan Ethic: work was not only necessary for survival, it was required for salvation. Conversely, leisure and recreation were sinful. Laws were made that provided for severe punishment of people caught engaging in recreation and leisure activities. As time passed and conditions improved, many of the laws and prohibitions against leisure were disbanded, but generations of Americans continued to be influenced by the Puritan Ethic."

Process: Present information on Puritan Ethic. Use visual aids such as pictures of the Puritans engaged in work and religious activities and the English engaging in recreation activities. Record key words on an easel. Show slides depicting this period in history.

5. Discussion

Content:
    a. Do you feel guilty if you engage in leisure before your work is done? If so, why do you think you feel this way?
    b. Do environmental and economic conditions still require that all of your efforts focus on work? If not, does it make any sense to be affected by the Puritan Ethic?
    c. What evidence of the influence of the Puritan Ethic exists in today's society?

Process: Conduct discussion using above questions. Emphasize idea that Puritan Ethic is good example of how conditions may be responsible for development of an idea or attitude to cope with those conditions. Emphasize that as time passes the conditions change, but the ideas and attitudes remain long after their usefulness has ended.

6. Presentation

Content: "Industrialization and its aftermath have also had a significant impact on American attitudes toward leisure. After the Industrial Revolution, machines performed most of the labor required to fuel the American economy. A belief developed that machines would release people from the toil and drudgery of labor, and workers would have a great deal of energy available to them. As industrialization progressed, a common work time was created for the majority of workers and a sense of time urgency emerged. Work sites were developed to make workers more efficient and productive. The American public was convinced to increase its consumption of the goods and services produced by the worker. The American economy was locked into cycles of production and consumption.

"Many American leaders believed that workers needed leisure and recreation during their nonwork hours. As a result, many urban parks were developed and opportunities for participation in recreation became widespread. American business leaders encouraged workers to participate in recreation, not because it was enjoyable and satisfying but because they believed that recreation would prepare workers to become even more efficient and productive. Thus, a cycle of work, recreation, work was begun. Leisure and recreation were not valued for themselves, but because they were believed to make better workers.

"Because the supremacy of work was not questioned, many people approached their leisure and recreation in the same way they did their work. People were unhappy unless their leisure and recreation were characterized by productivity, efficiency, and competition. Although a 40-hour work week became fairly standard and made greater quantities of nonwork time available, many Americans believed their leisure and recreation lacked quality."

Process: Present information on industrialization.

7. Discussion

Content:
a. Do you believe your attitude toward leisure has been influenced by our society's general attitude toward work and leisure? How so?
b. Have you had any experiences that can be related to a cycle of work, recreation, and more work? If so, what were they?
c. If leisure's only value is to prepare people to be better workers, how does this apply to people who do not work because of illness, disability, or retirement?

Process: Conduct discussion using above questions. Emphasize the relationship between societal attitudes and the way we feel about recreation and leisure. Review what is meant by industrialization. Encourage participants to recognize the different relationships between recreation and work.

8. Presentation

Content: "There have been several events in recent years that have had a significant impact on leisure in this country. Together, these events seem to signal a positive change in society's attitude toward leisure. Some of these events have been government actions, some have been from the business sector, and some are the result of general public opinion. For example, in the government, several laws have been passed that protect recreation resources, provide recreation programs and services, or ensure equality of opportunity, particularly for people with disabilities. In the business sector, there has been a great increase in the number of private businesses that offer recreation opportunities, and sales of recreation equipment and apparel have reached new heights. Public opinion polls in recent years have been consistent in reporting that the American public places a high value on leisure and recreation. It seems apparent that societal attitudes are undergoing a transformation regarding the significance of leisure in one's life."

Process: Present information on current events. Emphasize the impact recent events have had on our perception of leisure and the role it plays within our society. Use media to assist in the presentation by writing key words on an easel or chalkboard. The use of pictures or slides showing people engaging in various recreation activities may increase participants interest in the presentation.

9. Learning Activity

Content: "We have stated that several events of recent years have signaled a change in society's attitude toward leisure and its value. Each of you take a few minutes to think of an event or trend that is an indication of this change. For example, one could say the establishment of Great Basin National Park was an event signifying the federal government believes that leisure and recreation are important. Another example could be a statement to the effect that there has been a great increase in the number of private health and fitness clubs and that is evidence that people are willing to pay for leisure opportunities. Each of you will state the event or trend you think of with the group. Group members may ask questions or make comments related to the statements."

Process: Explain activity. Allow sufficient time for thinking. Provide each participant with opportunity to share event or trend. List all events or trends on board. Elicit discussion about each of the trends or events. If participants are unable to think of items, provide suggestions, such as:

- increase in number of public parks and playgrounds
- emphasis on physical fitness and culture
- three-day weekends
- popularity of theme parks
- increase in recreation opportunities for people with disabilities
- popularity of video games
- television commercials that depict recreation participation

10. Debriefing

Content:
    a. With which trends do you have personal experience?
    b. Have any of these events influenced your attitude about leisure? If so, which ones?
    c. Which events provide the best evidence that society's attitude toward leisure has changed?
        Why?
    d. Do you see any new trends that may affect societal attitudes about leisure?
        If so, what are they?

Process: Conduct debriefing using above questions. Encourage each participant to respond to at least one question.

11. Conclusion

Content: "We have seen how societal attitudes toward leisure have changed. This should help us understand that leisure now has a valued place in our culture. Because our own personal attitudes are often shaped by society's attitude, we should pause and reflect carefully on how we think and feel and about leisure."

Process: Make concluding statements. Provide opportunities for questions.

Objective 1.3: Demonstrate knowledge of the outcomes of leisure participation.

1. Orientation Activity

Content: "We are going to participate in an activity that will help us to know each other better and get us started in thinking about the benefits of engaging in leisure activities. A benefit is something good that is derived from participation. In addition, a benefit is something that serves to the advantage of an individual. Please arrange yourselves in a circle. As we go around the circle, individuals will take turns in stating their first name, a recreation activity he or she enjoys, and a benefit personally derived from participating in that activity."

Process: Explain activity. Arrange participants in a circle. Provide opportunity for each participant to have a turn. Move to debriefing.

2. Debriefing

Content:
- a. What did you learn from this about the benefits you obtain from leisure?
- b. Did anyone mention the same benefit as someone else, but indicate that it came from a different activity? If so, what was it?
- c. Did any one mention the same activity as someone else, but indicate a different benefit? If so, what was it?
- d. Can an individual obtain more than one benefit from a single activity? If so, how?

Process: Conduct debriefing using above questions. Emphasize diversity of benefits. Encourage each participant to respond to at least one of the questions.

3. Introduction

Content: "Engaging in leisure activities can result in a variety of outcomes, depending on the activity chosen, the reason for which it was chosen, and the manner in which an individual participates. For example, an individual may choose to go walking in order to relax and enjoy the sights and sounds of nature. The pace of the walk would not be hurried and there would probably be frequent stops along the way. At another time, an individual may choose to walk in order to release some tension and anxiety. The pace of the walk would probably be vigorous and nonstop. Having a knowledge of the outcomes of leisure can help an individual make decisions about participation."

Process: Introduce topic on the outcomes of leisure participation.

4. Presentation

Content: "The positive outcomes of leisure participation can be regarded as benefits that come to an individual. These benefits can, for the sake of discussion, be placed in one of four categories: social, emotional, mental, or physical. As we discuss these benefits, remember that many of them could fit into more than one category.

"Some benefits derived from leisure participation are regarded as social. Social refers to the relationships that exist among people and the things people do to shape those relationships. It ranges from the behaviors that influence an intimate relationship between two individuals in a familiar environment to the behavior of one person surrounded by a crowd of strangers in an unfamiliar place. Leisure participation can help you obtain skills that are of value in building social relationships of all kinds."

"Examples of social benefits derived from participation in leisure include: (a) ability to work toward a common goal as a member of a group, (b) ability to exert leadership as a member of a group, (c) ability to recognize group interests as opposed to individual interests, (d) develop confidence in capacity to meet and work with strangers, (e) opportunities to make new friends, (f) opportunities to gain acceptance and recognition by peers, (g) opportunities to develop respect for and understanding others, (h) develop confidence in ability to feel comfortable in unfamiliar surroundings, and (i) ability to recognize types of behavior required in diversity of circumstances.

The acquisition and development of social skills through leisure participation can lead to feelings of independence and control."

Process: Present information on social benefits of leisure participation. Use chalkboard or overhead projector to list benefits. Emphasize that the list is incomplete.

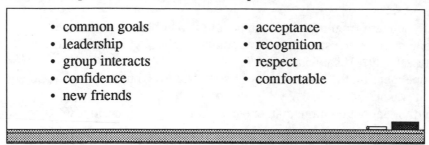

- common goals
- leadership
- group interacts
- confidence
- new friends

- acceptance
- recognition
- respect
- comfortable

5. Discussion

Content:
a. Are there other social benefits that we should list? If so, what are they?
b. Do you have any social skills that were acquired or enhanced through leisure participation? If so, what are they and how were they acquired or enhanced?
c. Are there any social benefits that you hope to gain from participating in this program? If so, what are they?
d. What will you have to do to gain these benefits?

Process: Conduct the discussion using the above questions. Encourage all the participants to contribute to the discussion.

6. Presentation

Content: "A second category of leisure participation outcomes is emotional benefits. Emotional refers to feelings that arise within us as a reaction to various kinds of external sensory stimuli, such as what we see, hear, smell, touch, or taste. Emotions may also be stimulated by internal sources, such as remembering a significant personal event or anticipating involvement in something that is yet to happen."

"It is important to recognize that all people experience a range of emotions and emotions cannot be categorized as 'good' or 'bad.' All feelings that exist are valid. The manner in which people respond to their emotions is an indication of their character and control.

"Examples of emotional benefits derived from leisure participation include: (a) happiness at being able to participate, (b) satisfaction of doing something well, (c) sense of reward from helping others participate, (d) opportunity to release tension and anxiety, (e) feelings of self-esteem from successful completion of project, (f) appreciation of the beauty and wonder of nature, (g) satisfaction of the urge to create, (h) opportunity to express oneself, and (i) contentment after a good physical workout.

Leisure is capable of providing the entire range of emotions known to us. If leisure is approached with a positive attitude, the emotional benefits are likely to be positive."

Process: Present information on emotional benefits. List benefits on chalkboard or use other visual aids. Move to discussion.

7. Discussion

Content:
   a. Should we specify additional emotional benefits? If so, what are they?
   b. What emotions have you experienced from leisure participation?
   c. In what other aspects of your life have you experienced this same emotion?
   d. Does leisure provide the best chance to feel emotions you like? Why or why not?
   e. Are most emotions you experience from leisure positive? If not, why not?

Process: Conduct discussion using above questions. Encourage all participants to contribute to the discussion.

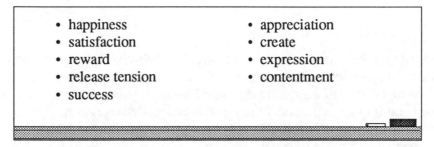

8. Presentation

Content: "A third category of benefits available through leisure participation is mental. Mental refers to the mind and the processes that are used to learn, remember, and solve problems. A common belief among many people is that learning is often unpleasant and required, leisure is enjoyable and the result of freedom of choice, and therefore, the two are incompatible. This does not have to be the case. Leisure provides many chances to obtain mental benefits in a pleasant and enjoyable atmosphere.

"Examples of mental benefits obtained by participating in leisure include: (a) learning the rules of a new activity, (b) opportunities to focus attention on the accomplishment of a single task, (c) learning to identify and make use of various community resources, (d) applying ideas learned in leisure to other aspects of living, (e) opportunities to set goals and determine how to best achieve them, (f) opportunities to participate in activities demanding timely decisions, (g) learning to devise and apply strategy in various activities, and (h) determining the best course of action from several possible options.

The mental benefits of leisure participation should not be overlooked   They are real and readily available."

Process: Present information on mental benefits. List benefits on chalkboard. Once presented, review the concepts and check them off the chalkboard as you review them. Move on to discussion.

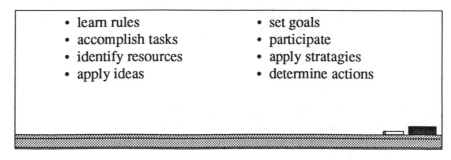

9. Discussion

Content:
    a.   Are there additional mental benefits we should list? If so, what are they?
    b.   Have you derived any mental benefits from leisure participation? If so, what were they
         and how did you do it?
    c.   Can you relate a leisure experience where you learned something that was useful in
         another aspect of your life? If so, what was it?

Process: Conduct discussion by using above questions. Encourage all participants to contribute to the discussion.

10. Presentation

Content: "The last category of benefits from leisure participation we will discuss is physical. Physical refers to the body and its operations. When most people think of the outcomes of leisure involvement, one of the first things that comes to their mind is physical benefits. Many Americans today do not have occupations that demand enough in the way of physical activity. Because exercise is important to health and fitness and, in many cases, is available primarily through leisure, the physical benefits of leisure participation are important. They are of equal importance with the other benefits of leisure.

"Examples of physical benefits that can be derived from leisure participation include: (a) an increase in the efficiency of the cardiovascular system, (b) improvement in muscle tone, (c) increase in strength, (d) improvement in eye-hand coordination, (e) increase in flexibility, (f) improvement in endurance, (g) increase in agility, and (h) improvement in weight control. The physical benefits of leisure are dependent on the type of activity chosen and the frequency and duration of participation. In an age of sedentary living for many Americans, vigorous participation in leisure is recommended and encouraged."

Process: Present information on physical benefits of leisure. List benefits on chalkboard. Show pictures or slides of people engaged in activities that appear to be providing physical benefits. Show these pictures or slides as you present the benefits.

- cardiovasclur
- muscle tone
- strength
- coordination
- flexibility
- endurance
- agility
- weight control

11. Discussion

Content:
    a. What are other physical benefits of leisure participation?
    b. Have you obtained physical benefits from leisure? How so?
    c. What physical benefits would you now like to obtain from leisure?
    d. What activities will help you obtain these benefits?

Process: Conduct discussion using above questions. Encourage all participants to contribute to the discussion.

12. Learning Activity

Content: "We are going to participate in an activity that will help us think about the benefits we can get from leisure involvement. I am going to divide you into two teams of equal numbers. I have a paper sack containing several slips of paper. On each slip of paper is written a recreation activity. The sack will be presented to one group and a member of that group will take one slip. The group will then have two minutes to say aloud all of the benefits that could be derived from participating in that activity. The benefits will be listed on the chalkboard. The sack will then be presented to the second group and the process will be repeated. Groups will alternate until each group has had five chances. We will then count the number of benefits identified by each group. We will see how many benefits we come up with as a total group. We are trying to beat the previous record set by the last group."

Process: Explain activity. Prepare slips prior to session. Examples of activities could include reading, going for a walk, visiting a sick friend, stitching on a quilt, baking a cake, bowling, and playing bingo. When slip is taken, do not return it to sack. Monitor listing of benefits to ensure fairness. Examples of benefits could include learning new things, relaxation, meeting new people, feeling good, fun, creating something, and sharing time with friends. Tally benefits and declare winner. Emphasize and summarize benefits generated by participants.

13. Debriefing

Content:
    a. What is your impression of the variety of benefits that were identified?
    b. Which of these benefits would you like most to obtain? Why?
    c. What will you need to do to obtain them?

Process: Conduct debriefing using above questions. Encourage each participant to answer at least one of the questions.

14. Learning Activity

Content: "You are going to have a chance to complete an open-ended questionnaire that will help you think about the benefits of leisure and, at the same time, learn something about your own leisure involvement. Please take the time to think carefully about your answers to the questions. There are no 'right' or 'wrong' answers. Be honest and write exactly what you feel. When the questionnaires are completed, we will use them as the basis for a group discussion."

Process: Explain activity. Distribute questionnaire and pencils. Provide sufficient time for completion. Move on to debriefing. Prepare questionnaire with the following items:

1. If I had a free weekend, I would want to:
2. I have decided to finally learn how to:
3. If I were to buy two magazines, I would choose:
4. I feel most bored when:
5. If I used my free time more wisely, I would:
6. I feel best when people:
7. On weekends, I like to:
8. I get real enjoyment from:
9. If I had a tankful of gas in a car:
10. What I want most in life is:
11. I have never liked:
12. When my family gets together:
13. I do not have enough time to:
14. I would consider it risky to:
15. My greatest accomplishment in leisure has been:

15. Debriefing

Content:
   a. How did you complete question 1? What benefits would you get from doing this?
   b. What is your answer to question 2? What benefits would you get from this?
   c. How did you answer question 3? Why did you to choose the magazines you did?
   d. How did you answer question 4? What could you do to keep from getting bored?
   e. What did you put for question 5? What category of benefits would your answer fit?
   f. How did you answer question 6? Is your answer a social or emotional benefit?
   g. What was your response to question 7? When was the last time you did this?
   h. How did you complete question 8? When was the last time you experienced this?
   i. How did you answer question 9? How would this benefit you?
   j. What did you say for question 10? What will you do to help you get it?
   k. What was your response to question 11? What does this say about you?
   l. How did you complete question 12? When was the last time your family was able to do this? Could you do anything to help in this area?
   m. How did you answer question 13? What could you do to have more time to do the things you want?
   n. What did you say for question 14? What could you do to change this?
   o. How did you complete question 15? Do you feel like your greatest accomplishments are yet to come? How can you help it happen?

Process: Conduct debriefing using above questions. Ask questions of each participant. Encourage more than one participant to respond to any given question.

16. Conclusion

Content: "There are many benefits available through participation in leisure but these benefits do not automatically come to everyone. It sometimes takes purposeful effort to obtain benefits. The benefits of leisure can play a very important role in our lives."

Process: Make concluding statements. Provide opportunities for questions.

Objective 1.4: Demonstrate knowledge of barriers to leisure participation.

1. Orientation Activity

Content: "I am giving each of you a card with a word or phrase that is relevant to leisure participation. Another person will have a card explaining how this word or phrase can be a barrier that inhibits or prevents leisure participation. You should try to find this person, introduce yourself, and discuss the barrier. After you have found the person and discussed the barrier, together the two of you should look for another pair of people that have succeeded in finding one another. When you find another pair, introduce yourselves and present your barrier to them and allow them to tell you about their barrier. Continue moving about the room, finding pairs of people until I give the signal to end the activity."

Process: Explain activity. Prepare cards prior to session. Agree on a signal (e.g., music starts) to end the activity. Distribute cards. Monitor activity. Provide assistance where needed. The first set of cards could include the following words or phrases:

- existing funds
- free time
- availability
- societal attitudes
- health
- skills

The second set of cards could include barriers such as:
- I want to go bowling but I do not have enough money.
- I would like to go for a walk tonight but I have to clean the house.
- I would like to play on a soccer team but there are no programs in the community.
- Theater owners do not want me to attend their movies because I use a wheelchair.
- I want to participate in the race but I do not have the stamina.
- I would like to go on the river trip but I do not know how to canoe.

2. Introduction

Content: "A barrier is something that stands in the way of our doing something we want to do. Therefore, a barrier may stop us from experiencing leisure as often as we would like. Sometimes we may plan or want to do something and we discover that, at that time, we are not able to engage in the activity. We may not be able to participate for many reasons. These reasons are 'barriers' to satisfying and enjoyable experiences. Each factor influencing leisure participation, such as existing funds, free time, availability, societal attitudes, health, and skills, may at some time or another be a barrier."

Process: Introduce topic of barriers to leisure participation.

3. Presentation

Content: "Lack of money can be a barrier to leisure participation. Many recreation activities require money to enjoy. This means that those of us wishing to participate must make sure we have enough money to pay for the activity. If we do not have enough money and are not permitted to participate as a result of this lack of resources, money has become a barrier to leisure participation for us."

Process: Present information on existing funds. List the first barrier on the chalkboard as "money."

4. Discussion

Content:
  a. What are some examples of how money may be a barrier to leisure participation?
  b. How do you feel when a lack of funds prevents you from engaging in an activity?
  c. Have you ever observed people being turned away from recreation activities because they did not have enough money? If so, how did that make you feel?

Process: Conduct discussion using above questions. Encourage all participants to contribute to the discussion.

5. Presentation

Content: "Lack of free time is another possible barrier to leisure participation. All activities require some amount of time. As a result, we must possess the time to participate. If we do not have sufficient time to participate in recreation activities, we may not experience leisure as frequently as we would like. In addition, there are instances when we do not manage our time very well and, as a result, we use time in ways that might not make us feel very good. We may feel that we 'wasted' time and missed out on opportunities for enjoyable, satisfying and meaningful experiences. When we do not have enough time or do not take advantage of the time we do have, time becomes a barrier to leisure participation."

Process: Present information on free time. Record the phrase "free time" on the chalkboard after the previous barrier of money.

6. Discussion

Content:
  a. Have you ever had problems finding enough time to enjoy yourself? If so, why do you think this happened?
  b. Are there instances when you have mismanaged your time? If so, when?
  c. Why do you think you have mismanaged some of your time in the past?
  d. What was the result of your mismanaged time?
  e. How do you feel when you have mismanaged time?

Process: Conduct discussion using above questions. Encourage all participants to contribute to the discussion.

7. Presentation

Content: "Lack of availability is another possible barrier to leisure participation. Sometimes there we would like to participate in activities but we cannot because we do not have adequate transportation. For example, a bus may not have a route running near a park you would like to go to. It also might be true that we want to participate in an organized activity that no one is providing in the community. For example, there does not seem to be an organized volleyball league in our community. Sometimes an activity can be present in a community and due to our work schedule and other responsibilities we can not get there at the times the activity is available. For example, because I work in the evening, I cannot participate in the evening bridge program. If you have limited mobility, you may encounter physical obstacles in the form of architectural barriers or ecological barriers. Architectural barriers are built by people, such as steps and heavy doors, while ecological barriers include those that are in the natural world, such as hills and snow. At times we encounter people whose attitudes towards us prevent us from having fun because they refuse to allow us to participate or they make us feel uncomfortable. For example, because you have a disability you can only use a specific section of the swimming pool at scheduled times."

Process: Present information on availability. List on an overhead projector or a chalkboard the major concepts discussed such as:

- Transportation
- Programs
- Scheduling
- Architecture
- Ecology
- Facilities

8. Discussion

Content:
    a. Are there activities in the community that are unavailable to you? What are they?
    b. Why do you think these activities are unavailable to you?
    c. Have you seen people that could not attend an activity because it was not available to them? If so, what happened?
    d. How do you feel when you want to do something and you can not participate because the activity is not available to you?

Process: Conduct discussion using above questions. Encourage all participants to contribute to the discussion.

9. Presentation

Content: "Societal attitudes can be another possible barrier to our leisure participation. We will now talk about attitudes that constitute barriers to participating in recreation activities. Sometimes people who provide programs refuse to let us participate because they think we will hurt ourselves or that we are not skilled enough to have fun. If we encounter these negative attitudes enough times, we may begin to believe we cannot do the things people keep telling us we cannot do. Other times, we might attend a program and the other participants may make us feel uncomfortable or actually tell us that we are not welcome. If enough people make us feel uncomfortable and not many people make us feel welcome, we may stop doing something we really enjoy."

Process: Present information of societal attitudes. Add the possible barrier of "societal attitudes" to the list of barriers on the chalkboard.

10. Discussion

Content:
    a.   Were there times when people's attitudes affected your participation? If so, how?
    b.   How did you feel when people's attitudes became a barrier to leisure expression?
    c.   What have you done in response to people's negative attitudes?

Process: Conduct discussion using above questions.

11. Presentation

Content: "A person's health can be another barrier to leisure participation. At times we may not be healthy. This lack of good health may inhibit our participation in recreation activities. Because of our temporary or permanent poor health, we may have to cope with limited physical abilities. For example, emphysema may prevent participation in aerobic activities, such as walking. In addition, we may have to deal with reduced mental awareness. For example, certain medications taken when we have an illness may result in confusion, preventing us from engaging in certain table games we enjoy. Social isolation may also result from health problems. For example, an observable disability may make some people feel uncomfortable, reducing chances for informal conversations. In addition, health problems may result in considerable pain and discomfort that may create barriers for us to concentrate on activities or have fun. For example, people receiving rehabilitation for severe burns may find concentration or reading difficult. All the examples we have just talked about are situations where poor health has become a barrier to leisure involvement."

Process: Present information on health. Add "poor health" to the list of potential barriers. Present pictures or slides of each example of health problems.

12. Discussion

Content:
    a.   Have there been times when health conditions have prevented your leisure participation? What were your problems?
    b.   What activities have you been unable to enjoy due to health problems?
    c.   How have you felt when you could not participate due to health reasons?
    d.   Are the health conditions creating barriers to you still present? If so, what are they?

Process: Conduct discussion using above questions. Encourage all participants to contribute to the discussion.

13. Presentation

Content: "Lack of skills can be another possible barrier to leisure participation. There are going to be times when you do not possess the skills required to participate in an activity. Sometimes, it is possible to work hard and acquire the needed skills, but there will be other times when the desired skills will not be attained despite the strongest efforts. Whether the lack of skills is temporary or permanent, if you do not have them, their absence creates a barrier for you. For example, if someone asks you to play tennis and you do not know how to hold a racquet, hit the ball, or keep score, your lack of skills will prevent you from sharing time with this person. Some activities will have prerequisite skills for participation. Therefore, you may need to demonstrate a certain level of competence to be eligible to participate. For example, water polo requires you to swim. If you do not possess these skills, an absence of these abilities becomes a major barrier to your leisure involvement. For example, because you cannot swim, you are not allowed to play water polo."

Process: Present information on skills as a barrier to leisure. Add the word "lack of skills" to the list of potential barriers to leisure participation. If possible, provide visual aids such as pictures or slides of people participating in the recreation activities (e.g., tennis, swimming) as they are presented in the discussion.

14. Discussion

Content:
    a. Have you been asked to participate in recreation activities but were not able to because of a lack of skills? If so, what activities?
    b. Have there been times when you knew people did not ask you to participate because they knew you were unable? If so, when?
    c. How did you feel when the absence of skills limited your participation?

Process: Conduct discussion using above questions. Encourage all participants to contribute to the discussion.

15. Learning Activity

Content: "We are now going to participate in an activity that helps us identify barriers to leisure participation. I am going to divide you into two teams: A and B. I have placed on the wall a number of pictures of people engaged in many different recreation activities. Team B will choose a picture. Team A must then identify a barrier that may prevent people from engaging in the activity. If Team A can identify a barrier, then Team B has the chance to identify a barrier. If Team B can identify a barrier, the teams will continue to take turns identifying barriers until one team runs out of ideas. When a team can no longer come up with any barriers, the other team will be awarded the picture. If at the beginning of the turn, Team A cannot identify a barrier, Team B can take a turn. If Team B identifies a barrier, they may take the picture off the wall and keep it. If neither team can identify a barrier, I will identify possible barriers. The picture will remain on the wall and can be chosen later. Team A will point to a new picture and Team B will begin. The game will proceed in this fashion until one team has obtained five pictures. Once a team has five pictures, we will go around the room and review the barriers we have identified during the game."

Process: Explain activity. Obtain pictures from magazines and mount on wall prior to session. Monitor activity, be prepared to assist if disagreements arise.

16. Debriefing

Content:
    a. Was it difficult for you to identify barriers?
    b. Have any barriers identified in the game been barriers to your leisure participation?
    c. Which of the pictures is your favorite? Why?
    d. Do you experience barriers limiting your participation in any of the activities in the pictures? If so, what are they?
    e. Did you like the game we just played? If so, why? If not, why not?
    f. Why do you think we did this activity?

Process: Conduct debriefing using above questions. Encourage each participant to respond to at least one of the debriefing questions.

17. Conclusion

Content: "A first step in solving any problem is to recognize that a problem exists. The same is true when we think about our leisure participation. If there are barriers to our participation, the first step is to identify what they are. We can then take steps to eliminate, reduce, or otherwise cope with those barriers."

Process: Make concluding statements. Provide opportunities for questions.

Objective 1.5: Demonstrate knowledge of strategies to overcome barriers to leisure.

1. Orientation Activity

Content: "We are going to look at ways we can overcome leisure barriers. Each of you has been given one third of a piece of colored paper. Find the other two people with the same color piece of paper, introduce yourself, and find out their names. Put together the pieces of paper to form one solid sheet. Use scotch tape on the side of the paper that does not have any words typed on it and fasten the three pieces together. Turn the paper over to discover two columns. In the left column is a list of barriers to leisure. In the right column is a list of possible solutions. One person from the group draw the first line to connect one barrier with one possible solution. The next player will match the next barrier and solution. Continue in this way until all barriers and solutions have been matched. Use only one barrier per solution and do not use a solution or barrier twice."

Process: Explain activity. Arrange participants in small groups. Distribute lists. Monitor activity. Follow with debriefing. Prepare lists prior to session. Include items such as:

```
 BARRIERS                        SOLUTIONS

I do not have enough money      Enroll in course teaching
   for activity.                   you a leisure skill.
I do not have enough time.      Save money and spend less
I do not know about com-          on other items.
   munity activities.           Call recreation professional
I do not have the skills.         on the telephone.
                                Get organized and budget
                                  your time.
```

2. Debriefing

Content:
    a   Was it difficult to match strategies to overcome the barriers that were presented?
    b. Did you have any problems in matching the items?
    c. Were there any strategies you did not understand? If so, what were they?
    d. What did you like about this orientation activity?

Process: Conduct debriefing using the above questions. Encourage all participants to contribute to the discussion.

3. Introduction

Content: "Strategies to overcoming leisure barriers are in demand. In order to participate actively in recreation activities, we must develop these strategies. In turn, we hope to reduce barriers that challenge us so that we can have more fun and be satisfied with our leisure participation. Strategies to overcome leisure barriers may include participating in recreation activities that are free of charge, developing time management skills, using leisure resources at home, learning necessary skills to participate in activities, and adapting materials to meet your needs."

Process: Introduce importance of strategies in overcoming leisure barriers.

4. Presentation

Content: "Participating in recreation activities that are free of charge is an excellent way to benefit from leisure and overcome the barrier of limited money. Free programs are offered by parks and recreation departments, community organizations, state parks, and cultural centers. The media, which includes television, newspaper and radio, advertise these programs and can be used to find free programs that meet your needs. Programs change over time, and new ones are offered that can be as interesting and exciting as those that charge fees. Lack of funds does not have to be a barrier to your leisure participation."

Process: Present information on free activity. List the phrase "free activity" on the chalkboard.

5. Discussion

Content:
  a. What agencies offer free recreation?
  b. What sources are available to find activities that are cost-free?
  c. Will free programs be offered to meet your needs?
  d. Are free programs as interesting and exciting as other programs?

Process: Conduct discussion using above questions. Encourage all participants to contribute to the discussion.

6. Presentation

Content: "Developing efficient time management skills is a positive approach to overcoming the barrier of not enough free time. Time management is a step-by-step process in which you prioritize and chart your responsibilities. In managing your time effectively, you include free time for recreation activities. If a situation arises where by your scheduled free time is no longer free, reschedule it as soon as you can. Once you have developed a high level of time management skills, it becomes a natural process and leisure time improves."

Process: Present information on developing time management skills. List "time management" on the chalkboard.

7. Discussion

Content:
  a. What are you doing when you are charting your responsibilities?
  b. When you develop a time management plan, do you schedule free time?
  c. How long must you use a schedule before free time becomes part of daily life?
  d. What happens when leisure is planned and situations occur that prevent it?

Process: Conduct discussion using above questions. Encourage all participants to contribute to the discussion.

8. Presentation

Content: "Using leisure resources at home is an easy way to overcome transportation barriers. Many leisure activities can be enjoyed at home and around your neighborhood. You may decide to use your basement or an extra room as a recreation area. It is easy to set up an area for games and hobbies that you enjoy. Just about any activity that you like can be done at home, if you get the equipment you need.

"There may be people in your neighborhood that are interested in these close-to-home activities. Talk with people in your area to see what they might be interested in doing. Whenever transportation is a barrier, use your home or yard as your facility for leisure."

Process: Present information on leisure resources at home. Record "leisure at home" on the chalkboard.

9. Discussion

Content:
   a. What are some recreation activities that can be done at home?
   b. What can you do at home to set it up for leisure?
   c. Can free time be enjoyable at home?
   d. What are some ways to get neighbors involved?

Process: Conduct discussion using above questions. Encourage all participants to contribute to the discussion.

10. Presentation

Content: "Acquiring needed skills to participate in activities reduces the skills barrier. There are many strategies to develop introductory skills without participating in the activity. These techniques can be practiced at home, with videotapes, with skilled peers, or with a private instructor.

"Videotapes are usually easy and fun to learn from. You can imitate the skills and review them many times. Skilled peers are enjoyable to work with. They tend to understand your position and they want to help you. They can tell you what you are doing wrong and offer you assistance when you need it. Private instructors are also willing to give you the help you need. They are skilled in the area, and they can teach you methods to improve your ability. Any strategy you choose will lead you toward participation."

Process: Present information on acquiring skills. Record the phrase "acquiring skills" on the chalkboard.

11. Discussion

Content:
   a. What is the benefit of acquiring needed skills?
   b. How can videotape instruction improve skills?
   c. What are some advantages of learning skills of experienced peers?
   d. How can private instruction help?
   e. How can practicing at home prepare you for the activity?

Process: Conduct discussion using above questions. Encourage all participants to contribute to the discussion.

12. Presentation

Content: "Materials required for leisure may be adapted or changed to meet your needs. Adaptive equipment is available for many recreation activities. Pools may have ramps or lifts to help you enter the water. Heavy or large equipment can be replaced by light or small equipment to help you learn skills. If you do not have access to these sources, you may contact people in the community to assist you in making special equipment or you may use substitute equipment.

"Rules can also be changed to allow you to participate in activities. Scores, distances, time limits, etc. can be altered to meet your needs. Lack of equipment or hard rules do not have to keep you from experiencing leisure."

Process: Present information on adaptive equipment. List "adaptive equipment" on the chalkboard.

13. Discussion

Content:
  a. Can substitutions be used to replace required materials?
  b. Is it possible to make special equipment on your own?
  c. Can equipment be adapted to meet your needs?
  d. What other ways are there to modify activities?

Process: Conduct discussion using above questions. Encourage all participants to contribute to the discussion.

14. Learning Activity

Content: "We are now going to participate in an activity that helps us develop strategies to overcome leisure barriers. First, I will help you get into pairs. Each pair will receive a card with a symbol of a leisure barrier pictured on it. Using your knowledge and imagination, develop a strategy to overcome the barrier. Then, try to explain your strategy on the other side of your card. After everyone is finished, we will join in a circle. One partner will be asked to share the symbol and explain the barrier to the group. The other partner will then describe the strategy to overcome the barrier. We will continue until everyone has taken a turn."

Process: Explain activity. Have leisure barrier symbols prepared before session. Monitor activity and assist when needed. Some possible symbols would be:

• No money– indicated by dollar sign.
• No time– indicated by clock face.
• No transportation– indicated by automobile.
• Lack of skills– indicated by wrecked bike.

15. Debriefing

Content:
  a. Was it hard to identify the leisure barrier by the symbol provided?
  b. What were some difficulties in developing a strategy to overcome the barrier?
  c. Do you think you can develop strategies to overcome barriers on your own?
  d. When faced with a leisure barrier, what is your first reaction?
  e. Do you think this activity helped you improve your skills to overcome barriers?

Process: Conduct debriefing using above questions. Encourage each participant to respond to one of the questions.

16. Conclusion

Content: "Leisure barriers do not always have to keep us from participating. We can use various resources to help us develop strategies to overcome them. We must first identify what the barrier is, and then start to think of solutions to overcome the problem. Developing strategies will allow us to participate in many fun activities that we may have thought were impossible."

LEISURE EDUCATION: AWARENESS OF SELF IN LEISURE

Purpose, Goal, and Objectives

Purpose: Provide opportunities for participants to become aware of their attitudes toward leisure, understand factors that may affect their leisure participation, examine their past recreation involvement, consider their current recreation involvement, and identify possible preferred future recreation activities.

Goal 2: Demonstrate an awareness of self in leisure.

Objective 2.1.   Demonstrate knowledge of personal attitudes toward leisure.
Objective 2.2.   Demonstrate knowledge of factors that may affect leisure participation.
Objective 2.3.   Demonstrate knowledge of past recreation involvement.
Objective 2.4.   Demonstrate knowledge of current recreation involvement.
Objective 2.5.   Demonstrate ability to identify possible preferred future recreation activities.

Goal, Objectives, and Performance Measures

Goal 2: Demonstrate an awareness of self in leisure.

Objective 2.1: Demonstrate knowledge of personal attitudes toward leisure.

Performance Measure A: Given paper and pencil, in 15 minutes the participant will:
- (a)   identify five recreation activities that you like to do (e.g., fishing, painting, cycling, reading, kayaking), and
- (b)   give one reason why you like each activity (e.g., fishing: peaceful; painting: creative expression; cycling: physical fitness; reading: choices of books; kayaking: adventure),

with 100% accuracy on two consecutive occasions.

Performance Measure B: Given paper and pencil, in 15 minutes:
- (a)   identify five recreation activities that you do not like to do (e.g., jogging, card playing, boating, football, opera), and
- (b)   give one reason why you do not like each activity (e.g., jogging: tiring; card playing: boring; boating: afraid of water; football: rough; opera: confusing),

with 100% accuracy on two consecutive occasions.

Objective 2.2: Demonstrate knowledge of factors that may affect leisure participation.

Performance Measure: Given five minutes, state six factors (e.g., existing funds, free time, availability, societal role expectations, health, and skills) affecting leisure participation, with 100% accuracy on two consecutive occasions.

Objective 2.3: Demonstrate knowledge of past recreation involvement.

Performance Measure: Given paper and pencil, in 15 minutes:
- (a)   list 10 past recreation activities resulting in enjoyment and satisfaction (e.g., horseback riding, jogging, basketball, reading, bird watching, bowling, volleyball, gardening, swimming, cross-stitch), and
- (b)   provide examples of participation in three of the activities listed (e.g., horseback riding) by identifying at least three of the following considerations:
  - (1) where: "When I lived in the country"
  - (2) when: "as a young adult"
  - (3) why: "I rode for pleasure"
  - (4) who: "with my sister"
  - (5) how often: "at least three times per week."

with 100% accuracy on two consecutive occasions.

Objective 2.4: Demonstrate knowledge of current recreation involvement.

Performance Measure A: Given paper and pencil, in 15 minutes:
- (a)   list ten current recreation activities resulting in enjoyment and satisfaction (e.g., watch television, attend sporting events, movies, visit art galleries, play video games, gardening, swimming, archery, fishing, macrame) and
- (b)   provide examples of participation in three of the activities listed (e.g., watch television) identify at least one of the following considerations:
  - (1) where: "When I am home"
  - (2) when: "at night,"
  - (3) why: "I watch television to relax"
  - (4) who: "by myself"
  - (5) how often: "every evening."

with 100% accuracy on two consecutive occasions.

Performance Measure B: Given a list of 10 past and 10 current recreation activities resulting in enjoyment and satisfaction, paper and pencil, in 15 minutes:
- (a)   identify all activities on the list previously engaged in but no longer doing so (e.g., horseback riding, jogging, basketball, reading, bird watching, bowling, volleyball, gardening, and cross-stitch),
- (b)   specify reasons why no longer engaging in those activities (e.g., jogging: "I now experience pain in my knees when jogging.")

OR
- (a)   identify that no discrepancies exist, and
- (b)   specify reasons for consistency ("Over the years, I have found ways to continue doing the things I like.").

with 100% accuracy.

Objective 2.5: Demonstrate ability to identify possible future recreation activities.

Performance Measure: Given paper and pencil, in 15 minutes: list 10 recreation activities in which future participation is desired (e.g., horseback riding, jogging, basketball, dating, traveling, bowling, volleyball, gardening, swimming, mountain climbing) with 100% accuracy on two consecutive occasions.

Goal, Objectives, Content, and Process

Goal 2: Demonstrate an awareness of self in leisure.

Objective 2.1: Demonstrate knowledge of personal attitudes toward leisure.

1. Orientation Activity

Content: "Please arrange yourselves in a circle so we can participate in an activity that will help us start to think about our attitudes toward leisure. We will introduce ourselves by our first names, state a leisure activity which we have enjoyed, and tell what it was about the activity that we liked. For example, a person could say: 'My name is Larry. I went on a camping trip and I enjoyed being in the natural environment.' Telling others what we like about something will begin to provide us with insight into our attitudes about it."

Process: Explain activity. Help arrange participants in circle. Provide each person with an opportunity to participate.

2. Introduction

Content: "Attitudes have a major effect on actions. This is as true of leisure as it is of other aspects of life. Your attitude toward leisure is important in deciding whether or not to participate in an activity, with whom, for how long, what is expected from it, and other factors. If leisure is valued, you will be willing to expend the resources and make the commitments necessary to have a chance to participate. If lcisure is not valued, you will make little or no effort to be involved in it. Developing an awareness of self requires clarification of your personal attitudes toward leisure."

Process: Introduce topic of personal attitudes toward leisure.

3. Presentation

Content: "Examining your attitude about leisure requires careful thinking. It calls for a high degree of honesty. It means that you must search yourself for your true feelings about leisure and attempt to develop an understanding of why you feel the way you do. One way this may be done is for you to ask yourself questions related to leisure. Care must be taken in answering questions to ensure that your response is an accurate reflection of your feelings and not merely what you believe others may expect to hear.

"Another way for you to investigate your attitudes is to place yourself in situations where you are confronted by choices regarding leisure. The choices that are made will be an indication of your attitude. Reflecting on why a choice was made may result in even better insight into to your attitude.

"There is nothing mysterious about gaining a knowledge of your attitudes toward leisure. It simply requires a little thought relative to some very basic questions. For example: (a) Is leisure valued? (b) Why is it (or is it not) valued? (c) Which activities are desired more than others? (d) Why is this so? (e) What types of leisure environments are preferred and why? and (f) How much involvement is preferred and with whom?

"Responding to these and similar questions will help individuals learn a great deal about their attitudes toward leisure."

Process: Present information on personal attitudes toward leisure. List the questions that can be asked of self on a chalkboard or easel.

- Is leisure valued? Why?
- Which activities are desired more than others? Why?
- What types of leisure environments are preferred? Why?
- How much involvement is preferred?
- With whom is involvement preferred?

4. Discussion

Content:
    a. Why is it important to understand your personal attitudes towards leisure?
    b. How does being confronted with choices help you learn about your attitudes?
    c. How can you be honest when you respond to questions you ask yourself?
    d. What additional questions can be asked to learn about one's attitude toward leisure?

Process: Conduct discussion using above questions. Encourage participants to contribute to the discussion. At the end of the discussion, inform participants that they will engage in several learning activities to investigate their attitudes towards leisure.

5. Learning Activity

Content: "We are going to begin to learn more about our attitudes towards leisure. Each of you has a pair of scissors, three envelopes, and several magazines. Browse through the magazines and cut out pictures of recreation activities. Select activities in which you have participated and experienced enjoyment and satisfaction, activities in which you have participated but had a negative experience, and activities in which you have not yet participated but think might interest you in the future. Label your envelopes in some way to reflect these three categories. For example, you could draw a happy face on the envelope that will contain pictures of activities you enjoyed, a sad face on the envelope containing activities that were negative experiences, and a question mark on activities you have not yet experienced. Try to get four or five activities in each envelope.

"When you are finished, I am going to put you in pairs and ask you to exchange envelopes with your partner. Your partner will select an envelope, withdraw one picture, and hand it to you. When you see the picture, tell your partner why you liked the activity, disliked it, or might be interested in it in the future. When you are finished, take a picture from one of your partner's envelopes and your partner will discuss the picture. Take turns drawing pictures from envelopes, making sure that you use all three envelopes during your discussion. As you participate in the discussion, think about why you liked or disliked an activity."

Process: Explain activity. Provide scissors, envelopes, and magazines. Divide into pairs. Allow ample time for discussion. Move about the room providing assistance as needed.

6. Debriefing

Content:
   a. Did you find pictures of your favorite activities? If so, what were they?
   b. Did you learn anything about your partner's attitude toward leisure? If so, what?
   c. What did you learn about your own attitude?
   d. Was it difficult to think of things to say during your discussion? If so, why?

Process: Conduct debriefing using above questions. Encourage each participant to respond to at least one of the questions.

7. Learning Activity

Content: "We are going to do an activity named 'Reaction.' I am going to give each of you five blank cards. Write the name of a different recreation activity on each of the cards. When everyone is finished, I will collect the cards and place them in a basket. Please get in a circle. I will withdraw a card, read aloud the name of the activity, and point to a person in the circle. That person will have five seconds to say aloud one word that describes his or her attitude toward the activity. We will then go clockwise around the circle and each person will have five seconds to state one word that describes his or her attitude toward the activity. For example, I may draw a card that has 'hang gliding' on it. The first person may say it is 'scary,' the second person may say it is 'exciting,' the third person may say it is 'dangerous.' When you respond, try to use a word that genuinely reflects your attitude toward the activity; it does not matter if someone else has already used that word."

Process: Explain activity. Provide cards and pencils. Arrange participants in a circle. When selecting a person to give first word, go around the circle so that everyone has an opportunity to be first to react.

8. Debriefing

Content:
   a. Do you think the words you used were an accurate reflection of your attitude?
   b. Did you use any words that, after reflecting on them, you would like to change?
       If so, what were they and with what activity were they used?
   c. Was it hard to react with a five second time limit? If so, why?
   d. Did you learn about your attitude toward leisure from this activity? If so, what?

Process: Conduct debriefing using above questions. Encourage each participant to respond to at least one question. Probe participants on the rationale for their answers.

9. Learning Activity

Content: "This is an activity named 'Either-Or.' Again, it is designed to assist you in knowing more about your attitude toward leisure. Please arrange yourselves in a circle. I will go around the circle and ask each of you a question: 'Is your leisure more like (*first choice*) or (*second choice*)?' I will point in one direction for the first choice and the opposite direction for the second choice. You will have 10 seconds to decide which choice your leisure is more like. You will then tell us why you made the choice you did. For example, I may say 'Is your leisure more like summer or winter?' and then you must choose."

Process: Explain activity. Arrange in circle. Ensure each participant has opportunity to respond to question. Go around circle as many times as desired. Prepare questions ahead of session. Questions could include the following. Is your leisure more like:

> • Los Angeles or the Rocky Mountains?
> • an ant or a grasshopper?
> • a mountain or a valley?
> • a seven course meal or fast food?
> • a saver or a spender?
> • a clothesline or a kite?
> • a window or a door?
> • a river or an ocean?
> • a bat or a ball?

10. Debriefing

Content:
    a. Was it difficult for you to make a choice? If so, why?
    b. Can you think of other pairs of choices that we could ask? If so, what are they?
    c. Did others make choices you thought they would? If not, what does this mean?
    d. Would you make changes in your choices? If so, what would they be and why?

Process: Conduct debriefing using above questions. Provide an example how you might change an original choice. Encourage participants to respond to the questions.

11. Learning Activity

Content: "Another way to learn something about your attitude toward leisure is to complete a Leisure Values Form. A Leisure Values Form is one that contains a rating scale and pairs of words that describe opposite feelings about leisure. A rating scale has several points on it, indicating different levels of agreement with the idea expressed by the word pair. For example, a rating scale might have five points on it, as follows:

1 = very   2 = slightly   3 = neutral   4 = slightly   5 = very

A word pair might be 'Exciting' and 'Relaxing' and would be shown as follows:

Exciting   1   2   3   4   5   Relaxing

"If a person was very positive about leisure and believed it was beautiful, then '1' would be circled. If a person had no feelings about it, '3' would be circled. The person would circle the number that most nearly resembled his or her feelings about leisure as indicated by the word pair. A number would be circled for every pair of words."

"Each of you has a Leisure Values Form. Read it carefully and complete it according to your feelings. When the forms are completed, you will be placed in groups of three or four and discuss your responses."

Process: Explain activity. Use board to show sample scale and word pair. When form is completed, put participants in small groups for discussion. Prepare following Leisure Values Form in advance of session:

LEISURE IS:

Exciting	1	2	3	4	5	Boring
Gratifying	1	2	3	4	5	Disappointing
Important	1	2	3	4	5	Trivial
Acceptance	1	2	3	4	5	Rejection
Bold	1	2	3	4	5	Timid
Positive	1	2	3	4	5	Negative
Action	1	2	3	4	5	Idleness
Growing	1	2	3	4	5	Stagnating
Expressive	1	2	3	4	5	Passive
Creative	1	2	3	4	5	Repetitious

12. Debriefing

Content:
   a. Did you feel the rating scale provided you with enough choices? If not, why not?
   b. Do you have any suggestions for additional word pairs? If so, what are they?
   c. As you look at your Leisure Values Form, are there more numbers on the left side of the sheet circled? On the right side? In the middle? What does this mean?
   d. What did you learn from this activity?

Process: Conduct debriefing using above questions. Possibly enlarge the instrument and make an overhead transparency to be used as a visual aid during the debriefing. Encourage all participants to contribute to the debriefing.

13. Learning Activity

Content: "Another pencil and paper exercise that can be used to learn about one's attitude toward leisure is the completion of a Leisure Satisfaction Form. A Leisure Satisfaction Form is a series of open-ended questions focused on what individuals like to do with their leisure. For example, a question might be stated as follows: 'When I am in the park, I like to_____.' Each individual completing the form would then write a response to that question."

"Each of you has been given a Leisure Satisfaction Form. Think carefully and complete each question on the form. When you finish, we will use the forms as a basis for discussion."

Process: Explain activity. Distribute forms and pencils. Allow sufficient time for completion. Move to debriefing. Prepare forms in advance of the session. The form could include the following questions:

LEISURE SATISFACTION

Complete the following sentences:

a. I am happiest when: _____

b. My favorite weekend is when:_____

c. If I could do anything I want, I would: _____

d. In the summer, I like:_____

e. My favorite evening activity is:_____

f. If I could go anywhere I want, I would go:_____

g. When I am alone, I like to:_____

h. If I had more time, I would:_____

i. I like holidays because:_____

j. The thing I like best about being with my friends is:_____

14. Debriefing

Content:

a. How did you respond to the statement (a through j)?

b. Are there additional statements that should be on the form? If so, what are they?

c. Was there a statement that was easier to answer than the others? If so, which one?

d. What did you learn from this activity?

Process: Conduct debriefing using above questions. Encourage each participant to respond to at least one of the questions.

15. Learning Activity

Content: "This activity is called 'Lose Your Marbles Over Leisure.' It is an activity designed to help you become more aware of your leisure attitudes and lifestyle and to help you interact with other members of the group. Each of you will receive five cards with a leisure-related question on each card. You will also receive five marbles. The cards will be face down on the table in front of you and there will be a cup in the center of the table. Play will begin with the person whose next birthday is closest to today's date and will rotate clockwise from that person. When it is your turn to play, draw one of your cards and answer the question on it within one minute. If you answer the question, place a marble in the cup and set the card aside. If you do not answer the question within one minute, return the card to your stack but do not place a marble in the cup. Play will proceed to the next person. Play will continue until one person has placed all five marbles in the cup."

Process: Explain activity. Prepare cards. Distribute cards and marbles. Monitor activity for compliance with one minute time-limit. Examples of questions could include:

- What does leisure mean to you?
- What leisure activity is your favorite and why?
- What leisure activity would you like to learn and why?
- What was your favorite thing to do as a child?
- Where would you like to travel next year?

16. Debriefing

Content:
a. What did you learn about your leisure involvement from this activity?
b. Was it awkward to answer questions in front of other group members?
c. What did you learn about other group members?
d. Why did we do this activity?

Process: Conduct debriefing using above questions. Refer back to the questions. List questions on an easel and point to the questions as they are addressed. Encourage each participant to respond to at least one of the questions.

17. Conclusion

Content: "We have participated in a variety of activities to help us learn about our attitudes toward leisure. Knowing what we like and dislike and why we feel the way we do is an important part of learning about ourselves. This knowledge can guide us in our choices and help us use leisure to our best advantage."

Process: Make concluding statements. Provide opportunities for questions.

Objective 2.2: Demonstrate knowledge of factors that may affect leisure participation.

1. Orientation Activity

Content: "We need to understand those things that affect our ability to participate in recreation activities. Each of you has a list of six questions focused on factors that affect leisure participation. Each of you also has a card that has one such factor on it. You cannot use your card to answer one of your own questions. Mingle among the other group members to locate someone who has a card that contains the answer to a question on your list. Make sure you introduce yourself and find out the person's name. When you are successful in finding such a person, record the factor on their card next to the question it answers on your list. Also, record their first name. Keep looking for persons who have cards that contain answers to your questions. Continue play until all questions have been answered or a signal to stop is given."

Process: Explain activity. Distribute list of questions and one card to each participant. Monitor activity. Prepare the following questions prior to the activity:

- What is a factor influencing leisure participation that affects most people who do not have much money?
- What is a factor influencing leisure participation that affects most people working?
- What is a factor influencing leisure participation that is affected by other people?
- What is a factor influencing leisure participation that affects most people's ability to feel comfortable?
- What is a factor influencing leisure participation that affects most people who are not physically fit?
- What is a factor influencing leisure participation that affects most people who have never tried an activity?

Prepare sufficient number of cards (one per participant) prior to session. Each card should contain one of the following:

- existing funds
- free time
- availability
- societal attitudes
- health
- skills

2. Debriefing

Content:

    a   Were you successful in obtaining answers to all of your questions?

    b.   Were you aware of these factors and their influence on leisure participation?

    c.   Are there other factors that should be considered? If so, what are they?

    d.   Why do you think we did this activity?

Process: Conduct debriefing using above questions. List the questions on a easel and refer to them as they are discussed. Encourage all participants to respond to at least one of the questions.

3. Introduction

Content: "There are many factors influencing people's decisions and abilities to participate in leisure. Examples of these factors include: money, free time, availability, societal attitudes, health, and skills. Acquiring knowledge about factors that affect leisure participation is an important part of developing an awareness of self in leisure."

Process: Introduce topic of factors that may affect leisure participation. Provide examples of these factors.

4. Presentation

Content: "*Money* is a factor that influences leisure participation. Although there are many recreation activities available that do not require money, there are also many that do. Many things in our lives require money. We may be required to pay rent, buy food and clothing, and meet expenses related to transportation, tuition, insurance, medical and dental care and a variety of other things. After these obligations have been met, there may not be any money remaining for other purposes such as recreation."

"Sometimes, there is money remaining after all obligations have been met. We can usually spend that money as we choose. This remaining money is discretionary money. Discretionary money can also be thought of as our existing funds. The amount of our existing funds influences the type of recreation activities in which we can engage. Some activities require a lot of money, some a moderate amount, and some activities require little or no money. When we think about participating in a recreation activity, we must consider how much money we have available and how much it costs to participate in that activity."

Process: Present information on money. Use the chalkboard or easel to record areas where money is required. Encourage participants to add to the following list:

> • food
> • clothing
> • transportation
> • tuition and membership fees
> • insurance
> • medical and dental care

5. Discussion

Content:
  a. What is discretionary money?
  b. What effect does money have on your recreation participation?
  c. What are some recreation activities you could do that do not require much money?
  d. Would you be willing to sacrifice one activity in order to accumulate money for another?
      If so, how would you do this?

Process: Conduct discussion using above questions. Refer back to the list on the chalkboard. Encourage all participants to contribute to the discussion.

6. Presentation

Content: "*Free time* also affects leisure participation. After our obligations to work, family, home, and self-maintenance are met, the time remaining is generally ours to do with as we please. Just as there is discretionary money, discretionary time also exists."

"Some recreation activities require fairly large blocks of time (e.g., a weekend at a ski resort). Some activities, however, can be enjoyed very quickly (e.g., a brief walk with a friend). Almost all recreation activities have a time component. The ability of people to make choices about their activities is influenced by the amount of free time they have and the amount of time required by the activity. Although many people complain about not having enough time to do the things they want or they do not have large enough blocks of time, there are many chances for participation in activities that do not demand large amounts of time. All it takes is a willingness to look for such activities."

Process: Present information on free time. Provide examples that are relevant to the participants. Emphasize the availability of activities that are brief and can facilitate leisure.

7. Discussion

Content:
  a. Do you feel you have enough or too much free time? Why?
  b. How can you use your free time to experience enjoyment and satisfaction?
  c. What kinds of things could you do if you had 30 minutes free during the day?
  d. What kinds of things could you do if you had all day free?

Process: Conduct discussion using above questions. A clock can be used as a visual aid during the discussion. Encourage participants to contribute to the discussion by responding to the questions.

8. Presentation

Content: "A third factor affecting leisure participation is *availability*. Availability refers to a number of elements that combine to determine if participation in a recreation activity is feasible. The opportunity to participate must be present in the community. For example, one cannot play tennis if there are no tennis courts available. The physical distance to the participation site cannot be too great. For example, the nearest tennis courts may be a day's drive from where one lives. If one has transportation, access to the tennis courts would be possible but the activity would not be readily available. The opportunity to participate must coincide with the time one is able to participate. If tennis courts were located in the community but open only in the mornings, people who worked during that time would not be able to participate. Activity sites must be accessible to those who want to use them. If the only tennis courts in the community are owned by a private club and their use is restricted to members, they are obviously not available to nonmembers. Tennis courts located in environments with physical barriers would not be accessible to people in wheelchairs. If tennis courts were open only to highly-skilled players, they would not be available to beginners or people wanting to learn how to play. These are examples of the kind of things that combine to determine if participation in a specific activity is available."

Process: Present information on availability. Record key points on the chalkboard or easel. Availability is related to the following points:

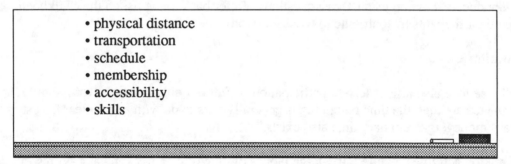

- physical distance
- transportation
- schedule
- membership
- accessibility
- skills

9. Discussion

Content:
    a.   What are some activities available to you in your neighborhood?
    b.   How does location of the facility affect your participation?
    c.   Why is it important to know what time activities are available at a particular agency?
    d.   What activities do you find are easy to access? Why?

Process: Conduct discussion using above questions. Encourage participants to contribute to the discussion by responding to the questions.

10. Presentation

Content: "*Societal attitudes* are another factor that affects participation in leisure. Some people may participate in certain activities because they think other people feel that is what they should be doing (e.g., playing bingo because they are older). In addition, some people may engage in, or refrain from, certain activities because of other prevalent societal attitudes (e.g., playing football because I am a boy; not building a tree house because I am a girl). At times some people may feel limitations are placed on them because of certain role obligations (e.g., spending all my free time doing things for my children rather than doing some things for myself). The presence of disabilities may influence participation of people who have them.   Individuals with disabilities may be denied the opportunity to engage in challenging adventure recreation activities because people think they may hurt themselves or that they do not possess the required skills. Societal attitudes can have a strong influence on our leisure participation."

Process: Present information on societal attitudes. Use slides and pictures depicting society's influence on leisure participation. Pictures and slides can be used to illustrate the examples mentioned above.

11. Discussion

Content:
a. What is an example of a societal role expectation?
b. Do you feel people expect you to do certain recreation activities? If so, which ones?
c. What are some characteristics of people that may result in others expecting them to behave a certain way?
d. Do you expect certain kinds of people to behave in certain ways? If so, describe the people and the type of behavior you expect from them?

Process: Conduct discussion using above questions. Encourage participants to contribute to the discussion by responding to each of the questions.

12. Presentation

Content: "A fifth factor affecting leisure participation is *health*. Some recreation activities are passive or sedentary, but many can be rigorous and demand a high level of health and fitness from participants. As people age, they may avoid certain activities because they feel they no longer have the levels of health and fitness required to participate. For example, they may feel they are lacking in strength and flexibility. Although aging is an inevitable process, it does not necessarily follow that it is always accompanied by drastic decreases in strength and flexibility. Many stretching and exercise programs can assist in increasing or maintaining strength and flexibility."

"Other examples of how health may affect participation could include slow recovery from injury, respiratory ailments that restrict the range of activities from which to choose, and illnesses that cause pain and discomfort. Some health conditions may cause a temporary change in one's leisure participation; other conditions may require a permanent change. In most cases, this could involve altering the level or intensity of participation in an activity or changing to another activity altogether. Individuals with health problems do not need to abandon interest or actual participation in leisure activities. They do need to recognize that health is a significant factor and to plan their leisure accordingly."

Process: Present information on health. Provide clear examples that are relevant to the participants. Emphasize how health does not have to be a barrier.

13. Discussion

Content:
a. How does health influence your participation?
b. Do you have health concerns influencing your leisure? If so, what are they?
c. How can you overcome health problems creating barriers to your leisure?
d. What suggestions do you have for other members of the group to overcome their health problems?

Process: Conduct discussion using above questions. Encourage participants to contribute to the discussion by responding to at least one of the questions. Stimulate problem solving to overcome the barrier of health.

14. Presentation

Content: "The sixth factor we are going to consider is *skill.* There seems to be a strong relationship between the level of skill one has and the amount of enjoyment that is experienced from participation in an activity. People with high levels of skill in an activity tend to continue to participate and enjoy that activity. People who work hard at developing skills in an activity but are not successful in doing so, tend to stop participating in that activity because there may be little or no enjoyment. Also, people usually enjoy participating in activities with other people who have similar levels of skill. Therefore, there should be many possibilities or choices within a single activity. For example, beginner, intermediate and advanced volleyball leagues could be offered."

"As you recognize skill as a factor that influences participation, you need to be able to improve your skills to meet the challenges of activities or adapt those activities to meet your skills. This means an effort must be made to find a reasonable match between skills and the activity. You must work toward participating in activities at a level that is good for you. You need to have the chance to develop more advanced skills as well as start new ones. Having many skills provides chances to express yourself in different ways and achieve leisure in various contexts. Skills, interests, and attitudes are very much related. Therefore, you must closely examine what you can do, what you want to do, and what you feel good doing. Skill is as significant as any of the other factors that affect participation."

Process: Present information on skill. Provide concise examples that are relevant to the participants. Encourage participants to think of ways to make a match with their skills and the requirements of various activities.

15. Discussion

Content:
   a.   What is one recreation activity skill you possess?
   b.   What recreation activity skill would you like to acquire?
   c.   Why is it useful to have a variety of recreation activity skills?
   d.   How can you increase your success in a recreation activity?

Process: Conduct discussion using above questions. Encourage each participant to contribute to the discussion by responding to at least one of the questions.

16. Learning Activity

Content: "We are going to do an activity that will help you apply what you have just learned about factors that affect leisure participation. I am going to divide you into small groups and ask each group to draw three cards from the box in the center of the table. Each card will contain a single recreation activity or event. Each group will hold a discussion about the impact of money, free time, availability, societal attitudes, health, and skill on each of the three events. After each small group has reached agreement about implications of the factors on each of the three events, it will present the results of its discussion to the larger group."

Process: Explain activity. List the six factors on the board. Divide participants into groups. Monitor activities. Prepare cards containing recreation activities or events prior to session. Examples of activities to write on cards could include:

- a weekend ski trip
- going for a walk with a friend
- competing in a 10 kilometer race
- going to the movies
- playing cards with the neighbors
- going on a picnic

17. Conclusion

Content: "Participation in a recreation activity requires more than interest or a desire to participate. There are several factors that must be considered and dealt with satisfactorily before participation is feasible. Being able to identify these factors and realizing how they influence participation is an important key to making decisions related to leisure."

Process: Make concluding statements. Provide opportunities for questions.

Objective 2.3: Demonstrate knowledge of past recreation involvement.

1. Orientation Activity

Content: "We are going to do an activity to introduce ourselves and to share our past recreation involvement with one another. On a sheet of paper, I want you to write one type of recreation that you enjoyed in the past. When all participants are finished, I will ask you to go around the room and introduce yourselves to each other and tell each other about your past recreation involvement. If you find someone with the same recreation involvement, pair up with them and introduce them to the next person. Once you have met each person and shared your experiences, sit down and wait for everyone to finish."

Process: Explain activity. Provide paper and pencils. Initiate introduction segment. Encourage participation and interaction.

2. Introduction

Content: "Past recreation involvement provides us with background information that can help us examine our awareness of self in leisure. Past experiences contribute to our knowledge and our present participation. By looking at our past involvement, we will increase our leisure awareness."

Process: Introduce topic of past recreation involvement.

3. Presentation

Content: "Our past recreation involvement can tell us our likes and interests. Several personal factors can cause changes in leisure. These factors can be determined by reviewing our past involvement. We need to look at those factors separately to see how and why they have changed. Personal factors may include age, health, free time, availability of recreation resources, and interest level. Any of these may change over time and cause a change in your recreation involvement.

"The amount of time you spent in recreation participation is also important. If you spent much of your time in recreation, it was probably important to you. You can gain a better understanding of the significance that leisure has had in your life by looking into the past."

Process: Present information on past recreation involvement. Provide examples that are appropriate for the participants.

4. Discussion

Content:
    a Why is your past recreation involvement important?
    b. What about your past involvement is important to remember?
    c. What factors can change over time and change your recreation involvement?
    d. How can you use your past experiences to increase awareness of your leisure?

Process: Conduct discussion using above questions. Encourage participants to contribute to the discussion.

5. Learning Activity

Content: "We are going to do an activity that will help us recall our past recreation involvement. Each of you will be given a paper bag, glue and magazines. Use the magazines to find pictures of recreation that you have enjoyed in the past and glue them to the bag. There will also be extra paper and markers available to draw pictures. Only choose pictures that are representative of activities that you have engaged in already. Once you have completed your projects, you will discuss your pictures with the rest of the group."

Process: Explain the activity. Distribute the supplies. Provide assistance to participants as necessary. Encourage all individuals to participate in the activity.

6. Debriefing

Content:
    a. How did this activity help you remember your past involvements?
    b. During this project, how did you become more aware of your past interests?
    c. How do your past experiences make you feel about your leisure lifestyle today?
    d. If you are not involved in some of these areas of recreation now, why not?

Process: Conduct discussion using above questions. Encourage participants to respond to at least one of the questions.

7. Learning Activity

Content: "We are going to do an activity to examine our past recreation involvement and the factors that were present. I am going to give you a handout that has been divided into several columns. In one column, you will make a list of your past involvements. Next to each item, you will describe personal factors considered during participation. These factors are headed: age, health, time, availability and interest level. Under each heading, record personal data during the time you participated in the recreation activity listed in the first column. Record as follows: your age at the time; your physical health in terms of being good, fair, or poor; hours per week you spent in this area; availability of resources in terms of good or poor; your interest level in this area in terms of high, medium or low. We will then take turns sharing one of our pastimes and our personal factors with the rest of the group. Each person will volunteer and present his or her data."

Process: Explain activity. Prepare handout with the following headings:

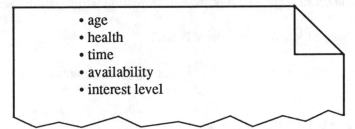

- age
- health
- time
- availability
- interest level

Distribute handout to the participants. Provide assistance as necessary. Encourage all participants to volunteer and share their data. Move to debriefing when activity is completed.

8. Debriefing

Content:

    a. Was it hard to remember the personal factors during your involvement? Why or why not?

    b. Do you think that some of your interests have changed because of these factors? If so, which ones?

    c. Would you like to change some factors so you can continue to be involved in these activities? If so, which ones?

    d. How did availability of the resource affect your participation?

    e. Has your interest level in the areas you listed changed over time, or has it remained the same? Why do you think it has or has not changed?

Process: Conduct debriefing using above questions. Encourage participants to contribute to the discussion by responding to at least one of the questions.

9. Learning Activity

Content: "We are going to see how much time we spent in recreation in the past. Again, we will look at our past involvements and the amount of time we spent in them. Each of you will receive a piece of paper with a circle drawn on it. I would like you to choose five of your past involvements and write them in the circle. Leave space between them. Under each word, write down the number of hours you spent each week in that area. Then make each activity into a piece of pie. Big pieces mean that you spent a great deal of time in that area, and little pieces mean that you spent a small amount of time in that area."

Process: Explain activity. Provide pictures of circles and writing utensils to each person. Provide assistance when necessary. Move to debriefing when activity is completed.

10. Debriefing

Content:
   a.   Did you spend an equal amount of time in each area, or more time in some than in others?
   b.   What do you think might be some reasons that you spent more time in some areas?
   c.   What are some reasons why you spent less time in some areas?
   d.   Do you feel like you spent a great deal of time in recreation participation, or a small amount of your time?
   e.   How would you change the circle to make it better?

Process: Conduct debriefing using above questions. Encourage participants to contribute by responding to the questions.

11. Learning Activity

Content: "We need to decide if leisure has been significant in our lives. Significance is how important it feels to us. We are going to make individual significance thermometers to show how important we feel leisure has been in our lives. I will give each of you a paper with a long narrow oval on it. If you feel recreation participation has little importance in your life, make a mark toward the bottom of the long oval. If you feel recreation has been of great importance, make a mark high on the oval. Color in red the area on the scale underneath the mark you made. The picture is now a thermometer of how important you think recreation has been in your life. Each of you will now show your thermometer and tell the group how important recreation participation has been to you."

Process: Explain the activity. Give each person a paper with a long narrow oval drawn on the sheet. Provide assistance as needed. Show two examples of thermometers drawn on an easel, one with a great deal of red to signify high and one with very little red to indicate low. Encourage participation. Move to debriefing.

12. Debriefing

Content:
   a.   How is the importance of recreation in your life influenced by past experiences?
   b.   Are you happy about the significance of leisure in your life? Why or why not?
   c.   How can you make recreation more important to you?
   d.   After looking at your scale, do you have a better understanding of the significance of recreation? In what way?

Process: Conduct debriefing using above questions. Encourage participants to contribute to the debriefing by responding to the questions.

13. Conclusion

Content: "Reviewing our past recreation involvement is a great way to look at our interests and is a method to use to find out how much time we have spent in recreation. We can see what has changed over time and what significance leisure has had in our lives. By looking at our past interests, we become more aware of the role that leisure has had in our lives."

Process: Make concluding statements. Provide opportunities for questions.

Objective 2.4: Demonstrate knowledge of current recreation involvement.

1. Orientation Activity

Content: "We are going to participate in an activity called 'I see you' to help us start thinking about our current participation in recreation activities. In my hand is a stack of cards. Each card contains the name of one person in this group. Each of you will be given the opportunity to draw one card from the stack. If you draw your own name, return the card and draw again. After everyone has drawn a card, arrange yourselves in a circle. We will start at one point in the circle and continue in a clockwise fashion. When it is your turn, look at the name on your card, use that person's first name, and try to guess what that person enjoys doing in his/her leisure participation. For example, the person who is guessing might say: 'Larry, in your leisure I see you flying model airplanes.' or 'Diane, in your leisure, I see you enjoying a walk through the park.' The person who was the subject of the guess must then tell the group whether the guess was correct or incorrect. Now it will be time for the person whose interest was guessed to guess about the person whose name is on his or her card. Continue guessing in this way until everyone has had a chance to guess what another person enjoys."

Process: Explain activity. Prepare cards, one for each person in the group. Select person to start activity. Emphasize necessity for guesses to be positive. Monitor process.

2. Debriefing

Content:
    a   Were you able to make an accurate guess of a leisure interest of the person whose name you drew? If so, on what did you base your guess?
    b. Was the guess made about your leisure interest accurate? On what basis do you think the guess was made?
    c. Did it make you uncomfortable to have someone guessing about your leisure activities? If so, why?
    d. What did you learn about the leisure interests of other members of the group?
    e. Were you surprised to learn this? If so, why?
    f. Why do you think we did this activity?

Process: Conduct debriefing using above questions. Emphasize how learning about recreation interests can help participants to get to know one another. Encourage all participants to contribute to the debriefing.

3. Introduction

Content: "Developing an awareness of leisure in your life requires an understanding of several related areas. We have spent some time in identifying our personal attitudes toward leisure and learning about factors that influence leisure participation. We have also thought about recreation activities in which we have engaged in the past. It is now time for us to think clearly and carefully about our current recreation involvement."

Process: Introduce topic of understanding your current recreation involvement.

4. Presentation

Content: "Thinking about our current recreation involvement seems easy. All we need to do is remember the recreation activities in which we participate. But sometimes we do not think as carefully as we should. For example, people might think of backpacking as a recreation activity in which they have recently been involved, but it has really been five years since their last backpacking journey. Would it be accurate to claim backpacking as a form of current recreation involvement? It is also difficult to be objective when we are thinking about ourselves. For example, people may not think of watching television as one of their current recreation involvements, when the truth is that this is how they spend a majority of their free time. It is not that these people are dishonest, they simply have not thought carefully.

"It can become easy to get from day-to-day without knowing how much or how little time is spent on specific activities, with whom time is spent, or how long it has been since participating in a favorite recreation activity. But there are several things you can do to arrive at a better understanding of how your time is actually spent. We are going to do several learning activities to help us understand our current recreation involvement."

Process: Present information on current recreation involvement. Gear examples to the needs and interests of the participants.

5. Discussion

Content:
    a   Why is it important to have knowledge of your current recreation involvement?
    b. How is it possible to not know precisely your current recreation involvement?
    c. What are some suggestions for determining your current recreation involvement?

Process: Conduct discussion using above questions. Encourage participants to respond to at least one of the questions.

6. Learning Activity

Content: "We are going to complete an exercise entitled 'Pie of Life.' It is a visual exercise designed to help individuals see how much of their time is spent on various activities during a typical day in their lives. You have each received a Pie of Life form. You can see the Pie of Life is represented by a circle and the circle has been divided into four equal quadrants. Each quadrant represents six of the 24 hours in a day. Take some time to think of how you spend a typical weekday. Choose any day, Monday through Friday. Divide the pie into segments (we will call them slices) that show how much time per day is spent on the things you typically do. For example, you may have a pie divided into: sleep, school, homework, household chores, self-maintenance (e.g., eating, personal hygiene), family obligations, and recreation.

"Another person may not have a slice that represents school but would have one that represents working to earn an income. The size of each slice depends on how much time is spent on the activity it represents. The more time that is spent on an activity, the larger the slice of pie; the less time that is spent, the smaller the slice. Try to be as accurate as possible in completing your Pie of Life. There is no predetermined right or wrong amount of time to spend on specific activities. Remember that the pie is to represent how you spend your time. Your pie may not resemble other pies in the group. When everyone has completed his or her pies,we will discuss what they depict."

Process: Explain activity. Prepare Pie of Life forms and distribute to individuals. Provide assistance as necessary. Move to debriefing.

7. Debriefing

Content:

    a. Which of your slices is the largest? Which is the smallest?
    b. How many different slices do you have?
    c. Are you satisfied with the relative size of your slices?
    d. If you could change the size of your slices, which ones would you change and what size would you make them?
    e. Is there a realistic possibility that you could change the size of some of your slices? If so, which ones?
    f. What would you have to do to bring about these changes?
    g. What did you learn from your Pie of Life?
    h. If you could step outside your Pie of Life and view it as someone else's, would you think that person had a balanced and interesting life? If not, why not?

Process: Conduct debriefing using above questions. Encourage participants to contribute to the discussion by responding to at least one of the questions.

8. Learning Activity

Content: "Now that you know how to do a Pie of Life, repeat the process, using a typical weekend day. Choose Saturday or Sunday and depict the way you typically spend your time. Again, be as accurate as possible and do not be concerned about what others' pies may look like. Your focus is to be on how you spend your time. When you are finished, compare your two pies."

Process: Explain activity. Distribute pie forms. Provide assistance as necessary.

9. Debriefing

Content:

    a. Did you have more free time available on a weekday or a weekend day?
    b. On which of the two days would you prefer to have free time available?
    c. If you could increase your free time on only one of the two days, which day would you choose? Why?
    d. What would you do with the increased free time?
    e. Are you satisfied with the way you spend your time, as depicted by both pies? If not, how would you change it?
    f. If you know how you would like to change the way in which you spend your time, is there anything preventing you from doing it? If so, what is it?

Process: Conduct debriefing using above questions. Encourage participants to contribute to the debriefing by responding to at least one of the questions.

10. Learning Activity

Content: "Another way to think about your current recreation involvement is to complete a recreation activity inventory. Each of you will be given an activity inventory form. The form will provide you with a place to list all of the recreation activities in which you have participated within the past year. The form will also contain columns in which you can respond to specified questions concerning those activities. Complete the form as correctly as possible. Do not include activities if you have not participated in them within the past calendar year. Again, the form should be a reflection of you and your recreation activities. Do not be concerned if it does not resemble other persons' forms. Use as many forms as needed to list your recreation activities in the past year."

Process: Explain activity. Prepare inventory form prior to session. Use lined paper. Provide space for 20-25 recreation activities on the left side of the paper. Remind participants to answer each of the following questions for each activity listed. On the remainder of the paper, prepare columns headed by the following questions:

- How often do I participate?
- When was the last time I participated?
- With whom did I participate?
- Where did I participate?
- How much did it cost?
- Was it fun?
- Do I want to do it again?
- Does this activity rank among my 10 most favorite activities?

11. Debriefing

Content:
a. Were you surprised at how many (or how few) activities are on your inventory?
b. Are you satisfied with the number of activities on your form?
c. What did you learn about your current recreation involvement?
d. What additional questions about the activities could be included on the form?

Process: Conduct debriefing using above questions. Encourage participants to participate actively in the debriefing by responding to at least one of the questions.

12. Conclusion

Content: "Thinking carefully about your current recreation involvement is a beneficial exercise. It can help you focus your thoughts on what you are now doing, rather than what you have done at times in the past. If you wish to make a change in your leisure participation, you must first know what your current status is. This type of exercise helps you to be objective and provides a good foundation for any decisions you may wish to make regarding your leisure."

Process: Make concluding statements. Provide opportunities for questions.

Objective 2.5: Demonstrate ability to identify possible future recreation activities.

1. Orientation Activity

Content: "We are going to play a type of 'leisure bingo' to help us get to know each other better and to start us thinking about recreation activities in which we would like to participate in the future. Each of you will be given a small piece of paper and a pencil. Write your name and one recreation activity in which you do not now participate but would like to try in the future. I will collect your slips of paper when you are finished and place them in a small basket.

"Each of you will also be given a sheet of paper that has been divided into 16 squares. Move about the room and meet other persons. Ask them their names and which activities they wrote on their slips of paper. Put the name of a person and his or her activity in one square. Continue this process until all the squares are filled.

"When everyone has finished, I will give each of you several poker chips. I will draw the slips of paper from the basket, one at a time. As I read the name and activity on the slip, look to see if it is on your sheet. If it is, place a poker chip on that square. The first person to cover four squares, vertically, horizontally, or diagonally, will call out 'bingo.' That person will be the winner."

Process: Explain activity. Distribute pencils and slips of paper. Prepare bingo sheets prior to session by dividing paper into 16 adjoining squares, four columns with four squares in each column. Distribute sheets and poker chips. Allow sufficient time for participants to fill squares. Draw and announce contents of slips. Confirm winner.

2. Debriefing

Content:
   a. Did you find anyone who had a future interest that matched yours? If so, who?
   b. By listening to others, did you get any ideas of activities in which you might become interested? If so, what were they?
   c. Did others list activities in which you already participate? If so, what were they?

Process: Conduct debriefing by using above questions. Encourage contributions from all participants by encouraging them to respond to the questions.

3. Introduction

Content: "Developing a comprehensive awareness of self in leisure is a task that includes several different components. We have examined four of these components. The remaining component is recreation activities in which we would like to participate in the future."

Process: Introduce topic of identifying possible future recreation activities in which they would like to engage.

4. Presentation

Content: "Thinking about which recreation activities you might like to do in the future is not just an exercise in wishful thinking, although dreaming about what you want to do is perfectly acceptable. Thinking about future recreation involvement should also be tempered with *realistic assessments* of the chances of participating in what you wish.

"Leisure, like life, is a dynamic process. It is not something that is static, but rather it changes and evolves as time passes. The things in which you are interested today might become things that are boring in a year's time. It is possible that some activities that may be widespread in the future have not yet been created and developed. Because change is inevitable, you should keep a *flexible attitude* about future recreation involvement.

"This is not to suggest that *long-term interests* should not be developed or that all interests and activities will be short-lived and eventually drop out of favor to be replaced by new ones. On the contrary, some activities that are favorites today may remain as favorites in the future. For example, nature walks are often a life-long interest for many people. There is no good reason for them to be otherwise, unless one becomes disinterested.

"The important focus is to *think seriously* about what you want in the future. Keeping interest and involvement in activities that bring joy and satisfaction is quite natural. But there should also be room for thinking about ideas of new activities that can be rewarding.

"Remember, it is fine to dream about what you want to do, but it often takes *purposeful effort* to make dreams come true. You should not be discouraged about future possibilities, but should understand that those things that are most likely to happen in the future are the things that you work to achieve."

Process: Present information on future recreation involvement. Use the chalkboard to record the following major points identified in the presentation

> • realistic assessments
> • flexible attitude
> • long-term interests
> • serious thought
> • purposeful effort

5. Discussion

Content:
    a. Why is it important to think about future recreation activities in which you want to participate?
    b. Do you participate in activities today that you did not do five years ago? Why?
    c. Which of your current recreation activities will still be of interest to you 10 years from now? Why?
    d. What can you do to increase your chances of participating in what you want in the future?

Process: Conduct discussion using above questions. Encourage all participants to contribute to the discussion by responding to at least one of the questions.

6. Learning Activity

Content: "A good way to begin thinking about future recreation involvement is to become aware of the many possibilities that exist. To start this process, we are going to participate in an activity known as 'Leisure Alphabet.' Get into groups of three. On a sheet of paper, list the letters of the alphabet in one or two columns. Now, try to think of recreation activities that begin with each letter of the alphabet, A through Z. If you think of an activity that begins with the letter A (e.g., archery), write that activity by the letter 'A.' Continue through the alphabet. Be as complete as possible but do not be discouraged if you do not think of an activity for a specific letter (e.g., 'Z'). You will have 15 minutes to complete this activity. Groups will then share results of their lists with the larger group."

Process: Explain activity. Provide pencil and paper. Put letters of alphabet on board. When groups are sharing, list activities by appropriate letter.

7. Debriefing

Content:
   a. Were any groups able to complete the entire alphabet?
   b. Were there any activities listed that were new to you? If so, what were they?
   c. What is your opinion of the diversity of activities?
   d. Do you see any activities that strike your interest as future possibilities? If so, what are they? What interests you about them?

Process: Conduct debriefing using above questions. Encourage participants to contribute to debriefing by having each person respond to at least one of the questions.

8. Learning Activity

Content: "Another way to think about possible future recreation involvement is to complete a 'Leisure Interest Finder.' Each of you will be given a form that has a list of words on the left-hand side, a column headed by 'By Myself' and a second column headed by 'With Others.' The two columns will be to the right of, but adjacent to, the list of words. For each of the words on the left-hand side, think of a recreation activity that you would enjoy doing by yourself in the future and record that activity in the column headed 'By Myself.' Think of another activity for that same word that you would enjoy doing with others in the future and enter it in the column headed by 'With Others.' Do not use an activity more than once. When everyone has finished, we will discuss the results."

Process: Explain activity. Prepare Leisure Interest Finder forms prior to session. Distribute forms and pencils. Encourage participants to complete both columns. Provide sufficient time to complete. Move to debriefing. Word list could include the following:

Active	Social
Passive	Cultural
Spring	Educational
Summer	Intellectual
Autumn	Entertaining
Winter	Creative
Indoors	Physical
Outdoors	Artistic

9. Debriefing

Content:

a. What activities were listed for 'Active' and 'By Myself?' (Use several combination of words and columns.)

b. Was it easier to think of activities for the 'With Others' column than the 'By Myself' column? If so, why?

c. Did you get any ideas for future participation from listening to the others? If so, what were they?

d. What are the possibilities that you will participate in several activities you listed?

Process: Conduct debriefing using above questions. Encourage each participant to contribute to the debriefing by having them respond to at least one of the questions.

10. Learning Activity

Content: "An additional way to think about recreation activities in which you might want to participate is to project yourself into the future to a time where you could do anything you wanted. Imagine that for a 48 hour period, you could do as you wish. The 48 hours could be next week, next month, next year, or any other time in the future. You have no physical or financial constraints; your only limit is the 48 hour time period. What would you do with that time? Construct an ideal 48 hours for yourself and put it in writing. Be as creative as you want; fantasize to your heart's content. When you are finished, be prepared to share your ideal 48 hours with the group."

Process: Explain activity. Distribute pencils and paper. Encourage creative thinking. Create an atmosphere of acceptance to innovative and different ideas.

11. Debriefing

Content:

a. What did your 48 hours look like?

b. What did you learn about yourself?

c. What did you learn about others?

d. Is there a chance some of your ideal 48 hours will come to pass?

e. What will you have to do to help it come true?

f. Was the process of fantasizing fun? How so?

Process: Conduct debriefing using above questions. Encourage participants to be active contributors to the debriefing by having them respond to at least one of the questions. Have as many participants as possible respond to the first question.

12. Learning Activity

Content: "Each of you now has the opportunity to create a future leisure collage. There are plenty of magazines, scissors, glue, and construction paper available to you. Browse through the magazines and cut out pictures of activities you will be doing or want to be doing in the future. Glue these pictures to the construction paper in any pattern you wish. Be as colorful and creative as you can, but remember your collage should represent you and what you want to do."

Process: Explain activity. Supply magazines, scissors, glue, and paper. Emphasize future orientation of collage.

13. Debriefing

Content:
    a. What do you like best about your collage? Why?
    b. How would you describe the majority of the depictions on your collage? Are they Physical? Social? Cultural? Solitary? Group?
    c. If you made a leisure collage five years from now, do you think it would be similar to this one?
    d. What will you do with your collage?

Process: Conduct debriefing using above questions. Encourage participants to contribute to the debriefing by responding to at least one of the questions.

14. Conclusion

Content: "Thinking about possible future recreation involvement is both healthy and necessary. How else will we know what we want to do? Although we have to do more than speculate about the future, speculating is the first step. Once we know where we want to go, then we can plan how to get there."

Process: Make concluding statements. Provide opportunity for participants to ask questions.

LEISURE EDUCATION: SELF-DETERMINATION IN LEISURE

Purpose, Goal, and Objectives

Purpose: Provide opportunities for participants to learn about their personal successes in leisure, understand the importance of personal growth and responsibility for leisure participation, learn to express preferences, and understand how to be assertive.

Goal 3: Demonstrate an understanding of self-determination in leisure.

Objective 3.1.   Demonstrate knowledge of personal successes in leisure.
Objective 3.2.   Demonstrate knowledge of the importance of personal growth associated with leisure.
Objective 3.3.   Demonstrate knowledge of the importance of personal responsibility for leisure participation.
Objective 3.4.   Demonstrate the ability to express preferences.
Objective 3.5.   Demonstrate knowledge of assertive behaviors.

Goal, Objectives, and Performance Measures

Goal 3: Demonstrate an understanding of self-determination in leisure

Objective 3.1: Demonstrate knowledge of personal successes in leisure.

Performance Measure: Given a list of 30 recreation activities (e.g., making friends, eating out, dancing, hiking, reading, skiing, playing cards, talking, swimming, writing, canoeing, jogging) with an additional three spaces identified as "other" to allow additions to the list, a paper and pencil, in five minutes:
  (a) identify three recreation activities where some level of success was achieved, and
  (b) specify a specific instance of success associated with each of the three recreation activities (e.g., making friends: "Last year I met this teacher and we see each other at least once a month and have a great time."; eating out: "Yesterday I had a terrific salad for lunch at that little Italian restaurant").
with 100% accuracy on two consecutive occasions.

Objective 3.2: Demonstrate knowledge of the importance of personal growth associated with leisure.

Performance Measure: Given a list of 30 recreation activities (e.g., making friends, eating out, dancing, hiking, reading, skiing, playing cards, talking, swimming, writing, canoeing, jogging), paper and pencil, in 10 minutes:
  (a) choose three activities from the list,
  (b) give an example of how people could focus on incremental improvements when participating in these three recreation activities (e.g., "Two weeks ago it took me 14 minutes to run a mile and a half, today I ran it in 13 minutes and 45 seconds."), and

(c)   provide a way people could reduce interpersonal comparisons when engaging in the three activities (e.g., "Rather than saying she ran faster than me today, I should talk about how I have reduced my time by 15 seconds in two weeks."),

with 100% accuracy on three consecutive occasions.

Objective 3.3: Demonstrate knowledge of the importance of personal responsibility for leisure participation.

Performance Measure: Upon request and within five minutes, state four possible reasons why personal responsibility for leisure participation is important (e.g., to allow change, to encourage learning, to avoid feelings of helplessness, to stimulate growth, to reduce impact of barriers, to gain control, to permit freedom, to facilitate engagement) with 100% accuracy on three consecutive occasions.

Objective 3.4: Demonstrate the ability to express preferences.

Performance Measure: Given four lists of five recreation activities (e.g., going to the movie theater, walking outside, talking to a friend on the phone, listening to music, volunteering to help someone, OR playing video games, chatting over dinner, playing tennis, painting, building models) in five minutes to speak:
  (a)   identify the most preferred recreation activity associated with each list (totaling four activities), and
  (b)   identify one reason why you chose each activity (going to the movie theater: "I like getting out of the house and seeing what many people are talking about." OR playing tennis: "I like to stay fit and enjoy the out-of-doors.") by using a different reason for each activity,

with 100% accuracy on three consecutive occasions.

Objective 3.5: Demonstrate knowledge of assertive behaviors.

Performance Measure A: Given five minutes to speak, identify three basic assertive rights (e.g., act to promote dignity and respect without violating others' rights, be treated with respect, say no without guilt, express feelings, change one's mind, ask for preferences, ask for information, make mistakes, feel good about self), with 100% accuracy on three consecutive occasions.

Performance Measure B: Given five minutes to speak, make distinctions among the following modes of interaction by identifying two characteristics of each:
  (a)   assertive behavior (e.g., honest, direct, respectful, accurate),
  (b)   aggressive behavior (e.g., illogical, hurts others, explosive, offensive), and
  (c)   nonassertive behavior (e.g., manipulative, dishonest, ulterior motives, hidden agendas, vague intentions),

with 100% accuracy on three consecutive occasions.

Goals, Objectives, Content, and Process

Goal 3: Demonstrate an understanding of self-determination in leisure.

Objective 3.1: Demonstrate knowledge of personal successes in leisure.

1. Orientation Activity

Content: "We are going to do an activity to help us meet each other and to help us think about personal successes in leisure. Please arrange yourselves in a circle. I want you to think about a personal success that was a result of a leisure experience. For example, during a visit to the park, you improved your appreciation for nature. When you have a success in mind, stand up in the circle. After every person stands, join hands with the person next to you. We will start with the last person who joined the circle and have this person state his or her name and the leisure success. We will continue clockwise until everyone has taken his or her turn."

Process: Explain activity. Arrange participants in a circle. Encourage each person to participate. If appropriate, ask participants to provide some additional detail related to their reported leisure experience.

2. Introduction

Content: "Our ability to determine what we want to do in leisure happens more easily when we become aware of our personal successes. Leisure provides an excellent opportunity for us to experience success. It is very important for us to realize when we are successful because this information will help us decide what we will do in the future. Our success is often related to how we feel about what we did in a given activity and the accomplishments we experienced. Personal successes are, therefore, defined by the individual and are unique to each individual. It is important to recognize your successes in leisure to increase your ability to determine what you will be in the future and gain control of your life. Leisure is a rewarding, self-fulfilling experience during which you can allow yourself the satisfaction of personal successes."

Process: Introduce topic of personal successes in leisure.

3. Presentation

Content: "Personal successes provide us with feelings of pride, self-worth, and personal satisfaction. Leisure gives us the opportunity to experience these qualities. If we allow ourselves to review our leisure experiences, we will become aware of our successes. The successes we experience in leisure are often internally rewarding. These experiences are not determined by external rewards or reinforcement from other people. The successes we experience are determined by the feelings of pride and satisfaction we derive from our participation. We can measure our leisure experiences by comparing our personal successes to the different values we feel are important. Our values include any personal beliefs we have that are related to our wanting to do something that is in the best interest of all people. Such values might include: appreciation of nature, respect for other people, making life fun for yourself and others, equal rights and opportunities for all people. These are just a few examples of values that you can think about when you participate in leisure."

Process: Present information on personal successes.

4. Discussion

Content:
a.   What are some of the feelings we get from personal successes?
b.   When can we experience personal successes?
c.   How are these experiences determined?
d.   How can we measure these successes?
e.   What are some of your values you use to measure success?

Process: Conduct discussion using above questions. Encourage participants to contribute to the discussion.

5. Learning Activity

Content: "We are going to look at our leisure experiences to determine what benefits we have felt as a result of leisure. I will give each of you a form to rate your feelings in different leisure experiences. I would like each of you to write five different recreation activities that you have participated in recently. There is a space on each form to record the activity. Under each activity, there are various benefits listed. Rate each from one to three. A rating of one means you felt this value strongly, a two means you felt it somewhat, and a three means you did not feel this value during this activity."

Process: Explain activity. Have forms prepared prior to activity session. Construct each form to have five activities to be rated according to the following benefits:

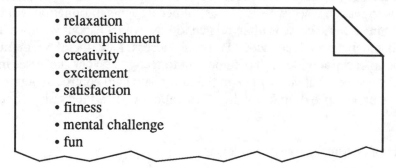

* relaxation
* accomplishment
* creativity
* excitement
* satisfaction
* fitness
* mental challenge
* fun

6. Debriefing

Content:
a.   Which benefits did you find you experienced during the activities? Why?
b.   Do you feel more of these values in some activities than others? If so, which ones?
c.   Do you think about these feelings when you are participating in these activities? If so, why? If not, why not?
d.   How do these feelings make your leisure experiences meaningful?
e.   What other benefits do you receive from leisure participation?

Process: Conduct debriefing using above questions. Encourage all participants to contribute to the debriefing. Provide a list of the benefits on the chalkboard and add additional benefits contributed by the participants to the list.

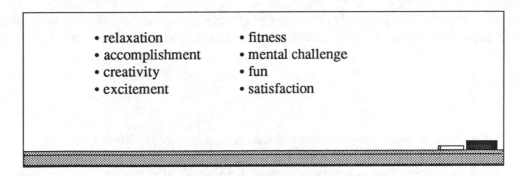

    • relaxation   • fitness
    • accomplishment • mental challenge
    • creativity   • fun
    • excitement   • satisfaction

7. Learning Activity

Content: "Now we are going to list possible successes in leisure. Each of us has our own ideas of success. Success can be anything that provides us with positive feelings. Some examples of success are: making new friends, building a bird house, and catching a ball. Together with three other participants, think of ten successes that can be achieved in leisure. Record these on the paper you have received. Once each group has identified ten activities, one person from each group will come to the easel and record one of the items from their list. We will take turns. Please try not to repeat any of the successes that are listed before yours. After we have had one contribution from each group, we will move to round two involving a different person from each group to record one response on the easel. We will continue in this way until everyone has had a chance to add to the list."

Process: Explain activity. Divide into groups. Provide paper, pencil and chalk. Assist participants when necessary. Encourage all individuals to participate and contribute to the list. After the paper becomes filled with responses, tear off the page and tape the paper to the wall with masking tape. Have participants continue to write on the next page of the easel. Encourage participants to write large enough for people to see but small enough to get at least a few successes listed on a given piece of paper. Draw lines to guide participants, if needed.

8. Debriefing

Content:
    a. Was it difficult to think of successes in leisure? If so, why? If not, why not?
    b. Is there a limit to possible successes during leisure? If so, why? If not, why not?
    c. Can one person's idea of success differ from another's idea? Why or why not?
    d. Do differences in ideas mean that one is a success and one is not? Please explain.

Process: Conduct debriefing using above questions. Encourage all participants to answer at least one question. Refer back to the items listed on the easel throughout the debriefing.

9. Learning Activity

Content: "We can now look at our own personal successes in leisure. Each of us has our own interests and we each reach different levels of success in these interests. On the piece of paper you have been given, I want you to use the paints on the table to paint a picture of what you have achieved in leisure recently. Include paintings of any feelings or improvements you have had that resulted from your leisure participation. You will be able to share the picture with the group."

Process: Explain the activity. Provide paper and paints. Assist participants when necessary. Move about the room to examine the paintings. Provide verbal encouragement and guidance when appropriate. After the paintings are completed, have participants sit in a circle and one at a time stand and describe their painting.

10. Debriefing

Content:
   a.   Was it difficult to paint your successes based on your interests? Why or why not?
   b.   Do your personal successes make you feel good about your leisure?
   c.   Do these successes make you a better person? If so, how? If not, why?
   d.   Can participating in leisure increase chances for you to succeed? Why or why not?

Process: Conduct debriefing using above questions. Prior to the debriefing, tape the pictures on the walls in the room so that they can be viewed by the participants. If needed, pictures can be referred to during the debriefing. Encourage all participants to respond to at least one of the debriefing questions.

11. Learning Activity

Content: "Personal successes in leisure contribute to our self-determination. This means that the more we succeed, the more likely we will independently choose what we like to do. If we experience success in leisure, we are more likely to be determined to participate in leisure. With this in mind, we are going to rate our level of determination in leisure based on our successes in leisure. I have a rating form for you to complete. Rate your level of determination on how strongly you wish to engage in leisure to achieve personal successes. Circle the word that best describes your rating."

Process: Explain the activity described above. Provide participants with the scale to rate determination level from high to low. An example of a possible scale is:

DETERMINATION LEVEL IN LEISURE

HIGH

MEDIUM

LOW

---

12. Debriefing

Content:
   a.   Do you feel more determined to engage in leisure because of the personal successes you achieved during leisure? If so, why? If not, why not?
   b.   Now that you have experienced some personal successes from leisure, will you be more determined for leisure? Why or why not?
   c.   How does the amount of determination you have in leisure affect your success?

Process: Conduct debriefing using above questions. Encourage all participants to contribute to the debriefing.

13. Conclusion

Content: "Personal successes are valuable to individual well-being and worth. We can experience successes during leisure that enhance ourselves and improve our personal qualities. Leisure provides us with the opportunity for self-accomplishment and reward."

Process: Make concluding statements. Provide opportunity for questions.

Objective 3.2: Demonstrate knowledge of the importance of personal growth associated with leisure.

1. Orientation Activity

Content: "We are going to do an activity to meet each other and to begin to look at personal growth in leisure. I have placed several large pieces of paper and markers around the room. Find another person in the room and introduce yourself. This person will now be your partner in this activity. Choose one person to go first. Those of you going first will tell your partner one way that you have grown in leisure. Your partner will illustrate this growth by drawing a picture on the paper. Your partner will have only a few minutes to complete the drawing while you watch and encourage him or her. When I give the signal, you will switch roles and your partner will now tell of personal growth associated with a leisure experience and you will illustrate this growth in a picture. After I give the signal, you will bring the pictures to the front of the room so we can tape them to the wall. Then we will look at each other's drawings for similarities and differences. Each of you will stand next to the picture that illustrates your personal growth in leisure and tell us your name. Then tell us how leisure has helped you grow."

Process: Explain activity. Divide into partners. Provide supplies and assistance when necessary.

2. Introduction

Content: "Personal growth is often associated with the leisure experience. During leisure we are able to do things that help us grow in many different ways. Each person's growth is different as a result of his or her leisure experience. Our personal growth also helps us increase our self-determination in leisure."

Process: Introduce topic of personal growth.

3. Presentation

Content: "It is often helpful for us to understand the importance of personal growth in leisure. Leisure gives us the chance to develop in many areas. These areas include physical growth to help our bodies become fit; social growth to help us develop relationships with friends, family members, and co-workers; mental growth to help us understand things, and emotional growth to help us feel good about ourselves and to show our feelings and express ourselves in ways that show we care about ourselves and other people. Physical development can include motor skills, fitness, stress reduction, and active participation. Social growth is related to communication skills, interaction with others, teamwork, sharing, and helping others. Mental development can include learning, listening, asking questions, thinking, and answering questions. Emotional growth can relate to controlling negative behaviors, showing positive emotions, and reacting to satisfying experiences. Leisure helps us grow in all these areas. To improve your knowledge about personal growth in leisure, we will look at each of these areas separately."

Process: Present information on personal growth in leisure. Write key words on an easel or chalkboard.

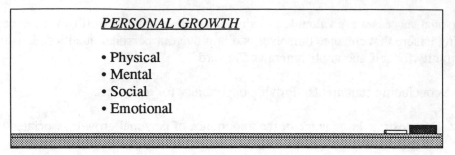

4. Discussion

Content:
    a. Is personal growth associated with leisure?
    b. In what areas do we grow in leisure?
    c. What are some characteristics of physical growth?
    d. What are some characteristics of mental growth?
    e. What are some characteristics of emotional growth?
    f. What are some characteristics of social growth?
    g. How can we improve our knowledge of personal growth?

Process: Conduct discussion using above questions. Encourage all participants to respond to at least one of the questions. Record responses on an easel for further clarification.

5. Learning Activity

Content: "Our physical growth can be reviewed by looking at our motor skills, fitness, if we are feeling good, and how actively we participate. We are going to describe each of these areas as they relate to our leisure experiences. These four areas of physical growth have been listed on a sheet of paper. Under each heading, circle the word that best describes how much you feel leisure has improved your growth in this area. Rate each one low, medium, or high. For example, if you feel your physical skills have improved greatly because of leisure participation, circle high after that category."

Process: Explain activity. Provide form and pencils. Provide assistance when necessary. Include the following categories on the paper.

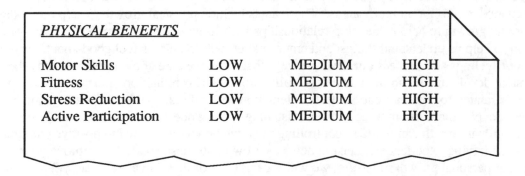

PHYSICAL BENEFITS			
Motor Skills	LOW	MEDIUM	HIGH
Fitness	LOW	MEDIUM	HIGH
Stress Reduction	LOW	MEDIUM	HIGH
Active Participation	LOW	MEDIUM	HIGH

6. Debriefing

Content:
    a.   What was the most common rating you gave to each of these areas?
    b.   Are some areas of physical growth improved more than others? If so, which ones?
    c.   Is leisure responsible for your physical growth in these areas? Why or why not?
    d.   Can you use leisure to improve your physical growth? If so, how? If not, why?

Process: Conduct debriefing using above questions. Encourage all participants to respond to at least one question.

7. Learning Activity

Content: "Mental growth is experienced during leisure every time we have to think, make decisions, and learn something. When we listen and respond to others, we are also using our mental skills. I want you to get into groups of three. Each group will receive a list of recreation activities. Look at each activity separately and write down two ways that you could grow mentally in each area. Write these on the paper next to each activity. After everyone is finished, we will ask each group to present its responses."

Process: Explain the activity listed above to the participants. Divide participants into groups containing three people. Distribute lists to each group. The following is an example of a possible list:

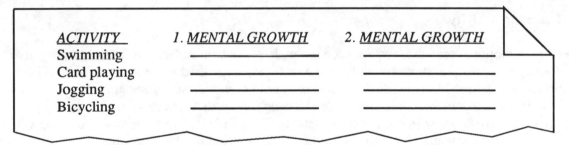

ACTIVITY	*1. MENTAL GROWTH*	*2. MENTAL GROWTH*
Swimming		
Card playing		
Jogging		
Bicycling		

8. Debriefing

Content:
    a.   Do all these activities help you grow mentally? If so, how? If not, why?
    b.   Were there different amounts of growth for you in the activities? What were they?
    c.   Do we improve our mental growth during recreation activities?
    d.   What are some recreation activities that are helpful to your mental growth?

Process: Conduct debriefing using above questions. Encourage each person to contribute to the discussion.

9. Learning Activity

Content: "Social growth is experienced during leisure when we interact with others. Teamwork, sharing, helping other people, and communicating with people improves our social skills. We will now divide into groups of four. Try to find three other people with whom you have yet to work. I will give each group an example of a leisure situation. Together, try to figure out what social skills you would use if you were in this situation. Make a list of all ideas. When everyone is finished, we will ask each group to share its list with the other participants."

Process: Explain the activity described above. Assist participants in getting into groups. Distribute paper with situations such as the following:

> *LEISURE SITUATION*
> 1. Volleyball game
> 2. Camping trip
> 3. White water rafting
> 4. Picnic with friends
>
> *SOCIAL SKILLS*
> 1._____
> 2._____
> 3._____
> 4._____

10. Debriefing

Content:
    a. Do some situations use more social skills than others? If so, which ones required the most and which ones required the least?
    b. What social skills are used when participating with groups?
    c. Can different leisure situations improve our social skills?
    d. Does leisure help us with our social growth? If so, how? If not, why?

Process: Conduct debriefing using above questions. Encourage all participants to respond.

11. Learning Activity

Content: "Emotional growth is experienced during leisure when we learn to control our negative behaviors, show positive emotions, and react to satisfying experiences. Leisure can help us improve our emotional expression. Please write down five of your leisure interests. Look at these and think about how you feel when you are involved in them. Now on five separate sheets of paper, draw a picture of the emotions you experience with each of the situations. For example, when you walk your dog you feel loved. You can draw yourself hugging your dog. After you are finished drawing your pictures, we will tape them at the front of the room and each person will describe his or her picture and what was felt during leisure."

Process: Explain the activity described above. Distribute five sheets of paper (for drawing), colored pencils, and a blank sheet of paper (for listing) to each participant. Provide assistance to the participants when necessary. Tape pictures on the walls. Encourage all participants to describe their pictures.

12. Debriefing

Content:
    a. How do you feel when you are involved in a leisure experience?
    b. Do you show positive emotions during leisure? If so, what are they? If not, why?
    c. Do you control negative behaviors during leisure? If so, how? If not, why?
    d. Do you react to satisfying experiences through your emotions? Please describe.
    e. Can leisure help you improve mental growth? If so, how? If not, why?

Process: Conduct debriefing using above questions. Encourage all participants to respond to at least one of the questions listed above.

13. Conclusion

Content: "We experience personal growth in leisure through four areas of development: physical, mental, social, and emotional. We can use our personal growth in leisure to make us more determined to participate in leisure."

Process: Make concluding statements. Provide opportunities for participants to ask questions and voice any concerns they may have.

Objective 3.3: Demonstrate knowledge of the importance of personal responsibility for leisure participation.

1. Orientation Activity

Content: "Let's do an activity to help us meet one another. Form two lines and face the person across from you. Shake your neighbor's hand and introduce yourself to him or her. With this person move to an area away from the other participants and sit on the floor. Have the person describe to you a time when he or she took responsibility for his or her actions. If he or she is having difficulty, try to assist this person by asking them helpful questions or make suggestions. If you both have difficulty, I will be available to assist you. After the person has identified a time that he or she was responsible it will be your turn to do the same. When you both have identified a time when you were responsible, stand up and go to different pairs to assist the people talking. After they have each identified a time when they were responsible, all four stand and find others. Continue until everyone is standing."

Process: Explain the activity described above. Help participants form two lines. Encourage participation. Move about the room assisting those individuals who have difficulty expressing themselves.

2. Introduction

Content: "It is important for us to take responsibility for our leisure participation. This means that each one of us is responsible for our own happiness and satisfaction. Therefore, if we are not enjoying ourselves, we must look closely at what we are doing and determine ways we can change. This means that we must take credit for our satisfaction and we must not blame others if we are not satisfied. Personal responsibility is taking control of a situation. We can control our leisure by learning about our responsibilities."

Process: Introduce topic of personal responsibility in leisure.

3. Presentation

Content: "To understand our personal responsibility in leisure, we can think about what we must do in a leisure situation. Each of us has responsibilities for leisure. Responsibility involves becoming more aware of what we enjoy and what we can do to help ourselves feel good. Trying to understand our skills and limitations is an example of showing responsibility. When we act in certain ways and accept the consequences of those actions, we are being responsible. We also may choose to develop skills and recognize that growth requires effort, time and practice. Responsibility in leisure requires us to know about resources associated with chosen recreation activities. When we take steps to ensure our physical health, we are setting the stage for ourselves to be able to experience leisure more easily and, therefore, we are being responsible for our actions. The following are just a few examples of ways we can be more responsible for our leisure participation.

"If we are to participate in an activity, it is our responsibility to learn the skills necessary for participation. We can develop skills before and during participation, but it is something we must each do. No one can do this for us. People may help and provide guidance, but when all is said and done, we must put forth energy and effort to gain skills. This is what responsibility is all about.

"It is our responsibility to gain knowledge of leisure resources. If we want to be able to participate in leisure, we have to know what is available to us. Not only do we have to know what is available, but we need to learn where the activity is going to take place. Once we determine where it is, we need to consider how to get there next. It is also useful to learn when the desired activity is going to occur. As we consider all of these issues and many other ideas, we are demonstrating responsibility for our leisure participation and, ultimately, our happiness.

"We must maintain our physical health to engage in leisure. Of course, there are some things over which we do not have control. There are, however, many actions we can take that keep us healthy as possible. We can try to get plenty of rest so that we have the energy to do the things that bring joy into our lives. Eating right and ensuring we receive proper nutrition is another action that demonstrates responsibility and can put us in position to experience leisure. Taking any medication we are on at the prescribed times with the recommended dosages is also very important. Staying fit by exercising regularly allows us to have the strength and stamina to do many things that we like. Doing all these things shows that we are acting responsibly and taking control of our lives.

"Each of us is responsible for initiating our own participation. If we have a desire to participate, we have to be the ones to do it. Therefore, we must learn to choose to participate in activities we enjoy without the prodding of other people. To be responsible for our leisure means we must initiate some of our participation. This means it is fine to talk with other people when we are thinking about doing something. We must, however, take responsibility for our choices and contribute to the decision-making process.

"Taking personal responsibility in leisure gives us control over what we do during leisure. Understanding our responsibilities and learning how to meet them makes us more self-determined in leisure."

Process: Present the information described above. Provide as many examples as possible. Expand the list to meet the unique needs of the participants. Present pictures of people demonstrating responsible actions that may lead to enhanced leisure participation. List key words on a chalkboard and write any additional phrases that may help participants retain information.

- learn leisure skills
- gain knowledge of leisure resources
- maintain physical health
- initiate participation

4. Debriefing

Content:
a. How do we have personal responsibility in leisure?
b. What are some of our responsibilities in leisure?
c. Who is responsible for developing our skills for participation? Why?
d. What is the benefit of having knowledge about leisure resources?
e. How can we become responsible for our physical health?
f. Do you control your participation in leisure? If so, how? If not, why?

Process: Conduct debriefing using above questions. Encourage all participants to respond to at least one of the questions. Refer to the key words listed on the chalkboard when discussing the concepts.

5. Learning Activity

Content: "We are going to do an activity to learn more about our responsibility in leisure. I want you to find two other people to work with during this activity. The three of you must choose what you all will do together this evening during your free time. You must come up with an activity that you all enjoy and includes one of the following: (a) it allows you to learn leisure skills, or (b) it provides you with an opportunity to gain knowledge of leisure resources, or (c) it increases your ability to maintain your physical health. After you choose the activity, devise a plan to make it possible for the three of you to participate in this recreation activity together. When the plan is completed, discuss why it is important to take personal responsibility for your leisure participation. Write your ideas on the paper you have been given. Each group will report to the entire group. One member of the group will describe the recreation activity the group chose. Another member of the group will describe the plan devised to allow them to participate. The final member of the group will state why it is important to take responsibility for leisure participation."

Process: Explain activity. Help participants get into groups of three. Provide paper and pencils to each group. Offer assistance as needed. Write group ideas on the board. List the criteria for the recreation activity on the easel or chalkboard.

> • enjoyable, and
> • learn leisure skills, or
> • gain knowledge of leisure resources, or
> • maintain physical health

6. Debriefing

Content:
a. Did you feel like it was your responsibility to help choose a recreation activity all of you liked?
b. By choosing the activity, how did you demonstrate responsibility?
c. Did you have control over the situation when working with the other people? If so, how? If not, why?
d. Will you be more likely to engage in leisure when you are responsible? If so, how? If not, why?

Process: Conduct debriefing using above questions. Encourage each person to respond. Refer to the criteria followed to choose the activity.

7. Learning Activity

Content: "We must take personal responsibility to learn the skills that are required for leisure participation. On the board, I have listed six different activities. We are going to list the skills that we would need to learn for each one. Then, we will discuss why it is our responsibility to develop these skills if we want to participate in these activities."

Process: Explain activity. Write the activities on the board and leave space for skills to be recorded under each activity. List activities appropriate for the participants. Some possible activities include:

> • swimming
> • gardening
> • playing volleyball
> • bowling
> • walking
> • playing softball

8. Debriefing

Content:
>   a.   How can a lack of skills prevent us from participating in recreation activities?
>   b.   How can we take responsibility and learn skills needed to experience leisure?
>   c.   If we learn the skills needed to participate in a desired recreation activity, are we more determined to participate in an activity? If so, how? If not, why?
>   d.   What could happen if we do not take responsibility to learn leisure skills?

Process: Conduct debriefing using above questions. Encourage all participants to respond to at least one of the questions.

9. Learning Activity

Content: "It is our responsibility to learn about leisure resources that are available to us. Pair up with one other person. Together, make a list of all the leisure resources you can think of that are available to you related to swimming, bowling, gardening, softball, walking, and volleyball. For example, if you would like to go swimming, there may be a pool in your neighborhood. After each group is finished, we will have each person read a resource from the list to the entire group."

Process: Explain activity. Help participants find partner. If there is an odd number of people, participate in the activity. Provide paper and pencils. Offer assistance when necessary. Ask each pair to share its list with the other participants.

10. Debriefing

Content:
    a. What are some leisure resources that are available?
    b. Why is it important to know about leisure resources?
    c. Who is responsible for knowing what is available?
    d. How can knowledge of leisure resources improve your self-determination?

Process: Conduct debriefing using above questions. Encourage all participants to respond to at least one of the questions.

11. Learning Activity

Content: "We are responsible for our physical health. I have a handout for each of you that divides physical health into several different areas of responsibility. These areas include: personal hygiene, exercise, diet, and health conditions. Personal hygiene is your daily self-care, dress, and appearance. Exercise includes any physical activity you engage in regularly. Diet is what you eat and drink each day. Health conditions include problems or illness of the body. Under each heading, write your responsibilities in each of these areas. For example, it is your responsibility to eat a balanced diet each day."

Process: Explain the learning activity described above. Provide assistance to the participants when necessary. Prepare handouts with the following heading and leave space below each heading for participants to record their responsibilities:

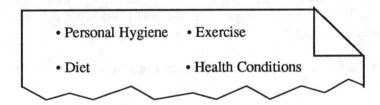

- Personal Hygiene   • Exercise

- Diet   • Health Conditions

12. Debriefing

Content:
    a. What responsibilities do you have for personal hygiene?
    b. How does personal hygiene relate to your leisure participation?
    c. How can exercise help your physical health and enhance your ability to enjoy life?
    d. How will maintaining a balanced diet assist you in becoming more self-determined?
    e. How does taking care of our health improve our ability to experience leisure?

Process: Conduct debriefing using above questions. Encourage each person to respond to at least one of the questions listed above.

13. Learning Activity

Content: "It is our personal responsibility to participate in leisure. Everyone sit down in a circle. I want each person to think of one reason why he or she should be responsible for his or her leisure participation. For example, I think that I should be responsible because sometimes I may be by myself and I will be the only person I can depend on. After you have thought of a reason why it is important to be responsible, fold your arms across your chest. When everyone has his or her arms folded, we will have one person at a time tell the group what he or she thought of. There are no wrong or right answers, we are just interested in what you are thinking."

Process: Explain the activity described above. Help the participants form a circle. Encourage participation. Assist participants in expressing their ideas if they encounter difficulty.

14. Debriefing

Content:
    a. Why is it our personal responsibility to participate in leisure?
    b. Will you be more likely to engage in leisure if you know it is your responsibility? If yes, why? If not, why not?
    c. How can you take control of your participation?
    d. Will you be more self-determined in leisure if you are responsible for participation? If so, why? If not, why not?

Process: Conduct debriefing using above questions. Encourage all participants to respond to at least one of the questions.

15. Conclusion

Content: "We have personal responsibilities in leisure. These responsibilities include, but are not limited to, the decisions we make, the skills we develop, the knowledge we gain about resources, the way we care for our physical health, and the amount of participation we have. It is important for us to take control of our lives in order to experience leisure throughout our lives."

Process: Make concluding statements. Provide sufficient opportunity for participants to ask questions and voice any of their concerns.

Objective 3.4: Demonstrate the ability to express preferences.

1. Orientation Activity

Content: "You have each been given a set of green chips, a set of brown chips, and a small paper bag. We are going to do an activity to help us meet each other and to start thinking about our preferences for leisure. Let's start by everyone finding a partner. Introduce yourself to this person and find out his or her name. Ask the person to tell you one thing he or she likes to do for leisure. If the activity or experience your partner describes is also one that you prefer, place a brown chip into your bag. If the activity of experience is not one that you prefer, place a green chip in your bag. Now it is your turn to state a preferred activity or experience and your partner will place the appropriate colored chip into his or her bag. Once you have both stated a preference, move to other people in the room and repeat the process. If you like, you may change the activity or experience for each person. When I give the signal stop, sit down and count how many brown and green chips you placed in your bag."

Process: Distribute a set of green chips, a set of brown chips, and a small paper bag to each person. Make sure you distribute enough chips to account for meeting each person in the room. Explain the above activity to the participants. Encourage their active participation. In advance determine a signal to stop the activity. When the activity is completed, move quickly to the debriefing.

2. Debriefing

Content:
    a.   What color chip do you have the most of in your bag?
    b.   Why do you think you ended up with more of that color?
    c.   How did you feel when you told the people what you like to do for leisure?
    d.   How did you feel when the others were telling you what they liked to do for leisure?

Process: Ask the questions listed above. Attempt to have each person respond to the first question by raising his or her hand while you say either "green" or "brown." Encourage each participant to answer at least one of the last two questions.

3. Introduction

Content: "Our ability to express preferences often determines what we do. Preferences are what we want to do the most, what we like to do, or what we enjoy doing. Learning to tell others what we prefer will help us do what we want."

Process: Introduce topic of expressing preferences.

4. Presentation

Content: "We can express preferences in a number of ways. To be most effective, we need to learn how to express ourselves to get the best results. Expressing preferences for leisure can be looked at in a number of ways.

"At one time or another you may be given a list of activities to choose from and you need to decide which one you want to do the most. The choices may come in the form of a list of movies in the newspaper, a list of classes or workshops you may enroll in, or a list of recreation activities at a recreation center. Even if you have a preference, you may not know how to tell someone what it is or why it is. First, you must attempt to communicate these preferences to people in positions to respond to your preferences.

"You may want to do an activity that is not readily available to you. The activity may not by considered by others as an option for you, but you prefer to participate in this activity over many other activities. After you communicate your preferences, you can support your preferences by providing reasons for wanting to participate. Although it should not be necessary, many people may be more cooperative if they become aware of the reasons you want to participate.

"It is your right to participate in recreation activities of your choice. Regardless of others' opinions or criticisms, if you have the necessary skills and knowledge to participate safely, you should be permitted to do so. Responsible recreation participation requires that your actions not bring physical or mental harm to others or yourself. We need to express our rights and our desires to be most effective. We should clearly communicate our leisure preferences to people in positions to respond to our requests."

"When we learn how to express preferences to others, we will be on our way to doing what we most want to do. We will also be more in control of our leisure when we do what we prefer. That is to say, we will enhance our ability to determine our leisure lifestyle. Therefore, another step in expressing our preferences is acting on the opportunities that are available to us to participate in our chosen leisure experiences."

Process: Present information on expressing preferences. Provide examples as needed. Present picture or slide of people demonstrating the four steps in communicating their preferences. Write the following key words on the board:

- Communicate preferences
- Provide reasons
- Express our rights
- Act on opportunities

5. Learning Activity

Content: "Effective communication is necessary to express our preferences. Let's do an activity to improve our communication skills. I want you to join in a circle. Each of you will be given a list of ten activities. Look at the list and choose one or two things that you would prefer to do. If you do not like any of them, pick something else you would like to do. We will go around the room and each person will have a chance to express his or her preference. Tell us exactly what you want to do."

Process: Explain the activity described above. Help participants form a circle. Provide assistance and examples when necessary. Encourage all individuals to participate.

6. Debriefing

Content:

    a. Did you like choosing your favorite activity and giving a preference? If yes, why?
        If not, why not?
    b. If a preference of yours was not on the list, did you choose a different activity? Why or
        why not?
    c. Why is it important to communicate our preferences to others about what we want to do?

Process: Conduct debriefing using above questions. Encourage all participants to answer at least one of the questions.

7. Learning Activity

Content: "We can support our preferences by giving reasons for them. For example, you may want to go on a walk because it makes you feel relaxed and allows you to enjoy the outdoors. You have a specific reason for wanting to take a walk and you can support it by stating the reason. In this activity, we are going to look at our preferences in leisure, and give reasons for them. On a piece of paper, list five leisure preferences. Next to each one, write down at least one reason why you want to do that activity. You may have only one reason or you may have several reasons. Write them on the piece of paper. After everyone is finished, I will ask each person to tell me one of his or her reasons and I will write them on the chalkboard."

Process: Explain the activity described above. Distribute paper and pencils to participants. Provide assistance when necessary. Write one reason for each individual on the board.

8. Debriefing

Content:

    a. Was it easy or hard to think of the reasons why you prefer certain activities? Why do you think it was this way?

    b Do you feel your reasons support your preferences?

    c. Did you see similarities between your reasons and reasons why other people participate? If so, what are they? If not, why do you think this is the case?

    d. What reasons do you think are acceptable for participating in a recreation activity?

Process: Conduct debriefing using above questions. Encourage each person to answer a question. Refer to the reasons listed on the chalkboard.

9. Learning Activity

Content: "Everyone has a right to engage in activities that he or she prefers. One way to stand up for our rights is to do what we want during leisure. Let's get into a circle. We are going to take turns and tell each other what rights we have in leisure. For example, you may feel you have the right to do what you enjoy. Share what you feel are your rights. I will write everyone's rights on the easel."

Process: Explain activity. Help form circle. Provide assistance when necessary. Encourage all individuals to engage in the activity and to make at least one contribution to the list on the easel. Write "RIGHTS" on the board and record each person's ideas.

10. Debriefing

Content:

    a. Why are our rights to engage in leisure important?

    b. Why is one of our rights to express preferences?

    c. How can these rights help us engage in leisure of our choice?

    d. If someone tries to take away our rights, how can we stand up for them?

Process: Conduct debriefing using above questions. Encourage all participants to contribute to the debriefing.

11. Learning Activity

Content: "Our self-determination in leisure is shown by our ability to express preferences. We can measure our self-determination by looking at the process of expressing preferences. If we know what we want to do, we tell others; we give reasons and we stand up for our rights to engage in leisure.

"To find out how determined we are in leisure, let's look at our ability to express preferences. Get with a partner. On a piece of paper, write one thing you want to do during leisure. Tell your partner what it is, give a reason why you want to do it, and state one of your rights in leisure. Then have your partner tell you what he or she wants to do."

Process: Explain the activity described above. Have participants choose partners. Distribute paper and pencils. Write key words on board:

> • Leisure Preferences
> • Reasons
> • Rights

12. Debriefing

Content:
    a.   If you have a preference, are you determined to engage in it? If yes, how do you communicate this preference? If no, why not?
    b.   How can you show someone that you are determined to do what you prefer?
    c.   How can your ability to express leisure preferences show your self-determination?

Process: Conduct debriefing using above questions. Encourage all participants to contribute the debriefing.

13. Conclusion

Content: "Our ability to express preferences often determines what we will do during leisure. To be most effective, communicate your preferences, provide reasons to support them, and stand up for your rights. The more determined you are to participate in an area of interest to you, the more likely you will participate."

Process: Make concluding statements. Provide sufficient opportunities for participants to ask questions and voice concerns.

Objective 3.5: Demonstrate knowledge of assertive behaviors.

1. Orientation Activity

Content: "To increase your knowledge about assertive behaviors, I am going to give you a chance to act out your responses to different daily situations. Each of you has been given a colored card with a situation written on it and a list of possible reactions. Please find the other three people that have the same color card as you. Sit in a group with the three other participants. Introduce yourselves to one another. One person will read the situation and possible reactions. Next, each person in the group will respond as if they were in that situation. Take turns reading the situation and responding to it."

Process: Explain the activity. Give a set of situations to each group. Move to debriefing when finished. Situations need to include possible reactions that represent aggressive, assertive, and nonassertive reactions to daily situations. A sample situation may be:

You are busy watching your favorite show on TV and you are asked to wash the dishes. Of the following, which response is the closest to the one you would make:
    1.   "Forget it. I'm watching TV"
    2.   "I will do the dishes if I can wait until this show is over."
    3.   No verbal response. You walk into the kitchen and wash them silently.

2. Debriefing

Content:
a. Was it hard to decide what you would do in these situations? Why or why not?
b. Have you ever felt bad when you did something just to please someone else? Why do you think you felt this way?
c. If people accuse you of being selfish and inconsiderate, how do you feel?
d. How can you be in control of your actions while being aware of your responses to others?
e. How could you change your behaviors to have a balance between your needs and the needs of others?

Process: Conduct debriefing using above questions. Encourage all participants to contribute the debriefing.

3. Introduction

Content: "Assertive behavior is an important component of self-determination in leisure. Indeed, it is as appropriate in a leisure context as it is in any other aspect of living. But before one can behave in an assertive manner, it is necessary to develop an understanding of assertiveness. This requires a knowledge of what is involved in assertiveness and, of equal importance, what distinguishes assertiveness from other types of behavior."

Process: Introduce topic of gaining knowledge about assertive behaviors.

4. Presentation

Content: "Being assertive is based on the assumption that every human being has certain fundamental rights. The manner in which individuals behave in relation to these rights can be placed in one of three categories: nonassertive, assertive, or aggressive. Being able to distinguish among these three types of behavior is essential. Behaving assertively is equally essential. People who learn how to respond in an assertive manner to various situations are accepting responsibility and taking control of their lives.

"Assertive behavior is behavior that helps you to act in your own best interests, to stand up for yourself without fear, to express honest feelings comfortably, and to exercise personal rights without denying the rights of others. It is a style of behavior that recognizes the extent of one's rights, the extent of the rights of others, and works to maintain a balance between the two. For example, you may have just purchased a new softball glove. A friend may ask to borrow it for a week to use in an out-of-town tournament. You could respond assertively by saying, 'I understand your desire to use a new glove, but I just bought this and want to break it in myself.' You would be recognizing both the right of your friend to ask to borrow your glove and your own right to refuse it.

"Nonassertive behavior occurs when individuals are unable to maintain a balance between their rights and the rights of others. Referring to the previous example of the softball glove, you could respond to the request in a nonassertive manner by loaning the glove because you were afraid if you refused, your friend would think you were being selfish and petty. You could then spend the next week worrying that your friend would damage your glove and it would not fit you properly. Nonassertive behavior occurs when an individual allows others to extend their rights by restricting his/her own.

"Aggressive behavior is the third style of responding or reacting to the fundamental rights that all humans possess. It occurs when an person invades the rights of others. In the matter of the softball glove, you could respond to your friend's request to borrow it by saying, 'You can't be serious!' or 'Absolutely not!' You would be acting aggressively because you would be ignoring your friend's right to be treated with respect and courtesy."

Process: Present information on assertive behavior described above. Use the chalkboard to list major points.

- Assertive
- Nonassertive
- Aggressive

5. Discussion

Content:
a.   What are the differences among nonassertive, assertive, and aggressive behaviors?
b.   What are some situations where you have observed others acting in a nonassertive manner? Assertive manner? Aggressive manner?
c.   What are some instances where you have behaved in a nonassertive manner? Assertive manner? Aggressive manner?
d   How did you feel when you behaved nonassertively?
e.   How did you feel when you behaved aggressively?
f.   Why is it important to learn how to engage in assertive behavior?

Process: Conduct discussion by using above questions. Encourage participation by everyone by having each participant respond to at least one of the questions.

6. Presentation

Content: "We have talked about the belief that all people have certain fundamental rights. Assertive behavior implies that individuals will take actions to stand up for and protect their rights. But before individuals can do that, they must be able to identify these rights.

"Within the context of assertive behavior, a fundamental right can be anything a person believes all other persons are entitled to do, or to be, or to have, simply because they are human beings. Fundamental rights are those things no individual should have to do without. The rights and freedoms that individuals claim for themselves should be extended to all others. The underlying rationale for fundamental rights is that all human beings are deserving of being treated with respect and dignity. When there are differences of opinion related to rights between individuals, any discussions or negotiations should be conducted in an atmosphere that reflects respect and dignity."

"Although there is no universal agreement about all the things that should be included in a list of fundamental human rights, the following are among the most important:

a. The right to act in ways that promote dignity and self-respect, as long as others' rights are not violated in the process. This means you have the right to be yourself and feel good about yourself, as long as you do not harm others.

b. The right to respect. You have the right to be treated courteously by salespersons, teachers, relatives, government employees, doctors, therapists, and all others. You also have the right to be treated as a capable human being and not be patronized.

c. The right to say no and not feel guilty about it. Many people have difficulty in saying no to others because they feel they should be unselfish. People who constantly place their wants and needs below the wants and needs of others are engaging in self-defeating behavior. Being assertive includes learning when to say yes and when to say no.

d. The right to express feelings. Instead of accepting the rights to have feelings, many individuals often tell themselves they should not feel the way they do about something. Because feelings and emotions are a natural part of being human, it is more logical to accept the right to experience them than to feel guilty about them.

e. The right to ask for what you want. A natural part of humanity is having wants. When you do not ask for what you want, you often (consciously or not) resort to other methods to get what you want in ways that violate others' rights.

f. The right to change one's mind. Changing your mind on the basis of new information demonstrates intelligence and flexibility. Refusing to change your mind when it is beneficial to do so demonstrates ignorance and obstinacy.

g. The right to make mistakes. It is not possible to be perfect. All individuals make mistakes; it is part of being human. Having the right to make mistakes includes accepting responsibility for them.

h. The right to get what one pays for. You have the right to expect to receive the product or the service which you purchased. Accepting less means you are allowing others to violate your rights.

i. The right to be left alone. There are times when you prefer to be by yourself, even when others are making demands on your time. Assertiveness includes taking the time to be alone and feeling good about it.

j. The right to have rights. This includes the right to behave in an assertive manner and the right to choose otherwise. There are times when you choose not to assert yourself because the cost of doing so demands too much in the way of time and effort. You have the right to make choices, including not being assertive in certain situations."

"This is not an exhaustive list of fundamental rights, but it is a good representation. It is important for you to know that a belief in fundamental rights may not be shared by all others. Aggressive individuals may attempt to ignore the rights of others. That is one reason why assertive behavior is necessary."

Process: Present information on fundamental rights. Use board to list examples of rights and associated examples.

• dignity	• change your mind
• respect	• make mistakes
• not feel guilty	• get what you pay for
• express feelings	• left alone
• ask for what you want	• have rights

7. Discussion

Content:
    a. How do you feel about standing up for the rights listed on the chalkboard?
    b. Which of the rights listed do you like best? Why?
    c. Which of the rights listed have you experienced being violated at one time or another?
        Please describe one situation associated with one right.

Process: Ask the questions listed above. Encourage all participants to contribute to the discussion by responding to each of the questions. The second question can be answered by people raising their hands as you point to the right listed on the chalkboard, state the right, and then allow them to explain why they chose that right.

8. Presentation

Content: "It is also important to know there is a difference between fundamental rights and role rights. Fundamental rights are related to all human beings, but role rights are reserved for people who accept certain responsibilities or occupy certain positions. For example, the coach of a team has the right to determine the starting line-up; a player does not. That is a role right. But coach and players have the right to be treated with respect. That is a fundamental right. An easy way to tell the difference between a fundamental right and a role right is to ask, 'Is this a right that all people should have?' If the answer is 'yes,' it is a fundamental right. The more you know about rights, the easier it is to identify them. Being able to identify fundamental rights is a first step in becoming assertive."

Process: Conduct discussion using above questions. Encourage all participants to contribute to the discussion.

9. Discussion

Content:
    a. What is a fundamental right?
    b. What is the justification for fundamental rights?
    c. What is the difference between a fundamental right and a role right?
    d. What is a way to tell the difference between fundamental rights and role rights?

Process: Conduct discussion using above questions. Encourage participants to respond to at least one of the questions.

10. Learning Activity

Content: "The fundamental rights that we have identified are not the only ones that exist. Please get into groups of four people and discuss additional rights to be added to the list. Each group must agree on adding five additional rights. When finished, each group will be given the opportunity to report its additional rights to the larger group."

Process: Explain activity. Provide "original" list of rights to each group. Use board to list additional rights as groups report them. After session is ended, revise original list by adding new rights. The list can be used in future activities. Move to debriefing.

11. Debriefing

Content:
a. Why did you choose the additional right?
b. Is your list now complete or are there others you believe should be added? If so, what are they?
c. Have you been in situations where you have exercised any of these rights? If so, please describe.
d. Why is it valuable to be able to identify fundamental rights?
e. How will you use this information?

Process: Conduct debriefing using above questions. Provide opportunities for each group to share its findings. Encourage each member of each group to make a contribution sometime during the debriefing.

12. Learning Activity

Content: "We are going to participate in an activity to help us distinguish between fundamental rights and role rights. Please get into groups of four. I am going to give each group a list of paired individuals that complement each other in some way. Each group will receive the same list. Each group will then generate a list of rights for each of the individuals in each pair. Try to identify at least six rights for each individual in a pair."

Process: Explain the activity described above. Divide participants into groups. Prepare list of paired individuals prior to session. Provide paper and pencil. Monitor activity. Move to debriefing when finished. Paired individuals could include:

> • Man and Woman
> • Coach and Player
> • Client and Therapist
> • Brother and Sister
> • Employee and Employer

13. Debriefing

Content:
a. What rights did you assign for the people in a particular pair?
b. Could any of the rights assigned to one person be generalized to the other person in the pair? If so, which ones?
c. Could any of the rights be generalized to the overall population? If so, which ones?
d. Would that make them fundamental rights?
e. If they can not be generalized to the overall population, what type of rights are they?

Process: Conduct debriefing using above questions. For the first question, choose a different pair for each group. Discuss each pair. Encourage participants to contribute to the debriefing by talking about a least one of the pairs.

14. Learning Activity

Content: "Part of learning how to be assertive is being confident of the right to have rights. Each of you will be provided with the list of fundamental rights we have generated in this class. Examine this list and select the five rights with which you feel most comfortable in accepting for yourself. When the selection process is completed, each of you will stand and, in a firm voice, read the five rights with which you feel most comfortable. Preface each of your statements with 'I have the right to _____.'"

Process: Distribute the list that was previously developed by the participants. Explain the activity. When participants are reading their rights, encourage firm voice, good posture, and eye contact. Provide support for them as they share their information. Assist their presentation by modeling some appropriate behaviors.

15. Debriefing

Content:
    a.   Of the five rights you selected, with which one are you most comfortable? Why?
    b.   Was it difficult for you to read your rights to the group? Why or why not?
    c.   If you had to add a right to your list of five, which one would it be?

Process: Conduct debriefing using above questions.

16. Presentation

Content: "Let us all get into a large circle. Each of you will go up to each person in the group and complete the following sentence: 'I have the right to _____,' stating the right which causes discomfort. The person spoken to will respond by saying 'Yes, you do have the right to _____,' or some other affirmation of the person to have the right. The person designated to begin the activity will travel around the circle, making the statement to each person in the circle and receiving a positive statement from each person. When the designated person returns to the starting point, the person on the left will begin a trip around the circle in the same manner as the designated person. The activity will continue until each person has completed the circle."

Process: Explain activity. Encourage eye contact, good posture, and firm voice from speakers. Emphasize that each participant is to provide a positive response to the speakers and to think of something different to say that would encourage the person to accept that right. Encourage participants to create a supportive environment for the person speaking.

17. Debriefing

Content:
    a.   Was this more difficult than the previous exercise? If so, why?
    b.   Did you feel different at the end of the circle than at the beginning? If so, why?
    c.   What can you do to increase your comfort with the right you chose for this exercise?

Process: Conduct debriefing using above questions. Encourage participants to respond to the question listed above. Respond to some of the questions and provide examples of some possible answers.

18. Learning Activity

Content: "The purpose of this activity is to help you distinguish among nonassertive, assertive, and aggressive behaviors. Each of you will be provided with a written description of four different situations, with three different responses to each situation. Identify each response as nonassertive, assertive, or aggressive."

Process: Explain activity. Provide assistance to any participants who are experiencing difficulty in distinguishing among behaviors. Prepare descriptions of situations prior to session. Descriptions could be as follows:

a. *Situation One.* You are sitting in the music room of a recreation center, listening to the stereo. Someone enters the room and changes the record.
   Possible responses:
   You say, "I was listening to that record. You may put on a different record when this one is finished." (Assertive response)
   You say, "Get your hands off that stereo. I don't want to listen to your lousy records." (Aggressive response)
   You angrily leave the room and decide to listen to your radio. (Nonassertive response)

b. *Situation Two.* You are in a crowded meeting room, waiting to get information on how to register for a volleyball league. Sitting next to you is someone whose cigarette smoke is bothering you.
   Possible responses:
   You squirm through the meeting, wishing that someone would tell the person to put out the cigarette. (Nonassertive response)
   You loudly tell the person how rude it is to not consider the nonsmokers in the room. (Aggressive response)
   You quietly say, "The smoke from your cigarette is making me uncomfortable. Would you please put it out?" (Assertive response)

c. *Situation Three.* A new friend has invited you to a small dinner party. Everyone else at the party seems to know each other quite well.
   Possible responses:
   You decide not to be left out and begin to monopolize the conversation, talking about your new job. (Aggressive response)
   You introduce yourself to the person sitting next to you and begin talking about where you met the host or hostess. (Assertive response)
   You listen quietly to the conversation at the table, wishing someone would talk to you. (Nonassertive response)

d. *Situation Four.* You want to spend your vacation relaxing at home and in the yard. Your spouse thinks it should be spent traveling and spending a few days at a resort.
   Possible responses:
   You think your spouse is tired of being at home and you agree to travel, but you really want to stay home. (Nonassertive response)
   You say, "All you want is to spend money and do what you want." (Aggressive response)
   You ask your spouse if you could discuss the vacation plans further, to determine if a part of the vacation could be spent at home and a portion at a resort. (Assertive response)

19. Debriefing

Content:
a. Have you been in similar situations as those just described? If so, how did you respond?
b. What are alternative assertive responses that could be given for each situation?
c. What did you learn from this activity?

Process: Conduct discussion using above questions. Encourage participants to talk about the different situations. Make sure that each participant contributes to the discussion.

20. Conclusion

Content: "Learning to be assertive is similar to learning anything else. It requires commitment and a willingness to practice, even when it feels uncomfortable. But persistence pays off. Acting in an assertive way allows you to be in control of your life and to assume responsibility. This is an important characteristic of living independently."

Process: Make concluding statements. Provide opportunity for questions. Allow participants to share any concerns or reservations related to acting assertively.

LEISURE EDUCATION: MAKING DECISIONS REGARDING LEISURE PARTICIPATION

Purpose, Goal, and Objectives

Purpose: Provide opportunities for participants to learn about the decision-making process needed for leisure participation, identify personal leisure participation goals and activities to achieve these goals, determine requirements of these activities and available personal resources needed for participation, and choose activities intended to achieve leisure goals.

Goal 4: Demonstrate ability to make decisions regarding leisure participation

Objective 4.1.   Identify personal leisure participation goals.
Objective 4.2.   Identify activities to achieve leisure goals.
Objective 4.3.   Determine requirements of activities identified to achieve leisure goals.
Objective 4.4.   Determine available personal resources needed for participation in activities intended to achieve leisure goals.

Goal, Objectives, and Performance Measures

Goal 4: Demonstrate ability to make decisions regarding leisure participation.

Objective 4.1: Identify personal leisure participation goals.

Performance Measure: Given a paper and pencil, in five minutes:
  (a) determine four personal leisure goals (e.g., control, mastery, freedom, competence, skill development, social interaction, self-esteem), and
  (b) state one reason for developing each of the four leisure goals (social interaction: "I would like to make more friends."; control: "Many times I feel powerless to change a situation."; mastery: "Since I have had so many failures, I need to feel like I can do something."; skill development: "I really want to learn to be able to do more for myself."),
with 100% accuracy on two consecutive occasions.

Objective 4.2: Identify activities to achieve leisure goals.

Performance Measure: Given a list of four personal leisure goals, paper and pencil, in 10 minutes:
  (a) identify four recreation activities to achieve each of the leisure goals (social interaction: join a church group, play softball, join a square dance club, volunteer at a hospital; control: learn to swim, learn to carve, take a self-defense course, learn to drive; skill development: attend a workshop to learn better communication skills, join and attend a fitness center, read a book, learn basic car maintenance), and
  (b) describe why the specific activities were chosen (e.g., social interaction: join a church group: "I know people who have met some of their best friends at church groups."; control: learn to swim:

"I often feel helpless around the water and I think learning to swim would help me feel more in control."),
with 100% accuracy on two consecutive occasions.

Objective 4.3: Determine requirements of activities identified to achieve leisure goals.

Performance Measure: Given a list of 16 activities (four activities per leisure goal) and a paper and pencil, in 20 minutes, determine the following five requirements for all 16 of the activities (e.g., learn to swim):
   (a)   prerequisite skills (e.g., none for beginners),
   (b)   cost requirements (e.g., money for swim suit, admission),
   (c)   equipment and apparel (e.g., swim suit (required), goggles (optional)),
   (d)   time needed for completion (e.g., lessons usually last an hour), and
   (e)   people with whom to participate (e.g., a teacher),
on two consecutive occasions.

Objective 4.4: Determine available personal resources needed for participation in activities intended to achieve leisure goals.

Performance Measure: Given a list of 16 activities (four activities per leisure goal) with associated requirements (skills, cost, equipment, time, people) and a paper and pencil, in 20 minutes, determine personal resources needed for participation in the 16 activities (e.g., play softball) relative to:
   (a)   skills (e.g., can catch but can't hit),
   (b)   money (e.g., have a few dollars to join a league if needed),
   (c)   equipment (e.g., have a glove and ball but no bat),
   (d)   time (e.g., only evenings free to play), and
   (e)   friends or family (e.g., I do not know anybody else who would like to play softball),
on two consecutive occasions.

Goal, Objectives, Content, and Process

Goal 4: Demonstrate ability to make decisions regarding leisure participation.

Objective 4.1: Identify personal leisure participation goals.

1. Orientation Activity

Content: "Please arrange yourselves in a circle for an activity that will help you begin to think about identifying personal leisure participation goals. Close your eyes and take two or three minutes to think of a recreation activity in which you are strongly interested in participating, but have not yet done so. It should be an activity in which you have a realistic chance to participate. We will go around the circle clockwise and you may take turns introducing yourselves by your first name and telling the group which recreation activity you would like to try. Remember, it should be an activity you sincerely are interested in doing."

Process: Explain the activity described above. Arrange participants in a circle. Allow time for participants to think of an activity. Ensure that each participant has an opportunity to introduce himself/herself and state activity.

2. Debriefing

Content:
    a. How long have you thought about about participating in the activity you named?
    b. Have you taken any steps toward actually participating? Why or why not?
    c. How soon do you see yourself participating in the activity?
    d. Do you daydream about participating in the activity or do you see it as a goal?
    e. Do you think there is a difference between daydreaming and having a goal?
       If so, what is it?

Process: Conduct debriefing using above questions. Encourage participants to contribute by responding to the questions.

3. Introduction

Content: "A personal goal is something you want to accomplish, acquire, or maintain. It is something you must be willing to take some action to achieve. You must have both the desire to achieve the goal and the willingness to expend the effort required to do so. Being able to identify personal leisure goals you want to accomplish is an important step in growth and development. As we develop skills and knowledge, we are in a better position to have a meaningful and rewarding leisure lifestyle."

Process: Introduce topic on identifying personal leisure participation goals.

4. Presentation

Content: "Identifying personal leisure goals is a process that requires concentration, the right mood, and energy. There are some guidelines available to help in the process. Following these guidelines should make the task of identifying personal leisure goals a rewarding process.

    a. *Your goals must be your own.* You are more likely to achieve goals you set for yourself than you are to achieve goals set for you by others. Goals should be based on your own values. This does not mean that you cannot adopt a goal that has been suggested by someone else. It does mean that if you are adopting the goal, you have thought it through carefully and consciously, determined it as something desired, and made a commitment to accomplish it. In general, however, the best goals for you are those you have identified for yourself.

    b. *Goals should be clear, precise, and written.* Writing goals tends to clarify them and make them more real. When a written goal is not stated clearly, it often means it has not been thought through clearly. Writing goals can reveal flaws and ambiguities. Goals are often revised as they are the subject of more thought. Putting them in writing helps the process of revision. When goals are written, individuals are also more likely to feel a commitment to accomplishing them. A written goal serves to remind you of its presence.

    c. *It is best to start with short-term goals.* A short-term goal is one that can be accomplished in a relatively short time, such as several days or a few weeks. Short-term goals that are easily attainable are very valuable. They can give you the confidence needed to tackle long-term and more challenging goals. Short-term goals are also more easily controlled. There are fewer chances of unforeseen circumstances interfering with the achievement of short-term goals.

d. *Goals should be based on moral and ethical values.* Most individuals have a belief system that places a high priority on morals and ethics. Goals should be identified in accordance with your belief system. An important consideration for you is how you will feel when the goal is accomplished. If the goal is achieved at the expense of your values, the feelings of reward and satisfaction that should come to you are often diminished by feelings of sorrow and guilt.

e. *Goals must be realistic and attainable.* Identifying goals is a necessary first step to accomplishing them, but if they are not realistic and attainable, they belong to the realm of fantasy. A common difficulty for people who are setting goals for the first time is that they set them too high. Realistic and attainable, however, does not imply that goals must be low; it simply means there must be a reasonable chance for accomplishment. Who is the best judge of what is realistic and attainable? You are. If it feels right to you, if it makes sense to you and trusted friends, then it can be regarded as realistic and attainable.

f. *Goals must be measurable.* Goals must be written in such a manner that individuals will know when they have been successful in attaining them. Goals should, therefore, be clear to you. Others should agree with you if you have attained your goals, if the goals are measurable.

g. *Establishing definite deadlines for achievement of goals is necessary.* Assigning target dates for the achievement of goals helps you maintain focus on what you need to accomplish. The achievement of goals by target dates results in feelings of satisfaction. Target dates can be altered if changing circumstances warrant it, but they should remain a part of every written goal.

"To summarize, the process of identifying goals is most effective when the goals are personal, clearly written, short-term (at least some of them), moral and ethical, realistic and attainable, measurable, and include deadlines for achievement."

Process: Present information on identifying goals and areas where personal leisure goals are often focused. List guidelines and areas on board.

> • Individuals' goals must be your own
> • Goals should be clear, precise, and written
> • It is best to start with short-term goals
> • Goals should be based on moral and ethical values
> • Goals must be realistic and attainable
> • Goals must be measurable
> • Establish deadlines for achievement of goals

5. Presentation

Content: "Personal goals vary greatly from one individual to the next, but they are usually focused on areas where individuals feel a need for improvement. In general, personal leisure goals are often established because of the desire to experience positive changes in control, mastery, competence, freedom, skill development, social interaction, or self-esteem.

"*Control* is related to the perception that individuals are able to take personal actions that will influence their environments. It also implies that individuals can manipulate their behaviors and that personal factors are more responsible for one's behavior than is one's environment. *Mastery* is closely related to the notion of control. It is a feeling of confidence in one's ability to exert some control and influence over a situation and that one does not have to be a victim of the whims of the environment. *Competence* is characterized by being adept, by having the ability to do something very well, by being 'good' at what one has chosen to do. *Freedom* is the presence of the element of choice related to participation in an activity. It is characterized by lack of obligation or any sense of compulsion. *Skill development* refers to the acquisition and refinement of the physical movements or cognitive abilities that enables one to perform well. It leads to feelings of competence. *Social interaction* refers to the establishment of relationships between or among individuals. It can range from general social contact in a large group to an intimate conversation with a friend. It includes all those things that require one to be attentive and responsive to others. *Self-esteem* is the assessment one makes about one's worth. It is related to the beliefs one has about one's abilities. Individuals with a healthy self-esteem are usually those who perceive themselves as competent and in control.

Process: Present information on positive experiences that encourage people to establish leisure goals. Identify the key points on a chalkboard or handout.

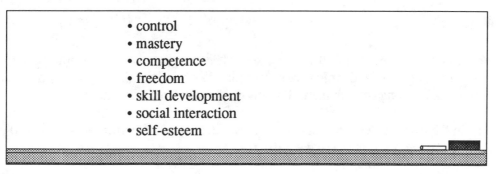

- control
- mastery
- competence
- freedom
- skill development
- social interaction
- self-esteem

6. Discussion

Content:
    a. Why is it recommended that individuals establish their own goals?
    b. What advantage is there to writing your goals?
    c. Have you ever written a personal goal? If so, please describe.
    d. Why is it feasible to have some short-term goals?
    e. Why should deadlines be a part of a goal?
    f. What are some of the areas in which individuals often establish personal goals?

Process: Conduct discussion using above questions. Encourage all participants to contribute to the discussion by responding to at least one of the questions. If participants are prepared to share some of their personal goals, you can record these on an easel. Record the areas presented by the participants in response to the last question on the easel.

7. Learning Activity

Content: "We are going to identify some personal leisure goals. Each of you will be provided with pencil and paper. Take a few minutes and think about some things you would like to accomplish. Don't worry about whether others will be impressed with your goals. The only individual that has to approve your personal goals is yourself. Remember, when you identify personal goals, it is important to be realistic. Try to identify a minimum of ten personal leisure goals. Write your goals on your sheet of paper. Do not be concerned at this point with the way your goals are written, just write them on the paper. When you are finished, you will have the opportunity to share some of your goals with the group. Take your time and have fun."

Process: Explain the activity described above. Provide participants with pencil and paper. Allow sufficient time for participants to identify their goals. Encourage each participant to share his or her goals with group.

8. Debriefing

Content:
   a. What process did you follow in identifying your personal leisure goals?
   b. Why did you identify the personal goals you did?
   c. Of the personal goals you identified, which two are the most important to you?
   d. What is your assessment of your chances to accomplish the goals you identified?

Process: Conduct debriefing using above questions. Encourage all participants to contribute by responding to at least one of the questions.

9. Learning Activity

Content: "Now that you have identified some personal leisure goals, take a few more minutes and determine which are long-term and which are short-term. Look at your list of goals and put an 'L' by those goals you think are long-term and an 'S' by those you think are short-term."

Process: Explain the activity described above. Provide an example if participants appear to be having difficulty. After a few minutes, move to debriefing.

10. Debriefing

Content:
   a. Did you have both long-term and short-term goals on your list?
   b. How did you decide which was which?
   c. How can achieving short-term goals lead to the accomplishment of long-term goals?
   d. Which short-term goal do you want to accomplish first?

Process: Conduct debriefing using above questions. Encourage all participants to contribute by responding to at least one of the questions.

11. Learning Activity

Content: "Look at your list of goals and see which of them can fit into any of the following categories: control, mastery, competence, freedom, skill development, social interaction, or self-esteem. After each goal, write the category into which it most closely fits."

Process: Explain the activity described above. Record the categories on the chalkboard. Move to debriefing after participants stop writing on their papers.

- control
- mastery
- competence
- freedom
- skill development
- social interaction
- self-esteem

12. Debriefing

Content:
    a. Was it difficult to determine which goals might fit with which categories?
    b. Is there a specific category into which most of your goals fit? If so, which one?
    c. Do you feel like you should have goals in each of the categories? Why or why not?

Process: Conduct debriefing using above questions. Encourage all participants to contribute by responding to at least one of the questions.

13. Conclusion

Content: "You have been given some guidelines to follow in the process of identifying personal leisure goals. Applying these guidelines will be very helpful. Identifying goals is simply a matter of deciding what you want to accomplish in the near- or long-term future. Identifying goals is the first step to achieving them."

Process: Make concluding statements. Provide opportunities for questions.

Objective 4.2: Identify activities to achieve leisure goals.

1. Orientation Activity

Content: "We are going to participate in an activity that will help us become aware of the wide variety of recreation activities that exists. Please arrange yourselves in a circle. I will select a person to begin the activity. That person will introduce himself or herself and name a recreation activity that begins with the letter 'A' (e.g., archery). The first person to the left will introduce himself or herself and name an activity that begins with the letter 'B' (baseball). The next person to the left will introduce himself or herself and name an activity that begins with the letter 'C' (e.g., crossword puzzles). Play will continue clockwise around the circle. If a person gets stuck on a letter, the group may help by suggesting activities. If the group gets stuck, we will proceed to the next letter. Let's try to get through the alphabet twice. The second time around, the activity named for a letter must be different from that which was named the first time around."

Process: Explain the activity described above. Arrange participants in a circle. If a participant is unable to name activity after one minute, ask the group to help. If group cannot help after one minute, proceed to next letter. Create a relaxed atmosphere by encouraging participants to contribute to the activity and supporting those individuals that may be having difficulty identifying an activity.

2. Debriefing

Content:
    a.   Were there any activities named which were new to you? If so, which ones?
    b.   Discounting troublesome letters (e.g., 'Z'), how many times do you think the group could have gone around the alphabet?
    c.   Did this exercise help you think of any activities you might choose to help you meet a personal leisure goal? How so?
    d.   Did your favorite activity get mentioned? What is it?

Process: Conduct debriefing using above questions. Encourage all participants to contribute by responding to at least one of the questions.

3. Introduction

Content: "Identifying personal leisure goals is only a first step in arriving at decisions regarding leisure participation. When personal leisure goals have been identified, it then becomes necessary to examine recreation activities that will contribute to achievement of those goals. There are numerous activities that have the potential to contribute to goal achievement. The more possibilities one is aware of, the more choices one has."

Process: Introduce topic of identifying activities to achieve leisure goals.

4. Presentation

Content: "After you determine the personal leisure goals you would like to achieve, the next step is to consider which activities could help this process. It is likely that several different activities could contribute to the achievement of each specific personal leisure goal. You do not need to participate in, or even identify, all of these possible activities. You should, however, be aware of a variety of activities from which you can identify those you wish to use to achieve a goal."

Process: Present information on identifying activities to achieve goals.

5. Discussion

Content:
    a.   Of what value is it to be aware of a wide variety of recreation activities?
    b.   How extensive is your knowledge of possible recreation activities?
    c.   What could you do to broaden your knowledge of possible recreation activities?

Process: Conduct discussion using above questions. Encourage all participants to contribute to the discussion by responding to at least one of the questions.

6. Learning Activity

Content: "We are going to play a type of bingo to help us think about the wide variety of recreation activities that exists. Each of you will be provided with a sheet that has been divided into 25 equal squares, five across and five down. Each square contains the name of a recreation activity. Each of you also will be provided with a pair of scissors, glue, and several magazines. Look through the magazines for pictures that match the recreation activities in the squares. When you find a picture that matches, cut it out and glue it to the appropriate square. The first person to fill five squares horizontally, vertically, or diagonally will be declared the winner."

Process: Explain activity. Prepare forms by dividing a sheet of paper into 25 equal squares. Put name of one recreation activity into each square. Activities could include angling, bowling, checkers, dining out, exercising, fishing, golfing, and hiking. Distribute sheets. Provide scissors, glue, and magazines. Give signal to begin.

7. Debriefing

Content:
    a. Of the pictures you found, how many showed activities in which you participate?
    b. Did you find activities you have not tried but are interested in? If so, which ones?
    c. What did you learn about possible activities available to you?
    d. Of all the pictures you found, which is the most interesting to you? Why?

Process: Conduct debriefing using above questions. Encourage all participants to contribute by responding to at least one of the questions.

8. Presentation

Content: "To help you think about different recreation activities you can take part in, I will describe some ways to categorize recreation activities. I hope these categories will help you identify activities you participate in for fun and enjoyment.

"It may be helpful to think about the *social context* that you arc in when engaged in different recreation activities. For instance, there are some activities that you can enjoy while you are alone, such as reading. There are other activities you may enjoy with only one other person, like walking in the park. Perhaps there are activities that you enjoy with many people, such as dancing. The social context is an important consideration for us in regard to our desire to participate in a given activity.

"The *physical requirements* associated with a particular recreation activity may influence your choice of activities. In addition, thinking about the physical aspects of activities can help stimulate ideas about what activities you enjoy. There are times when you may not enjoy a lot of physical exertion and, therefore, you may gravitate to more sedentary activities, such as writing. On the other hand, you may be concerned about fitness or simply enjoy the exhilaration associated with some physical recreation activities and choose to do these types of activities on other occasions.

"There may be times when you want to be *mentally challenged,* so you choose recreation activities that may be educationally oriented, like learning to speak a foreign language, or you may chooses activities involving mental competition such as chess. On other occasions, however, you may want to simply relax and do something that is not mentally challenging, like sit outside and watch the sun set.

"Another way to help you think about recreation activities you may enjoy is to think about how you feel during your participation. Some recreation activities have strong *emotional aspects* to them. For instance, you many enjoy watching sad, funny, or even scary movies. These movies may strongly influence the mood you are in. Music can also have a powerful impact on how you feel. There may be other activities, such as walking, that may not demand a great deal from you emotionally."

Process: Present the information described above. Show pictures of people participating in different recreation activities related to the various categories. List the four categories on an easel or chalkboard.

```
• social context
• physical requirements
• mental challenges
• emotional aspects
```

9. Discussion

Content:
   a. What recreation activity comes to mind when you think of the category of social context?
   b. What recreation activity comes to mind when you think of of physical requirements?
   c. What recreation activity do you think about when you think of being or not being mentally challenged?
   d. What recreation activity comes to mind when you think of when you are strongly influenced emotionally or times when you are not?
   e. How does thinking about the social, emotional, physical or mental aspects of participation help you identify recreation activities you may enjoy?

Process: Conduct discussion using above questions. Encourage all participants to contribute to the discussion by responding to at least one of the questions.

10. Learning Activity

Content: "We are going to do an activity to help you look at the different categories involved in recreation. With a group of three other individuals, I want you to make a list of four recreation activities. For each activity, write down its social context, physical requirements, mental challenges, and emotional aspects. When each group is finished, it will present its list to the rest of the group. I will write all the ideas on the board."

Process: Explain activity. Provide pencil and paper. Put headings on the board, and record information below.

- social context
- physical requirements
- mental challenges
- emotional aspects

11. Debriefing

Content:
- a. Can one activity include all these categories? In what ways?
- b. What are some of the social aspects involved in activities?
- c. Name some physical requirements in your activities?
- d. What are some of the mental challenges you face during participation?
- e. How are emotions involved in activities?

Process: Conduct debriefing using above questions. Encourage each of the participants to respond to at least one of the questions.

12. Presentation

Content: "To help you think about different recreation activities you can participate in, I will describe another way to categorize recreation activities. I hope this way of categorizing will help you identify more activities you could participate in for fun and enjoyment.

"Thinking about the *type of competition* that one enjoys may spark an idea related to a favorite recreation activity. There are times when we enjoy competing against a record or previous achievement. This means we have to know what we have done in the past in a given activity and then strive to do better. The only person you should compare yourself to is you. For instance, you may enjoy hiking and wish to hike on a trail that you have never hiked on before or you may enjoy bird watching because each time you go out you hope to see a bird you have never seen before. At other times, you may want to compete against other people. There are many traditional recreation activities, such as softball and bridge, that pit you against other people."

Process: Present the information on types of competition. Differentiate between the activities that primarily focus on competition against a personal achievement and those that involve competition with other people.

13. Discussion

Content:
- a. What is another way to categorize activities?
- b. Do you enjoy a feeling of competition during participation? Why or why not?
- c. Do you like to compete against yourself, or others? Why?

Process: Conduct discussion using above question. Encourage individuals to respond to at least one of the questions.

14. Learning Activity

Content: "Let's take a look at recreation activities we engage in and try to determine if they involve competition. Choose a partner. Sit together and tell each other about an activity that you enjoy. Then, try to decide if it involves some type of competition, either against your past performance or against others. Help each other evaluate the activities. Choose another partner, and a different activity, and consider its competition with him or her. After discussion with two individuals, sit in the circle of chairs at the front of the room. We will then talk about what you discovered."

Process: Explain the activity describe above. Help participants find partners. Encourage their active participation in the learning activity. Place a circle of chairs at the front of the room with one for each participant.

15. Debriefing

Content:
    a. Tell us an activity you chose and whether it involves competition.
    b. Do you enjoy competitive activities against yourself, or against others? Why?
    c. Do you prefer activities that are noncompetitive over those that are competitive? Why or why not?
    d. How does competition make you feel?

Process: Conduct debriefing using above questions. Encourage all participants to respond to the first question and as many as possible to the remaining questions.

16. Presentation

Content: "Being familiar with many activities can be a great benefit to you. Not only does it provide greater choice when it comes to identifying activities to help achieve leisure goals, it allows you the luxury of being able to select alternatives when original plans cannot be carried out. For example, if you plan to spend a Saturday on an outing in the park but the weather turns bad, then you could examine other things to do that would also bring enjoyment and satisfaction. Alternative activities could include reading a novel, making something in the kitchen, going to a movie or a shopping mall, or doing crafts. For those times that something interferes with your original plans, knowledge of many activities will help provide you with fun alternatives."

Process: Present information on alternatives described above. Provide examples that are appropriate for the age and interests of the participants.

17. Discussion

Content:
    a. What is an alternative?
    b. How does knowledge of various activities help you choose alternatives?
    c. What was an experience you have had when a planned recreation activity could not be carried out? Did you come up with an alternative. If so, what was it? If not, what would have been a possible alternative you could have followed?

Process: Conduct discussion using above questions. Encourage all participants to contribute to the discussion by responding to at least one of the questions. If time permits have each person respond to the last question. Listing different phases of this question on a handout and allowing participants time to think of a response may facilitate more active participation in the discussion.

18. Learning Activity

Content: "We are going to do an activity that will help you think about alternatives. Please form a large circle. I will now describe a variety of situations related to your becoming involved in a recreation activity that did not actually go as planned. I want you to listen to these situations and think of possible alternatives that you could follow that would still allow you to have a good time.

"Situation One: Assume that you plan to attend a concert. On the day of the concert, the star performer is injured in an accident and the concert is cancelled. Take a few minutes and think of what you could do as an alternative. We will go around the circle and each of you will state what you would do as an alternative to attending the concert.

"Situation Two: Assume you and a friend are planning a trip to go camping and fishing. On the day you are to leave, your friend becomes ill and cannot go. As we go around the circle, tell us what you would do as an alternative.

"Situation Three: Assume you are on a limited, fixed income. You have saved enough money to go out to dinner and a movie tomorrow night. Today, after a walk through the neighborhood, you discover you have the lost the money you were going to use for the dinner and movie. You cannot afford your night out. As we go around the circle, tell us what you would do as an alternative."

Process: Explain the activity described above. Create as many scenarios for alternative choices as necessary. Gear the scenarios to the characteristics of the individual participants. Provide each participant with an opportunity to state alternatives to at least one of the scenarios.

19. Debriefing

Content:
  a. Was it difficult to think of alternatives? If so, why? If not, why not?
  b. What did you learn from the alternatives suggested by others?
  c. What was one leisure experience where you had to think of alternatives?
  d. Why do you think we did this learning activity?

Process: Conduct debriefing using above questions. Encourage all participants to contribute by responding to at least one of the questions. Try to have as many participants as possible respond to the third question.

20. Learning Activity

Content: "Another way to think of alternatives is to prepare a list of several different activities that can fit into predetermined categories. Place yourselves in small groups of three or four persons each. Each group will be given the same set of five categories. Think of as many activities as you can for each category. When finished, the small groups will share their results with the large group."

Process: Explain activity. Determine the five categories in advance of the learning activity. When groups are finished with their lists, provide them with the opportunity to share their lists with the large group. Put results on the chalkboard. The categories could include the following:

> • Things to do on a weekend in this community
> • Things to do by myself
> • Ways to make new friends through leisure
> • Things to do without spending any money
> • Ways to have fun after school or work

21. Debriefing

Content:

    a. How did having categories help you focus your thinking on alternatives?
    b. For which category was it easiest to think of activities?
    c. How will you use this information?
    d. Can you think of additional categories that could be used? If so, what are they?

Process: Conduct debriefing using above questions. Encourage all participants to contribute by responding to at least one of the questions.

22. Conclusion

Content: "Identifying activities that can lead to the achievement of personal leisure goals is an important part of making decisions relative to leisure participation. The more knowledge one has, the easier it is to identify activities. It also makes it easier to think of alternatives when that becomes necessary. Being able to identify activities as stepping stones to achieve goals is a characteristic of a competent person."

Process: Make concluding statements described above. Provide opportunities for participants to ask questions.

Objective 4.3: Determine requirements of activities identified to achieve leisure goals.

1. Orientation Activity

Content: "We are going to do an exercise to help us begin to think of the different requirements associated with recreation activities. Each of you will be given a card with the name of a recreation activity written on it and three numbered, blank spaces. You will also receive three other cards, each containing the name of one piece of equipment or apparel needed to participate in activities other than the one on your first card. Mingle with the group and try to find three different people who have a card that contains a piece of equipment or apparel needed to complete the activity on your first card. When you find someone, introduce yourself, record on your first card their name and the item of equipment or apparel on one of their cards that you need to participate in your activity. People will also ask you what items are contained on your cards that they might need. After you have obtained the names of three different people with items you need, you must still mingle because you may have cards with items other people need."

Process: Explain activity. Prepare cards ahead of session. Ensure availability of sufficient number of cards containing items of equipment or apparel to enable participants to be successful in their quest. Prepare cards in sets. For example, if softball is used as an activity on one card, prepare three other cards to go with it, one containing the word "bat," one "ball," and one "glove." Put cards in groups of four, ensuring that the three cards containing items of equipment or apparel do not match the card with the recreation activity on it. Distribute sets of four cards at random to participants.

2. Debriefing

Content:

    a. Were you able to find three items needed to participate in your activity?

    b. Were you uncertain about what items you might need? If so, please explain.

    c. How many people did you talk with before you found three items needed to participate in your activity?

    d. Why do you think we did this activity?

Process: Conduct debriefing using above questions. Encourage all participants to contribute by responding to at least one of the questions.

3. Introduction

Content: "When you have identified several activities that might contribute to the achievement of your personal leisure goals, an important step has been completed. But, there are several equally important tasks remaining to be done. A major task is to consider the activities identified in light of their requirements. Knowledge of activity requirements is necessary before intelligent decisions regarding leisure participation can be made."

Process: Introduce topic on determining requirements of activities intended to achieve leisure goals.

4. Presentation

Content: "Different activities have different requirements for successful participation. Some activities require physical skills, others intellectual skills, and still others a combination of the two. Some require physical endurance, some require none. Some involve a significant expense, others a moderate sum, and still others none at all. The variety that exists is as broad in scope as the types of recreation activities that exist. Having a general framework to serve as a guide in determining the requirements of various activities would be very helpful. One such framework for determining requirements of activities would include the following elements:

    a. prerequisite skills

    b. costs

    c. equipment and apparel

    d. time needed for completion

    e. people with whom to participate

"Using this framework as a guide should enable one to gather the information necessary to make choices among activities.

"*Prerequisite skills* are essential considerations when weighing choices among activities. It is necessary to know what kinds of skills (e.g., physical, mental, social, or a combination) are required for participation. It is also necessary to know what level of skills is required (e.g., a potential participant may have to demonstrate a certain level of proficiency in swimming before being allowed to play water polo). Prerequisite skills also include any knowledge base or prior experience that may be used as a qualification for participation (e.g., familiarity with the rules of bridge may be required before entering a bridge tournament or prior overnight camping experience may be required before one is eligible to go an an extended tent-camping trip). Knowing what is required in the way of skills allows potential participants to recognize their own status and feel confident in their abilities or encourage them to take steps to acquire what is needed.

"The financial *cost* associated with participating in a recreation activity is also an important consideration. Although there are many activities available that do not have a direct participation fee, there has been a marked increase in the number of activities offered which public agencies charge. Direct participation fees may constitute only a portion of the costs associated with a recreation activity. There may be costs related to transportation, equipment purchase or rental, clothing, food, or entertainment. Costs may be assessed to individual participants or to groups of which they are members. Some costs may be due at the moment of participation, others may be due in advance. Learning as much as possible about the costs involved in participating in a specific activity is an important part of the decision-making process.

"*Equipment and apparel needs* are another significant factor in making decisions related to recreation participation. Many activities require little or nothing in the way of equipment, and ordinary clothing is sufficient for participation. But some activities (e.g., fishing, bowling, or softball) require specialized equipment. If specialized equipment is necessary, must it be purchased or can it be obtained on a rental basis? If it cannot be rented and one cannot afford to purchase it, can it be borrowed? Can participants share equipment during the activity or must each participant have his or her own? Is there a chance that substitutions can be made for some items of equipment? The preceding questions also apply to apparel. When thinking of apparel, there is an additional consideration. Is the apparel really necessary for the performance of the activity or is it desired because of its costume effect? For example, does one need a fancy, colorful outfit to jog or will plain old sweat-clothes do?

"The *time* required to participate in an activity is an important consideration for most individuals. Some activities (e.g., a scheduled league basketball game) are governed by the clock, some are governed by the interests and desires of the individual participant (e.g., going for a walk). The actual length or duration of participation may be only part of the time requirement. Must one take into account the travel time to and from the site of participation? Is changing into and out of special apparel or showering after the activity a factor that must be considered? Is the activity something that lends itself to participation on a spur-of-the-moment impulse or must time be spent in detailed planning? Does participation require commitment for an extended period of time (e.g., a ten-week oil painting class) or can it be accomplished in a short time period (e.g., attending an art show)? Time is an essential ingredient of life. Spending it wisely calls for very careful thinking.

"The last element of the suggested framework is *people* with whom to participate. Many activities can be enjoyed by oneself, but others require the participation of more than one person. Participation with others also creates an atmosphere where social interaction, with all its possibilities for fun and enjoyment, can occur. If the activity requires the participation of other people, how are such arrangements made? For example, if one wants to participate in an organized volleyball league, does one have to be part of an official team or can one join as an individual and then be placed with other individuals to form a team? Is one required to have a partner before being allowed to enter a doubles tennis tournament, or will the sponsoring agency or organization provide assistance in locating a partner?

"There may be a need to learn about other requirements of specific activities that have been identified to help achieve leisure goals, but the aforementioned ones will provide a framework that can serve as a general guide. Utilizing this framework will enable participants to make good decisions relative to specific activities."

Process: Present information on requirements of activities. Use the chalkboard to outline framework. Summarize the major points addressed in the presentation.

- prerequisite skills
- cost
- equipment and clothes
- time needed to finish
- people with whom to participate

5. Discussion

Content:
    a. Why is it necessary to know requirements of activities identified to achieve leisure goals?
    b. If you are not familiar with requirements of an activity, what can you do to learn what they are?
    c. Are there other factors that should be added to our general framework? If so, what are they?
    d. If you determine that you do not currently meet the requirements of an activity, what options are available to you?

Process: Conduct debriefing using above questions. Encourage all participants to contribute by responding to at least one of the questions.

6. Learning Activity

Content: "We are going to do an exercise that will help you focus on the requirements of activities. Get into groups of three or four persons each. Each group will be given the same set of five recreation activities and asked to determine the requirements of each activity in terms of (a) prerequisite skills, (b) cost, (c) equipment and apparel, (d) time needed for completion, and (e) people with whom to participate. When each group has determined what it believes to be the requirements for all five activities, it will share its results with the larger group. The larger group may make suggestions or ask questions for purposes of clarification."

Process: Explain the learning activity described above. Determine five activities to supply to small groups. Activities could include:

- playing softball in a recreation league.
- weekend ski trip.
- bowling.
- playing racquetball.
- dining out.

Help formation of small groups. Provide ample time to determine requirements. Provide each group an opportunity to present requirements to the larger group. List requirements on board. Encourage feedback from large group.

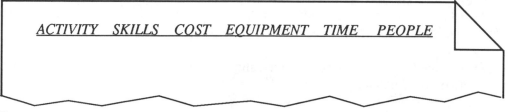

REQUIREMENTS

- prerequisite skills
- cost
- equipment and apparel
- time needed for completion
- people with whom to participate.

7. Debriefing

Content:

    a.   What did you learn about requirements of activities from the group discussions?

    b.   Could your group have changed its list of requirements after listening to feedback from the entire group? If so, in what way?

    c.   If your group was given a different set of five recreation activities, would the framework still be applicable? Why or why not?

Process: Conduct debriefing using above questions. Encourage all participants to contribute by responding to at least one of the questions.

8. Learning Activity

Content: "Now I want you to look at some activities that you want to participate in to see what their requirements include. On a sheet of paper, write three of your leisure interests. Beside each one, list the prerequisite skills associated with the activity, the cost, equipment and apparel needed to participate, time required for involvement, and people with whom to participate. After each of you has completed your chart, you can share it with the group."

Process: Provide paper and pencils to the participants. Provide assistance when necessary. Encourage each person to present his or her chart to the entire group. On the handout include the following column headings:

ACTIVITY   SKILLS   COST   EQUIPMENT   TIME   PEOPLE

9. Debriefing

Content:

    a.   What requirements did one of your leisure interests have?

    b.   Why will you be more prepared to meet requirements after writing them on paper?

    c.   Each time you want to do an activity, is it good to think about what it involves? Why or why not?

    d.   Does an activity's requirements sometimes keep you from participating in it? If so, please identify an activity and one such requirement.

Process: Conduct debriefing using above questions. Encourage all participants to contribute to the discussion by responding to at least one of the questions. Ensure that the participants have the handout as you work through the debriefing questions.

10. Learning Activity

Content: "At times we are prevented from participating in an activity because of its requirements. To overcome this barrier, we can develop alternatives to these activities and do something less demanding. For example, I may want to go to the swimming pool, but I do not have the money to pay the admission fee. So, I decide to go to a lake to swim instead. When I chose to go to the lake I overcame the barrier of cost and was able to enjoy my chosen recreation activity. Now look at the list you made for the last learning activity. For each activity you listed, write one alternative activity you could do if you could not meet the requirements for the first one. After everyone is finished, we will take turns telling each other our alternatives."

Process: Distribute the lists developed during the previous learning activity. Provide clear and concise directions. Attempt to have each participant identify at least one activity and an associated alternative.

11. Debriefing

Content:
    a. What is one of your activities and one alternative activity ?
    b. What options do you have if you can not meet the requirements for an activity?
    c. What are some decisions you must make about an activity that has too many demands?
    d. What are some activities for which you had difficulty finding an alternative?

Process: Conduct debriefing using above questions. Encourage responses by all the participants.

12. Conclusion

Content: "Determining the requirements of activities that might assist in the achievement of personal leisure goals is an important responsibility. Having a framework to use as a reference helps to ensure that the right kinds of questions are asked relative to the requirements. When individuals know a lot about the requirements of activities, they can feel confident about their decisions regarding recreation participation."

Process: Make concluding statements. Provide participants with opportunities to ask questions.

Objective 4.4: Determine available personal resources needed for participation in activities intended to achieve leisure goals.

1. Orientation Activity

Content: "We are going to do an activity to help us think about some of the personal resources that can be used in leisure participation and are available to each of us. Our homes can be used as a leisure resource. Please arrange yourselves in a circle. One person will begin the activity by introducing himself or herself by first name and telling of recreation activity that he or she does at home. For example, one might say, 'My name is Marilyn and I do knitting at home.' Introductions will proceed clockwise around the circle. When the first round is completed, the participant who started the activity will begin a second round by stating his or her last name and a second leisure activity done at home. For example, 'My last name is Smith and I also listen to classical music at home.' Last name introductions will also move clockwise around the circle."

Process: Explain the activity and provide needed examples. Help arrange participants in circle. Select someone to begin introductions. If participants have difficulties, provide verbal assistance as needed. Gear examples to the individual interests of the participants.

2. Debriefing

Content:
    a.   Was it difficult to think of leisure activities you do at home? Why or why not?
    b.   Did you hear of some activities done at home that you did not expect? If so, what were they?
    c.   Did you get some ideas about additional things you can do at home? If so, what were they?
    d.   Had you thought of your place of residence as a personal leisure resource?
    e.   Why do you think we did this activity?

Process: Conduct debriefing using above questions. Encourage all participants to contribute by responding to at least one of the questions.

3. Introduction

Content: "Being aware of your personal resources will greatly enhance your ability to make decisions regarding leisure participation. Although personal resources vary from individual to individual, each of us has things we can use to our advantage. Sometimes we even have things of which we are unaware that could be used as resources. Reflecting about ourselves will help us to identify our personal resources."

Process: Introduce topic of determining available personal resources useful in achieving leisure goals.

4. Presentation

Content: "Personal resources can be divided into two major categories, internal and external. We will now take the time to discuss the personal resources associated with those that are internal.

"Internal personal resources consist of the way you creatively express your *feelings and emotions*. You may have talents and interests in this area that can help you make express decisions regarding your leisure participation patterns. For example, based on your interest to express your emotions, you may pursue activities related to the performing arts such as drama or music.

"Another internal resource involves your *mental or intellectual skills*. Your ability to take part in activities requiring mental abilities and your interest in developing your intellectual skills can help you make leisure-related decisions. For instance, you may decide that you would like to play table games, such as Trivial Pursuit™, that require recall of information and can result in new knowledge.

"Perhaps you have some *physical competencies* that can be applied to your leisure participation. Physical skills are required in many active events including a variety of sports. You may have such skills. If you enjoy demonstrating your physical talents in the outdoors during winter, you may decide to participate in cross-country skiing or ice skating.

"You may be an extremely personable individual. Some people have very strong *social skills*. All of us can work on developing these skills. You, however, may have a natural aptitude for activities that involve social interaction. If you have strengths in this area, you may enjoy attending parties and meeting new people.

"There are many different personal resources we possess. These include ingenuity, resourcefulness, a sense of adventure, a sense of humor, a willingness to try new things, and many, many more. Internal resources vary from one individual to another. There is no suggestion that one resource is better than another, only that individuals possess them in varying degrees."

Process: Present information on personal resources. List examples of internal personal resources on the easel or chalkboard.

> *INTERNAL*
>
> - feelings and emotions
> - mental or intellectual skills
> - physical competencies
> - social skills
> - resourcefulness
>
> - ingenuity
> - sense of adventure
> - sense of humor
> - willingness to try new things

5. Discussion

Content:
    a. What are personal leisure resources?
    b. Why is it important to know what they are?
    c. How can you learn what your personal resources are?
    d. When you know what your personal resources are, what will this help you to do?
    e. What additional internal resources do you have that are not listed on the easel/chalkboard?

Process: Conduct discussion using above questions. Write on the easel/chalkboard additional internal resources that participants identify. Encourage all participants to contribute to the discussion by responding to at least one of the questions.

6. Presentation

Content: "Personal resources can be divided into two major categories, internal and external. We will now take the time to discuss the personal resources associated with those that are external.

"External personal resources consist of such things as *personal finances*. Knowing how much money you have will help you decide what activities you can pursue. You need to make sure that you have enough money to participate in your desired activity. If you do not have sufficient funds, you have a couple choices. Either you can choose another leisure pursuit or you can find ways to earn additional money.

"Your *physical possessions* may allow you to enjoy many different recreation activities. For instance, if you own a car you can easily get to the facilities you wish to attend. If you do not have a car, you might be able to use a bicycle. The sporting equipment you own may provide you with resources needed to participate. For instance, if you were interesting in playing baseball, having a baseball glove would be helpful to you.

"The *people* you know are resources that can help you decide which recreation activities you will enjoy. Members of your family can be very useful when you would like to talk to someone or play a table game at home. If you like to go bowling, going with friends can enhance the experience for you. Your friends may help with transportation, directions, and can help you with the activity. Your friends and family members can also make any activity more fun. Sometimes, whom you do something with is more important than what you are actually doing.

"External resources vary from one individual to another. Being able to recognize your personal resources is necessary, but not always easy. Thinking about your own external resources can give you a more complete picture of what they are. But thinking about your internal resources is more difficult. It is not easy to be objective when we are thinking about ourselves. It sometimes results in failure to recognize a characteristic as a resource. It is often helpful to talk with a trusted friend when trying to identify one's internal resources."

Process: Present information on personal resources. List examples of external personal resources on the easel or chalkboard.

EXTERNAL

• personal finances
• physical possessions
• people: family and friends

---

7. Discussion

Content:
    a.   What are external personal leisure resources?
    b.   Why is it important to know what they are?
    c.   How can you learn what your external personal resources are?
    d.   When you know what your external personal resources are, what will that knowledge help you to do?

Process: Conduct discussion using above questions. Encourage all participants to contribute to the discussion by responding to at least one of the questions.

8. Learning Activity

Content: "We are going to take an inventory of the external personal resources we have that allow us to participate in recreation activities. Each of you will be provided with pencil and paper. Take the time to reflect seriously about yourself and make a list of your most positive external resources. Think of how much money you have or might be able to make. Think of the different possessions you have, and remember the people close to you who can assist you and share in the fun. Try to list at least six or seven external resources. When you are finished, you will be given the chance to share your list with all the participants."

Process: Explain the activity described above. Provide participants with a pencil and paper. Allow time for reflective thinking. Provide each participant with opportunity to share list with group. Move to debriefing once participants complete task.

9. Debriefing

Content:
   a. What do you feel is your strongest internal resource? Why?
   b. Did listening to the lists of others remind you of resources you may have overlooked? If so, what were they?
   c. What are some things you could do to increase your arsenal of resources?

Process: Conduct debriefing using above questions. Encourage all participants to contribute by responding to at least one of the questions.

10. Learning Activity

Content: "Now that you have a list of personal internal resources, take some time to think about how you have used those resources in the past to participate in leisure activities. Also, think about how you could use them in the future to participate in new activities. For each resource on your list, name one activity which it was used for in the past and one for which it can be used in the future. When you are finished, you will be asked to share your results with the group."

Process: Explain the activity described above. Provide sufficient time for participants to complete the activity. Ask participants to share their findings with the group.

11. Debriefing

Content:
   a. Was it difficult to think of how you might use your internal resources in the future? If so, why?
   b. Did listening to others give you new ideas for using your internal resources in the future? If so, how?
   c. Do you feel you are getting the maximum value from your internal resources? If not, what can you do above it?

Process: Conduct debriefing using above questions. Encourage all participants to contribute by responding to at least one of the questions.

12. Learning Activity

Content: "Think about the external personal resources you have. What physical possessions do you have that can be used for leisure activities? How can family and friends help you in this? Each of you make a list of your external resources. Be as thorough as you can. When you are finished, you will share your results with the group."

Process: Explain the activity described above. Allow time for participants to complete the task. Provide an opportunity for participants to share results.

13. Debriefing

Content:
    a.   What is your best external resource? Why?
    b.   Do you feel that you have adequate external resources? Why or why not?
    c.   Do you have things you had not thought of as resources? If so, what are they?
    d.   What can you do to enhance your external resources?

Process: Conduct debriefing using above questions. Encourage all participants to contribute by responding to at least one of the questions.

14. Learning Activity

Content: "Now that you have a list of your external personal resources, think about the ways you have used them for leisure participation in the past and how you can use them for different activities in the future. For each external resource on your list, name an activity for which it was used in the past and a different one for which it can be used in the future. When everyone is finished, we will share results."

Process: Explain the activity described above. Allow participants sufficient time to complete the activity. Encourage participants to share their results.

15. Learning Activity

Content: "We began with an activity that asked you to think of two leisure activities that you have done at your residence. Let us further pursue that activity. Each of you has pencil and paper. Draw the basic dimensions of your home. Label the rooms and furnishings. Think of how you could use different areas for leisure activities. For example, a kitchen could be used for gourmet cooking, sharing a cup of coffee with a friend, or baking a cake as a surprise for a neighbor. A living area could be used for reading a novel, playing cards, or hosting a small, informal gathering of friends to discuss items of interest. Be both creative and realistic. Identify as many activities as you can by writing their names in the areas where they could take place. When you are finished, you may share your work with the group."

Process: Explain the activity described above. Provide participants with pencils and paper. Encourage participants to share their results with the group.

16. Debriefing

Content:
    a.   Is there more or less to do where you live than you initially thought? How so?
    b.   What can you do to enhance your place of residence as a personal resource?
    c.   Regarding the activities you can do at home, is there a balance between those you would do alone and those that would involve other people? If not, what could you do to create a balance? Do you have to have a balance?

Process: Conduct debriefing using above questions. Encourage all participants to contribute by responding to at least one of the questions.

17. Conclusion

Content: "When individuals have discovered the personal resources available to them for leisure participation, they are then in a position to make responsible decisions about which activities are feasible and to make plans for future action. Knowledge of what one's personal resources are and the confidence to use them increases one's feelings of independence and sense of control."

Process: Make concluding statements. Provide opportunities for participants to ask questions and express any concerns they have regarding their retention of the material associated with this objective and the entire goal of decision making.

LEISURE EDUCATION: KNOWLEDGE AND UTILIZATION OF RESOURCES FACILITATING LEISURE

Purpose, Goal, and Objectives

Purpose: Provide opportunities for participants to learn how to locate and identify sources of information about leisure opportunities, identify specifics to solicit advice from information sources about leisure, and use printed/human/agency resources that facilitate leisure participation.

Goal 5: Knowledge and utilization of resources facilitating leisure participation.

Objective 5.1.   Identify information to solicit from leisure resources.
Objective 5.2.   Use printed resources facilitating leisure participation.
Objective 5.3.   Use human resources facilitating leisure participation.
Objective 5.4.   Use agency resources facilitating leisure participation.

Goal, Objectives, and Performance Measures

Goal 5: Knowledge and utilization of resources facilitating leisure participation.

Objective 5.1: Identify information to solicit from leisure resources.

Performance Measure: Given a paper and pencil, in 10 minutes:
- (a) identify seven specifics to solicit from sources of information about leisure opportunities: (1) activities, (2) facilities and location, (3) schedules, (4) cost, (5) equipment and apparel, (6) people, and (7) transportation, and
- (b) provide a brief explanation of why they should obtain this information: (1) activities (e.g., determine what is offered), (2) facilities and location (e.g., determine where it is), (3) schedules (determine when it is offered), (4) cost (determine how much it is), (5) equipment and apparel (determine what needs to be done), (6) people (determine who is available), and (7) transportation (determine how to get there),

identifying six of the seven specifics with associated explanations on two consecutive occasions.

Objective 5.2: Use printed resources facilitating leisure participation.

Performance Measure: Given a newspaper, telephone book, directories and pamphlets, and a paper and pencil, in 30 minutes:
- (a) choose a recreation agency, and
- (b) determine the following about the agency: (1) activities, (2) facilities and location, (3) schedules, (4) cost, (5) equipment and apparel, (6) people, and (7) transportation,

identifying six of the seven specifics on two consecutive occasions.

Objective 5.3: Use human resources facilitating leisure participation.

Performance Measure: Given the opportunity to speak with neighbors, experts associated with a recreation activity, and friends, and a paper and pencil, in 30 minutes:
  (a)   choose a recreation agency, and
  (b)   determine the following about the agency: (1) activities, (2) facilities and location, (3) schedules, (4) cost, (5) equipment and apparel, (6) people, and (7) transportation,
identifying six of the seven specifics on two consecutive occasions.

Objective 5.4: Use agency resources facilitating leisure participation.

Performance Measure: Given the opportunity to speak with personnel at the chamber of commerce, parks and recreation, and youth group, and a paper and pencil, in 30 minutes:
  (a)   choose a recreation agency, and
  (b)   determine the following about the agency: (1) activities, (2) facilities and location, (3) schedules, (4) cost, (5) equipment and apparel, (6) people, and (7) transportation,
identifying six of the seven specifics on two consecutive occasions.

Goal, Objectives, Content, and Process

Goal 5: Knowledge and utilization of resources facilitating leisure participation.

Objective 5.1: Identify information to solicit from leisure resources.

1. Orientation Activity

Content: "Pretend that you have just moved to a home in a new community. Choose a recreation activity. Write this activity at the top of the paper I have given each of you. Next, write one question you would like answered about this activity in order for you to participate in the community. For example: I choose basketball and I would like to know 'Where is the closest court to my home?' After you have completed this step, stand up and begin walking around the room. Find someone who is standing and not talking with anyone. Introduce yourself to the person and find out the person's name. Share your activity and your need for information. Find out the person's activity and the question he or she would like answered. Together, come up with an additional question to which you need the answer and one question helpful for the other person. Record the additional question and write the name of the person who helped you think of the question immediately after the question. Continue meeting with other participants, trying to make your list of questions related to your recreation activity as long as possible."

Process: Distribute paper and writing instruments to the participants. Encourage them to generate as many questions as possible. If some participants are reluctant to approach others, assist them by walking with them and modeling the desired behavior.

2. Debriefing

Content:
  a.   What are some questions you wanted answered about your activity?
  b.   Now that people shared some of their questions, what questions can you add to your list?

c.   Why do you think we did this orientation activity?

Process: Conduct debriefing using above questions. Provide opportunity for each person to respond to at least one of the questions.

3. Introduction

Content: "Knowing sources of information about leisure opportunities is an essential step in becoming independent and accepting the responsibility for taking control of one's life. But knowing sources of information is only a first step. It is not the responsibility of these sources to think of everything potential participants might want to know about a leisure opportunity. Rather, it is the responsibility of the individual to ascertain the information they need to know and to take the steps necessary to acquire that information."

Process: Introduce topic of identifying specifics to solicit information from sources of information about leisure.

4. Presentation

Content: "The types of information that would be of benefit to potential leisure participants may vary from activity to activity and from person to person. For example, the issue of crowding or numbers of participants might be of concern to one person and a matter of indifference to another. One person might wish to know if the hiking trails are heavily used on the weekends and another person may not care whether or not the beaches are crowded on weekends. Thus, one person feels a need to have a specific item of information relative to a leisure opportunity, while another person is not interested in that kind of information regarding the activity in which they are interested. In general, however, the types of information that are most useful concerning leisure opportunities include cost, transportation, equipment, skill required, location, hours of operation, and any unique requirements, such as membership or reservations.

"The costs associated with a leisure activity should be among the first things a potential participant investigates. Often, there is a direct cost assessed to participants. Direct costs usually take the form of *admission* or *user fees*. Examples of direct costs would be the the price of admission to a movie theater or a swimming pool, the team entry fee for a volleyball league, the price of lift tickets at a ski area or the entrance fee to a national park.

"Admission or user fees are often not the only cost associated with participation in a leisure activity. Some activities may have additional costs related to *transportation, lodging, meals, equipment, and clothing*. These costs may be greater than the price of direct participation in the activity. When one is attempting to determine the cost of participating in an activity, all of these factors must be carefully considered.

"When considering cost, it is important to keep abreast of the changes that are occurring among many leisure service providers. Public park and recreation agencies, in particular, now have a fee for many activities that used to be free. Efforts must be made to determine if there is a fee and how much it is. Other leisure service providers periodically increase their participation fees in order to keep up with the expenses of operating and to realize a reasonable profit. Determining the costs of participation in an activity must be based on current information."

Process: Present information on cost. Use easel or chalkboard to illustrate examples of costs.

- admission
- user fees
- transportation
- lodging
- meals
- equipment
- clothing

5. Discussion

Content:

    a. What is a direct cost associated with leisure participation?

    b. Can you give some examples of direct costs? If so, please do.

    c. What other kinds of costs might be associated with leisure participation?

    d. Why is it important to have current information related to cost of participation?

    e. How do you feel about having to pay to participate in an activity provided by the municipal park and recreation department?

Process: Conduct debriefing using above questions. Encourage all participants to contribute by responding to at least one of the questions.

6. Learning Activity

Content: "We are going to do an exercise to start us thinking about costs associated with participation in a leisure activity. Think of an activity in which you have not yet participated, but are eager to try. Identify the types of things which cost money. After you have done this, determine the total amount it would cost you to participate in this activity. When you are finished, be prepared to share your results with the rest of the group."

Process: Explain activity. Emphasize necessity to be thorough. Move to debriefing when finished.

7. Debriefing

Content:

    a. What activity did you choose?

    b. What kinds of expenses are associated with your activity?

    c. Are there any additional expenses? If so, what are they?

    d. What was the total amount of your expenses?

    e. What was the most expensive item?

    f. Were you surprised by the number of things that must be considered when trying to determine costs of participation? If so, how?

    g. Of what value was this exercise to you?

Process: Conduct debriefing using above questions. Encourage all participants to contribute by responding to at least one of the questions.

8. Presentation

Content: "Transportation is another factor about which specific information is needed. Opportunities for participation in many activities depend on the ability of the participants to get to specific locations, but these sites may not be accessible by all modes of transportation. If there are several modes of transportation that could be utilized, which mode is the most feasible? There may be many modes of transportation, but not all of them may be available to some individuals. Determining specifics about transportation is an important task.

"When considering transportation relative to participation in a leisure activity, there are several questions to which one must find the answers. For example:
   a. Is the location of the activity within walking distance?
   b. Is walking the best form of transportation to use?
   c. If it is too far to walk, what other modes of transportation are available?
   d. Am I able to use all the modes that are available?
   e. What are the advantages and disadvantages of the different modes of transportation?

"Answering these questions will provide information that is helpful in making decisions about participating in a specific leisure activity."

Process: Present the material on using transportation to get to a recreation activity. Develop a handout containing the following questions:

> • Is activity within walking distance?
> • Is walking the best transportation?
> • If too far to walk, what are other modes?
> • Am I able to use all available modes?
> • What are advantages and disadvantages of different modes?

9. Presentation

Content: "Knowledge of the advantages and disadvantages of common modes of transportation may help individuals identify questions they wish to ask regarding participation in specific leisure activities. In general, the following information appears to be relevant:

Walk. There is no direct cost involved and it is a beneficial exercise. It requires extra time, is sometimes fatiguing, and poses the risk of being caught in inclement weather.

Cycle. A bicycle is more efficient than walking, is fairly speedy, and is also a healthful exercise. Bicycles must be securely locked when not in use and also put the rider at the mercy of the weather.

Taxi. A taxi leaves the responsibility of driving and dealing with the traffic to another person, eliminates a parking problem, and provides door-to-door service. They can be fairly expensive compared to other modes of transportation and sometimes necessitate a lengthy wait until one is available.

Automobile. Your car is convenient, allows independence, and usually is a great time-saver. Operating a car can be expensive and requires a safe, secure parking area.

Bus. Using the public transportation system is usually inexpensive, eliminates parking problems, and removes the responsibility of driving. You must be familiar with the bus schedules and adapt your transportation needs to it. Buses do not necessarily operate all hours of the day or on both days of the weekend. Some neighborhoods are not well-served by buses.

Train. For some people, trains provide a nice alternative to flying. They are not as expensive as flying but are more expensive than many other forms of transportation. Their schedules are often inconvenient and sometimes they have trouble staying on schedule.

Airplane. Flying is a fast, convenient method to travel great distances. It is relatively expensive and often requires the traveler to arrange for other modes of transportation after the destination is reached.

"There may be other, more exotic modes of transportation, but the above are most relevant for traveling in and between communities and recreation areas in our country."

Process: Present information on modes of transportation. List modes on chalkboard; list advantages and disadvantages of each.

> • Walking
> • Cycling
> • Taxi
> • Private automobile
> • Bus
> • Train
> • Airplane

10. Discussion

Content:
    a.   What modes of transportation are available to you within your community?
    b.   Are they available and accessible to all citizens?
    c.   Are there recreation areas in your vicinity that are not served by public transportation? If so, what are they?
    d.   What other modes of transportation can be used to reach these areas?

Process: Conduct discussion using above questions. Encourage all participants to contribute to the discussion by responding to at least one of the questions.

11. Presentation

Content: "The mode of transportation about which the most questions are asked appears to be the bus. What does one need to know in order to use a bus system effectively? Basically, one needs to know the following:
    a.   What does it cost?
    b.   Are passes or tokens available for purchase?
    c.   What is the schedule (i.e., routes; time of arrival and departure)?
    d.   Where can one obtain schedules?

e. With which bus stops does one need to be familiar?
f. What are the days and hours of operation?
g. Where can one call for information?

"Other helpful information concerning buses includes: (1) in most cases, either the exact fare or a pass or token is required because drivers do not carry or make change, (2) buses are equipped with devices (cords or buttons) that passengers may use to notify to the driver that they wish to get off at a certain point, (3) the types of areas that are typically served by buses include shopping malls, athletic facilities, urban parks, and downtown areas, and (4) transfers are available to allow individuals to change buses to get to a desired location."

Process: Present information on buses. Write on the chalkboard the following abbreviated questions:

- • Cost?
- • Passes or tokens?
- • Schedule?
- • Where are schedules?
- • Bus stops?
- • Operation times?
- • Call for information?

12. Discussion

Content:
   a. What do you need to know to use the bus?
   b. Have you used the bus system? If so, when did you use it and where did you go?
   c. Did you experience any difficulty in using the bus? If so, how?
   d. Would you use the bus again?
   e. Are you familiar with any recreation areas or facilities that are easily accessible by bus?
       If so, what are they?
   f. Are the buses in this community accessible to all people with disabilities?

Process: Conduct discussion using above questions. Encourage all participants to contribute to the discussion by responding to at least one of the questions.

13. Learning Activity

Content: "Knowing about the bus system should give one the confidence needed to use it when the occasion arises. This activity will help you gain confidence in using the bus system. Each of you has been given pamphlets describing the services offered by the bus system. These pamphlets provide information concerning fares, schedules, routes, and hours of operation. Select a recreation area or facility as your destination and find the answers to the following questions:
   a. Where do I go to meet the bus?
   b. When do I need to be there?
   c. What is the fare?
   d. Where will I get off the bus?
   e. Where will I go to board the bus to return home?

    f.   What time will the bus be there?
    g.   What time does the last bus leave?
    h.   What is the closest bus stop to my home?
    i.   What time will I get home?

"Write your answers to the questions on the paper that will be provided to you. Be prepared to share your answers with the group. When you do, the group will be asked to judge your responses for accuracy."

Process: Explain activity. Provide pencil, paper, and bus information. Provide individual assistance as necessary. Give each participant opportunity to share answers with group and receive feedback during debriefing.

14. Debriefing

Content:
    a.   What was your destination?
    b.   Did you find answers to all the questions?
    c.   Could you select other destinations and still find the answers?
    d.   Did you find several options related to arrival and departure times for your destination?
    e.   How will you use this information?

Process: Conduct debriefing using above questions. Encourage all participants to contribute by responding to at least one of the questions.

15. Presentation

Content: "Equipment is another area for which answers to specific questions must be obtained. Knowing what to ask about equipment is a step toward independence and control. If one is thinking about participating in a recreation activity, questions about equipment should include the following:
    a.   What equipment, if any, is required to participate in the activity?
    b.   Does the organization that provides the opportunity also provide any equipment?
    c.   If participants must supply the equipment, is it available on a rental basis?
    d.   If equipment is available, from whom and for how much can it be rented?
    e.   If the equipment must be purchased, where can it be bought and at what cost?
    f.   Is special clothing required? If so, what kind and from where?"

Process: Present information on equipment. List abbreviated questions on board.

• What equipment?   • Buy where?
• Does organization provide equipment?   • What cost?
• What equipment rental?   • What special clothing?
• Who rents?
• How much is rental?

16. Discussion

Content:
    a. In what activities have you participated that required some type of equipment?
    b. Where and how did you obtain the equipment?
    c. What are additional questions related to equipment, other than the ones presented?

Process: Conduct debriefing using above questions. Encourage all participants to contribute by responding to at least one of the questions.

17. Presentation

Content: "Skill level is also a factor about which specific information must be obtained. If individuals are in the process of determining the feasibility of participating in a particular activity, their skill level or readiness should be a primary consideration. Questions to be asked could include the following:
    a. What are the prerequisites, if any, for this particular activity?
    b. Do I meet those prerequisites?
    c. Does the activity require the same level of skill from all participants or are allowances made for people with different levels of skill?
    d. Is some type of demonstration or proof of skills required?
    e. Is a minimum level of knowledge and basic physical skills required?
    f. Is instruction in required skills available from some source?

"Learning the answers to these and similar questions will enable participants to make intelligent decisions regarding leisure participation."

Process: Present information on skill level. Use board to list abbreviated questions.

> • What prerequisites?
> • Do I meet prerequisites?
> • Allowances for different levels?
> • Skill demonstration?
> • Knowledge and physical skills?
> • Is instruction available?

18. Discussion

Content:
    a. In what activities have you participated that required more than beginning skills?
    b. Where and how did you obtain those skills?
    c. Could you have participated without them?
    d. Are there other questions regarding skill that should be asked? If so, what are they?

Process: Conduct discussion using above questions. Encourage all participants to contribute to discussion by responding to at least one of the questions.

19. Presentation

Content: "There are other factors about which specific information must be obtained to determine the feasibility of participation in a particular activity. These include the physical location of the areas or facilities where the activity is offered, the hours the activity is available, and whether participation is available to the general public on a first come-first served basis or if there are some kinds of restrictions in place. For example:

    a. Is the activity available in more than one place?
    b. Where are these places and can I get to them?
    c. When I get to them, can I participate freely or must I have a reservation or be a member of a group or the facility?
    d. If I need a reservation or a membership, how can I obtain one?
    e. What are the days and hours when the activity is available?
    f. Can I be there sometime during those days and hours?

"These are the types of questions to which you must have answers. Obtaining the answers removes any uncertainty about the possibility of participating in a leisure activity."

Process: Present information on other factors. Use board to list abbreviated questions.

> • Is activity available?
> • Where are places?
> • Do I need reservation or membership?
> • How can I get reservation or membership?
> • What is schedule?
> • Can I be there then?

20. Discussion

Content:

    a. Have there been instances where you have had to find answers to the above questions? If so, for what activity?
    b. Why is it necessary to have answers to these questions?
    c. Are there other questions that need to be asked? If so, what are they?

Process: Conduct debriefing using above questions. Encourage all participants to contribute by responding to at least one of the questions.

21. Learning Activity

Content: "You are going to be given an opportunity to apply all that you have learned about identifying the specific kinds of information needed to determine the feasibility of participating in a particular leisure activity. This is an exercise that you can do in groups of three or four. There are several slips of paper in the container in the middle of the table. Each slip of paper has an activity written on it. Each group will draw a slip of paper from the container and identify specific questions that must be answered regarding the activity on it. Questions should be grouped into the following categories:

    a. cost
    b. transportation
    c. equipment
    d. skill
    e. location
    f. hours of operation
    g. other requirements

"You are not required to find the answers to the questions. The purpose of this exercise is to identify the questions. When you are finished, you may share your questions with the larger group."

Process: Explain activity. Divide into groups. Provide each group with the opportunity to share with larger group. Prepare slips with activities in advance of the session. Activities could include:

> • take a weekend ski trip
> • enroll in oil painting class
> • learn to play racquetball
> • enroll in basic automobile maintenance class
> • take SCUBA lessons
> • learn to bowl
> • enroll in glass-blowing class
> • learn archery

22. Debriefing

Content:
    a. Did you generate questions you wanted to ask that we had not identified in class? If so, what were they?
    b. What is your opinion regarding the number of questions that need to be answered?
    c. Why do you think we did this exercise?
    d. What use will you make of what you learned from this?

Process: Conduct debriefing using above questions. Encourage all participants to contribute by responding to at least one of the questions.

23. Conclusion

Content: "No one can know everything necessary for participation in all leisure activities. But knowing what questions to ask about participation is a major step toward independence and being in control of one's own life in leisure. After one knows which questions to ask, time and energy can then be focused on obtaining answers."

Process: Make concluding statements. Provide opportunity for questions.

Objective 5.2: Use printed resources facilitating leisure participation.

1. Orientation Activity

Content: "Each of you has been given three cards containing three different types of printed resources that could help you take part in enjoyable recreation activities. The three types of printed sources are (a) pamphlets and brochures, (b) newspapers, and (c) phone books. Fan your three cards out as if you were playing a card game so that only you can see them. Find a person, introduce yourself, and find out the person's name. Then, using the person's name, ask the person to take one of your cards. The other person will then do so. Now the person can call you by name and offer you one of his or her cards. You accept and take a card. Once you have each swapped cards, go to another person and repeat the process. The object is to get three cards that list the same printed sources. Once a person gets three of a kind, he or she will hold up the cards and state the type of printed sources. All participants must then participate in a brief discussion about that source of information. Once we finish talking about that source of information, we will resume the orientation activity until another person gets three of a kind."

Process: Walk around the room and help any participants having trouble. Once a person gets three of a kind, the debriefing questions can be asked. In advance, make up three cards per person with the following written on each card.

• pamphlets and brochures
• newspapers
• phone books

2. Debriefing

Content:
    a. How can the printed sources help you to participate in leisure?
    b. What other printed materials could we use to find out about the recreation activity?
    c. Why do you think we did this orientation activity?

Process: Conduct debriefing using above questions. Provide opportunity for each person to respond to at least one of the questions.

3. Introduction

Content: "There is a lot of information about opportunities for leisure participation in and near most communities. Much of the information is in printed form and is a valuable resource for those who utilize it. The information is available from many sources. Tapping this resource benefit those of you who want to make the most of your leisure."

Process: Introduce topic of using printed resources facilitating leisure participation.

4. Presentation

Content: "To take full advantage of one's leisure it is necessary to be well-informed about several aspects of leisure participation. For example, one needs to know what kinds of opportunities are available, who provides such opportunities, when and where can one participate, how much it costs, and eligibility requirements. Much of this information is available in printed form. Some of it appears in *pamphlets and brochures* that are focused on the offerings of a specific agency, such as a municipal park and recreation department; some of it is in publications that cover a variety of topics, such as *newspapers;* and some of it appears in sources that are harder to find and use, such as the yellow pages of a *telephone book.* Knowing where to look and what to look for will help you benefit from the printed information that is available."

Process: Present the information on the many different types of printed resources available to facilitate leisure participation. List the key points on an easel or chalkboard:

> • pamphlets and brochures
> • newspapers
> • telephone book

5. Presentation

Content: "A telephone directory is a valuable source of information. If one knows the name of a specific agency, organization, or other leisure service provider, the white pages will provide the telephone number where they can be called and be put in direct contact. If one does not know the name of a specific agency or organization, the yellow pages will provide categories of goods and services providers. Searching through the yellow pages sometimes requires a little effort because they are often organized in a manner that is different from what we expect. But after a person has become familiar with how they are organized, they can assist one in obtaining a considerable amount of information. Many telephone directories also have a section of pages that is colored blue. The blue pages provide information about local government agencies, such as the municipal park and recreation department. One can find the telephone numbers for the recreation centers, swimming pools, special facilities (e.g, the zoo), and the administrative offices of the park and recreation department. The blue pages also provide information about state and federal offices located in the local community."

Process: Present information about telephone directories. Have directory on hand to use as demonstration model.

6. Discussion

Content:
    a.   How can printed information be of value to you?
    b.   What are examples of printed material you used to learn about leisure opportunities?
    c.   How can a telephone directory assist you in learning about leisure opportunities?
    d.   What are examples of how you have used the yellow pages to help you find information about a particular leisure activity?.
    e.   How have you used the blue pages to learn about a leisure opportunity?

Process: Conduct discussion using above questions. Encourage all participants to contribute to the discussion by responding to at least one of the questions.

7. Learning Activity

Content: "We are going to participate in an activity that will help us feel confident about our ability to use effectively the yellow and blue pages. Each of you will be given a telephone directory and a sheet of paper that contains a list of areas, facilities, organizations, or other suppliers of goods and services that have the potential to provide opportunities for leisure participation. Use the directory to locate an example of each item on the list. Record the specific name, address, and telephone number of each example. Also record the page number where you found the information. When you are finished, we will go around the group and ask each of you to give your example for a particular item. When you respond, give the page number in the directory where you found it so that all may turn to it and see it for themselves."

Process: Explain activity. Distribute directories and list of entities. Remind participants to record name, address, telephone number, and relevant directory page number. Provide opportunity for each participant to give an example. Prepare list prior to session. The list could include the following items:

- recreation centers
- parks
- movie theaters
- swimming pools
- shopping malls
- restaurants
- museums
- health clubs
- bowling alleys
- sight-seeing tours

8. Debriefing

Content:
  a. Did you have difficulty finding an example for each item? If so, which ones?
  b. Which of the sections, (white, yellow or blue), is easiest to use? Why?
  c. What kinds of information can the directory supply you with?
  d. Do you feel confident in using the telephone directory to help locate information?
  e. What is an example of how you will use this information in the future?

Process: Conduct debriefing using above questions. Encourage all participants to contribute by responding to at least one of the questions.

9. Presentation

Content: "Newspapers are another valuable source of printed information and can be of great help in learning about leisure opportunities. Although they sometimes carry feature stories that give information on particular activities, such stories do not appear on a regular basis. But newspapers contain other features that can be used to one's advantage.

"Newspapers often provide information about registration procedures and deadlines for activities sponsored by the municipal park and recreation department. They also often print a schedule of local sporting events. Daily papers also provide television listings and advertisements for what is playing at the theaters, along with their starting times and price of admission. Sunday newspapers usually have an entertainment section devoted to leisure opportunities in the local community. Many newspapers perform a public service by printing the local park and recreation department's program offerings (e.g., Winter, Spring, Summer, and Fall) and providing it as a special insert in a Sunday paper.

"The information provided by newspapers includes what is happening, where it is located, and what it costs to participate. Newspapers have the advantage of being current, thus one can usually rely on the information obtained from them to be accurate."

Process: Present information on newspapers. Use daily and Sunday papers as demonstration models. List key points:

- registration procedures
- schedule of sporting events
- television listings
- movie advertisements
- entertainment section
- recreation department's programs

10. Discussion

Content:
    a. What can you learn about chances for leisure participation from a local newspaper?
    b. What sections of a newspaper are likely to provide you with pertinent information?
    c. What is an example of how you used a newspaper to learn about a leisure opportunity?

Process: Conduct debriefing using above questions. Encourage all participants to contribute by responding to at least one of the questions.

11. Learning Activity

Content: "We are going to use pencil and paper to make a list of all the leisure opportunities we can find in a Sunday newspaper. Please get into groups of three or four. Each group will be given a Sunday paper. Look through the paper carefully and make a record of each source of information you find concerning a leisure opportunity. Record the section, page number and, if available, headline or heading. When you are finished, we will compare results."

Process: Explain activity. Provide paper, pencil, and Sunday paper. Examine paper and prepare list of opportunities prior to session. Provide each group with the opportunity to share its list.

12. Debriefing

Content:
    a. In how many different sections did you find information?
    b. In which section did you find the most information?
    c. Is there some information that is more easily understood than the rest? If so, what is it? Why is it?
    d. What is your opinion of the variety of information?
    e. What did you learn from this activity?
    f. How will you use this information?

Process: Conduct debriefing using above questions. Encourage all participants to contribute by responding to at least one of the questions.

13. Presentation

Content: "Pamphlets and brochures are another source of printed information available to those who want to learn more about leisure opportunities. They are usually organized to provide information that is easy to read and understand. Pamphlets and brochures may be organized around a single topic such as public fishing areas, the range of programs and services offered by the local park and recreation department, the geographic location of specific facilities such as the street addresses of municipal recreation centers, or in some other manner.

"Pamphlets and brochures are usually published by park and recreation departments and agencies such as YMCA, YWCA, Jewish Community Centers, Boys' Clubs, and Girls' Clubs. Private organizations, such as health and fitness clubs, may also describe their programs and services in such publications. In addition, travel agencies use them to illustrate their services.

"Where can one get these publications? They are available, at no cost, from the agency or organization that produces them. Usually all you have to do is make a request by a telephone call, letter, or personal visit and you'll be given what you want. They are available from local chambers of commerce and are often distributed in Welcome Wagon kits provided to newcomers. Church groups will sometimes obtain and distribute such publications to their congregations, particularly those pamphlets and brochures provided by public agencies.

"State and federal agencies also publish pamphlets and brochures describing areas and facilities under their control and the programs and services which they provide to the public. They give such information as where to go, how to get there, what to bring, and what to do after you arrive. They also are available upon request and at no cost."

Process: Present information on pamphlets and brochures. Bring demonstration models to session. Distribute samples to participants.

14. Discussion

Content:
    a. Have you obtained pamphlets or brochures to learn about leisure opportunities? If so, please describe. Did you find them useful?
    b. Who provides pamphlets and brochures?
    c. How can you get them?
    d. What can you learn from such publications?

Process: Conduct debriefing using above questions. Encourage all participants to contribute by responding to at least one of the questions.

15. Learning Activity

Content: "This is a two-part exercise designed to help you use pamphlets and brochures as resources to facilitate your leisure participation. This exercise will be done in groups of three. During the first part each group will generate a list of the kinds of information that should be included in a pamphlet or brochure. When each group is finished making its list, we will combine them to make a master list.

"After the master list is compiled, each group will use it to judge the value or effectiveness of pamphlets and brochures with which it will be supplied. This will be the second part of the exercise. Each group will be given the opportunity to express its judgment of the pamphlets and brochures given it."

Process: Explain activity ahead of the session. Devise list of types of information for brochures. List could include:

- What is being offered?
- Who is offering it?
- Where is it offered?
- When is it offered?
- What is the cost?
- Who can participate?
- What is required to participate?
- Is there a telephone number to call for additional information?

Use list to supplement lists from participants, if necessary. Compile master list and distribute. Provide each group with the same five or six pamphlets and brochures. Emphasize task is to judge information provided, not appearance of brochures. When finished, move to debriefing.

16. Debriefing

Content:
    a. Which brochure provided the best information? Why?
    b. Which provided the least information?
    c. Are you confident you can use brochures to help learn about leisure opportunities?
    d. How will this exercise be helpful to you?

Process: Conduct debriefing using above questions. Encourage all participants to contribute by responding to at least one of the questions.

17. Conclusion

Content: "Printed information can be a great asset in learning about leisure opportunities and making decisions relative to participating in them. Knowing how to obtain printed information and how to use it after it is acquired enables one to be less dependent on others and more self-reliant. Learning how to utilize such sources is an indication of the acceptance of greater responsibility."

Process: Make concluding statements. Provide opportunity for questions.

Objective 5.3: Use human resources facilitating leisure participation.

1. Orientation Activity

Content: "Each of you has been given three cards containing three different types of *human resources* that could help you participate in enjoyable recreation activities. The three human resources are (a) using a telephone, (b) writing letters, and (c) making visits. Fan your three cards out as if you were playing a card game so that only you can see them. Find a person, introduce yourself, and find out the person's name. Then using the person's name, ask the person if he or she would like to take one of your cards.

The other person will then take a card. Now the person will call you by name and offer one of his or her cards. You then accept and take a card. Once you have swapped cards, move on to another person and repeat the process. The object is to get three cards that list the same human sources that could help you participate in a recreation activity. Once a person gets three of a kind, he or she will hold up the cards and state the type of human resources. All participants must then participate in a brief discussion about that source of information. Once we finish talking about that source of information, we will resume the orientation activity until another person gets three of a kind."

Process: Walk around the room and assist any participants encountering difficulty. Once a person gets three of a kind, the debriefing questions can be asked. In advance, make up three cards per person with one of the following written on each card.

- use telephone
- write letters
- go and visit

2. Debriefing

Content:
    a. How can the human resources help you participate in leisure?
    b. What other materials could we use to find out about the recreation activity?
    c. Why do you think we did this orientation activity?

Process: Conduct debriefing using above questions. Provide opportunity for each person to respond to at least one of the questions.

3. Introduction

Content: "People who are attempting to gather as much information as possible in order to make decisions about their leisure participation must learn to use as many sources of information as they can. Printed sources of information are excellent, but may not always be available. Often the quickest and most efficient method of gathering information will be to get it from other people. Developing the ability to get information from leisure service providers is an important task."

Process: Introduce topic of using human resources facilitating leisure participation.

4. Presentation

Content: "In general, there are three methods by which you can get information about opportunities for leisure participation from other people. One common method is by using the *telephone,* another is to request information through written *letters*, and a third method is to *visit* in person and speak directly to individuals from whom one is seeking assistance. People who know how to use human resources to facilitate their leisure participation are skilled at these three ways of obtaining information."

Process: Present information on the different ways participants can access human resources. List key points on an easel or chalkboard:

- use telephone
- write letters
- talk in person

5. Presentation

Content: "Using a telephone is a quick and efficient way to obtain information from a leisure service provider. It is quick in that it usually provides instant answers to questions. It is efficient in that it allows one to speak directly with others without having to be in their presence. This saves travel time and expense. Successive telephone calls enable a person to communicate with several other individuals in several other locations, all in a short time-period. This is a major advantage of the telephone.

"To use the telephone successfully and efficiently, one needs to know who to call and precisely what information one is seeking. The following procedure would be appropriate:
  a. Obtain the telephone number of the agency or facility you wish to call.
  b. If possible, know the name of the person to whom you wish to speak.
  c. Know in advance the questions you wish to ask and what information you are seeking. For example, what hours are they open, how much does it cost, where are they located, or what kinds of services do they provide? If it is helpful, write down the questions you wish to ask.
  d. Dial the desired number.
  e. When the phone is answered, greet the person and say you are seeking information.
  f. Ask your questions. If necessary, make written notes of the answers.
  g. When you have all the information you need, thank the person, say 'good-bye,' and hang up the receiver.

"It is important to speak clearly, in a moderate tone and with sufficient volume. Use good telephone manners. Be polite. Do not chew gum, eat, or drink while using the telephone. Turn down or off the volume of radio or television sets that would create unnecessary interference. Try to call at a time when there will be little or no noise from other people at your end of the line.

"If the person who answers the phone asks you with whom you would like to speak and you don't know a name, tell them you want to speak with someone who can answer your questions. If you are asked if you can 'hold,' that means you are being asked to wait before someone will come on the line to speak to you. You decide if you want to 'hold' or if you want to call back at a later time. When you are polite and use good telephone manners, you have the right to expect the same from those with whom you are speaking. If you are unhappy with the way you are being treated on the phone, you have the right to ask for better treatment."

Process: Present information on use of the telephone. Outline procedure on chalkboard.

> - Obtain telephone number
> - Know name of person
> - Know questions
> - Dial number
> - Greet person
> - Say you are seeking information
>
> - Ask your questions
> - Make notes of answers
> - Thank person
> - Say 'good-bye'
> - Hang up receiver

6. Discussion

Content:

    a. What advantages does use of the telephone have over writing or visiting in person when one is seeking information?

    b. What are possible additions to the telephone procedure outlined on the board?

    c. Have you used the telephone to seek information related to leisure participation? If so, please describe.

    d. What is included in good telephone manners?

Process: Conduct discussion using above questions. Encourage all participants to contribute to the discussion by responding to at least one of the questions.

7. Learning Activity

Content: "Each of you will be given the chance to use the telephone to seek information about an opportunity for leisure participation. Each of you will prepare a leisure-related question to which you want an answer. You will then determine the agency or leisure service provider that is best suited to provide the answer. Outline, in writing, the procedure you will follow to ask the question and receive the answer. When you are finished, you will tell the group about your procedure. The group may make suggestions for change. When you are satisfied with the outline, you will then make the call and obtain the information."

Process: Explain activity. Provide pencil and paper. Remind participants they may use procedure on board as model for their outline. Provide each participant with opportunity to share outline with large group. After calls are made, move to debriefing.

8. Debriefing

Content:

    a. To what question were you seeking an answer?

    b. Who did you call for the answer?

    c. Did you have difficulty in reaching the right agency or service provider? If so, please explain.

    d. What answer did you receive?

    e. What was your impression of the agency or person that gave the answer? Why?

    f. How confident are you about using the phone to get information about leisure services?

    g. For what other purposes will you use the telephone?

Process: Conduct debriefing using above questions. Encourage all participants to contribute by responding to at least one of the questions.

9. Presentation

Content: "There are times when seeking information by writing is the most feasible method to use. A letter may be used when you do not have access to a telephone, lack transportation to the information source, or do not have time to make a personal visit. It may be that you simply prefer to write. Whatever the reason, acquiring information by writing and asking for it is one more way of being able to use human resources to facilitate leisure participation.

"When writing a letter, you must be very careful in explaining what information is being sought. This means you must think clearly and be sure that the questions being asked are easily understood and are asking for the right information. Unlike the telephone, where clarification can be sought and received instantly, a letter that is not clear can result in unnecessary delay and additional correspondence.

"There is a format to follow that is helpful in organizing a letter. If a writer uses a format similar to the following, the reader will find it very helpful:
    a. Write the date near the top and at the left margin.
    b Put your address and telephone number under the date.
    c. Next, put the name and address of the person or agency to whom you are writing.
    d. Write the salutation (Dear _____:).
    e. Write the body of the letter.
    f. Close by thanking the person or agency.
    g. After the body of the letter, write 'Sincerely.'
    h. Sign your name.

"Using this format will help you organize your letter, but remember that to be very clear about what you are asking is the most important feature. The more specific the questions, the more likely they will be answered to your satisfaction."

Process: Present information on writing a letter. Prepare and distribute sample letters to demonstrate as models. Put suggested format on chalkboard.

- Write date near top at left margin.
- Put your address and telephone number under date.
- Put name and address of person or agency to whom you are writing.
- Write salutation (Dear _____:).
- Write body of letter.
- Thank person or agency.
- Write 'Sincerely.'
- Sign name.

10. Discussion

Content:
   a. Why should we make letters clear and accurate?
   b. Have you written letters to get information about leisure participation opportunities?
       If so, please describe.
   c. Are there questions or suggestions related to the sample format?
       If so, what are they?

Process: Conduct discussion using above questions. Encourage all participants to contribute by responding to at least one of the questions.

11. Learning Activity

Content: "Each of you will be given the chance to practice writing letters to seek leisure-related information. You will select three different agencies or leisure service providers and decide what information you wish to seek from each of them. Write a letter to each of them, asking them what you want. When you finish writing, you will read each of your letters to the group. The group will listen and, if needed, make suggestions for improvement. You will then choose one of your letters and send it. If you wish, you may mail all three."

Process: Explain activity. Provide pen and paper. Ensure each participant has opportunity to read letters to group. Encourage constructive suggestions.

12. Debriefing

Content:
   a. To whom did you write?
   b. What did you ask?
   c. Was it difficult to express clearly what you were asking for?
   d. How do you feel about your ability to write a clear letter?
   e. How else will you use your letter-writing ability?

Process: Conduct debriefing using above questions. Encourage all participants to contribute by responding to at least one of the questions.

13. Presentation

Content: "The third method that is commonly used to obtain information from other individuals or agencies is to visit with them face-to-face. There may be several reasons why one would prefer to obtain information in this manner. Visiting a leisure service agency or facility enables one to see the place, talk directly with the people who are answering questions, and pick-up any free materials they may have.

"There is a pattern of behavior that is appropriate when visiting a leisure-service provider for the purpose of obtaining information. Usually the first thing you find when entering the agency is a reception desk. Go directly to the desk. If you are looking for a specific person, it is best to have made an appointment with that person. Tell the receptionist you are there to see that person. If you do not have an appointment, the receptionist can help you get the information you need or direct you to people who can help you. Be clear in stating what you are seeking. After you have what you came for, thank those who helped you, and leave."

Process: Present information on visiting in person. Demonstrate behaviors while they are being discussed.

14. Discussion

Content:
    a. Have you visited a leisure agency to ask for information? If so, please describe.
    b. Where are some places you could visit to seek information?
    c. Can you describe the appropriate behavior for visiting a place to ask for information? If so, please do.
    d. Why should one go directly to a receptionist's desk or counter?
    e. Why is it important not to loiter after you have what you came for?

Process: Conduct debriefing using above questions. Encourage all participants to contribute by responding to at least one of the questions.

15. Learning Activity

Content: "This activity is like a homework assignment. Each of you will select a leisure service provider and make plans to visit that person sometime within the next week. Before you visit, decide what it is you want to find out. You may have many questions you want to ask. If you wish, you may write these questions to remind yourself of what they are. Each of you will tell the group what you are asking before making the visit. If appropriate, the group may make suggestions for additions or changes. After your visit, you will share the results with the group."

Process: Explain activity. Provide each participant with opportunity to share questions with group prior to making visit. Emphasize deadline of one week for visit to occur. Debrief after visit.

16. Debriefing

Content:
    a. Where did you visit?
    b. What were you trying to learn?
    c. What did you learn?
    d. Were you comfortable during the visit?
    e. Where are some other places you could visit?

Process: Conduct debriefing using above questions. Encourage all participants to contribute by responding to at least one of the questions.

17. Conclusion

Content: "Developing the ability to utilize human resources to facilitate leisure participation is a necessary task. Dealing with others should always be done in a polite and courteous manner. Doing so will enable one to take full advantage of all the resources available to obtain information and make intelligent decisions related to leisure."

Process: Make concluding statements. Provide opportunity for questions.

Objective 5.4: Use agency resources facilitating leisure participation.

1. Introduction

Content: "Each of you has been given a colored sheet of paper with a question written on the top of it. Find a person, introduce yourself, and find out the person's name. Ask the person the question written at the top of your paper. If the person is able to answer it, write the response on the paper and record his or her name immediately following the answer. If someone else has already provided that answer, write the new name beside the name of the last person that provided you with that information. If the person is unable to answer the question, read him or her whatever information, if any, is recorded on your paper. Now the person will ask you his or her question. Try to answer it as best you can. The person will respond in the same way you did to him or her. The object is to get as many answers as possible to your question. Once you have both tried to answer each other's questions, thank the person and find another person and begin the process again. Continue until you speak with everyone in the room or I provide the signal to stop."

Process: Walk around the room and assist any participants having difficulty. Once a person gets three of a kind, the debriefing questions can be asked. Establish a signal to stop the activity, such as flickering of the lights. In advance, make up sheets of paper with the following written on different sheets of paper.

1. What are examples of state and national facilities and areas that can be used for recreation purposes?
2. What are examples of voluntary or youth-serving agencies that can be used for recreation purposes?
3. What are examples of facilities that are available through the public schools that can be used for recreation purposes?
4. What are examples of commercial or private facilities that can be used for recreation purposes?

2. Debriefing

Content:
    a. How can the agency sources help you to utilize your leisure?
    b. What other agencies could we use to find out about the recreation activity?
    c. Why do you think we did this orientation activity?

Process: Conduct debriefing using above questions. Provide opportunity for each person to respond to at least one of the questions.

3. Introduction

Content: "Most communities contain a variety of agencies, organizations, and enterprises that exist for the primary purpose of making leisure opportunities available to the general public, or to certain segments of it. These entities can be a very valuable resource for most of us. The greater your knowledge of such resources, the broader your options for taking part in enjoyable and satisfying activities."

Process: Introduce topic of using agency resources facilitating leisure participation.

4. Presentation

Content: "The leisure service providers that exist in a community cannot always be neatly categorized. They are sometimes quite diverse and what exists in one community may not exist in another. But, in general, the providers can be placed in one of the following categories:

   a. public
   b. voluntary
   c. school
   d. religious organizations
   e. private/commercial

"Developing an understanding of each of these categories can help individuals take better advantage of their services."

Process: Present information on public agencies. Use board to list major points.

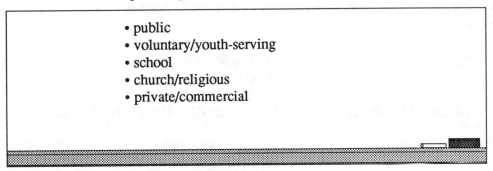

• public
• voluntary/youth-serving
• school
• church/religious
• private/commercial

5. Presentation

Content: "*Public agencies* are supported by some level of government. They are agencies that are funded primarily by tax dollars. In our country, the city, county, state, and federal governments all have agencies that manage areas and facilities for the purpose of providing leisure opportunities for their citizens. The most common of these public leisure-service agencies is the municipal (city) park and recreation department.

"Municipal park and recreation departments, because they are supported by public taxes, provide programs and services for all segments of the public within their jurisdiction (the city limits). Some of their programs are designed to appeal to specific groups, such as youth, elderly, or people with disabilities. Some are designed to appeal to specific interests, such as athletic competition, arts and crafts, or outdoor recreation. Some of their programs are designed to accommodate large groups of people and some are designed to appeal to small groups and individuals Some programs are highly structured and require formal leadership. Some are informal and allow for direction to come from the participants. Although it is not possible for municipal departments to provide all things to all people, they do attempt to provide a diversity of offerings that will appeal to a diversity of people. They operate on a year-round basis and provide facilities and services in most geographic areas of the community.

"Although municipal departments are funded primarily with public monies, they often assess a participation fee or admission charge. The fees are usually very reasonable and are collected to defray expenses, rather than to generate a profit. Thus, the fees are generally less than one would pay for a similar program or service in the private sector.

"Because municipal departments are public agencies, they are obligated to provide for the public and are prohibited from discriminating against any groups or individuals. They are the major, and in some instances the only, provider of leisure services for some segments of the population, including the economically disadvantaged and people with disabilities.

"Information about their programs and services is available through a variety of sources. Newspapers often carry their program schedules, along with information related to registering and participating. Radio and television stations sometimes provide coverage. Pamphlets and brochures may be obtained at most recreation centers, special facilities (such as a zoo or observatory), and their administrative offices. Employees of municipal park and recreation departments are public servants. It is their obligation to serve the public by aiding its participation in their programs.

"State and federal government agencies also provide leisure opportunities, although they are less involved than municipal departments in offering direct programs. State and federal agencies are more likely to provide areas and facilities, such as *state and national parks, forests, wildlife refuges,* and other *outdoor recreation areas.* State and federal agencies do provide direct programming in their *hospital, prison,* and *military* facilities."

Process: Present information on public agencies. Use board to list examples of state and federal facilities and programs that can be used for recreation purposes.

STATE AND NATIONAL AREAS	*STATE AND NATIONAL PROGRAMS*
• parks	• hospitals
• forests	• prisons
• wildlife refuges	• military bases
• other outdoor recreation areas	

6. Discussion

Content:
  a. Why are municipal departments obligated to serve the public?
  b. In which programs provided by the municipal department have you participated?
  c. Did you have to pay to participate? If so, how much?
  d. How did you learn about their programs?
  e. How else can one learn about their services?
  f. In which programs would you like to take part but have not yet done so?
  g. What has prevented you from participating?

Process: Conduct discussion using above questions. Encourage all participants to contribute to the discussion by responding to at least one of the questions.

7. Presentation

Content: "*Voluntary agencies/youth-serving* make an important contribution to the spectrum of leisure opportunities available in most communities. Voluntary/youth-serving agencies are entities such as the *YWCA, YMCA, Jewish Community Centers, Campfire Girls, Girl Scouts, Boy Scouts, Girls' Clubs* and *Boys' Clubs*. Because they are not government agencies, they have the option of choosing what kinds of programs to offer and to whom they wish to offer them. These agencies generally focus on a specific segment of the public and direct their programs and services toward it. Some agencies, such as the Y's, serve a broader portion of the public than other agencies, such as the Scouts. The Scouts focus on a limited age-group and, often, on one gender. The Y's offer a wider variety of programs to more age-groups and usually to both genders.

"Voluntary agencies/youth-serving agencies often offer instructional classes in recreation activities as part of their programs. Most of these classes are designed to accommodate beginners. Learning about these classes and how to participate in them can provide individuals with broader choices related to their leisure.

"These agencies depend on contributions, membership dues, program participation fees, and support from organizations such as the United Way. They do not receive support from tax dollars and are responsible for generating their own funds. The fees assessed for participating in their programs are usually moderate and within the reach of most of us.

"Voluntary agencies/youth-serving agencies are eager to provide leisure opportunities to as many participants as possible. They publicize their programs through the mass media and their own printed pamphlets and brochures. Information concerning their programs is also available by telephoning or visiting them. Individuals who are interested in acquiring the skills and knowledge needed to participate in a variety of activities can consider the offerings of voluntary agencies/youth-serving agencies as part of the total leisure package available in a community."

Process: Present information on voluntary/youth-serving agencies. Use board to list examples of agencies and major points.

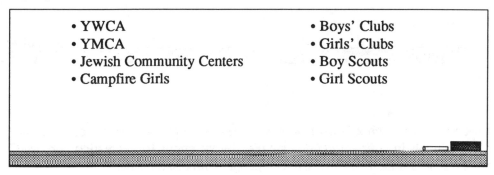

* YWCA   • Boys' Clubs
* YMCA   • Girls' Clubs
* Jewish Community Centers   • Boy Scouts
* Campfire Girls   • Girl Scouts

8. Discussion

Content:
    a.   Which voluntary/youth-serving agencies exist in our community?
    b.   How do voluntary/youth-serving agencies differ from municipal park and recreation departments? How are they alike?

    c. Have you participated in leisure programs provided by a voluntary/youth-serving agency?
        If so, please describe.
    d. Have you ever wanted to participate in one of their programs, but were unable?
        If so, please describe.
    e. How can one learn about their programs?

Process: Conduct debriefing using above questions. Encourage all participants to contribute by responding to at least one of the questions.

9. Presentation

Content: "In many communities the *public schools* are a major provider of leisure opportunities. In some instances, the public recreation program is offered through the schools; in other instances, the schools cooperate closely with the municipal park and recreation department. A major way in which schools cooperate with municipal agencies is by allowing the use of school facilities. Most schools have facilities such as *outdoor playing fields, playgrounds, gymnasiums, auditoriums, shops,* and *multi-purpose rooms* that can support a wide variety of recreation activities.

"Some schools are involved in community education programs that offer a wide range of activities to all segments of the population, not just the school-age population. The program offerings are similar to those that would be found in a municipal park and recreation department or some voluntary/youth-serving agencies. They serve to increase the richness of leisure opportunities in a community."

Process: Present information on schools and leisure opportunities. List examples on an easel or chalkboard of possible facilities available through the public schools.

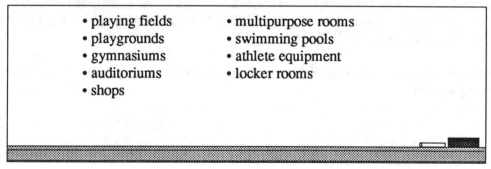

    • playing fields   • multipurpose rooms
    • playgrounds   • swimming pools
    • gymnasiums   • athlete equipment
    • auditoriums   • locker rooms
    • shops

10. Discussion

Content:
    a. What role can the school play in enhancing leisure opportunities in a community?
    b. Which schools in your community are used by the public for recreation purposes?
    c. Are the school's facilities accessible to people with disabilities?
    d. Are there any school-sponsored leisure programs that are open to the public?
        If so, what are they?
    e. If you wanted to participate in one of these programs, what steps would you take?
    f. Have you ever participated in any of these programs? If so, which ones?

Process: Conduct discussion using above questions. Encourage all participants to contribute to the discussion by responding to at least one of the questions.

11. Presentation

Content: "*Religious organizations* sometimes sponsor recreation activities. Often, these activities are for members of their own parish or congregation, but sometimes they are open to nonmembers. Such programs usually stress fellowship and social interaction.

"In some communities, religious organizations cooperate with the municipal agency by offering to share facilities, if appropriate, and by attempting to avoid duplication of the municipal program. If an individual is seeking a specific type of leisure activity and cannot find it in other places, there is a possibility it can be found through a program sponsored by a religious organization."

Process: Present information on church and religious organizations.

12. Discussion

Content:
    a. Are you aware of any leisure programs sponsored by religious organizations?
       If so, what are they?
    b. Have you participated in such a program? If so, please describe.
    c. Are there programs in the community in which you have wanted to participate but were unable?
       If so, what prevented you?
    d. How can one learn about leisure programs sponsored by religious organizations?
    e. If such a program existed and you wanted to participate, what would you do?

Process: Conduct debriefing using above questions. Encourage all participants to contribute by responding to at least one of the questions.

13. Presentation

Content: "*The private/commercial sector* offers a very wide variety of leisure opportunities. The breadth of opportunities is so great that it is sometimes difficult to grasp. The private/commercial sector comprises all enterprises that offer leisure opportunities for the purpose of making a profit. This would include *movie theaters, bowling establishments, restaurants, health and fitness clubs, arcades, resorts, amusement parks,* and a host of other enterprises.

"The private/commercial sector uses many methods to inform the public of its offerings. It advertises extensively through newspapers, radio and television, and signs and billboards. Because they are in business to make a profit from the public, they make a strong effort to keep abreast of current trends and to offer those activities that are popular.

"Becoming aware of all the possibilities available through the private/commercial sector is a task that requires some effort. The effort, however, will result in the reward of having a vast array of possibilities from which to choose. The possibilities of the private/commercial sector further enrich the local leisure opportunities."

Process: Present information on the private/commercial sector. List examples of private or commercial recreation opportunities on an easel or chalkboard.

COMMERCIAL/PRIVATE FACILITIES

- movie theaters
- bowling alleys
- restaurants
- health and fitness clubs

- arcades
- resorts
- amusement parks

14. Discussion

Content:

    a.   What is an example of a leisure opportunity available from the private/commercial sector?

    b.   What was your last leisure experience through the private/commercial sector?

    c.   How can you learn what is available through the private/commercial sector?

    d.   If you could choose any activity available from the private/commercial sector, what would it be?

Process: Conduct discussion using above questions. Encourage all participants to contribute by responding to at least one of the questions.

15. Learning Activity

Content: "We are going to participate in an extended activity to learn as much as we can about the leisure opportunities available to us. This is an activity that will require several days to complete and can be best approached by working in groups. We are going to divide into five groups of equal numbers. One group will be assigned to each of the categories we just examined. We are then going to make an inventory of the leisure opportunities in each category in this community and create a resource file for each of us.

"We must first agree about what we want to know about entries in each category. Each group will generate a list of the kinds of information that would be helpful to include about all of the agencies, organizations, and enterprises in our resource file. The lists will be compared to see that we have not overlooked anything and a master list will be created. After we have agreed on the content of the master list, each group will use all the means at its disposal to gather the information desired. The information will be duplicated so that each of you will have your own leisure resource file."

Process: Explain activity. Divide into groups. Assign one group to each of the following:

- Public
- Voluntary/youth-serving
- School
- Religious organizations
- Private/commercial

Create master list of types of information desired. List could include:

> • Name, address, and phone number of agency
>   or organization
> • Programs and activities offered
> • Transportation available to reach activity sites
> • Costs of participation, if any
> • Special equipment required, if any
> • Membership or eligibility restrictions, if any

Provide telephone directories, brochures, pamphlets, newspapers, and other tools to groups. Obtain information and duplicate, collate, and distribute.

16. Debriefing

Content:
    a. Did you have difficulty in getting information you desired? If so, how did you cope with the difficulty?
    b. What is your opinion of the variety of resources that have been identified?
    c. Of what value will this resource file be to you?

Process: Conduct debriefing using above questions. Encourage all participants to contribute by responding to at least one of the questions.

17. Conclusion

Content: "Each of the categories of leisure-service providers that we have examined makes a contribution to the total resources available in a community. To effectively utilize those resources, one must know something about them. Knowing differences and similarities that exist among these categories can provide valuable guide posts in arriving at intelligent decisions related to leisure participation."

Process: Make concluding statements. Provide opportunity for questions.

LEISURE EDUCATION: SOCIAL INTERACTION

Purpose, Goal, and Objectives

Purpose: Provide opportunities for participants to learn the dynamics of social interaction, gain knowledge about the appropriateness of social interaction behaviors, demonstrate verbal and nonverbal behaviors encouraging attention to speakers and exhibit verbal behaviors required of an effective speaker.

Goal 6: Demonstrate knowledge of effective social interaction skills.

Objective 6.1. Demonstrate knowledge of the dynamics of social interaction.
Objective 6.2. Demonstrate knowledge of considerations for appropriateness of behaviors during social interaction.
Objective 6.3. Demonstrate verbal behaviors encouraging attention to speaker.
Objective 6.4. Demonstrate nonverbal behaviors encouraging attention to a speaker.
Objective 6.5. Demonstrate verbal behaviors required of an effective speaker.

Goal, Objectives, and Performance Measures

Goal 6: Demonstrate knowledge of effective social interaction skills.

Objective 6.1: Demonstrate knowledge of the dynamics of social interaction.

Performance Measure A: Upon request and within two minutes, identify two modes of social interaction (e.g., verbal and nonverbal interaction skills), with 100% accuracy on three consecutive occasions.

Performance Measure B: Upon request and within two minutes identify two roles associated with social interaction [e.g., speaking (sender) and listening (receiver)], with 100% accuracy on three consecutive occasions.

Performance Measure C: Upon request and within two minutes specify importance of determining appropriateness of behaviors when engaging in social interaction, with 100% accuracy on three consecutive occasions.

Objective 6.2: Demonstrate knowledge of considerations for appropriateness of behaviors during social interaction.

Performance Measure A: Given a paper and pencil, in five minutes write the definitions of the following:
  (a) paying attention (e.g., staying focused on the individuals with whom one is interacting is fundamental to the establishment and maintenance of good relationships), and

(b)　empathy (e.g., act of projecting one's own consciousness into the situation of another person, act of putting oneself into the position of another in an attempt to understand that person's feelings),

on two consecutive occasions.

Performance Measure B:　Upon request and within five minutes describe the steps involved in the following:

(a)　initiating an interaction by exhibiting the following behaviors:　(1) approach person,　(2) get other person's attention,　(3) make an opening statement, and (4) engage in a conversation, and

(b)　interrupting properly by exhibiting the following behaviors:　(1) raise index finger, or motion with the entire hand, (2) wait until acknowledged, (3) speak, and (4) if speaker does not acknowledge, say "Excuse me..."

identifying at least three of the four steps per behavior on two consecutive occasions.

Objective 6.3:　Demonstrate verbal behaviors encouraging attention to speaker.

Performance Measure:　Given a paper describing a situation (e.g., Person A is having difficulty with learning a recreation activity skill and is telling Person B about the situation), and with 15 minutes to engage in interchange:

(a)　assume the role of Person B

(b)　demonstrate attentiveness to person by eliciting each of the following verbal behaviors at least once:　(1) agree (e.g., uh-huh, yes) or disagree (e.g., no), (2) paraphrase ("You said that you are having difficulty kicking the soccer ball into the net."), (3) clarify ("I am confused as to how this relates to your brother.　Could you help me understand?"), (4) perception checking ("You appear frustrated.　Am I correct? "),

with 100% accuracy on three consecutive occasions.

Objective 6.4:　Demonstrate nonverbal behaviors encouraging attention to a speaker.

Performance Measure A:　Given a paper describing a situation (e.g., Person A is having difficulty with learning a recreation activity skill and is telling Person B about the situation) and with 10 minutes to engage in interchange:

(a)　assume the role of Person B

(b)　demonstrate attentiveness to person by exhibiting each of the following nonverbal behaviors: (1) looking directly at speaker, (2) sitting or standing upright, (3) gesturing comprehension (e.g, head nods, head shakes), (4) making supportive facial expressions (e.g., smile or frown as appropriate for discussion), (5) maintaining proximity (staying within three yards of speaker), (6) using voice effectively (volume, tone),

80% of the time on two consecutive occasions.

Performance Measure B:　Given a paper describing a situation (e.g., Person A is having difficulty with learning a recreation activity skill and is telling Person B about the situation) and with 10 minutes to engage in interchange,

(a)　assume the role of Person A

(b)　demonstrate being an effective speaker by exhibiting each of the following nonverbal behaviors: (1) looking in direction of audience, (2) sitting or standing upright, (3) using gestures (e.g, supportive hand movements), (4) making supportive facial expressions (e.g., smile or frown as appropriate for discussion), (5) maintaining proximity (staying within three yards of audience), (6) using voice effectively (volume, tone),

80% of the time on two consecutive occasions.

Objective 6.5: Demonstrate verbal behaviors required of an effective speaker.

Performance Measure: Given a paper describing a situation (e.g., Person A is having difficulty with learning a recreation activity skill and is telling Person B about the situation) and with 15 minutes to engage in interchange,
   (a)   assume the role of Person A
   (b)   demonstrate effective speaking skills by exhibiting the following verbal behaviors: (1) use appropriate vocabulary (avoid slang and offensive terminology), (2) enunciate clearly (pronounce words properly), (3) avoid distracting fillers (e.g., "ummm," "like ya know," "ahh"), (4) present information in a logical sequence, and (5) present relevant content,
90% of the time on two separate occasions.

Goal, Objectives, Content, and Process

Goal 6: Demonstrate knowledge of effective social interaction skills.

Objective 6.1: Demonstrate knowledge of the dynamics of social interaction.

1. Orientation Activity

Content: "Form a circle by linking your arms with each other. After the circle is formed, drop your arms. Extend your right arms into the circle and join hands with someone across the circle from you. Without releasing your right hand, extend your left arm into the circle and grasp the left hand of someone other than the person whose right hand you are holding. The result of these actions should be a giant human knot. Now, it is your task to untie the knot by directing one person at a time to release first the right hand, then the left hand. After we have untied the knot, form a line. Introduce yourself to the person to the right and left of you."

Process: Explain activity. Help form circle. Monitor joining of hands to ensure that no person is joined with only one other person. Emphasize untying of knot by one person at a time. Refrain from giving directions to specific individuals to release hands.

2. Debriefing

Content:
   a.   How did the giant knot resemble the linkages present in group communication?
   b.   How did communication help untie the knot?
   c.   Was the communication that occurred easy to understand or was there some confusion on the part of the speakers, listeners, or both? How so?
   d.   Were you a speaker, a listener, or both? Give examples.

Process: Conduct debriefing by using above questions. Encourage all participants to contribute to the debriefing by responding to at least one of the questions.

3. Introduction

Content: "An important aspect of participating in leisure activities is having the skills necessary to interact with other people. It is essential that one be able to establish and maintain friendships, socialize with others, and feel competent to cope with different types of social situations. Having good communication skills is an integral part of the dynamics of social interaction."

Process: Introduce topic on the dynamics of social interaction.

4. Presentation

Content: "Most of us have already acquired some interpersonal skills, simply by the process of having lived among and interacted with other people. But most of us could also improve our interpersonal skills and become more open, more understanding, more caring, and more genuine in our relationships with each other. Communication is the foundation upon which interpersonal skills are based. It is the essential ingredient in all relationships. When clear, caring communication occurs, relationships grow; when communication is incomplete, hostile, or ineffective, relationships deteriorate. Few things are more important in social interaction than good communication."

"Communication is the process of *sending and receiving* messages. At a personal level, communication may be *verbal* or *nonverbal*. It is important to understand that words are not always needed to send messages. Clear messages are often conveyed by body position (stance) and facial expression. Examples of sending messages without using words include the following: (1) an individual standing with hands on the hips and a frown on the face can clearly send a message of anger or disapproval, (2) an individual can smile broadly to communicate approval or happiness, or (3) a person can wink and use a hand to cover the mouth to communicate the idea of a secret or a shared feeling. There are many other forms of nonverbal communication.

"Sometimes, individuals send unclear messages because their body postures and facial expressions do not fit the words they are using. For example, an individual could emphatically pound a table and frown while saying, 'I am not angry.' Or an individual could have a pinched facial expression and state, 'I am really quite happy about this.' These individuals would be sending mixed signals to their listeners. The likelihood is that clear communication is not present.

"In addition to speakers (senders) sometimes failing to transmit clear messages, listeners (receivers) sometimes fail in hearing and interpreting messages. Misunderstandings can happen when individuals think they have received a clear message but they have not been careful in listening to the message or they have misinterpreted nonverbal clues coming from the speaker. Failure to listen with understanding can result in some serious communication problems. For example, if a listener is preoccupied with something else, it may appear that total attention is being given to the speaker, but in reality, little is being heard. The message did not get through to the receiver. Sometimes, listeners can assume they know what speakers are trying to tell them and they do not bother to listen carefully or check to see if their assumptions are correct. If their assumptions are wrong, there is miscommunication. Sometimes senders and receivers interpret common words or sayings differently. For example, a speaker might say, 'I will be back in a few minutes.' A listener might interpret the phrase 'a few minutes' to mean less than 10 minutes. The speaker might mean anything up to 30 minutes. In this situation, the potential for miscommunication is very high."

Process: Present information on communication. Demonstrate nonverbal messages. Use board to illustrate major points.

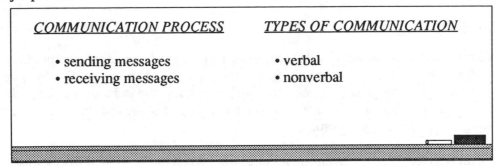

5. Discussion

Content:
 a. What are some examples of how you use communication in your everyday routine?
 b. Have you been in situations that were unexpected because of miscommunication with someone? What were the circumstances?
 c. Have you sent nonverbal messages to someone? Please demonstrate.
 d. Have you received nonverbal messages from someone? How were you able to tell if you interpreted them correctly?
 e. What are examples of words or phrases that people might interpret differently?
 f. Have you been in conversations where the speaker or the listener made incorrect assumptions about what was being said? Did the incorrect assumptions affect the immediate conversation or did they affect later events? How so?

Process: Conduct debriefing using above questions. Provide opportunity for each person to respond to at least one of the questions.

6. Learning Activity

Content: "We are going to do an activity using verbal and nonverbal communication. Stand, link arms, and form a circle. After the circle is formed, drop your arms. We will go around the circle clockwise. The first player will state his or her name, identify a favorite recreation activity, and briefly act out the activity. When the player is finished, the entire circle will repeat the name, the activity, and the actions of the player. The next player will then state his or her name, a favorite activity, and act out the activity. The group will follow suit. Play will proceed until everyone in the circle has had a turn."

Process: Explain activity. Help form circle. Make sure each player has a turn. Move to debriefing when activity is completed.

7. Debriefing

Content:
 a. Was the verbal communication clear? Did you clearly understand what the activities were before they were acted out?
 b. Were the nonverbal actions used to illustrate the activities appropriate? Would you have been able to identify the activities if you did not already know what they were?
 c. Why do you think we did this activity?

Process: Conduct debriefing using above questions. Provide opportunity for each person to respond to at least one of the questions.

8. Learning Activity

Content: "We are going to do an activity that will focus on the use of nonverbal communication. Form another circle. Now, without speaking or writing, arrange yourselves in a straight line by order of month of birth. Figure out some way to have those people whose birthdays are in January to be in the first part of the line, those with birthdays in February to be in the second part of the line, etc. Remember, do this without speaking or writing a single word."

Process: Explain activity. Monitor to ensure no speaking. When line is formed, check to see if order is correct. Move to debriefing.

9. Debriefing

Content:
    a.   Was the line in the right order? If not, how far off was it?
    b.   How many strategies did you use to form the line?
    c.   Which strategies were the most successful?
    d.   How can nonverbal communication be used in leisure participation?

Process: Conduct debriefing using above questions. Provide opportunity for each person to respond to at least one of the questions.

10. Presentation

Content: "Verbal communication can be divided into the processes of *encoding* and *decoding*. Encoding is the process by which a speaker forms a mental image of a message and translates it into words. Decoding is the process which a listener uses to interpret the meaning of the words that have been spoken. By decoding, the listener is able to form mental images of what the speaker said. If the decoding has been accurate, the message has been correctly understood. Sometimes, the encoding or the decoding process (or both) can be faulty. When this happens, miscommunication is the result.

"Encoders and decoders can check the accuracy of their efforts by seeking feedback related to their communication. Feedback allows speakers and listeners to be confident that messages have been sent and received correctly. Feedback often takes the form of questions related to the communication. For example, speakers can ask listeners to paraphrase what they have just heard and listeners can ask speakers to repeat the message. Feedback is used for clarification and the enhancement of mutual understanding."

Process: Present information on encoding, decoding, and feedback. Write the words and definitions on the easel or chalkboard:

> ### *VERBAL COMMUNICATION*
>
> Encoding: speaker forms mental image of message and translates
>   into words
> Decoding: listener interprets meaning of spoken words

11. Discussion

Content:
    a. Do you believe you are a better encoder than a decoder or vice versa? Why?
    b. What can you do to be better at these processes?
    c. Have you used feedback to clarify communication? How so?

Process: Conduct discussion using above questions. Provide opportunity for each person to contribute to the discussion by responding to at least one of the questions.

12. Learning Activity

Content: "We are going to do an activity that will require careful speaking and listening skills. Each of you has paper and pencil. One of you will be selected to study the arrangement of a set of squares and verbally direct the others to duplicate (by drawing) the same arrangement of squares. The person giving the directions will be the only person allowed to see the arrangement of squares and will also be the only person to speak. The person giving the directions should stand with his or her back to the group. The listeners, who will try to duplicate the arrangement as directed, will not be allowed to ask questions about the directions. This activity requires the speaker to be careful and precise in describing the squares and it requires the listeners to be very attentive to the speaker."

Process: Explain activity. Provide paper and pencils. Prepare arrangement of squares ahead of session. Monitor activity to ensure that listeners do not ask questions or seek clarification of directions. If desired, prepare several different arrangements of squares and provide each participant with opportunity to be the speaker. An example of an arrangement of the squares could involve three squares in a diagonal with the top square's bottom left corner touching the middle square's upper right corner and the middle square's lower left corner touching the bottom square's upper right corner.

13. Debriefing

Content:
    a. How close was your drawing to the original set of squares?
    b. What was the most difficult part of doing this activity?
    c. Was it easier to give directions or to listen to them? Why?
    d. What conclusions can you draw from this regarding communication?

Process: Conduct debriefing using above questions. Provide opportunity for each person to respond to at least one of the questions.

14. Learning Activity

Content: "We are going to repeat the previous activity, but with two important differences. The squares will be in different arrangements and the listeners may ask questions of and seek clarification from the speaker. The speaker may face the listeners, repeat directions, and answer questions. The speaker will still be the only person who can see the arrangement of squares that is being described."

Process: Explain activity. Prepare squares ahead of session. Prepare sufficient number of different arrangements to provide each person the opportunity to be the speaker.

15. Debriefing

Content:
    a.   How close were your drawings to the squares that were being described?
    b.   Were the directions easier to follow this time? If so, why?
    c.   What conclusions relative to communication can you draw from this activity?

Process: Conduct debriefing using above questions. Provide opportunity for each person to respond to at least one of the questions.

16. Conclusion

Content: "Communication is a process that requires careful attention from both senders and receivers. If careful attention is given, there is a great likelihood that the communication will be accurate and easily understood. Communication can be verbal, nonverbal, or a combination of both. Being adept in communication is usually a prerequisite for establishing comfortable relationships with others. Communication improves social interaction."

Process: Make concluding statements. Provide opportunities for participants to ask questions and raise concerns.

Objective 6.2: Demonstrate knowledge of considerations for appropriateness of behaviors during social interaction.

1. Orientation Activity

Content: "Everyone please sit in a circle. I have given each of you a description of something that you could do that would be appropriate and would communicate that you care about the person. If your card is green, turn to the person on your left; if your card is purple, turn to the person on your right.

"Introduce yourself and find out the person's name. Then read the statement to the person and allow him or her to read the statement to you. Once you have completed this, turn to your other side and wait for that person to finish talking and then repeat the process. After you have introduced yourselves to the people on both sides of you, we are going to watch a skit that presents a brief interaction between two people. Observe closely and be prepared to share your observations at the end of the skit."

Process: Explain activity. Prepare cards in advance containing the following statements (one per card).

- Pay attention to the person.
- Be empathetic to the person.
- Initiate interaction with the person.
- If necessary, interrupt the person properly.

Select and rehearse two participants ahead of session. Prepare script to show interaction. Script could be as follows:

> Speaker 1: Let me tell you about my weekend. It was so wonderful.
>
> Speaker 2: Oh, I had a good time on the weekend too.
>
> Speaker 1: Yes, well, I've been waiting a long time for this, but I finally got to go to San Francisco. The weather was just beautiful...
>
> Speaker 2: I really like good weather. I can play tennis in good weather.
>
> Speaker 1: Good. Oh, I want to tell you about the Golden Gate Bridge. It was my first experience on a suspension bridge and...
>
> Speaker 2: I haven't had much experience with tennis, but I'm getting better, especially with my backhand.
>
> Speaker 1: That's nice. Anyway, in San Francisco we drove to the top of Nob Hill and we could see the boats in the bay and...
>
> Speaker 2: I like boating too, but tennis is even more exciting.
>
> Speaker 1: Yes. Well, I hope you get to play soon. So long.

Instruct Speaker 2 to abruptly interrupt Speaker 1 at indicated times. Move to debriefing at conclusion of skit.

2. Debriefing

Content:
a. How would you characterize Speaker 2's behavior? Why?
b. If you believe Speaker 2's behavior was inappropriate, in what ways was it inappropriate?
c. How would you have felt if you were Speaker 1? Why
d. What was the quality of the interaction between the two speakers? Why?
e. Based on this observation only, what do you think the quality will be of any future interactions between these two people?

Process: Conduct debriefing using above questions. Emphasize Speaker 2's interruptions and inability to pay attention to Speaker 1. Encourage all participants to contribute to the debriefing.

3. Introduction

Content: "Behaving appropriately is an important part of social interaction. When an individual behaves inappropriately, a negative influence is introduced into the environment in which the interaction is taking place. If the behavior is mildly inappropriate, the interaction may be disturbed but it may also continue. If it is markedly inappropriate, the interaction may simply cease. Making decisions about behavior requires intelligent judgments because what may be inappropriate for one situation may be acceptable in a different situation. The best rule of thumb to follow is to always be conservative in behavior until one learns more about the situation."

Process: Introduce topic on gaining knowledge of considerations for appropriateness of behaviors during social interaction.

4. Presentation

Content: "Although there may be some uncertainty regarding the appropriateness of behavior in certain situations, there are some basic considerations related to behavior that merit attention. These considerations are not all-inclusive, but adherence to their spirit will work to one's advantage. These considerations include (a) paying attention (staying focused), (b) being empathetic, (c) initiating interaction, and (d) interrupting properly.

"*Paying attention,* or staying focused, on the individuals with whom one is interacting is fundamental to the establishment and maintenance of good relationships. If one is self-absorbed, unfocused, or inattentive in other ways, one is sending a clear message to the other individuals present that what they are saying is not worth the effort it takes to listen to them. Such behavior is inappropriate and makes it difficult, if not impossible, to engage in meaningful social interaction with others."

Process: Present information on paying attention. List key points on an easel or chalkboard.

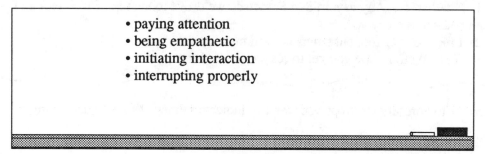

- paying attention
- being empathetic
- initiating interaction
- interrupting properly

5. Discussion

Content:
    a. Have you attempted to interact with others who would not pay attention to you?
    b. How did you feel when this happened?
    c. After this happened, did you make other attempts at interaction with them? Why?
    d. Have you been in situations where you ignored others who were trying to interact with you? If so, why?

Process: Conduct discussion using above questions. Provide opportunity for each person to contribute to the discussion by responding to at least one of the questions.

6. Presentation

Content: "*Empathy* is the act of projecting one's own consciousness into the situation of another person. It is an act of putting oneself into the position of another in an attempt to understand that person's feelings. It does not mean that one has to have the same intensity of feeling or emotion that another person is experiencing, but it does mean that one cares enough to listen to the concerns of the other. Empathy is associated with the saying 'Walk a mile in my shoes.' Being empathetic can be an important form of interaction."

Process: Present information on empathy. Use examples as needed.

7. Discussion

Content:
    a.   What is empathy?
    b.   Why is it important?
    c.   Are there empathetic persons among your friends?
    d.   Are you an empathetic person? If so, can you provide an example of when you were empathetic?

Process: Conduct discussion using above questions. Provide opportunity for each person to contribute to the discussion by responding to at least one of the questions.

8. Presentation

Content: "*Initiating interaction* is usually an easier thing to do with friends than it is with strangers or people you have just met. Yet, someone must take the first step if interaction is to take place. If you are faced with the prospect of initiating interaction with a stranger, following some simple guidelines will be a great help. These guidelines include:

    a.   Approach the other person.
    b.   Get the other person's attention. Do this by saying 'Excuse me,' gently tapping on his or her shoulder, etc.
    c.   Have an opening statement. A question such as 'How are you today?,' a statement such as 'My name is Margaret,' or a request such as 'Can you please tell me the time?' would be appropriate.
    d.   Engage in conversation.

Making the initial effort to start some interaction will be easier if these simple guidelines are followed."

Process: Present information on initiating interaction. List guidelines on chalkboard.

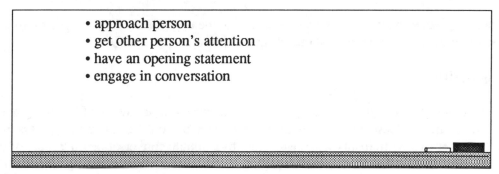

    • approach person
    • get other person's attention
    • have an opening statement
    • engage in conversation

9. Discussion

Content:
    a.   When you meet someone for the first time, do you wait for them to start a conversation? Why?
    b.   What is an example of when you took the first steps to start an interaction?
    c.   What can you do to improve your ability to initiate interaction?

Process: Conduct discussion using above questions. Provide opportunity for each person to contribute to the discussion by responding to at least one of the questions.

10. Presentation

Content: "As a general rule, it is inappropriate to interrupt others when they are speaking. But there are times when it may be necessary. In those situations, there is a procedure to follow that is appropriate. The procedure for *interrupting properly* in any nonemergency situation is as follows: (a) the listener may raise an index finger or motion with the entire hand to let the speaker know he or she has something to say, (b) the listener waits until he or she is acknowledged and then speaks, (c) if the speaker does not acknowledge the listener and continues speaking, the listener may say 'Excuse me, but I need to say...' This needs to be done politely but firmly. If there is an emergency, one does not need to worry about interrupting improperly but should immediately take whatever action the emergency requires."

Process: Present information on interrupting properly. List key points on the easel or chalkboard.

> - raise index finger
> - motion with the entire hand
> - wait until acknowledged
> - speak
> - if speaker does not acknowledge, say "Excuse me..."

11. Discussion

Content:
    a.   How do you feel when you are abruptly interrupted?
    b.   What are some times when it would be appropriate to interrupt a speaker?
    c.   What procedure should be followed when interrupting a speaker?

Process: Conduct discussion using above questions. Provide opportunity for each person to contribute to the discussion by responding to at least one of the questions.

12. Learning Activity

Content: "We are going to do an activity that will help us become more aware of behaving appropriately during social interaction. Please get into groups of three. One person in each group will assume the role of observer; the other two participants will engage in a five-minute conversation on a topic of their choosing. The conversationalists will focus on paying attention to each other, being empathetic, and interrupting properly. The observer will make notes about how the conversation was initiated and by whom, any indications of empathy, and if interruptions were made properly. When five minutes have elapsed, the conversation will end and all three participants in each group will use the next five minutes to discuss the notes. The observer will then change roles with one of the conversationalists and the process will be repeated. The activity will continue until each group member has had the opportunity to be the observer."

Process: Explain activity. Divide group into threes. Provide paper and pencil for observers. Monitor five-minute time periods.

13. Debriefing

Content:
    a. What clues did you use to determine if the conversationalists were paying attention to each other?
    b. What evidence of empathy did you observe?
    c. Were the interruptions done properly?
    d. As a speaker, how did you feel when you were interrupted?
    e. How did you feel when you interrupted the speaker?

Process: Conduct debriefing using above questions. Provide opportunity for each participant to respond to at least one of the questions.

14. Conclusion

Content: "Appropriate behavior is important to social interaction. It is something that can be practiced and perfected. People who genuinely try to behave appropriately are generally successful."

Process: Make concluding statements. Provide participants with the opportunity to ask questions.

Objective 6.3: Demonstrate verbal behaviors encouraging attention to a speaker.

1. Orientation Activity

Content: "Everyone please sit in a circle. Now that we are seated in a circle, I have given each of you a procedure that you could follow to show you are paying attention to a person and that you care about the person. If your card is brown, turn to the person on your left; if your card is yellow, turn to the person on your right. Introduce yourself and find out the person's name. Then read the statement to the person and allow him or her to read the statement to you. Once you have completed this, turn to your other side and wait for that person to finish talking and then repeat the process. After we have introduced ourselves to the people on both sides of us, we are going to watch a brief skit to help us become aware of the importance of verbal behaviors a listener can use to encourage a speaker. Watch and listen carefully to the interaction between two people."

Process: Explain the activity. Develop cards with the following procedures written on different cards.

• listening to the speaker
• paraphrasing what the speaker said
• clarifying responses of the speaker
• checking the perception of the speaker

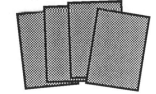

Preselect and rehearse two people to engage in following interactions:

- First person to talk for one or two minutes about participating in an upcoming recreation activity; the other person to sit silently and make no reaction to what is being said.
- Same person to repeat comments in first situation; second person to respond in timely fashion with comments such as 'I see,' 'That's interesting,' or 'Tell me more about that.' First person to speak with more enthusiasm after hearing listener's comments.

2. Debriefing

Content:
    a.   What differences did you see between the first and second situations?
    b.   What do you think the speaker was feeling in the first situation?
    c.   What else could the listener have done to encourage the speaker in the second situation?

Process: Conduct debriefing using above questions. Provide opportunity for each person to respond to at least one of the questions.

3. Introduction

Content: "Most people would benefit from an improvement in their listening skills. It is important to be an effective listener because of the amount of time most of us spend in listening. The quality of our relationships with others is often dependent on our ability to listen. It may be helpful to think about the difference between listening and hearing. Hearing has been described as a process whereby sound is received by the ears and sent to the brain. It is a physiological process. Listening is a process that involves interpreting and understanding the significance of the sounds. Listening is more than hearing."

Process: Introduce topic on verbal behaviors encouraging attention to a speaker.

4. Presentation

Content: "Learning to be a good listener can be a difficult task for some people. Although most of us spend more time in listening than we do in speaking, we receive very little, if any, training in how to be good listeners. Yet, it is possible to acquire and develop skills that will enhance our abilities as attentive and effective listeners.

"There are five major skills involved in being an active listener. These skills may be categorized as (a) attending, (b) paraphrasing, (c) clarifying response, (d) perception checking and (e) listening response. Attending is nonverbal behavior that tells the speaker the listener is paying attention to the speaker and is interested in the message. Attending is the focus of the next objective in this program.

"*Paraphrasing* is a good way for a person to demonstrate active listening skills. A paraphrase is a response by a listener to a speaker, wherein the listener uses his or her own words to state the essence of the speaker's message. A paraphrase has four basic characteristics.

"The first characteristic of a good paraphrase is that it is brief. It should never be longer than the speaker's message. Otherwise, it can result in the listener interrupting the speaker's train of thought and erecting a barrier to communication. Good listeners learn to make brief paraphrases.

"The second characteristic of a good paraphrase is that it is concise. It reflects accurately the essence of the speaker's message and cuts through the nonessential details that are present in many conversations. A good listener develops the ability to be attentive to the heart of the message.

"A third characteristic of a good paraphrase is that it focuses only on the content of the speaker's message and disregards the emotions with which the message is spoken. Even though nonverbal clues provided by the sender are important, the paraphrase should state only the facts or ideas being communicated. The nonverbal clues can be received and processed in another manner. A good listener learns to focus on the content of the message.

"The fourth characteristic of a good paraphrase is that it is stated in the listener's own words, rather than by repeating the words of the speaker. A paraphrase summarizes the listener's understanding of the message in his or her own words. If a listener simply repeats the words of the speaker, the result is parroting, not paraphrasing. Parroting can be a barrier to communication; paraphrasing can enhance it."

Process: Present information on paraphrasing. Use chalkboard to list four major characteristics.

> - brief
> - concise
> - focuses only on the content of the speaker's message
> - state in the listener's words

5. Discussion

Content:
    a. What is a paraphrase?
    b. What are some instances when you have found paraphrasing to be useful?
    c. How do you feel when someone paraphrases something you have just said?
    d. In your opinion, what is the most difficult thing about paraphrasing?
    e. How can you improve your ability to paraphrase?

Process: Conduct discussion using above questions. Provide opportunity for each person to contribute to the discussion by responding to at least one of the questions.

6. Presentation

Content: "Another skill that active listeners can employ to improve communication is the *clarifying response.* A clarifying response is sought from the speaker when a listener is confused or has an inadequate understanding of the message. Listeners can accomplish this by asking speakers to repeat part of the message, to use different words, to illustrate their meaning with an example, or to respond to questions from the listener. A clarifying response can be an integral part of communication but it must be used in a wise manner. If a listener constantly interrupts a speaker to seek clarifying responses, communication will probably be greatly impeded.

"It is usually best to enhance understanding by asking for one clarifying response at a time. When two or more clarifying responses are sought in quick succession, it sometimes means the listener is not attending to the speaker and the communication process is needlessly inhibited."

Process: Present information on clarifying response. Provide examples as the information listed above is presented.

7. Discussion

Content:
    a.   What is a clarifying response?
    b.   What are some examples of a clarifying response?
    c.   Can you give some instances when you have asked for a clarifying response?

Process: Conduct discussion using above questions. Provide opportunity for each person to contribute to the discussion by responding to at least one of the questions.

8. Presentation

Content: "*Perception checking* is another tool that can be used by active listeners. Sometimes it is difficult for people to say precisely what they want to say and sometimes others find it equally difficult to listen without distraction to what is being said. Because this is a rather common occurrence, there needs to be a check for accuracy in communication. Effective listeners frequently reflect back the essence of what they have heard. This process is referred to as perception checking.

"Perception checking is basically a three-step process used by effective listeners. It involves (a) the listener paraphrasing the message from the speaker, (b) asking the speaker if the paraphrase is accurate, and (c) providing the speaker with an opportunity to correct any misperception. Perception checking provides a channel through which accuracy of communication is determined and controlled."

Process: Present information on perception checking. List the three steps on the easel or chalkboard.

> • paraphrase message from speaker
> • ask speaker to confirm or deny accuracy of paraphrase
> • provide speaker with opportunity to correct any inaccurate perception

9. Discussion

Content:
    a.   What is perception checking?
    b.   Why is it necessary?
    c.   When have you used perception checking?
    d.   How can you improve your ability in perception checking?

Process: Conduct discussion using above questions. Provide opportunity for each person to contribute to the discussion by responding to at least one of the questions.

10. Presentation

Content: "*Using a listening response* is another way to be an attentive listener. A listening response is a very brief comment or action made to the speaker that indicates the listener is interested and wishes the speaker to continue. It is made quietly and briefly to ensure there is no interference with the speaker's train of thought.

"There are at least five types of listening responses. One type is simply nodding the head slightly and waiting for the speaker to continue. A second type is to pause and look at the speaker expectantly, without saying or doing anything. A third is using a casual remark, such as 'I see', 'Mmmm,' or 'That's interesting', to demonstrate interest in the speaker and the message. A fourth is the echo, or repeating the last few words of the speaker. A fifth listening response is known as a mirror, which is the listener reflecting his or her understanding of the message back to the speaker."

Process: Present information on listening response. Use board to list types of listening responses.

> • nodding head slightly and waiting for speaker to continue
> • pause and look at speaker expectantly
> • using a casual remark, such as "I see."
> • repeat last few words of speaker
> • reflect your understanding of the message back to speaker

11. Discussion

Content:
    a. What is a listening response?
    b. Are there listening responses that you commonly use? If so, what are they?
    c. What is your feeling when you are speaking and someone provides you with a listening response?
    d. How can you improve your ability to give listening responses?

Process: Conduct discussion using above questions. Provide opportunity for each person to contribute to the discussion by responding to at least one of the questions.

12. Learning Activity

Content: "We are going to do an activity that will help you become more aware of listening responses. Please get into groups of three. One person in each group will assume the role of speaker, one the role of listener, and one the role of observer. The speaker will think of a problem he or she has experienced while participating in a recreation activity and relate it to the listener. The listener will make listening responses, as appropriate. The observer will record notes about the listening responses. When five minutes have elapsed, the speaker will end his or her comments and the next five minutes will be spent with all three members discussing the listening responses that were recorded. The three group members will then change roles and repeat the process. The activity will continue until each group member has had the opportunity to act in all three roles."

Process: Explain activity. Divide group into threes. Provide paper and pencil for observers. Monitor five minute time periods.

13. Debriefing

Content:

    a. What listening responses were commonly used?

    b. As a speaker, how did you feel when you received a listening response?

    c. As a listener, was it difficult to find an appropriate moment to make a listening response? If so, how did you deal with it?

    d. How will you use your knowledge of listening responses in your recreation participation?

Process: Conduct debriefing using above questions. Provide opportunity for each person to respond to at least one of the questions.

14. Learning Activity

Content: "We are going to do another activity that will allow you to use paraphrasing, clarifying response, and perception checking. Please get into groups of three again, with one person being the speaker, one the listener, and one the observer. The process will be repeated three times so that each person has the opportunity to fill each role. The speaker and listener will engage in a five minute exchange, with the speaker giving his or her thoughts about a specified topic and the listener using the techniques of paraphrasing, clarifying response, and perception checking as often as appropriate. The observer will record each use of these skills. A five minute discussion, focused on these skills, will occur among the three members of each group before the roles are rotated."

Process: Explain activity. Help divide into groups of three. Provide pencil and paper. Ensure each participant has opportunity to play each role. Move to debriefing.

15. Debriefing

Content:

    a. Were the listening skills of paraphrasing, clarifying response, and perception checking used at appropriate moments?

    b. Were they used at inappropriate times? If so, how could a sense of timing be improved?

    c. Which skill was used most often?

    d. As a listener, which skill seemed to be the most effective? Why?

    e. As a speaker, what was your reaction when the listener utilized these skills?

Process: Conduct discussion using above questions. Provide opportunity for each person to contribute to the discussion by responding to at least one of the questions.

16. Conclusion

Content: "Becoming a good listener requires purposeful effort; it is not something that occurs just by chance. Like most other skills, becoming a good listener takes practice. Consciously utilizing different listening responses and the techniques of paraphrasing, clarifying response, and perception checking will result in being a better listener."

Process: Make concluding statements. Provide participants with the opportunity to ask questions.

Objective 6.4: Demonstrate nonverbal behaviors encouraging attention to a speaker.

1. Orientation Activity

Content: "We are going to do an activity where each of you will use nonverbal behavior in an attempt to convey the meaning of a word. There are several slips of paper in the little box in the center of the table. Each slip contains one word that describes a feeling or emotion which people often have. One at a time, each of you will draw a slip from the box and go to the front of the group. Introduce yourself to the group and then do not speak. Use actions or facial expressions, but no words, to demonstrate the meaning of the word on your slip. The rest of the group will have one minute to guess the word that is being demonstrated. The activity will continue until each person has had the opportunity to use nonverbal behavior to demonstrate a word."

Process: Explain activity. Prepare slips of paper prior to session. Slips could contain words such as bored, curious, preoccupied, confused, sad, excited, happy, relaxed, or impatient. Ensure that each participant has opportunity to demonstrate word.

2. Debriefing

Content:
    a.   Were different facial expressions used by group members? If so, describe some?
    b.   What were some other physical actions used to convey meanings of words?
    c.   Were some words easier to guess than others? If so, which ones?
    d.   Were some nonverbal messages particularly strong? If so, which were they?

Process: Conduct debriefing using above questions. Provide opportunity for each person to respond to at least one of the questions.

3. Introduction

Content: "Nonverbal behaviors are ways that attitudes and feelings can be conveyed without speaking. They can send strong messages and have a significant impact on others. Some experts believe it is not possible to speak without also sending a nonverbal message to the listener. It is also believed that listeners always send nonverbal messages back to speakers. There is a considerable amount of agreement that the nonverbal behavior of a listener can have a powerful influence on a speaker."

Process: Introduce topic of nonverbal behaviors encouraging attention to a speaker.

4. Presentation

Content: "Nonverbal behavior is an essential component of communication. It is behavior that is displayed by speakers and listeners. It can be used by either to enhance or retard communication. When nonverbal behavior is used by listeners to enhance communication, it is often referred to as attending to the speaker. Attending means listeners are giving their physical attention to speakers. It is sometimes referred to as listening with the whole body. It indicates that the listener is paying careful attention to the person who is talking. Attending behavior includes eye contact, facial expressions, posture and gestures, body orientation, and physical proximity.

"In our culture, good *eye contact* on the part of the listener expresses interest in what the speaker is saying. Poor eye contact is usually interpreted in a negative way, such as embarrassment, dishonesty, lying, shame, hostility, lack of respect, or disinterest. It is important to know that poor eye contact includes more than a refusal to look at the speaker or looking away whenever the speaker looks at the listener. It also includes staring constantly at the speaker or looking at the speaker in a blank, unfocused manner. Good eye contact means a soft focusing of the eyes on the speaker's eyes, with an occasional shifting to other parts of the face or body, such as a gesturing hand, and then returning to the eyes.

"Some individuals have a difficult time in making eye contact, just as some individuals have a difficult time in knowing what to do with their hands during conversation. Good eye contact is a skill that may require some hard work to achieve, but it is necessary for effective social interaction. It allows speakers to judge how their message is being received and what steps they may have to take to make their communication more meaningful."

Process: Present information on eye contact. Demonstrate examples of poor and good eye contact. Encourage participants to repeat your behaviors.

5. Discussion

Content:
  a. Why is good eye contact important in a listener?
  b. How does good eye contact enhance communication?
  c. What is involved in good eye contact?
  d. How is poor eye contact perceived?
  e. What are some examples of poor eye contact?

Process: Conduct discussion using above questions. Provide opportunity for each person to contribute to the discussion by responding to at least one of the questions.

6. Learning Activity

Content: "Establishing eye contact is a skill that can be learned like any other skill. We are going to engage in a brief activity to help us get started. Please pair up with a partner. Face each other at a distance of six feet. Look in the direction of your partner for one minute. Decrease your distance by half. Look at your partner's hair, forehead, ears, chin, and eyes for one minute. You may shift your gaze in a random manner, but return to your partner's eyes every other shift. Try to look at specific features for at least three seconds at a time."

Process: Explain activity. Help divide into pairs, if necessary. Announce beginning and end of one minute periods. Remind participants that this is a skill they can practice whenever they are with another person.

7. Debriefing

Content:
    a. From a distance of six feet, could you tell if your partner was looking at your eyes?
    b. How difficult was it to look into the eyes of your partner?
    c. How difficult was it to distinguish between your partner looking at your eyes and looking at your forehead?
    d. When can you practice using eye contact?

Process: Conduct debriefing using above questions. Provide opportunity for each person to respond to at least one of the questions.

8. Presentation

Content: "*Facial expression* is another important component of nonverbal behavior in communication. The expression on a listener's face should convey a message of interest and attentiveness to the speaker. It is the expression on a listener's face that indicates the speaker is receiving the psychological as well as the physical attention of the listener.

"Attending to a speaker also implies that the facial expression of the listener is appropriate to what is being heard. For example, if a coach called a meeting of the volleyball team and announced that one of the players had suffered a broken leg in an automobile accident on the way to practice, it would be inappropriate to receive that news with a smile on one's face. On the other hand, it is equally inappropriate to receive happy and joyous news with a grim expression on one's face. The expression on a listener's face should tell the speaker the message is not only being heard, it also is being understood and processed in a manner that is appropriate to its content. Facial expressions, like other forms of nonverbal behavior, can enhance or inhibit communication."

Process: Present information on facial expression. Demonstrate examples.

9. Discussion

Content:
    a. How is facial expression important in attending to a speaker?
    b. Do facial expressions reveal the attitude of the listener? How so?
    c. When have you observed inappropriate facial expressions on listeners?
    d. Do you believe your facial expressions when listening are always appropriate?
    e. If your facial expressions are inappropriate at times, what can you do to improve?

Process: Conduct discussion using above questions. Provide opportunity for each person to contribute to the discussion by responding to at least one of the questions.

10. Learning Activity

Content: "We are going to do an activity to make us more aware of facial expressions. I have placed a large sheet of construction paper on the wall. The sheet of paper is divided into four major columns. One column is headed by the word *happy,* one by *sad,* one by *angry,* and one by *determined.* There is a large group of magazines on the table in front of you. Browse through the magazines. When you come to a picture that depicts one of the four facial expressions listed on the sheet of paper, ask another person if he or she agrees with you about what the face is expressing. If the two of you agree on the expression, remove the picture from the magazine and paste it in the appropriate column on the construction paper. We will do this activity for 15 minutes."

Process: Explain activity. Place paper on wall. Provide magazines, scissors, and paste. If necessary, demonstrate directions by looking through a magazine, finding a picture of a face, removing it, and pasting it in the appropriate column of the paper.

11. Debriefing

Content:
   a. Select one of the pictures on the paper and identify some possible reasons for the facial expression. (Repeat this item as often as desired.)
   b. Is there any disagreement about any expression in any of the columns? If so, which one(s)?
   c. Which expression(s) seemed to be easy to identify? Why?

Process: Conduct debriefing using above questions. Encourage all participants to respond to the first question. Provide opportunity for each person to contribute to the debriefing by responding to at least one of the questions.

12. Presentation

Content: "*Posture and gestures,* like facial expression, can contribute to or detract from communication. Maintaining a posture that combines being relaxed and alert at the same time is an excellent way for a listener to attend to a speaker. The listener should adopt a posture that indicates a balance between feeling comfortable with the speaker and the purpose of paying very careful attention to what is being said. A very effective listening stance can be achieved by blending these two important body messages. Elements of a good listening posture include standing or sitting reasonably erect, facing the speaker, and refraining from fidgeting.

"Gestures from a listener may be as important as the listener's posture in attending to a speaker. Gestures can be a good nonverbal indication of the reaction of the listener to the message. For example, nodding or shaking the head can convey agreement or disagreement with what is being said. Shrugging the shoulders, combined with facial expressions, can indicate ignorance or indifference. Rubbing the chin or scratching the head can indicate thoughtfulness."

Process: Present information on posture and gestures. Demonstrate positive and negative postures and gestures and encourage participants to model your behaviors.

13. Discussion

Content:
    a. How does posture contribute to attending to a speaker?
    b. What two messages should a listener's posture attempt to convey?
    c. Describe what is included in a good listening posture.
    d. How would you describe your own listening posture?
    e. What can you do to improve your listening posture?
    f. What role do gestures play in attending to a speaker?

Process: Conduct discussion using above questions. Provide opportunity for each person to contribute to the discussion by responding to at least one of the questions.

14. Presentation

Content: "*Body orientation* is closely associated with posture. It refers to the positioning of the listener's body relative to that of the speaker's. The body orientation of a listener can include such elements as slightly leaning toward the speaker, squarely facing the speaker, and maintaining an 'open' stance.

"When listeners incline their bodies toward a speaker, it communicates more attentiveness than does leaning back or slumping in a chair. When listeners are totally engrossed in what they are hearing, they are often said to be on the edge of their seats. This conjures a picture of listeners that not only are sitting erectly, but also leaning forward. This is not to suggest that listeners adopt an exaggerated posture of tilting toward a speaker, but a slight forward bend would be appropriate.

"Listeners can also squarely face a speaker without being confrontational. For example, a listener who squares his or her right shoulder with a speaker's left shoulder can communicate a high level of attentiveness and involvement with what is being said. Listeners who turn their shoulders away from a speaker can be seen as disinterested or rejecting the message. In our culture, people who reject others are said to be giving them a cold shoulder. This expression may illustrate the importance of squarely facing a speaker.

"Body orientation also includes being at approximately the same eye level with a speaker. This is particularly important in one-to-one conversations if there is a distinct difference in the amounts of authority ascribed to the speaker and the listener. If a speaker has to bend his or her head back at a severe angle in order to look a listener in the eye, it is a major barrier to communication.

"Maintaining an open posture is also an important part of body orientation. An open posture means a listener is willing to accept the message being conveyed by the speaker. An open posture generally means the listener does not have crossed arms or legs. A closed posture, where the arms and legs are tightly crossed, usually indicates the listener is unwilling to accept the message being conveyed. Picture the manager of a softball team arguing with an umpire over a call made at first base. In addition to verbal expression, the manager may be very animated and engaging in all types of movements. The umpire generally stands with arms tightly folded across the chest. The posture of the umpire clearly indicates rejection of the manager's message."

Process: Present information on body orientation. Demonstrate examples of positive and negative body orientation. Encourage participants to repeat your behavior. Record key points on an easel or chalkboard.

> ### BODY ORIENTATION
>
> • slightly lean toward speaker
> • squarely face speaker
> • maintain open stance

15. Discussion

Content:
- a.   What is meant by the term "body orientation"?
- b.   What is included in the body orientation of a listener to a speaker?
- c.   Why is it important for speakers and listeners to be at approximately the same eye level in one-to-one conversations?
- d.   Can you adopt a body orientation that indicates you are willing to listen to what is being said? Please do so.
- e.   Can you adopt a body orientation that indicates you are unwilling to listen to what is being said? Please do so.
- f.   How can you make yourself aware of your body orientation when you are a listener?

Process: Conduct discussion using above questions. Provide opportunity for each person to contribute to the discussion by responding to at least one of the questions.

16. Presentation

Content: "The *physical proximity* of listeners to speakers is another component of nonverbal behavior that influences communication. Too much distance between listener and speaker inhibits communication. On the other hand, when a listener gets to close to a speaker, the result is often anxiety, which also inhibits communication. How can one tell what is an appropriate distance? There is considerable evidence that a distance of three feet is comfortable in our society. Obviously, this distance may vary, depending on the level of intimacy that exists between listener and speaker."

Process: Present information on physical proximity. Demonstrate positive and negative examples of physical proximity. Encourage participants to repeat your behaviors.

17. Discussion

Content:
- a.   How does physical proximity influence communication?
- b.   How can a listener determine an appropriate physical distance from a speaker?
- c.   At what distance do you feel comfortable when listening to a friend?
- d.   Does the distance needed for comfort change when you are listening to someone you just met? How so?

Process: Conduct discussion using above questions. Provide opportunity for each person to contribute to the discussion by responding to at least one of the questions.

18. Learning Activity

Content: "We are going to divide into groups of three and make some observations about nonverbal behavior. In each group of three, one person will begin as the sender, one as the receiver, and one as the observer. The sender will speak for approximately three minutes, telling the receiver about a favorite leisure activity. The receiver will respond nonverbally as he or she feels appropriate. The observer will watch the receiver and record any nonverbal behaviors that are being demonstrated. After the end of a three-minute period, the roles in the group will change. The person who was the receiver will become the sender, the observer will become the receiver, and the sender will become the observer. The exercise will be repeated for three minutes and the roles will again rotate. Each person will have the opportunity to fulfill each role. We will then come back together as the full group and share our observations."

Process: Explain activity. Divide into groups of three. Provide paper and pencils for observers to record. Encourage observers to make notes of anything that seems interesting to them. Give signal to change roles after three-minute periods have elapsed.

19. Debriefing

Content:
    a. What were some of the nonverbal behaviors that were observed?
    b. Were some of these behaviors common to most of the receivers? If so, which ones?
    c. How aware were the senders of the nonverbal behaviors of the receivers? Can you provide examples?
    d. What did you obtain from this activity? How will you use it?

Process: Conduct debriefing using above questions. Provide opportunity for each person to respond to at least one of the questions.

20. Conclusion

Content: "Nonverbal behaviors are a very important part of communication. They include eye contact, facial expressions, posture, gestures, body orientation, and physical distance between sender and receiver. The receiver can use nonverbal behavior to tell the sender if the message is being heard and processed. Nonverbal behavior can also tell the sender what the receiver thinks of the message and the sender. It is a powerful tool and one to which all of us should be in tune."

Process: Make concluding statements. Provide participants with an opportunity to ask questions. Attempt to respond to concerns by the participants.

Objective 6.5: Demonstrate verbal behaviors required of an effective speaker.

1. Orientation Activity

Content: "We are going to engage in an activity that is sometimes known as the gossip game. Please form a circle. First introduce yourself to the person on each side of you and find out each person's name. One person will begin by whispering a message to the person on his or her right, who will repeat the message to the person on his or her right, until the message has returned to the point where it started. The object of the activity is to repeat the message accurately so that it arrives back at its start exactly as it began. This activity requires both careful listening and accurate repetition of the message. We will repeat this process several times, choosing a different starting point for each message."

Process: Explain activity. Help form circle. Select various participants to start activity. Emphasize necessity of listening and speaking carefully. Prepare several messages prior to the session. Examples of messages could include:

- Peter Piper picked a pumpkin from the preacher's porch.
- Robin Red Breast is the best dressed robin.
- Little Bo Peep uses her Jeep to shepherd a heap of sheep.
- Little Jack Horner became a mourner when his Turbo Z failed to corner.

2. Debriefing

Content:

    a.   Which of the messages was the most difficult to repeat accurately? Why?

    b.   What could you have done to ensure that you were repeating a message accurately?

    c.   What does this tell you about the communication process?

Process: Conduct debriefing using above questions. Provide opportunity for each person to respond to at least one of the questions.

3. Introduction

Content: "Just as effective listening is more than the physiological process of receiving sound and sending it to the brain, effective speaking is more than the process of uttering words. There are many things individuals can do to help themselves become effective speakers. Those who make an effort to become more effective speakers are also enhancing their ability to engage in meaningful social interactions."

Process: Introduce topic on verbal behaviors required of an effective speaker.

4. Presentation

Content: "Among the things you can do to become a more effective speaker is to focus on verbal behaviors that enhance your ability to communicate. The verbal behaviors required of an effective speaker include (a) the use of appropriate vocabulary, (b) clear enunciation, (c) avoidance of distracting fillers, (d) the presentation of information in a logical sequence, and (e) the presentation of relevant content. Although there are other verbal behaviors that can influence one's effectiveness as a speaker, mastery of these five behaviors is necessary. Such mastery will have a positive impact on one's ability to communicate.

"The *use of appropriate vocabulary* is fundamental to good communication. Appropriate vocabulary includes the avoidance of slang or offensive terminology. Although slang words are very popular among some people, they are not universally understood or accepted. Slang words are often ambiguous and nebulous, and obscure communication rather than clarifying it. Speakers using slang may have a clear idea of what they wish to say, but if the listeners are unfamiliar with its usage, they will be forced to guess at the meaning and the intent of the speaker. Such a situation does not contribute to the effectiveness of the speaker; in fact, it gets in the way of good communication.

"The use of offensive terminology also detracts from one's effectiveness as a speaker. Offensive terminology includes obscenities and words and phrases that are construed as derogatory comments focused on race, ethnicity, gender, age, religion, disability, or other factors. Speakers who use such words may claim that they do not intend to be offensive but that has little impact on how the words are perceived by listeners. Offensive terminology generally does nothing but erect unnecessary barriers to effective communication.

"*Clear enunciation* is another verbal behavior that contributes to being an effective speaker. Enunciation refers to the clear and full pronouncement and articulation of words. Words that are not pronounced clearly and correctly not only fail to contribute to clarity of meaning; they may contribute to just the opposite–uncertainty and misunderstanding. When listeners are forced to focus intently on deciphering mispronounced words, they may lose sight of the message of the speaker. It is the responsibility of speakers to do more than speak so they can be understood; they must speak so they cannot be misunderstood.

"*Avoiding distracting fillers* is a third verbal behavior that can contribute to being an effective speaker. A filler is a word, phrase, or sound employed by speakers to cover lapses in their trains of thought or to use as a substitute for carefully thinking through what they wish to say. Examples of fillers are sounds such as 'errr' or 'ahhh' and phrases such as 'you know.' Some speakers make such liberal use of fillers that their communication efforts are distorted and difficult to follow. Listeners usually find it very annoying when they have to filter the message of the speaker through an excessive number of fillers. Speakers who use fillers are relying on the listener to dig out the content of the message, rather than making the effort to ensure the message is clear and unable to be misunderstood.

"Another verbal behavior that contributes to being an effective speaker is to *present information in a logical sequence*. Information that has a logical progression from one point to the next is usually easily followed and understood. It provides listeners with opportunities to use appropriate listening skills to monitor the accuracy with which they are receiving messages. Speakers that jump from one point to another, with no apparent pattern or connecting threads between thoughts, are difficult to follow and often appear incoherent. Listeners have to work very hard to receive the messages being sent and there is very little assurance that the messages being received are what the speakers intend.

"A fifth basic verbal behavior that speakers can employ is to *present relevant content*. Information that is not pertinent to a conversation is pointless, even though it may be accurate. Such information is not helpful to communication. It is distracting and can lead both speakers and listeners on a path that moves away from the topics that should be central to the conversation. Adhering to the verbal behavior of presenting relevant content requires speakers to think carefully before they open their mouths. Although this is a process that is widely admired, it is also one that is seldom practiced by those who would benefit most from it. Presenting relevant content is a process that requires constant self-monitoring."

Process: Present information. Use board to list five major verbal behaviors.

- use appropriate vocabulary
- enunciate clearly
- avoid distracting fillers
- present information in logical sequence
- present relevant content

5. Discussion

Content:

    a.   Do you feel that you need improvement in any of the verbal behaviors we have identified? If so, which ones?

    b.   What will you actually do to enhance your performance in those verbal behaviors needing improvement?

    c.   Can you provide examples of how you have used any of these verbal behaviors to become a more effective speaker? If so, what are they?

    d.   How will you use this information?

Process: Conduct discussion using above questions. Provide opportunity for each person to contribute to the discussion by responding to at least one of the questions.

6. Learning Activity

Content: "This activity is a version of the gossip game. Some of you will be asked to listen to a message and to correctly repeat it to others. Remember, when you are repeating a message, enunciate carefully, confine yourself to relevant information, and do not add extraneous material such as fillers. Four of you will be asked to leave the room and be ready to repeat a message that will be given to you. The rest of you will act as observers. One of the four persons who left the room will be asked to return and listen to a message I will read to him. A second person will be asked to return and listen to the message, which will be related from memory by the first person. A third person will be asked to return and will listen to the message from the second person. The fourth person will then enter, listen to the message from the third person, and repeat it to the group. We will then select four more people to leave the room and the process will be repeated with a different message. This process will continue until each person has had the opportunity to be among a group of four that leaves the room."

Process: Explain activity. Select four participants to leave room. Read message to first person asked to return. Participants can be given opportunity to make up messages for the groups of four. Emphasize need for speakers to enunciate clearly, avoid fillers, have a logical progression, and use relevant content. Examples of messages could include:

- Go to your room, put on your hat, coat, and mittens, then return and sit on the sofa.
- Trace each pattern on the paper. Cut out each pattern, then sit with your hands folded and wait for further instructions.
- Yes, you can get to the library from here. Go through the double doors at the end of this hallway. Turn to the right and start down that hallway. The library will be the first door on your left.
- Mary and Beth were playing basketball. They each jumped for the ball just as Jim walked by. They bumped into each other and fell into Jim. He was knocked down. He was angry, but he was not hurt. It really was accidental.

7. Debriefing

Content:
a. What did you do to help yourself remember the message you were given?
b. What did you do as speaker to help the listener understand the message?
c. Did you notice changes in the messages when they were repeated from one person to the next? If so, provide examples.
d. Why do you think changes occurred?
e. What does this indicate about the process of communication?

Process: Conduct debriefing using above questions. Provide opportunity for each person to respond to at least one of the questions.

8. Learning Activity

Content: "We are going to do an activity that will provide each of you with the chance to give verbal directions to the rest of the group for drawing a picture. Each of you will be given paper and pencil. Go someplace in the room and draw a simple picture, but do not show it to anyone. Return to the group, place the picture face down in a pile, and form a circle around the pile of pictures. One person will take a picture from the pile, not allow anyone else to look at it, and give directions to the group that will enable them to duplicate the picture as nearly as possible. The group will listen carefully and try to follow the directions that are given. The directions should be as clear and simple as possible. For example, if the person giving directions is looking at a picture of a house, the directions could begin by saying 'Draw a long line across the bottom of your paper. Draw a parallel line in the middle of the paper. Connect the ends to make a box. Put a door on the middle of the bottom line.' The directions would continue until all parts of the house were described. Each person will be given the chance to look at a picture and give directions to the group."

Process: Explain activity. Provide pencils and sufficient paper. Ensure that only the person giving directions can see the picture being described. Provide opportunity for each participant to be a describer. Emphasize necessity of providing relevant content in a logical sequence.

9. Debriefing

Content:
   a.   What difficulties did you have in giving directions?
   b.   What difficulties did you have in receiving directions?
   c.   Was it more difficult to give or receive directions? Why?
   d.   Other than looking at the picture, how could receiving directions be made easier?

Process: Conduct debriefing using above questions. Provide opportunity for each person to respond to at least one of the questions.

10. Learning Activity

Content: "This activity is similar to a mouse finding its way through a maze. We will use chairs, books, coats, and other objects to make a maze in this room. One person in the group will be blindfolded; another will be selected to give directions to guide the blindfolded person through the maze. The directions must be simple and accurate. After the blindfolded person has been successfully directed through the maze, a new person will be blindfolded and the shape of the maze will be changed. A new person will be selected to give directions. This process will be repeated until each person has had the opportunity to be blindfolded and to give directions. Remember, directions should have a logical sequence, be easily understood, and have no unnecessary content."

Process: Explain activity. Use objects to make maze. Monitor activity to ensure safety of blindfolded person. Emphasize clarity of directions.

11. Debriefing

Content:
   a.   Did the presence of a blindfolded listener make you a more careful speaker? If so, how so?
   b.   Did wearing a blindfold make you a more careful listener? If so, how so?
   c.   Did the inability of the blindfolded listener to see any gestures you wanted to make have an influence on your ability to give effective directions? If so, how so?
   d.   What is your assessment of the importance of presenting relevant information in a logical sequence, without distracting fillers?

Process: Conduct debriefing using above questions. Provide opportunity for each person to respond to at least one of the questions.

12. Conclusion

Content: "The ability of people to engage in meaningful social interaction is often dependent on their communication skills. An integral part of communication is effective speaking. Utilization of basic verbal skills can help one become a more effective speaker. Practicing the use of these skills requires purposeful effort and attention; the result should be improvement in communication and social interaction."

Process: Make concluding statements. Provide participants with an opportunity to ask questions and voice concerns. Attempt to respond to all questions and concerns.

Section C

Specific Leisure Education Programs:
Activities

Section C   Specific Leisure Education Programs: Activities

1. Leisure Education Swimming Program: Provide opportunities for participants to become aware that swimming can be a leisure experience; learn about beginner-level swimming and what skills are needed to be a participant; learn about swimming resources; and become an active and cooperative member of a swimming group.

2. Leisure Education Walking Program: Provide opportunities for participants to gain insight into the process of walking as a leisure experience, increase their understanding of leisure resources associated with walking, learn to apply effective health and fitness techniques associated with walking, and be assertive when walking.

3. Leisure Education Gardening Program: Provide opportunities for participants to gain insight into the process of gardening as a leisure experience, acquire knowledge about planting and harvesting a vegetable garden, increase their understanding of leisure resources associated with gardening, learn skills associated with gardening, and learn about plant maintenance.

4. Leisure Education Bowling Program: Provide opportunities for participants to learn to bowl, learn the rules of bowling, become aware of self-improvements, and increase their ability to develop realistic self-expectations and effective problem solving strategies.

5. Leisure Education Softball Program: Provide opportunities for participants to become aware of personal responsibilities and self-determination associated with softball, learn to make decisions to participate successfully in softball, become aware of resources for softball and how to access them, and acquire social interaction and physical skills needed to play softball.

6. Leisure Education Volleyball Program: Provide opportunities for participants to learn the skills required for volleyball, increase their understanding of leisure resources associated with volleyball, develop their ability to cooperate with others, be assertive, and enhance their ability to establish realistic goals in volleyball.

LEISURE EDUCATION SWIMMING PROGRAM

Purpose, Goals, and Objectives

Purpose: Provide opportunities for participants to become aware that swimming can be a leisure experience; learn about beginner-level swimming and what skills are needed to be a participant; learn about swimming resources; and become an active and cooperative member of a swimming group.

Goal 1: Demonstrate an awareness of swimming as a leisure experience.

Objective 1.1. Demonstrate knowledge of the benefits of swimming.
Objective 1.2. Demonstrate the ability to choose swimming as a leisure experience.

Goal 2: Demonstrate knowledge of and skills needed to participate in beginner-level swimming activities.

Objective 2.1. Demonstrate knowledge of major safety rules related to swimming.
Objective 2.2. Demonstrate the ability to enter/exit water safely and independently.
Objective 2.3. Demonstrate the ability to be independent in the water.

Goal 3: Demonstrate knowledge of swimming resources.

Objective 3.1. Demonstrate knowledge of facilities where swimming may occur.
Objective 3.2. Demonstrate knowledge of equipment used in swimming.
Objective 3.3. Demonstrate knowledge of how to obtain swimming equipment.
Objective 3.4. Demonstrate knowledge of transportation to swimming facilities.

Goal 4: Demonstrate the ability to be an active and cooperative member of a swimming group.

Objective 4.1. Demonstrate the ability to comply with group decisions.
Objective 4.2. Demonstrate the ability to share swimming equipment with others.
Objective 4.3. Demonstrate the ability to participate in group decision-making.

Goals, Objectives, and Performance Measures

Goal 1: Demonstrate an awareness of swimming as a leisure experience.

Objective 1.1: Demonstrate knowledge of the benefits of swimming.

Performance Measure: Upon request and within 10 minutes, participant will demonstrate knowledge of the benefits of swimming by verbally identifying five of the following 12 benefits:
    (a) cardiovascular endurance,
    (b) enhancing self-image,
    (c) muscle endurance,

(d)   strength and power,
(e)   emotional outlets,
(f)   flexibility,
(g)   peer-group interaction,
(h)   experiencing success,
(i)   learning social skills,
(j)   safety,
(k)   muscle tone, and
(l)   weight maintenance,
on two consecutive occasions.

Objective 1.2: Demonstrate the ability to choose swimming as a leisure experience.

Performance Measure: Given the opportunity to choose between swimming and some other recreation activity, within two minutes participant will demonstrate the ability to choose swimming as a way to experience leisure by requesting it, on two consecutive occasions.

Goal 2: Demonstrate knowledge and skills needed to participate in beginner-level swimming activities.

Objective 2.1: Demonstrate knowledge of major safety rules related to swimming.

Performance Measure: Upon request and within 10 minutes, participant will demonstrate knowledge of major safety rules by verbally stating five of the following rules:
(a)   never swim alone,
(b)   always swim in a supervised area,
(c)   know how to seek assistance for self and others,
(d)   refrain from horseplay,
(e)   refrain from running on deck,
(f)   rescue equipment is always present,
(g)   be familiar with the area in which you are swimming, and
(h)   dive only in deep water,
on two consecutive occasions.

Objective 2.2: Demonstrate the ability to enter/exit water safely and independently.

Performance Measure: Given a swimming pool, in two minutes participant will demonstrate the ability to enter and exit the water safely and independently by entering and exiting the pool from the deck at a point where the water is chest high, on three consecutive occasions.

Objective 2.3: Demonstrate the ability to be independent in the water.

Performance Measure: Given a swimming pool at least 30 feet in length, participant will demonstrate the ability to be independent in the water by traversing the length of the pool and back, using the front crawl stroke without touching the sides or bottom of the pool or the ropes and without flotation devices, on three consecutive occasions.

Goal 3: Demonstrate knowledge of swimming resources.

Objective 3.1: Demonstrate knowledge of facilities where swimming may occur.

Performance Measure: Upon request and within five minutes, participant will demonstrate knowledge of facilities where swimming is available by verbally naming four such facilities in the community, on two consecutive occasions.

Objective 3.2: Demonstrate knowledge of equipment used in swimming.

Performance Measure: Upon request and within five minutes, participant will demonstrate knowledge of equipment used in swimming by verbally identifying five of the following seven types of equipment:
- (a) swimsuit,
- (b) ear and nose plugs,
- (c) swim cap,
- (d) goggles,
- (e) towel,
- (f) snorkel,
- (g) flotation devices, and
- (h) fins,

on two consecutive occasions.

Objective 3.3: Demonstrate knowledge of how to obtain swimming equipment.

Performance Measure: Upon request and within 10 minutes, the participant will demonstrate knowledge of how and where to obtain equipment used in swimming by verbally identifying three of the following five sources to assist in purchasing swimming equipment:
- (a) catalogs,
- (b) department stores,
- (c) sporting goods stores,
- (d) telephone directory, and
- (e) newspapers,

on two consecutive occasions.

Objective 3.4: Demonstrate knowledge of transportation to swimming facilities.

Performance Measure: Given paper and pencil, within 10 minutes participant will demonstrate knowledge of sources of transportation providing access to swimming facilities by listing four of the following six sources:
- (a) walking,
- (b) taxi,
- (c) bicycling,
- (d) riding with parent,
- (e) bus, and
- (f) riding with a friend,

on two consecutive occasions.

Goal 4: Demonstrate the ability to be an active and cooperative member of a swimming group.

Objective 4.1: Demonstrate the ability to comply with group decisions.

Performance Measure: Given a group consisting of three to eight people, participant will demonstrate the ability to comply with group decisions by freely participating in the group's choice of activities, on five consecutive occasions.

Objective 4.2: Demonstrate the ability to share swimming equipment with others.

Performance Measure: Given one kick board, a snorkel, pair of fins, and instructions to have each person in the pair swim for at least four minutes during a 10 minute swim, participant will demonstrate the ability to share swimming equipment with other participants by ensuring that the other participant in the pair has the kick board, snorkel, and fins for at least four minutes, on two consecutive occasions.

Objective 4.3: Demonstrate the ability to participate in group decision-making.

Performance Measure: Given at least two feasible options from which to choose within 15 minutes, the participant, as a member of a group, will demonstrate the ability to participate in group decision-making by verbally expressing an opinion about the options and allowing others the opportunity to express their opinions, on three consecutive occasions.

Goals, Objectives, Content, and Process

Goal 1: Demonstrate an awareness of swimming as a leisure experience.

Objective 1.1: Demonstrate knowledge of the benefits of swimming.

1. Orientation Activity

Content: "You have been given a list of possible benefits that may be associated with swimming. Read the list and identify the three benefits listed that are most important to you and rank them, giving the number 1 for the most important, number 2 for the second, and number 3 for the third. On the space at the bottom of the sheet, list any additional benefits you could see coming from swimming.

"Now that you are finished, move about the room and find someone who is not talking with anyone, introduce yourself, find out the other person's name, and ask him or her what his or her top three benefits are and why they chose them. After the person replies, share your benefits with him or her. Once completed, continue to move about the room, trying to talk to as many people as possible to find out what benefits they chose. When I give the signal to stop, we will talk about swimming and share additional benefits we could add to the list."

Process: Develop a handout with the following list of possible benefits from swimming: endurance, strength, flexibility, success, positive self-image, emotional outlet, group interaction, social skills, safety). List the benefits on an easel or chalkboard. Establish a signal for stopping prior to starting the activity. Provide clear and concise directions. Move about the room, assisting participants as needed. Conduct a brief discussion following the activity and record any new benefits on the easel or chalkboard to expand the original list.

2. Introduction

Content: "Swimming can provide a chance for many people to experience leisure. Once learned, swimming is something that can be done for a lifetime. Depending on the availability of a swimming pool, it is also an activity in which participants can engage throughout the entire year. In addition to the physical benefits that you can get, swimming can open the door to many fun and enjoyable activities."

Process: Introduce topic on the benefits of swimming.

3. Presentation

Content: "The benefits of swimming can be put into two categories: physical and mental. Among the physical benefits are the following:
   a.   Cardiovascular endurance: active and frequent swimming can increase the ability of the heart, lungs, and circulatory system to sustain activity.
   b.   Muscular endurance: muscle use over a long period of time in a regular swimming program can increase one's endurance.
   c.   Strength and power: power requires one to release force with sudden exertion and swimming can increase an individuals' ability to exert force.
   d.   Flexibility: Swimming can improve an individual's ability to bend, stretch, and move through a normal range of motion.

"Among the mental benefits of swimming are:
   a.   Experience success: swimming can provide individuals with the opportunity to do something well and to enjoy the feeling of success.
   b.   Enhance self-image: being successful in anything, including swimming, enhances one's self-image.
   c.   Provide positive emotional outlets: swimming can be fun. For many people, it is an activity that can be done easily. Swimming can provide a chance to release frustration safely. Water can be slapped, kicked, and thrashed around in without causing harm. This can be an acceptable way of removing stress, anxiety, and excessive energy.
   d.   Group interaction: swimming programs can provide numerous opportunities for group interaction and acceptance by one's peers. Interaction with peers on the basis of equality is important. Water can be an equalizer in many ways.
   e.   Learning social skills: swimming programs provide a great environment for learning social skills. Swimming programs can teach sharing, cooperation, group decision-making, and other skills that are important.
   f.   Safety: a program that teaches swimming and safety skills will increase your ability to accept the responsibility to take care of yourself. Teaching safety should be a goal of all swimming programs."

Process: Present information on benefits of swimming. Use chalkboard to list each benefit. Provide the list of benefits as follows:

- success
- self-image
- emotional outlet
- interaction
- social skills
- safety

4. Discussion

Content:
    a. What physical benefits are available through swimming?
    b. What mental benefits are available through swimming?
    c. Are there benefits which we have not yet considered? If so, what are they?
    d. What benefits do you personally anticipate from swimming?

Process: Conduct discussion using above questions. Encourage all participants to contribute to the discussion.

5. Learning Activity

Content: "We need to think a little bit further about the benefits of swimming and what they mean to us personally. In this jar are small slips of paper; each paper has one benefit from swimming written on it. Each of you will take a slip from the jar and be prepared to state how you will gain from that benefit. We will take turns doing this until every swimmer has had the chance to talk about a benefit."

Process: Explain activity. Prepare slips in advance, one for each swimmer. A benefit can be written on more than one slip, if necessary. Give equal emphasis to each benefit.

6. Debriefing

Content:
    a. Has your understanding of swimming benefits increased? If so, how?
    b. What did you learn from this activity?
    c. How do you plan to use this information?
    d. Which benefits do you want most to get from swimming? Why?

Process: Conduct debriefing using above questions. Encourage all participants to respond to at least one question.

7. Conclusion

Content: "Gaining the benefits that are possible through swimming does not happen automatically. It requires effort. Accepting the responsibility to try to get the benefits is an important step for swimmers. The rewards to be gained are worth every effort."

Process: Make concluding statements. Provide opportunity for questions.

Objective 1.2: Demonstrate the ability to choose swimming as a leisure experience.

1. Orientation Activity

Content: "Half of you have been given hats with a sign on the front that says 'Ace Reporter.' The other people have been given a name tag that says 'Joe' or 'Jane Public.' With paper and pencil, each reporter should approach a Joe or Jane, introduce himself or herself, find out the person's name and interview the person about what things he or she considers when deciding to take a part in leisure. Reporters should find out some things that prevent Joe or Jane from participating in some activities and things that attract them to other activities. The reporter should record the responses of the person and then move on to interview another person. When I give the signal, everyone stop. Exchange your hat for a name tag with the person closest to you. Now, those of you who have hats must interview the others. See how many people you can talk to. When I give the signal, we will stop and share some of your findings."

Process: Distribute hats, name tags, paper and pencils. Prior to beginning the activity establish a signal to stop. Provide clear and concise directions. Move about the room assisting people who are having difficulty. Once participants have finished interviewing, have them form a circle to share their findings.

2. Introduction

Content: "Developing the ability to choose swimming as a way to experience leisure is a desired outcome of this program. It requires a conscious intent to make a deliberate choice. It means weighing the benefits of choosing swimming against the benefits of choosing some other activity. It does not mean that swimming must always be the choice. It means that if an individual wants to choose swimming, the necessary skills and knowledge are in place to make it a feasible decision."

Process: Introduce topic of choosing swimming as a way to experience leisure.

3. Presentation

Content: "When this program is ended, you will have gained a basic level of swimming and safety skills and a knowledge of community swimming resources and how to get to them. Your new skills and knowledge will allow you to continue enjoying swimming as a way to experience leisure. Whether you choose to continue swimming is a decision you will make in the future.

"It will be your responsibility to make this decision, rather than to allow someone to make it for you. Among the things that you will probably consider when making your decision are such things as availability, cost, convenience, influence of family and friends, and your personal level of enjoyment. When thinking about these and other factors, it might also be helpful to remember that maintaining your swimming skills is a sign of accepting responsibility. Being able to care for yourself in and around water means that others do not need to take responsibility for you.

"You may choose to swim as a recreation activity because it is fun and enjoyable. You need no other reason. The joy of being independent in the water, the physical feeling of movement, the companionship of good friends, and the belief that you are doing something you want to do are rewards in themselves."

Process: Present information on choosing swimming as a way to experience leisure. Use chalkboard to list major points as follows:

> - availability
> - cost
> - convenience
> - family and friends
> - enjoyment

4. Discussion

Content:
   a. What is considered when you make a decision to participate in leisure?
   b. Why is the maintenance of swimming skills regarded as a social responsibility?
   c. How can an activity be justified on the basis that it is fun and enjoyable?
   d. Will you plan to continue swimming when this program is over? Why or why not?

Process: Conduct discussion using above questions. Encourage all participants to contribute to the discussion.

5. Learning Activity

Content: "Almost every skill we have is a result of practice. Making choices is a skill that can be practiced. Each of you will be given a list of 20 games or activities that are related to swimming. Each game or activity has a short description. Choose the 10 activities in which you would most like to participate and rank them in order of priority. Place the number '1' by your first choice, '2' by your second choice, etc. When you are finished, I will collect and keep your lists. As we go through the program, we will check each list and, when you are ready, provide chances for participation in activities you want."

Process: Explain activity. There are numerous books available that describe various types of games and activities. Use these to compile list and descriptions prior to session. Collect finished lists. Follow through on promise to periodically check lists and provide opportunities for participation in activities.

6. Debriefing

Content:
   a. Which activities did you choose?
   b. Why did you make your choices?
   c. What skills will you need to participate in the activities you chose?
   d. Can you continue to participate in your chosen activities after this program is ended? How so?

Process: Conduct debriefing using above questions. Encourage all participants to respond to at least one question.

7. Conclusion

Content: "Most of us are regularly confronted with the need to make choices. Making leisure choices is as important as making choices in other areas of our lives. Choosing swimming as a way to experience leisure can be rewarding to us and benefit everyone."

Process: Make concluding statements. Provide opportunity for questions.

Goal 2:   Demonstrate knowledge of and skills needed to participate in beginner-level swimming activities.

Objective 2.1: Demonstrate knowledge of major safety rules related to swimming.

1. Orientation Activity

Content: "We are going to see if we can learn how to be safe while participating in swimming. On the chalkboard, I have listed 9 major safety rules and numbered them 1 through 9. Scattered on the bottom of the shallow end of the pool are 30 stones. Two of the stones are marked with a '1,' two are marked with a '2,' etc., through '9.' The remaining 12 stones are blank. After being divided into two teams, enter the water. You are not permitted to touch another swimmer. If you come in contact with another swimmer, you must move to the edge of the pool and remain there for one minute. When given the signal to start, each team will retrieve as many of the stones as possible. When given the signal to stop, the team with the most complete set of stones will be the winner. It makes no difference how many duplicate or blank stones a team has. The important thing is to have as nearly a complete set of consecutive numbers as possible. I will then ask each person to introduce himself or herself, show one stone he or she collected and then recite the rule associated with that number."

Process: Explain activity. Mark stones (or any object that will remain submerged) with magic marker. Place stones close to deck at shallow end of pool. At end of activity when checking each team for completeness of set, read each rule for which they have a stone and then for which they retrieved no stone.

2. Introduction

Content: "Safety is important in all activities, including swimming. The reason for this is because the possible results of breaking a swimming safety rule can be very damaging. It even may result in death. Every year there is a loss of life in swimming accidents and not all of the victims are people who could not swim. In fact, many of them are swimmers who did not follow basic safety practices. Water can be a very comfortable and enjoyable place for people at leisure, but it can also be a dangerous one and must be respected."

Process: Introduce topic of major safety rules related to swimming.

3. Presentation

Content: "There are some basic safety rules that should be followed with all swimming programs and by all swimmers, regardless of whether they are participating in an organized program or not. These rules are summarized as follows:
    a. Swimmers should never swim alone.
    b. Swimming should always be done in a supervised area where a lifeguard is present.
    c. Swimmers who lack lifeguarding skills should know how to seek assistance for swimmers in distress or danger.
    d. Pushing people who are standing on the deck or floor into the water is prohibited.
    e. Running on the deck is prohibited. Deck areas can be slippery; people can injure themselves on the deck's hard surface or the pool's edge.

    f.   Rescue equipment should always be present and available.

    g.   Swimmers should know the area in which they are swimming. In an unfamiliar environment, caution is the wisest course of action.

    h.   Diving should be done only in deep water.

    i.   Supervisory staff should be skilled in first-aid and CPR techniques.

"There are other rules that apply to swimming programs, beginning or otherwise. They also have safety and health implications. Examples of these rules include:

    j.   Participants must respond quickly to signals. If a whistle is used to clear the pool in emergency situations, participants must know what it means and what to do.

    k.   Toilets and showers should be used before entering the pool.

    l.   Beginning swimmers should not enter the pool until given permission.

"Rules and regulations sometimes seem to limit fun and enjoyment for some people. But the rules and regulations associated with a swimming program are made to increase fun, fairness, and safety for everyone. Obeying the rules means individuals are being responsible for their own safety and the safety of others."

Process: Present information on safety rules. Explain each rule carefully. Have rescue equipment available (e.g., flotation devices, reaching pole, rope) and demonstrate their use. Provide swimmers opportunity to handle equipment. List each rule in prominent letters on chalkboard as follows:

1. never swim alone	6. know swimming area
2. swim with lifeguard	7. dive only in deep water
3. know where to get help	8. know first-aid
4. no pushing	9. know rescue equipment
5. no running	

4. Discussion

Content:

    a.   Are there any rules which you want more fully explained? If so, which ones?

    b.   Are there any rules with which you disagree? If so, which ones and why?

    c.   What is the purpose of having rules in any program or activity?

    d.   Why are rules important in a swimming program?

Process: Conduct discussion using above questions. Encourage all participants to contribute to the discussion.

5. Learning Activity

Content: "We are going to play Swimming Safety Rules Charades. Please be seated. I will whisper to each of you a swimming safety rule. You will act out your rule while the rest of the group attempts to guess what it is. After your rule has been identified, you will join the group and I will select the next actor or actress. Each swimmer will have the opportunity to act out a rule."

Process: Explain activity. After each rule has been identified, ask if it is clearly understood and emphasize its importance.

6. Debriefing

Content:
    a. Do you think any one rule is more important than the others? Why or why not?
    b. What did you learn from this activity?
    c. How will you make use of this information?
    d. How successful will our group be in obeying all the rules?
    e. How can you add to the success of the group?

Process: Conduct debriefing using above questions. Encourage all participants to respond to at least one question.

7. Conclusion

Content: "Rules are not made to be broken. They are made to protect people from making mistakes or having mistakes made by other people. Rules guiding a swimming program must be obeyed. Following the rules not only helps provide a safe environment but also adds greatly to the fun and enjoyment that is available through swimming."

Process: Make concluding statements. Provide opportunity for questions.

Objective 2.2: Demonstrate the ability to enter/exit the water safely and independently.

1. Orientation Activity

Content: "We are going to participate in an activity that does not allow running. I am going to divide you into two teams, with the same number of players on each team. At the shallow end of the pool, each team will be at one corner, seated on the deck. I will be in the pool at an equal distance from the two sides, standing in water up to my waist. In each hand, I will have a cup with marbles in it. When given the signal to begin, one person from each team will enter the water, wade out to me, introduce themselves to me (I will then give the person one marble from the cup), wade back, get out of the pool, and sit down. When that person is seated, the next player will enter the water for a marble. The team whose players are first to each have a marble will be the winner. Moving quickly in the water is permissible but there can be no running on the deck. Players who run must return to their starting point and begin again."

Process: Explain activity. Have marbles and cups on hand. Divide into teams. Emphasize the ban on running. Encourage participants to cheer for one another.

2. Introduction

Content: "Entering and leaving the water in a swimming area are skills that must be mastered before any other swimming instruction can occur. Swimmers use various methods to accomplish this. We are going to start at the beginning and allow individuals to proceed at their own pace."

Process: Introduce topic of entering and exiting the water safely and independently.

3. Presentation

Content: "There are three primary ways to enter a pool. One method is not better than others; the important thing is to be able to get into and out of the water safely and independently. The design and construction of the pool will have an influence on your entry and exit but the three methods we will learn can generally be used anywhere.

"The first method of entry is wading. Beginners usually start by getting into the shallow end of the pool and moving to areas where the water depth is approximately waist to chest level. If a pool has a ramp or steps, you simply walk into the water. If a pool has a ladder, you usually go down the ladder facing it, because that position offers more stability and balance. If a pool does not have ramps, steps, or ladders, you sit on the deck with your feet dangling in the water, use your arms to push yourself up and off the deck, and wade into the water.

"A second method of entering the water is by jumping in with the feet first. The water depth should be at least at chest level to accommodate this way of getting into the water. You stand on the deck and face the water, bend slightly forward at the waist, and jump. While jumping, your arms can be extended out to maintain balance and slow the downward movement of the body. Swimmers entering the water in this way must remember to bend the ankles, knees, and hips to help absorb the impact of landing on the bottom of the pool.

"The third method of entry is diving. This method should be used only in deep-water areas and by individuals with good swimming skills. Diving for this program refers to entering the water from the deck; it does not refer to athletic feats from a diving board. Diving from a board is possible after you have the necessary swimming skills, but becoming a good diver requires training that is beyond the scope of a beginning swimming program.

"You may dive into the water from a crouched position on the poolside by placing both feet on the edge of the deck, curling your toes over the edge, and falling forward into the water, extending your legs as you fall. Another way to enter the water by diving is to follow the progression for the crouched position but have one foot 12 to 18 inches behind the other. As you fall forward into the water, the rear foot is tossed up and backward. A third diving method is to be in the crouched position, fall forward, and push off by bending the knees, then forcefully extending the legs. This lifts the hips and legs and allows you to enter the water in an extended position.

"Unless otherwise instructed, the way a swimmer enters the water is unimportant, as long as basic safety precautions are observed. As swimmers become more comfortable in a water environment, jumping and diving may be the more prevalent method. Whatever the method utilized, only one swimmer at a time should enter the water from any given point. Swimmers entering from steps, ramps, ladders, deck, or diving board should be allowed to get into the water and clear the entry area before the next swimmer starts.

"You can leave a pool by using steps, ramps, ladders, or pulling yourself up by your arms on the deck. Leaving a pool should be done with as much care as entering. Again, there should be no more than one swimmer attempting to leave a pool at any given point."

Process: Present information on entering and getting out of a pool. Demonstrate each method, emphasizing safety and required depth.

4. Discussion

Content:
   a. What are the three accepted methods of entering the water?
   b. What are the accepted water depths for each of the methods?
   c. Who should determine what method is used to enter the water?
   d. What do you think would happen if more than one swimmer tried to get into the water at the same time from the same place?

Process: Conduct discussion using above questions. After the discussion, swimmers should be provided the opportunity to practice various methods of entering the water, guided by their skill level, degree of comfort, and approval of the instructors.

5. Learning Activity (after swimmers are familiar with entry and exit methods)

Content: "We are going to do an activity to help us practice getting in and out of the swimming pool. We will stay in the shallow end, where all of you will sit on the edge of the deck, facing the water, legs dangling in the pool, and ready to push off into the water. None of you will be in water that is more than waist-deep. On a signal to start, enter the water, wade as fast as you can to the other side of the pool, submerge, come up, turn around, wade back to the starting line, pull yourself out of the pool, and sit on the deck."

Process: Explain activity. Ensure adequate spacing between swimmers seated on deck. Monitor activity to prevent pushing and shoving among swimmers. Emphasize safety.

6. Debriefing

Content:
   a. Did you have any difficulty getting into the water? If so, how?
   b. Did you have any difficulty getting out of the water? If so, how?
   c. Which was easiest, getting in or out of the water?
   d. Why did we make sure there was space between swimmers before we started?

Process: Conduct debriefing using above questions. Encourage all participants to respond to at least one question.

7. Conclusion

Content: "Swimmers need to be able to get in and out of the water in a safe and responsible manner. Doing so helps make their time in the pool fun and enjoyable and does not reduce the positive experience of other swimmers."

Process: Make concluding statements. Provide opportunity for questions.

Objective 2.3: Demonstrate the ability to be independent in the water.

1. Orientation Activity

Content: "We are going to have a relay using Ping-Pong™ balls. You will be divided into two teams, each team having the same number of swimmers. At the shallow end, half of each team will be on one side of the pool and half will be on the other side. Each team will have one Ping-Pong™ ball. Each half-team will be in single file, with the first person in each line sitting on the edge of the deck. On one side of the pool, the first person for each team will have a Ping-Pong™ ball. When given the signal to start, the two swimmers with the Ping-Pong™ balls will enter the water, give their names, place the balls in front of them, and blow the ball toward the waiting team member on the other side of the pool. You will have to move yourself after your ball in whatever way you can. When the ball touches the opposite side of the pool, the player on that side will announce the person's name who completed the task, and then state his or her own name. This person will then enter the water and blow, directing the ball back toward the other side. Once each person has had the chance to complete the task, repeat the process until I give the signal to stop. The object is to have as many people complete the task as possible."

Process: Explain activity. Demonstrate blowing ball from one side to other. Provide adequate space between teams to avoid interference. Monitor activity for fairness. Remind participants of the importance of announcing their names so everyone can learn.

2. Introduction

Content: "The primary purpose of a beginning swimming program is to teach people to be independent in the water. Developing the ability to swim can open the door to many wonderful leisure experiences that would not otherwise be available. Knowing that one is able to move in the water and care for oneself is very satisfying. That knowledge, combined with the physical sensations of movement and floating, can be fun."

Process: Introduce topic of being independent in the water.

3. Presentation

Content: "There are many ways to learn how to swim. We are going to introduce a single skill and provide opportunities for you to master it before moving on to a new skill. Each skill that is introduced will be based on your mastery of the previous skills.

"The first skill we will focus on is breathing and breath control. Breath control is important in learning how to swim. The presence of water is the major factor in breath control. The best way to achieve breath control is to inhale while the face is above water and to exhale while the nose and mouth are in the water. It is not as good to hold the head out of the water to do both. Some people are uncomfortable when they feel water entering their nostrils as they swim. Exhaling in the water through the nose helps prevent this."

Process: Present information on breath control.

4. Learning Activity

Content: "We are going to do some bobbing to get us started on breath control. Wade into the pool until the water is as high as your chest and extend your arms to the side for balance. Keep your back straight but raise and lower your body by bending your knees. Inhale above the water and exhale below the water. You may exhale through the nose, the mouth, or a combination of the two, whichever you find is most comfortable. Repeat this motion for 10 trials, inhaling when you are above the water and exhaling into the water.

"Now try it for 20 trials and then continue until you feel comfortable with the rate of breathing. You should exhale enough air so that when you come out of the water, you are immediately ready to inhale."

Process: Explain activity. Get swimmers into the water, with adequate spacing among them. Demonstrate bobbing and breathing. Swimmers count their own bobbing but monitor to see that all complete the required number of trials. Emphasize purpose of activity is breath control, not to see who can finish first.

5. Debriefing

Content:
    a. Did you have any difficulty with the exercise? If so, how?
    b. Was it easier to inhale or exhale? Why?
    c. Why should exhaling be done into the water?
    d. Did you begin to feel comfortable with the rate of breathing?

Process: Conduct debriefing using above questions. Encourage all participants to respond to at least one question.

6. Learning Activity

Content: "We are going to do another activity to help us with breath control. You may stay in the same depth of water. Bend forward and turn your head so that one ear is on the water, pointing toward the bottom of the pool. Use either ear. Inhale and then turn your face into the water and exhale. Repeat this for 10 trials or until you are comfortable with your breathing. When you inhale, do not lift your bottom ear from the water."

Process: Explain activity. Demonstrate breathing. Swimmers can do this activity by holding onto the side of the deck, if they wish.

7. Debriefing

Content:
    a. Was this easier or more difficult than bobbing? Why?
    b. Which ear was your bottom ear?
    c. Did you try the exercise with the other ear as the bottom one?
    d. Which ear was most comfortable?
    e. How comfortable were you inhaling with one ear in the water?

Process: Conduct debriefing using above questions. Encourage all participants to respond to at least one question.

8. Presentation

Content: "Most people can float, if they will take the time to learn how. Our bodies enable us to float when we inflate our lungs to the fullest and relax all our muscles. This will allow most of us to float, if only we will allow the water to support us. Some people may have to help their buoyancy by moving their hands and wrists in a relaxed manner known as sculling. In sculling, the arms are close to the body and the hands are open and flat, with the fingers extended and together. There are many movements the hands can make in sculling, such as up and down, right to left, and figure eights, but in floating the major idea is to use just enough pressure to help the body with its buoyancy."

Process: Present information on buoyancy and floating. Demonstrate sculling.

9. Learning Activity

Content: "We are going to learn to float in different positions. The first position we are going to try is the jellyfish float. In water that is about chest high, take a deep, full breath and bend forward, putting your face in the water. Place your hands on your knees and 'walk' your fingers down your legs, as if you were going to touch your toes. As you near your toes, the water will lift your feet off the bottom of the pool. Your head will be in the water, but some of your body will be at or near the surface of the water. This is an example of buoyancy; your body will float. To return to an upright position, 'walk' your fingers back up your legs. Your head will emerge from the water. Repeat this action for five trials."

Process: Explain activity. Demonstrate jellyfish float. Monitor activity. Encourage swimmers to continue activity until they are comfortable.

10. Debriefing

Content:
   a. What is buoyancy?
   b. What is the purpose of taking a deep breath before doing a jellyfish float?
   c. What is sculling? Did you do any?
   d. Did you feel like any part of your body was above the water? If so, what part?

Process: Conduct debriefing using above questions. Encourage all participants to respond to at least one question.

11. Learning Activity

Content: "The second float we are going to learn is the prone float. Get in the water about chest high, take a deep breath, and assume a jellyfish floating position. Slowly extend your arms straight out past your head and your legs straight out behind. You should be floating in a prone position. To regain an upright position, slowly return to the jellyfish floating position and then stand up. Repeat this for five trials, or until you feel comfortable."

Process: Explain activity. Demonstrate prone float. Monitor swimmers as they attempt this float. Encourage swimmers to persevere until they feel at ease.

12. Debriefing

Content:
a. How does a prone float feel compared to a jellyfish float?
b. Which do you prefer?
c. Which was more difficult to do? Why?

Process: Conduct debriefing using above questions. Encourage all participants to respond to at least one question.

13. Learning Activity

Content: "The third buoyancy exercise we are going to do is the back float. Start in a standing position in chest high water and bend your knees until your shoulders are under the water. Take a deep breath and tilt your head back until your ears are also under the water. Put an arch in your back and slowly extend your arms out to the side. Some of you may float almost horizontally, some of you vertically, and some of you in between those two positions. This is due to differences in your bodies. You may have to do some sculling to remain afloat. If you wish, you may have a partner support your head during your first few attempts. To return to an upright position, push water toward your feet, bring your knees to your chest, and lift your head, all at the same time. Do this for five or more trials, continuing until you feel comfortable."

Process: Explain activity. Demonstrate prone float and how to regain feet. Use a volunteer swimmer and demonstrate how to support by placing hand under back of head. Emphasize that different people will float differently.

14. Debriefing

Content:
a. How do you compare the difficulty of a prone float with a back float?
b. Did you float horizontally or vertically or in between?
c. Did you need help from a partner during your first few attempts?
d. Did you try sculling? Did it help you stay afloat?

Process: Conduct debriefing using above questions. Encourage all participants to respond to at least one question.

15. Presentation

Content: "The next skill we are going to learn is how to glide through the water. We will learn how to glide in a prone position and also do a back glide. We will begin both glides by pushing off the wall of the pool. It is easier to get our bodies in motion by doing this than it is to try to get them moving from a stationary position."

Process: Present information on gliding.

16. Learning Activity

Content: "Get into the water between waist and chest high. To do a prone glide, stand with your back to the wall and raise one foot and place it against the wall. Extend your arms above your head, squeezing your ears with your upper arms, and take a deep breath. Place your arms and face in the water and forcefully push off with the foot that is against the wall. Stretch your body out by extending your legs behind you and pointing your toes. Feel your body move through the water. To regain an upright position, push your hands toward the bottom, lift your head and curl your knees, and stand up."

Process: Explain activity. Demonstrate prone glide and how to recover. Assure swimmers that they will be able to end the glide by standing up. Encourage them to find out how far they can glide. Practice this action for several minutes.

17. Debriefing

Content:
   a. How did your body feel, gliding through the water?
   b. What is the purpose of stretching out and pointing the toes?
   c. How far were you able to glide?
   d. Do you feel comfortable doing this?

Process: Conduct debriefing using above questions. Encourage all participants to respond to at least one question.

18. Learning Activity

Content: "The second glide we will learn is a back glide. In water that is chest high, face the side of the pool, reach out, and grab the edge of the gutter with both hands. Curl your feet and place their bottoms against the wall. Put your shoulders under the water and tilt your head back until your ears are on the water. Take a deep breath and push off the wall with a gentle motion by extending your legs, keeping your arms by your sides. This is a back glide. After you have done this a few times, you can increase the force with which you push off. To regain an upright position, push water toward your feet, bring your knees toward your chest, lift your head, and stand up."

Process: Explain activity. Demonstrate back glide and recovery. Provide several minutes for practice.

19. Debriefing

Content:
   a. Is a back glide easier to perform than a front glide? Why or why not?
   b. Could you go farther in a front glide than a back glide? Why?
   c. Are you comfortable with a back glide? If not, why not?

Process: Conduct debriefing using above questions. Encourage all participants to respond to at least one question.

20. Presentation

Content: "The next skill we need to master is leg motion. In swimming, the legs stabilize the body, help maintain its position in the water, and assist in pushing the body forward. We are going to combine leg motion with the prone and back glides. In a stretched prone glide position, you should relax your legs and feet and move them alternately with an up and down motion from the hips. Your knees may be slightly bent at the beginning of the motion but should be straightened during the downward kick. Your feet should be extended throughout the motion. The heels of your feet may just break the surface of the water. In a back glide position, the leg motion is the same, with a little more emphasis on the upward kick. Again, the motion originates in the hips and not at the knees."

Process: Present information on leg motion.

21. Learning Activity

Content: "We are going to combine leg motion with the prone and back glides. In water that is chest high, alternate pushing off the pool wall in the prone and back glide positions and use leg motion to propel your body through the water. In the prone glide position, keep your arms extended in front of your head; in the back glide position, keep them at your sides."

Process: Explain activity. Demonstrate leg motion with both glide positions. Provide opportunity for extended period of practice.

22. Debriefing

Content:
   a. Were you able to power your leg kicks with your hips, rather than your knees?
   b. Did you keep your feet from totally coming out of the water during your leg kicks?
   c. Which position, prone or back, was easier to combine with leg motion? Why?
   d. Which position allowed you to travel farther in the water?

Process: Conduct debriefing using above questions. Encourage all participants to respond to at least one question.

23. Presentation

Content: "In swimming, it is the arms that provide the major force. The motion of the arms varies, depending on the type of stroke that is being performed. We are going to concentrate on the front crawl stroke, which is a basic swimming stroke. Arm motions must be coordinated with the rest of the body movements and with breathing patterns.

"In the front crawl stroke, the arms are in continuous alternating movement, one arm moving from front to back in the water and one arm moving from back to front in the air. One or the other should always be in the underwater pull. The hand enters the water well in front of the head, with the elbow raised and the forearm sloping downward. When the hand enters the water, the fingers are held firmly together and the tips enter the water first. The hand, wrist, and elbow are held firmly as the arm is used as a paddle to propel the body forward. The arm pushes back in a direct line under the body, with the elbow slightly raised, until the thumb brushes the thigh. The elbow clears the water first and is lifted over the water to move to the entry point and start the motion again. When one arm is in the recovery motion, the other arm is in the underwater pull.

"When you are doing the front crawl, breathing can be timed to the arm motion. The action is the same as you learned in the breathing exercise. Roll your head sideways and inhale; do not lift your head. You can breathe to the right or left side, whichever makes you comfortable."

Process: Present information on arm action in front crawl. Demonstrate arm positions and movements.

24. Learning Activity

Content: "We are going to put all the things we have learned into use. In water that is chest high, stand with your back to the pool wall, push off in a prone glide, using both leg and arm motion. Do not expect to make the movements perfectly. Learning to swim is mostly a matter of repetition of basic skills. As you go through this exercise, you may work with a partner. We will repeat this activity until you are able to cover 10 feet, using these motions."

Process: Explain activity. Encourage swimmers to persevere. Stress importance of practice. Extra instructional staff to provide one-on-one assistance is suggested. Repetition of any skill in sequence should be made when necessary. Several sessions will be required for most swimmers to learn skills.

25. Conclusion

Content: "Learning to swim is an important skill. It contributes to our ability to look after ourselves when we are in or near the water. Swimming is an excellent exercise and enhances our physical well-being. It is also a great way to have fun and enjoy our leisure hours."

Process: Make concluding statements. Provide opportunity for questions.

Goal 3: Demonstrate knowledge of swimming resources.

Objective 3.1: Demonstrate knowledge of facilities where swimming may occur.

1. Orientation Activity

Content: "Some of you have been given a microphone, a badge that says 'TV News Reporter,' and a list of questions. Others of you have been given a badge that says 'Expert' and a list of questions with answers. Now that we are in a circle, one reporter will begin by standing up, going over to one expert, introducing himself or herself, and finding out the person's name. The reporter will then face the other participants pretending they are the camera and begin the news report. First, the reporter should introduce the person to the viewing audience and then ask him or her one of the questions on the list. The expert can then read the answer and briefly add other comments, if desired. Once the interview is completed, the reporter will say 'back to you' and then say another reporter's name. At this time the first reporter will sit down and the second reporter will begin interviewing a different expert. We will continue until all experts have been interviewed. If time allows, we will change roles. Reporters should make sure that they turn over the mike to a reporter who has yet to do an interview."

Process: Obtain objects that can be used as microphones. Develop badges and handouts in advance of the activity. The questions should include the following: Where are the swimming pools in this community? Which swimming pools are open to the public? What are the community swimming pool's days and hours of operation? How much is the fee for swimming? What are the rules of the local swimming pool's operation? Are there eligibility requirements for attending the swimming pool? If so, what are they? Help participants who are having difficulty. Encourage participants to "ham it up" and have fun.

2. Introduction

Content: "Swimming should be done in a safe, supervised place. Generally, swimming pools are safer than rivers and lakes because they are smaller areas with known depths and dimensions and with water that you can see in fairly well. Knowing where such places are located and when and how they may be used is an important part of swimming."

Process: Introduce topic of facilities where one can swim.

3. Presentation

Content: "Swimming pools are specialized facilities. They are expensive to build, maintain, and operate. As a result, most pools in a community are controlled and operated by municipal recreation departments, YMCAs, YWCAs, schools, private country clubs, and commercial fitness centers. Some pools are open to the public; some are not. Almost all pools charge a fee for swimming.

"Swimmers need to have information about the swimming pools in a community to make decisions on when, where, and how they can swim. When this program is ended, swimmers will want to know how to get the information they need to continue swimming as a recreation activity. Among the things swimmers need to know are the following:
  a.   Where are the pools in this community?
  b.   Which ones are open to the public?
  c.   What are there days and hours of operation?
  d.   How much is the fee for swimming?
  e.   What policies govern their operation?
  f.   Are there eligibility requirements regarding participation? If so, what are they?

"Having this kind of information will enable swimmers to make informed decisions regarding their swimming."

Process: Present rationale for needing information relative to swimming facilities. Put questions needing answers on chalkboard.

4. Discussion

Content:
  a.   Why are swimming pools better places to swim than rivers and lakes?
  b.   What information do you need to make decisions about community swimming?
  c.   How can swimmers make use of this information?

Process: Conduct discussion using above questions. Encourage all participants to contribute to the discussion.

5. Learning Activity

Content: "We are going to learn as much as we can about the swimming facilities in this community. The first thing we will do is to get in groups of five or six and think of all the questions we want answered. Each small group will report to the larger group, and from these reports we will select a single set of questions to which we want answers.

"When we have determined what the set of questions will be, we will use the telephone directory, program brochures, material from the chamber of commerce, and any other means we can think of to identify the pools in this community. Each group will select pools to telephone to obtain answers to our questions. When we have the information we need, we will compile a master list of pools and the answers to our questions. Each of you will then receive a copy of the master list."

Process: Explain activity. Divide into groups. Groups should focus on questions previously presented. If necessary, provide any questions that are missing. List questions on chalkboard. Ensure that each identified pool is included in telephone survey. Have groups collate information. Make and distribute master list.

6. Debriefing

Content:
   a. Does the master list contain everything we need to know about swimming facilities in this community? If not, what more is needed?
   b. What did you learn from this exercise?
   c. Do you feel you could get this information on your own?
   d. How will you use this list?

Process: Conduct debriefing using above questions. Encourage all participants to respond to at least one question.

7. Conclusion

Content: "Having this information about available swimming facilities will allow you to make decisions about swimming and how you wish to spend your leisure. Making informed decisions is a sign of responsibility. This is true for swimming, as it is for all other aspects of our lives."

Process: Make concluding statements. Provide opportunity for questions.

Objective 3.2: Demonstrate knowledge of equipment used in swimming.

1. Orientation Activity

Content: "Several items of equipment used by swimmers are displayed on the table. Please come to the table and look at the equipment. As you look at the equipment, think about how each piece might be used and which items you would like to try. Once you have finished doing this, I will ask you to stand, introduce yourself, go over to a piece of equipment, hold it up, and tell us one thing this piece of equipment may be used for."

Process: Explain activity. Arrange display of items on table (e.g., swimsuits, towels, swim caps, flotation devices, ear and nose plugs, goggles, snorkels, and fins). Assist participants having difficulty thinking of things to do with the equipment.

2. Introduction

Content: "Swimming equipment is designed to help swimmers feel more comfortable in the water, learn more quickly, and have fun. Such equipment may be thought of as tools that make the job easier. Understanding the uses of this equipment will help you make decisions about your swimming activity."

Process: Introduce topic of equipment used in swimming.

3. Presentation

Content: "Swimming equipment may be divided into that which is necessary and that which is optional. The necessary equipment consists only of swimsuits and towels. Suits must be worn for purposes of comfort, hygiene, and public acceptability. Towels are also necessary for comfort and hygiene. Suits and towels should not be shared; this is not a selfish act, but rather a good health and hygiene practice. Optional equipment and their uses include the following:

    a. Flotation devices: include flutter or kick boards, life rings, life jackets and water wings of various kinds. Their purpose is to help you stay afloat while learning.

    b. Swim caps: are used to keep hair dry and to prevent loosened hair from clogging pool drains. Some public facilities require swimmers with long hair to wear caps to protect drainage systems.

    c. Ear and nose plugs: are used to keep water from entering the ears and nostrils. Their use makes some swimmers more comfortable in the water.

    d. Goggles and masks: are used to keep water out of the eyes and to allow swimmers to see underwater without discomfort.

    e. Snorkels: are used for breathing without lifting one's face from the water.

    f. Fins: are used for better propulsion from the feet.

"It is generally acceptable to share flotation devices, goggles, snorkels, and fins. Swim caps and ear and nose plugs should not be shared."

Process: Present information on swimming equipment. Identify and demonstrate use of each piece of equipment.

4. Discussion

Content:
    a. What is the difference between necessary and optional equipment?
    b. What piece of equipment could be considered both necessary and optional?
    c. Why are swimsuits and towels necessary?
    d. What is the purpose of ear or nose plugs? fins? snorkels? flotation devices?

Process: Conduct discussion using above questions. Encourage all participants to contribute to the discussion.

5. Learning Activity

Content: "Each of you will be given the chance to use flotation devices, goggles, a snorkel, and fins. Get into the water and take turns using each item. Each of you may use an item for five minutes. When I give the signal, exchange items with another swimmer. We will continue exchanging items after five minute periods, until each swimmer has had the chance to try each type of equipment."

Process: Explain activity. Have four or five items of each kind of equipment. Give signal for exchange every five minutes. Monitor activity to see that each swimmer has chance to try each type of equipment.

6. Debriefing

Content:
   a.   Which items were easiest to use?
   b.   Which items were the most fun?
   c.   If you could choose only one piece of equipment, which would it be? Why?
   d.   Could you learn to swim without this equipment?

Process: Conduct debriefing using above questions. Encourage all participants to respond to at least one question.

7. Conclusion

Content: "All swimmers must wear swimsuits, have their own towels, and in some cases their own swim caps. We have used other equipment that makes learning to swim easier or more fun, but is not necessary. Ownership and use of this equipment is a personal decision left to the judgment of each individual."

Process: Make concluding statements. Provide opportunity for questions.

Objective 3.3: Demonstrate knowledge of how to obtain swimming equipment.

1. Orientation Activity

Content: "Each of you has been given an item of swimming equipment. Find the person who has been given the same equipment as you. When you find this person, introduce yourself and find out his or her name. Together, you are going to make a poster displaying various kinds of swimming equipment. Each pair will have scissors, glue, poster paper, and sporting goods and swimming catalogs. Place your name on your poster paper and then cut out pictures of the equipment you find in the catalogs and glue them to the paper. When your posters are finished, we will save them for use with a later activity."

Process: Distribute swimming equipment to participants, being sure that two pieces of the same equipment are distributed. Explain the activity. Distribute the materials. Collect posters for use with learning activity at later time.

2. Introduction

Content: "The equipment used in swimming (both necessary and optional) is generally such that it can be used for several seasons, with the possible exception of swimsuits. New suits are often purchased each year to keep up with growth or changing styles. Knowing where to obtain equipment is very helpful."

Process: Introduce topic on how and where to obtain equipment used in swimming.

3. Presentation

Content: "Locating sources of equipment and acquiring items you want is part of the fun of the swimming experience. Swimsuits and towels can be purchased in most department and sporting goods stores. The telephone directory can supply information on the addresses of these stores. Another source of information about such stores is in the advertisements they place in newspapers. The advertisements often supply pictures and prices of swimsuits and towels. Optional equipment, such as snorkels and fins, is usually found in sporting goods stores or large department stores with sporting goods sections. Mail-order catalogs are another source of both necessary and optional equipment. Catalogs are available from companies by requesting them. Readers often find coupons or addresses for catalogs in magazines and newspapers."

Process: Present information on how to obtain swimming equipment. Demonstrate use of yellow pages in telephone directory. Bring several catalogs to session.

4. Discussion

Content:
    a.   Where can you get swimming equipment?
    b.   How can the yellow pages help you locate places where you can buy equipment?
    c.   How can you get a sporting goods catalog?
    d.   What department and sporting goods stores might have swimming equipment?
    e.   Which kind of store is most likely to carry optional swimming equipment?

Process: Conduct discussion using above items. Encourage all participants to contribute to the discussion.

5. Learning Activity

Content: "We are going to visit a local store that sells swimming equipment. Examine the posters you made and remember to look for examples of the equipment on your posters when we are in the store. A member of the store's staff will guide us through the store, show us equipment, tell us what it costs, and answer any questions we have."

Process: Explain activity. Prearrange visit and transportation. Distribute posters to swimmers.

6. Debriefing

Content:
    a.   Did you find all the equipment on your poster? If not, what was not found?
    b.   Which equipment did you like best? Why?
    c.   What did you learn from the visit? How can you use what you learned?
    d.   What other stores in the community could we have visited?

Process: Conduct debriefing using above questions. Encourage all participants to respond to at least one question.

7. Conclusion

Content: "Buying equipment can be done by visiting local stores and making purchases there or by buying through a mail-order catalog. Knowing where, when, and how to buy equipment is a necessity for independent swimmers."

Process: Make concluding statements. Provide opportunity for questions.

Objective 3.4: Demonstrate knowledge of transportation to swimming facilities.

1. Orientation Activity

Content: "I want you to think about how you would get to this swimming pool if you could not come by your usual method. For example, if you usually come here by riding with a parent, think about how you could come if your parent's car was at the repair shop for several days. Each of you has a paper and pencil. List all the ways you could expect to get to this program if your usual method was no longer available. When you are finished, we will have you describe the various ways you have listed. We will sit in a circle and have you stand, introduce yourself, and tell one way you might come to the swimming pool. Everyone will get a chance to suggest one way. It is fine if you repeat what someone else has already said. However, if you do repeat what someone has said you must, after you introduce yourself, identify the last person who has given this method of transportation by stating his or her name."

Process: Explain activity. Distribute pencil and paper to swimmers. Ask swimmers for methods they listed. Write the methods on the chalkboard. Arrange participants in a circle to share information on paper. Assist participants having difficulty.

2. Introduction

Content: "Because swimming facilities are not present in every neighborhood, most of us have to know how to get to pools that are some distance from us. This knowledge is even more valuable if we know several ways to get to the same place. This helps us to be prepared for unforeseen events."

Process: Introduce topic of sources of transportation providing access to swimming facilities.

3. Presentation

Content: "There are several options available for traveling to and from a swimming facility. Among these options are:
    a.   Walking: if facilities are close and the route is not dangerous in any way.
    b.   Bicycling: if the route is safe, you own a bike, and there is a safe place to park it.
    c.   Bus: if a bus route runs near the facility and the cost is affordable.
    e.   Taxi: if the cost is affordable.
    f.   Ride with parent: if parent is willing and available.
    g.   Ride with friend: if friend is willing and available.

Having more than one way to get to a swimming pools makes good sense. Failure of one method will not mean failure to participate. You will simply switch to another method."

Process: Present information of methods of transportation.

4. Discussion

Content:
    a.   What are different methods of transportation you can use to get to a swimming pool?
    b.   How many options do you personally have?
    c.   Which ones make the best sense to you personally?
    d.   Which is the least expensive? Which is the most expensive?

Process: Conduct discussion using above questions. Encourage all participants to contribute to the discussion.

5. Learning Activity

Content: "We have learned which facilities are available to us and where they are located. Each of you will be given a list of these facilities and a map of the community. Determine where these pools are located on the map. Make a plan that shows the best way for you to get from your home to each pool on the list. For example, Pool A might be close enough to reach by walking, Pool B might be on a bus route, and Pool C might be best reached by bicycling. Use the pencil and paper you have been given. List each pool by name and state the best way for you to get to it."

Process: Explain activity. Distribute pencil and paper. Have maps of the community, bus routes, and schedules available. Provide assistance for those experiencing difficulty.

6. Debriefing

Content:
    a. How many pools are within walking distance of where you live?
    b. Are any pools in the community near a bus route? If so, which ones?
    c. Are some pools just too far away for you to consider going there?
    d. How will you use this information?

Process: Conduct debriefing using above questions. Encourage all participants to respond to at least one question.

7. Conclusion

Content: "Being familiar with several different ways of reaching the same place is helpful. It is your responsibility to learn what these ways are, how to use them, and the expense involved in using them. Having command of this knowledge enables you to make good judgments about getting to places where you can enjoy swimming."

Process: Make concluding statements. Provide opportunity for questions.

Goal 4: Demonstrate the ability to be an active and cooperative member of a swimming group.

Objective 4.1: Demonstrate the ability to comply with group decisions.

1. Orientation Activity

Content: "We are going to do an activity named 'Animal Get-Together.' The purpose of this activity is to break down barriers and help us to know each other better. I am going to divide you into two equal groups and have the two groups face each other at a distance of 10 feet. Each person in one group will receive a slip of paper with the name of an animal written on it; the animals will be different for each person. Persons in the second group will receive slips of paper with the same animals as those in the first group. Thus, an animal will be represented by one person in each group. After seeing the animal name on the slip of paper, each person will be blindfolded. When given the signal to begin, each person will make the noise that is commonly associated with their animal. For example, a horse's neigh, a duck's quack, a cat's meow. The object is for each person making an animal noise to find the other person making the same noise. When two 'animals' have been paired, they can stop making the noise and remain silent until the last pairing has been made. Once everyone has found a partner, remove your blind folds and introduce yourself to your partner."

Process: Explain activity. Prepare sufficient blindfolds and animal slips and bring to session. Monitor activity carefully for safety since the participants will be blindfolded much of the time. Make sure you clear the area of objects that could create injuries. Prevent any participants from walking into objects.

2. Introduction

Content: "All of us are members of groups. We belong to groups consisting of family, neighborhood friends, schoolmates, athletic teams, people from church, or any of several other associations. To be a successful member of a group means learning to follow group decisions and not always being able to have our own way in everything. Giving up what you want for the good of the larger group is important when involved with a group."

Process: Introduce topic of complying with group decisions.

3. Presentation

Content: "A group, like a chain, is only as strong as its weakest link. Groups with cooperative members are able to achieve greater things for the good of the group than those whose members simply go their own way. When groups are successful, every member shares in that success. When group members fail to cooperate and to comply with group decisions, the entire group suffers from the consequences.

"Complying with group decisions is important in a beginning swimming group. Although we each learn at different rates and have different likes and dislikes, cooperation within the group is necessary for both safety and learning. In the future, this group will be given the chance to make decisions about which activities to do in a session, in what order the activities will be done, the depth of water in which to do them, and other factors that require consideration. When the decisions are made, all will be expected to comply with them. Learning this lesson and living by it is an attribute of a responsible person."

Process: Present information on complying with group decisions.

4. Discussion

Content:
    a. Why is it not possible to always have our own way?
    b. What happens when group members cooperate and comply with group decisions?
    c. What happens when members of a group refuse to cooperate with others?
    d. What use will you make of this information?

Process: Conduct discussion using above questions. Encourage all participants to contribute to the discussion.

5. Learning Activity

Content: "Pass the Can is an activity that requires cooperation from everyone in order to be completed successfully. Please arrange yourselves in a circle. I want you to pass a can around the circle by using your feet instead of your hands. The object is to pass the can without letting it hit the floor. I am going to place an empty can at the feet of one of you. That person will pick up the can, using both feet but no hands, and pass it to the person sitting on the left. The person on the left will receive the can with both feet and pass it to the left. If the can is dropped, I will place it beneath another person's feet, and we will begin again. Each person must contribute to the success of this activity by receiving and passing the can without dropping it."

Process: Explain activity. Use an empty gallon can. Provide opportunity for several trials. After successful trial, use different starting points and reverse direction.

6. Debriefing

Content:
    a. What did you do to help make this activity successful?
    b. With whom did you cooperate most closely?
    c. What would happen in an activity if a person did not cooperate?

Process: Conduct debriefing using above questions. Encourage all participants to respond to at least one question.

7. Conclusion

Content: "It is important that groups work together in order to succeed. Being a member of a group means working for the success of that group. One way to be a good group member is to learn to cooperate and comply with group decisions."

Process: Make concluding statements. Provide opportunity for questions.

Objective 4.2: Demonstrate the ability to share swimming equipment with others.

1. Orientation Activity

Content: "Each of you has been given a piece of poster board to make a collage of swimming. Some of you have been given scissors, others have been given paste, and others have been given a box of magazines and pictures related to swimming. First, find two people who have different materials from each other and from you. For example, if you have scissors, find one person with paste, and another with swimming pictures. Introduce yourself to the two people and find out their names. Next go to a work table. Each of you then will work on your own collage. You must share the scissors, paste, and pictures."

Process: Distribute poster board to each person. Distribute one pair of scissors, one jar of paste and swimming pictures and magazines to every third person. Encourage the participants to share the equipment. Move about the room and model sharing behaviors. Assist participants as needed.

2. Introduction

Content: "Sharing is an important part of being in a group. It is behavior that is highly desired in everyone. It is part of being a polite and courteous person, one who is considerate of the feelings of others. People who share generally feel very good about themselves."

Process: Introduce topic of sharing swimming and pool equipment with other participants.

3. Presentation

Content: "Swimmers can share in many different ways. Sharing means allowing others to touch equipment, regardless of whether the equipment is provided by the program (e.g., kick boards) or owned by you (e.g., a pair of fins). Sharing also means allowing others a chance to use the equipment. Other examples of sharing include letting others be first to use the steps to get into the pool, first to jump off the board, or to sit in a favorite place on the deck. Sharing is being unselfish. Learning to share also means treating borrowed or shared items with respect and seeing that they are not damaged in any way.

"Refusing to share is being selfish. It means keeping equipment to yourself, not allowing others to see or use it. It means saying 'no' when someone asks to borrow something. Crowding in line and always demanding to be first are examples of not sharing.

"Sharing is not restricted to just equipment or physical space. The nicest thing to share is the easiest thing to share–yourself. Giving others a smile or a pat on the back is sharing yourself. The best group members are those who share their equipment and themselves."

Process: Present information on sharing.

4. Discussion

Content:
    a.   What things have you shared with someone in your family?
    b.   What things have you shared with someone in this program?
    c.   What things in this program could we do a better job of sharing?
    d.   How would you feel if you asked someone to share and you were refused?
    e.   Will you make an effort to begin or continue to share things with others?

Process: Conduct discussion using above questions. Encourage all participants to contribute to the discussion.

5. Learning Activity

Content: "It is easy to share things we do not care about, but sometimes it is a little more difficult to share things we really like. When you return for the next session, bring an item that is a favorite of yours. It must be something that is small enough for you to bring here. It could be a book, picture, baseball, model plane, or any other object. When everyone has brought a personal favorite item, we will pass them around and let everyone handle them."

Process: Explain activity. Make request for swimmers to bring items at least one session prior to date when activity is to occur. Monitor activity to see that all items are treated with care.

6. Debriefing

Content:
    a.   How did it feel to share your special item?
    b.   Do you feel good about yourself, knowing that you can share?
    c.   How did you feel about seeing and handling other people's favorite items?
    d.   Do you have any other feelings about sharing?

Process: Conduct debriefing using above questions. Encourage all participants to respond to at least one question.

7. Conclusion

Content: "Sharing helps us to get along with each other. It contributes to the common good because it shows that you are willing to help the group. Sharing is showing that you trust others."

Process: Make concluding statements. Provide opportunity for questions.

Objective 4.3: Demonstrate the ability to participate in group decision-making.

1. Orientation Activity

Content: "We are going to participate in an activity in which everyone must decide to act in a timely fashion for the good of the group. Each of you has been given a kick board with a number on it. Find the other participants who have the same number on their kick boards. Introduce yourself and find out their names. You are now divided into groups of five but we will do this activity in groups of six. I will be the sixth person in each group. The first group of five may get into the pool in waist-deep water and we will form a circle by holding hands. I will squeeze the hand of the person on my left. That person will go under the water and then squeeze the hand of the next person on the left, who will submerge and squeeze the hand on the left. This action will continue until it travels around the circle and returns to me. I will again squeeze the hand of the person on my left, who will come out of the water and squeeze the hand of the next person on the left. This will continue until all are out of the water. You must clearly squeeze the hand of the person on the left in order for the group to do this activity successfully."

Process: Explain activity. Divide swimmers into groups of five. When activity is finished, ask swimmers what the result would be if one or more persons in a group decided not to participate in the hand squeeze.

2. Introduction

Content: "Being a good group member means accepting the responsibility to be active in the group and participate in group decision-making, rather than withdrawing and letting others make all the decisions. Each individual in a group has something to contribute and should be willing to share that contribution with the others."

Process: Introduce topic of participating in group decision-making.

3. Presentation

Content: "Participating in group decision-making can be relatively simple. All it requires of an individual is to focus attention on the issue at hand and a willingness to give an opinion or suggestion regarding the issue. It is important for people to realize that their thoughts are as valuable as the thoughts of others in the group. The expressed opinions of one person in a group may help others in forming their own thoughts about an issue."

"Participation in group decision-making means more than a willingness to express an opinion about an issue or to state thoughts about what course of action should be taken. It also means that an individual does not try to dominate a group. Opportunities should be provided for all members of the group to express their thoughts. The courtesy and consideration that occurs during a conversation between two individuals who respect each other should also be present in group decision-making."

Process: Present information on participating in group decision-making.

4. Discussion

Content:
    a.   What does it mean to be an active participant in group decision-making?
    b.   Why is it important to be an active participant in group decision-making?
    c.   Do you regard yourself as an active or passive participant?
    d.   What have you learned that will assist you as an active participant?

Process: Conduct discussion using above questions. Encourage all participants to contribute to the discussion.

5. Learning Activity

Content: "We are going to conduct an exercise that will help us be better participants in group discussions. You will be divided into small groups of five or six persons each. Each of you will think of a topic related to swimming that you would like discussed by your group. The topic may be anything that interests you about swimming, but it does not have to pertain to swimming. You will introduce that topic to the group and make one statement about it. Each person in the group will also make one statement about the topic. While the activity is in progress, everyone must remain quiet and allow the person who is speaking to finish without being interrupted."

Process: Explain activity. Divide into small groups. Move from group to group to ensure that all are participating as directed.

6. Learning Activity

Content: "You know the basic approach to group discussion of a topic, now you will have the opportunity to make group decisions regarding the following: (a) what activities should we do in the pool at our next session? and (b) in what order should we do these activities? We will not divide into smaller groups. You can make your decisions as a large group and we will implement them for our next session. I will be the monitor for your discussion."

Process: Explain activity. List suggestions as they are made. Elicit comments from each swimmer. Let swimmers decide how to decide (e.g., majority vote, group consensus, show of hands).

7. Debriefing

Content:
    a. What did you decide to do?
    b. How did you make your decisions?
    c. Did each of you participate in the process? If not, why not?
    d. Do you feel your participation was appropriate?
    e. Will you feel comfortable about participating in group decision-making in the future?

Process: Conduct debriefing using above questions. Encourage all participants to respond to at least one question.

8. Conclusion

Content: "Learning how to participate in group decision-making is an important lesson for us. There are many situations in our lives that are influenced by decisions made by groups of which we are members. Being able to participate in and influence those decisions increases our feelings of independence."

Process: Make concluding statements. Provide opportunity for questions.

LEISURE EDUCATION WALKING PROGRAM

Purpose, Goals, and Objectives

Purpose: Provide opportunities for participants to gain insight into the process of walking as a leisure experience, increase their understanding of leisure resources associated with walking, learn to apply effective health and fitness techniques associated with walking, and be assertive when walking.

Goal 1: Demonstrate knowledge of walking as a way to enhance leisure.

Objective 1.1.   Demonstrate knowledge of the benefits of walking.
Objective 1.2.   Demonstrate knowledge of recreation activities associated with walking.

Goal 2: Demonstrate knowledge of leisure resources associated with walking.

Objective 2.1.   Demonstrate knowledge of equipment useful for walking.
Objective 2.2.   Demonstrate knowledge of leisure resources within walking distance of home.

Goal 3: Demonstrate the ability to apply health and fitness techniques to walking.

Objective 3.1.   Demonstrate the ability to monitor one's heart rate.
Objective 3.2.   Demonstrate the ability to perform warm-up and cool-down exercises associated with walking.
Objective 3.3.   Demonstrate the proper technique used for walking.

Goal 4: Demonstrate the ability to be assertive while walking.

Objective 4.1.   Demonstrate the ability to ask a question while walking.
Objective 4.2.   Demonstrate the ability to conduct a discussion with walking partners.
Objective 4.3.   Demonstrate the ability to share feelings about the walking experience.

Goals, Objectives, and Performance Measures

Goal 1: Demonstrate knowledge of walking as a way to facilitate leisure.

Objective 1.1: Demonstrate knowledge of the benefits of walking.

Performance Measure: Upon request, participant will demonstrate knowledge of the benefits of walking by verbally stating, within two minutes, four of the following benefits derived from walking:
  (a) increased aerobic capacity,
  (b) maintain weight,
  (c) lower resting heart rate,
  (d) reduce stress,
  (e) stronger heart,

- (f) release tension,
- (g) lower blood pressure,
- (h) feel good,
- (i) lose weight,
- (j) relax,
- (k) tone muscles, and
- (l) have fun,

on two consecutive occasions.

Objective 1.2: Demonstrate knowledge of recreation activities associated with walking.

Performance Measure: Upon request, participant will demonstrate knowledge of recreation activities associated with walking by verbally stating, within two minutes, four of the following:
- (a) orienteering,
- (b) hunting,
- (c) backpacking,
- (d) golf,
- (e) nature hikes,
- (f) walking to a store,
- (g) walking to where a recreation activity is being conducted (e.g., movie theater), and
- (h) walking with a pet,

on two consecutive occasions.

Goal 2: Demonstrate knowledge of leisure resources associated with walking.

Objective 2.1: Demonstrate knowledge of equipment useful for walking.

Performance Measure: Given pencil and paper, within five minutes participant will demonstrate knowledge of equipment useful for walking by identifying three items that would be useful for an extended neighborhood walk or a walk through the countryside:
- (a) comfortable shoes with support,
- (b) socks,
- (c) timepiece,
- (d) compass,
- (e) map,
- (f) decent, comfortable layers of clothes,
- (g) food and liquid containers,
- (h) pedometers, and
- (i) walking stick,

on three consecutive occasions.

Objective 2.2: Demonstrate knowledge of leisure resources within walking distance of home.

Performance Measure: Upon request, participant will demonstrate knowledge of leisure resources within walking distance (approximately 45 minutes) of own home by verbally stating, within three minutes, four such resources (examples:
- (a) municipal parks,
- (b) theaters,
- (c) museums,

    (d)   restaurants,
    (e)   shopping malls,
    (f)   libraries,
    (g)   swimming pools,
    (h)   tennis courts,
    (i)   bowling alleys,
    (j)   arcades,
    (k)   zoos,
    (l)   flower gardens,
    (m) community centers, and
    (n)   health and fitness clubs),
on two consecutive occasions.

Goal 3: Demonstrate the ability to apply health and fitness techniques to walking.

Objective 3.1: Demonstrate the ability to monitor one's heart rate.

Performance Measure: Given pencil and paper, within five minutes, participant will demonstrate the ability to monitor own heart rate by:
    (a)   placing second, third, and fourth fingers of one hand on the thumb side of the wrist of the other hand,
    (b)   locating the pulse,
    (c)   counting the number of beats for six seconds,
    (d)   adding a zero to that number to determine the heart rate, and
    (e)   recording the number,
on three consecutive occasions.

Objective 3.2: Demonstrate the ability to perform warm-up and cool-down exercises associated with walking.

Performance Measure: Upon request, participant will demonstrate the ability to perform warm-up and cool-down exercises for walking by correctly executing, within five minutes, each of the following:
    (a)   sitting toe-touch,
    (b)   head flexor,
    (c)   calf stretcher,
    (d)   head turn,
    (e)   side stretch,
    (f)   trunk twister, and
    (g)   arm circle,
on two consecutive occasions.

Objective 3.3: Demonstrate the proper technique used for walking.

Performance Measure: Given the opportunity to walk, participant will demonstrate ability to use proper walking technique, within five minutes by
    (a)   keeping back erect and holding head high,
    (b)   allowing natural arm motion,
    (c)   touching ground with heel first, and
    (d)   rolling forward on toes, while walking distance of 60 feet,
on three consecutive occasions.

Goal 4: Demonstrate the ability to be assertive while walking.

Objective 4.1: Demonstrate the ability to ask a question while walking.

Performance Measure: Given a 10-minute walk with at least one other person, participant will demonstrate the ability to ask a question by
- (a)   looking toward a fellow walker,
- (b)   asking a question,
- (c)   waiting for the person to respond, and
- (d)   acknowledging the person's contribution,

on two consecutive occasions with two different walkers.

Objective 4.2: Demonstrate the ability to conduct a discussion with walking partners.

Performance Measure: Given a 15-minute walk with the group, participant will demonstrate the ability to conduct a discussion with a walking partner by:
- (a)   initiating eye contact with a fellow walker,
- (b)   engaging in conversation for a minimum of five minutes,
- (c)   not interrupting the partner's remarks, and
- (d)   concluding the discussion in a polite manner,

on two consecutive occasions.

Objective 4.3: Demonstrate the ability to share feelings about the walking experience.

Performance Measure: In a 15-minute group discussion, participant will demonstrate the ability to share feelings about the walking experience by voluntarily describing feelings and making statements that do not bring harm to other participants and themselves, on two consecutive occasions.

Goals, Objectives, Content, and Process

Goal 1: Demonstrate knowledge of walking as an activity that can facilitate leisure participation.

Objective 1.1: Demonstrate knowledge of the benefits of walking.

1. Orientation Activity

Content: "We are now going to do an activity to help you get to know each other and to begin thinking about the value of walking as a leisure experience. Now that I have divided you into two groups, I would like one group to line up at the end of the room and face the members of the other group who are at the other end of the room. Each team must choose half its team members to be volunteer walkers.

"Now that we have volunteers, when I say 'begin' you will walk toward the other team, find a person you do not know, introduce yourself to him or her, and talk about the times you have walked for fun. Begin.

"Since you have not all had a chance to walk, now the other people in the group are the walkers and you will walk down to the other end of the room and introduce yourself to someone and talk about walking for fun. Begin."

Process: Divide participants into two groups. Have one group line up at one end of a room or open field and another group line up at the other end. Instruct the participants to face each other across the field or room. At a signal, half of the participants from each of the groups will be instructed to walk across the field or room and find a person to whom they will introduce themselves or, if they already know the other participants, to engage in a brief conversation about walking. After a few minutes, instruct the participants who were not among the first groups of walkers to walk down to meet a person. Now have the participants divide into small groups of two or, if an uneven number, a group of three. Have half the participants from each line walk down in pairs and speak with another pair. Continue with different combinations of people until interest wanes.

2. Introduction

Content: "Many medical and fitness experts agree that most of us do not get enough exercise. We live in a world that often demands little physical activity of us. Our bodies are designed to be active. A healthy body needs exercise. Because many of us are not very active, we may experience some health-related problems. Many of these problems can be prevented, or at least reduced, by proper exercise and diet.

"To become healthy and fit, you can run, cycle, lift weights, swim, work out on apparatus, join health clubs, and do any number of other things. Each of these is good, but one of the simplest and easiest ways to become healthy and fit is also the most natural and inexpensive way–by walking. The act of placing one foot in front of the other and then alternating that motion can bring great benefits to us.

"A regular and frequent program of walking can result in many benefits. We are going to focus on walking as (1) a means of healthy exercise for the heart, lungs, and blood vessels, (2) a way to control weight, (3) a method of relieving stress and tension, and (4) an enjoyable recreation activity."

Process: Have participants seated where they can see and hear you. Introduce topic. Speak clearly, with appropriate volume. Use chalkboard, transparency on overhead projector, printed handout, or other means to outline four major points listed above.

3. Presentation

Content: "Walking can be an aerobic exercise. 'Aerobic' simply refers to the presence of oxygen and is related to the amount of oxygen the body can use when involved in physical activity. Aerobic capacity refers to more than just the amount of air that can be inhaled; it means how much oxygen can be carried by the blood to the muscles of the body, where it is used to burn fuels to supply energy for physical activity.

"One of the purposes of exercise is to increase aerobic capacity. Walking frequently at a moderate-to-fast pace and for a good length of time can increase aerobic capacity. The larger one's aerobic capacity is, the better the heart, lungs, and blood vessels work. The key to good health is the heart. Aerobic capacity is a measure of your heart's fitness.

"Walking produces positive effects on the heart. Continuous participation in a walking program can result in a lower resting heart rate (the heart gets to rest longer between beats), an increase in stroke volume (the heart pumps more blood with each beat), and a lowering of blood pressure (less pressure on the interior walls of blood vessels). Walking can make the heart muscle stronger and better able to withstand stress. An added physical benefit of walking is that it helps the muscles pump blood. As muscles contract in exercise, they help push the blood through the veins back to the heart. Walking is simply good for the heart."

Process: Present information on benefits to cardiovascular system of walking. If available, use anatomical chart to illustrate points. Allow participants to ask questions as you proceed. Repeat any information you think necessary.

4. Discussion

Content:
    a.   What are some examples of aerobic exercise other than walking?
    b.   If walking is less active than these exercises, why is it considered aerobic?
    c.   Why do you think doctors often recommend walking as an exercise for people who have had a heart attack?
    d.   Do you know of anyone who has been placed on a walking program by a doctor? Can you tell us anything about it?

Process: Conduct discussion by asking above questions. Create friendly, informal atmosphere by using first names of participants, smiling, providing positive feedback and support for responses. Questions are discussion starters and may lead to other questions and comments. Provide each participant with opportunity to respond to questions. If appropriate, guide discussion by providing supplemental information to participant responses. Use discussion to remind participants of material presented above.

5. Presentation

Content: "Walking can serve as a good means of weight control. Extra weight is due as much to sedentary living as it is to eating too much. Many people who are overweight eat as little as slim people do; the slim people, however, burn up a greater percentage of the calories they consume. Calories that are not expended are stored as fat. Weight gain is the result of eating more calories than are expended and is usually a gradual process.

"Walking for weight control is usually easier than going on a stringent diet. A 30-45 minute walk at a moderate pace may expend 200-225 calories. A person who engaged in a daily walking program could lose 15 pounds in a year (weight loss, like weight gain, should be gradual). A reduction in food intake, coupled with a daily walk, would result in a greater weight loss. There are activities that would take off weight quicker, but walking is something that most people find easy to stick with."

Process: Present information on walking as means of weight control. Illustrate caloric expenditure for walking at specific pace for specific lengths of time on a large chart.

6. Discussion

Content:
    a.   Why would it be easier to stick to a walking program than other exercise programs?
    b.   Can you walk for weight control and leisure at the same time? Why or why not?
    c.   Should you walk for weight control if you do not need to lose weight? Why or why not?

Process: Conduct discussion by asking above questions. Attempt to have each participant make some contribution to the discussion.

7. Presentation

Content: "Walking is an excellent means of easing stress and nervous tension. Many people lead lives that have a lot of hurry and worry, a fast pace, demanding deadlines, too much to do and too little time to do it in, and very little or no time to relax and get a better grip on their lives. These people often bottle up their frustrations and anxieties. Your emotional state can affect your physical well-being and vice versa. Walking can be effective in relieving stress and tension and improve physical and mental states.

"There are many benefits of walking. In certain instances, walking has been better than medication in reducing stress and tension. Regular walking has worked in reducing hypertension. Walking may be an effective way to rid a person of the unpleasantness of stress and tension and restore balance to living."

Process: Present above information on walking as means to reduce stress and tension.

8. Discussion

Content:
    a. Do you ever feel too rushed to take a walk? If so, what can you do about it?
    b. How do you think walking reduces stress and tension?
    c. Have you ever experienced a walk that made you feel especially good?
       If so, please describe the experience.

Process: Conduct discussion using above questions. Encourage all participants to contribute to the discussion.

9. Presentation

Content: "Walking can be a very enjoyable recreation activity. It can be done by yourself, if that is what you wish. It can be done in pairs or in groups and, if so desired, it can be sociable. You can engage in conversation while walking at a comfortable pace. It is noncompetitive; participants regulate their own involvement.

"Walking is generally painless. It does not place undue stress on feet, ankles, knees, and hips. Often, walkers feel good during and after the exercise; they feel recharged. Walking is an easy activity. It can be done almost anywhere at anytime by anybody. It requires only wanting to participate."

Process: Present above information on walking as recreation activity.

10. Discussion

Content:
    a. Do you prefer walking alone or with a companion? Why?
    b. If you have a pet, do you enjoy walking with it?
    c. Have you previously thought of walking as a source of enjoyment? Why?
    d. Can you describe an enjoyable walking experience? Please do so.

Process: Conduct discussion using above questions. Encourage all participants to contribute to the discussion.

11. Learning Activity

Content: "Now that you are in four groups and have been given a large piece of cardboard and several large felt tip markers, I would like each team to draw a different picture about walking. Group A will depict walking as an aerobic activity, Group B will depict walking as a way to control weight, Group C will show walking as a way to remove stress, and Group D will illustrate walking as fun."

Process: Divide participants in groups of four. Distribute large magic markers of various colors and a large piece of poster board to each group. Emphasize team work and cooperation. Walk around to each group as they are drawing and provide encouragement and answer questions as needed.

12. Debriefing

Content:
    a.   Did you enjoy depicting walking? Why or why not?
    b.   Why do you think we did this activity?
    c.   Now that we have completed the activity, what are the benefits of walking?
    d.   What would you have added to any of the pictures?

Process: Conduct debriefing using above questions. Encourage all participants to contribute to the discussion.

13. Conclusion

Content: "We have now discussed the value of walking as a recreation activity. Walking can be aerobic and help us be more fit, it can help us control our weight, it can assist us in relieving stress, and most important, walking can help us experience leisure by being an enjoyable, satisfying and meaningful experience."

Process: Present the above material. Provide an opportunity for participants to ask questions.

Objective 1.2: Demonstrate knowledge of recreation activities associated with walking.

1. Orientation Activity

Content: "In this bag are pictures of recreation activities that often require people to walk. Each one of you will have a chance to reach into the bag without looking and pull out a picture. Look at the picture and then show it to the other participants. First, introduce yourself and then describe why walking may be important to the person participating in the recreation activity presented on the picture. Once the person has completed his or her presentation, not to exceed three minutes, the other participants will have a chance to add to the discussion. After ideas have been shared about the activity, the next person will choose a picture from the bag."

Process: Cut out pictures from magazines and paste them to index cards. There should be at least one picture that depicts each of the following activities: (a) orienteering, (b) backpacking, (c) hiking, (d) hunting and fishing, (e) golf, and (f) walking a pet. Many other activities that involve walking could be added to this list. Place the pictures into a bag. Create a relaxed atmosphere. It may be useful for you to go first, choose a picture, and describe it. Your example may set the tone for the discussion and provide an opportunity for participants to model your response and your enthusiasm.

2. Introduction

Content: "There are many recreation activities that are directly dependent on walking. Whatever the focus of the activity, it is walking that enables it to be done. Being fit to walk enhances enjoyment of these activities. Walking truly can open the door for participation in a number of recreation activities."

Process: Introduce above topic of recreation activities associated with walking. Check to be certain participants understand the concept of fitness.

3. Presentation

Content: "Orienteering is a walking activity based on skill with map and compass. It involves finding your way in the outdoors and moving (walking) from point to point. It provides chances for traveling through woods and fields, over hills and mountains, across rivers and lakes, and throughout the natural environment. Orienteering is a way to get pleasure and fitness from walking in the outdoors.

"Backpacking is a popular outdoor activity. It allows you to walk into remote areas, carrying enough provisions to stay for several days. Backpacking can be done individually, in pairs, or with groups. It provides opportunities to leave the beaten path and experience adventure. Backpackers can view scenes that are not visible from the road. Backpacking routes can vary from easy to quite difficult. Good judgment can help develop an outing that is good for everyone.

"Nature hikes are another way to enjoy walking and the outdoors. A nature hike may be a structured walk provided by a local leisure service agency or it can be done by an individual. If it is a structured activity, a guide will point out different things and provide information about them. An informal hike can be equally beneficial. It is not necessary to know the names of trees, birds, flowers, and other objects in order to enjoy them. A nature hike can occur on a marked nature trail in a local park or it can be a walk around the neighborhood. The pace can be slow or rapid. All that is required for a successful nature hike is the willingness to walk, look, listen, pause and enjoy.

"Many people who like the outdoors use walking to participate in their favorite activity or arrive at their favorite outdoor area. Hunters and fisherman often hike into their preferred spots. Their enjoyment is increased by the effort required to reach their spot. It is fun to be in a place that can be reached only by walking.

"One reason why many people enjoy golf is because it provides them the chance to walk in a pleasant place. Golf courses are designed to create an enjoyable place for the golfers. Although some people use golf carts when playing golf, most golfers walk.

"Walking can provide individuals with a means to get to a destination. Many people choose to walk to the store. Other people may choose to walk to a place that provides recreation activities such as flower gardens, municipal park and recreation areas, movie theaters, local community centers, or fitness clubs.

"Finally, walking may be done to provide the animals you own, such as a dog, with the chance to exercise. Many veterinarians suggest that one way to help your dog get plenty of exercise is to walk him or her on a regular basis. These are just a few examples of recreation activities that are dependent on walking. Other activities may range from walking on a lunch break to walking to a movie."

Process: Present information on recreation activities dependent on walking.

4. Discussion

Content:
    a. Have you ever backpacked, orienteered, or hiked to a favorite spot? If so, please describe the experience.
    b. What are some other recreation activities that require walking?
    c. How can walking be incorporated into our daily activities?
    d. Why would you walk your pet?

Process: Conduct discussion using above questions. Encourage all participants to contribute to the discussion.

5. Learning Activity

Content: "I have written different recreation activities on slips of paper and have placed them in this container. Each one of you will have a chance to come and pick one of the pieces of paper and read it without showing anyone else. Once you know what activity it is, you are to act out that activity while walking around in a large circle. While you are walking, you can not say anything. The other people will watch the person and not say a word. After 60 seconds the person in the center can stop and everyone must write their guesses of the activity on their index card. After everyone has finished writing, we will have you turn over your card and show everyone, so that we can discuss the activity."

Process: Prior to the activity, write various recreation activities that involve walking on slips of paper (e.g., hiking, hunting, golfing, walking a pet). Have participants arrange themselves in a large circle. Establish a relaxed atmosphere. Perhaps the leader can be the first person in the middle to provide a clear example. Distribute one index card and a pencil to each individual before the person in the center begins to act out his or her activity. Remind participants to be silent while person is acting.

6. Debriefing

Content:
    a. How did you feel while acting out the learning activity?
    b. How important is walking to the recreation activities covered in this learning activity?
    c. Why do you think we conducted this learning activity?
    d. What would be your first choice of a recreation activity that involved walking and was covered during this learning activity?
    e. Are there other recreation activities that involve walking that we did not act out?

Process: Conduct debriefing using the above questions. Encourage all participants to contribute to the debriefing.

7. Conclusion

Content: "We completed a learning activity that focused on various recreation activities you can do that involve walking. Prior to the learning activity, I talked about some possible recreation activities we could do while walking. We spent this discussion time today to help show you how valuable walking is in our lives and how it can be an important part of many different recreation activities."

Process: Present concluding statements above. Provide the participants opportunities to ask questions. Attempt to answer relevant questions and clarify or redirect those questions that are not relevant or are inappropriate.

Goal 2: Demonstrate knowledge of leisure resources associated with walking.

Objective 2.1: Demonstrate knowledge of equipment useful for walking.

1. Orientation Activity

Content: "You have been divided into small groups. In the room there are many hidden slips of paper, each with an item of clothing or equipment written on it. When the signal to begin is given, each group is to search for and collect as many slips of paper as possible. The object is to collect slips of paper with the right clothing and equipment to outfit a person for a walk around the neighborhood and a person for a walk through the woods. At the end of a five minute search period, each group will have five minutes to examine its slips of paper and assemble an outfit for each walk. Some groups will have incomplete outfits, so each group will then be given an opportunity to trade no more than two slips of paper with each of the other groups. When the trading period is over, we will record the outfits for cach walk from each group."

Process: Prepare a list of items of clothing and equipment that would be appropriate for a walk around the neighborhood (e.g., left walking shoe, right walking shoe, left sock, right sock, walking shorts, T-shirt, sun visor) and for a walk through the woods (e.g., left hiking boot, right hiking boot, left sock, right sock, long trousers, loose-fitting shirt, knapsack, hat, canteen). Write the names of items of clothing and equipment on slips of colored paper, one item per slip. Prepare as many sets of slips of paper as there are groups participating in the activity. Scatter the slips in hiding places around the room (e.g., behind curtains, under the furniture, in plants).

Divide participants into small groups and give the signal to begin. Stop the search at the appropriate time, allow an opportunity to assemble the outfits, and provide time for the trading period. End the activity by asking each group to report what it was able to assemble for each excursion.

2. Introduction

Content: "The type of clothing and equipment used in walking can enhance or reduce the pleasure derived from the activity. The kind of walking to be done will help determine what is correct. The weather will also affect our decisions about to what to wear."

Process: Introduce topic. Provide some pictures or slides of different clothing and equipment used when walking.

3. Presentation

Content: "Shoes are the most important piece of equipment needed for walking. They are the foundation of success. Ordinary street shoes can be used for walking in many circumstances, but they are generally not good for long and frequent periods of walking, even at a moderate pace.

"Shoes made for running or jogging are good for walking. Although they are designed for speed, they work well at a slower pace. The cushioning that is built into a running shoe softens the shock when the foot hits the ground. Such softening is important for walkers. Running shoes are lightweight and that makes them less tiring than ordinary footwear. They work well on paved surfaces and are good on dry, grassy surfaces.

"Walkers who choose to walk on rugged, natural ground need to pay attention to their footwear. Some ankle protection is needed; this means a good pair of hiking boots.

"Lightweight wool socks are helpful with either running shoes or hiking boots. Cotton socks are also good."

Process: Present information on footwear. Use running shoe and ordinary street shoe as visual models. Emphasize difference in cushioning. Use white wool or cotton socks for demonstration. If available, have a pair of hiking boots on hand. Compare with street shoes; point out ankle protection and difference in sole pattern. Items can be passed around for participants to inspect.

4. Discussion

Content:
   a.   Have you unexpectedly had to walk a long distance, such as after a car broke down? Can you remember what type of shoes you were wearing and if your feet hurt before you were finished? Please describe the situation.
   b.   Why are running shoes also recommended for walking?
   c.   Would tennis shoes or sneakers be good for walking? Why?

Process: Conduct the discussion using the above questions. Encourage all participants to contribute to the discussion.

5. Presentation

Content: "Weather will be the major factor in determining the kind of clothing to wear while walking. Within the boundaries of decency and comfort, the general rule of thumb is: the less clothing, the better.

"Walking in warm or hot weather should be done in loose, light-colored clothing. Cotton is good because it 'breathes,' allowing moisture to pass freely from the surface of the body to outside the clothing. Light-colored clothes help to reflect rather than absorb the sun's rays and assist in cooling the body. Shorts are good; tight-fitting jeans are not.

"Walking in cold weather can be fun if you are dressed properly. The key to dressing for cold weather is to dress in layers. Layers of clothing help to 'trap' air that has been warmed by your body heat. If you become too warm, outer layers can be removed until you are comfortable. Wool garments that fit loosely are excellent.

"Depending on the circumstances, some type of headgear may be advisable. The hot glare of the sun can be eased by wearing a sun visor or a cap with a bill. A hat in wintertime can slow the escape of body heat through the head.

"One of the attractive features of walking for exercise is that expensive and specialized clothing is not necessary. Headbands, wristbands, running suits, and other things can be worn, if you like, but a successful walking program does not require it."

Process: Present information on clothing. Use appropriate items (e.g., walking shorts, shirt, visored cap) as demonstration models. Provide opportunity for participants to inspect the clothing.

6. Discussion

Content:
   a. What kind of clothing do you prefer when you walk?
   b. What features do you believe are most important in clothing for walking?
   c. How might the weather influence your choice of clothing for walking?

Process: Conduct discussion using above questions. Encourage all participants to contribute to the discussion.

7. Presentation

Content: "Additional types of equipment are available and, in some circumstances, may be convenient. An all-day walk in the countryside might call for a knapsack. A flask or canteen may be appropriate; insect repellent could be handy. Depending on the land, maps and compass could be used. Many walkers use pedometers (devices to measure mileage), but they are often inaccurate. Some people like to walk with a walking stick. Many items could be used while walking, but good judgment is needed to keep you from becoming unnecessarily burdened."

Process: Present information on additional equipment available. Use demonstration models when able. Emphasize equipment is optional.

8. Discussion

Content:
   a. Do you have any favorite items you like to carry with you when you walk? If so, what are they?
   b. Would walking in the city affect the type of equipment a walker might choose, as compared to in the country? How so?
   c. Would a personal stereo headset add or detract from your sense of pleasure while walking? Why or why not?

Process: Conduct discussion using above questions. Encourage all participants to contribute to the discussion.

9. Learning Activity

Content: "We are now going to engage in an activity to help us apply what we have just learned. Each group has an identical set of three sheets of paper. Each sheet has a heading on it that describes conditions in which a walk may be taken. On each sheet, list the kind of clothing and equipment that would be good for a walk under the conditions described. When you are finished, we will compare results."

Process: Divide participants into groups of three or four. Provide each group with a set of three sheets of paper, headed respectively with "Walk in a park on a hot summer day," "Hike in the woods on a crisp autumn day," and "Walk in the neighborhood on a cold winter day." Prepare sheets ahead of time. Have sufficient sheets of paper and pencils on hand. Be available for assistance, if requested. When lists are completed, move on to debriefing.

10. Debriefing

Content:
   a. What items of clothing/equipment did you list for the conditions described?
   b. Were there items the same for each condition described? If so, what were they?
   c. Were there items different for the conditions described? If so, what were they?

Process: Conduct debriefing. Provide each group with opportunity to respond. List responses on chalkboard. Provide feedback relative to appropriateness of responses. If necessary, supply essential items that were omitted.

11. Conclusion

Content: "The correct type of clothing and equipment can increase the pleasure from walking. Almost any kind of clothing can be worn but there are some circumstances where a particular type is better. The right footwear is very important. Remember to avoid carrying unnecessary items. The walk is the thing, not the costume."

Process: Make concluding statements. Provide opportunity for questions.

Objective 2.2: Demonstrate knowledge of leisure resources within walking distance of home.

1. Orientation Activity

Content: "Each of you has a sheet of paper with 10 items related to walking on it. Following each item is a blank line. Find someone who has done what is described in an item and get that person's signature on the line following the item. Do not use the same person for more than two of the items. When the items are completed (or nearly so), we will share the results of our sheets with the group."

Process: Conduct orientation activity. Prepare handout of 10 items. Handout will be headed with "Find someone who..." Examples of items:

- ...walks to a neighborhood park. _____
- ...walked to this class. _____
- ...walked to school, rather than rode a bus. _____
- ...walks with a pet. _____
- ...walked to a movie. _____
- ...walked to a shopping mall. _____

Create 10 items. Have sufficient handouts and pencils. Allow approximately 10 minutes for completion. Bring participants together to share results. Provide each participant opportunity to name the people whose signatures were obtained.

2. Introduction

Content: "Walking for leisure can be combined with other purposes. Walking can be done for fitness, for weight control, and for reducing stress and tension. It can also be done for the purpose of getting to other leisure resources. If alternate forms of transportation to those resources are available, walkers have the option of using them. If there are no other means of transportation, those resources may still be accessible by walking. Sometimes, walking lets you be in control and less dependent on others."

Process: Introduce topic on resources associated with walking.

3. Presentation

Content: "There are a number of leisure resources scattered throughout a community. Depending on where you live, many of these resources may be within reasonable walking distance of your home. Knowing where leisure resources are located in a community and how to get to them is important. Leisure resources enrich our lives."

Process: Present information emphasizing the importance of knowing resources associated with walking.

4. Discussion

Content:
    a. Do you do any walking for multiple purposes? If so, what are they?
    b. Do you regularly walk to any leisure resources in the community? If so, what is the resource and why do you walk to it?
    c. Why is it important to know where leisure resources are in a community?

Process: Conduct the discussion using the above questions. Encourage all participants to contribute to the discussion.

5. Learning Activity

Content: "We are going to participate in a three-part activity designed to help us learn more about our community and to allow us to use what we learned in our walking program. The first thing we are going to do is identify as many community leisure resources as we can. We are going to do this in small groups of three or four persons. Each group has a pencil and paper. Make a list of all the community leisure resources of which you are aware (e.g., parks, theaters, museums, restaurants, shopping malls, libraries, recreation centers, swimming pools, tennis courts, bowling alleys, arcades, zoos)."

"Using the list of resources we have generated, place them on a city street map by writing their names at the proper locations. Draw stars on the map to indicate where each of you lives. Write each person's name by his or her star. Each of you make a map of the resources identified and where you live. Starting with where you live, draw a route that connects your home with at least three of the community resources and then returns to where you live. Your return route does not have to follow your outward bound route. Draw another route from your residence to three more community resources and back to your residence. Let us examine what we have and see what use we can make of it."

Process: Divide participants into small groups. Provide each group with paper and pencil. Ask each group to share the resources identified. Put list on chalkboard. Obtain city street map (perhaps from chamber of commerce or AAA) or create one using simple grid system. Provide telephone books for addresses of resources identified. Use colored ink for stars. Provide sufficient number of maps. Circulate among participants and offer individual help, if needed. Ask participants to share maps with group. Comment on resources connected with routes from individual places of residence.

6. Debriefing

Content:
    a.   How can we tell if the resources are within walking distance of where we live?
    b.   If all of the resources are too far, how can we map out several walking routes?
    c.   Start in a central location and draw a route that connects all the resources in your neighborhood. How long do you think it would take for you to walk this route?
    d.   Are there people in this program who live close to you? Could you walk these routes together?

Process: Conduct debriefing using above questions. Encourage all participants to contribute to the discussion.

7. Conclusion

Content: "Walking to community leisure resources is a good way to combine fitness, stress reduction, weight control, and fun. Please remember, however, accomplishing more than one purpose in the same amount of time may be efficient but it is not required. Walking can be done for no other purpose than it is pleasurable. Having a reasonable estimate of the time required to walk to certain places allows you to be a better planner. It is easy to glance at a planned route and have an idea of what it requires. Remember that you may change routes at any time or walk only a portion of a route. Planned routes should not take the fun out of a walking program."

Process: Conclude session using above statements. Encourage participants to ask questions.

Goal 3: Demonstrate the ability to apply health and fitness techniques to walking.

Objective 3.1: Demonstrate the ability to monitor one's heart rate.

1. Orientation Activity

Content: "We are going to do a brief physical activity to increase the rate our hearts are beating. Jump up and down on both feet (or run in place or walk up a flight of steps) for one minute. Place a hand firmly over your heart and feel its beat. Also, notice if your rate of breathing is faster and if you are breathing more deeply."

Process: Conduct orientation activity. Use sweep hand on watch or wall clock, or digital watch display; give signal to start and stop. Ask if anyone had trouble feeling heartbeat. Seek reaction to changes in respiration.

2. Introduction

Content: "When we exercise, our hearts beat more times per minute than they do when we are not exercising or working hard at physical labor. Our hearts beat more often when we work hard because the muscles of our bodies need more blood (oxygen) to work. Although walking is not an exercise that normally elevates our heart rate, we still need to be able to know how fast it is beating. We can check our heart rate by taking our own pulse."

Process: Introduce the topic of monitoring one's heart rate. Emphasize the value of monitoring your heart rate.

3. Presentation

Content: "When we exercise, our muscles require an adequate supply of oxygen-rich blood. Our hearts meet this demand by beating faster and circulating more fresh blood. As our muscles demand even more oxygen, our heart rates increase even more. Each of us has a maximum heart rate, which can be thought of as the rate our heart would beat if we engaged in an all-out muscular effort for a three- or four-minute period.

"We do not want to exercise at our maximum heart rate and walking will not raise our heart rate to that level. Depending on your individual level of fitness, walking will increase your heart rate some, but not to anywhere near its maximum rate. It is important to be able to listen to our heart rates because they can be a measure of how we feel. Our heart rates can tell us whether we should increase our pace of walking or choose a steeper path, if that is what we want to do. They can also tell us if we should stop and take a rest (e.g., on a hot day).

"Measuring our heart rate is simple. We can do this by counting our pulse. An easy place to do this is at the wrist. To take your pulse at the wrist, use the second, third and fourth fingers of one hand to feel for the pulse on the thumb side of your other hand's wrist. Your fingers will feel a thump or a push. That is your pulse.

"After you have found your pulse, you will need an accurate way to measure time. A watch with a sweep second hand will do fine. You can count your pulse beats for six seconds and add a 0 to the number of beats you counted. This will tell you how many times your heart is beating per minute. If you have difficulty finding your pulse at the wrist, you can place your hand firmly over your heart and count the beats there. It is important to take your pulse immediately after you have stopped exercising because your heart rate will diminish fairly rapidly."

Process: Present information on pulse. Demonstrate correct spot on wrist. Provide example of counting beats for six seconds and adding a zero. Demonstrate on self.

4. Discussion

Content:
    a. Why do our hearts beat faster during exercise?
    b. How can we tell how fast our hearts our beating?
    c. Why is it important to know how fast our hearts are beating during exercise?
    d. Have you ever taken your pulse when you are at rest?
    e. Have you ever taken your pulse after you have exercised?
    f. Is exercise the only thing that can make our hearts beat faster? If not, what are some other things that can increase our heart rate?

Process: Conduct discussion using above questions. Encourage participants to contribute to the discussion.

5. Learning Activity

Content: "You are now going to practice taking your own pulse. Pair up with a partner. Take your own pulse before doing any exercise. Tell your partner what your heart rate per minute is. Now jump up and down on both feet for one minute. Take your pulse again. Tell your partner what your new heart rate per minute is."

Process: Conduct learning activity. Divide participants into pairs. If uneven number of participants, have one group of three. Give start and stop signal for exercise. Move among participants; be sure each is able to find and count own pulse. Repeat exercise if necessary.

6. Debriefing

Content:
    a. Did you have any difficulty in finding your pulse?
    b. What method did you use?
    c. What was your heart rate at rest?
    d. What was your heart rate after the exercise?

"Take your pulse one more time to see how much your heart rate has slowed since ending the exercise."

Process: Conduct debriefing using above questions. Provide opportunity for each participant to state resting heart rate and rate immediately after exercise. Give signal for taking final pulse. Have each person report results.

7. Conclusion

Content: "Taking our pulse is a wise thing to do. It helps us to keep track of how our bodies are responding to exercise. It is something we can do on our own, without the help of anyone else. Knowing what our heart rate is helps us to make judgments about whether we want to exercise longer or harder or whether we want to slow down."

Process: Conclude session. Ask for questions or comments.

Objective 3.2: Demonstrate the ability to perform warm-up and cool-down exercises associated with walking.

1. Orientation Activity

Content: "Stand sideways to a wall with your arm extended, your palm flat on the wall and your feet flat on the floor. Stay erect, keep your feet flat on the floor and move them away from the wall until your fingers are extended. Continue to inch away from the wall as far as you can but still remain in physical contact with it (probably by the tip of your middle finger). Repeat this action a time or two. Ask yourself if it felt easier the second or third time you did it."

Process: Conduct orientation activity. Make sure adequate wall space is available. If outside, use telephone pole, tree, or similar object. Seek reactions from participants.

2. Introduction

Content: "Before beginning to exercise, do some stretching. Stretching helps prepare the body for active exercise by loosening muscles and lubricating joints. Use of cold or stiff muscles in active exercise can result in aches and pains or lead to more serious injuries. We respond to exercise better after we have gone through a warm-up period.

"The best way to stretch is to gradually move until you first feel the muscle begin to pull, hold that position for a few seconds, and then relax. Do not jerk or bounce while stretching– that can cause pain and injury. Stretching as a warm-up activity does not need to last a long time; five minutes is generally enough. After the warm-up is completed, begin the walking immediately. A short cool-down period of recovery after exercise is equally important. This allows our breathing and body temperature to return gradually to their normal resting levels. Engaging in the same set of stretching exercises done for warm-up is a good way to cool-down."

Process: Introduce topic. Emphasize proper procedures designed to avoid injury and result in a safe and enjoyable experience.

3. Presentation

Content: "We are now going to consider some stretching exercises used for warming-up that prepare us to receive the most benefits from walking. I will demonstrate each of the exercises to you and identify which part(s) of the body it is stretching.

  a. *Sitting toe touches:* Sit on the floor with your legs extended in front of you and your feet together. Slowly reach for your toes with both of your hands, bending at the waist and bringing your forehead as close to your knees as possible. Hold this position for a few seconds and then return to a sitting position. Repeat this action for a minute or so. This exercise stretches the back of your thighs and your lower back.

  b. *Calf stretchers:* Stand facing a wall and place your palms on it at about eye level. Lean forward, keeping your body straight and supporting your weight with your arms. Step backwards, keeping your feet flat on the floor until you feel your calf muscles beginning to stretch. Hold this position for a few seconds and then return to an upright position. Repeat this action four or five times. This is a good exercise to stretch your calf muscles and tendons.

c. *Side stretch:* Stand erect with your feet a little more than shoulder-width apart. Raise your right arm, with the elbow bent, over your head. Bend your upper body to the left until you feel the muscles pull. Hold this position for a few seconds, return to an upright position, raise your left arm with the elbow bent and bend to the right. Alternate bending to the left and the right a few times. This is a good exercise to stretch the lateral portions of your torso.

d. *Arm circles:* Stand erect with your feet shoulder-width apart and pointing forward. Extend one arm straight over your head and the other arm straight down by your side. Rotate both arms forward in big circles for a few seconds, keeping your arms straight. Reverse directions and rotate both arms backwards in big circles. Alternate directions every 10 seconds or so. This exercise loosens your shoulder joints and stretches your upper arm and shoulder girdle muscles.

e. *Head flexor:* Stand comfortably erect with your arms at your sides. Move your head forward by slowly dropping your chin to your chest. Try to move your chin down as far as possible. Return your head to an upright position and then tip it as far back as you can. Repeat these movements for a few seconds. Do this exercise slowly. This exercise helps to increase neck flexibility and it can also help firm the muscles in front of your neck.

f. *Head turns:* Stand comfortably erect with your arms at your sides. Turn your head slowly to the left and look over your left shoulder. Return your head to a forward position and then turn to the right and look over your right shoulder. Alternate looking left and right for a few seconds. This exercise is also good for neck flexibility.

g. *Trunk twisters:* Stand erect with your feet shoulder-width apart, heels flat on the floor and arms extended to the side at shoulder height. Slowly twist your upper body to the right as far as you can and then twist it to the left. Do not hold the twisted position but keep your upper body moving. Keep your heels flat on the floor. This exercise stretches your back muscles and your torso."

Process: Present material. Arrange participants so they have unobstructed view of you. Name each exercise and clearly state which body part(s) it is for. While describing each exercise, demonstrate it. After completing all seven stretches, demonstrate them again.

4. Discussion

Content:
a. What is the purpose of doing stretching exercises?
b. Why are these exercises done slowly?
c. Why are bouncing and jerking not recommended during stretching?
d. Do you wish to see any of the exercises demonstrated again?
e. Are you ready to try them yourself?

Process: Conduct discussion using above questions. Encourage participants to contribute to the discussion.

5. Learning Activity

Content: "We are now going to go through the stretching routine together. I will demonstrate each exercise again and then you will repeat it while I observe you. Remember to avoid bouncing or jerking. Do the exercises slowly. Stop if you feel pain or discomfort." (Go through the set of exercises.)

Process: Conduct learning activity. Use proper technique when demonstrating. Emphasize avoidance of bouncing. Move among participants. Offer individual assistance when appropriate.

6. Debriefing

Content:
   a. How did it feel?
   b. Did any exercise feel particularly good?
   c. Was there any one exercise that was more difficult to do than the others?
   d. Do you feel there should be an established sequence for the exercises?

Process: Conduct debriefing. If people are having difficulty expressing themselves, encourage them to demonstrate the exercise.

7. Conclusion

Content: "Stretching each time is recommended before and after walking. The set of stretching exercises you have just learned can be completed in a few minutes. You should start walking immediately after stretching. When you have completed your walk, repeat the exercises to cool-down and avoid any muscle stiffness or soreness."

Process: Make concluding statements. Emphasize the importance of injury prevention.

Objective 3.3: Demonstrate the proper technique used for walking.

1. Orientation Activity

Content: "When walking, one of the things we should try to do is walk with an erect posture. We are going to do an activity that emphasizes posture; it is something you have probably tried before. You are divided into two teams, each with a book. Each member of each team will balance the book on his/her head, walk 10 feet, return to the starting point, and hand the book to the next member of the team. Try to walk without having the book fall or having to grab it to keep it from falling. Count each time it falls or is touched to keep it from falling. The object of each team is *not* to finish first but to finish with the least number of times the book fell or was touched to keep it from falling. In the case of a tie, the team that first completes the task will be declared the winner. Remember to walk erect and without excessive movement of the head."

Process: Conduct orientation activity. Divide group into two teams. If uneven number of participants, you can act as "counter." Use tape or chalk for starting line and line 10 feet away. Use same size and weight of book for each team. Emphasize posture. Conclude with acknowledgment that stillness of head may be somewhat unnatural but the purpose was to walk erect.

2. Introduction

Content: "The correct form should be used when walking in order to get the most out of the exercise. If you walk with poor posture, your body will not get the most benefits. Try to use the following techniques if they do not feel uncomfortable or unnatural. You will know what feels right and what does not."

Process: Introduce topic. Emphasize proper techniques but remember to accommodate for different individual styles.

3. Presentation

Content: "There are correct walking techniques that ensure optimum benefits but do not place unnecessary strain on your body. Utilization of these techniques should add to the pleasure you derive from walking.
   a. Keep your back straight and walk erect, hold your head high as you walk.
   b. Do not exaggerate your arm motion. Allow your arms to hang loosely at your sides. When you stride, they will swing in opposite action to your legs.
   c. Let your hands, hips, knees, and ankles relax. Do not be concerned about the length of your stride; do whatever feels comfortable to you.
   d. Each foot should strike the ground at the heel. As you move forward, your weight is transferred from the heel along the outer border of your foot towards the toes. When you push off with your toes, you complete your foot strike pattern.
   e. As you move from heel to toe, you will get a rolling motion that propels you forward. Avoid landing flat-footed or on the balls of your feet.
   f. As you walk, breathe normally. If you feel more comfortable with your mouth closed, close it; if you feel better with your mouth open, open it. The faster you walk, the more air you will need.
   g. Remember, you are walking for enjoyment and leisure. There is no need to worry excessively about form and style."

Process: Present material. Use visual aids to present the seven techniques. Ttechniques written on an easel or listed on a handout may be useful. Provide demonstrations of the appropriate techniques while describing them.

4. Discussion

Content:
   a. Are you comfortable with your walking style? If not, why not?
   b. Do you have any habits of style that you would like to change? If so, what are they and what will you do to change them?
   c. Have you observed the walking style of others that would not be comfortable for you? Why would it be uncomfortable?
   d. Do you have any suggestions related to walking style or techniques that you would like to add to the discussion?

Process: Conduct discussion using above questions. Encourage participants to contribute to the discussion.

5. Learning Activity

Content: "We are now going to practice by doing our stretching exercises and going for a 15 minute walk. We will walk as a loose knit group. If you want to walk with a partner within the group, that is fine. As you walk, make a conscious effort to practice the technique(s) you wish to improve (e.g., holding your head high, having your heels touch the ground first, letting your arms swing in a natural manner). If you try something that makes you uncomfortable, you do not need to keep trying it. When we have finished our walk, we will stretch again as a cool-down exercise. Remember, you are walking for fun."

Process: Conduct learning activity. Move among group, walking with people in lead, in the rear, and all other places. Provide encouragement. When an aspect of walking is not being performed effectively by an individual, make a correction to the entire group rather than singling out one person. If a person is alone, you can walk beside him/her and encourage modeling of your behaviors.

6. Debriefing

Content:
   a. How did the walk feel?
   b. What specific walking techniques did you try?
   c. Did anything feel unnatural?
   d. How did the warm-up and cool-down stretching feel?

Process: Conduct debriefing. Provide opportunities for participants to identify any problems they may have experienced during the walk.

7. Conclusion

Content: "Using proper walking techniques is of great benefit to us. All it requires is effort on our part. The use of proper walking techniques places less strain on our bodies and increases our enjoyment of walking. It allows us to enjoy many other activities that are associated with walking such as bird watching, golf, marching, and hiking. Walking can be a source of great pleasure in our lives."

Process: Make concluding statements. Provide opportunity for questions.

Goal 4: Demonstrate the ability to be assertive while walking.

Objective 4.1: Demonstrate the ability to ask a question while walking.

1. Orientation Activity

Content: "We are going do an activity to demonstrate the value of questions. I am going to pin a name tag on the back of your collar. It will contain the name of a well-known figure; the figure may be a real person or a character from a book or movie. You will be able to move around and see the names on the back of everyone else but you will not know the name on the tag on your own back. Try to discover the identity of the figure on your tag by asking questions of the people in the group. The questions must be such that they can be answered with a 'yes' or 'no.' You may ask no more than three questions of any one person. When you have learned the identity of the figure on your tag, you may sit down and observe the remainder of the activity."

Process: Prepare name tags prior to session. Have sufficient number of tags and pins available. Names on tags must be well-known (e.g., Martin Luther King, Bob Hope, Tarzan, President Lincoln, Winston Churchill, Mickey Mouse, Mahatma Ghandi, Albert Einstein). Move among participants. As activity nears end, provide hints to anyone having particularly difficult time. Ensure that no one is embarrassed.

2. Introduction

Content: "Asking questions is an important part of communication. Asking a question of another person in a polite and respectful way shows that you are interested in the opinion of that person. You may be participating in this walking program with some people you already know or you may be meeting some people for the first time. By asking questions, you may learn new things about your old friends and become better acquainted with your new friends. Also, by asking questions, you are indicating that you are willing to respond to questions asked of you."

Process: Introduce topic. Emphasize relationship between the orientation activity and the importance of asking questions in an attempt to provide a clear transition into the material.

3. Presentation

Content: "Asking questions should be a gentle art. The way questions are asked may be as important as the questions themselves. Questions should be asked politely and firmly, but without aggression. Eye contact without staring for long periods of time is also an important factor. Questions should not interrupt a person who is speaking, but should be held until that person has finished.

"There are some guidelines related to formulating questions that can be of assistance:
   a.   Be sure the question is worded in question form. Otherwise, it may not require a response
        by another person.
   b.   Keep the question short and simple to ensure that the question is easily understood.
   c.   Word the question so that it does not show a bias. A question that indicates it has an
        expected conclusion or response may not be discussed honestly and openly.
   d.   In most cases, a question should be worded so that it cannot be answered with only a 'yes'
        or 'no.' They should be worded to allow for many responses.

"Judgment must be used relative to the timing and the appropriateness of questions. Timing refers both to not interrupting and being in keeping with the content of the discussion. Appropriateness refers to the degree of intimacy or privacy that should be present. Questions that are appropriate for close friends would not be suitable for casual acquaintances and even less so for strangers. Judgment is important."

Process: Present material. Use chalkboard or other forms of media to outline major points. For example:

```
• use a polite manner
• be sure question is in question form
• use short, simple questions
• avoid questions with predetermined answers
• avoid questions with "yes" or "no" answers
• use good timing
• avoid too much familiarity
```

4. Discussion

Content:
   a. Of what value are questions?
   b. How do you respond to questions from people you have just met?
   c. Do you feel comfortable asking questions of people you have just met?
   d. How can you judge if it is appropriate to ask a question?

Process: Conduct discussion using above questions. Include in your discussion information about the timing and appropriateness of effective questioning. Encourage participants to contribute to the discussion.

5. Learning Activity

Content: "We are going to divide into small groups of two or three people each. The task of each group will be to generate two separate lists of questions: (1) What questions would you ask while walking with a friend? (2) What questions would you ask while walking with a new acquaintance? When lists are completed, each small group will share its questions with the entire group."

Process: Conduct learning activity. Divide group into small groups. Provide each group with pencil and paper. Move among groups to answer questions and provide assistance. After they have completed their lists, provide opportunities for each group to share its questions. Write questions on chalkboard. If inappropriate questions are generated, suggest ways to make them better.

6. Debriefing

Content:
   a. Is there a difference between questions asked of a friend with whom you were walking and those asked of a new acquaintance? If so, what are they?
   b. Are there questions with which you feel uncomfortable? If so, what are they and why do you feel uncomfortable?
   c. What difference, if any, would there be in the way questions were asked of a friend, compared with those asked of a new acquaintance?
   d. How would you react if you asked a question and received no response?

Process: Conduct debriefing. Focus on differences between a close friend and a new acquaintance. Encourage participants to contribute to the debriefing.

7. Conclusion

Content: "Questions, asked in a courteous manner, can add to the fun of walking with others. They can enable us to get information we need, tell others we care about what they think and feel, add zest to conversations, or serve a number of other purposes. Walking can be a good time for asking questions."

Process: Make concluding statements. Demonstrate enthusiasm and interest in the idea of asking questions while walking. Provide opportunity for questions.

Objective 4.2: Demonstrate the ability to conduct a discussion with walking partners.

1. Orientation Activity

Content: "Each pair of you has an identical set of interview cards. One of you select the first card and ask your partner the question on it. After the question has been answered, your partner will select the next card and ask you the question on it. Alternate asking and answering questions until all the cards have been used. Each of you will have asked and responded to an equal number of questions, but you will not have asked the same questions of each other. Now that you have completed the questions, each of you can tell the rest of us what you learned about your partner."

Process: Conduct orientation activity. Divide the group into pairs. If uneven number of participants, instructor can serve as a partner. Prepare set of 10 interview cards in advance and duplicate sufficient number. Use 3" x 5" cards; place one question on each card. Examples of questions:

- What is your favorite recreation activity that involves walking?
- What new activity would you like to learn that involves walking?
- Name a place to where you would like to walk?
- Where would you like to go for a long walk?

Conclude by having each participant relate what was learned by asking the questions.

2. Introduction

Content: "Engaging in a discussion with another person is a social activity. It is an activity that is necessary for good communication, which is required for community living. Although questions and answers can be a foundation, discussions can be much broader. The skills needed to participate in a satisfactory discussion are within reach of all of us. A good discussion can increase the fun we get from walking."

Process: Introduce topic of conducting a discussion while walking. Relate content of introduction to the orientation activity to provide an effective transition to the material.

3. Presentation

Content: "A good discussion with another person can provide a chance for learning some things about that person and sharing some things about yourself. It can lead to an understanding of issues and formation of opinions. A discussion can help to develop or reaffirm personal values. There are a number of good things associated with discussions. Following a few guidelines can increase our ability to engage in discussions.

"If you know the person with whom you wish to engage in discussion, you have already accomplished the first step. If not, introduce yourself or ask to be introduced to that person. Making light conversation can help break the ice.

"The next thing that needs to be accomplished is to establish a feeling of mutual trust. This can be accomplished by being honest, open, and respectful. The sense of trust can be maintained by continuing to act in that manner. Each person must accept the responsibility of contributing to the discussion, listening carefully to what is being said, and then providing feedback. If this is not done, the discussion may become a monologue.

"There are additional things to be aware of when engaging in a discussion while walking. Eye contact is still necessary, but may not be required as frequently as in other situations. It is also important to maintain appropriate physical proximity to your walking partner. This means walking close, but not too close, to your partner. Most people have a 'bubble of personal space' around them that they do not like to have broken in the normal course of events. The size of this 'bubble' varies from person to person and from situation to situation but a good rule of thumb is to regard it as 2 1/2 to 3 feet. Walking at this distance should be appropriate in most cases.

"Remember that a discussion is a cooperative event. Express yourself openly and politely, listen carefully, do not interrupt, and provide feedback relevant to what your partner is saying. These are the ingredients necessary for a successful discussion."

Process: Present material. Demonstrate proper techniques as they are being discussed. Use chalkboard or other media to outline major points. For example:

> *IMPORTANT GUIDELINES:*
>
> • make acquaintance   • maintain appropriate physical distance
> • contribute to conversation   • listen and converse politely
> • make eye contact   • provide feedback to partner's comments
> • establish trust

4. Discussion

Content:
    a. Why is it important to engage effectively in discussion with others?
    b. In what ways can a person contribute to a discussion between two people?
    c. What are some possible topics of discussion with a walking partner?

Process: Conduct discussion using above questions. Encourage participants to contribute to the discussion.

5. Learning Activity

Content: "We are going to go through our set of stretching exercises and then take a 15-20 minute walk. You will be paired with a partner. During the walk, carry on a discussion with your partner. You do not need to have a discussion for the entire time of the walk, but make an honest effort to have one for at least 50 percent of the walk. When we return we will go through our cool-down exercises and then share our discussions with the group."

Process: Conduct learning activity. Do stretching exercises. Divide group into pairs. All pairs walk the same route. Move among the pairs during the walk. Assist any person experiencing difficulty with the conversation. Do stretching exercises when the walk is completed. Move on to debriefing session.

6. Debriefing

Content:
    a. Did you find it easy or difficult to engage in a discussion as you walked? Why?
    b. What can you do to make it easier to engage in a discussion the next time you walk?
    c. Did you talk about more than one topic? What did you talk about?
    d. What are some things you would like to talk about the next time you go for a walk?   Will you try to talk about them?

Process: Conduct debriefing session with above questions. Provide participants with an opportunity to ask additional questions and make other comments.

7. Conclusion

Content: "Being able to engage in discussion helps us have more control over our lives. Having a discussion with a walking partner can be a pleasant experience. You can discuss many topics, ranging from politics to what you have seen while walking. All it takes to feel comfortable about participating in a discussion is practice. We can all do that and we can all have more fun while walking."

Process: Make concluding statement. Thank participants for their contributions and encourage them to practice conducting discussions. Provide opportunity for questions.

Objective 4.3: Demonstrate the ability to share feelings about the walking experience.

1. Orientation Activity

Content: "Each of you has a pair of scissors. There are several magazines available to you. Browse through the magazines and find pictures or cartoons that contain at least two people. Cut out two or three pictures or cartoons. Take a minute and think about what the people in your pictures might be feeling. Each of you may select one picture and tell us what you think the people in it might be feeling."

Process: Conduct orientation activity. Have sufficient scissors and magazines. Ensure quiet environment suitable for discussion. Provide each participant with opportunity to speak. If desired, have participants select a second picture and repeat the process.

2. Introduction

Content: "Sometimes we feel uncomfortable when we are asked to share our feelings with others. This feeling of unease can reduce our enjoyment of an activity and cause us to experience stress and tension. Learning to share feelings with others can reduce anxiety and increase our sense of pleasure."

Process: Introduce topic by describing the value of sharing one's feelings.

3. Presentation

Content: "Individuals have the right to express themselves and feel good about it as long as they do not hurt others in the process. Although we recognize this as a right everyone should have, we sometimes hesitate to claim it for ourselves. We may hesitate because we may be very reserved or fearful that we will be ridiculed; we may be nervous about speaking in a group or think that what we have to say is not worthwhile. There may be many other reasons why we do not express ourselves. In spite of any problems that might exist, each of us can overcome them. We can learn to exercise our right to express ourselves comfortably without denying the rights of others. There are some simple guidelines available to help us.

"The most important thing to remember about self-expression is to be honest and open about what we are feeling. This is necessary because it allows us to feel good about ourselves, it allows others to be honest when expressing themselves, and it does not require anyone to make guesses about what others are feeling.

"When expressing oneself, it is necessary to be firm and direct but respectful of others. We can express opinions that are quite different from the opinions of others without being offensive. If we act in a respectful manner, others will act that way toward us.

"Another guideline to be aware of is that the substance of what we say and the manner in which we say it are both important. The nonverbal style with which words are expressed may say as much as the words themselves. Nonverbal style includes such things as eye contact, facial expression, gestures, and the tone, volume, and inflection of our voices.

"If we are somewhat nervous about expressing ourselves, we can help overcome our anxiety by making positive self-statements about the worth of our feelings and our ability to state them. It is also worthwhile to remember that self-expression is like many other things in our lives—the more often we do it, the easier it becomes."

Process: Present material on guidelines to follow when expressing oneself. Provide opportunities for participants to make additional points. Use the easel or chalkboard to list the following key points:

> - honesty
> - firmness
> - directness
> - respect
> - effective nonverbal statements
> - positive self-statements

4. Discussion

Content:
    a. What are your attitudes about expressing yourself?
    b. Are you more comfortable in some situations than in others? If so, what are they?
    c. What obstacles are in the way of expressing yourself?
    d. Are you fearful you will hurt someone's feelings when you talk? Why or why not?
    e. Are you fearful someone will hurt your feelings when you talk? Why or why not?

Process: Conduct discussion using above questions. Encourage all participants to contribute to the discussion.

5. Learning Activity

Content: "Each of you has a blank sheet of paper. Please draw a square (approximately three inches per side) in the middle of the sheet. Inside the square, at the top, write your name. Still inside the square, write three things you learned about walking by participating in this program (e.g., importance of stretching, proper techniques, walking can be fun). Now draw a straight line from the top left corner of your square to the top left corner of the sheet of paper. Connect the remaining corners of your square with their corresponding corners on the sheet of paper. You now have four sections on your paper.

"In the top part, write three things you liked best about this program (e.g., the exercise, my walking partner, the pace we walked). In the bottom section, write three things you liked least about this program (e.g., time of the day, the route(s) we walked, the noise from the streets). In the right-hand section, write three things you like to do when walking (e.g., whistle, listen to the birds, watch the sunset). In the left-hand section, write three things that can prevent you from enjoying a walk (e.g., fear of dogs, too cold and windy, too crowded). We are now going to take turns and share our responses with the group."

Process: Conduct learning activity. Have sufficient paper and pencils available for participants. Draw model on chalkboard of the way the paper should look after directions are completed. Allow a few minutes for completion of each section of paper. Attempt to stimulate a response from each participant.

6. Debriefing

Content:
    a.   Was it easier to write your responses to the items than to say them aloud? Why?
    b.   What are your reactions to the responses of others about the walking program?
    c.   Would you recommend changes in the walking program? If so, what are they?
    d.   Are you pleased with your efforts in the walking program?
    e.   Did you get the benefits you wanted from this program?

Process: Conduct debriefing. Provide an opportunity for questions and comments.

7. Conclusion

Content: "It is important for you to examine your feelings about your involvement in the walking program. This will help you make decisions regarding your future participation in walking for leisure. It is equally important that you share your feelings about the walking program with us. If we know the things you liked and disliked about the program, we can make improvements in it that will benefit future participants."

Process: Make concluding statements. Provide an opportunity for participants to ask questions. Thank walkers for their input and participation in the program.

LEISURE EDUCATION GARDENING PROGRAM

Purpose, Goals, and Objectives

Purpose: Provide opportunities for participants to gain insight into the process of gardening as a leisure experience, acquire knowledge about planting and harvesting a vegetable garden, increase their understanding of leisure resources associated with gardening, learn skills associated with gardening, and acquire knowledge about plant maintenance.

Goal 1: Demonstrate knowledge of gardening and its potential as a leisure experience.

Objective 1.1.   Demonstrate knowledge of the meaning of gardening.
Objective 1.2.   Demonstrate knowledge of personal attitudes relative to gardening.
Objective 1.3.   Demonstrate knowledge of gardening as a leisure experience.

Goal 2: Demonstrate knowledge related to planting and harvesting a vegetable garden.

Objective 2.1.   Demonstrate knowledge of vegetables that can be grown in a garden.
Objective 2.2.   Demonstrate the ability to decide what to grow in a vegetable garden.
Objective 2.3.   Demonstrate knowledge about using a garden harvest.

Goal 3: Demonstrate knowledge of gardening equipment and resources.

Objective 3.1.   Demonstrate the ability to identify gardening equipment.
Objective 3.2.   Demonstrate knowledge of the use of gardening equipment.
Objective 3.3.   Demonstrate knowledge of locating gardening materials/resources.
Objective 3.4.   Demonstrate knowledge of desired characteristics of a garden plot.
Objective 3.5.   Demonstrate knowledge of where plants and seeds can be obtained.

Goal 4: Demonstrate the ability to perform skills associated with vegetable gardening.

Objective 4.1.   Demonstrate the ability to use a hoe.
Objective 4.2.   Demonstrate the ability to use a trowel to uproot weeds or dig holes.
Objective 4.3.   Demonstrate the ability to place seeds in a furrow and cover with soil.
Objective 4.4.   Demonstrate the ability to use a watering can to water planted seeds.

Goal 5: Demonstrate knowledge of basic plant maintenance required for vegetable gardening.

Objective 5.1.   Demonstrate knowledge of how to water a garden.
Objective 5.2.   Demonstrate knowledge of how to fertilize vegetable plants.

Goals, Objectives, and Performance Measures

Goal 1: Demonstrate knowledge of gardening and its potential as a leisure experience.

Objective 1.1: Demonstrate knowledge of the meaning of gardening.

Performance Measure: Upon request and within three minutes, participant will demonstrate knowledge of the meaning of gardening by providing a verbal definition of a garden, including the following three elements:
  (a)   a plot of ground,
  (b)   manipulated by a human being, and
  (c)   to produce what that person wants,
on two consecutive occasions.

Objective 1.2: Demonstrate knowledge of personal attitudes relative to gardening.

Performance Measure: Upon request and within three minutes, participant will demonstrate knowledge of personal attitudes relative to gardening by verbally expressing two different feelings related to the activity (e.g., Gardening seems fun. I am afraid I will not succeed at gardening. Gardening has many rewards.), on two consecutive occasions.

Objective 1.3: Demonstrate knowledge of gardening as a leisure experience.

Performance Measure: Given pencil and paper, within 10 minutes participant will demonstrate knowledge of gardening as a leisure experience by identifying, in writing, five benefits of leisure that can be experienced through gardening (e.g., sense of freedom, happiness, increased self-esteem, enjoyment, social interaction, physical or mental fitness, stress reduction, skill development, and change of pace), on two consecutive occasions.

Goal 2: Demonstrate knowledge related to planting and harvesting a vegetable garden.

Objective 2.1: Demonstrate knowledge of vegetables that can be grown in a garden.

Performance Measure: Within five minutes, given a list of five vegetable families (e.g., beans, cabbages, corn, eggplant, greens, okra, onions, peanuts, peas, peppers, perennials, potatoes, root crops, sunflowers, tomatoes, and vine crops), participant will demonstrate knowledge of the types of vegetables by verbally stating two specific vegetables from each of the five families, on two consecutive occasions.

Objective 2.2: Demonstrate the ability to decide what to grow in a vegetable garden.

Performance Measure: Given pencil and paper, within 10 minutes participant will demonstrate knowledge of decision-making related to gardening by writing five questions that should be considered when planting a vegetable garden (e.g., What vegetables would I like to grow? Why would I like to grow these vegetables? Will my garden plot be suited to these vegetables? How much money will this require? What equipment is needed to plant and sustain these vegetables? Will I have the time to nurture what I plant? What use will I make of the harvest?), on two consecutive occasions.

Objective 2.3: Demonstrate knowledge about using a garden harvest.

Performance Measure: Given pencil, paper, and a list of five harvested vegetables (e.g., corn, pumpkin, peas, carrots, tomatoes), within 10 minutes participant will demonstrate knowledge relative to use of a garden harvest by writing two specific uses for each of the vegetables (e.g., eat them, use them as ornamentals, freeze them, can them, give them to others), on two consecutive occasions.

Goal 3: Demonstrate knowledge of gardening equipment and resources.

Objective 3.1: Demonstrate the ability to identify gardening equipment.

Performance Measure: Given pictures of nine different garden tools (e.g., square-ended spade, pointed shovel, rake, hoe, trowel, file or sharpening stone, garden hose, watering can, and wheelbarrow), within five minutes participant will demonstrate the ability to identify gardening equipment by correctly naming seven of the nine tools, on two consecutive occasions.

Objective 3.2: Demonstrate knowledge of the use of gardening equipment.

Performance Measure: Given pictures of nine different garden tools, within 10 minutes participant will demonstrate knowledge of the tools by correctly stating the intended function of seven of the nine tools, on two consecutive occasions.

Objective 3.3: Demonstrate knowledge of locating gardening materials/resources.

Performance Measure: Given paper, pencil, and a telephone directory, within 10 minutes participant will demonstrate knowledge of how to locate gardening materials and resources by making a list of the names, addresses, and telephone numbers of five retail and/or rental sources found in the directory, on two consecutive occasions.

Objective 3.4: Demonstrate knowledge of desired characteristics of a garden plot.

Performance Measure: Given paper, pencil, within 15 minutes, participant will demonstrate knowledge of the desired characteristics of a garden plot by listing four of the five basic requirements of plants (e.g., light, nutrients, water, reasonable temperatures, and freedom from pests and disease) and identifying and describing four of the six major soil types (e.g., clay, silts, loams, sand, chalks and limestone soils, peat and fen soils), on two consecutive occasions.

Objective 3.5: Demonstrate knowledge of where plants and seeds can be obtained.

Performance Measure: Upon request and within five minutes, participant will demonstrate knowledge of where to obtain plants and seeds by verbally identifying three local stores and two seed catalog companies where such material is available, on two consecutive occasions.

Goal 4: Demonstrate the ability to perform skills associated with vegetable gardening.

Objective 4.1: Demonstrate the ability to use a hoe.

Performance Measure: Given a hoe, within 10 minutes participant will demonstrate the ability to use the hoe by chopping weeds and tilling the soil to a depth of two inches in an assigned three-foot square plot, on two consecutive occasions.

Objective 4.2: Demonstrate the ability to use a trowel to uproot weeds or dig planting holes.

Performance Measure: Given a trowel, within 10 minutes, participant will demonstrate the ability to use the trowel by: (a) uprooting five weeds, (b) replacing the disturbed soil, and (c) digging two planting holes by removing the soil to a depth of six inches and piling it by the holes, on two consecutive occasions.

Objective 4.3: Demonstrate the ability to place seeds in a furrow and cover with soil.

Performance Measure: Given a prepared furrow and five minutes, participant will demonstrate the ability to plant an appropriate number of seeds by placing seeds one inch apart and covering them with one inch of soil, on two consecutive occasions.

Objective 4.4: Demonstrate the ability to use a watering can to water planted seeds.

Performance Measure: Given a watering can and five feet of planted furrow, participant will demonstrate the ability to water newly planted seeds adequately by: (a) applying water to the furrow from a height of less than one foot, (b) avoiding mud splatters, and (c) watering until the water no longer soaks into the ground, on two consecutive occasions.

Goal 5: Demonstrate knowledge of basic plant maintenance required for vegetable gardening.

Objective 5.1: Demonstrate knowledge of how to water a garden.

Performance Measure: Upon request and within five minutes, participant will demonstrate knowledge of how often and how much to water by verbally identifying six of the following eight conditions that influence the amount of water needed by a garden: (a) amount and frequency of rainfall, (b) temperature, (c) level of relative humidity, (d) amount of sunshine, (e) amount of wind, (f) porosity of soil, (g) type of plants and stage of growth, and (h) amount of mulch used, on two consecutive occasions.

Objective 5.2: Demonstrate knowledge of how to fertilize vegetable plants.

Performance Measure: Upon request and within three minutes, participant will demonstrate knowledge of how often and how much to fertilize vegetable plants by verbally stating that a weak application of fertilizer every other watering is appropriate, on three consecutive occasions.

Goals, Objectives, Content, and Process

Goal 1: Demonstrate knowledge of gardening and its potential as a leisure experience.

Objective 1.1: Demonstrate knowledge of the meaning of gardening.

1. Orientation Activity

Content: "To introduce us to the topic of gardening, we are going to play Gardening Word Scramble. In this activity, each of you will use the letters in the word GARDENING to make as many words of three or more letters as possible. In any one word, you may not use a letter any more times than it appears in GARDENING. You may use the letters 'g' and 'n' twice in any one word, but you may not repeat any other letters. Examples of words you can create out of G-A-R-D-E-N-I-N-G include 'grade,' 'red,' and 'drag.' There are many more you can create.

"Each of you has paper and pencil. Spell out the word GARDENING at the top of your paper. When I give you the signal to start, you will have 10 minutes to make as many words as you can. Are there questions? If not, you may begin."

Process: Distribute pencil and paper to each participant. Write GARDENING in large letters on chalkboard. Give signal to begin. When time has expired, ask participants for words they have created and put them on chalkboard. Give each participant opportunity to provide words. Commend participants with most words.

2. Introduction

Content: "Gardening is an extremely popular activity in this country and throughout the world. There are many forms of gardening, from plots in backyards and vacant lots to containers on patios and balconies. People garden, not only for the products they can grow and utilize, but also for the pleasure and satisfaction they derive from it. Gardening is considered by many to be the most popular pastime in the world. Millions of people garden. It is an activity that can be demanding and rewarding at the same time. It can be done so that it requires only a moderate amount of time or it can be expanded to demand a great deal of time. It can be planned to yield a few simple products or an extensive array of items. Gardening has the ability to accommodate all levels of skill and interest."

Process: Introduce topic on gardening as a leisure experience.

3. Presentation

Content: "A garden, by definition, is a plot of ground that has been manipulated by a person to produce what that person wants. This means the person has intervened to change the character of what would grow on a plot of ground, if that plot were left to its own devices. The intervention could include removing the natural vegetation, changing the composition of the soil, planting and nurturing different vegetation, harvesting the product, and reaping the benefits of the harvest. The most common garden is an area that produces vegetables, fruits, herbs, or flowers. But it can include trees, bushes, shrubs, and other forms of vegetation. Gardens can include arrangements of rock, bodies of water, and other landscaped features. In short, gardening means the altering and rearranging of the landscape to render it more useful or pleasing in some manner to humans. Although there are numerous types of gardens, the focus of this program is on vegetable gardens."

Process: When presenting material, speak clearly and with appropriate volume. Use pictures (slides, overhead transparencies, posters, or other means) to illustrate comments. Highlight the characteristics of gardening as follows:

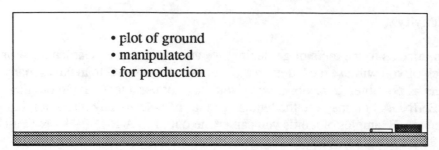

4. Discussion

Content:

    a. Define what is meant by gardening.

    b. How many kinds of gardens have you seen? What can you tell us about them?

    c. What did you like best about the gardens you have seen?

    d. If you have gardened, what kind of garden did you have?

    e. What would your ideal garden look like?

Process: Conduct discussion using above questions. Elicit comments from participants.

5. Learning Activity

Content: "We are going to make collages about gardens and gardening. Each of you will be given poster paper, scissors, paste, and several magazines about gardening. Cut pictures from the magazines, arrange them as you like, and paste them on the poster paper. When you are finished with your collages, we will look at and discuss each of them."

Process: Distribute magazines, scissors, paste, and poster paper. Give instructions for activity. Walk among participants, answer any questions that may be asked. Provide individual assistance, if requested.

6. Debriefing

Content:

    a. What do you see in the collage that relates to gardening?

    b. Can you identify any of the plants in the collage? If so, which ones?

    c. If there are people in the collage, what do they appear to be doing?

    d. Do they look as if they are enjoying themselves?

    e. Could they be experiencing leisure? How so?

Process: Conduct debriefing using above questions. Encourage participants to ask questions. Attempt to have all participants make a contribution.

7. Conclusion

Content: "With gardening we can spend much time with it as a full-time hobby or it can be something we use for a few minutes as a break from our normal daily routine. It can be a major recreation activity or one of many in which we participate. It will almost certainly be a source of pleasure and satisfaction. As you learn about gardening, you will have the opportunity and the responsibility to decide how you want to use your knowledge."

Process: Make concluding statements. Provide adequate opportunity for participants to ask questions.

Objective 1.2: Demonstrate knowledge of personal attitudes relative to gardening.

1. Orientation Activity

Content: "I am giving each of you a magic marker and a cardboard name tag. Please write your first name in bold letters across the top of the card. Under your name, draw a picture of how you feel about gardening. When you are finished, raise your hand and I will help you pin the card to your shirt. After you have your tag on, please mingle with the others and see if you can guess what feelings each person's drawing represents. Make sure that you say each person's first name before you try to guess how he or she feels about gardening."

Process: Obtain magic markers and cardboard name tags. Arrange participants in a circle. Move about the room providing assistance as needed.

2. Introduction

Content: "The attitude of a person is affected by many factors. Present circumstances, past experiences, level of energy, time and money available, feelings of families and friends, level of knowledge, and social approval or disapproval are some of the factors that affect the way we think and feel about specific things in our lives. We are going to explore our attitudes toward gardening and share them with each other."

Process: Introduce topic on personal attitudes relative to gardening. Emphasize the relationship between attitudes and behaviors.

3. Presentation

Content: "In exploring attitudes toward gardening, it may be helpful to begin by trying to identify the attitude and interest of the public. What do you think about the following:
   a.   How common is gardening in this country?
   b.   What evidence do you see that indicates gardening's popularity?
   c.   Why do you think people garden?
   d.   Do urban Americans do much gardening?
   e.   What do you think they get out of it?
   f.   Can you see anything that might change people's attitudes toward gardening?

"Your personal attitude toward gardening might be similar to the public attitude or it might be different in some ways. How do you respond to the following:
   a.   Have you done any gardening in the past?
   b.   If so, how has that influenced the way you feel about gardening?
   c.   How do you feel about gardening?
   d.   What do you expect to derive from a gardening experience?
   e.   Where does gardening rank in your list of favorite things to do?
   f.   What would have to happen to cause you to change your ranking of gardening?"

Process: Use above questions to encourage participants to share opinions and attitudes with group. Give each participant an opportunity to contribute.

4. Discussion

Content:
    a. Are there other questions we should consider in order to learn more about our attitudes? If so, what are they?
    b. Are you comfortable sharing your attitude about gardening? Why or why not?
    c. Has your attitude toward gardening changed in the past several years? If so, how has it changed?
    d. How do you think participation in this class will influence your attitude?

Process: Conduct discussion using above questions. Encourage all participants to make a contribution.

5. Learning Activity

Content: "We are going to have small group discussions to further explore our attitudes toward gardening. I will describe three different situations to you. Imagine you are in each situation as it is described. For each situation, think about what your attitude and feelings about gardening would be.

    a. *Situation One.* You are a member of a family of seven and you work in a factory. You are the only family member that receives an income. You live in a house that sits on a double lot. There is a space for a garden.

    b. *Situation Two.* There are four people in your family and both parents work full-time, one as a retail salesperson in a shopping mall and the other in a downtown office building. You live in a house in a suburban area, on a lot that has an adequate backyard. Part of the backyard could provide space for a garden.

    c. *Situation Three.* You are single and work in the data processing center for an insurance company. You live in a high-rise apartment building. There is a balcony that runs the length of your apartment. The balcony has space for planters."

Process: Divide participants into small groups. Describe situation one. Allow ample time for discussion. Move from group to group to observe, intervene if necessary to get dialogue started. Encourage everyone to participate. Repeat process for situations two and three.

6. Debriefing

Content:
    a. Did your attitudes toward gardening remain the same from situation to situation?
    b. If your attitude changed, why do you think it changed?
    c. In which situation would you have felt most comfortable? Why?
    d. In which situation would you have felt least comfortable? Why?

Process: Conduct debriefing using above questions. Encourage all participants to make a contribution.

7. Conclusion

Content: "Some of you may be in the process of forming your attitudes about gardening. Some of you may have attitudes that are changing. Your attitudes are your own property and should be based on your feelings and experiences. If gardening is fun for you, if it is an activity that allows you to make choices and exercise responsibility, if it gives you a feeling of reward and satisfaction, these things will be reflected in your attitude."

Process: Make concluding statements. Allow participants to ask questions.

Objective 1.3: Demonstrate knowledge of gardening as a leisure experience.

1. Orientation Activity

Content: "We are going to do an activity to get us thinking about gardening as a recreation activity. We will take turns trying to complete the statement: 'My name is _____ and I like gardening because it is _____.' We will try to complete the statement by using our first name and a word that begins with the same letter as our first name. For example, 'My name is Susan and I like gardening because it is satisfying.' If you have trouble thinking of only one word, you may use a phrase. Be creative."

Process: Have participants seated in a circle. Give directions for activity. Provide example using own name. When participants have responded, ask question: "Is the reason you like gardening associated with fun or leisure? If so, how? If not, why not?"

2. Introduction

Content: "Although gardening, like many other things, has the potential to be a recreation activity, it is the attitude and feelings of the individual that determines whether it actually is. We know that many people consider gardening to be a prime recreation activity. It will be helpful to consider gardening's potential as a recreation activity for us."

Process: Introduce topic of gardening as a recreation activity.

3. Presentation

Content: "We know that leisure can be a state of mind, characterized by feelings of satisfaction and enjoyment from experiencing an activity that is freely chosen. It is associated with a sense of competence and good feelings when participating. We also know that leisure is a matter of individual preference and varies among people. An activity that one person considers leisure may be considered as work by the next person. An activity may be considered as leisure by an individual at one time but not at another time.

"Gardening is an activity that requires planned, purposeful action by the gardener. Gardening is started with a specific purpose in mind and requires involvement over an extended period of time. Gardening also brings rewards of various kinds to its participants. Our purpose is to examine both leisure and gardening."

Process: Present information on leisure and gardening. Provide opportunities for participants to make comments and ask questions.

4. Discussion

Content:
   a.   What is leisure?
   b.   Why is there a difference when people think about whether specific activities are leisure?
   c.   How can we determine if gardening is leisure for some individuals?

Process: Conduct discussion using above questions. Attempt to have all participants contribute to the discussion.

5. Learning Activity

Content: "How can gardening fit into the framework of leisure? We can begin to answer this question by making a list of benefits that are related to leisure participation. Please get into groups of three or four and make a list of the things you think people get from engaging in leisure. You can include benefits you have personally experienced from leisure. What will be on your list? Now compile a list of the benefits that can be attributed to gardening. You can draw from your personal experience for this list, too. Let us compare the two lists."

Process: Divide participants into groups. Provide pencil and paper. For comparison, put lists on chalkboard. If necessary, add to lists. Leave lists on chalkboard and move to debriefing. Possible benefits of leisure could include the following list:

• sense of freedom	• stress reduction
• happiness	• skill development
• increased self-esteem	• change of pace
• enjoyment	
• social interaction	
• physical or mental fitness	

Possible benefits of gardening could include the following:

- enjoyment of nature
- freedom to choose what to plant and grow
- satisfaction derived from nurturing
- enjoyment of harvest
- change from regular routine
- aesthetic satisfaction
- relaxation, feeling of calmness

6. Debriefing

Content:
   a.   Do you see any similarities between the two lists? If so, what are they?
   b.   Do you see why many people consider gardening to be a prime recreation activity?
   c.   Do you feel gardening is a recreation activity for you? Why or why not?

Process: Conduct debriefing using above questions. Attempt to have all participants contribute to the discussion.

7. Conclusion

Content: "Gardening is leisure for people throughout the world. It has the potential to be leisure for you. It will be your attitude that determines whether it is or is not. If gardening is approached with the appropriate frame of mind, it can provide rewards that are as satisfying as any other activity. For some individuals, it can provide rewards that are not available anywhere else."

Process: Make concluding statements. Encourage participants to ask questions about gardening as a recreation activity.

Goal 2: Demonstrate knowledge related to planting and harvesting a vegetable garden.

Objective 2.1: Demonstrate knowledge of vegetables that can be grown in a garden.

1. Orientation Activity

Content: "We are going to play Upset the Vegetable Garden. If you have ever played Upset the Fruit Basket, you will know how to play this game. Please arrange your chairs in a circle. When we begin the activity, we will remove one chair. This activity requires one less seat than there are players.

"I will assign each of you the name of a vegetable. You must remember this name. We will begin by one person being designated as 'IT' and going to the center of the circle. When 'IT' calls out the name of a vegetable, all persons who have been assigned that name must leave their seat and find a new place to sit. 'IT' will also try to sit in a seat that has just been vacated. If 'IT' is successful, the person who is left without a place to sit becomes the new 'IT.' If 'IT' is unsuccessful, the process repeats itself with the name of a new vegetable being called out. When 'IT' says "Upset the Vegetable Garden," everyone must get up and find a new seat, while 'IT' also tries to be seated. Do you have any questions about this activity? After I assign you names, we will play a practice round."

Process: Seat participants in a circle. After "IT" has been designated, remove one chair from the circle. Assign vegetable names to participants, distributing them evenly. There must be at least two participants per vegetable. Monitor activity to encourage participation and to settle disputes.

2. Introduction

Content: "Gardens can produce a variety of vegetables. Some vegetables can be harvested early in the gardening season, some midway through the season, and some at the end. Good planning can help the gardener get a fairly steady harvest throughout the season. Gardens can also produce vegetables for more than one purpose. Having knowledge regarding the possibilities of what can be included in a garden is important."

Process: Introduce topic of vegetable gardening.

3. Presentation

Content: "Most people agree that the primary purpose of a garden is to produce edible vegetables. Edible simply means it can be eaten as food. A few people, however, see the growing of ornamentals as the major purpose of their gardens. Ornamentals are vegetables that are often used as display items. Examples of ornamentals include cucumbers, pumpkins, squash, watermelons, and ears of corn. Most edibles could be displayed as ornamentals, and ornamentals are also edible.

"Garden vegetables can be roughly grouped as follows: (a) bean family (includes snap, shell, and soy beans), (b) cabbage family (includes broccoli, brussel sprouts, cabbage, cauliflower, and kohlrabi, (c) corn, (d) eggplant, (e) greens family (includes celery, chard, collard, endive, kale, lettuce, mustard, and spinach), (f) okra, (g) onion family (includes garlic, leeks, onions, and shallots), (h) peanuts, (i) peas, (j) peppers, (k) perennials (includes asparagus, rhubarb, horseradish, and strawberries), (l) potatoes, (m) root crop family (includes beets, carrots, parsnips, radishes, rutabagas, and turnips) (n) sunflowers, (o) tomatoes, and (p) vine crop family (includes cucumbers, melons, pumpkins, squash, and zucchini). It is evident that there is a wide variety of vegetables from which to choose. Part of the fun of gardening is getting to choose the mix of vegetables to plant."

Process: Present information on vegetable families. Use pictures of vegetable with associated names to illustrate comments. Prepare handout of vegetable families to distribute to participants. Have as many actual vegetables as possible available for participants to see and hold.

 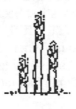 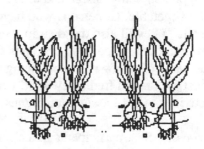

4. Discussion

Content:
    a. What is the difference between an edible and an ornamental?
    b. Can you identify three different families of garden vegetables?
    c. Can you identify a specific member of those families?
    d. What is the advantage of planting different kinds of vegetables?
    e. What is your favorite garden vegetable? Why?

Process: Conduct discussion using above questions. Encourage all participants to contribute to the discussion.

5. Learning Activity

Content: "To become more familiar with the variety of vegetables available, we are going to make some pictures of the vegetable families we discussed and of the vegetables that did not fit neatly into family categories. I am going to divide you into small groups and give each group a list of the garden vegetables we have discussed. I am also going to supply each group with seed and gardening catalogs. Search through the catalogs and cut out as many examples of vegetables you can find that are on the list. On poster paper, write the name of the vegetable (or its family) and paste a picture of it next to the name. For example, you might write CABBAGE FAMILY on the poster and then find pictures of broccoli, cabbage, and cauliflower to paste by it. Try to find at least one example for each vegetable on the list. When we are finished, we will display each of the posters."

Process: Prepare handouts of vegetable list ahead of session. Divide into groups. Supply scissors, paste, and pencils to each group. Move among groups to give assistance where needed.

6. Debriefing

Content:
   a. What vegetables were unfamiliar to you before we started this activity?
   b. Which vegetables are most difficult to identify?
   c. Is there enough variety from which to choose?

Process: Conduct debriefing using above questions. Encourage all participants to answer the questions.

7. Conclusion

Content: "If variety is the spice of life, the same may be said of vegetable gardens. There is an abundance of vegetables that can be planted, tended, and harvested. Knowing the possibilities adds to the fun and enjoyment of gardening."

Process: Make concluding statements. Provide the chance for participants to ask questions.

Objective 2.2: Demonstrate the ability to decide what to grow in a vegetable garden.

1. Orientation Activity

Content: "Each of you will be given a sheet of paper containing a list of vegetables, an empty vegetable seed package which will be pinned to your shirt, and a pencil. You must find people with a seed package on their shirt that is included in the list on your sheet. After you find a person, ask the person his or her name and write it in the column to the the left of the vegetable. You will be required to complete the sheet as quickly as possible."

Process: Make up sheets with vegetables listed in the left column and a column to the right that is blank. The blank side will be the area that participants will record the name of the people they find. Make sufficient copies of sheet for participants. Collect enough empty seed packets, pins and pencils prior to the activity to accommodate all participants.

2. Introduction

Content: "Given the many vegetables available, the gardener must make careful decisions about which to plant. The decisions that are made will have consequences that are felt throughout the gardening season. They will influence planting times, cultivation practices, time of harvest, and enjoyment of the harvest. Decisions should be the result of a reasoned process, rather than haphazard guesses."

Process: Introduce topic of making decisions about what to grow in a garden.

3. Presentation

Content: "Deciding what to plant in the garden is a fundamental first step that must be accomplished. There are many factors that affect gardening decisions but the focus here is on which vegetables to plant. It is the gardener's responsibility to make these decisions. The way decisions are made is important. The following suggestions should help:
   a.   Identify all possibilities.
   b.   Weigh value and benefits of each possibility against other possibilities.
   c.   Narrow the choices.
   d.   Choose the best possibilities.
   e.   Evaluate the choices at the appropriate times.

"There are some specific questions that should be considered when deciding which vegetables to plant in the garden. Examples of such questions include:
   a.   What vegetables would I like to grow?
   b.   Why would I like to grow these vegetables?
   c.   Will my garden plot be suited to these vegetables?
   d.   How much money will this require?
   e.   What equipment is needed to plant and sustain these vegetables?
   f.   Will I have the time to nurture what I plant?
   g.   What use will I make of the harvest?

Answering these and similar questions will be helpful in making decisions regarding which vegetables to plant."

Process: Present information on making decisions regarding which vegetables to plant. List decision-making suggestions on chalkboard. Use above questions to stimulate dialogue among participants.

4. Discussion

Content:
   a.   Who should decide what to plant in a garden? Why?
   b.   How should decisions be made regarding what to plant in a garden?
   c.   How will you choose the vegetables that will be planted in your garden?
   d.   What vegetables will you choose?
   e.   What vegetables would be in your ideal garden?
   f.   If there is a difference between what your ideal planting would be and what you will actually plant, what accounts for the difference?

Process: Conduct discussion using above questions. Encourage all participants to respond to the questions.

5. Learning Activity

Content: "Each of you will decide what you are going to plant in your garden. I am going to give each of you some seed and gardening catalogs. Your task is to look through these catalogs to help you decide what you want to plant. Make a list of the vegetables you want to have in your garden. Then make a drawing of your garden plot and show where each type of vegetable will be planted. Remember to allow for enough space between plants and between rows. Seed catalogs will provide you with that information. When you are finished, we will look at each of your garden plots and discuss your decisions."

Process: Distribute seed and gardening catalogs, pencil, and paper. Monitor participants to see if they need assistance. When drawing of garden plots is completed, move to debriefing.

6. Debriefing

Content:
    a. What vegetables did you decide to plant?
    b. How did you make your decision?
    c. How confident are you that you can raise the vegetables you chose?
    d. Can your garden plot hold everything you want to plant?
    e. If you had to remove a vegetable from the list of those you wanted to plant, which one would it be? Why?

Process: Conduct debriefing using above questions. Provide each participant with an opportunity to respond. Provide corrective feedback where appropriate.

7. Conclusion

Content: "Deciding what to plant in a garden is part of the fun of being a gardener. It is also an opportunity to exercise the freedom to choose and to demonstrate responsibility for your own actions. Making good planting decisions in gardening is the first step to a good harvest, with good things to eat and give to neighbors and friends."

Process: Make concluding statements. Provide opportunity for participants to ask questions.

Objective 2.3: Demonstrate knowledge about using a garden harvest.

1. Orientation Activity

Content: "Each of you is receiving a handout. The sentence on the handout reads 'If I grow vegetables, I most prefer to: (a) eat them fresh, (b) display them, (c) can them, (d) freeze them, (e) give them away, or (f) store them.' Choose one of the six choices that best describes your feelings. We will go around the group and ask you to introduce yourself, give your answer and tell why you choose that answer. We will continue around the room so we can get to know more about each other."

Process: Make up handouts in advance that contain the different options for using vegetables. Arrange participants in a circle. Provide sufficient time for them to choose a response. Help participants who may have difficulty expressing their ideas.

2. Introduction

Content: "Many people believe that nothing tastes as good as the food they have grown themselves. Garden produce can be harvested when it is at its freshest and eaten without unnecessary delays. But it does not have to be eaten immediately. Some garden products can be stored or processed to last for an extended period of time following the harvest."

Process: Introduce topic of using a garden harvest.

3. Presentation

Content: "Deciding how to use the harvest from a vegetable garden is related to why the garden was planted. If you wanted to grow fresh vegetables to eat, that option is available. If the purpose was to grow ornamentals, the vegetables can be used in that manner. If there was a desire to freeze or can vegetables for eating at a later time, that can also be done. Other options include giving the harvest to friends, neighbors, the needy, or storing it for later use. A nice thing about a garden harvest is that all of these things can be done. Choosing to do one thing does not stop you from doing others.

"There are other things that will affect decisions about use of the harvest. Whether a gardener has a freezer, storage space, or the resources to do some canning are important considerations. Time and money play a role in decision-making. Whatever decisions are made, they are usually a source of great satisfaction and pleasure to the gardener."

Process: Present information on use of harvest. List options for use on chalkboard. List factors that influence decisions. Identify primary ways as listed below:

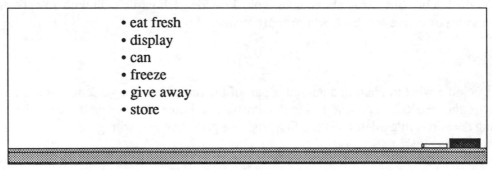

- eat fresh
- display
- can
- freeze
- give away
- store

4. Discussion

Content:
    a. What different uses can be made of a garden harvest?
    b. How will you decide what use to make of your harvest?
    c. When do you have to decide how to use a harvest.
    d. At this time, what use do you think you will make of your harvest?
    e. Do you have all the resources necessary to use your harvest as you wish?

Process: Conduct discussion using above questions. Encourage all participants to answer the questions.

5. Learning Activity

Content: "Let us think ahead about how we will use the harvest from our gardens. Make a list of the types of vegetables you plan to harvest. For each type of vegetable, indicate what you plan to do with it. You can plan several uses of any garden product. For example, pumpkin: make pumpkin pie, make Halloween jack-o-lantern, give to neighbor, enter in county fair. When the lists are finished, we will share them with each other."

Process: Distribute pencil and paper for lists. Encourage participants to be creative but realistic. Provide each participant with opportunity to share by moving on to debriefing.

6. Debriefing

Content:
    a.   How do you plan to use your garden harvest?
    b.   How did you make your decisions?
    c.   What rewards do you anticipate?
    d.   How confident are you that you will be able to do as you plan?

Process: Conduct debriefing using above questions. Ensure all participants contribute to the discussion.

7. Conclusion

Content: "Harvesting a garden is the end of many weeks of effort. Although there is joy in harvesting, there also is satisfaction in doing the things necessary to get to the point where harvesting is possible. Deciding how to use the harvest is another example of how gardening provides freedom of choice and the chance to be responsible for our actions."

Process: Make concluding statements. Provide opportunity for questions.

Goal 3: Demonstrate knowledge of gardening equipment and resources.

Objective 3.1: Demonstrate the ability to identify gardening equipment.

1. Orientation Activity

Content: "I am going to attach a tag on the back of each of you. Each tag will contain the name of a garden tool or a piece of gardening equipment. By moving around and looking, you will be able to read the tags of everyone else, but you will not know what is on your tag. The object of this activity is to find out what is written on your tag. You may do this by asking questions of others in the group. The questions must be able to be answered with 'yes' or 'no.' Ask no more than three questions of any one person. When you identify what is on your own tag, have someone remove your tag, place it in the box in the front of the room and continue to mingle with the others, attempting to help them discover their garden tool."

Process: Prepare tags prior to session. Make sure sufficient tags and pins are available. Write the names of tools or pieces of equipment that will be topic of today's presentation. Examples: hoe, rake, trowel, hose. Names may be repeated. Move among players as they participate. When fewer players remain, provide helpful hints to avoid any embarrassment about being unable to identify tag.

2. Introduction

Content: "Gardening tools help gardeners perform their tasks in the most efficient manner. There is a wide variety of tools available and buying all of them can be expensive. It pays to know something about gardening equipment and which pieces of equipment are necessary to start and maintain a garden."

Process: Introduce topic of gardening tools.

3. Presentation

Content: "Garden tools are somewhat like clothes; they should be tried on for size before they are purchased. Tools should fit the height, weight, and body strength of the gardener. For example, long-handled spades should be used by tall people, but they are difficult for shorter folks to use. Like-wise, short-handled spades would require tall persons to work in an uncomfortable bent position, causing back strain and making the work unnecessarily difficult.

"All tools should be well-balanced and the gardener's grip on the tool should feel comfortable. The working end of the tool (for example, a shovel blade, rake teeth, or fork tines) should be sturdy but it does not have to be heavy. Many tools are available in stainless steel. They are a little more expensive but worth the extra cost. They are very durable and easy to use.

"Only basic equipment is needed to start and maintain a garden. The following items are considered to be the most essential: (a) square-ended spade, (b) pointed shovel, (c) rake, (d) hoe, (e) trowel, (f) file or sharpening stone, (g) garden hose, (h) watering can, and (i) wheelbarrow (depending on distance of garden). There are many other items available, such as sprayers, tillers, and weed forks. They all have their uses but can be acquired gradually. The above list is what is needed to get started."

Process: Present information on garden tools and equipment. Have samples of each available. Give participants opportunity to handle the items. Display items while discussing their use.

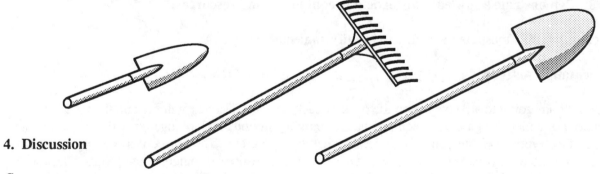

4. Discussion

Content:
   a. Why should garden tools "fit" the gardener?
   b. How can you tell if a tool is "right" for you?
   c. Why should gardeners consider getting stainless steel tools?
   d. What are five tools or pieces of equipment used for starting and maintaining a garden?

Process: Conduct discussion using above questions. Attempt to have each participant contribute to the discussion.

5. Learning Activity

Content: "We are going to do an activity that will allow us to identify various kinds of garden tools and equipment. Each of you has a pencil and paper. I am going to show you pictures of garden tools and equipment. Each picture is numbered and will contain only one tool. Put the number on your paper and then identify the tool that was pictured with that number. For example, if a picture is numbered with '1' and you think the tool shown with it is a hoe, put the number '1', followed by the word 'hoe' on your paper."

Process: Prepare pictures in advance. Use tools and equipment that have just been discussed. Distribute pencil and paper. Use overhead transparencies, enlarged pictures from books or catalogs, drawings on poster boards, or whatever is available. Ensure that participants can see picture and number. Allow 30-45 seconds per picture before showing next one. Repeat showing of any picture requested. Collect papers when finished.

6. Debriefing

Content:
  a. What did you learn from this activity?
  b. Were there any items that were difficult to identify? If so, why?
  c. Do you want to see any of the pictures again?

Process: Conduct debriefing using above questions. Encourage participants to contribute.

7. Conclusion

Content: "Gardening does not require many tools but the tools it does require make gardening much easier. They aid in completing tasks that help you develop a healthy and productive garden. Knowledge of basic gardening tools is essential for success."

Process: Make concluding statements. Provide opportunities for questions.

Objective 3.2: Demonstrate knowledge of the use of gardening equipment.

1. Orientation Activity

Content: "Each of you is receiving five cards. Do not allow the other participants to see your cards. If you see someone standing alone go up to that person and introduce yourself. Ask the person for a specific card that matches one of yours. If the player has such a card, then he or she will give you that card and ask you for a different one that matches one in his or her hand. If the person does not have the card for which you asked, they will then ask you for one. Once each of you has had a chance to ask each other for a card, look for another person with whom to talk."

Process: Make up several cards of each of the nine gardening tools. Have a picture and the name of the tool on each card. Monitor the group and assist participants as needed.

2. Introduction

Content: "Garden tools are designed to perform specific functions. When used as designed, they make the gardener's job easier and contribute to a healthy and productive garden. Like all tools, they should be used only for their specific function and not be abused. For example, the end of a spade or shovel should not be used as a hammer. Garden tools used properly and kept in good working order will last indefinitely."

Process: Introduce topic of using gardening tools.

3. Presentation

Content: "Gardening tools have not changed much in a long time. They make gardening possible. Knowing how and why to use garden tools contributes to the pleasure of the gardener and the health of the garden. The functions of garden tools are, briefly:
   a.   Spade: dig holes or divide soil, usually has tread for foot to force blade into earth.
   b.   Shovel: dig many different size holes.
   c.   Rake: break up and smooth soil, gather pulled weeds, clippings, and other items.
   d.   Hoe: cultivate and aerate soil, dig small weeds between rows of vegetables.
   e.   Trowel: dig weeds and small planting holes, harvest small, underground vegetables.
   f.   File or sharpening stone: keep a keen edge on tool blades.
   g.   Garden hose: deliver water to plants, usually over a large area.
   h.   Watering can: water seedlings or dispense dissolved nutrients.
   i.   Wheelbarrow: transport equipment or items, such as fertilizer, soil, or compost."

Process: Present information on use of garden tools. Have samples of tools available. Demonstrate use of each tool as it is discussed. Use cards with names of tools. Place the cards in front of the tools.

- spade
- shovel
- rake
- hoe
- trowel

- file or sharpening stone
- garden hose
- watering can
- wheelbarrow

4. Discussion

Content:
   a.   How long can you expect garden tools to last?
   b.   What can you do to help garden tools last?
   c.   Why is it important to know the proper use of garden tools?
   d.   What is an example of the proper use of (select any tool described above)?
   e.   What is an example of an inappropriate use of (tool used in previous question)?

Process: Conduct discussion using above questions. Encourage all participants to contribute to the discussion.

5. Learning Activity

Content: "Gardeners need to know the appropriate use of tools available to them. We are going to do a pencil and paper exercise that will help us find out how much we know and what we have yet to learn. This is a matching exercise. I am going to give you a sheet of paper that has two columns. The left-hand column contains names of garden tools and equipment; each tool is preceded by a number. The right-hand column contains functions of these items but in a random order; each function is preceded by a blank space (_____). Match each tool with its function by placing its number in the appropriate blank."

Process: Prepare sheets with matching exercise ahead of session. Ensure pencils are available. Use names of tools discussed in this session. Allow an appropriate amount of time for this exercise, depending on skill level of participants. Collect and correct papers. Provide feedback during debriefing.

6. Debriefing

Content:
    a.   Are there any tools whose use you wish to review? If so, which ones?
    b.   How comfortable are you with your level of knowledge on the use of garden tools?
    c.   Did you enjoy the learning activity. If so, why? If not, why not?

Process: Conduct debriefing using above questions. Check papers to see if more attention should be given to specific tools.

7. Conclusion

Content: "Making appropriate use of garden tools is a characteristic of good gardeners. Using tools properly protects the investment that was made in them and enhances the satisfaction that comes from gardening."

Process: Make concluding statements. Allow participants to ask questions.

Objective 3.3: Demonstrate knowledge of locating gardening materials/resources.

1. Orientation Activity

Content: "We will divide into groups of no more than nine participants. Each of you will receive a picture of a garden tool and a number beside the tool. All those with number 1 on their cards go to this group forming a circle, those with the number 2 on them will be in this group forming a circle. Now that you are divided into groups, I want each of you to think of a physical action that best reflects the use of your tool. We will then go around the group and each of us will say our first name and use our action and say the name of the tool. I will begin by stating my name, using my action and then making the action of another person in the group. This person must shout his or her name, make the action and then make someone else's action. The game will continue in this way. If someone is having difficulty remembering his or her action, we will all wait for 10 seconds and then remind the person."

Process: Make up cards with pictures of tools and their names recorded on the cards. Make sure participants are arranged in a circle so that they are visible to one another. Assist any individuals having difficulty. Assist participants in developing recognizable signs. Continue the activity until interest wanes.

2. Introduction

Content: "Individuals who have done some lawn and yard work in the past may already have most of the equipment needed to start and maintain a garden. Others, who are just beginning, may need to know where to start looking for such equipment. Veteran gardeners and beginners alike can benefit from knowing where to look for help and find additional information relative to gardening."

Process: Introduce topic of locating gardening materials and resources.

3. Presentation

Content: "There are many places available to look for gardening equipment. A good place to start is in the yellow pages of the telephone directory. Nurseries and garden stores advertise in the yellow pages, giving their location, hours of operation, types of things carried, and telephone number. Hardware stores are also good places to look for gardening equipment. The yellow pages will list discount department stores. Such stores usually have a gardening section or carry a range of gardening equipment.

"Another place to look for gardening tools is in mail-order catalogs. Large retail chains, such as Sears, publish catalogs that include gardening equipment, along with the information necessary to order such equipment through the mail. Smaller stores that focus exclusively on lawn and garden materials also have catalogs.

"If a gardener needs a specific tool on occasion but does not need it regularly, an equipment rental store is a good place. Most rental stores have gardening equipment of various kinds. Using rental equipment requires careful, advanced planning.

"Another possible source of equipment is friends and neighbors. Depending on the relationship, a gardener can sometimes borrow equipment from friends or neighbors. It is probably a good idea to avoid borrowing equipment as a regular practice, but there may be occasions when it is appropriate to do so.

"In addition to equipment, gardeners also want information relative to common gardening practices or to special problems that arise. People employed by nurseries and gardening stores are often very helpful in supplying information. They can help identify problems and recommend solutions to those problems.

"Another source of information is the county extension agent. Every county has one. The county extension agent is the local representative of the U.S. Department of Agriculture and is also affiliated with the land grant university of the state. County extension agents provide a wide variety of services, including advice and information related to gardening. County extension offices also provide pamphlets and other printed material related to gardening. These materials are usually available free of charge."

Process: Present information on where to obtain tools and information. Have telephone directory and a variety of catalogs available. Provide address of county extension office. Use chalkboard to list main sources:

- telephone book
- hardware stores
- mail-order catalogs
- rental stores
- friends
- people at nurseries
- county extension agent

4. Discussion

Content:

   a. How can a telephone directory help you locate places to get gardening equipment?
   b. What are three sources of equipment that are likely to be in the telephone directory?
   c. What kind of information can you obtain over the telephone?
   d. Other than purchasing, what other options are there for getting gardening tools?
   e. Where can you get information or answers to questions regarding gardening?

Process: Conduct discussion using above questions. Encourage all participants to contribute to the discussion.

5. Learning Activity

Content: "We are going to compile a handy reference list of places where gardening tools and equipment can be obtained. I am going to place you in groups of three or four and give each group a telephone directory. Each group will use the directory to identify both retail and rental outlets for garden tools. Make a list of the sources you find by including their name, location, telephone number, days of the week they are open, hours of operation, types of equipment they have, whether they sell or rent, and if they accept charge cards. When each group has finished, we will compare results and make a master list. We will make copies of the master list and make sure each of you receives one."

Process: Divide into groups, with a telephone directory for each group. Provide a handout that lists all the information that participants should be collecting. Circulate among groups to provide assistance as needed. If more information is needed than is available in directory, consider having group member telephone to obtain it.

6. Debriefing

Content:

   a. Are there additional commercial outlets to add to the list?
   b. What other sources are there that are not included on the list?
   c. How will you make use of the list?
   d. Can you get the tools and information needed to get started?

Process: Conduct debriefing using above questions. Encourage all participants to contribute to the debriefing.

7. Conclusion

Content: "Gardeners often encounter situations where they need a tool they do not yet have or need an answer to a question. Knowing where to go to get the correct tool or the correct answer to a question allows you to demonstrate control and responsibility."

Process: Make concluding statements. Provide opportunity for questions.

Objective 3.4: Demonstrate knowledge of desired characteristics of a garden plot.

1. Orientation Activity

Content: "You are each being given a clear plastic bag containing soil. The object of this activity is to find the other people in the group that have the same type of soil. Once you have found the other people, introduce yourself and move to this table. Look on the wall in front of the table and you will see a chart of the different soils and their identifying characteristics. With the help of the chart, label the bags of soil. Once you have completed labeling the soil, tape the label to the bag and return to your seat. Once everyone is seated, each group will stand, introduce themselves, show the others their soil and identify the type of soil contained in the bags."

Process: Make up a chart of the different types of soil. Staple a small plastic bag of the soil to the chart. List the name and characteristics of the soil on the chart. Begin the activity with everyone seated in chairs in a circle and end the activity in this same formation. Obtain ink markers, paper labels, and tape prior to the session. Place the materials on a large table positioned in front of the soil chart. Assist participants as needed.

2. Introduction

Content: "Some plots of land are good for growing vegetable gardens; some are not. If you are going to expend time, money, and energy in gardening, a reasonable degree of success should follow. Choosing a good garden site is important to success. If a poor site is chosen, success may never come. Knowing what to look for in a plot of land is important."

Process: Introduce topic of desired characteristics of garden plots.

3. Presentation

Content: "Vegetable plants, like all other plants, have basic needs that must be met if they are to survive. The plot of ground that is selected must be able to meet these needs. Plants need light, nutrients, water, reasonable temperatures, and freedom from pests and disease.

"Careful location of a plot can provide the right amount of sunshine. Planting at the right time of the year can help us get reasonable temperatures. Cultivation, regular monitoring, and preventive measures can assist in the control of disease and pests. Watering at appropriate times is expected of the gardener, as is supplying fertilizers containing nutrients. Supplying water and nutrients is dependent on soil characteristics. The top layer of soil is most capable of supporting plant life. It is called the topsoil and may vary in depth from two inches to two feet. The topsoil is exposed to the sun and the air and is the most enriched by plant remains. There are many types of soil, but in general soils can be classified as follows:

a. *Clays*. When wet, clay soil is very sticky. When dry, it can be very hard, shrink, and crack. Its mineral particles are very small. This slows the movement of air and water. Thus, clay soils do not drain well. Clay soils can be improved by adding and mixing organic matter into them.

b. *Silts*. Silty soils have mineral particles that are just a little bit larger than those of clay soils, but they lack the chemical qualities of clay. They are less fertile than clay. After silts receive moisture, the surface tends to meld together; this slows the air and makes the soil more likely to erode.

c. *Loams*. These are the best soils for gardening. They contain a good mixture of different size particles. This means they have good drainage and aeration; they also hold plant nutrients well. Loams also contain good reserves of organic matter.

d. *Sands*. Sandy soils are composed of grains of silica and contain no plant nutrients. Their fertility depends on the other substances (e.g., clay and organic matter) mixed with it and their nutrients. Drainage is very rapid, resulting in the loss of nutrients. Sandy soils can be improved by mixing in clay and organic matter.

e. *Chalks and limestones*. They are generally very shallow and lack some elements. They are well-drained. Chalky and limestone soils can be improved by importing topsoil to increase their depths.

f. *Peat and fen soils*. These soils are comprised of partially decomposed organic matter and have little mineral content. When they are drained, they can be very fertile if the right nutrients are added.

"The best garden soil is loamy, dark and rich in color, and when formed into a ball, holds it shape but crumbles when touched. If the soil in a garden lacks these characteristics, it can be improved by adding materials. How can you tell what a soil needs for vegetable plants? Soils can be tested. Soil-testing kits can be purchased and the gardener can perform the tests or samples of soil can be sent to county extension offices or some nurseries, where experts will do the job and recommend the items to be added to the soil."

Process: Present information of garden needs and soil characteristics. Use chalkboard to list major requirements of gardens and major soil types. If possible, bring in soil samples. Provide participants opportunity to feel soil. Show soil testing kit.

4. Discussion

Content:
a. What basic requirements must plants have to survive?
b. What is topsoil and why is it important?
c. What are some of the different types of soil?
d. How do the soils differ from each other?
e. Which soil type is the best for gardening? Why?
f. How can you learn about the soil in your garden plot?

Process: Conduct discussion using above questions. Encourage participants to contribute to the discussion.

5. Learning Activity

Content: "Imagine where the best place in the entire world would be to have a garden. Think about this for a couple of minutes and then be prepared to finish this statement: 'The best place in the whole world where I could garden would be _____.'   Be creative and also be ready to tell us why you want to garden there. Examples of 'best places' could include the Garden of Eden, the White House Garden, or your backyard."

Process: Allow participants time to think. Make sure each participant has an opportunity to finish his or her sentences. After participants have identified their best place to garden, move immediately to debriefing.

6. Debriefing

Content:
    a.   Why did you choose the place you did?
    b.   Do you think it will receive enough sunlight and moisture?
    c.   What kind of soil characteristics do you think it will have?
    d.   Do you think the soil will be easy to cultivate?
    e.   What might you grow there?

Process: Conduct debriefing using above questions. Elicit responses from each participant.

7. Conclusion

Content: "Soil fertility is one of the most important signs of whether a plot of ground can support a good garden. Gardeners can enhance fertility by learning about the soil and taking steps to add elements that are lacking. Being a good gardener means knowing some basic facts about soil."

Process: Make concluding statements. Provide opportunities for asking questions.

Objective 3.5: Demonstrate knowledge of where plants and seeds can be obtained.

1. Orientation Activity

Content: "Please get into a circle. We are going to do an activity called 'Telephone.' I will whisper a message into the ear of a person in the circle. That person, in turn, will whisper the message into the ear of the person on the right. This process will repeat itself until the message makes its way around the circle and returns to me. We will see how close it is to the original message."

Process: Form participants into circle. Prepare several messages ahead of time (e.g., 'The best place to get watermelon seeds to grow the biggest, sweetest watermelons is not at a seed store, but in the middle of a watermelon.'). Messages should pertain to seeds and gardening. Start each message at a different point in the circle. Conduct a brief discussion after each message has gone around the circle.

2. Introduction

Content: "Getting plants and seeds to put in the ground is useful to gardening. Knowing where and how to get plants and seeds is important and can be fun. Some gardeners gather seeds from plants, with the intent of planting them during the next gardening season. But most gardeners find it easier and inexpensive to buy packaged seeds."

Process: Introduce topic of where plants and seeds can be found for planting in a garden.

3. Presentation

Content: "When buying packaged seeds and bedding plants, there are options. Local nurseries, gardening specialty stores, hardware stores, and department stores with gardening sections generally carry a wide selection. Bedding plants should always be purchased from local stores. They are more likely to be healthy and, if problems with them arise, gardeners can go directly to the source for help in solving problems or replacing them. Before making a trip to a local store, information about varieties available can be obtained by telephone.

"Packaged seeds can be purchased locally or from mail-order supply houses. Mail-order businesses that sell packaged seeds produce and distribute colorful and attractive catalogs. They also advertise, providing information about how to get their catalogs. When a gardener buys something through a catalog or simply requests the catalog, the gardener's name is usually placed on a mailing list and catalogs are automatically mailed in the future."

Process: Present information on where to obtain seeds and bedding plants. Have samples of seed packets, bedding plants, and seed catalogs available.

4. Discussion

Content:
    a. Where can you get seeds and plants for your garden?
    b. Why is it best to buy bedding plants from local sources?
    c. How can you get a catalog from a seed company?
    d. How can you get on the mailing list for catalogs from seed companies?

Process: Conduct discussion using above questions and encourage all participants to contribute to the discussion.

5. Learning Activity

Content: "We are going to take a field trip to a local nursery. While we are there, one of their staff will visit with us and answer questions we have about seeds and bedding plants. Begin to think of questions you want to ask when we are there. We will have time to see the bedding plants and seed packets, and other things that interest us."

Process: Prearrange visit with local nursery. Take necessary steps for transportation to and from nursery. Prepare participants to ask questions. Monitor class for attentiveness.

6. Debriefing

Content:
    a. What did you like best about the visit to the nursery?
    b. What did you learn about bedding plants and seeds?

    c.   What did you learn about how to use a nursery?
    d.   What other nurseries can you visit?
    e.   Did you get your question answered at the nursery?
    f.   Do you have any new questions?

Process: Conduct debriefing using above questions and encourage all participants to contribute to the debriefing.

7. Conclusion

Content: "Buying seeds and bedding plants is much easier than growing your own. Beginning gardeners should purchase seeds and plants from commercial outlets where you can shop as early as you would in a supermarket."

Process: Make concluding statements. Provide opportunity for questions.

Goal 4: Demonstrate the ability to perform skills associated with vegetable gardening.

Objective 4.1: Demonstrate the ability to use a hoe.

1. Orientation Activity

Content: "Each of you has been given a hoe with a brightly colored picture of a square or a circle. Find the colored picture attached to your hoe. Once you have found your colored shape, find the other person in the group that has a hoe with the same colored shape attached to it. When you find the person with the matching hoe, introduce yourself and conduct a brief discussion of what you think a hoe is used for. Use demonstrations. Once each of you has had a turn, it is time to find the other pair that has the same color picture attached to their hoe that is in a different shape. For example, one pair may have a green circle and the other pair may have a green square. When you find the group, introduce your partner and have your partner introduce you. After everyone has been introduced, talk about what you think the hoe is used for."

Process: Obtain sufficient hoes for all participants. If you can not obtain enough hoes, use pictures of hoes to supplement the actual hoes. Construct cards with colored shapes in advance. Move about the room providing assistance for people having difficulty.

2. Introduction

Content: "A hoe is a very valuable garden tool. Properly used, a hoe can assist a gardener in starting a garden and maintaining it until it is time to harvest. It can do things that other garden tools cannot and it can do so in a manner that is not physically demanding on the gardener. Knowing how to use a hoe can help you to become a better gardener."

Process: Introduce topic of using a hoe for gardening.

3. Presentation

Content: "There are two basic purposes of cultivating a garden with a hoe. One is to remove weeds; the other is to till the soil.

"Although chemical weed killers are widely used, there are instances when their use is inappropriate. In some cases, gardeners simply do not wish to use chemicals around vegetable plants whose produce they plan on eating. In other cases, a garden bed may be densely covered with vegetable plants and it would not be possible to apply a weed killer without also treating some of the vegetable plants. In situations like these, the alternative to chemical weed killers is the hoe. A hoe can be used to cut weeds slightly below the soil surface and reduce their ability to take light and nutrients away from the vegetable plants.

"A second purpose of using a hoe is to till the soil. A hoe can be used to prevent or break up soil crusting. When soil crusts, it slows air and water to the roots of plants. This, then, slows the growth of a garden and leads to a limited harvest. A hoe can be used to break up the crust into loose soil, which allows air and water to enter.

"Hoeing correctly is easy on the gardener. Hoeing is easier if the hoe blade is kept sharp. Running a file over the edge of the blade will keep it sharp. When hoeing, you should hold the middle of the handle with your dominant hand and the end of the handle with your nondominant hand. You should not bend over but stand erect, place the edge of the blade just under the soil surface, and use a fluid, sweeping motion to draw the hoe toward your feet. Hoeing should stir the soil lightly, not more than two inches deep. To avoid fatigue, you can change body positions by reversing the position of your hands on the hoe. It is best to walk backwards while hoeing; this prevents you from tramping down the soil that has just been tilled."

Process: Present information on use of a hoe. Use chalkboard to emphasize major points. Demonstrate proper use of a hoe at appropriate time in presentation. Demonstrate how to sharpen a hoe.

4. Discussion

Content:
    a.   What are the basic uses of a hoe?
    b.   How can a hoe be used to deal with soil crusting?
    c.   Why should soil crusting be removed?
    d.   Why and how should a gardener keep a hoe blade sharp?
    e.   How deep should a gardener hoe?
    f.   What is proper hoeing stance and action?
    g.   Why should a gardener walk backwards when hoeing?

Process: Conduct discussion using above questions. Encourage all participants to contribute to the discussion.

5. Learning Activity

Content: "Each of you will be given an opportunity to practice with a hoe. We will go into the garden to practice two skills. One will be to use the hoe to chop weeds from their roots. The second skill will be to break up the soil into small chunks, about two inches deep. Use the hoe only as instructed and in a safe manner. Use the proper posture and walk backward as you work."

Process: Have sufficient number of hoes available, at least one for every two gardeners. One can hoe while one observes. Begin with chopping weeds. Give each gardener an opportunity to chop several weeds, plus till small areas of soil. Monitor posture, hoeing action, and walking backward. Make corrections as needed.

6. Debriefing

Content:
   a.   Were you able to cut through the weeds easily?
   b.   If not, how could you make it easier?
   c.   Did you have difficulty moving backwards while working? If so, how?
   d.   Did you develop any tender spots or blisters? If so, how can they be avoided?

Process: Conduct debriefing using above questions. Encourage all participants to contribute to the debriefing.

7. Conclusion

Content: "Hoeing is a basic gardening skill. Using a hoe properly helps keep a garden free of weeds, the soil able to readily absorb moisture, and you free from unnecessary strain."

Process: Make concluding statements. Encourage participants to ask questions.

Objective 4.2: Demonstrate the ability to use a trowel to uproot weeds or dig holes.

1. Orientation Activity

Content: "Each of you has been given a trowel with a brightly colored square or circle attached to it. Find the colored shape attached to your trowel. Once you have found your colored shape, find the other person in the group who has a trowel with the same colored shape attached to it. When you find the person with the matching trowel, introduce yourself and conduct a brief discussion of what you think the uses of a trowel are. Use demonstrations. Once each of you has had a chance, it is time to find the other pair who has a trowel with a different shape of the same color attached to it. For example; one pair may have a green circle and the other pair may have a green square. When you find the group introduce your partner and have your partner introduce you. After everyone has been introduced, talk about what you think the uses of a trowel are."

Process: Obtain sufficient trowels for all participants. If you cannot obtain enough trowels, use pictures of trowels to supplement the actual trowels. Construct cards with colored shapes in advance. Move about the room providing assistance for people having difficulty.

2. Introduction

Content: "A trowel is a small garden implement often referred to as a hand shovel. It is a small tool to be used for small tasks. It is easier to use than a garden spade. A trowel allows a gardener to be more precise when precision is necessary."

Process: Introduce topic of using a trowel for gardening.

3. Presentation

Content: "A trowel can be used for several purposes in gardening. It can be used to uproot weeds in areas where a hoe would not be handy. A trowel can penetrate the soil several inches deep and allow you to remove all of the root of a weed or it can cut the root at a depth that makes regeneration difficult.

Trowels can also be used to dig planting holes for seedlings or bedding plants. A narrow trowel is especially good for planting bulbs. Another purpose of trowels is for use in harvesting small root crops, such as radishes.

"Trowels are simple to use. Because they are short implements and their function is to dig, you can crouch, squat, kneel, or sit on the ground. Kneeling is the preferred position. You should hold the trowel in the dominant hand by holding the handle at its end, with your thumb on the top side of the handle. The point of the trowel is placed on the ground where you wish to dig and force is used to push the trowel into the ground. The trowel should be lifted up and away from your body to remove the soil from the hole, eject a weed, or harvest a small root crop. The soil on the trowel blade should be placed on the ground beside the newly dug hole, if you are planting. If you want to dig weeds or harvest crops, the soil should be removed from the roots and placed back in the hole."

Process: Present information on trowels. Have sample trowels available for participants to use. Demonstrate proper use.

4. Discussion

Content:
    a.   What uses are there for a trowel?
    b.   Why would you use a trowel, rather than a shovel or spade?
    c.   What is proper troweling action?

Process: Conduct discussion using above questions. Encourage all participants to contribute to the discussion.

5. Learning Activity

Content: "We are going to go into the garden and practice using trowels. Each of you will have a trowel. The first thing we will practice will be digging a hole to receive a bedding plant. When you have completed digging such a hole, call me and I will look at it. The second thing we will practice will be uprooting small weeds with the trowel. I will watch each of you as you do this."

Process: Ensure that each participant has a trowel. Inspect each digging hole, with careful attention to appropriate depth. Soil should be piled beside each hole. Provide feedback, make corrections as necessary. Check uprooted weeds to see if all of the root has been extracted.

6. Debriefing

Content:
    a.   Did you find the trowel easy to use? Why or why not?
    b.   If you used both a sitting or a kneeling position, which was most comfortable?
    c.   Do you feel a trowel gives you more control for digging than other tools? Why?

Process: Conduct debriefing using above questions. Encourage all participants to respond to the questions.

7. Conclusion

Content: "Trowels are useful tools. They can be used for a variety of purposes and do not require a great deal of skill. They can be used throughout the gardening season."

Process: Make concluding statements. Provide opportunity for questions.

Objective 4.3: Demonstrate the ability to place seeds in a furrow and cover with soil.

1. Orientation Activity

Content: "Each of you has been given 10 seeds and a name tag. The name tag is either green or yellow. Those people who have green tags will go with even numbers and those given yellow tags will go with odd numbers. The object of the game is to put either two seeds or one seed in your right hand and keep the remaining seeds in your left hand. Go up to someone who has a different colored badge than you. Introduce yourself and find out the other person's name, then each of you will hold out your right hand that contains either one or two seeds. At the count of three, open your hands. If the total number of seeds is two or four the person with the green tag keeps all the seeds. If the total number of seeds is three, then the person with the yellow tag will keep all three seeds. Once you have exchanged the seeds, separate and put either one or two seeds into your right hand and find another person with a different colored badge to repeat the process. Continue doing this until I give you a signal to stop."

Process: Obtain at least 10 seeds per person prior to the activity. Position yourself so that everyone in the group can hear and see you while you give directions. Move about the room listening to participants and assisting them as needed. Decide on a signal to stop the activity in advance and tell the group what signal you will use to end the activity. When the activity is completed, you can announce which participants have the most seeds.

2. Introduction

Content: "Some vegetables can be started in containers indoors and then transplanted in gardens as very small plants referred to as seedlings. Some gardeners like to raise their own seedlings and others like to purchase them from nurseries. Other vegetables (e.g., carrots and parsnips) must have their seeds placed directly into the ground. Most gardeners enjoy planting seeds in the soil and caring for the plants until harvest time."

Process: Introduce topic of placing seeds in a planting furrow and covering them in soil.

3. Presentation

Content: "Planting seeds requires the garden to be prepared to receive them. This means the plot should be dug, enriched with some organic material, fertilized, and have any foreign objects, such as stones, removed. Before sowing the seeds, planting rows should be laid out with stakes at each end, connected with a length of string or twine to provide a straight planting line. Furrows should be laid out along each string. The depth of the furrow is very important. Instructions on seed packets provide the depth at which seeds should be planted. Generally, furrows should be 1/2 inch deep for small seeds and one inch deep for larger seeds. Small seeds should be spaced evenly but close together. Larger seeds can be placed about one inch apart. Follow directions on the packet. After seeds have been sown in the furrow, they should be covered with soil, gently tamped down, and watered. Each furrow should be marked with a plant label and planting date. This helps to identify the contents of a furrow after it has been covered and tells you when sprouts can be expected."

Process: Present information on planting seeds. Demonstrate correct technique.

4. Discussion

Content:
    a. What options are available when planting seeds for a vegetable garden?
    b. What work must be done before a garden plot is ready for seeds or seedlings?
    c. What is the purpose of using string to connect planting stakes?
    d. How can a gardener tell how deep to plant a seed?
    e. After seeds are sown, what is the next step for the gardener?
    f. What is the purpose of marking furrows with plant labels and dates?

Process: Conduct discussion using above questions. Encourage all participants to answer at least one question.

5. Learning Activity

Content: "We are going to prepare planting furrows and plant seeds in our garden. The group will be divided into teams of three or four persons. Each group will prepare a planting furrow, label it, place seeds in it, and cover the seeds with soil. Each member of each group will prepare part of the furrow, place seeds in that part, and cover them with soil. This is an important step and must be done carefully."

Process: Garden plot must be prepared prior to session. Have available sufficient furrow end-stakes, string, trowels, hoes, seed packets, and means of watering newly planted seeds. Supervise each team paying special attention to the depth of the furrow made. Watch each person plant and cover seeds. Provide feedback as necessary. If you do not immediately move to next objective, you should water the seeds.

6. Debriefing

Content
    a. What did you do to make straight furrows?
    b. How did you mark or label your furrow when planting was done?
    c. How deep did you make your furrow?
    d. What did you plant in your furrow?

Process: Conduct debriefing using above questions.

7. Conclusion

Content: "A garden with straight, evenly-spaced furrows is attractive and functional. Preparing furrows for receiving seeds is a time of hope. We enjoy the look, feel, and smell of newly-turned earth and look forward to 'working' in the garden in the coming weeks."

Process: Make concluding statements. Provide opportunity for questions.

Objective 4.4: Demonstrate the ability to use a watering can to water planted seeds.

1. Orientation Activity

Content: "Each of you has been given a watering can with a brightly colored picture of a square or a circle. Find the colored picture attached to your watering can. Once you have found your colored shape, find the other person in the group that has a watering can with a picture the same color and shape attached to it. When you find the person with the matching watering can, introduce yourself and conduct a brief discussion of what you think a watering can is used for. Use demonstrations. Once each of you has had a turn, it is time to find the other pair that has the same color picture as yours, but in a different shape attached to their watering can. For example, one pair may have a green circle and the other pair may have a green square. When you find the group, introduce your partner and have your partner introduce you. After everyone has been introduced, talk about what you think the uses of a watering can are."

Process: Obtain enough watering cans for all participants. If you cannot obtain enough watering cans, use pictures of watering cans to supplement the actual watering cans. Construct cards with colored shapes in advance. Move about the room providing assistance for people having difficulty.

2. Introduction

Content: "Newly planted seeds require careful attention. The soil containing seeds should be constantly moist until the seeds sprout. But caution must be taken to avoid over-watering. If the soil seems dry, it should be watered lightly. The soil should be damp, not waterlogged. Too much water can cause seeds to rot."

Process: Introduce topic of watering, emphasizing problems associated with too little and too much water.

3. Presentation

Content: "Newly planted seeds should be watered with a watering can rather than from a garden hose. Garden hoses can give too much water with too much force. Watering cans allow you to have much better control than garden hoses. The spout of the watering can should be fitted with a rose, a cap with holes in it that allows a gentle spray, and aimed directly at the soil. The water should be poured from a height of a few inches, rather than from a few feet. Watering from too great a height wastes water, bounces water away from the target area, washes soil away, splatters mud, and increases the chance of exposing seeds."

Process: Present information on watering newly planted seeds. Display watering can with hose. Demonstrate correct techniques.

4. Discussion

Content:
   a. After seeds are planted, what should the moisture condition of the soil be?
   b. What happens to newly planted seeds if they do not receive enough moisture?
   c. What happens if plants receive too much?

    d.   Why is a watering can recommended for watering newly planted seeds?

    e.   How can a gardener ensure a gentle spray from a watering can?

    f.   What can happen if you water newly planted seeds from too great a height?

Process: Conduct discussion using above questions. Encourage all participants to contribute to the discussion.

5. Learning Activity

Content: "We are going to practice watering newly planted seeds. We will begin by watering some furrows that are like those that contain newly planted seeds. After we have practiced on these furrows, we will water those that do have seeds in them. You will be divided into pairs. While one waters, the other will watch and provide feedback. The roles will then be reversed."

Process: On edge of garden or any available space, prepare practice furrows ahead of session. Have watering can with rose for each pair. Provide opportunity for each person to practice. Monitor technique and make corrections as needed. When each pair has demonstrated readiness, assign seed-containing furrow or portion of furrow to be watered in garden. Continue to monitor watering techniques.

6. Debriefing

Content:
    a.   Were you able to water without excessive splashing of mud or water?

    b.   From what height did you water?

    c.   Why is it important to water from a low height?

    d.   What was the moisture condition of the soil after you finished watering?

    e.   What advantages does a watering can provide? What disadvantages?

Process: Conduct debriefing using above questions. Encourage all participant to contribute to the debriefing.

7. Conclusion

Content: "Correctly watering newly planted seeds helps them grow. A watering can is better for this purpose than a garden hose. Be careful that too much water is not applied. When plants begin to sprout, the amount of water can be increased."

Process: Make concluding statements. Provide opportunity for questions.

Goal 5: Demonstrate knowledge of basic plant maintenance required for vegetable gardening.

Objective 5.1: Demonstrate knowledge of how to water a garden.

1. Orientation Activity

Content: "You have all been given a handout and a pencil. The handout contains a question: What are things that affect the amount of water needed by a garden? Below this question are two columns. The first column contains spaces for recording a person's name. The second column has spaces for recording the person's answer. Walk around the room and find people who are not talking to any one else and find out their name and one thing they feel affects the amount of water needed by a garden. Once you obtain this information, move to another person. Attempt to speak with every person in the room."

Process: Develop handouts in advance. Distribute the handout to participants as they enter the room. Have the directions typed at the top of the handout. Circulate among the participants, assisting them as needed. Participate in the activity, recording names and responses to allow you to interact with participants. Collect the sheets and review them after factors influencing the amount of water needed for a garden are presented.

2. Introduction

Content: "People and plants are similar in their need for water. Just as people need water to help meet their physical needs, so do plants. Just as we will die without water, so will plants. Some plants need more water than others, but all plants need water to live. During long periods of hot, dry weather, extra water is needed to keep gardens alive and healthy."

Process: Introduce topic of plants need for water.

3. Presentation

Content: "Comparing people and plants is a good way to understand the need for water. People and plants need water throughout their entire lives. Consider the following:

a.   Water is the major component of our bodies. There is a need for us to constantly replace water that has been used to perform physical functions and eliminated from the body. Plants also lose water through their leaves and need to have more water often.

b.   Water helps dissolve and move nutrients throughout our bodies. It performs the same function in plants. When we take vitamin pills, we do so with water to help dissolve the pills. Water helps dissolve plant fertilizer and move it to parts of the plant.

c.   When we need water, we are sluggish and have trouble standing and walking. Plants also have difficulty in staying upright if they do not get enough water. That is why they wilt and lose their firm shapes.

d.   As humans mature and continue to live, their bodies are constantly replacing skin cells and producing chemicals. These actions are dependent on water. Vegetable plants produce blossoms, vegetables, and new leaves. These actions also are dependent on water.

"Knowing how often to provide water to vegetable plants is important. Plants need water throughout their growing season but there are two times when watering is especially necessary: at germination and when harvest time nears. How often to water is closely related to how much water to apply. There are several things that affect the amount of water needed by a garden. Among these are:

a.   the amount and frequency of rainfall that occurs. A general rule of thumb is that gardens need one inch of water per week.

b.   the temperature. Plants lose more water during very hot periods than they do during periods of moderate or cool temperatures; they need water accordingly. Too much water may cause plants to rot during prolonged periods of cool temperatures.

c. the level of relative humidity. When the humidity is low, plants lose more water.

d. the amount of sunshine. Usually, the sunnier the days, the more water is needed.

e. the amount of wind. Wind increases the amount of water that plants lose.

f. the drainage of the soil. Some soils have poor drainage and retain water for a long time; some soils retain water for a very short time.

g. the type of plant and its stage of growth. Some plants need water more often than others. Plants especially need water during their early stages of growth.

h. the amount of mulch used around plants. Mulches retain moisture and help reduce the need for watering.

"Knowing how much water to apply to a garden is as important as knowing how often to water. When watering, you should always soak the soil three to five inches below the surface. If water is applied in this amount, a once-a-week watering is usually best. Avoid frequent application of small amounts of water. This tends to promote shallow root growth. This, in turn, encourages roots to come to the surface to seek water, where they may be damaged by the sun or other forces. Too much water can kill plants. Another factor that influences the amount of water needed is the types of plants in the garden. Follow instructions that are given on the seed packets or included in the material that accompanies bedding plants."

Process: Present information on watering. Use chalkboard to show major points.

4. Discussion

Content:
a. How does water help plants survive?
b. What happens when plants are deprived of water?
c. How often should a garden be watered?
d. How do high temperatures influence the amount of water a garden needs?
e. What happens to roots of plants when they get some moisture but it is not enough?

Process: Conduct discussion using above questions. Encourage all participants to contribute to the discussion.

5. Learning Activity

Content: "Imagine we have planted a vegetable garden and carefully tended it. Seedlings have emerged. All the young plants are off to a healthy start. You are responsible for seeing that the garden is watered throughout the growing season.

"You each have pencil and paper. This is an individual exercise. Write your reactions on how the following situations would affect your decisions to water. When you have finished writing, we will share the responses.

a. *Situation One.* Temperatures have been moderate and seasonable. Rainfall has been normal, averaging one inch per week. How much would you need to water?

b. *Situation Two.* Temperatures have been moderate and seasonable. It has rained a little bit every day for the past week, but not much more than a trace on several of those days. How much would you need to water?

    c. *Situation Three*. Both the temperature and the relative humidity have been high for the past week. There was a little rain five days ago. How much would you need to water?

    d. *Situation Four*. The temperatures have been high, hot winds are blowing, and it has been weeks since the last rain. How much would you need to water?"

Process: Distribute pencils and paper. Describe each situation, allow ample time for participants to write after each description. Repeat any description requested. When writing is finished, move immediately to debriefing.

6. Debriefing

Content:
    a. What was your response to Situation 1?
    b. What was your response to Situation 2?
    c. What was your response to Situation 3?
    d. What was your response to Situation 4?
    e. What else would you like to know when deciding how much to water?

Process: Conduct debriefing using above questions. Encourage all participants to contribute to the debriefing.

7. Conclusion

Content: "Watering is one of the most important tasks of the gardener. Knowing when and how much to water is important to success. Provided at the right time and in the right amount, water helps make a good harvest."

Process: Make concluding statements. Provide opportunity for questions.

Objective 5.2: Demonstrate knowledge of how to fertilize vegetable plants.

1. Orientation Activity

Content: "You have been given a can with an amount of fertilizer in it and a handout that contains the following questions: What are fertilizers? Why are fertilizers needed? What types of fertilizers are there and how are they applied? How often is fertilizer needed? Some people in the group have cans with a great deal of fertilizer; others have very little. You will now attempt to find other people who have similar amounts of fertilizer as you. When you find the other person who has a similar amount of fertilizer, begin a discussion on fertilizer. Introduce each other and try to answer the four questions listed on your handout."

Process: Place different amounts of fertilizer in clear plastic containers. Filling the container 1/4, 1/2, 3/4, or totally full may be a useful way to distribute the fertilizer. Provide participants with writing utensils. Make up sufficient handouts for the group.

2. Introduction

Content: "Fertilizing plants is an important part of garden maintenance. A fertilizer is a food; fertilizing means feeding. All living things need food to stay alive and healthy. Many vegetable plants need frequent feedings to grow as they are intended to do, and produce food. Knowing about fertilizers will help you be a better gardener."

Process: Introduce topic of fertilizing a garden.

3. Presentation

Content: "What are fertilizers? Simply stated, fertilizers are plant food or plant nutrients. Why are fertilizers needed? There are many elements known to be necessary for plant growth. Three of these are absorbed from the air and water. The rest are obtained from the soil. Most are needed in such small quantities that they are not likely to be used up. But nitrogen, phosphorous, and potassium are required in larger amounts and can be more quickly depleted from the soil. Therefore, they need to be replaced regularly. This is especially true during the main growing season.

"What types of fertilizers are there and how are they applied? Fertilizers may be purchased in liquid form. They are diluted with water and generally applied to the soil for root feeding. Sometimes, liquid fertilizers are diluted with water and applied directly to the leaves of the plant. Fertilizers may also be purchased in granular form. They may be mixed in water and applied to the soil or they may be scattered directly on the soil and then have water applied. Liquid fertilizers are easily applied, but they are more expensive than granular fertilizers and do not remain in the soil as long.

"How often is fertilizer needed? This depends on the 'natural' fertility of the soil and other factors. In general, most plants will benefit from a mild start-up application in the early stages of growth. During the growing season, a weak solution every other watering can help. Underfeeding may prevent a vegetable crop from producing at the desired rate, but overfeeding may burn or kill the crop."

Process: Present information on fertilizers. Use chalkboard to present the four questions.

4. Discussion

Content:
    a. What is a fertilizer?
    b. What are the three major elements contained in most commercial fertilizers?
    c. Why do fertilizers need to be applied?

d.   What advantages do liquid fertilizers have? What disadvantages?
e.   How often should fertilizers be applied?
f.   What happens to plants when too little fertilizer is applied?
g.   What happens when too much fertilizer is applied?

Process: Conduct discussion using above questions. Encourage all participants to respond to at least one of the questions.

5. Learning Activity

Content: "We are going to have an open-ended, round-table discussion about fertilizers. This is a chance for you to ask questions about any information that was presented or new information that you may want. You may relate any experiences you have had with fertilizers or make any comments you wish."

Process: Seat participants in circle or around table. Allow time for participants to feel comfortable and volunteer questions or comments. If no questions are forthcoming, initiate discussion. For example: Are there any personal health concerns about handling fertilizers? Are there any environmental concerns? Are there alternatives to commercial fertilizers? Do you prefer liquid or granular forms?

6. Debriefing

Content:
a.   What did you learn from the discussion?
b.   How will you make use of what you learned?
c.   Did you have a chance to ask everything you wanted? If not, what is your question?
d.   Are you comfortable with what you know about fertilizers?

Process: Conduct debriefing using above questions. Encourage all participants to respond to at least one question.

7. Conclusion

Content: "Fertilizers are needed in most gardens. Applied according to directions, they are safe and help a garden. Knowing about fertilizers is the mark of a good gardener."

Process: Make concluding statements. Provide opportunity for questions.

LEISURE EDUCATION BOWLING PROGRAM

Purpose, Goals, and Objectives

Purpose: Provide opportunities for participants to learn to bowl, acquire knowledge about rules of bowling, gain an awareness of self-improvements, and increase their ability to develop realistic self-expectations and effective problem solving strategies.

Goal 1: Demonstrate the ability to bowl.

Objective 1.1.   Demonstrate knowledge of bowling lanes.
Objective 1.2.   Demonstrate the ability to perform a four- or five-step approach.
Objective 1.3.   Demonstrate the ability to correctly release the bowling ball.
Objective 1.4.   Demonstrate the ability to release different types of balls.

Goal 2: Demonstrate knowledge of rules related to bowling.

Objective 2.1.   Demonstrate knowledge of key terms used in bowling.
Objective 2.2.   Demonstrate the ability to keep score.
Objective 2.3.   Demonstrate knowledge of common bowling courtesies.

Goal 3: Demonstrate self-awareness in bowling.

Objective 3.1.   Demonstrate the ability to set realistic goals.
Objective 3.2.   Demonstrate the ability to recognize capabilities.
Objective 3.3.   Demonstrate use of constructive self-evaluation techniques.

Goal 4: Demonstrate decision-making skills related to bowling.

Objective 4.1.   Demonstrate knowledge of correct target pin for picking up a spare.
Objective 4.2.   Demonstrate the ability to adjust target mark to hit the strike pocket.
Objective 4.3.   Demonstrate the ability to correctly choose a bowling ball.

Goals, Objectives, and Performance Measures

Goal 1: Demonstrate the ability to bowl.

Objective 1.1: Demonstrate knowledge of bowling lanes.

Performance Measure: Given five minutes, participant will demonstrate knowledge of bowling lanes by verbally giving the correct location of six of the following eight features: deck area, gutters, approach area, ten pins, bowling lane, pin setter, foul lights, and pin lights, on three consecutive occasions.

Objective 1.2: Demonstrate the ability to perform a four- or five-step approach.

Performance Measure: Given a bowling platform, in five minutes participant will perform a four- or five-step approach without crossing the foul line on six out of eight trials, on four consecutive occasions.

Objective 1.3: Demonstrate the ability to correctly release the bowling ball.

Performance Measure: Given a bowling ball, bowling platform, in two minutes participant will demonstrate the ability to correctly release the ball by performing at least four of the following:
- (a)   push ball forward to extended elbow,
- (b)   swing ball down and back, keeping elbow straight and close to the body,
- (c)   swing ball forward, keeping elbow extended and arm close to the body,
- (d)   release ball with a roll (no throwing), and
- (e)   keep thumb pointed up,

on three consecutive occasions.

Objective 1.4: Demonstrate the ability to release different types of balls.

Performance Measure: Given a bowling ball, platform, within five minutes participant will demonstrate the ability to release different types of balls by rolling a straight ball on four out of five trials and then a hook ball on four out of five trials, on three consecutive occasions.

Goal 2: Demonstrate knowledge of rules related to bowling.

Objective 2.1: Demonstrate knowledge of key terms used in bowling.

Performance Measure: Within 30 minutes, on a written examination with 30 questions (15 questions provide terms and ask for definitions, and 15 questions provide definitions and ask for terms. Examples include:
- (a)   *strike:* all pins knocked down with first ball in a frame;
- (b)   *spare:* all pins knocked down with second ball in a frame;
- (c)   *miss:* when pins are standing after two balls rolled in a frame;
- (d)   *split:* combinations of two or more pins standing after first ball rolled in a frame;
- (e)   *foul:* when bowler touches beyond foul line with a part of the body as ball is delivered;
- (f)   *washout:* split with the head pin standing;
- (g)   *frame:* one of 10 frames in a game, with two deliveries constituting a frame;
- (h)   *approach:* runway or platform bowler moves to deliver ball or actual steps and movements made by bowler;
- (i)   *double:* two strikes in a row;
- (j)   *gutters:* troughs on each side of lane;
- (k)   *head pin:* number 1 pin;
- (l)   *king pin:* number 5 pin;
- (m)   *lane:* long, narrow area where ball is bowled;
- (n)   *line:* game of 10 frames;
- (o)   *mark:* a strike, spare or a spot on the lane used for aiming;
- (p)   *pocket:* usually strike pocket, that is between 1 and 3 pins for right-handers and 1 and 2 pins for left-handers;

(q)   *series:* total pins knocked down in a specific number of games;

(r)   *turkey:* three consecutive strikes),

participant will demonstrate knowledge of key terms by correctly answering 24 (80%) questions.

Objective 2.2: Demonstrate the ability to keep score.

Performance Measure: Given a blank score sheet with 10 frames, a bowling game with at least one partner, within 10 minutes participant will demonstrate the ability to keep score by recording the correct score for the partner's game, on three consecutive occasions.

Objective 2.3: Demonstrate knowledge of common bowling courtesies.

Performance Measure: Upon request and within five minutes, participant will demonstrate knowledge of common bowling courtesies by verbally stating five of the following seven courtesies:
  (a)   when two bowlers are ready to bowl at the same time, bowler on the right should
        go first,
  (b)   take turn immediately,
  (c)   wait for ball near the return rack,
  (d)   respect foul line,
  (e)   do not use powder or other materials on shoes,
  (f)   refrain from conversation with bowlers preparing to deliver the ball, and
  (g)   refrain from commenting on other bowlers' styles,
on three consecutive occasions.

Goal 3: Demonstrate self-awareness in bowling.

Objective 3.1: Demonstrate the ability to set realistic goals.

Performance Measure: Given paper, pencil, within 10 minutes participant will demonstrate the ability to set realistic goals by formulating and recording four such goals to be accomplished in the next four sessions, and achieving two of the four goals, on two consecutive occasions.

Objective 3.2: Demonstrate the ability to recognize capabilities.

Performance Measure: Given paper, pencil, within 10 minutes participant will demonstrate the ability to recognize capabilities by recording three accomplishments that were direct results of participant's actions, on three consecutive occasions.

Objective 3.3: Demonstrate use of constructive self-evaluation techniques.

Performance Measure: Upon request and within five minutes, participant will demonstrate use of constructive self-evaluation techniques by verbally identifying a problem encountered in the day's session and a possible solution to that problem, on three consecutive occasions.

Goal 4: Demonstrate decision-making skills related to bowling.

Objective 4.1: Demonstrate knowledge of correct target pin for picking up a spare.

Performance Measure: Given an examination consisting of 20 pictures of various spare situations within 30 minutes participant will demonstrate knowledge of the correct target pin at which to aim by drawing a ball path to the correct pin on 80% of the pictures, on two consecutive occasions.

Objective 4.2: Demonstrate the ability to adjust target mark to hit the strike pocket.

Performance Measure: Given two lanes with different surface conditions, participant will demonstrate the ability to adjust the target mark by hitting the strike pocket on each lane on two out of five trials, on two consecutive occasions.

Objective 4.3: Demonstrate the ability to correctly choose a bowling ball.

Performance Measure: Given a choice of six balls with various finger settings and weight within five minutes participant will demonstrate the ability to correctly choose a proper bowling ball by selecting a ball and verbally expressing three of the following criteria:
   (a)   while thumb is completely in thumbhole, other two holes are immediately under the
          second knuckle of the second finger,
   (b)   finger hole spaces are not greater than the distance between the first knuckles of the first
          and third fingers,
   (c)   thumb and finger holes allow for easy grip, but smoothly slide off, and
   (d)   weight of the ball is at least 10% of participant's weight,
on three consecutive occasions.

Goals, Objectives, Content, and Process

Goal 1: Demonstrate the ability to bowl.

Objective 1.1: Demonstrate knowledge of bowling lanes.

1. Orientation Activity

Content: "Each of you has been given two colored cards with a part of the bowling lane listed on each card. Find the three people that have the same color card as you, introduce yourself, and find out their names.

"I am giving each group a drawing of a bowling lane with eight slots. Each of you should take turns and place the cards you have been given in the slot that points to the areas on the picture that corresponds with the word on the card. As you do this, look to the other group members and tell them what part of the lane is listed on your card. Once you have all the cards in place, we will get into a circle and see if all the pictures have the same labeling system."

Process: Prior to the activity, construct several pictures of bowling lanes and cut slots in the pictures. Write on different colored index cards the eight different parts of the lane (deck area, gutters, approach area, ten pins, bowling lane, pin setter, foul lights, and pin lights). Distribute cards to each participant. Once they have formed groups of four, distribute the pictures of the lanes. Move about the room as the participants insert the cards into the slots. Arrange participants in a large group after the small groups have inserted their eight cards.

2. Introduction

Content: "Learning to bowl requires familiarity with the physical environment in which bowling occurs. Most of us probably have some idea of what a bowling lane looks like, but it will be to our advantage to become more knowledgable about them."

Process: Introduce topic of bowling lanes.

3. Presentation

Content: "Each bowling lane usually includes the following:
 a. *deck area.* The space that contains the score table, ball rack, and seating for the bowlers. It is usually set a little bit below the approach area.
 b. *approach area.* The area in which the bowler walks to deliver the ball.
 c. *bowling lane.* The area in which the ball is rolled to the pins.
 d. *foul lights.* A light at each side of the lane where the foul line separates the approach area from the bowling lane. It is used to detect illegal deliveries.
 e. *gutters.* A trough on each side of the lane that runs the entire length of the lane and delivers errant balls into the pit behind the pins.
 f. *ten pins.* Arranged in a triangle and numbered as follows:

$$7 \ 8 \ 9 \ 10$$
$$4 \ 5 \ 6$$
$$2 \ 3$$
$$1$$

 h. *pin setter.* An automatic machine that sets and/or removes pins and can be seen only when it is raising or lowering the pins.
 i. *pin lights.* A lighted board on the end wall above the pins designed to inform the bowler of the pins that are left standing after the first ball.

These are the major features of each lane. Becoming familiar with them will make it easier to understand instructions and the special terminology related to bowling."

Process: Present information. Use chalkboard to list each feature. Diagram correct setting for ten pins.

4. Discussion

Content:
 a. Why is it important to know what a typical lane looks like?
 b. What is the difference between the deck area and the approach area?
 c. What is the purpose of the foul lights?
 d. What is the purpose of the pin lights?

Process: Conduct discussion using above questions. Encourage all participants to contribute to the discussion.

5. Learning Activity

Content: "I am going to give each of you a blank sheet of paper and a pencil. Please draw and label a bowling lane that contains the eight features we have learned about today. Include the correct arrangement of the 10 pins. When you are finished, we will check your paper for accuracy and make any necessary corrections."

Process: Explain activity. Provide paper and pencil. When activity is completed, move to debriefing.

6. Debriefing

Content:
- a. Did you get all eight features on your lane?
- b. Were there any parts that were difficult to remember?
- c. Where are the gutters? Foul lights? Pin lights? Approach area? Deck area?
- d. Did you get the pins numbered correctly?
- e. How will you make use of this information?

Process: Conduct debriefing using above questions. Put correctly labeled diagram on board or overhead projector screen. Identify correct location of each feature. Provide opportunity for participants to correct their diagrams. Encourage all participants to respond to at least one of the questions.

7. Conclusion

Content: "Learning the parts of a bowling lane is the first step in learning how to bowl. It will help you begin to understand bowling terms and future instructions will be easier to follow. Knowing what a typical bowling lane looks like will help you be comfortable in any bowling center you choose to frequent."

Process: Make concluding statements. Provide opportunity for questions.

Objective 1.2: Demonstrate the ability to perform a four- or five-step approach.

1. Orientation Activity

Content: "You have each been given a bowling shoe. Find the person that has the shoe that completes the pair. Look at the size of your shoe. You should find the person with the same size but the opposite foot. Once you find the person, introduce yourself and find out the person's name.

"Now we need to discover which of our feet is our favorite. This will help us when we begin to practice our approach. Stand any place where there is room for you to walk in a straight line for several steps. Your feet should be side by side, with the toes pointed ahead and your body weight equally distributed on both feet. Take a few steps and then stop while your partner watches. After a few seconds, take some more steps and stop again. The number of steps you take is not important. Repeat this action several times until you see which foot you naturally start on. This is your favorite foot. Check to see if your partner is in agreement with you. Remember it, because it will be the foot you start with when you learn how to make an approach in bowling. Now switch roles."

Process: Explain activity. Allow several minutes for participants to determine which foot is their favorite. Encourage them to remember their favorite foot because that is how they will start their approach.

2. Introduction

Content: "Bowling is an activity in which everyone can participate. If a bowler can coordinate taking a few steps in a straight line with the swinging of a bowling ball, a fundamental skill will be mastered. This skill is referred to as the approach. It is the base upon which other skills are built and, as such, has a great impact on performance."

Process: Introduce topic performing a four- or five-step approach.

3. Presentation

Content: "In considering the approach, there are some things of which you must be aware. These considerations include (a) the strike pocket, (b) targeting, and (c) the track. The strike pocket is the most effective place for the ball to strike the pins with a chance to knock down all 10 of them. For right-handed bowlers, the strike pocket is the area between the 1 and 3 pins. For left-handed bowlers, it is the area between the 1 and 2 pins.

"Targeting is the process of developing a focus of aim. There are two types of targeting: pin bowling and spot bowling. Pin bowling means that you aim at the pins. A pin bowler tries to throw the ball directly at the pins. Most beginners use this method but very few skilled bowlers do. Spot bowling means you aim at a spot (target) on the lane. Approximately 16 feet beyond the foul line on each lane is a set of spots (arrows or darts) that represents the way the pins are set. Experienced bowlers aim at these spots, rather than at the pins. Beginning bowlers should use this method of targeting.

"The track is an area between the second and third target spots on the lane. Most bowlers are right-handed and most use the area between the second and third spots as their point of aim. The effect of so many bowling balls being rolled over that spot is a slight wearing down of the surface, which results in a very small groove or track. The track is where a ball can be most effective. Right-handed bowlers that detect and use the track generally enhance their performances. Because the left side of the lane does not receive as much use, there is no track for left-handed bowlers to use.

"The approach you use should be a natural, rhythmic step pattern. The number of steps a bowler takes should be based on what feels most natural. Most bowlers use a four- or a five-step approach. To determine the best distance from the foul line for the start of the approach, place both heels about two inches in front of the foul line, facing away from the pins. You should then take four or five steps away from the line, and then take another half-step. This is the place where the approach should begin.

"Your stance at the beginning of the approach is important. The arm that is carrying the ball should have its elbow tucked into the side. Your feet should be close together, with the soles firmly planted on the floor. One foot can be slightly ahead of the other, depending on whether you are right- or left-handed and use a four- or five-step approach. Experience will tell you the number of steps that feels best. Regardless of the number of steps in the approach, the last step is a slide-lunge with the forward foot. Your forward leg is bent at the knee, the trailing leg may have the toe on the floor or the foot slightly elevated. While the approach is being executed, the arm holding the ball swings like a pendulum and the release of the ball is coordinated with the slide-lunge. We will focus on the release a bit later."

Process: Present information on approach, using demonstrations throughout presentation. Put explanation of strike, targeting, and track on the chalkboard. Emphasize difference between pin and spot bowling. Demonstrate four- and five-step approaches.

4. Discussion

Content:
   a.   What is the strike pocket for a right-handed bowler? What is it for a left-hander?
   b.   What is the difference between pin bowling and spot bowling?
   c.   Which of the two, pin bowling or spot bowling, is suggested for beginning bowlers?
   d.   On a bowling lane, what is the track?
   e.   Why is there no track for left-handed bowlers?
   f.   How can you determine the appropriate starting distance from the foul line?
   g.   What is the last step in the approach?

Process: Conduct discussion using above questions. Encourage all participants to contribute to the discussion.

5. Learning Activity

Content: "We are going to practice three exercises to help us learn an approach with which we are comfortable. First, stand with your feet together. Starting with your favorite foot, take four or more steps and slide-lunge on the last one. The number of steps you take is not a concern if you take at least four and slide-lunge on the last one. If you are right-handed, you should end with your left knee forward and bent, your right arm reaching forward, and your right leg trailing. If you are left-handed, you should end in an opposite position to that of a right-handed bowler. Repeat this action several times.

"Second, if you are right-handed and your left foot is your favorite, take five steps and slide-lunge on the fifth step. If your favorite foot is the right, take four steps and slide-lunge on the fourth. Swing your right arm forward on the slide-lunge. If you are left-handed, take five steps if your right foot is the favorite; slide-lunge on the fifth step. If your left foot is your favorite, take four steps and slide-lunge on the fourth one. Swing your left arm forward on the slide-lunge. Repeat this several times until you settle on a four-step or five-step approach.

"Third, now that you have determined the number of steps in your approach, practice it with a partner. Your partner is your target. Put enough space between the two of you and alternate practicing your approach. Approach your partner directly. The partner can observe the entire movement and offer suggestions. As you go through your approach, keep your shoulders and torso level and your hips and pelvis pointed toward the target. On the slide-lunge, swing your bowling arm toward the target. Repeat this action several times."

Process: Explain activities. Provide ample time for each participant to go through each movement several times. Repeat directions as participants are practicing. Observe and provide corrective feedback.

6. Debriefing

Content:
   a.   Which approach is the most comfortable for you?
   b.   If your approach does not feel comfortable, what will you do to make it so?
   c.   What questions or suggestions do you have about the approach?

Process: Conduct debriefing using above questions. Encourage all participants to respond to at least one of the questions.

7. Conclusion

Content: "You can learn a good approach without ever having a ball in your hand. Continue to practice your approach at every opportunity. Once you feel natural and comfortable with it, you can begin to add other skills. A good approach is the foundation for the other things you will learn."

Process: Make concluding statements. Provide opportunity for questions.

Objective 1.3: Demonstrate the ability to correctly release the bowling ball.

1. Orientation Activity

Content: "Each of you has been given a piece of a picture of a bowling ball. Find the person with the other piece that completes the picture. Introduce yourself and find out the person's name.

"Now that you are in pairs, we are going to combine a perpendicular arm swing with the foot movements of our approach. Pair off so that partners can help each other. Face away from your partner and go through your approach. As you move through your approach, swing your arm backward in a straight line. At the midpoint of your swing, your arm should be directly under your shoulder joint and perpendicular to the floor. The backward swing should continue until your arm is about at shoulder height. From the top of the backswing, your arm should swing forward in the same straight line. Keep your arm completely extended throughout the swing. Do not let your elbow bend. Alternate this action between partners. Partners observe form and provide feedback to each other. Repeat this action until each partner has had 10 trials. The arm swing is critical to releasing the ball properly."

Process: Explain activity. Help participants find their partners, if necessary. Demonstrate correct arm swing. Talk and walk through motion. Observe each bowler and make suggestions. Emphasize relationship between swinging the arm and learning how to correctly release a ball.

2. Introduction

Content: "It requires coordination and practice to correctly release a bowling ball. A good pendulum swing of the bowling arm and release of the ball is part of a rhythmic approach. Coordinating the swing and release with the foot movements of the approach requires practice. Mastery of these skills is important to becoming a good bowler."

Process: Introduce topic of correctly releasing the bowling ball.

3. Presentation

Content: "Releasing a bowling ball is part of a set of moves that begins with the first step of the approach. The movement of the bowling arm should look like a smooth pendulum swing. The arm that holds the ball should swing without benefit of muscular force. When the move is started with the ball being pushed away from the body, gravity should move the ball into the backswing. At the top of the backswing, gravity should again move the ball down and forward to its point of release. The ball does not have to be forced.

"When the arm is swung, it should be kept fairly close to the body, with the elbow always extended. After the ball is released, the follow-through is critical. The swing should end with the bowling arm extended along the side of the head. This will help the ball stay on its intended course of travel. The ball should be delivered over the foul line. The ball should leave the thumb first, then the fingers."

Process: Present information on ball release. Demonstrate pendulum arm swing and follow-through. Use slow movements to make points. Encourage questions; respond accordingly.

4. Discussion

Content:
   a.   What is a pendulum arm swing?
   b.   What supplies the force for a pendulum swing?
   c.   What should be the motion of the arm after the ball is released?
   d.   Why is the follow-through important?

Process: Conduct discussion using above questions. Encourage all participants to contribute to the discussion.

5. Learning Activity

Content: "We are going to practice an approach and release that will help us deliver the ball past the foul line. A towel, rolled lengthwise, will be placed over the foul line. Each of you will have 10 opportunities to approach and release the ball. The ball should pass over the towel without touching it and make contact with the floor a few inches past it. Keep track of how many times you deliver the ball past the foul line without touching the towel."

Process: Explain activity. Use several lanes. Place towels. Monitor activity and provide suggestions for improvement.

6. Debriefing

Content:
   a.   Did you hit the towel on any of your tries?
   b.   If you hit the towel, what did you do to correct your delivery on your next try?
   c.   Where did your bowling arm complete its follow-through?
   d.   Did you deliver the ball without supplying muscular force? How did it feel?

Process: Conduct debriefing using above questions. Encourage all participants to respond to at least one of the questions.

7. Conclusion

Content: "You now know how to approach, swing, and release. These three actions are all part of a continuous series of movements. Mastery of these movements will allow you to enhance your performance and increase your enjoyment of bowling."

Process: Make concluding statements. Provide opportunity for questions.

Objective 1.4: Demonstrate the ability to release different types of balls.

1. Orientation Activity

Content: "Some of you have been given colored construction paper and a pair of scissors. Others of you have been given a protractor and a colored pencil. Those of you with construction paper find the person with the pencil color that matches your paper, introduce yourself, and find out the person's name.

"Now, together we are going to practice some arm swings that will make us aware of the position of the thumb at the time of release on the bowling hand. Draw as large a circle as you can on the paper. Put numbers 1 through 12 on the circle, as though it were a clock face. Cut the clock face out of the paper. Face each other at a distance of about five feet. One partner should hold the clock face with both hands at shoulder level, with the arms extended and the face of the clock pointing toward the other partner. The partner without the clock will make 10 pendulum swings with the bowling arm and end the follow-through with the thumb pointing at 12:00 o'clock and then take 10 swings and end with the thumb pointing at 10:00 o'clock. Partners will then alternate roles."

Process: Explain activity. Provide materials. Demonstrate arm swings ending at 12:00 o'clock and 10:00 o'clock. Monitor activity and provide corrective feedback to bowlers.

2. Introduction

Content: "Having the ability to release different kinds of balls can be useful to a bowler. There are times when one type of delivery is more useful than others but beginning bowlers are usually taught two types and then focus on the one with which they feel most comfortable."

Process: Introduce topic of throwing different types of balls.

3. Presentation

Content: "There are four types of balls that may be used by a bowler: (a) straight ball, (b) curve ball, (c) hook ball, and (d) reverse hook ball. The most common and useful types are the straight ball and the hook ball. Beginning bowlers should ignore the curve ball and the reverse hook ball. Releasing a straight ball and a hook ball are very much alike. Learning how to do one type makes it easy to learn how to use the other.

"The thumb acts as a lever in releasing a bowling ball. The position of the thumb and fingers at the point of release determines what the ball will do. Picture a clock face. If, at the time of release, the thumb is pointing at 12:00 o'clock and the fingers are directly behind the thumb, the ball will go *straight*. If the thumb is pointed toward 10:00 o'clock at the time of release, the ball will *hook*. Most bowlers throw a hook ball for strikes. A straight ball is sometimes used to pick up certain spares."

Process: Present information on types of balls. Demonstrate straight and hook balls, emphasizing difference in position of thumbs.

4. Discussion

Content:
    a.   Which is the most common type of delivery in bowling? Why?
    b.   What role does the thumb of the bowling hand play in releasing a hook ball?
    c.   What role does it play in releasing a straight ball?
    d.   Do you have any questions?

Process: Conduct discussion using above questions. Encourage all participants to contribute to the discussion.

5. Learning Activity

Content: "We are going to practice throwing straight and hook balls. In groups of four at each lane, take turns until each bowler in each group has thrown 10 straight and 10 hook balls. Watch closely to see the curving motion of the hook."

Process: Explain activity. Demonstrate each type. Monitor activity and provide instructional hints, as necessary.

6. Debriefing

Content:
    a.   Which ball did you prefer to use? Why?
    b.   Was it easy to see the hook on your ball?
    c.   How can you perfect your preferred delivery?
    d.   Are you ready to practice your delivery whenever you have the opportunity?

Process: Conduct debriefing using above questions. Encourage all participants to respond to at least one of the questions.

7. Conclusion

Content: "Even though most bowlers use a hook delivery, there are no hard and fast rules as to which type of delivery you should use. Learning to use a straight ball and then progressing to a hook is a common process for many bowlers. Use what feels best for you."

Process: Make concluding statements. Provide opportunity for questions.

Goal 2: Demonstrate knowledge of rules related to bowling.

Objective 2.1: Demonstrate knowledge of key terms used in bowling.

1. Orientation Activity

Content: "Each of you has been given a card with a number of colored bowling pins on it. Find the person who has a picture with the same color of pins and whose number, when added to your number, results in 10. When you find your partner, introduce yourself and find out the other person's name.

"One of the tasks facing beginning bowlers is making sense of bowling terms. To help you get started, I am going to give each pair a sheet of paper that lists 15 bowling terms, but each term has its letters scrambled. For example, you might see 'WINGLOB' on the sheet. Unscramble 'WINGLOB' to form the word 'BOWLING.' At the end of the exercise, we will see how well each pair did."

Process: Explain activity. Prepare list of 15 scrambled terms prior to session (e.g., miss, frame, strike, spare, split, foul, approach, pocket, mark, line). Help bowlers get in pairs, if necessary. At end of exercise, provide correct answers on handouts or on the chalkboard.

2. Introduction

Content: "Bowling, like many other activities, has a language all its own. In order to fully understand the activity and to communicate with others about it, you need to know the meaning of terms and symbols that are specific to bowling. Having such knowledge will also increase your level of comfort and enjoyment of the activity."

Process: Introduce topic of key terms used in bowling.

3. Presentation

Content: "There are several terms that have a particular meaning when used in reference to bowling, a meaning that is different than when used to refer to things other than bowling. If an individual wishes to have a comprehensive grasp of bowling, especially the scoring procedures, a knowledge of those terms is necessary.

"I am going to provide you with a list of bowling terms and their meaning. The first seven are particularly important for gaining a knowledge of the scoring process. Learning the meaning of these terms is essential to understanding bowling. The list is as follows:

  a. *strike.* When all the pins are knocked down with the first ball rolled in a frame.
  b. *spare.* When all the pins are knocked down with the second ball rolled in a frame.
  c. *miss.* When pins are still left standing after two balls have been rolled in a frame.
  d. *split.* When combinations of two or more pins remaining standing after first ball has been rolled in a frame.
  e. *foul.* This occurs when a bowler touches anywhere beyond the foul line with any part of the body as the ball is delivered.
  f. *washout.* This is a split with the head pin still standing.
  g. *frame.* This is one of the 10 frames in a game, with two deliveries constituting a frame.
  h. *approach.* A runway or platform on which the bowler moves to deliver the ball or the actual steps and movements made by the bowler.
  i. *double.* When two strikes appear in a row.
  j. *gutters.* These are the troughs on each side of the lane, sometimes referred to as channels.
  k. *head pin.* This is the number 1 pin.
  l. *king pin.* This is the number 5 pin.
  m. *lane.* This is the long, narrow area on which the ball is bowled, sometimes referred to as the alley.
  n. *line.* This is a game of 10 frames.
  o. *mark.* It refers to a strike or a spare or a spot on the lane used for aiming.
  p. *pocket.* It is usually the strike pocket, the area between the 1 and 3 pins for right-handed bowlers, the 1 and 2 pins for left-handers.

q. *series*. This is the total number of pins knocked down in specific number of games, usually three.
r. *turkey*. When three consecutive strikes occur.

There are other words found in the terminology of bowling, but the terms listed are important for building an understanding of the game and its scoring."

Process: Present information on terms. Prepare list of terms and definitions for distribution to class. Use chalkboard or overhead projector to explain each term.

4. Discussion

Content:
    a. Why is it necessary to know the meaning of bowling terms?
    b. What will you do to come to an understanding of these terms?
    c. Are there any terms you would like to have reviewed? If so, which ones?
    d. How soon will you be able to use these terms when you discuss bowling?

Process: Conduct discussion using above questions. Encourage all participants to contribute to the discussion.

5. Learning Activity

Content: "We are going to see how well we have learned our bowling terms. This is a two-part exercise. I am going to give each of you a sheet of paper with 15 bowling terms on it. Please put your name on the paper. Following each term is enough space for you to write a brief definition of the term. When you are finished with this part of the exercise, I will collect your papers and you will do the second part.

"The second part of the exercise is very similar to the first. This time you will each be given a sheet of paper that has 15 definitions on it. There is a blank space before each definition. Write the appropriate terms in those spaces. When you are finished, raise your hand and I will bring you your first paper. Check your answers to see how well you did. The numbers on the two handouts correspond. That is, the first term on the first handout goes with the first definition on the second handout."

Process: Explain activity. Prepare terms and definitions. Encourage bowlers to do their best but to avoid stress. As they are correcting their papers, observe them and provide extra help, as needed.

6. Debriefing

Content:
    a. Are there any answers you would like to change? If so, which ones?
    b. When your paper is corrected, what will you do with it?
    c. What other ways can we learn and remember bowling terms?

Process: Conduct debriefing using above questions. Encourage all participants to respond to at least one of the questions.

7. Conclusion

Content: "Knowing and using bowling terms correctly will help you become a good bowler. It will also help you learn how to score bowling games, which is important in understanding the game."

Process: Make concluding statements. Provide opportunity for questions.

Objective 2.2: Demonstrate the ability to keep score.

1. Orientation Activity

Content: "You have been given a scoring sheet with five names on the sheet, including yours. Move about the group introducing yourself to each person and asking their names. When you find a person who is on your score sheet, have him or her autograph the sheet beside his or her name. Once you have all signatures, get together with the other four people on your sheet and tell each person one bowling term and its definition. Continue doing this until I give you the signal to stop."

Process: Make up score sheets with five names on them prior to the session. Establish a signal for stopping. Distribute sheets to correct participants. Observe group discussion and provide assistance as needed.

2. Introduction

Content: "It is important for you to know how to keep score in bowling. Although many bowling centers are equipped with automatic scoring machines, there are some centers that do not have them. There may also be times when scoring machines are broken. You should be able to score games without having to depend on a machine to do it for you."

Process: Introduce topic of keeping score.

3. Presentation

Content: "A game of bowling consists of 10 frames. Scoring requires you to continuously add. The score in each frame includes the score from all previous frames. In other words, the scorer must add the score made in each frame to the scores in the preceding frames.

"There are five symbols or markings used for recording scores. A strike is represented by an X, a spare by a / (slash), a foul by an F, a split by a O (circle), and a miss by a – (dash). Each frame on a score sheet has two recording boxes in the upper-right corner. The first box is for recording the results of the first ball; the second box is for the results of the second ball, if a second ball is necessary.

"If a bowler makes a strike, the scorer records an X in the first box. If a strike is not made, the number of pins knocked down with the first ball are recorded in the first box. If the first ball is a gutter ball and no pins are knocked down, a – is placed in the first box. If a foul is made, an F is placed in the first box.

"If the second ball results in a spare, a / is recorded in the second box. If a spare is not made, the number of pins knocked down with the second ball is recorded. If the second throw results in a gutter ball or a foul, a – or an F is recorded.

"A strike is worth 10 pins *plus* the total number of pins knocked down with the next two balls. A spare is worth 10 pins *plus* the total number of pins knocked down with the next ball. No score is recorded in a frame when there is a strike or a spare *until* the next two balls for a strike have been delivered or the next ball for a spare has been thrown. Remember, every strike is worth 10 plus two more balls; every spare is worth 10 plus one more ball.

"Three strikes in a row is worth 30 pins in the frame where the first strike was thrown. A strike followed by a spare, or a spare followed by a strike, is worth 20 points for the first of the two frames.

"The tenth frame is the end of the game and is scored as follows:
   a. If you do not make a strike or a spare, you simply add the number of pins knocked down in the tenth frame to the score in the ninth frame. This becomes the tenth frame score and the score for the game.
   b. If you throw a strike, two more balls are allowed. The total number of pins knocked down by all three balls is added to the ninth frame score. This becomes the tenth frame score and the score for the game.
   c. If you throw a spare, one more ball is allowed. The number of pins (10) knocked down in the spare and by the one extra ball is added to the ninth frame score. This becomes the tenth frame score and the score for the game.

"Scoring a game does not need to be complex. Study and practice will make scoring much easier."

Process: Present information on scoring. Prepare handout of scoring rules. Distribute rules and sample score sheets to bowlers. Put scoring rules on chalkboard or overhead. Provide examples with each rule. Encourage questions.

4. Discussion

Content:
   a. Why should you know how to score a game?
   b. What is the symbol used to indicate a strike? A spare? A split? A foul? A miss?
   c. How many pins is a strike worth? How many is a spare worth?
   d. If you throw a strike in the tenth frame, how many more throws are allowed?
   e. How many more throws are allowed if a spare is thrown in the tenth frame?

Process: Conduct discussion using above questions. Encourage all participants to contribute to the discussion.

5. Learning Activity

Content: "Each of you has a score sheet. Lets 'talk through' and score an imaginary game. I will describe the results of each frame and give you the opportunity to mark your score sheet accordingly. Then we will discuss what the marking should be. If you have made the wrong mark, you can correct it and then we will go on to the next frame. We will check the results at the end of this exercise and correct any mistakes we encounter.

"The results of each frame are as follows:

Frame 1: is a strike. Put an X in the first recording box of the first frame. Do not record anything else at this time.

Frame 2: the first ball knocks down seven pins and the second ball knocks down two pins. Put a 7 in the first recording box and a – and a 2 in the second box. Put the 2 under the –. Because a strike is worth 10 pins plus the total knocked down with the next two balls, go back to the first frame and record 19. Add the number of pins (9) knocked down in this frame to the total of the first frame (19) for a score of 28.

Frame 3: eight pins are downed with the first ball and the two remaining pins are downed with the second ball. This is a spare. Put an 8 in the first recording box and a / in the second one. Do not put anything else in the frame at this time.

Frame 4: is a strike. Put an X in the first recording box. Because a spare is worth 10 pins plus the number knocked down with the next ball, go back to frame 3. Add 20 points to frame 2 and put a 48 in frame 3. Do not put anything else in frame 4 now.

Frame 5: is a strike. Put an X in the first recording box. Do not put anything else in the frame at this time.

Frame 6: seven pins are downed with the first ball and the remaining three pins are downed with the second ball. Put a 7 in the first recording box and a / in the second box. Go back to frame 4. Remember, a strike is worth 10 pins plus the number downed with the next two balls. Therefore, add 27 pins to total in frame 3 (48 pins). This makes a cumulative score of 75 pins for frame 4. Go to frame 5 and apply the scoring rule for strikes. This will result in 20 pins being added to the total of frame 4. Frame 5 will now have a cumulative score of 95 pins.

Frame 7: six pins are knocked down with the first ball and two pins with the second ball. This is a miss. Put a 6 in the first recording box and a 2 under a – in the second box. Go back to frame 6 and apply the scoring rule for a spare. This means 16 pins should be added to the total in frame 5 (95 pins). The cumulative total for frame 6 is 111 pins. The eight pins knocked down in this frame should be added to the total of frame 6. This makes an accumulative score of 119 for frame 7.

Frame 8: eight pins are bowled over with the first ball, leaving the 9 and 10 pins standing. This is a split. Put an 8 in the first recording box and the split symbol (a 0) in the second box. The second ball knocks over the 9 and 10 pins. Put the symbol for a spare (a /) through the split symbol in the second box.

Frame 9: the first ball knocks over five pins. Put a 5 in the first box. The second ball knocks over the remaining five pins but the bowler committed a foul on the delivery. An F should be recorded in the second box and no points awarded for the five pins downed by the second ball. Go back to frame 8 and apply the scoring rule for a spare. This results in adding 15 pins to the total of frame 7 (119). The cumulative score for frame 8 is 134 pins. The score for frame 9 is 139 pins.

Frame 10: the first ball is a strike. The first extra ball is also a strike. The second extra ball knocks down seven pins. The first ball strike is worth 27 pins. Add 27 to the total in frame 9 (139). The cumulative score for frame 10 and the game is 166 pins.

This is the end of the game."

1	2		3		4	5	6		7		8		9		10			TOTAL
☒	7	2̄	8	/	☒	☒	7	/	6	2̄	8	Ø	5	F	☒	☒	7	
19	28		48		75	95	111		119		134		139		166			166

Process: Explain activity. Explain each frame carefully. Use chalkboard or overhead projector to demonstrate scoring for each frame. Provide opportunity for questions at each frame. Make sure all participants have correct number of pins or recording marks for each frame before proceeding to the next.

1	2		3		4	5	6		7	8	9	10	TOTAL
☒	7	2̄	8	/	☒	☒	7	/					
19	28		48		75	95							

6. Debriefing

Content:
  a. Are there any rules you would like to review? If so, which ones?
  b. Are there any symbols you would like to review? If so, which ones?
  c. Do you feel comfortable with your ability to score a game? If not, what will it take to help you feel comfortable?
  d. How will you improve your ability to keep score?

Process: Conduct debriefing using above questions. Encourage all participants to respond to at least one of the questions.

7. Conclusion

Content: "Knowing scoring procedures is a valuable asset for you. It can help you be independent and not have to rely on others. It can also help you to explain the game to others who might be interested. It is another part of being in control of your own leisure."

Process: Make concluding statements. Provide opportunity for questions.

Objective 2.3: Demonstrate knowledge of common bowling courtesies.

1. Orientation Activity

Content: "Each of you has been given a picture of bowling equipment. Find the other two people who have the same equipment, introduce yourself, and find out the other people's names.

"We are now going to give you each a chance to practice being a mime for a few minutes. Each trio is being given six slips of paper that have been folded and placed in a small box. Someone begin and take one slip of paper. Read the paper and then silently act out the courtesy written on the slip of paper while one other member (the observer) watches with a checklist of the six courtesies. Without speaking, you can position the third person (helper) to help with the role play. The observer will watch silently until you are finished. When completed, the observer will guess which courtesy you were role playing. Once this has been completed, switch roles until each person has role played two courtesies each."

Process: Make up three pictures of each piece of bowling equipment (e.g., shoes, towel, ball, pins, score sheet, pencil). Prepare sufficient slips in advance with six of the courtesies listed below. Place them in small boxes. Remind participants not to speak during the role play. Move about the room providing assistance as needed.

2. Introduction

Content: "If bowling is to be enjoyed by all participants and spectators, there are some common bowling courtesies that must be observed. These courtesies are as important to the game as knocking down the pins. Basically, they are unwritten rules that provide equal consideration and respect for all."

Process: Introduce topic of common bowling courtesies.

3. Presentation

Content: "There are not many unwritten rules to which bowlers should adhere, but they are important. Bowlers who break these rules often have a negative impact on the enjoyment of others. Following the rules is a sign of a good sport.
   a. When two bowlers approach the ball rack at the same time to pick up a ball, the bowler on the right should bowl first. This means you should check lanes on both sides to ensure that two bowlers who are side-by-side do not make their approach and delivery at the same time. This prevents bowlers from disturbing each other.
   b. You must be ready to take your turn immediately. This helps the game go smoothly and without delay. This is important during league and tournament play.
   c. When you take your turn, always stay on the approach runway. After you make your first delivery, step back from the foul line and wait for your ball by the return area.
   d. Always stay behind the foul line. Nothing is gained by doing otherwise.
   e. Do not use powder or other materials on your shoes, even if you do not like the surface conditions of the approach area. Other bowlers may like it as it is.
   f. There should be no conversation with a bowler who is on the approach area and ready to make the delivery. That bowler should be allowed to concentrate. Conversation can take place after the bowler has made the delivery.
   g. You should not make comments about the style of others. Good sportsmanship requires that all bowlers have the opportunity to enjoy the game, without having to experience negative comments from others.

"These rules are simple and basic. They are not difficult to follow nor are they hard to remember. Practice these rules so that no one is offended by your actions."

Process: Present information on courtesy. Put rules on chalkboard. Prepare list of rules prior to session and distribute to bowlers. Carefully explain each rule and rationale for it.

4. Discussion

Content:
    a.   Why are rules of courtesy necessary?
    b.   Are there any rules you wish reviewed? If so, which ones?
    c.   How will you practice these rules?
    d.   How will you monitor your adherence to the rules?

Process: Conduct discussion using above questions. Encourage all participants to contribute to the discussion.

5. Learning Activity

Content: "I have prepared a checklist of the rules for each of you. We are going to bowl some practice games. As the games are bowled, practice the courtesies that are listed on your sheet. You are responsible for your own behavior and that is the way it should be. Therefore, you are on the honor system for monitoring your own behavior. If you adhere to a rule throughout the practice games, make a note to that effect by that rule on your sheet. If you slip up and break a rule, make a note of that also. When the practice games are over, we will check and see how well we did."

Process: Explain activity. Prepare checklist and distribute to bowlers. Emphasize use of honor system. Monitor activity.

6. Debriefing

Content:
    a.   Did you observe the rules most of the time? All of the time? None of the time?
    b.   Did anyone have to remind you when you failed to follow a rule?
    c.   Which rule seemed to be the most difficult to follow? Why?
    d.   What will you do to get better at observing the rules?

Process: Conduct debriefing by using the above questions. Encourage all participants to respond to at least one of the questions.

7. Conclusion

Content: "Bowling is more than just knocking down pins. It is a time to participate in an activity with friends and experience enjoyment and satisfaction. Observing the rules and treating everyone with respect and consideration adds to the enjoyment."

Process: Make concluding statements. Provide opportunity for questions.

Goal 3: Demonstrate self-awareness in bowling.

Objective 3.1: Demonstrate the ability to set realistic goals.

1. Orientation Activity

Content: "As each of you entered the room, I pinned a sign on your back that you were not permitted to either look at or ask anyone what is written on it. On the sign is written the name of a famous person. The objective of this activity is for you to figure out whose name you are wearing. Go up to a person who is not talking to anyone, introduce yourself, and find out his or her name. Then ask the person to name one goal I have or had in my life (if I were the person indicated by my sign). The person should look at your name tag and tell you a goal you would probably have if you were that person. For example, you may have the name Abraham Lincoln and the person may say that one of your goals is to end slavery. Begin to move about the room trying to find out who you are. You could be a man or woman of any race or religion. If you do not recognize the person's name, please come see me and I will tell you about the person and why he or she is famous. Once you have guessed the name of the person on your sign, have the person who identified the goal take the name tag off your back and place it on your shoulder. Continue moving about the room, providing goals for other people."

Process: Write out sufficient number of name tags for each participant (e.g., Mahatma Gandhi, Helen Keller, Martin Luther King Jr., Meryl Streep, John Glenn, Gloria Estefan, Albert Einstein, Princess Diana, Bill Cosby, Steffi Graf). Pin the tags on the people as they enter the room. Solicit assistance from participants if needed. Move about the room helping participants who do not recognize or are unable to guess the name.

2. Introduction

Content: "When we participate in an activity, we should have some idea of what we expect to get from it. If we expect nothing, then it makes no difference what we do, whether we participate or not. If we expect more than we can obtain, we may be discouraged and disappointed. If we expect less than we are able to achieve, we may feel bored. But if we set realistic, challenging goals and put forth our best effort, we should feel good about ourselves, whether we achieve them or not. Setting realistic goals is important."

Process: Introduce topic of setting realistic goals.

3. Presentation

Content: "Setting realistic goals is something each of us can do. There are goal-setting processes that can help in this effort. A simplified version of such a process is as follows:
   a. Identify what you wish to accomplish (your goal).
   b. Brainstorm possible actions that could help you achieve your goal. In brainstorming there are no right or wrong answers.
   c. Evaluate each action. Is it possible? Is it realistic? What are its advantages? What are its disadvantages? How does it compare to the other possible actions?
   d. Select the best action and implement it.
   e. Evaluate your action and make any modifications required.

"Following such a process can work to our advantage. It requires us to approach goal-setting with an objective attitude. If we think carefully about what we want to do and how we can do it, we can set realistic goals for ourselves."

Process: Present information on goal-setting. Use chalkboard to list steps in process. Explain each step. Provide an example.

4. Discussion

Content:
    a.   Why is goal-setting something we should do?
    b.   What is the likely result if our goals are unreasonably difficult?
    c.   What is the likely result if our goals are too easy?
    d.   What is the value of having a goal-setting process to follow?

Process: Conduct discussion using above questions. Encourage all participants to contribute to the discussion.

5. Learning Activity

Content: "Each of you has a pencil and paper. Please take a few moments to think of some goals you want to accomplish when you bowl your next game. Your goals do not need to be like any one else's. Use the process you have learned. Write at least four goals.

"Examples of some possible goals include:
    a.   to throw a strike,
    b.   to keep score accurately,
    c.   to observe all the bowling courtesies,
    d.   to keep my temper under control,
    e.   to choose an appropriate bowling ball,
    f.   to use bowling terms correctly in conversation,
    g.   to interact with other bowlers, and
    h.   to score better than my last game.

"Remember, your goals should be your own. Put your names on your papers. After you have bowled today, assess how well accomplished your goals. We will then meet and discuss how we did."

Process: Explain activity. Put possible goals on board but emphasize that goals are individual's choice. Allow sufficient time. Provide opportunity to bowl before debriefing.

6. Debriefing

Content:
    a.   How realistic were the goals that you set for yourself?
    b.   How many of your goals were you able to achieve?
    c.   Do you think you should modify any of your goals? If so, which ones?
    d.   If the goal-setting process worked for bowling, where else can it work?

Process: Conduct debriefing using above questions. Encourage all participants to respond to at least one of the questions.

7. Conclusion

Content: "Setting goals provides us with a direction for our energy and helps us to focus our efforts. If we set reasonable and challenging goals for all aspects of our lives and if we sincerely try to achieve them, we can be satisfied with ourselves. We can get pleasure and enjoyment from bowling, as well as other aspects of our lives."

Process: Make concluding statements. Provide opportunity for questions.

Objective 3.2: Demonstrate the ability to recognize capabilities.

1. Orientation Activity

Content: "You have each been given a pencil, paper, and a sheet of paper with two headings. The headings are 'name' and 'something you could teach'. Go up to a person who is not talking with someone, introduce yourself, and find out the person's name.

"Write the person's name in the first column. Then ask the person to tell you a skill he or she has and could teach others. Once you record the skill, provide the same information to that person. Once completed, move to another person, trying to speak with as many people as possible before I give the signal to stop. The skills can be anything, from tying your shoes to playing tennis, from shaking a tambourine to playing the guitar, from playing 'Go Fish' to Bridge. Remember, the skill does not have to be complex."

Process: Develop the handouts with the two columns prior to the session. On the handouts, write at the top on the left side the word "name" and on the right side "something you could teach." Then make a series of lines under the two columns for participants to record the information. Distribute the handouts providing clear and concise directions. Move about the room providing assistance as needed. Identify a signal to stop.

2. Introduction

Content: "We should be realistic when setting goals and thinking about what we want to gain from our participation in an activity. We should be realistic in assessing our ability to reach our goals or improve on our performances. This is good. But we should be equally realistic when it is time for us to recognize the things we do well and what we have been able to accomplish."

Process: Introduce topic of recognizing capabilities.

3. Presentation

Content: "Recognizing your own abilities is a positive step forward. You have the right to take pride in your accomplishments. Your self-esteem should increase when you know that your successes are the result of your actions. When you set goals for yourselves and work hard to achieve those goals, one of your rewards should be the satisfaction of knowing that you are a success.

"Reflect on your participation in bowling. What can you do now that you could not do before you entered this program? Can you deliver a bowling ball and knock down some pins with it? Do you know about bowling terms and are you able to use them in your conversation? Can you throw a strike or a spare? Do you know how to score a game? Do you understand the handicap system? Can you observe common bowling courtesies? Do you interact with your fellow bowlers?

"Think about these things. If you can do some of these, or other things you learned in this program, it is because of your own efforts and abilities. No one accomplished them for you. You demonstrated that you were capable of being successful."

Process: Present information. Use chalkboard to list possible successes.

4. Discussion

Content:
    a.   Of what value is it to recognize your capabilities?
    b.   If you achieve a goal, do you think it was because of hard work or luck? Why?
    c.   Do you feel you need to achieve 100% of a goal before you feel successful? Why?
    d.   If you recognize your abilities in one activity, how can it help you in other activities?

Process: Conduct discussion using above questions. Encourage all participants to contribute to the discussion.

5. Learning Activity

Content: "Please take a few moments and think about the specific things you can do as a result of participating in this program. Each of you has pencil and paper. Record five things you are capable of doing as a result of being in this program. Think further about the five things you recorded and write a brief explanation of what you did that allowed you to do each of them. When you are finished, we will ask each of you to share some of your results with the group."

Process: Explain activity. Provide sufficient time for thinking and writing. Provide opportunity for each participant to share one item from paper. Repeat process for second or subsequent items, depending on time.

6. Debriefing

Content:
    a.   Was it difficult to think of five things you can do as a result of this program?   Why?
    b.   Were all of the things you thought of related to the physical or mental aspects of bowling? If not, what were some of the other things?
    c.   How can we keep recognition of our capabilities and limitations in perspective?
    d.   Why should we try to keep them in balance?

Process: Conduct debriefing using above questions. Encourage all participants to respond to at least one of the questions.

7. Conclusion

Content: "Recognizing our capabilities is as much a result of growth and responsibility as is recognizing our limitations. Knowing that we are capable of being successful should make us feel good about ourselves. Bowling can provide us numerous opportunities to recognize our capabilities. We can learn from this and recognize our abilities in other aspects of our lives as well."

Process: Make concluding statements. Provide opportunity for questions.

Objective 3.3: Demonstrate use of constructive self-evaluation techniques.

1. Orientation Activity

Content: "Some of you have been given a colored card with three questions written on the card. Others have been given a colored piece of paper and a pencil. Persons with the colored card should find someone who has paper that matches the color of the card, introduce themselves, and find out the person's name.

"Persons with cards should ask those with paper the questions on the card. After the person reads the first question, the person with the paper should write down a brief, one-sentence answer to the question. Once the person has answered all three questions, the pair should signal me by raising their hands. Once all pairs have completed the three questions, we will form a circle and share our responses with the entire group."

Process: Prepare cards in advance of the session with questions (e.g., What is self-evaluation? Why do we do self-evaluation? How does self-evaluation relate to bowling?). Move about the room and help participants read the questions and write the responses, if needed. Once completed, arrange participants into a circle and assist them in a sharing their responses. Facilitate a brief discussion.

2. Introduction

Content: "We are going to identify some problem areas you may have had while bowling and talk about possible causes and solutions to those problems. When you have finished this program, it will be your responsibility to deal with various problems that may arise as you continue to participate in bowling. Asking questions of yourself is a good way to begin to identify problems and start action to solve them."

Process: Introduce topic of constructive self-evaluation techniques.

3. Presentation

Content: "As you think about your performance and participation in this bowling program, there are several questions you could consider that help you in identifying and solving problems. For example:
  a. Did anything happen during this session that disturbed my ability to bowl?
  b. Did anything happen that increased my frustration level?
  c. Was I as successful in bowling today as I hoped to be? If not, why not?
  d. How can I learn more about a specific aspect of bowling? Who can help me?
  e. What areas of my game or participation do I need to improve?
  f. Have I done anything to cause problems for myself?
  g. What can I do next time to correct or avoid problems?
  h. What did I do today in bowling that was a source of satisfaction to me?

"Questions such as these can help us evaluate our performance and find ways to improve."

Process: Present information. List questions on chalkboard. Solicit additional questions from bowlers.

4. Discussion

Content:
    a. Why should you be concerned about monitoring your own performance?
    b. Of what value is it to ask questions of yourself?
    c. How can you be sure you are asking yourself the right questions?
    d. How can you be sure you are responding honestly to your questions?

Process: Conduct discussion using above questions. Encourage all participants to contribute to the discussion.

5. Learning Activity

Content: "I am going to provide each of you with pencil and paper. Please take a few minutes and think about any problems you have had while bowling. List two of these problems on your paper. Take a few more minutes to think and then write the best solution you can think of for each of the problems. When you have finished writing, each of you will be asked to tell the class about a problem you identified and your solution to that problem. After each problem and solution is presented, the class will discuss it to see if there are any helpful suggestions they can make."

Process: Explain activity. Provide pencil and paper. Allow sufficient time for thinking and writing. Provide each person with an opportunity to present a problem and solution. Encourage group to make positive suggestions. If time allows, repeat process with second problem.

6. Debriefing

Content:
    a. Were there problems similar to any you have experienced? If so, what were they?
    b. Were there suggestions made that may help you? If so, what were they?
    c. Did anyone have a problem that no else has had? If so, what is it and what can you do about it? Does anyone have any suggestions for it?
    d. What did you learn from this activity? How will it help you?

Process: Conduct debriefing using above questions. Encourage all participants to respond to at least one of the questions.

7. Conclusion

Content: "The best person to help you improve is yourself. In fact, no one can do it for you. Self-improvement requires patience, practice, and hard work. By asking questions of yourself and thinking of solutions, you can make progress toward self-improvement."

Process: Make concluding statements. Provide opportunity for questions.

Goal 4: Demonstrate effective decision-making skills related to bowling.

Objective 4.1: Demonstrate knowledge of correct target pin for picking up a spare.

1. Orientation Activity

Content: "Each of you has been given two cards that are pictures of colored bowling pins. Find the person who has the cards with the same colored bowling pins as you, introduce yourself, and find out the person's name.

"Together, you now have four different cards that show a lane with pins on one end. The number of pins standing will range from 2-9. With your partner, decide where the ball should be thrown for the best chance of getting a spare. Draw a line from the penalty line to the spot you would try to hit. Each of you do this on two of the pictures. Make sure you talk it over with your partner before you draw the line. We will then get into a circle and share our results with the group. Be sure to introduce yourself, describe two of the pictures, and allow your partner to describe the other two pictures."

Process: Make up several different combinations of pins remaining and draw them on cards. Make sure there are at least two cards per participant. Distribute the pictures and pencils. Move about the room assisting participants as needed. After participants complete the drawing, arrange them in a circle. Have each person speak.

2. Introduction

Content: "In bowling, a spare means the bowler downed all 10 pins with two shots in one frame. Bowlers often fail to pick up spares because they are unaware of which pins to use as targets and where the ball should make contact with the pin. Having knowledge of how to score spares will help you become a better bowler and increase your enjoyment of leisure through bowling."

Process: Introduce topic of identifying the correct target pin at which to aim for picking up a spare.

3. Presentation

Content: "Bowlers must consider several actions when they are preparing to shoot for a spare. To be successful, bowlers should:
  a. determine which pin is the target pin and where the ball should make contact with it,
  b. select the required angle and target on the lane,
  c. select the approach position,
  d. identify any special problems (e.g., pins off spot),
  e. line up on the selected approach and squarely face the target,
  f. recheck the approach position, target, and point of contact,
  g. concentrate and make the shot,
  h. follow-through with the shot, and
  i. watch and evaluate the shot.

"This may seem like too many steps to remember but, with practice, they will become second nature. "In bowling, there are many possible combinations of pins to form a spare. In general, these combinations can be grouped into spares where pins are left standing on (a) the right side of the lane, (b) in the middle of the lane, or (c) on the left side of the lane. Each of these groups requires a different approach.

"In spares where pins are left on the right side of the lane, you should start with a left side approach and use the third arrow from the right as the lane target. Left-handed bowlers should use the second arrow from the left as the lane target. In spares where pins are left in the middle of the lane, you should start with a center approach and use the second arrow from the right as the lane target. Left-handed bowlers should use the second arrow from the left as the lane target. In spares where pins are left on the left side of the lane, you should start with a right side approach and use the second arrow from the right as the lane target. Left-handed bowlers should use the third arrow from the left as the lane target. This is known as the cross-lane principle. The cross-lane principle allows you to use the full width of the lane. This is important to remember when shooting for spares.

"Every combination of pins in a spare has a key or target pin. This is generally the pin that is closest to the bowler and is the one that must be struck first in order to pick up the spare. Each target pin has an area on it that is known as the *spare zone*. This is the actual spot on the pin where the ball should make contact. For right-handed bowlers, the spare zone is usually located on the right side of the pin, for left-handed bowlers it is usually on the left side of the pin. Some spares result in pins having *head on spare zones*. This refers to the area directly in the middle of the pin and is the same for right- or left-handed bowlers. Using these zones on the 1, 2, 3, 4, 6, 7, and 10 pins covers all possible spares."

Process: Present information on spares and target pins. Use chalkboard to list nine major actions when picking up spares. Demonstrate application of cross-lane principle. Emphasize and illustrate concept of target pins and spare zones.

4. Discussion

Content:
    a.   What is a spare and how many possible combinations of pins for spares are there?
    b.   What is the cross-lane principle and how can it be useful to a bowler?
    c.   In a spare, what is the target pin?
    d.   On a target pin, what is the spare zone?

Process: Conduct discussion using above questions. Encourage all participants to contribute to the discussion.

5. Learning Activity

Content: "We are going to look at several possible spare combinations. I am going to illustrate them one at a time on the chalkboard. For each spare combination that is illustrated, I will ask one of you to identify the target pin and its spare zone. All bowlers will have the same number of opportunities to identify target pins and spare zones."

Process: Explain activity. Illustrate spares on chalkboard. Use enough combinations to provide each participant with four or five opportunities to identify target pins and spare zones.

6. Debriefing

Content:
    a.   Why is the target pin the one that is usually nearest to the bowler?
    b.   Which spares appear to be the most difficult to pick up?
    c.   How can the cross-lane approach make it easier to pick up spares?
    d.   How can this knowledge help you become a better bowler?

Process: Conduct debriefing using above questions. Encourage all participants to respond to at least one of the questions.

7. Conclusion

Content: "Knowing how to pick up spares and having the physical skills to do so will improve your performance. It will also allow you to be a valuable asset to friends and fellow bowlers by sharing that knowledge with them and encouraging them to improve their skills. Bowlers usually have to work hard to acquire and develop skills in picking up spares but the resulting improvement will increase the satisfaction and fun of the game."

Process: Make concluding statements. Provide opportunity for questions.

Objective 4.2: Demonstrate the ability to adjust target mark to hit the strike pocket.

1. Orientation Activity

Content: "You each have been given two pictures of a person thinking. The first light yellow picture represents you when you were four years old thinking about what you most like to do. Draw a picture inside the cloud above your head that best represents what you most liked to do then. Once you have finished, turn to the green picture representing you today, thinking about what you most like to do. Draw this activity in the cloud above your head. When everyone is finished, we will get into a circle to share our work. When it is your turn to share with us, be sure to tell us your name, show us the pictures, identify the activities, and tell us if you have changed."

Process: Make a picture of a person thinking. Place on the bottom part of the paper the top of someone's head and have the cloud consume the majority of the paper to allow participants space to draw. Copy the picture on two different colors. Distribute crayons, markers or colored pencils with the two copies to each participant. If there are not enough writing implements, then have participants sit at small tables and share the pencils or markers. Move among the participants as they draw, providing encouragement and commenting on the pictures.

2. Introduction

Content: "Although efforts are made to insure lane uniformity and consistency among bowling centers, lane conditions vary from center to center. Sometimes, conditions can vary from lane to lane within the same center and even on the same lane during a game. Because of variation in lanes, it is important to know how to adjust the target mark in order to hit the strike pocket."

Process: Introduce topic of adjusting the target mark to hit the strike pocket.

3. Presentation

Content: "Remember that the strike pocket for right-handed bowlers is the area between the 1 and 3 pins; for left-handed bowlers, it is the area between the 1 and 2 pins. The first ball of every frame is aimed at the strike pocket. Right-handed bowlers use a right-of-center approach and the second arrow from the right edge of the lane as the target mark. Left-handed bowlers do the opposite. But differences in lane conditions may require you to change the target mark.

"When adjusting the target mark, you must carefully observe and track the course of the first ball thrown. If the ball travels too much to the left, you should shift the approach to the left. If the ball is going to the right, then the approach should be shifted to the right. Lane conditions will dictate how much of a shift should be made. The ability to adjust target marks comes only with experience and practice.

"Some bowlers use the boards that make up the bowling lane to adjust the target marks. Boards are counted from right to left; the head pin is always set on board number 20. From whatever board you stand on to throw strikes, you can count and move three boards to the right or left to hit one pin to the right or left of the head pin. For each succeeding pin to the right or left of the head pin, three more boards should be counted. This is a skill that also comes with practice, but it will help you adapt to different lane conditions."

Process: Present information on changing target marks. Use chalkboard or overhead projector to present diagrams of moving mark to right or left.

4. Discussion

Content:
    a. Why do you need to know how to adjust your target marks?
    b. Why is it important to follow the course of the first ball thrown on a lane?
    c. If a ball travels too much to the left, what adjustment can be made in the approach?
    d. On what board does the head pin sit?

Process: Conduct discussion using above questions. Encourage all participants to contribute to the discussion.

5. Learning Activity

Content: "The best way to develop skill in adjusting target marks is to practice on several different lanes. We have arranged for each of you to throw eight consecutive balls on each lane. Take your ball with you from lane to lane. When you get to a new lane, watch the course of your first delivery and begin to make necessary adjustments in your target marks. This activity requires that you make adjustments. Remember what you have learned."

Process: Explain activity. Players change lanes after every eight throws. Monitor activity. Answer questions and provide hints, as necessary.

6. Debriefing

Content:
    a. Did you notice variations among lanes? Which lanes seemed the most different?
    b. Were eight throws enough to help you make the adjustment you wanted?
    c. How did you adjust your approach?
    d. How will you continue to improve your ability to adjust your target marks?

Process: Conduct debriefing using above questions. Encourage all participants to respond to at least one of the questions.

7. Conclusion

Content: "Being able to adjust target marks in response to variations in lane conditions makes it possible for you to enjoy this activity in a variety of bowling centers. You do not have to bowl in the same place every time or on the same lanes every time. Variety increases your chances for enjoyment."

Process: Make concluding statements. Provide opportunity for questions.

Objective 4.3: Demonstrate the ability to correctly choose a bowling ball.

1. Orientation Activity

Content: "Half of you have been given a list of five things that we consider when choosing a bowling ball. The other half of the group has been given a bowling ball. Those of you with the lists should find a person with a bowling ball. Approach the person, introduce yourself, and find out the person's name. Do not show the person what is written on your paper. Ask the person to tell you one thing he or she thinks about when choosing a bowling ball. Once the person answers, write his or her name beside the consideration listed on your paper. Approach another person, introduce yourself and find out the person's name. Ask this person to share what he or she considers when choosing a bowling ball and, in addition, tell the person that he or she must give you a different consideration than the first person with whom you spoke. Read this consideration to the person and have him or her suggest another one. If the person cannot think of another consideration, move to another person. Continue moving about the room trying to get people's names recorded for each of the five considerations listed on the paper."

Process: On a paper list five things considered when choosing a bowling ball (e.g., grip, pitch of finger holes, span of finger holes, width of finger holes, and weight of the ball). Put a space after these considerations for participants to record names of other participants. Move about the room assisting people as needed. Possibly participate in this activity. A discussion could be conducted after the activity.

2. Introduction

Content: "Choosing a bowling ball that fits well and is comfortable reflects your knowledge of bowling. It is also an indication of your willingness and ability to be responsible for yourself. Awareness of factors that influence the choice of a ball will help you make appropriate and independent decisions."

Process: Introduce topic of correctly choosing a proper bowling ball.

3. Presentation

Content: "A bowling ball that is comfortable and properly fitted can significantly impact a bowler's performance. There are several factors to be considered when fitting a ball to a bowler. The most important factors are:
    a. grip,
    b. pitch of finger holes,
    c. span of finger holes,
    d. width of finger holes, and
    e. weight of the ball.

"There are two types of finger grips: conventional and finger tip. The conventional grip is the most comfortable and is usually the one adopted by most new bowlers. In this grip the middle and ring fingers go into the ball to the second joint. The conventional grip gives a feeling of control and security. With the finger tip grip, the middle and ring fingers go into the ball only to the first joint. It is up to you to decide which grip is best for you.

"Pitch also contributes to proper fit of a bowling ball. Pitch refers to the angle at which holes are drilled into the balls. Too much or too little pitch can give a feeling of loss of control and not being comfortable. It can cause you to release the ball too soon or too late. New bowlers should find a ball which they do not have to squeeze tightly with their fingers in order to feel in control of the ball. The fit should be comfortable and allow you to release the ball with as little tension in the arm as possible.

"Span refers to the distance from the inner edge of the thumb hole to the inner edge of each of the finger holes. To test for a proper span, the thumb should be completely inserted into the thumb hole. Then, the middle fingers should be stretched over the finger holes. If the ball has a good span for you, the second joint of the second finger will be directly over the finger holes.

"Another factor that should be considered when fitting a ball is the width of the finger holes. This refers to the distance between the finger holes. The finger hole spaces should not be greater than the distance between the first knuckles of the first and third fingers.

"The last factor to be considered in fitting a ball is its weight. Bowling balls range in weight from less than 10 pounds to a maximum of 16 pounds. The weight of the ball, which is usually stamped next to the finger holes, should be at least 10 percent of the bowler's body weight. The following formula can be used to determine the weight of a ball for you: Body weight x .10 = minimum weight of ball. For example, a bowler who weighs 109 pounds would have a formula as follows: 109 x .10 = 10.9 (rounded to 11). In this case, the bowler should use an 11 pound ball."

Process: Present information on fitting a ball. Use chalkboard to emphasize five major factors. Demonstrate difference between conventional and finger tip grips. Emphasize that pitch is a matter of personal comfort. Use bowling ball to demonstrate how to test for span and width. Provide two or more examples of using formula to determine weight of ball.

4. Discussion

Content:
     a.   Why is proper fit of a ball important to a bowler?
     b.   What factors are important in fitting a ball to a bowler?
     c.   What is meant by pitch? By span? By width?
     d.   How can a bowler determine how much a ball should weigh?

Process: Conduct discussion using above questions. Encourage all participants to contribute to the discussion.

5. Learning Activity

Content: "Please get into pairs and get ready to choose a ball that has a proper fit for you. You each have paper and pencil. Use the formula that you have been taught to determine the weight of a ball that would be proper for you. Show your partner how you calculated the ball weight. Partners will check each other's calculations to see that they are correct. Partners will then have five minutes to go to the ball racks and, using the criteria presented in this lesson, choose a ball for each that fits properly. Partners will explain to each other how they made their choice and then bring the ball to me and explain their choice."

Process: Explain activity. Provide pencil and paper. Monitor calculations. Provide opportunity for each bowler to explain choice of fit.

6. Debriefing

Content:

    a. What weight did you choose? How did you determine that?
    b. How did you determine the width of the finger holes?
    c. How did you determine the span?
    d. What grip did you use?
    e. The next time you bowl, will you be able to choose a ball that fits you properly?

Process: Conduct debriefing using above questions. Encourage all participants to respond to at least one of the questions.

7. Conclusion

Content: "We have examined the factors that should be considered when you choose a bowling ball. Knowing what these factors are and how to apply them will help you to choose a properly fitting ball. You can now be responsible for making that choice."

Process: Make concluding statements. Provide opportunity for questions.

LEISURE EDUCATION VOLLEYBALL PROGRAM

Purpose, Goals, and Objectives

Purpose: Provide opportunities for participants to learn the skills required for volleyball, increase their understanding of leisure resources associated with volleyball, develop their ability to cooperate with others, be assertive, and enhance their ability to establish realistic goals in volleyball.

Goal 1: Demonstrate ability to play volleyball.

Objective 1.1.   Demonstrate ability to serve.
Objective 1.2.   Demonstrate ability to perform a forearm pass.
Objective 1.3.   Demonstrate ability to set a volleyball.
Objective 1.4.   Demonstrate ability to spike a volleyball.
Objective 1.5.   Demonstrate knowledge of the rules of volleyball.

Goal 2: Demonstrate knowledge of volleyball resources.

Objective 2.1.   Demonstrate knowledge of equipment needed for volleyball.
Objective 2.2.   Demonstrate knowledge of facilities where volleyball can be played.
Objective 2.3.   Demonstrate knowledge of stores that sell volleyball equipment.

Goal 3: Demonstrate ability to cooperate with others during volleyball.

Objective 3.1.   Demonstrate ability to follow rules.
Objective 3.2.   Demonstrate ability to take constructive criticism.
Objective 3.3.   Demonstrate ability to comply with group decisions.

Goal 4: Demonstrate ability to be assertive during volleyball.

Objective 4.1.   Demonstrate ability to ask questions.
Objective 4.2.   Demonstrate ability to offer suggestions.

Goal 5: Demonstrate ability to establish realistic goals for volleyball.

Objective 5.1.   Demonstrate ability to establish achievable, challenging goals.
Objective 5.2.   Demonstrate ability to modify goals.

Goals, Objectives, and Performance Measures

Goal 1: Demonstrate ability to play volleyball.

Objective 1.1: Demonstrate ability to serve.

Performance Measure: Given a volleyball, net, and court, in five minutes participant will demonstrate ability to serve a volleyball by executing an underhand serve and having the ball pass over the net and land in the opponents' court, on eight out of 10 consecutive attempts.

Objective 1.2: Demonstrate ability to perform a forearm pass.

Performance Measure: Given a volleyball, net, and court, participant will demonstrate ability to perform a forearm pass by passing the ball back and forth with the instructor for 60 consecutive seconds without letting the ball touch the floor.

Objective 1.3: Demonstrate ability to set a volleyball.

Performance Measure: Given a volleyball, participant will demonstrate ability to set a volleyball by setting the ball back and forth with the instructor for 30 consecutive seconds without letting the ball touch the floor.

Objective 1.4: Demonstrate ability to spike a volleyball.

Performance Measure: Given a volleyball, net, and court, participant will demonstrate ability to spike a volleyball by forcefully hitting a ball set above the net by the instructor and driving it downward into the opponents' court on six out of 10 consecutive attempts.

Objective 1.5: Demonstrate knowledge of the rules of volleyball.

Performance Measure: Upon request and within 10 minutes, participant will demonstrate knowledge of the rules of volleyball by verbally providing the correct response to eight of the following 10 questions:
  (a)   How many points does it take to win a game?
  (b)   How many points must a team win by?
  (c)   How many games are there in a match?
  (d)   How many hits per team are allowed when the ball is on their side of the net?
  (e)   What is a foot fault?
  (f)   What parts of the body may come in contact with the ball?
  (g)   What should happen when a player touches the net when the ball is in play?
  (h)   What should happen when a player catches the ball?
  (i)   Are players allowed to change positions after the ball is served?
  (j)   When can a player hit the ball twice in succession?
on two consecutive occasions.

Goal 2: Demonstrate knowledge of volleyball resources.

Objective 2.1: Demonstrate knowledge of equipment needed for volleyball.

Performance Measure: Given pencil and paper within 10 minutes participant will demonstrate knowledge of equipment needed for volleyball by writing any five of the following seven items:

  (a) volleyball,
  (b) socks,
  (c) net,
  (d) shorts or sweat pants,
  (e) shoes,
  (f) T-shirt or sweatshirt, and
  (g) knee pads,

on two consecutive occasions.

Objective 2.2: Demonstrate knowledge of facilities where volleyball can be played.

Performance Measure: Given pencil and paper within five minutes participant will demonstrate knowledge of facilities where volleyball can be played by listing three facilities (e.g., fitness club, park, municipal recreation department) in the community, on three consecutive occasions.

Objective 2.3: Demonstrate knowledge of stores that sell volleyball equipment.

Performance Measure: Given pencil and paper within five minutes, participant will demonstrate knowledge of community retail outlets that sell volleyball equipment by listing four retail outlets in the community, on three consecutive occasions.

Goal 3: Demonstrate ability to cooperate with others during volleyball.

Objective 3.1: Demonstrate ability to follow rules.

Performance Measure: Given five volleyball games, participant will demonstrate the ability to follow rules by adhering to established program rules:

  (a) points may be scored by the serving team only,
  (b) server cannot step on the service line,
  (c) the ball cannot come to rest on any part of a player's body,
  (d) players cannot hit a ball twice in succession unless the ball is touched while blocking or the ball is contacted twice in rapid succession while in the act of blocking,
  (e) a team is allowed three contacts of the ball with the exception that a touch by a blocker does not count,
  (f) players cannot touch the net while the ball is in play,
  (g) players must be in their correct rotation positions at the moment the ball is served but after the ball is in play, players may move to any position on the court,

for five consecutive games, as observed by the instructor.

Objective 3.2: Demonstrate ability to take constructive criticism.

Performance Measure: Given constructive criticism by the instructor when warranted, participant will demonstrate the ability to take such criticism by thanking the instructor and attempting, within five minutes, to change behavior as suggested by the criticism, on three consecutive occasions.

Objective 3.3: Demonstrate ability to comply with group decisions.

Performance Measure: The player, as a member of a group given the opportunity to choose its practice drills, will demonstrate the ability to comply with group decisions by participating in all such drills for three consecutive sessions.

Goal 4: Demonstrate ability to be assertive during volleyball.

Objective 4.1: Demonstrate ability to ask questions.

Performance Measure: Given a 10 minute discussion on volleyball, participant will demonstrate the ability to ask questions by making two volleyball-related inquiries of the instructor, on three consecutive occasions.

Objective 4.2: Demonstrate ability to offer suggestions.

Performance Measure: Given a volleyball game, participant will demonstrate the ability to offer suggestions by making two volleyball-related suggestions to teammates, on three consecutive occasions.

Goal 5: Demonstrate ability to establish realistic goals for volleyball.

Objective 5.1: Demonstrate ability to establish achievable, challenging goals.

Performance Measure: Given paper, pencil, within 20 minutes, participant will demonstrate ability to establish goals by listing 10 goals to be achieved in the volleyball program.

Objective 5.2: Demonstrate ability to modify goals.

Performance Measure: Given paper, pencil, and a previously prepared list of 10 personal goals, within 10 minutes participant will demonstrate ability to modify goals by reviewing the list and altering two of the goals to make them easier or more difficult to attain.

Goals, Objectives, Content, and Process

Goal 1: Demonstrate ability to play volleyball.

Objective 1.1: Demonstrate ability to serve.

1. Orientation Activity

Content: "I have given some of you balls with different colored dots on them. Those of you who have been given colored cards are to now find the person who has the volleyball with dots that are the same color as your card. Once you have located the person, introduce yourself and find out his or her name. Now you are ready to try a wall serving game. There is a strip of tape on the floor about 30 feet from the wall. On the wall there is a strip of tape at a height of eight feet. Stand behind the tape line on the floor, hit the ball in any way you wish, and hit it above the tape on the wall without first touching the ceiling, floor, or a side wall. Have your partner keep track of the number of consecutive hits you make. Try to extend your streak as long as possible. You are permitted three hits that do not hit the wall above the eight foot strip. Once you have made three such hits, switch places with your partner and continue in this way until I give you the signal to stop."

Process: Prepare dots on balls and cards to allow you to pair participants together. Explain activity. Have one ball for every pair. Encourage players who are counting to call out the numbers of consecutive hits and cheer for the player who is hitting the ball. At the end of the activity, ask players for demonstrations of their hitting techniques.

2. Introduction

Content: "Serving is the act of putting the volleyball into play by striking it so that it goes into the opponents' court. Only the serving team can score points in volleyball, so the serve is a skill that must be learned by all players. Basically, there are two types of serves in volleyball–the underhand serve and the overhand serve. We are going to concentrate on the underhand serve because it is easier to learn. Having command of the underhand serve will allow us to move more quickly to other parts of the game."

Process: Introduce topic on serving the volleyball.

3. Presentation

Content: "Players must be consistent and accurate in serving a volleyball. Consistency means serving the ball into the opposing team's court as often as possible. If you do not do so, you lose your chance to score a point. Accuracy means serving the ball to a specific location in the opponents' court. Once consistency and accuracy are achieved, you may consider serving with more power or putting movement on the ball. But beginning players must learn consistency first and then accuracy.

"The underhand serve is usually the serve beginning players find most consistently gets the ball into the opponents' court. This is important in games because it keeps the opportunity to score, but it is also important in practices because it is necessary to start play so other parts of the game can be learned.

"The underhand serve is begun by the server standing in stride position behind the service line; that is, the leg opposite the hitting arm should be forward. The ball should be held with the nonhitting hand about waist-high in front of the lead leg. The hitting arm should be extended at the elbow and drawn back in preparation for striking the ball. The hitting motion for the underhand serve is similar to tossing a ball underhanded or pitching a horseshoe. At the same time the hitting arm is moving forward, the server should step forward, transferring body weight from the rear leg to the lead leg. The ball should be contacted behind the service line and in front of the body at a point just below the waist. The ball should be released by the nonhitting hand just prior to contact by the hitting arm. The ball should be contacted just below its center by the heel of the open hand of the hitting arm. The hitting arm should complete its follow-through motion and the server should move onto the court, ready to play the ball if it is returned over the net.

"A serve is deemed illegal if you serve while in contact with the floor outside the service area. It is also illegal if the ball is thrown or pushed instead of struck, if the server hits it with two hands or arms, and if it is not released before it is hit for service. These actions are known as service faults.

"A served ball must get in the opponents' court by passing over the net without touching it. Only the server can put the ball in play; it cannot be touched by any other player on the server's team prior to passing over the net. The ball cannot pass under the net and it cannot land outside the boundaries of the opponents' playing area."

Process: Present information on serving. Prepare diagram of court and service area ahead of session; distribute to players. Point out service area on diagram and on court. Demonstrate underhand serve and service faults. Serve to opponents' court and ask players if serve is in or out.

4. Discussion

Content:
    a.   What is the difference between consistency and accuracy in serving?
    b.   Which would you choose for your volleyball skills, consistency or accuracy? Why?
    c.   What is a service fault?
    d.   What are some examples of service faults?
    e.   What are some things that could happen that would make a serve illegal?

Process: Conduct discussion using above questions. Encourage all participants to contribute to the discussion.

5. Learning Activity

Content: "We are going to practice the underhand serve. Pair up with a partner and take a volleyball. Get on opposite sides of the net. One partner should get behind the service line and try 10 underhand serves; the other partner will retrieve and return the ball. After 10 serves, switch roles but stay on your own side of the net. The server becomes the retriever and the retriever becomes the server. Continue changing roles. Concentrate on consistency."

Process: Explain activity. Have sufficient volleyballs on hand. Emphasize correct serving technique and consistency. Move among players and offer assistance when needed.

6. Learning Activity

Content: "We are going to divide into two groups to do this activity. The two groups will be on opposite sides of the net, behind the service lines on their respective sides. Line up in single file. The first person in one line will make an underhand serve. If the ball passes over the net and lands in the opponents' court, the serving side will shout "1." If the ball does not pass over the net or lands out-of-bounds, the serving side will remain silent. In either case, the server will go to the end of the line. The first person in the other line will then try an underhand serve, with the same rules. Serves will alternate from line to line. I will judge whether the ball lands in- or out-of-bounds. After each good serve, the serving side will shout out its count of good serves. The first side to reach 10 will be the winner."

Process: Explain activity. Divide players into two groups. Use only one ball. After one side reaches "10," repeat activity.

7. Debriefing

Content:
    a.   What common errors were made in serving?
    b.   How can these errors be corrected?

    c.   What was the relationship between consistency and the side that won the contest?

    d.   Do you feel like you need more practice time?

Process: Conduct debriefing using above questions.

8. Conclusion

Content: "Serving is a skill that must be learned because points can only be scored by the serving team. The underhand serve is usually the best serve for beginning players. As you become more experienced in serving, you may think about using an overhand serve, but for now the underhand serve is best."

Process: Make concluding statements. Provide opportunity for questions.

Objective 1.2: Demonstrate ability to perform a forearm pass.

1. Orientation Activity

Content: "Everyone sit down in a circle and take off one shoe. Throw the shoe in the box in the center of the circle. Now I will tie pairs of shoes together. Once I have tied all shoes in pairs, I will lay them on the floor. Find your shoe and your partner will be the person who owns the shoe tied to yours. Introduce yourself to the person and find out his or her name. Untie the shoes and put your shoe on.

"We are going to practice passing a volleyball to ourselves, so I am giving each pair a volleyball. One player in each pair will begin by hitting the ball six to eight feet in the air by use of the forearms. As the ball comes down, the player will again use the forearms to hit the ball back into the air. The player will continue until the ball has been hit 10 consecutive times. The player's partner will count the number of consecutive hits. If the player uses the hands to hit the ball or is unable to reach the ball to hit it again, the partner will become the passer to self and the first player will become the counter. Players will alternate their turns trying to become the first to pass the ball to themselves 10 consecutive times."

Process: Obtain a box large enough to hold one shoe per participant. Explain activity. Allow sufficient space per pair. Use one ball per pair. Emphasize use of forearms, not hands. At conclusion of activity, ask players if they successfully avoided using their hands.

2. Introduction

Content: "The forearm pass is one of the most important skills in volleyball. It is used for receiving serves and digging hits from opponents. The forearm pass, after receiving a serve, helps begin the next sequence of passes by the offensive team. A good pass usually leads to a good set; a poor pass usually means a poor set."

Process: Introduce topic on forearm pass. Demonstrate correct form.

3. Presentation

Content: "To get ready to receive the ball, the passer must be both alert and relaxed. Your weight should be on the balls of your feet to help you react quickly to the incoming ball. The passer should try to get directly in line with the incoming ball by taking small, quick sliding steps with the knees bent.

"You should contact the ball with the forearms just above the wrists. When the ball is contacted, your arms should be straight with your elbows fully extended and your thumbs pointed downward. The power for the forearm pass comes from a combination of factors: the speed of the incoming ball, the extension of your legs and hips, and the force of your shoulder elevation and flexion. When the ball is contacted, your forearms are used in a controlled hit. There should be little follow-through with your forearms.

"The forearm pass can be thought of in terms of providing a passing platform for the ball. When your elbows are locked and your thumbs and hands pointed downward, your arms can be raised, lowered, or turned to a side to give the ball a flat surface to contact and rebound in the direction you want. The forearm pass requires concentrated effort and practice. It is the basis for successful volleyball and worth the effort it takes to master it."

Process: Present information on forearm pass. Demonstrate proper technique.

4. Discussion

Content:
    a.   Why is the forearm pass considered to be the most important skill in volleyball?
    b.   How does a player get into position to make a forearm pass?
    c.   Where does the ball contact the body in a properly executed forearm pass?
    d.   What is the position and action of the arms in a forearm pass?

Process: Conduct discussion using above questions. Encourage all participants to answer at least one of the questions.

5. Learning Activity

Content: "Pair up for a forearm passing practice game. Partners should face each other at a distance of ten feet. Practice passing a volleyball back and forth by bumping it with your forearms to a height of no more than 10 feet. Count your own passes. See which pair can be the first to make 15 consecutive passes without an error."

Process: Explain activity. Have one ball per pair. Use tape marks to ensure distance of 10 feet between players. Allow sufficient space per pair. Monitor activity for fairness in counting.

6. Learning Activity

Content: "Get into groups of three for another passing game. One person in the group will start as the passer, one as the setter, and one as the thrower. The passer and setter will be on one side of the net and the thrower will be on the other side. The thrower will toss the ball over the net to the passer. The passer will make a forearm pass to the setter. The setter will catch the pass and return the ball to the thrower. After 10 tries, rotate. The thrower will move to the passer's position, the passer to the setter's position, and the setter to the thrower's position. Rotate until each player has had three chances to be the passer."

Process: Explain activity. Divide players into groups of three, if necessary. Many groups can participate simultaneously in this activity.

7. Debriefing

Content:
    a. What movements do you make to prepare yourself to perform a forearm pass?
    b. Are you feeling better using your forearms and not your hands in passing the ball? If not, are you ready for more practice?
    c. Are you gaining confidence in your ability to pass the ball accurately? If not, what needs to be done to increase your confidence?
    d. What questions or comments do you have about the forearm pass?

Process: Conduct debriefing using above questions. Encourage all participants to respond to your questions.

8. Conclusion

Content: "Learning the forearm pass may seem difficult because volleyball is the only sport that uses it. Most of us want to use our hands until we learn to use our forearms. Practice is necessary, especially in learning to receive serves from the opponent. If we cannot successfully receive a serve, we cannot get the ball back for our team to serve and score."

Process: Make concluding statements. Provide opportunity to ask questions.

Objective 1.3: Demonstrate ability to set a volleyball.

1. Orientation Activity

Content: "All your names have been taped on the wall. Find your name and lift it up to see another name under yours. This person will be your partner for this activity. Find the person. Introduce yourself, find out the person's name, and begin the activity.

"We must learn to make high overhead passes. On the wall there is a tape line at a height of 12 feet. One of you will pass the ball to a spot on the wall above the tape line and hit the rebound back to a spot above the line. The rebound must be contacted at a point above your head. The ball cannot touch the floor and the player can have only momentary contact with the ball. Your partner will count how many consecutive passes you make. Once the ball hits the ground three times, the counter will become the passer. Continue in this way, remembering the most consecutive hits completed by a player."

Process: Prepare duplicate cards of each player's name. Take two names and put one name (A) on top of the other name (B) and put the remaining name of B and place it on top of A's name. Tape them to a wall, making sure to only tape the top side to allow players to look under their names. Explain activity. Have sufficient number of volleyballs on hand.

2. Introduction

Content: "Setting a volleyball is making an overhead pass. It is used to put the ball in position for an attack. It must be accurate and made at the correct height and distance. Setting must be performed consistently for a team to take the serve from the opponents."

Process: Introduce topic of setting a volleyball. Demonstrate correct form.

3. Presentation

Content: "Setting, like all other volleyball skills, requires good execution in order for a team to be successful. Performing the set consistently is an ability that comes with practice. You must pay attention to technique.

"In preparing to perform an overhead pass for a set, you should move under the ball as it is passed from a teammate. Your knees should be bent and ready to be extended as soon as the ball comes in contact with your fingers. Your legs provide much of the power for the overhead pass. At the same time you are moving under the ball, your hands should be placed above your head, with your elbows pointing outward. Your wrists should be extended or bent backwards, your fingers spread, and your thumbs pointing slightly at each other. The ball should be contacted only by your thumbs and fingertips, never by your palms. As the ball is contacted, your wrists and fingers should be flexed forward, your arms extended at your elbows, and your legs straightened by extending your knees. The ball must be contacted at the same time by both hands. It must not touch your palms or be directed by your fingers. If it is, it will be ruled an illegal hit. The ball must be hit, not caught and thrown, and set at a height that allows the next player to hit the ball forcefully.

"The positioning of your feet is an important part of setting a volleyball. Your feet should be in a stride position, one foot placed ahead of the other, rather than in a square position, one foot even with the other. The stride position prepares you to move in the direction of the set as it is made. Accurate sets are easier to make when your body is in line with the direction of the set."

Process: Present information on setting. Describe and demonstrate technique. Divide setting into separate positions and movements. Use slow, exaggerated movements to demonstrate each facet.

4. Discussion

Content:
   a.   Why is setting an important skill?
   b.   What is the proper body position and movement for performing a set?
   c.   Why are the legs bent at the knees prior to making a set?
   d.   What happens if the ball is contacted by the palms in making a set?

Process: Conduct discussion using above questions. Encourage all participants to contribute to the discussion.

5. Learning Activity

Content: "We are going to do some setting while sitting. Pair off and sit on the floor, facing each other. Your feet should be about five feet from your partner's feet. Practice setting the ball back and forth from this position. The more accurate your sets are, the less your partner will have to move. The goal of each pair is to make 15 consecutive sets without making an error."

Process: Explain activity. Help players pair off, if necessary. Have one ball for each pair.

6. Learning Activity

Content: "Pair up for a passing and setting activity. One player in each pair will begin by bumping a low forearm pass to himself or herself and then setting a high pass for the partner. The partner will catch the ball and return it to the first player. After 10 tries, the players will change roles. Continue changing until each of you has had 30 chances at setting."

Process: Explain activity. Have one ball per pair. Provide each pair sufficient space.

7. Debriefing

Content:
   a. What is the purpose of practicing setting while sitting?
   b. Do you think it helped in improving your accuracy? If so, how? If not, why not?
   c. What were the movements you went through to set the ball?
   d. Can you teach another player to properly set the ball? If so, how? If not, why not?

Process: Conduct debriefing using above questions. Encourage all participants to respond to at least one of the questions.

8. Conclusion

Content: "Setters need to have good overhead passing skills. They must also have a feel for the position of players on both sides of the net. Setting is used when a team tries to score or take the serve from the opponent. It is an important play in volleyball."

Process: Make concluding statements. Provide opportunity for questions.

Objective 1.4: Demonstrate ability to spike a volleyball.

1. Orientation Activity

Content: "Timing is very important when spiking a volleyball. In this activity the emphasis is on timing. Line up in single file at a distance of 10 feet from the net. I will stand by the net and toss the ball into the air. The first player in line will approach the net in a controlled run, jump, and catch the ball at its peak with both hands. The player will then turn to the group, introduce himself or herself, return the ball to me and go to the end of the line. The other players will advance one place toward the head of the line. We will repeat this action until each of you has gone through the line five times. Timing your jump to catch the ball at its peak is the object of this activity."

Process: Explain activity. Toss ball to appropriate height. If you err on the toss, repeat it so each player has chance to perform activity properly.

2. Introduction

Content: "The spike is considered by many to be the most exciting play in volleyball. It is similar to the slam-dunk in basketball, in that everyone would like to be able to do it well."

Process: Introduce topic of spiking a volleyball.

3. Presentation

Content: "Spiking a volleyball is the result of a combination of several skills: approaching the net, swinging the arms, jumping, hitting the ball, and following through. Most players can do these things separately. Putting them together should result in a spike. A good spike is difficult to return.

"In performing a spike, a three- or four-step approach is enough. As your final steps are taken, your arms should be swung back, your feet should come together, and your arms swung forward as part of your vertical jump. When in the air, your back should be arched, your shoulder girdle rotated, and your hitting arm cocked in readiness. The ball should be struck forcefully with an open hand. The heel of your hand should strike the ball and your wrist should be snapped forward. This action will put top spin on the ball and make it more difficult to return."

Process: Present information on spiking. Demonstrate actions while describing them. Repeat demonstrations, if necessary.

4. Discussion

Content:
a. Why is the spike a favorite play of the fans?
b. What is the purpose of the spike?
c. What is the combination of skills necessary to perform a good spike?
d. What is the relationship between a good set and a good spike?

Process: Conduct discussion using above questions. Encourage all participants to contribute to the discussion.

5. Learning Activity

Content: "We are going to repeat what we did in the orientation activity, except this time, after you catch the ball, throw it down into the opponents' court with both hands. Staying in the air long enough to catch and throw the ball will be similar to the length of time you have to be in the air while actually spiking a ball."

Process: Explain activity. Be consistent in tossing ball above net. Provide each player with an opportunity for 10 attempts.

6. Learning Activity

Content: "This time we are not going to catch the ball. At the peak of your jump, forcefully hit the ball with one hand and drive it down into the opponents' court. Hitting the ball hard is important, but hitting it so hard that control is lost is useless."

Process: Explain activity. Provide each player with 10 attempts. Emphasize force as well as control.

7. Debriefing

Content:
- a. With what part of your hand did you contact the ball?
- b. What is the purpose of snapping your wrist forward in spiking?
- c. Were you able to hit the ball at its peak? If not, why not?
- d. Are you confident in spiking the ball? If not, what will increase your confidence?

Process: Conduct debriefing using above questions. Encourage all participants to respond to at least one of the questions.

8. Conclusion

Content: "The spike can be a nice way to score points or take the serve away from the opposing team. Practicing the spike will bring its rewards during games."

Process: Make concluding statements. Provide opportunity for questions.

Objective 1.5: Demonstrate knowledge of the rules of volleyball.

1. Orientation Activity

Content: "Everyone please sit close together in a circle on the floor with your legs straight. I will spin the volleyball in the center of the group. Once I begin to spin the volleyball, no one can move. The person whose feet are first hit with the volleyball will stand up while everyone moves closer together to fill up the space made by the person standing. This person will then come to the center, tell everyone his or her name, and spin the volleyball. The person whose feet are then hit by the volleyball will move to the center. The person who previously spun the ball will step outside of the circle. The first four people standing outside the circle will be the first group. Continue spinning until only four players remain. These players will be in a group together. Once you are in your group, introduce yourselves and find out the names of the other players in your group. After introductions are made, give as many rules as you can think of about volleyball. Have one person record the rules."

Process: Obtain a volleyball. Observe and assist as needed. Once each group has identified a few rules, give them one minute to complete their list and end the discussion. Have each group report on a rule they recorded. Write the rule on a chalk board. Continue asking each group for a rule until the groups run out of ideas. Provide encouragement for contributions. If an incorrect rule is given, thank the group for the contribution and make changes to the rule so it is listed on the chalkboard correctly.

2. Introduction

Content: "Volleyball players need to have knowledge of the rules of the game. Such knowledge allows the game to be played without confusion, disruption, and delay. Knowing the rules also helps players and influences their strategy. As players become more experienced, they may progress to a more detailed knowledge of the rules, but a basic knowledge is enough for beginning players to get enjoyment from their play."

Process: Introduce topic of knowledge of volleyball rules.

3. Presentation

Content: "Volleyball rules have been established by various organizations that have an interest in the game. Chief among these organizations are the United States Volleyball Association, the National Association for Girls and Women in Sport, and the National Federation of State High School Associations. Each of these organizations has a set of rules for volleyball that varies slightly from the others. Our intention is to become familiar with a set of rules that are as common as possible. Rules that provide structure to the game and allow us to enjoy it are as follows:

   a. Net height for women and girls is 7 feet 4 1/8 inches and 7 feet 11 5/8 inches for men and boys.
   b. Games are played to 15 points.
   c. A team must win by at least two points.
   d. A match is the best two out of three games.
   e. Points may be scored by the serving team only.
   f. When serving, the server cannot step on the service line. This is called a foot fault.
   g. The ball may be played by any part of the body above the waist.
   h. It is illegal for the ball to noticeably come to rest on any part of a player's body.
   i. It is illegal for players to hit a ball twice in succession, except players touching the ball while blocking the next play on the ball if it stays on their side of the net. If players contact the ball twice in rapid succession while in the act of blocking, this counts as one hit only.
   j. A team is allowed three contacts of the ball, except a touch by a blocker does not count as one of three allowable contacts.
   k. Players can not touch the net while the ball is in play.
   l. Players must be in their correct rotation positions at the moment the ball is served.
   m. After the ball is in play, players may move to any position on the court."

Process: Present information on basic rules. Use chalkboard or handout to list each rule. Explain each rule as it is presented. Ask players if clarification is needed.

4. Discussion

Content:
   a. Why is knowing the rules important?
   b. Are there rules you don't understand? If so, which are they?
   c. What suggestions do you have for getting more information on the rules?
   d. How will knowledge of the rules help you personally?

Process: Conduct discussion using above questions. Encourage all participants to contribute to the discussion.

5. Learning Activity

Content: "The best way to know and understand the rules of the game is to see them in action. I am going to divide you into two teams and we will play some practice games. As the games are played, I will monitor the action and stop the game to point out rules. You can also stop and ask questions at any time. Remember, these are practice games and their purpose is to help you understand the rules better. Winning the game is not the object."

Process: Explain activity. Divide group into teams. Observe game closely. Stop and instruct when appropriate. Encourage players to ask questions.

6. Debriefing

Content:
  a. How did this activity help you better understand the rules?
  b. Which rules seemed most difficult to follow? Why?
  c. Do you have questions about any of the rules? If so, which ones?

Process: Conduct debriefing using above questions. Encourage all participants to respond to at least one of the questions.

7. Conclusion

Content: "There are several volleyball rules that players should know. You can get information about these rules from the rule book, but your understanding will be more complete when you see them in a game. Knowing the rules makes the game more fun."

Process: Make concluding statements. Encourage participants to ask questions.

Goal 2: Demonstrate knowledge of volleyball resources.

Objective 2.1: Demonstrate knowledge of equipment needed for volleyball.

1. Orientation Activity

Content: "Most games require some things that are unique to that game and generally not used in other games. For example, certain mallets, balls, and wickets are required for croquet but are not used in other games. On the tables before you are pieces of equipment and pictures of courts and playing fields. Each item of equipment and each picture has a number attached to it. Each of you will be given a pencil and a sheet of paper. Put your name on your paper and go to the tables. When you see a picture of a field or court or an item of equipment that is used for volleyball, write the number of that object on your paper. When 10 minutes have passed, I will ask you to arrange your numbers in order. You can then compare your lists to a correct list. I will ask each of you to stand, introduce yourself, and identify one piece of equipment you listed. As people identify objects, place a check mark in front of that item listed on your sheet. If you missed it, add the item to your list."

Process: Explain activity. Provide pencil and paper. Put numbers on items. For example, have pictures of basketball, badminton, tennis, and volleyball courts numbered. Number a basketball, soccer ball, beach ball, and volleyball. Put numbers on various items of gym clothes, such as shorts, sneakers, and knee pads. Have enough volleyball items so that each person can identify at least one piece of equipment.

2. Introduction

Content: "Volleyball can be played in a very relaxed, informal manner as part of a picnic or a day at the beach. It can also be played in a more formal, competitive manner. Volleyball always requires the use of a net, ball, and court of some kind, but the environment in which the game is played and the social circumstances surrounding the activity can influence the type of clothing that is worn. Having knowledge of the equipment needed to play volleyball is necessary to make informed decisions about participation."

Process: Introduce topic of equipment needed for volleyball.

3. Presentation

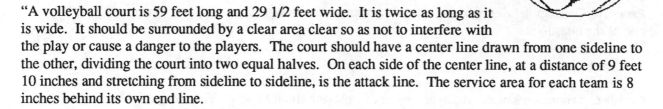

Content: "To play volleyball, certain basic equipment is required. A court, net, and ball must be available.

"A volleyball court is 59 feet long and 29 1/2 feet wide. It is twice as long as it is wide. It should be surrounded by a clear area clear so as not to interfere with the play or cause a danger to the players. The court should have a center line drawn from one sideline to the other, dividing the court into two equal halves. On each side of the center line, at a distance of 9 feet 10 inches and stretching from sideline to sideline, is the attack line. The service area for each team is 8 inches behind its own end line.

"A regulation volleyball net is 32 feet in length and 39 inches in width. It should be placed at a height of 7 feet, 11 and 5/8 inches for men and 7 feet, 4 and 1/8 inches for women for competitive play. The height of the net can be adjusted to the age group or the physical abilities of the participants.

"Volleyballs are round and laceless. They are made of leather or leather-like material in 12 or more segments. They must be from 25 to 27 inches around and weigh 9-10 ounces.

"Personal clothing should include gym clothes, sneakers, and knee pads if the activity is to take place on a hard-surfaced court. Playing in a backyard or park or on a beach requires no special clothing.

Process: Present information on equipment. Prepare and distribute diagram of court with proper markings. Put up net prior to session. Have ball for demonstration model. Emphasize need for knee pads for hard-surface court. Point to lines on court and diagram.

4. Discussion

Content:
   a. In what way can clothing vary from one playing environment to another? Why?
   b. Do nets always have to be placed at regulation heights? Why or why not?
   c. Why are knee pads necessary equipment on some courts?
   d. How will you make use of this information?

Process: Conduct discussion using above questions. Encourage all participants to contribute to the discussion.

5. Learning Activity

Content: "To get a better idea of the equipment needed to play volleyball, we are going to divide into three groups and assume that each group is responsible for determining the kind of equipment that would be needed in three different circumstances. Each group will be given pencils and three sheets of paper. On one sheet, list the equipment needed if a game were to be played for a league championship at a local recreation center. On a second sheet, list the equipment needed if a group of people at the beach decided they wanted to play. On the third sheet, list the equipment needed if people at a backyard barbecue decided they wanted to play. When you have completed your lists, we will compare them."

Process: Explain activity. Divide participants into three groups. Provide pencil and paper. Circulate among participants to answer questions or provide assistance, if necessary. When lists are completed, put each group's response on chalkboard and move to debriefing.

6. Debriefing

Content:
    a. What items of equipment are common to all three environments?
    b. What clothing should be worn at a recreation center as compared to a beach?
    c. What clothing would be worn when playing at a beach as compared to a backyard?
    d. What differences are there in the court at a recreation center as compared to the beach or the backyard?

Process: Conduct debriefing using above questions. Encourage all participants to contribute to the discussion.

7. Conclusion

Content: "We have learned that some items of equipment are always necessary, regardless of the environment in which volleyball is played. We have also learned that the personal clothing needed to play can vary. Knowing what is appropriate for various circumstances allows us to make correct decisions with confidence."

Process: Make concluding statements. Provide opportunity for questions.

Objective 2.2: Demonstrate knowledge of facilities where volleyball can be played.

1. Orientation Activity

Content: "You are being given a handout that contains a list of places where you could play volleyball. Next to the places listed are three columns. The first column is to be used to record whether a person has actually played at a specific place. The second column is to be used to record whether a person would like to play at that place. The third column has been provided to record a person's name. Move about the room and find a person who is not talking with someone. Ask the person the two questions related to the first facility listed on your paper. Record the person's name once he or she has answered the two questions. Find another person and ask the two questions related to the next facility. Continue talking with people until you have answers to all questions. Make sure you introduce yourself to each person you talk to."

Process: Develop a handout containing a list of facilities where volleyball could be played (e.g., municipal recreation center courts, municipal park courts, private health and fitness club courts, Boys' and Girls' Club courts, religious club courts, public school courts). Move about the room assisting students experiencing difficulties. Obtain a handout and take part in the activity if possible.

2. Introduction

Content: "In some instances, volleyball can be played almost anywhere there is open space. But at other times, a regulation court is needed to play the game in order to follow all the rules. Knowing where these courts are located in a community and how to make arrangements to use them allows you to be responsible for your leisure."

Process: Introduce topic on volleyball facilities.

3. Presentation

Content: "Most communities have regulation volleyball courts or courts that can be marked for regulation play. These courts are provided by public or private agencies.

"Community recreation departments usually have both indoor and outdoor courts. Outdoor courts are often available at no cost and on a first come-first served basis. Some indoor community courts are also available at no cost, but some do have a user's fee. Most indoor community courts are managed by a reservation system. Many recreation departments sponsor volleyball leagues and tournaments as part of their ongoing programs. Participation in these programs is usually fee-based, and playing times and space are set.

"Private health and fitness clubs often have courts that can be used for regulation volleyball play. Most of these are indoor courts, but a few may have outdoor courts. A fee is charged for the use of either type of court. Sometimes, the fee is less if players are members of the club. These courts are also available by reservation.

"YMCAs, YWCAs, Jewish Community Centers, Boys' Clubs, Girls' Clubs, and similar agencies often have courts available on a limited basis. The first concern of these organizations is to serve their membership, but after these needs are met, their facilities are sometimes made available to nonmembers for a reasonable fee.

"Public schools, colleges and universities, and sometimes churches are other community groups that generally have courts that can be used for volleyball. You will have to find out whether these courts are open to you and on what basis.

"Most communities have courts to meet the demand for volleyball. Knowing where these resources are located and how to arrange for their use is the key to their accessibility."

Process: Present information on facilities. Use chalkboard to list community organizations that might be able to provide courts. Explain how reservation systems work.

4. Discussion

Content:
    a. What community groups are likely to have courts where volleyball is played?
    b. What opportunities for play are offered by community recreation departments?
    c. How does a reservation system work?
    d. Have we overlooked facilities for volleyball in the community? If so, which ones?

Process: Conduct discussion using above questions. Encourage all participants to contribute to the discussion.

5. Learning Activity

Content: "Now that we know the types of places to look for volleyball courts, we need to gather some specific information. But I want you to determine what specific information is needed in order for us to have a good understanding of volleyball facilities and their availability in this community. I am going to divide you into three groups and give each group pencil and paper. It will be the task of each group to identify the questions to which we need answers. Once we agree on the questions, we will then try to find answers to them."

Process: Explain activity. Divide players into three groups. Provide pencil and paper. Be available to answer questions. When players are finished, use chalkboard and proceed to debriefing to compile list of questions related to facilities and their availability.

6. Debriefing

Content:
    a.   What things do we need to know?
    b.   How can we find the answers to these questions?
    c.   What is the best way for us to start?
    d.   Once we have answers to the questions, what shall we do with the information?

Process: Conduct debriefing. Ensure that responses to question "a" include name, location, phone number, fee, reservation system, and contact person. Question "b" should include use of telephone directory and direct visit to contact organizations. Question "c" should include arrangements for division of responsibility in information-gathering. Question "d" should suggest collating and distributing information after it is gathered. Devise form with all questions that must be answered and move to next learning activity.

7. Learning Activity

Content: "Now that we know what information we want, our next step is to gather it. The first thing we need to do is select the organizations in our community that we want answers from. After we have identified those organizations, we will divide them among your three groups and have each group obtain the necessary information. This can be done by the telephone or by a direct visit. When we have all the information we need, we will make a list of all the available facilities and the information they provided and see that each of you receives a copy."

Process: Explain activity. Prepare list of community facilities before session. Add to players' list, if needed. Assign organizations to groups. Compile information when gathered. Make and distribute master list.

8. Debriefing

Content:
    a.   How did you find your information? Could you have found an easier way to get it?
    b.   Which organization was the easiest to deal with? Why?
    c.   How will you use this information?

Process: Conduct debriefing using above questions. Encourage each participant to respond to at least one of the questions.

9. Conclusion

Content: "We have just taken a look at the facilities available for playing volleyball in this community. This information can help when we are making decisions about our leisure. Playing volleyball can be fun and enjoyable; having the knowledge to make informed decisions can be equally satisfying."

Process: Make concluding statements. Provide opportunity for questions.

Objective 2.3: Demonstrate knowledge of stores that sell volleyball equipment.

1. Orientation Activity

Content: "Each of you has been given a colored card that indicates you are either a store clerk or a volleyball player. If you are a player, find the person who has a clerk card that is the same color as your card. Once you find this person, introduce yourself and find out the other person's name. The clerk will identify at least two pieces of volleyball equipment the store sells. The player will then decide what item to purchase. Once everyone has had a chance to do this, we will get together as a group and tell what the players bought."

Process: Make up matching colored cards for "clerks" and "players." Distribute cards and provide clear directions. Assist any participants having difficulty finding their partners. Conduct a brief discussion after the orientation by arranging participants in a small circle.

2. Introduction

Content: "If you know where and how to get volleyball equipment, you will become more responsible for your leisure. Knowing where to get what you need and not having to depend on others to get it for you helps you control your own life."

Process: Introduce topic on the value of knowing where to purchase volleyball equipment.

3. Presentation

Content: "There are many sources in a community where you can get the equipment and clothing needed to play volleyball. Most department stores have sportswear sections that carry all of the personal clothing that is required, with the possible exception of knee pads. Sporting goods stores and discount stores that have sporting goods sections also carry the clothing needed, including knee pads. They also carry volleyballs and nets. If such stores do not carry what you want, they are usually willing to order it."

Process: Present information on sources of equipment in community.

4. Discussion

Content:

a. What type of stores are likely to have volleyball equipment and clothing?
b. Have we overlooked any types of stores that might also sell this kind of equipment?
c. Which type of store is most likely to have volleyballs and nets?
d. What can you do if you want an item that the store does not currently have in stock?

Process: Conduct discussion using above questions. Encourage all participants to contribute to the discussion.

5. Learning Activity

Content: "We need to know specifically which stores in this community sell volleyball equipment. To help us find this out, I am going to divide you into three groups and give each group several 3 inch by 5 inch cards. By using the telephone directory, each group will identify on a card the name of a store it thinks handles volleyball equipment. Each store a group can think of will be listed on a separate card. When the groups cannot think of any other possibilities, I will collect the cards and remove duplicates. The remaining cards will be placed in a box and the groups will take turns drawing them out one at a time. Each group will then contact the stores on its cards and ask if they sell sportswear and volleyball equipment. The groups will record the addresses and telephone numbers of those stores that carry such goods. When this activity is completed, we will have a useful list of the stores in this community that sell the equipment and clothing we need. We will make and distribute a list of these stores to each of you."

Process: Explain activity. Divide into groups and distribute cards. Prepare master list of stores ahead of session to see that none are overlooked. After information is compiled, make and distribute list.

6. Debriefing

Content:

a. Is our list complete? Have we overlooked any stores? If so, which ones?
b. What is the value of a list such as this?
c. How can you maintain this list and keep it current?

Process: Conduct debriefing using above questions. Encourage participants to respond to at least one question.

7. Conclusion

Content: "You now have a list of the stores in this community that sell volleyball equipment. You also know to develop and maintain such a list. If you can do this for volleyball, you can do it for any number of things in your life."

Process: Make concluding statements. Provide an opportunity for questions.

Goal 3: Demonstrate ability to cooperate with others during volleyball.

Objective 3.1: Demonstrate ability to follow rules.

1. Orientation Activity

Content: "Each of you has a balloon with a string attached to it. Tie the string around your ankle. Try to step on other participants' balloons while you protect your own. When a balloon has been broken, everyone must stop. If it was your balloon that was broken, pick up the slip of paper, introduce yourself, and read the rule to the others. Once you have completed reading the rule, say 'go' and the action continues."

Process: Make of slips of paper containing rules for volleyball such as:

- points may be scored by the serving team only,
- server cannot step on the service line,
- the ball can not come to rest on any part of a player's body,
- players can not hit a ball twice in succession unless the ball is touched while blocking or
    the ball is contacted twice in rapid succession while in the act of blocking,
- a team is allowed three contacts of the ball with the exception that a touch by a blocker
    does not count,
- players cannot touch the net while the ball is in play,
- players must be in their correct rotation positions at the moment the ball is served but after
    the ball is in play players may move to any position on the court.

Put them in balloons. Blow up the balloons and tie a string to each of the balloons. Emphasize stepping on balloons, rather than kicking at them.

2. Introduction

Content: "Volleyball players must be able to follow the rules of the game. We are going to look at why rules are necessary and what often happens when rules are not followed."

Process: Introduce topic of the need to follow rules.

3. Presentation

Content: "All games have rules that must be followed. Rules provide structure and guidance for our actions and ensure that all participants are treated equally. The rules are the same for everyone in the activity. Activity without rules can become disorderly and confusing. Having the ability and the will to follow rules is a requirement for participation in a team activity. Following the rules means everyone has a chance to enjoy the activity.

"Rules are also established to protect participants from injury and harm. Sometimes, rules are intended to protect players from their own actions and sometimes they are intended to protect others. Safety is important in the conduct of activities.

"Programs may have at least two sets of rules. One set of rules governs the activity. The rules of volleyball guide the playing of the game. There is also likely to be another set of rules. These rules are set to guide the behavior and actions of players in all aspects of the program. For example, there may be rules that do not allow smoking, swearing, playing in the shower room, and other behaviors. Adherence to each set of rules is important.

"People sometimes fail to follow the rules because they do not know what the rules are. This is easily corrected. There are also times when people deliberately choose to not follow the rules. This is usually a selfish and inconsiderate act. When rules in the game of volleyball are broken, a penalty is assessed, meaning a team loses the opportunity to score a point or allows the other team to score. When program rules are broken, there should also be a penalty of some type. The purpose of the penalty should not be regarded as punishment for players, but rather as encouragement for them to change their behavior."

Process: Present information on following the rules.

4. Discussion

Content:
    a.   Why are rules needed for a game?
    b.   Why are rules need for all aspects of a program?
    c.   What is the result of a rule violation in a game?
    d.   What should you expect to happen to you if you break a program rule?
    e.   What is the purpose of assessing a penalty for breaking a program rule?

Process: Conduct discussion using above questions. Encourage all participants to contribute to the discussion.

5. Learning Activity

Content: "We have looked at some rules of volleyball. I have several slips of paper in my hand. Each contains a volleyball rule. I am going to divide you into groups of three and have each group take a slip of paper. Groups will then have 10 minutes to plan a demonstration of how the rule is violated during play and a demonstration of how it is followed."

Process: Explain activity. Prepare the following slips prior to session:

- points may be scored by the serving team only,
- server cannot step on the service line,
- the ball cannot come to rest on any part of a player's body,
- players cannot hit a ball twice in succession unless the ball is touched while blocking or the ball is contacted twice in rapid succession while in the act of blocking,
- a team is allowed three contacts of the ball with the exception that a touch by a blocker does not count,
- players cannot touch the net while the ball is in play,
- players must be in their correct rotation positions at the moment the ball is served but after the ball is in play players may move to any position on the court.

Divide into groups and provide assistance to groups, if necessary.

6. Debriefing

Content:
    a. Has this activity helped you to follow the rules? If so, how? If not, why not?
    b. Are there other things we could do to learn to follow rules? If so, what are they?
    c. Which rules seem to be the easiest to follow? Why?
    d. Which rules seem the most difficult to follow? Why?

Process: Conduct debriefing using above questions. Encourage all participants to respond to at least one question.

7. Conclusion

Content: "Following the rules of volleyball means the game progresses smoothly and everyone has a chance for fun and enjoyment. Following the rules of the program is a sign of respect and consideration for your fellow players."

Process: Make concluding statements. Provide opportunity for questions.

Objective 3.2: Demonstrate ability to take constructive criticism.

1. Orientation Activity

Content: "You have been in this program long enough to have formed some opinions about it and the way it is operated. Take a few minutes to think of a suggestion as to how the program could be improved. Each of you will write your suggestion on a card, but you will not write your name. I will then collect the cards, shuffle them and give them back to you. Each of you will then introduce yourself and read the suggestion on the card."

Process: Distribute pencils and cards. Provide opportunity for each player to read a suggestion. After each suggestion, ask if the suggestion seems helpful and in what spirit did it seem to be made.

2. Introduction

Content: "We are going to give some consideration to the area of constructive criticism. None of us is a perfect volleyball player and each of us has areas in which we could improve. Oftentimes, it is the suggestions and assistance from others that allows us to improve our performance and increase our enjoyment of the game. That is the essence of constructive criticism."

Process: Introduce topic of taking constructive criticism.

3. Presentation

Content: "Constructive criticism is an evaluation of your performance and the provision of feedback to you, with the intent of helping you further develop. Constructive criticism is a very positive act. It is offered in the spirit of friendship. It is not meant to embarrass or demean anyone. We should remember this when we receive constructive criticism.

"The focus of constructive criticism is on a specific aspect of performance. It has nothing to do with the kind of person we are or our value as people. Examples of constructive criticism related to performance of volleyball skills could include the following: 'You are improving your serving technique, but if you hit the ball a little harder, your serves would be more accurate. When you are returning the ball, it would go farther if you kept your hands together when you hit it. When you play the front line, you sometimes stand too close to the net. As a result, it is hard for the ball to clear the net when you try to return it.' All of these examples focus on a specific aspect of performance, not on the player.

"When criticism is offered in a friendly, helpful manner, it should be received in a similar spirit. The recipient should be gracious, acknowledge the suggestions, and thank the other person for providing them. Remember that the other person is not trying to hurt your feelings, but rather is trying to help you improve as a player."

Process: Present the information on constructive criticism. Encourage questions and comments from participants. Provide additional examples if participants appear confused. Emphasize the value of constructive criticism.

4. Discussion

Content:
   a.   What is the purpose of constructive criticism?
   b.   Have you ever been harshly criticized? If so, how did you feel?
   c.   How should we react to constructive criticism?
   d.   Make up an example of constructive criticism. How would you react if this were said to you?

Process: Conduct discussion using above questions. Encourage all participants to contribute to the discussion.

5. Learning Activity

Content: "We are going to play some practice games, during which time we will also give and receive constructive criticism. I will be the referee and those players who are not in the game will sit behind me. They will observe players and my performance as referee. After five minutes of playing time, we will stop play. At that time, the observers will offer constructive criticism to the players and to me. A player may receive criticism only once, but I will accept as much criticism as you think I need. We will then rotate observers into the game and participants who were players will become observers. We will continue this process until everyone receives some constructive criticism."

Process: Explain activity. Play for five minutes. Maintain a list of players, keep track of criticism of players. Rotate players in and out of game. Emphasize friendly, helpful spirit.

6. Debriefing

Content:
   a.   For what part of your performance did you receive criticism?
   b.   How did you feel? How did you react?
   c.   Was there a difference between your feelings and your reaction? If so, what was it?
   d.   What suggestions do you have for the manner in which criticism was offered?
   e.   What are other ways we could learn to accept constructive criticism?

Process: Conduct debriefing using above questions. Encourage participants to respond to at least one of the questions.

7. Conclusion

Content: "Being able to accept constructive criticism without becoming angry is a sign of maturity. We should be grateful that others are interested in us and are willing to help us improve. As our performance improves, so should our fun and enjoyment."

Process: Make concluding statements. Provide the opportunity for questions.

Objective 3.3: Demonstrate ability to comply with group decisions.

1. Orientation Activity

Content: "You have each been given a colored piece of paper with five recreation activities listed on it. Take time now to read the five activities. There is a space to the left of the activities. Rank the five activities. Assign the number 1 to the activity you feel is best and the number 5 to the activity you feel is the least desirable. Now that all of you have assigned a rank to each of the activities, notice that your form is colored. Find the other participants who have the same color paper as you, introduce yourself, and find out everyone's name. Your task is to come up with a group list of the best and least desired activities. This list should be fairly close to each person's individual list. You are going to have to compromise and work together. If you have problems, raise your hands and I will come to your group."

Process: Develop sheets of paper with five recreation activities listed on them (e.g., walking, Ping-Pong™, dancing, talking, reading, traveling). Make sure that you have different colored sheets so that groups can be made. Groups should be two to four people in size.

2. Introduction

Content: "In any group, decisions are usually made for the good of the group, rather than the good of the individuals that make up the group. This is as it should be. Groups could not function as groups if it were any other way. This is as true of volleyball teams as it is of any other group. Being a good member of a group means following group decisions."

Process: Introduce topic of complying with group decisions.

3. Presentation

Content: "Many groups reach a decision by using consensus. This means the group arrived at a decision that reflects the thinking and desires of the majority of the group. It does not necessarily mean that every individual in the group agrees with the decision. Responsible group members, however, comply with group decisions regardless of whether or not they agree with them, unless the decision calls for violation of morals or ethics.

"Volleyball teams often make group decisions. Good team members follow those decisions and they do so in a positive spirit. A cooperative spirit boosts everyone's morale. Team members that disagree with a team decision and express their displeasure by negative actions are disruptive. We should all work to avoid being disruptive."

Process: Present information on complying with group decisions. Encourage questions and comments from participants.

4. Discussion

Content:
    a. What is the meaning of "group consensus?"
    b. What is meant by complying with a group decision?
    c. What would be the effects on a team if players did not comply with team decisions?
    d. What is one example of your complying with a group decision with which you disagreed?

Process: Conduct discussion using above questions. Encourage all participants to contribute to the discussion.

5. Learning Activity

Content: "We are going to divide into teams and play some practice games. Each team will make decisions about its participation in the games. Teams will decide who will start the game, what the rotation will be, what warm-up drills to conduct, and all other matters pertaining to the game. Each player on each team will comply with team decisions and act accordingly, even if he or she disagrees with the decisions."

Process: Explain activity. Divide players into teams and provide opportunity for all other decisions to be made by teams. Monitor behavior of players.

6. Debriefing

Content:
    a. Did you agree with all the decisions that were made?
    b. If you did not agree, what did you do?
    c. How do you feel about your behavior?
    d. Do you think this activity helped you to learn how to comply with group decisions?

Process: Conduct debriefing using above questions. Encourage each participant to respond to at least one of the questions.

7. Conclusion

Content: "None of us always gets to do what we want to do. Players who cooperate for the benefit of the team are often referred to as 'good sports.' That is a nice compliment and one to which we should all aspire."

Process: Make concluding statements. Provide the opportunity for questions.

Goal 4: Demonstrate ability to be assertive during volleyball.

Objective 4.1: Demonstrate ability to ask questions.

1. Orientation Activity

Content: "You have all been given a large index card and a pencil. On the top line write down one question you have about volleyball that you would like answered. Now that everyone has a question to ask, move about the room. Find someone who is not talking with another person, introduce yourself, and find out the person's name. Now that you know the person's name, ask him or her your question. The person should try to answer the question or tell you that he or she does not know. After you have received a response, have the person ask his or her question and attempt to answer the question. Once both of you have asked your questions, move on to another person and repeat the process. Continue asking questions until you have visited with everyone or I give you the signal to stop."

Process: Distribute an index card and pencils to each participant. Encourage the participants to speak with as many people as they possibly can. Move about the room listening to the questions. Provide assistance to participants having difficulty. Prior to beginning the activity, establish a sign that will signal to the participants to stop.

2. Introduction

Content: "Asking questions is a part of any day. We often experience situations in which we have not been given enough information or that, for a variety or reasons, we do not fully understand. Some of us may be somewhat shy, and as a result, are unwilling to ask questions. We need to develop the ability to assert ourselves. One way to do this is to ask questions in a polite but firm manner. Asking questions helps us to be more assertive."

Process: Introduce topic of being assertive during volleyball by asking questions.

3. Presentation

Content: "All people have questions at one time or another. This is true when people encounter a situation with which they are unfamiliar or are faced with a new learning task. For example, people who are first learning to play volleyball may have many questions they would like to ask. They may have questions related to the rules of the game, how to perform a specific physical task, how points are scored, what kind of clothing to wear, where they can play volleyball after the program is finished, or any number of other items.

"Asking questions is a way to gather information. Sometimes people hesitate to ask questions because they think their questions are not worthwhile. Please know that no question is too simple. Any question you ask of me about this program will be treated with respect and given a courteous answer.

"Sometimes we may have a question we wish to ask but are not willing to do so in a crowd because we do not want to call attention to ourselves. This may be understandable but it is also a feeling we should work to overcome. There is no simple way to overcome the fear of asking questions. The only way to get comfortable with asking questions is to ask questions. Just like doing a forearm pass, it is something that will come with practice."

Process: Present information on asking questions. Use a moderate tone that indicates you are open to questions. Emphasize courteous response to questions.

4. Discussion

Content:
    a. Why do we ask questions?
    b. What was the last question you asked of anyone?
    c. Have you been in a situation where you were unwilling to ask a question?
        Why were you unwilling? Did you ask the question anyway?
    d. How can a person overcome an unwillingness to ask questions?

Process: Conduct discussion using above questions. Encourage all participants to contribute to the discussion.

5. Learning Activity

Content: "We are going to have a question and answer session. During the first part of the session, each of you will ask me a volleyball-related question. I will respond to each question. For the second portion of the session, I will put each of your names on slips of paper. You will draw a slip of paper and direct a volleyball-related question to the person whose name is on your slip."

Process: Explain activity. Arrange players in circle or semicircle formation. Respond to questions in open, courteous manner. Prepare slips ahead of session. Provide players time to think of questions.

6. Debriefing

Content:
    a. Was it easy or difficult to ask me a question? Why?
    b. Was it easy or difficult to ask a fellow player a question? Why?
    c. Do you think this activity helped you to ask questions? Why or why not?
    d. What do you plan to do to become more comfortable in asking questions?

Process: Conduct debriefing asking above questions. Encourage each participant to respond to at least one of the questions.

7. Conclusion

Content: "Developing the ability to ask questions is an important task. We need to learn to rely on ourselves to get the information we want. We need to be responsible for ourselves and see to it that we obtain what we need. We can do this by asking questions. This will allow us to be more assertive."

Process: Make concluding statements. Allow participants to ask questions.

Objective 4.2: Demonstrate ability to offer suggestions.

1. Orientation Activity

Content: "Half of you have been given paints and an easel. Please begin to paint a picture of the objects I have placed on the table. The other half of you begin to walk around the room and observe the other people paint. After five minutes, go up to one of the painters, introduce yourself and find out the person's name. Then provide them with one suggestion on how to improve their painting. Once this has been done, continue walking around the room and find another person to meet and provide suggestions. Continue in this way until you have given every painter a suggestion. Once everyone has had a chance to provide suggestions, we will switch roles and allow the painters to become the observers."

Process: Obtain enough easels and paints for half the participants. Place the easels as far apart from each other in the room as possible. Move about the room listening and providing assistance as needed.

2. Introduction

Content: "It may be more difficult for some of us to offer suggestions to others than it is to ask questions of them. This may be because we feel that we have no suggestions of value, or that our suggestions will be rejected. Learning to offer suggestions, when appropriate, is part of being assertive."

Process: Introduce topic of being more assertive by offering suggestions.

3. Presentation

Content: "Offering suggestions to others should be the result of an interest in improving a specific situation. Most of us have probably been the recipients of suggestions that have helped us improve our performance, understand an issue better, or perhaps gain greater acceptance by changing our behavior. Most of us are probably grateful for having been given the suggestions. If we have suggestions for others, based on an interest in helping them improve or change, should we not then share those suggestions with them?

"There is a difference between sharing a suggestion with someone and telling that person what to do. The manner in which a suggestion is offered is often the key as to whether or not it is accepted. Suggestions should be offered in a friendly, open style. The person offering the suggestion should clearly communicate that the motivation for making the offer is based on care and concern for the other person. It should also be communicated that the person receiving the suggestion has the right to decide what to do with it.

"Another critical factor in offering suggestions to others is timing. Good judgment tells us that there are times when people are not in the right frame of mind to accept suggestions and there are other times when their mood is such that they welcome suggestions. We have to be sensitive to tell the difference between those times. There are also times when the situation calls for immediate suggestions and instances where suggestions can be delayed."

Process: Present information on offering suggestions.

4. Discussion

Content:
   a.   Why is the manner in which suggestions are offered important?
   b.   What should be the motivation for offering suggestions?
   c.   Are you sometimes reluctant to offer suggestions? Why? How can you change?
   d.   How can you develop a sense of timing for offering suggestions?

Process: Conduct discussion using above questions. Encourage all participants to contribute to the discussion.

5. Learning Activity

Content: "We are going to have a session where we can offer suggestions to each other. Take some time and think of a suggestion related to this program that you would have for me. You may offer suggestions related to my teaching style, the content of lessons, the practice drills, the rules of the program, or anything else you think needs some change or improvement. Each of you will be asked to offer one suggestion to me"

Process: Explain activity. Provide ample time for players to think of suggestions. Ensure that each player offers a suggestion. Receive suggestions in affable manner.

6. Debriefing

Content:
   a.   Were you comfortable offering a suggestion to me? Why or why not?
   b.   Do you have any other suggestions for me? If so, what are they?
   c.   What will you do to continue to offer suggestions to others in the future?

Process: Conduct debriefing using above questions. Encourage each participant to respond to at least one of the questions.

7. Conclusion

Content: "For some of us, a big obstacle to overcome is our unwillingness to offer suggestions. Being a team member means accepting an obligation to help the team and its members improve performance and enjoy what they are doing. One of the ways to do this is to offer suggestions. Offering suggestions allows us to be more assertive."

Process: Make concluding statements. Provide opportunity for questions.

Goal 5: Demonstrate ability to establish realistic personal goals in volleyball.

Objective 5.1: Demonstrate ability to establish achievable, challenging goals.

1. Orientation Activity

Content: "Each of you has been given a handout. Please set one leisure goal that you would like to achieve, record this goal at the top and then respond to the remaining questions. If you need some help, let me know and I will be around to help you. Once you have completed answering the questions of the handout, move about the room and find a person who is not talking to anyone. Introduce yourself and find out his or her name. Then ask the person his or her goal and tell yours. If you find a person with a similar goal, you two then become a pair and continue to move around the room talking with other people. If you find another person with a goal similar to your team's, the two of you then become a three-person team. Continue this until you have spoken to everyone in the room."

Process: Develop handouts with a place for participant to record a goal. Collect the handouts for use in another orientation activity. The handouts can contain some of the following questions:

> • What could keep me from meeting this goal?
> • What are some things I could do so that these
>   things do not stop me from reaching my goal?
> • Who can help me?
> • What are my chances of achieving this goal?
> • Why do I feel this way?
> • What are some good things that might happen if I succeed?
> • What are some bad things that might happen if I succeed?
> • How can I prevent bad things from happening?
> • What is the first step I should take to reach this goal?

2. Introduction

Content: "When we establish goals, we focus on what we hope to achieve. We think about what we want from participation in a program or activity and how we can get it. Goals help to keep us on task and set a target at which to aim. Having goals and striving to attain them can add to feelings of satisfaction and enjoyment we get from volleyball."

Process: Introduce topic of establishing meaningful goals.

3. Presentation

Content: "Goals are long-range, desirable outcomes. Objectives are often referred to as short-range outcomes or the stepping stones used to reach goals. For the purposes of this program, we are going to think of goals as simply the things you want to do as a result of this program. The goals we wish to attain should be set as the result of careful thought and many of them should stretch our abilities to perform. For the most part, our goals should make us work hard to attain them. It is through concentrated effort that we grow as individuals. The achievement of goals that do not challenge us does not help us grow. Most of our goals should be challenging to achieve, but not impossible.

"When we set a goal, we think about what we want to accomplish. Goals are personal and may vary from person to person. Although people in the same program may have some goals that are similar, it is equally possible that you have some goals that are quite different. For example, in a volleyball program one player's goals may focus on becoming physically fit and developing sport skills, while another player's goals may focus on making new friends and developing leisure interests. Both players have set good goals for themselves.

"When we set goals for ourselves we should think about what we want to accomplish and have a reasonable chance of doing. Setting goals that are achievable but challenging is a skill that comes only with practice. It requires that we be honest with ourselves and make realistic assessments of our abilities, neither overestimating or underestimating them."

Process: Present information on setting goals. Use chalkboard to list major points. Emphasize the need for realistic goal-setting.

4. Discussion

Content:
    a. What is a goal?
    b. How can goals differ between two people who are in the same program?
    c. How can you set "achievable" and "challenging" goals for yourself?
    d. In what other areas of your life do you establish goals?

Process: Conduct discussion using above questions. Encourage participants to contribute to the discussion.

5. Learning Activity

Content: "I want you to take some time and think about what you want to get from this program. Each of you will be given a pencil and paper. Please put your name on your paper. After careful consideration, write five goals that you hope to achieve by the end of this program. Examples of goals might include: 'I want to be able to play three consecutive games without becoming tired,' 'I want to learn the rules of volleyball,' 'I want to learn how to do a forearm pass,' or 'I want to make three new friends.' Do your best to write your goals so that, at the end of the program, you will be able to tell whether you were able to achieve them. When you are finished, I will collect your papers and keep them for later use."

Process: Explain activity. Provide pencil and paper and ample time for thought. Be available to answer individual questions. Collect and save papers.

6. Debriefing

Content:
    a. Was it difficult for you to think of five goals for volleyball? If so, why?
    b. Which of your goals do you think will be the most difficult to attain?
    c. What must you do to achieve the goals you established?
    d. How will you be able to tell if you reached your goals?

Process: Conduct debriefing using above questions. Encourage each participant to respond to at least one of the questions.

7. Conclusion

Content: "You have set some goals for yourselves for volleyball. Now you have to take steps to see that you reach those goals. Having goals does not assure success. Successful attainment of goals requires purposeful effort. Postponement of effort usually means failure to achieve goals. Concentrating on the tasks you have set for yourselves will help assure success in volleyball."

Process: Make concluding statements. Provide an opportunity for questions.

Objective 5.2: Demonstrate ability to modify goals.

1. Orientation Activity

Content: "Each of you is now receiving the form you completed related to establishing a leisure goal. Pretend you have changed in some way to affect the way you play volleyball (for example: you have learned some volleyball skills, you have lost a lot of weight, you have grown a foot taller). Write how you have changed beside the goal and then modify the goal to correspond with your new abilities or disabilities. Once you have completed this, move about the room to see how the other people have modified their goals. Make sure that you greet each person by name. If you have forgotten someone's name, please ask them."

Process: Distribute the handouts that the participants had previously completed. Provide directions and move about the room assisting people having difficulty. Provide examples of how people could have changed.

2. Introduction

Content: "After goals have been set, they should not be regarded as rigid and unchangeable. People often review their circumstances and their goals to see if any changes should be made. Modifying goals is a normal procedure. Acquiring and developing this ability is an important aspect of learning to be in control of our lives."

Process: Introduce topic of modifying goals.

3. Presentation

Content: "It is difficult, if not impossible, to look into the future. When we set goals, we are looking into the future and assessing our chances of being able to accomplish what we want to do. Sometimes, our assessments are accurate and events progress as we thought. Other times, our assessments turn out to be inaccurate and we discover that we cannot reach all of our goals or that our goals were too easy.

"There may be many reasons for setting goals that turn out to be unrealistic. We may honestly fail to accurately assess our abilities. Circumstances beyond our control, such as illness, injury, weather, or economic difficulties, may arise. Any number of things could happen. When we know that our goals are unrealistic, either too difficult or too easy, we should reassess our situation and modify our goals. This is an ordinary action."

Process: Present information on modifying goals.

4. Discussion

Content:
    a. Why do goals sometimes need to be modified?
    b. What are some possible reasons for modifying goals?
    c. Have you ever established a goal and later modified it? If so,why and how?
    d. How do you tell if you should modify your goals?

Process: Conduct discussion using above questions. Encourage all participants to contribute to the discussion.

5. Learning Activity (to be conducted after goals have been established)

Content: "Each of you has previously written a list of five goals you wished to accomplish as a result of participating in this volleyball program. I am going to give your lists back to you and ask you to review them. Examine each goal and determine if it should be modified. Only you can make this determination. If you think a goal should be changed, rewrite it to reflect your new thinking. When you finish, return your papers to me."

Process: Explain activity. Return original lists to players. Provide ample time for activity. Encourage each player to think carefully about modifying at least one goal.

6. Debriefing

Content:
    a. Which goal(s) did you modify? In what way?
    b. What caused you to modify them?
    c. Is modifying a goal easier or more difficult than first establishing a goal? Why?
    d. How can this activity help you in other parts of your life?

Process: Conduct debriefing using above questions. Encourage each participant to answer at least one of the questions.

7. Conclusion

Content: "We should never be reluctant to modify goals that we have set. We need to be comfortable with ourselves that we have given our best effort to attain our goals as we established them, but there are times when goals must be changed. Knowing when to do this, and acting accordingly, is an indication of our maturity and responsibility. Setting goals for volleyball can help you gain more satisfaction from the sport."

Process: Make concluding statements. Provide opportunity for questions.

LEISURE EDUCATION SOFTBALL PROGRAM

Purpose, Goals, and Objectives

Purpose: Provide opportunities for participants to gain an awareness of personal responsibilities and self-determination associated with softball, learn to make decisions to participate successfully in softball, become aware of resources for softball and how to access them, and acquire social interaction and physical skills needed to play softball.

Goal 1: Demonstrate an awareness of personal responsibilities and self-determination in softball.

Objective 1.1.	Demonstrate knowledge of personal responsibility to a softball team.
Objective 1.2.	Demonstrate knowledge of the benefits of a competitive team sport.
Objective 1.3.	Demonstrate knowledge of psychological barriers to team participation.

Goal 2: Demonstrate the ability to make appropriate decisions to participate successfully in softball.

Objective 2.1.	Demonstrate the ability to understand and follow rules.
Objective 2.2.	Demonstrate the ability to make group decisions to reach a goal.

Goal 3: Demonstrate knowledge of leisure resources and how to access them to play softball.

Objective 3.1.	Demonstrate knowledge of transportation to and from softball.
Objective 3.2.	Demonstrate the ability to access facilities for softball.
Objective 3.3.	Demonstrate the ability to acquire and maintain softball equipment.
Objective 3.4.	Demonstrate knowledge of the cost involved in playing softball.

Goal 4: Demonstrate the ability to engage in social interaction skills needed to play softball.

Objective 4.1.	Demonstrate knowledge of softball positions.
Objective 4.2.	Demonstrate knowledge of the value of communication to softball.
Objective 4.3.	Demonstrate the ability to organize a group of people to play softball.
Objective 4.4.	Demonstrate the ability to accept constructive criticism.

Goal 5: Demonstrate the ability to actively play softball.

Objective 5.1.	Demonstrate the ability to throw a softball.
Objective 5.2.	Demonstrate the ability to catch a softball.
Objective 5.3.	Demonstrate the ability to hit a softball.
Objective 5.4.	Demonstrate the ability to run bases.

Goals, Objectives, and Performance Measures

Goal 1: Demonstrate an awareness of personal responsibilities and self-determination in softball.

Objective 1.1: Demonstrate knowledge of personal responsibility to a team.

Performance Measure: Upon request and within five minutes, participant will demonstrate knowledge of personal responsibility to a team by verbally identifying three such responsibilities, as exemplified by:
    (a) supporting and encouraging other players,
    (b) recognizing different roles on a team,
    (c) cooperating for the achievement of a common goal,
    (d) sharing experiences of winning and losing, and
    (e) communicating with the team members,
on two consecutive occasions.

Objective 1.2: Demonstrate knowledge of the beneficial effects of a competitive team sport.

Performance Measure: Upon request and within one minute, participant will demonstrate knowledge of the beneficial effects of a competitive team sport by verbally identifying three such benefits, as exemplified by:
    (a) experience team unity,
    (b) having fun,
    (c) feeling team spirit,
    (d) making new friends, and
    (e) improving skills,
on two consecutive occasions.

Objective 1.3: Demonstrate knowledge of the psychological barriers to participation on a team.

Performance Measure: Upon request and within five minutes, participant will demonstrate knowledge of the psychological barriers to participation on a team by verbally identifying two such barriers, as exemplified by:
    (a) emphasis on winning rather than having fun,
    (b) emphasis on performance rather than participation,
    (c) feelings of inadequacy associated with failure, and
    (d) pressures of performing in front of large groups,
on two consecutive occasions.

Goal 2: Demonstrate the ability to make appropriate decisions to participate successfully in softball.

Objective 2.1: Demonstrate the ability to understand and follow rules.

Performance Measure: Given a pencil and a 10 item test on the rules of softball, participant will demonstrate the ability to understand and follow rules by correctly answering eight of the 10 questions within 15 minutes (e.g., How many innings are there in the game of softball? How many outs are there in an inning? How does a player make an out? What is the ten-run rule? What is a walk?), on two consecutive occasions.

Objective 2.2: Demonstrate the ability to work and make decisions in a group to reach a common goal.

Performance Measure: Given a group of nine people, within 20 minutes participant will demonstrate the ability to make decisions in a group by conferring with the group and selecting two warm-up activities that are acceptable to the majority of players as demonstrated by a vote, on two consecutive occasions.

Goal 3: Demonstrate knowledge of leisure resources and how to access them to play softball.

Objective 3.1: Demonstrate knowledge of methods of transportation to and from the softball field.

Performance Measure: Given paper and pencil, within 10 minutes participant will demonstrate knowledge of methods of transportation to and from the softball field by submitting a list of three possible methods of transportation, such as:
- (a) walking
- (b) riding in a car with a parent or friend,
- (c) bicycling, and
- (d) riding a bus,

on three consecutive occasions.

Objective 3.2: Demonstrate the ability to access facilities for softball.

Performance Measure: Given paper and pencil, within 10 minutes participant will demonstrate the ability to access facilities for softball by writing
- (a) the names of three different fields,
- (b) the organization that controls each field, and
- (c) who to call to reserve them,

on two consecutive occasions.

Objective 3.3: Demonstrate the ability to acquire and maintain equipment needed to participate in a softball game.

Performance Measure: Upon request, participant will demonstrate the ability to acquire and maintain equipment needed to participate in a softball game by bringing or wearing to practice:
- (a) playing shoes (e.g., tennis shoes, rubber spikes),
- (b) a glove, and
- (c) comfortable clothes (e.g., sweatshirt or T-shirt, sweat-pants or jeans, sweatsocks, ball cap),

on five consecutive sessions.

Objective 3.4: Demonstrate knowledge of the cost involved in playing softball.

Performance Measure: Given a list of at least seven items, within 15 minutes participant will demonstrate knowledge of the cost involved in playing softball by writing a figure within 20% of the price for each item, including:
- (a) glove,
- (b) ball,
- (c) shoes,

(d)   field reservation,
(e)   bat, and
(f)   umpire fees,
on two consecutive occasions.

Goal 4: Demonstrate the ability to engage in social interaction skills needed to play softball.

Objective 4.1: Demonstrate knowledge of the various positions and their spatial relationships with each other.

Performance Measure: Given a diagram of a softball field, within 10 minutes participant will demonstrate knowledge of the various positions and their spatial relationships with each other by correctly locating and labeling each defensive position on the diagram.

Objective 4.2: Demonstrate knowledge of the value of communication to softball.

Performance Measure: Upon request and within five minutes, participant will demonstrate the ability to communicate by verbally stating two purposes and two benefits of communication, on three consecutive occasions.

Objective 4.3: Demonstrate the ability to organize a group of people to play softball.

Performance Measure: Given directions to be captain of a team, within 20 minutes the player will demonstrate the ability to organize a group of people to play softball by:
(a)   assigning a player to each position,
(b)   determining the batting order, and
(c)   writing the batting order in the scorebook with the associated position,
for two consecutive games.

Objective 4.4: Demonstrate the ability to accept constructive criticism.

Performance Measure: Given constructive criticism on three separate occasions when warranted and within a five minute time-frame, participant will demonstrate the ability to accept criticism by
(a)   refraining from crying, yelling, fighting, stomping feet, or running away, and
(b)   acknowledging the criticism and attempting to change behavior,
on two consecutive occasions.

Goal 5: Demonstrate the ability to actively play softball.

Objective 5.1: Demonstrate the ability to throw a softball.

Performance Measure: Given a ball and mitt, within five minutes participant will make a catchable, overhand throw to a partner on at least eight out of 10 attempts, on five consecutive occasions.

Objective 5.2: Demonstrate the ability to catch a softball.

Performance Measure: Given a mitt, five ground balls and five fly balls thrown by the instructor, participant will catch the softball in the mitt at least eight out of 10 tries, on three consecutive occasions.

Objective 5.3: Demonstrate the ability to hit a softball.

Performance Measure: Given a bat and 10 underhand pitches by the instructor, participant will hit a softball in fair territory at least five times, on five consecutive occasions.

Objective 5.4: Demonstrate the ability to run bases.

Performance Measure: Given a ground ball hit through the infield with no runners on second or third and no outs, participant will demonstrate the ability to run the bases as characterized by immediately:
    (a)   running in the base line to second base,
    (b)   stepping on second base,
    (c)   looking toward the third base coach for signal to hold up or advance,
on three consecutive occasions.

Goals, Objectives, Content, and Process

Goal 1: Demonstrate an awareness of personal responsibilities and self-determination in softball.

Objective 1.1: Demonstrate knowledge of personal responsibility to a team.

1. Orientation Activity

Content: "You have all been given either a bat or a softball with a number taped to it. Those of you with bats may remain in your current positions and wait for the person with the ball to locate you. Those of you with a ball move about the group and find the person with the bat who has the number that matches yours. Once you have found the person, please introduce yourself.

"Now that you each have partners, I want you to stay together and form a line. Each partner face the other and take 10 steps backward. Those people with bats lay them on the ground. The person with the ball should roll the ball and try to hit the bat. The other person should stand behind the bat and catch the rolling ball. After catching the ball, run up to the person who threw the ball and tag the person. The person who threw the ball will then run and stand behind the bat. The new thrower will then attempt to roll the ball and hit the bat. Continue until I give you a signal to stop."

Process: Prepare for the activity by obtaining balls and bats. Construct two sets of cards with numbers, or pictures, or colors, and tape them to the balls and bats. Observe and assist individuals as needed. Allow the activity to proceed until each participant has rolled the ball at least two times. Conduct the activity in a large open area.

2. Introduction

Content: "Softball requires team effort. A team is a group that works together to accomplish a common goal. A successful team is one in which individuals, confronted with a choice, are willing to pass up personal accomplishment for the sake of team success. Softball can provide a chance for enjoyment and satisfaction through a team effort."

Process: Introduce topic of personal responsibility in softball, emphasizing the positive aspects of team sports.

3. Presentation

Content: "Being a member of a team can be a valuable experience by providing you with chances to be with friends and make new ones. Teams encourage cooperation and commitment to goals. Team members can offer support and encouragement for each other. Success depends on all members doing their parts. Membership requires communication, which is a key ingredient in working toward success. Members of softball teams can share the joy of working and winning together. They can be supportive when they are defeated. In addition to being fun, membership on a softball team can foster feelings of belonging.

"There are many team roles for softball players and a player has to fill different roles at different times. Players have to hit and they have to field. They have to support and encourage other players and allow others to encourage them. They have to practice and help others practice. They have to talk and they have to listen. They have to give pats on the back. Sometimes, they just have to be a friend.

"Team members learn to play together by being together. This means being faithful in attending practice, running drills together, concentrating on playing ball, making good plays together, and winning and losing together. Being a team member means working cooperatively to solve problems. Problems could include poor communication among team members, difficulty in getting along with coaches, players not coming to practice, and many other possibilities. Solving problems requires a real commitment from the players, but it is all part of being on a team."

Process: Present information on being a member of a team. Arrange players sitting in semicircle facing instructor. Encourage comments and questions from players.

4. Discussion

Content:
    a.   What does being on a team mean to you?
    b.   What are some of the different roles team members play?
    c.   Describe some ways that you can encourage and support other players.
    d.   What are some problems that can arise on a team?
    e.   How can you work toward solving problems with your team mates?

Process: Conduct discussion using above questions. Allow players to ask questions. Encourage all participants to contribute to the discussion.

5. Learning Activity

Content: "We are going to do an activity that requires teamwork. There is a log anchored to the ground. Everybody get in a single file standing on the log. Your task is to rearrange yourselves without talking and without falling or stepping off the log. The person at the head of the line on the log must get to the end of the line on the log, to be followed by the next person and the next until everyone is back in their original position. Players that talk or fall off must return to their position and start again."

Process: Explain activity. If a log is unavailable, use long bench or draw two lines separated by a relatively narrow space. Monitor activity by watching players closely. Encourage participants to work together.

6. Debriefing

Content:
    a.   What did you learn from this activity?
    b.   What roles did you play?
    c.   How did the group work together?
    d.   What did you do to solve any problems?

Process: Conduct debriefing using above questions. Encourage participants to respond to at least one of the questions.

7. Conclusion

Content: "Being a member of a team often makes you feel good. It requires responsibility to the team. One of the rewards of being on a team is the satisfaction that results from meeting that responsibility."

Process: Make concluding statements. Ask players if they have any questions.

Objective 1.2: Demonstrate knowledge of the beneficial effects of a competitive team sport.

1. Orientation Activity

Content: "Each of you has a card with a phrase written on it. Find the other person whose card has the same phrase, introduce yourself to the person and find out the person's name. The two of you will work together on this activity. Look through the box you have been given and choose pictures you feel best represent your phrase. Take the pictures and glue them to the poster board. When completed, I will help you tape the poster board to the wall. After all posters are up, I will give each pair a paper and pencil. I want everyone to write the phrase that first comes to mind when looking at the collage to which I point. Once everyone has recorded his or her responses, I will ask you to tell me what you recorded. When everyone has had a chance, we will have the artists of the collage under consideration show us their phrase."

Process: Write two sets of cards with phrases describing the positive aspects of softball (e.g., team unity, working together, team spirit, getting better, having fun, being satisfied). Cut out of magazines a variety of pictures of people and place them in boxes. Once the group is arranged in pairs, give each pair a box of pictures, a piece of cardboard and some glue. Tape collages up on an acceptable surface. Distribute a pencil and paper to each person to record his or her phrases.

2. Introduction

Content: "Playing in a competitive team sport can be beneficial to participants. But these benefits do not just automatically happen. Players should be aware of what these benefits are and strive to bring them about."

Process: Introduce topic and communicate the value of being aware of benefits.

3. Presentation

Content: "One benefit from being on a team is a feeling of team unity. Players spend time together doing the same drills and sharing the experience of practices and games and soon begin to identify with the team.

"Another benefit that can be derived from participation in a competitive team sport is the lesson of what can be achieved by working together. Being part of a productive group requires players to put forth their best efforts. The combination of every player's best effort results in an outcome with which everyone can be satisfied and happy.

"Team spirit that emerges among players should be highly valued. This spirit helps players to encourage fellow players when they are upset or when they make mistakes. Players will offer suggestions for improvement and congratulations for good performance.

"Playing a competitive team sport is motivating for many players. Some players try hard because they want to have the experience of winning; other players try just as hard because they want to please their fellow players and coaches. Some are motivated to impress their family and friends and some because they want to improve and become better players.

"Although playing a game against a rival team is a highlight, practice for such competition is also valuable. It provides game situations without actually being a game. It allows players to learn from their mistakes and improve their performances. It gives opportunities to grow as a player in a supportive environment."

Process: Present information about benefits of participation in a team sport. Use chalkboard to illustrate main points. Encourage questions and comments from players.

4. Discussion

Content:
     a.   What are some of the benefits of participating in a team sport?
     b.   What do you hope to gain from participating?
     c.   What do you think is meant by team unity?
     d.   What are some of the reasons players motivate themselves?
     e.   What are ways players can get as much from practice as they do from a game?

Process: Conduct discussion using above questions. Encourage each person to make at least one contribution to the discussion.

5. Learning Activity

Content: "We are going to divide into groups and do an activity to remind us of the benefits we can gain from softball. Each group will do the same activity. I will pick a person, who will start the activity by naming one benefit that can be gained. The person to his or her immediate left will repeat the benefit and add a new one. The next person on the left will repeat the first two benefits and add one more. This process will continue until it arrives back with the person who started the activity."

Process: Explain activity. Divide into groups of no more than five or six people each. Help players who have difficulty.

6. Debriefing

Content:
  a. Were there any benefits that were new to you? If so, what were they?
  b. What will you have to do to see that you receive these benefits?
  c. How can you help someone else receive these benefits?
  d. Do you have any suggestions to offer to the team? If so,what are they?

Process: Conduct debriefing using above questions. Allow participants to ask questions. Attempt to answer questions. When needed, provide participants with more information.

7. Conclusion

Content: "Competition can be fun and enjoyable. Softball provides many people with benefits that result from testing themselves against others and against themselves."

Process: Make concluding statements. Emphasize good sportsmanship. Provide opportunities for participants to ask questions.

Objective 1.3: Demonstrate knowledge of the psychological barriers to participation on a team.

1. Orientation Activity

Content: "Each of you has a colored card. Find the other two people who have the same color card and introduce yourselves. Each trio will then designate a 'carrier,' 'loader,' and 'guider.' The carrier will attempt to carry as many of these large card board boxes as possible through the path marked by the orange cones. The loader will attempt to place as many boxes on the carrier as possible. Once the carrier begins the walk, the loader may not touch any of the boxes and must cheer the person on. The guider will tell the carrier where to go. The object is for the group to get as many boxes to the end of the path as possible. Once the carrier arrives at the end of the path, the carrier becomes the new loader, the loader becomes the new guider and the guider becomes the new carrier. Continue until each person has been the carrier. Once completed, call me and I will help you add up the total number of boxes at the end of the path."

Process: Obtain large cardboard boxes. Write on each of the boxes in large magic marker a psychological barrier (e.g., wanting to win at all costs, dwelling on mistakes, feeling foolish, being afraid of groups). Possibly conduct a discussion of the problems with balancing psychological barriers and the value of the guider and loader helping the carrier.

2. Introduction

Content: "There are times when mental barriers exist and work against participation in a competitive team sport. If these barriers can be identified, efforts can be made to cope with them. Some barriers can be removed; others have to be dealt with in other ways."

Process: Introduce topic on psychological barriers.

3. Presentation

Content: "There are several things that can serve as mental barriers to participation on a team. The actions of other people can produce barriers, as well as your own attitudes and perceptions. A barrier for one person may not be a barrier for another person.

"Sometimes players feel there is a barrier to their participation because they believe there is too much focus on performance. They do not feel comfortable in such circumstances and prefer an environment that emphasizes improvement and having fun, not necessarily in that order.

"Players sometimes experience barriers because of the intensity of competition among team members for playing positions and starting roles. Such competition can work against team spirit and foster disunity.

"Some players feel inadequate, that they are not contributing enough to the team. They dwell on their mistakes. If they are not starters and do not get much playing time, they feel inferior. Such barriers may be of their own making, but they are real nonetheless.

"Barriers may exist because of a lack of social interaction skills. Some people may be overwhelmed by being part of a group of 15-20 people. The group may be too large for them at the present time. They may work quite well in smaller groups and need assistance in coping with larger groups.

"Depending on the nature of the barrier, players can take action to attempt to overcome them. One way is for persons to begin a new activity with an already established friend. Sometimes it is advisable to enter a noncompetitive situation first and gradually become prepared to engage in competition. It might also be a good idea to enter a program that involves smaller numbers and then progress to larger groups. There are other steps to take, depending on the circumstances."

Process: Present information on barriers. List major barriers on chalkboard. Emphasize concept that barriers can be reduced or removed.

4. Discussion

Content:
    a.   What is a mental or psychological barrier?
    b.   What are some examples of barriers to participation on a team?
    c.   How can barriers be overcome?
    d.   Can you think of any barriers that might exist in this program?

Process: Conduct discussion using above questions. Keep a positive attitude while conducting the discussion and encourage all participants to make a contribution.

5. Learning Activity

Content: "People who believe there are barriers to their participation in an activity often do not tell anyone. They simply do not enter the activity. Perhaps we can do something to address these unspoken concerns by making some posters that show why someone might want to join a softball team. For example, a poster might show players having fun playing ball, a player and coach talking in a friendly manner, or two friends joining a team together. Get into small groups and use construction paper, poster board, colored pencils or crayons, glue, and pictures from magazines. Each group will make a poster. When you are finished, we will ask each group to tell us about their poster."

Process: Explain activity. Divide into groups and distribute materials. When posters are finished, conduct debriefing.

6. Debriefing

Content:
    a. Did you attempt to depict a particular barrier? If so, tell us about it.
    b. How did you show a barrier being reduced or removed?
    c. What other things does your poster show?
    d. How can we make use of these posters? How can we provide opportunities for other people to benefit from them?

Process: Conduct debriefing using above questions. Provide opportunities for participants to ask questions. Encourage all participants to respond to at least one of the questions.

7. Conclusion

Content: "Barriers exist for most of us at one time or another in our lives. Sometimes they are of our own making. Recognizing barriers, deciding how to cope, and working toward solutions is a characteristic of a responsible person."

Process: Make concluding statements. Provide an opportunity for questions.

Goal 2: Demonstrate the ability to make appropriate decisions to participate successfully in softball.

Objective 2.1: Demonstrate the ability to understand and follow rules.

l. Orientation Activity

Content: "We are going to play Simon Says Play Softball. Get into two lines about 20 feet apart, with five to six feet separating each player in each line. I will give you instructions to do something, after the phrase 'Simon Says.' For example, 'Simon says to get in a batting stance.' Each of you will assume a batting stance. But if I give you a direction that does not follow 'Simon Says' and you follow the direction, you must play from within this large circle drawn on the ground until we start a new round. We will start a new round when all but one player is in the circle area."

Process: Explain activity. Form lines and have ample space. Use as many softball-related directions as possible. For example: (a) touch your nose as a signal to bunt, (b) swing the bat, (c) pull your hat down to shade the sun, (d) twist your trunk to loosen up, and (e) pound the pocket in your glove. Play two or three rounds.

2. Introduction

Content: "Softball is a structured game, with rules that are followed so players can enjoy participation. The rules, which focus on procedures for playing the game and equipment used, are designed to make the game easy to understand and fair. Rules are designed to protect players."

Process: Introduce topic of following rules in softball.

3. Presentation

Content: "There are organizations that promote softball. One such agency is the Amateur Softball Association, known as ASA. It publishes a rule book which we will follow. The rule book tells how the game is structured, including how many innings in a game, how many outs in an inning, how many players on a team, how players make outs, rules for pitching, rules for running the bases, and many other areas. Knowing the rules helps us understand the game. The rules of the game are necessary to prevent confusion, help the game go at a good pace and protect players. Rules help good sportsmanship and provide penalties for problems.

"In addition to rules that govern the playing of the game, most softball programs have other rules to guide your conduct. For example, some programs prohibit profanity by players or ban alcohol, drugs, or tobacco. Some programs have rules on the number of practices a player can miss or that require all players to play at least a portion of the game. Violation of rules usually calls for players to sit out some practice time or a game. In extreme cases, players are prohibited from participation on the team for a season.

"Rules should not be arbitrary and often can be established with the help of the players. Once established, they are to be obeyed. They are established with the best interests of the players in mind. Players who cannot adhere to the rules find their enjoyment, and often their participation, severely restricted."

Process: Present information on rules. Emphasize need for knowing and following rules of program and for playing the game.

4. Discussion

Content:
    a.   Why is there a need for rules in a team activity?
    b.   Why do players need to obey the rules?
    c.   How can players get clarification of a rule they do not understand?
    d.   What are some possible penalties for violation of rules in a softball program?
    e.   What suggestions do you have for rules or rules changes for this program?

Process: Conduct discussion using above questions. Encourage all the participants to contribute to the discussion.

5. Learning Activity

Content: "We need to know and understand the rules for playing softball. I am going to divide you into small groups, give each group a rule book, and each player a set of written questions concerning the rules of the game. Each player will have the same set of questions. Use the rule book to find the answers to the questions. When you are finished, we will go over your answers and see that everyone has the correct ones."

Process: Explain activity. Divide into groups. Use *The Official ASA Guide and Playing Rules*. Prepare written questions prior to session. Examples of questions could include: How many innings are there in the game of softball? How many outs are there in an inning? How does a player make an out? What is the ten-run rule? What constitutes a walk? Give players ample time to look up answers. Provide help, if necessary.   When finished, provide answers to questions and move to debriefing.   After debriefing, each player keeps questions and answers.

6. Debriefing

Content:
    a.   Did you find answers to all questions? If not, which ones were you unable to find?
    b.   Do you understand each question and answer? If not, which need clarification?
    c.   How will you use the questions and answers you now have?

Process: Conduct debriefing using above questions. Encourage participants to respond to at least one of the questions.

7. Conclusion

Content: "Following rules ensures fairness for all players. Knowledge of the rules and willingness to play by them is required of all participants. This makes the game more enjoyable and satisfying for everyone."

Process: Make concluding statements. Provide opportunities for questions.

Objective 2.2: Demonstrate the ability to work and make decisions in a group to reach a common goal.

1. Orientation Activity

Content: "You have been given a partial picture of a bat, softball, glove, cap, or base. Find the other two people who have partial pictures that will allow you to complete the picture of the piece of softball equipment.   Once you find the other two people, introduce yourself and get acquainted.

"I am now giving seven strips of cardboard with Velcro™ on the back to each trio. Written on each slip of paper is a step involved in the decision-making process. Please order them in the correct sequence, placing the first step at the top and the last step at the bottom of the piece of cardboard with seven strips of Velcro™ glued on it. Once each trio has completed the task, we will have each trio present their process."

Process: Draw large pictures of brightly colored softball equipment on poster board. Cut the pictures into three pieces. Make several sets of the decision-making process by writing the steps on a piece of poster board, cutting them into strips and pasting Velcro™ on the backs. Prepare poster boards with seven strips of Velcro™ glued to them to allow participants to attach the steps in their desired order.

2. Introduction

Content: "Decision-making is an important skill in softball. Results of decisions have an impact on the team and, in some cases, the outcomes of games. Players in the field need to decide what to do with a ball they might field, batters need to decide whether to swing at a pitch, and runners need to decide how to run the bases. You also need to make decisions about your conduct as a team member. In all instances, options must be considered and choices made."

Process: Introduce topic of decision-making related to softball. Answer questions about decision-making.

3. Presentation

Content: "There is a framework within which decisions should be made. In general, decisions need to be compatible with the interests and skills of the decision-maker and within legal and social boundaries. Decisions should not harm or damage others or self.

"Several models exist for decision-making and the components of most models are compatible with each other. A generic model would include the following: (a) identify the need for a decision to be made, (b) collect all information that may influence decision, (c) identify all possible options, (d) evaluate potential outcomes of each option, (e) select the best option, (f) implement decision, and (g) evaluate outcome.

"There are many situations in a softball game where decisions must be made. For example, an outfielder who has just caught a fly ball, with runners on base and one out, must decide what to do with the ball. The decision will be influenced by where the runners and infielders are in relation to each other, the strength of the player's throwing arm, what will happen if the ball is thrown to a specific base, or if the ball is run in from the outfield. The game situation will affect the decision and probably dictate that it be made quickly. The more experienced a player becomes, the easier it is to make correct decisions."

Process: Present information on decision-making. Use easel or chalkboard to list major components of decision-making model.

- Identify need for decision.
- Collect information.
- Identify options.
- Evaluate potential outcomes.
- Select best option.
- Implement decision.
- Evaluate outcomes.

4. Discussion

Content:
  a. What are the characteristics of an appropriate decision?
  b. What are the steps, in sequence, of a good decision-making process?
  c. Identify some situations in softball that require decision-making?
  d. How did you decide to participate in this program?

Process: Conduct discussion using above items. Assist participants by uncovering steps to decision-making listed on the easel.

5. Learning Activity

Content: "We are going to give each of you an opportunity to participate in small-group decision-making. For each of the next several practices, three players will be selected to decide which warm-up drills the team will use and in what order they will be used. Three different players will be used for each practice. We will do this until all of you have had an opportunity to help decide. The three players selected for each practice must meet as a group and make their decision. At the end of each practice, I will meet with the three decision-makers of the day."

Process: Explain activity. Meet with group prior to practice to provide assistance, if necessary. Meet after practice to debrief.

6. Debriefing

Content:
   a. How difficult was it to make a decision?
   b. Did you have to make any compromises?
   c. Did your group vote or reach a consensus?
   d. What considerations did you have to make before reaching a decision?

Process: Conduct debriefing using above questions. Encourage all participants to respond to at least one of the questions.

7. Conclusion

Content: "Softball constantly provides situations in which decisions must be made. Decisions in a team game affect more than the player making the decision; they also affect the player's teammates and the game itself. Selecting the right course of action often means the difference between success and failure."

Process: Make concluding statements. Provide opportunity for questions.

Goal 3: Demonstrate a knowledge of leisure resources and how to access them to play softball.

Objective 3.1: Demonstrate the ability to use transportation to and from the softball field.

1. Orientation Activity

Content: "You have been given a large paper and some colored markers. Divide the paper into three sections, drawing lines down the page. On the left hand side of the paper, draw a softball field. On the right hand side, draw your home. In the center section draw, the way you would enjoy getting from your home to the softball field.

"Once you have completed the picture, look on your green marker to find a small picture of a piece of softball equipment. Find the two other people in the group with the same picture and introduce yourself. Place your seats facing each other in a triangle. Share with the other two people what your picture is about and why you chose the method of transportation recorded on the paper."

Process: Obtain sufficient number of markers and paper for participants. Place a small picture of a piece of softball equipment on each green marker, making certain to have three pictures of each piece of equipment. If the number of participants is not evenly divisible by three, have one or two groups have only two people. As participants begin their discussion, move among groups assisting participants and facilitating discussion.

2. Introduction

Content: "How you get back and forth between your home and the softball field for practice and games is a matter of importance to us. We want you to arrive here and return home safely and without difficulty. Some of you may live within walking distance, some may arrive on bicycles, some may have rides from parents or friends, and some may use public transportation. We are concerned about all of you."

Process: Introduce the topic of transportation to the softball field.

3. Presentation

Content: "There are several ways that you can travel between your home and the field. If you live nearby, you can walk or bicycle. If you live some distance away, you can bicycle or catch a ride with family members or neighbors. Using the bus may be a good choice for some of you. You should think carefully of the options that are available to you.

"One option to consider is car pooling. Car pooling simply means a group of players take turns getting rides with each other. Advantages of car pooling include saving time for parents and saving money and gasoline. It also saves wear on automobiles.

"Another option to consider is riding the bus. If the bus schedule is convenient and the route passes near your home and the field, riding the bus might be a wise choice for you.

"It is your responsibility to think of the safest and most efficient way to get to practice and games and get back home. It is also your responsibility to tell us how you are doing this, so that we will know when to expect you and with whom you will be riding. We need to know this so we will know what to do in an emergency."

Process: Present information on transportation. Ask players how they are getting to and from the field.

4. Discussion

Content:
    a.   What options are available to you for getting here and returning home?
    b.   Why do your instructors need to know this?
    c.   What is car pooling?
    d.   What advantages does car pooling offer?

Process: Conduct discussion using above questions. Encourage all participants to contribute to the discussion.

5. Learning Activity

Content: "We are going to do an activity that will help us find the best way to get to and from the softball field. I am going to give each of you a map and a red pencil. I want you to locate your address on the map and the softball field. Then draw the best route for you to take to get from your home to the field. At the bottom of the map, write whether you are walking, cycling, riding with family or friend, or using the bus. Mark all the stops on the map. When you are finished with the drawing, we will look at each of your maps."

Process: Explain activity. Obtain maps from local source (e.g., chamber of commerce, AAA). Provide red pencils. Observe any difficulty and offer assistance.

6. Debriefing

Content:
    a. Where do you live?
    b. How far away from the field do you live?
    c. What method of transportation do you use to get here?
    d. Do you usually follow the route you drew on the map? If not, why not?
    e. If your usual method of transportation failed, could you give directions to someone to take you home?

Process: Conduct debriefing using above questions. Require every player to supply home address, telephone number, and method used to get to practice and games and return home.

7. Conclusion

Content: "Knowing and using the best ways to get to the field and back home is a sign of responsibility. It demonstrates the ability to be in control of an important aspect of your life."

Process: Make concluding statements. Provide opportunities for questions.

Objective 3.2: Demonstrate the ability to access facilities for softball.

1. Orientation Activity

Content: "I have divided a cardboard picture of a softball field into 10 pieces associated with each of the defensive positions. You each have a brightly colored piece. When I call your name, please come up to the picture taped to the wall that has an outline of a softball field drawn on it. Tape your picture to the spot where it belongs. After you place the piece on the designated spot, turn to the group, introduce yourself, and tell the others what player would play in this area of the field. You then may sit down and we will continue with the remaining participants."

Process: Sketch two identical pictures of a softball field. One picture should be colored and then cut into 10 pieces. Distribute one piece to each person. If there are fewer than 10 participants, you can begin by identify the remaining sections. If there are more participants, repeat the process until all people have had an opportunity to participate. Arrange participants in a semicircle facing the large uncut sketch of the field. Place the picture on an easel stand. Assist participants who do not know the correct response.

2. Introduction

Content: "Softball needs a place where it can be played. Finding a place to play can sometimes be a problem. One of the things you need to know is how to locate softball fields and how to get the opportunity to play on them."

Process: Introduce topic of accessing facilities for softball.

3. Presentation

Content: "Softball requires a large playing area. Often, parks have large open spaces where informal games are played, but most developed softball fields are maintained by municipal recreation departments, schools, or similar organizations. Teams can show up at a field and hope it is not in use; however, there may be teams playing on it. A way to make sure a field is open when you want to use it is to call the organization that controls the field and make a reservation. If your team is playing in a league, games and practices are usually scheduled. If your team is not in a league, it will probably have to use the fields when league teams do not need it. Softball fields provided by schools and recreation departments can be reserved for little or no cost. Other organizations' fields usually have fees."

Process: Present information on accessing fields.

4. Discussion

Content:
    a.   What is a developed softball field?
    b.   What organizations in a community usually have developed softball fields?
    c.   How can you make arrangements with these agencies to get to use their fields?

Process: Conduct discussion using above questions. Encourage all participants to contribute to the discussion.

5. Learning Activity

Content: "We are going to make a directory of the softball fields in our area. I am going to divide you into groups and supply each group with pencils, paper, a map, and a telephone directory. The map contains parks, playgrounds and other spaces where softball fields are generally located. The telephone directory will provide information about the agencies that control these fields. We can contact those agencies and learn what procedures we need to follow to use their fields. Each group will contact a separate agency for information. We will then combine all the information we have gathered and make a directory of the softball fields and how to access them."

Process: Explain activity. Obtain maps from local chamber of commerce, AAA, or other source. Have group collate information gathered and make directory. Distribute directory.

6. Debriefing

Content:
    a. Was it difficult to obtain information from the agencies? If so, why?
    b. Do the agencies differ in their policies? If so, how?
    c. Did we overlook any potential sources for fields? If so, which ones?
    d. How will you use your directory?

Process: Conduct debriefing using above questions. Encourage participants to respond to at least one of the questions.

7. Conclusion

Content: "Knowing where and how to access softball fields is an important piece of information for you. When this program is finished, you will know where you can go to continue playing softball."

Process: Make concluding statements. Provide opportunities for questions.

Objective 3.3: Demonstrate the ability to acquire and maintain equipment needed to participate in a softball game.

1. Orientation Activity

Content: "Each of you will be given the opportunity to make a mobile depicting the equipment that is used in a softball game. Each of you will have scissors, glue, yarn, construction paper, magazines and catalogs, and a wire hanger. Cut pictures from the magazines and catalogs, trace their outline on the construction paper, glue the picture to the outline, and tie it to the hanger with the yarn. Be as creative as you wish. When we are finished participants will stand, introduce themselves, and show the group their mobiles."

Process: Explain activity. Distribute materials. Move about the room as participants make their mobiles, providing assistance and encouragement as needed. Encourage participants to show their appreciation for the work of others by applauding after participants have made their presentations.

2. Introduction

Content: "Softball can require special equipment. Most sporting goods stores carry softball equipment. In addition, most equipment is available through mail-order catalogs. Knowing what equipment is needed and how to care for equipment is an important part of learning about softball. Having the equipment and keeping it in good repair helps people play the game better, have fun, and prevent unnecessary expense."

Process: Introduce topic of acquiring and maintaining equipment needed to participate in a softball game.

3. Presentation

Content: "Softball requires a lot of movement, so footwear is an important factor. Street shoes are not suitable. A pair of athletic shoes (sneakers), cleated shoes if playing on grass, or turf shoes with plastic tips is recommended, depending on the playing surface. Regular gym clothes or a sweat suit, depending on the time of the year, will be fine. A cap is also recommended. All of these items should fit and be comfortable.

"A softball glove, a bat, and a ball are also needed. The type of glove used by a player is somewhat dependent on the player's position. In general, a glove should have the fingers in one grouping, the thumb in another, and should be separated by a wide pocket. The glove should be of a size that the player can easily control.

"When a player selects a bat, there are several factors that need to be considered. The length of the bat, its weight, and the feel of the grip must be right for the player. The distribution of the weight is also important. Although wood bats are still available, most bats are now aluminum. The bat must be controlled by the hitter.

"It may be necessary for players to supply balls but usually softballs are provided by the sponsoring agency. A regulation softball with a cork center is needed.

"Using equipment properly and with care will extend its life and usefulness. Players should never sit on their gloves. If gloves become dirty, they should not be allowed to remain so. Dirt and mud should be removed promptly. A leather conditioner and protector should be used regularly to prevent damage from water. Players should form pockets in their gloves to help catch and contain the ball.

"Bats should be used only for hitting a softball. They should never be thrown or used to pound the ground. They are not substitute hammers and should not be used to pound stakes to hold bases or secure in place the pitching rubber or home plate."

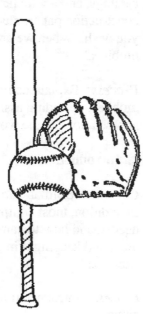

Process: Present information on equipment and its maintenance. Use samples of equipment as demonstration models. Demonstrate how to oil a glove.

4. Discussion

Content:
    a.   Where can softball equipment be purchased?
    b.   What kinds of shoes are commonly worn by softball players?
    c.   How can you determine which shoes are appropriate for softball?
    d.   What are some important factors to consider when selecting a bat?
    e.   Why is proper maintenance of equipment important?
    f.   What are some tips for the care of gloves?

Process: Conduct discussion using above questions. Pass equipment around the group as questions are asked and participants discuss the possible answers. Encourage all participants to contribute to the discussion.

5. Learning Activity

Content: "The more we know about equipment, the better decisions we can make in selecting it. I am going to divide you into four groups and give each group several sporting-goods catalogs, scissors, paste, and poster paper. Each group will use the catalogs to compile descriptions about a specific item of equipment. Cut the descriptions and pictures of the item from the catalog and paste them on the poster board. One group will be assigned to softball bats, one to gloves, one to balls, and one to shoes. Gather as many descriptions as you can about your assigned item. When we are finished, each group will share its information with the entire group."

Process: Explain activity. Divide participants into groups and supply them with catalogs, scissors, paste, and poster paper. Have groups share finished product with each other. Post on bulletin board.

6. Debriefing

Content:
    a. How similar are the descriptions for bats? Balls? Gloves? Shoes?
    b. How believable are the descriptions?
    c. What characteristics are emphasized in the descriptions?
    d. What did you learn about equipment?

Process: Conduct debriefing using above questions. Attempt to have every participant make some contribution to the debriefing.

7. Conclusion

Content: "Careful consideration should be given to the selection of softball equipment. Knowing something about selection of equipment helps make you an educated consumer. Taking good care of equipment is a characteristic of a responsible person."

Process: Make concluding statements. Emphasize individual responsibility for equipment care. Provide participants with the opportunity to ask questions.

Objective 3.4: Demonstrate knowledge of the cost involved in playing softball.

1. Orientation Activity

Content: "Each of you has been given $200 in play money. I have placed on the table pictures of softball equipment, with a range of typical prices for each item recorded on the back of the cards. Each of you will have a chance to take a turn. When it is your turn, place the amount of money you wish to spend beside the equipment card. Then turn toward the group, introduce yourself, identify what piece of equipment you want to purchase and state the amount you intend to pay. Then turn the picture over. If you are within the designated range, you may pick up the picture, state the range to the group, give the money you want to spend to me, and return to your seat. If your guess does not fall within the designated range, return the card to the table and return to your seat and wait for another turn."

Process: Make cards with pictures of equipment on one side and the range of typical costs for the equipment on the reverse side. To allow people more practice, make up several copies of cards and place them in stack so when a person chooses the picture of a softball, there will be another copy under it. Assist participants who are having difficulty. Allow people to repeat their attempts later if they were initially unsuccessful.

2. Introduction

Content: "There are costs in playing softball. Unless you have sponsors, you must pay for clothing, shoes, gloves, bats and balls. Sometimes, you have to help pay for a field and pay the umpires. Transportation to and from the field is also an expense. Knowing the cost of items is a factor in decision-making. Softball is no exception."

Process: Introduce topic of cost involved in playing softball.

3. Presentation

Content: "Softball equipment is available at varying prices. Deciding what to pay for an item is an important consideration. If you are just learning the game, it is not advisable to spend a lot of money on equipment until it is clear that you will continue to play in the future. In that case, inexpensive equipment is a good decision. On the other hand, if you are experienced and know that your participation will continue for years, spending money to purchase quality equipment is a good investment.

"The cost of shoes can range from $___ to $___, depending on type and quality. The average cost range for gloves is $___ to $___. Aluminum bats range from $___ to $___. Wood bats are much less expensive. Softballs are generally available at prices ranging from $___ to $___.

"Sometimes, there is a cost involved in reserving a field. Most municipal recreation departments and schools do not assess a fee for using their fields. Other organizations may charge from $___ to $___ for the use of a field. Umpires may be available for as little as $___an hour to as much as $___ an hour.

"Transportation may also be an expense. The expense may be covered by parents, but it does exist. It might be bus fare or it might be the costs involved in using an automobile to get players to and from the field."

Process: Present information on costs. Check local sporting good stores and catalogs for price information. Include prices in the spaces provided that are appropriate for your area. List items and associated costs on chalkboard.

4. Discussion

Content:
    a.   Were you aware of the costs associated with playing softball? If so, how?
    b.   Identify the items which cost money.
    c.   Why is it wise for beginning players to delay the purchase of costly equipment?
    d.   Which is the best decision, (1) to buy inexpensive items with an expected short life span or (2) to buy costly items with expected long life span? Why?

Process: Conduct discussion using above questions. Contact a sporting goods shop and obtain the price ranges for the equipment described above. Include these amounts in the above content.

5. Learning Activity

Content: "To help us better understand the cost of playing softball, I want each of you to keep an account of how much money you spend related to softball next week. Keep an account of each day. If you spend money on a piece of equipment, record it. Keep track of what is spent on transportation. If you ride with parents or friends, ask for an estimate of the cost. Be complete. At the end of a week, we will look at the accounts."

Process: Explain activity. Emphasize accuracy. Give reminders during the week. Establish date for players to bring accounts to practice and debrief.

6. Debriefing

Content:
   a.   How much did the activity of softball cost you last week?
   b.   On what did you spend money?
   c.   Do you feel the money was well spent? If so, why? If not, why not?
   d.   Is an account of one week representative of all weeks? If not, why not?

Process: Conduct debriefing using above questions. Encourage all participants to respond to at least one question.

7. Conclusion

Content: "There are costs involved in playing softball but they can be held to a reasonable level. Deciding how much to spend is dependent on many things, one of which is related to the extent of future participation."

Process: Make concluding statements. Provide opportunities for questions.

Goal 4: Demonstrate the ability to engage in appropriate social interaction skills needed to play softball.

Objective 4.1: Demonstrate knowledge of the various positions and their spatial relationships with each other.

1. Orientation Activity

Content: "We are going to make some 'free-form sculptures' by using softball-related words. We are going to divide into pairs, with each pair having several sheets of paper and pencil. In the middle of a sheet of paper, write the word SOFTBALL. Think of another softball-related word that contains one of the letters S-O-F-T-B-A-L-L and write that word so that it connects vertically with SOFTBALL. Continue to think of softball-related words that connect with the words on your paper like STRIKE. Your paper could now look like:

You may use a word only once. If a word's letters connect horizontally and vertically with other letters, they must form legitimate softball-related words in both directions. Now choose a spokesperson. Introduce your partner and yourself and show the group your paper and state how many different words the two of you came up with."

Process: Explain activity. Divide into pairs. Distribute paper and pencil. Put example on board. Move among pairs to clarify directions, if necessary. Emphasize letters have to be in correct position to make sense; spatial relationship is critical. Post sculptures so everyone can see them.

2. Introduction

Content: "An important part of playing softball is knowing where all players should be positioned on the field. Being in the right place at the right time enables players to help each other and to make their greatest contributions to the team."

Process: Introduce topic of various positions and their relationship to each other.

3. Presentation

Content: "There are 10 positions on conventional softball teams. Knowing something about where they should be on a softball field is a responsibility of every player. The positions are as follow:
  a. *Pitcher:* plays 40 feet in front of home plate. The pitching rubber is located in the middle of the infield between first, second, third, and home. The pitcher throws the ball across home plate toward the batter.
  b. *Catcher:* position is three feet behind home plate. The catcher squats, catches pitches, tries to prevent passed balls and returns the ball to the pitcher.
  c. *First Base:* plays five feet area around first base, usually in front. First base is located on the right point of the diamond, off the right foul line.
  d. *Second Base:* position is played half-way between first and second, usually behind the base line. Second base is located behind the pitching rubber, at the point of the diamond opposite home plate.
  e. *Third Base:* plays five feet area around third base, usually in front of base. Third base is located on the left point of the diamond, off the left foul line.
  f. *Shortstop:* plays half-way between second and third base, usually behind baseline.
  g. *Right Fielder:* plays right field, which is the area behind the baseline between first and second base to the outfield fence. It extends from right foul line to center field.
  h. *Center Fielder:* plays behind second base to the fence, from right field to left field.
  i. *Left Fielder:* plays left field, which is the area behind the baseline between second and third base to the outfield fence. It extends from the left foul line to center field.
  j. *Short Field or Rover:* Position played anywhere in outfield but usually in area between center field and second base."

Process: Present information on team positions. List positions on chalkboard. Prepare handout of diagram of softball field with player positions on it. Point to the positions as they are being discussed. Have participants place a mark on the portion of the field on which the person is positioned.

4. Discussion

Content:
    a. Where does the shortstop play?
    b. What is the function of the catcher?
    c. What are the outfield positions called and where are they?
    d. Where does the rover play?
    e. How many players are there on a team?

Process: Conduct discussion using above questions. Encourage all participants to contribute to the discussion.

5. Learning Activity

Content: "We are going to do an activity to help us learn where all players should be on a softball field. In my hat are 10 folded pieces of paper. Each paper contains the name of one position. Ten of you will draw a piece of paper from my hat but do not look until I tell you. When I give you the signal to start, everyone will look at the position on the paper and run to it on the field. When everyone has found the correct position, return papers to my hat and 10 more players will draw and run through the activity."

Process: Explain activity. Prepare papers ahead of session. Accompany each group as it runs to the field. Provide assistance as necessary. Repeat exercise until every player participates five times.

6. Debriefing

Content:
    a. Which positions are easiest to remember? Which are most difficult? Why?
    b. Do you know where all positions are? If not, which ones should we review?
    c. Are you ready to tell someone where all the positions are?
    d. What are the 10 positions?

Process: Conduct debriefing using above questions. Encourage each participant to respond to at least one of the questions.

7. Conclusion

Content: "Knowing where everyone should be on the field is a characteristic of a knowledgeable player. It makes the game easier to play and prevents situations from arising that could detract from the fun and enjoyment."

Process: Make concluding statements. Provide opportunity for questions.

Objective 4.2: Demonstrate understanding of the importance of communication to softball.

1. Orientation Activity

Content: "Please sit in the seats arranged in a circle. Look at the person to your right and think of a brief phrase associated with softball that the person brings to mind. Once everyone has a phrase in mind, I will ask each of you to introduce yourself and the person to your right and provide us with the softball-related phrase that reminds you of this person (e.g., Marty is a powerful hitter. Gloria is a quick base runner.)"

Process: Arrange the group to sit in a circle. Provide examples or begin the activity by taking a seat in the circle and introducing the person to your right.

2. Introduction

Content: "Communication skills are important. They are needed when relating to another person or to an entire group. A structured group activity such as softball requires communication in order to be played properly and provide maximum benefits."

Process: Introduce the topic of communication. Emphasize the relationship and importance of communication to playing softball.

3. Presentation

Content: "Communication can be used to persuade other people to do what you want, to let other people know what you are doing, to learn what others are doing, to negotiate differences, and to make a foundation supporting cooperative efforts. Teams that communicate increase their chances of success and enhance their enjoyment.

"There are a few things to consider to be successful in communicating. Communication must be clear and concise. You must know what you want to say, think it through clearly, and state it simply. The message to be conveyed should not be too complicated. If a message is complex, it should be divided into components and delivered carefully. Words should be enunciated clearly and not run together. Remember that in communication, listening carefully is as important as speaking.

"Communicating without speaking is also common; it is known as nonverbal communication. Posture, eye contact, facial expression, speed of movement, sighing, laughing, and crying are included among ways that messages can be conveyed without words. A good communicator is alert to both verbal and nonverbal communication."

Process: Present information on communication. Use chalkboard to list important points. Demonstrate examples of nonverbal communication. Encourage participants to expand list of types of nonverbal communication.

4. Discussion

Content:
   a.   What are some purposes of communication?
   b.   What are some benefits of communication?
   c.   Why is listening as important as speaking in communication?

    d. What are some examples of nonverbal communication?
    e. How can communication be helpful to a softball team?

Process: Conduct discussion using above items. Encourage all participants to contribute to the discussion.

5. Learning Activity

Content: "We are going to do a mime activity to illustrate how we can communicate without words. A player will take a slip of paper from my hat and act out what is contained on it. The rest of us will try to guess what is being acted out. Each player will have an opportunity to mime for the rest of us."

Process: Explain activity. Prepare adequate number of slips with softball-related actions. For example: "I just hit a home run," "I'm looking for my glove," "I just fielded a hot grounder," "I legged out an infield single," "I just caught a high fly ball." "I just took a called third strike." Help players understand message on paper, if needed.

6. Debriefing

Content:
    a. Which mime action was easiest to understand? Why?
    b. Is it sometimes difficult to communicate without words?
    c. Why is nonverbal communication useful?
    d. Do we sometimes communicate nonverbally when we are not aware of it?

Process: Conduct debriefing using above questions. Encourage each participant to respond to at least one of the questions.

7. Conclusion

Content: "Clear communication requires hard work. Softball is a team game and, as such, is best played when team members know what other players are thinking and doing. Communication leads to cooperation, and cooperation is necessary for the achievement of team goals."

Process: Make concluding statements. Provide opportunity for questions.

Objective 4.3: Demonstrate the ability to organize a group of people to play softball.

1. Orientation Activity

Content: "In this box is a variety of softball equipment. Without looking, reach into the box and pull out one piece of equipment. Find the other people who have the same type of equipment (e.g., bats, balls, bases). Introduce yourself to the other members of your group and choose a group leader.

"All of you are being given a bat and a blindfold. Everyone, except the leader, put on your blindfold. The leader must organize the group so that together they are holding up the leader's bat. Each player's bat must be touching the leader's bat. Once the bat is being supported by all the player's bats, the leader must state all the player's names. Once the leader completes this task, blindfolds can be removed and you may now select another leader. Continue this process until all participants have been the leader."

Process: Obtain a large box and cut a hole in the bottom that is large enough to allow someone to remove the items from the box. Place a dark cloth over the hole attached to the box at the top of the hole. Insert into the box one piece of equipment per person. Cut pieces of cloth long enough to use as blindfolds. Obtain a softball bat for each player. Encourage leaders to problem solve. Assist only when necessary. Move among groups, insuring activity is running smoothly.

2. Introduction

Content: "Helping a group of people play softball requires organizational skills. These skills can be learned and applied. If used correctly, they prevent disappointment and confusion and enhance enjoyment derived from playing."

Process: Introduce topic of organization related to softball. Determine if participants understand the concept of "organization."

3. Presentation

Content: "Organizational techniques help you get things done efficiently and effectively. They save time, prevent disorder, and allow effective use of resources. Applied in a democratic manner, they help people enjoy their time and activities.

"Organizational skill is needed when dealing with a group of people who want to play softball. One of the first things to accomplish is dividing the group into two teams. Communication must occur to inform the group of the organizational technique that will be used to form the teams. For example, the following technique could be communicated to the group:

> Please form a single line. Starting with the person on the left, count off by twos. That is, the first person says 'one,' the second person says 'two,' the third person says 'one,' the fourth person says 'two,' etc. When counting is finished, the 'ones' will be a team and the 'twos' will be a team.

"This is an organizational technique. But it does have a potential problem. If it is used excessively, people will space themselves in line to be on the same team as the best players. This results in unfair competition. Techniques such as the instructor placing individuals on teams, allowing two players to choose teams, drawing cards, or other methods could be employed to prevent this from happening.

"After players are on teams, the team to bat first must be determined. One way to decide is to spin the bat. The bat should be spun on its end, away from the handle. There is a number on the end of the bat. A player from one team spins the bat; a player from the other team calls 'up' or 'down.' If the bat lands with the number more than halfway up, it is 'up' that wins. If the number is more than halfway down, 'down' wins. If it is too close to call, the bat is spun again. The team that wins the call gets to choose to bat first or take the field. A coin toss or choosing a number closest to a number known only by a trusted third party are other ways of deciding which team will bat first.

"In addition to deciding which team will bat first, there must be a decision made regarding the order in which the players on a team will bat. This can be decided by a team leader on the basis of batting skill, the positions can be numbered one through ten and players bat in numbered succession, a coin flip, or other means."

Process: Present information on organizational skills. Put players in line and demonstrate methods to divide into two teams. Demonstrate bat spin and coin toss.

4. Discussion

Content:
   a.   How are organizational skills used to help a group get ready to play softball?
   b.   How does the count-off method work to decide teams?
   c.   What other methods could be used to decide who will be on what team?
   d.   How does the bat spin work to decide which team will bat first?
   e.   How can a batting order be determined?

Process: Conduct discussion using above items. Ask if they have any questions. Encourage all participants to contribute to the discussion.

5. Learning Activity

Content: "We are going to do an activity that will help get us organized to play softball. I am going to divide you into groups of ten. The groups will do this activity independent of each other. Each group will be given a hat containing three folded pieces of paper. One paper will have 'form teams' written on it, one will have 'decide which team bats first' on it, and the final one will have 'determine the batting order.' A player from each group will draw a paper from the hat and describe how the direction will be achieved. The paper will then be returned to the hat and the next player will draw. If a paper is drawn that has previously been used, the player must describe how the direction will be accomplished, using a method that has not yet been described."

Process: Explain activity. Prepare sufficient sets of papers ahead of session. Divide players into groups. Have sufficient number of hats. Have adequate physical distance separating groups. Move from group to group or enlist monitor for each group. If player draws a paper used more than three times, allow new paper to be drawn.

6. Debriefing

Content:
   a.   Which organizational technique was the most difficult to describe? Why?
   b.   What can be done to make it easier to communicate directions?
   c.   Do you feel confident in your ability to organize a group of people to play softball? If not, what more needs to be done?

Process: Conduct debriefing using above questions. Encourage each participant to respond to at least one of the questions.

7. Conclusion

Content: "Knowing how to use organizational skills is a valuable asset. Applying them in a friendly and democratic manner facilitates the accomplishment of goals."

Process: Make concluding statements. Review any material that created problems for participants. Provide sufficient opportunities for questions and answers.

Objective 4.4: Demonstrate the ability to accept constructive criticism.

1. Orientation Activity

Content: "You now will assume the role of an art critic. I am distributing pictures of softball scenes that I have drawn. Please examine the picture. Soon I will ask you to stand, introduce yourself, show the picture to the other participants, and then critique the picture. That is, I want you to tell us about the things you like and those things that could be improved. When providing the critique, please begin and end with something positive about the picture. Who would like to volunteer to begin the activity?"

Process: Draw picture of softball scenes prior to the activity. Draw sufficient copies for each participant. Distribute the pictures to each participant and provide directions to the activity. Assist individuals with critiques as needed.

2. Introduction

Content: "A first step in improving one's skills and competencies is to be aware of the need for improvement. But it is sometimes very difficult to recognize one's own limitations. It is often necessary to have these areas pointed out by others. Identifying areas of need and informing individuals of those areas is a form of criticism. The manner in which criticism is offered and received is very important."

Process: Introduce topic of accepting criticism. Emphasize the value of criticism.

3. Presentation

Content: "Criticism that is offered in a friendly, nonthreatening manner is referred to as constructive criticism. Its purpose is to point out weaknesses and offer suggestions so improvements can be made and to persuade individuals to see things from a different perspective. Constructive criticism is not person-specific but rather it is behavior-specific. It is focused on actions, not on personalities.

"Constructive criticism should be delivered in a calm manner and with a moderate tone of voice. The reason for the criticism should be explained and tips for improvement should be made. Criticism without suggestions for action has limited value.

"Constructive criticism should be received in a calm but alert way. The person should acknowledge the criticism, ask for clarification, assess its helpfulness, and, if appropriate, indicate a willingness to act. Inappropriate reactions to constructive criticism include yelling, stomping, kicking, fighting, cursing, and running away."

Process: Present information on criticism. Provide demonstrations to illustrate appropriate delivery of constructive criticism and acceptance of constructive criticism.

4. Discussion

Content:
  a.   Do you think constructive criticism is beneficial? If so, how is it?
  b.   What is meant by the phrase "behavior-specific rather than person-specific?"
  c.   Is the style in which criticism is delivered important? If so, in what way?
  d.   Describe an appropriate reaction to constructive criticism.
  e.   Describe an inappropriate reaction to constructive criticism.

Process: Conduct discussion using above items. Encourage participants to contribute and ask questions.

5. Learning Activity

Content: "We are going to watch a skit based on giving criticism. One of our players will assume a batting stance. A second player will offer criticism in a particular manner. A third player will offer criticism in a different manner. Think about the styles of giving criticism. When the skit is finished, we will discuss it."

Process: Explain activity. Preselect three willing players and assign roles. First criticizer will be aggressive and abusive, with no thought for the feelings of the batter, will focus on batter, and offer no help for change. Second criticizer be calm, friendly, and helpful, explain what is wrong, and offer suggestions for improvement, including a demonstration of correct stance. When skit is finished, move to debriefing.

6. Debriefing

Content:
   a. Which person do you think was the most helpful? Why?
   b. Which person would you want to give you criticism? Why?
   c. How would you offer criticism to another person?
   d. How would you feel if you were criticized by an abusive person?

Process: Conduct debriefing using above items. Encourage participants to ask questions and respond to at least one of the questions.

7. Conclusion

Content: "Criticism is helpful if used properly. It can lead to improvement of skills and better performance by players. If used improperly, it can have a negative impact on individuals and a team. If criticism must be offered, it must be done constructively."

Process: Make concluding statements. Review any material that created problems for participants. Provide opportunity for questions.

Goal 5: Demonstrate the ability to actively participate in the game of softball.

Objective 5.1: Demonstrate the ability to throw a softball.

1. Orientation Activity

Content: "We are going to have a little target practice. The target is on the fence, with different point values for different areas of the target. The object is to stand behind this line and throw a softball at the target, hitting the area with the highest number of points. I will judge where the target is hit. Once you have thrown the ball, you must go pick up the ball and give it to a player who has yet to throw the ball. When giving the ball to the player, you must introduce yourself and ask for the person's name. Then return to me to find out how many points you scored."

Process: Explain activity. Construct target prior to session and attach to fence or wall. Target can be old sheet or large piece of cardboard. Make bull's eye and concentric circles, assign point values to each. You can model it on a dart board or the shape of a softball diamond, with different areas worth different points. Instructor judges where ball hits. Players throw from behind a line that is a challenging distance from the target, yet permits some degree of success. Emphasize accuracy, not force.

2. Introduction

Content: "Throwing is a fundamental skill necessary for success in softball. It is a defensive skill. Accurate throwing can enable a defensive player to assist in putting out players from the opposing team, preventing them from advancing on the base paths, and keeping them from scoring runs. Throwing forcefully and accurately is a very desirable characteristic in a player."

Process: Introduce the topic of throwing a softball.

3. Presentation

Content: "Throwing can be perfected by practicing, but the correct techniques must be practiced before you can become skilled in throwing. Throwing can be divided into four steps.

"Step one focuses on the grip. The ball should be in contact with all fingers of the throwing hand. The index, middle, and ring fingers should grasp the ball at the top; the little finger is placed at the side of the ball and serves as a guider rather than a gripper. The thumb stabilizes the grasp and is the first to leave the ball on release. Do not let the ball fall into the palm of your hand; grip the ball firmly with the fingers to prevent this. If there is too much contact with the palm, the throw is likely to be inaccurate and without much force.

"Step two is the first part of the throwing motion. Bring the ball behind your head, passing it near your ear and cocking your wrist back. The majority of the thrower's weight should be placed on the back foot (the right foot if throwing right-handed, the left foot if throwing left-handed). When weight is shifted to the back foot, the front foot may come slightly off the ground. The front foot is positioned comfortably forward and pointed toward the target. The hips and shoulders should be in an open position, with a slightly arched back. The front arm should be out and away from the body for balance.

"Step three is the middle part of the throwing motion. Your hips should begin to close, followed by shoulders. The upper part of the throwing arm starts forward. As hips and shoulders close, the throwing arm comes through. Hand and ball come through last, and the wrist snaps forward as the ball is released. Weight is transferred to the front foot and the front arm swings back, allowing the torso to rotate.

"Step four is the final part of the throwing motion. After the ball is released, the back foot should come forward to the side or in front of the lead foot to complete the weight transfer. Throwing arm continues forward, following a path downward to the opposite knee."

Process: Have players in front of instructor, with a clear view. Demonstrate throwing motion, without ball, as each step is described. Slow down or exaggerate specific movements to make point. Repeat movements as necessary. Give each player a ball and have them model your demonstration.

4. Discussion

Content:
    a. How should the ball be gripped?
    b. Why is it necessary to keep the ball off the palm of your hand?
    c. What is the first step in throwing? Second? Third? Fourth?
    d. Are there any motions you would like to have repeated?

Process: Conduct discussion using above questions. Encourage participants to demonstrate the skill as they answer the questions.

5. Presentation

Content: "There are two types of throws that are generally used by softball players, the overhand throw and the three-quarters throw. In the overhand throw, the ball is released at the top of the head, directly above the shoulder of the throwing arm. The arm is almost fully extended at the highest point of the throwing motion. The spin of the ball on release is vertical. This helps it travel in a straight line and not curve or tail away from the target. The glove hand is extended in front of the body for balance. When the arm is drawn back to throw, the back is slightly arched. As the ball is released, the back straightens and body weight is transferred from the back foot to the front foot. The follow-through is on a line to the opposite knee.

"In the three-quarters throw, the ball is released at a point beside the head. Imagine your arm fully extended straight above your head. Now imagine it extended straight out from your shoulder, parallel to the ground. Midway between those two positions is the line of travel for the throwing arm in a three-quarters throw. The throwing arm is not drawn as far back as in an overhand throw. Body rotation is especially important in a three-quarters throw because it helps the ball to be thrown with more force.

"Overhand throws are used most often by outfielders, catchers, and shortstops. They are used when long, forceful throws are needed. They are also the most accurate type of throw. The three-quarters throw is the basic throw used by infielders, with the exception of the shortstop. It can be a quick, forceful throw but generally is not capable of as much distance as an overhand throw."

Process: Demonstrate both throwing motions. Use slow or exaggerated movements to make specific points. Repeat as necessary. Provide participants with balls while talking. Have them model your behaviors. Encourage them to go through the motions without releasing the ball.

6. Discussion

Content:
    a. What is the major difference between the overhand throw and the three-quarters throw?
    b. What players are the major users of the overhand throw? Why?
    c. What players are the major users of the three-quarters throw? Why?

Process: Conduct discussion using above questions. Encourage all participants to contribute to the discussion.

7. Learning Activity

Content: "We are going to pair up and practice each of the two throws we have just discussed. Concentrate on making the correct throwing motion. We are not now concerned with throwing for distance, just with the right motion. As you throw back and forth, divide your throws evenly between overhand and three-quarters. Keep track of how many throws you catch in a row without dropping one. I will be around to ask what your record is so far."

Process: Have at least one ball for every two players. Help players pair up, if necessary. Pairs should face each other at a distance of approximately 25 feet. Help players find proper distance, if necessary. Caution players not to throw hard. Move among players and give feedback. Allow 10-15 minutes for throwing activity.

8. Debriefing

Content:
    a. Did you have difficulty gripping the ball? If so, what changes did you make?
    b. Did the footwork involved in throwing seem natural?
    c. Was one throw more difficult than the other? If so, which one?
    d. What questions or comments do you have about throwing?

Process: Conduct debriefing. Allow each player to describe and demonstrate any difficulties experienced. Encourage continuing practice to improve throwing motion.

9. Conclusion

Content: "Practicing throwing skills will make you a better thrower. Being able to throw well will enhance your enjoyment from playing softball. It increases your ability to contribute to the team and it makes you feel better, knowing that that you are doing the best you are able."

Process: Make concluding statement. Encourage participants to ask questions. Provide additional practice and demonstrations as needed.

Objective 5.2: Demonstrate the ability to catch a softball.

1. Orientation Activity

Content: "Catching or fielding requires your hands to yield to help absorb the impact of the thrown object. Please get into pairs and face each other at a distance of about eight feet. Here is a balloon filled with water for each pair. Using an underhand toss, throw the balloon back and forth. The player who catches the balloon may take one step backward before tossing it back. The object is to see the greatest distance that can be covered without breaking the balloon. Breaking the balloon has an obvious penalty. Once your balloon breaks, go over to others who are still throwing and cheer them on."

Process: Explain activity. Use small balloons, fill with enough water to make them somewhat fragile. Caution against throwing with too much force. If desired, have enough balloons to offer each pair two opportunities.

2. Introduction

Content: "Control of the ball is one of the most important aspects of softball. Defensive players must be ready to take control of the ball at any given moment. With each pitch, defensive players prepare themselves to field the ball if it is hit into their area. Good fielding is critical to the success of a softball team."

Process: Introduce the topic of catching a softball.

3. Presentation

Content: "Players can develop the ability to field a ball by practicing. The first thing to master is getting into a 'set' position. This is done by having the feet shoulder-width apart, knees bent, body crouched, head up, and shoulders relaxed. The weight is forward on the balls of the feet. The glove is held open in a low position in front of the body and the throwing hand is placed to the side of the glove. The eyes are on the ball at all times. The set position is one that enables a player to spring toward the ball, whether it is hit on the ground or in the air.

"Being in a set position has some advantages. In fielding ground balls, it can limit the number of errors committed because it allows the fielder to play the ball, rather than the ball playing the fielder. That is, the player can move quickly to the ball and field it, rather than having to react to the ball movement at the last possible moment and trying to field it in an awkward position. The set position also allows the arms to give with the force of the ball, thus softening the impact. Placing the glove in a low position allows easier and quicker movement when the ball takes an unexpected hop.

"Your hands should work together with your eyes. When you field a ball, it should be watched until it enters the glove. The throwing hand should be partially behind the glove to help stop the ball and then it should cover the ball in the glove. This helps prevent the ball from spinning out of the glove and it enables the fielder to get a grip on the ball in preparation for throwing it.

"When fielding a ball, the impact of the catch and the give of the arms should be directed toward the throwing shoulder. At the same time, the upper body should rotate to an open position and the feet pivot-hop, distributing the weight over the back foot. This movement positions the player to throw the ball.

"Some players develop poor habits in catching. For example, some players wait until the last moment before flipping their gloves downward to catch a grounder. Often, they do not get the glove down in time and the ball gets by them. This means they have made an error. Other players turn their heads and do not watch the ball into the glove. They fail to catch or hold on to the ball, thus committing an error. Still other players will field a ball cleanly but then flip the ball with their gloved hand into their throwing hand, often dropping it. All of these habits can be avoided by concentrating on the correct way to field a ball."

Process: Present information on physical position in preparing to field ball, with emphasis on ground balls. Position participants where they can clearly see and hear instructor. Demonstrate physical position. Field grounders as part of demonstration.

4. Discussion

Content:
    a.   What are the steps to follow in a good "set" position?
    b.   Why is the weight on the balls of the feet?
    c.   What is meant by the saying: "Play the ball before the ball plays you"?
    d.   What role does the nonglove hand play in fielding a ball?
    e.   What are some common physical errors related to fielding a ball?

Process: Conduct discussion using above questions. Encourage all participants to contribute to the discussion.

5. Presentation

Content: "Players must also be able to catch balls hit into the air. A set position is also used in this process, but the glove hand is not held as low as it is in preparing to field a grounder. The set position enables the player to quickly move toward the ball. The player must also judge the flight of the ball. This is best done by reacting to the ball as soon as it leaves the bat. This is a learned skill and takes practice to master.

"Judging a ball in flight means assessing its direction, speed, height, and spin, as well as environmental factors such as strength and direction of wind and the angle of the sun. Players usually must adjust from a set position to a running position to get under the ball. Good players try to get into a position where they can catch the ball and immediately throw it with force and accuracy. The glove and cover hand should be raised to approximately shoulder height and positioned under the ball. Just before catching the ball, players frequently step forward so there is momentum at the time the ball is caught. This adds force to the throw. If a strong throw is needed, these players put themselves into a position where they can take two steps before catching the ball. This allows them to charge into the ball and have greater momentum to help in the throw.

"When a fly ball enters the glove, the glove and cover hand should give toward the throwing shoulder. This should happen simultaneously with the feet getting into position to throw. If a player cannot get into position to catch a ball with two hands, the ball must be grasped and controlled with the glove. The player must then recover body position quickly and throw the ball."

Process: Present information on catching a fly ball. Demonstrate techniques in "slow motion" without the ball, then by actually catching fly balls. Emphasize throwing after the catch.

6. Discussion

Content:
    a.   What factors must a player consider when judging a ball in flight?
    b.   How can a player get maximum force on a throw after catching a fly ball?
    c.   In catching a fly ball, why do the glove hand and cover hand give in the direction of the throwing shoulder?

Process: Conduct discussion using above questions. Encourage all participants to contribute to the discussion.

7. Learning Activity

Content: "We are going to play 'pepper' to help sharpen our fielding skills. Get into groups of five or six players. One player in each group bats, another catches for the batter, and the others field. Batter and fielders face each other at a distance of 18-20 feet. The batter starts play by swinging gently and hitting a soft grounder to a fielder. The fielder will throw the ball back to the player catching for the batter with just enough force to be accurate. The player will then give the ball to the batter. The batter will hit the ball on the ground back to the fielders. This process can continue until the batter hits a 'pop-up' that is caught on the fly by a fielder. The fielder then comes in and catches for the batter, the catcher for the batter becomes the batter, and the batter goes to the field. Remember not to throw hard and not to swing the bat forcefully. The purpose of this activity is to practice fielding ground balls."

Process: Divide players into groups. Players provide own gloves. Have a bat and at least one ball for each group. Emphasize throwing and hitting with appropriate restraint. If desired, ensure that each player gets opportunity to bat by rotation scheme, rather than by who catches pop-up.

8. Debriefing

Content:
   a.   Were you able to be in a set position for fielding? If not why not?
   b.   Did you watch the ball into your glove? If not, why not?
   c.   Did you use both hands to field? If not, why not?
   d.   Why would you adjust the distance between batter and fielders?

Process: Conduct debriefing using above questions. Encourage each participant to respond to at least one of the questions.

9. Learning Activity

Content: "We are going to participate in an activity to catch fly balls. Everyone needs a glove. Pair up with a partner. Each pair should be separated from other pairs by about 10 yards so people do not run into each other. Partners should face each other at a distance of about 20 feet. Practice throwing fly balls to each other. Throw at half-speed to a height of approximately 35-40 feet. Throw some so that your partner will have to run forward to catch the ball and some where running back will be needed. Focus on doing things right. Keep track of how many consecutive catches you both make without dropping the ball. When I come around to you, tell me your best record."

Process: Help players pair up. Provide each pair with a ball. Move among the players and give feedback where appropriate. Demonstrate a desirable throw.

10. Debriefing

Content:
   a.   Did you watch the ball into the glove? If not, why not?
   b.   Did you use both hands to catch the ball? If not, why not?
   c.   Was running forward or backward easier? Why?
   d.   Are you ready for higher fly balls? If not, are you ready to practice some more at this height?

Process: Conduct debriefing using above questions. Attempt to have each participant make a contribution.

11. Conclusion

Content: "Being able to catch is absolutely essential to being a good fielder. Defense depends on a team being able to field grounders and fly balls. Concentrating on the fundamentals is the best way to become a good fielder and contribute to the success of the team. As in all other skills, the road to mastering the fundamentals is practice."

Process: Make concluding statements. Encourage participants to ask questions. Provide opportunities for additional practice as needed.

Objective 5.3: Demonstrate the ability to hit a softball.

1. Orientation Activity

Content: "We are going to pair up for a hitting game. Each pair needs a bat, ball, and glove. The player with the bat will stand 10 feet from the fence, in a position to hit a ball toward the fence. Place the glove on the ground, as though it were home plate. The other player will stand to the side of the batter, out of reach of the swing (6-7 feet) and use an underhand motion to toss the ball so it will land in the glove. The batter will use a controlled swing to hit the ball. If the ball lands high on the fence, the batter has undercut it. If it goes into the ground, the batter has topped it. After the batter has had 10 swings, the players will exchange positions."

Process: Explain activity. Have bat and ball for each pair. Emphasize safety. Move among pairs to provide assistance and feedback. Make sure everybody gets to hit.

2. Introduction

Content: "Hitting requires careful practice. Although there are recommended steps to follow in developing this skill, remember that no two batters are exactly alike. Different batters may have different styles. If a batter is comfortable with a particular style and if it works well, there is no need to attempt to change the style."

Process: Introduce the topic of hitting a softball.

3. Presentation

Content: "Hitting a softball can be separated into five components: grip, stance, stride, swing, and follow-through. Mastering the techniques associated with each of these components can enable players to become better hitters.

"The first step in becoming a better hitter is to grip the bat for good control. The bat should be held firmly but not tightly. The hands should be placed on the bat in such a way that the middle knuckles of the hands are aligned with each other. This tends to prevent the wrists from locking. The bat should be held in the fingers and finger pads, not in the palms. This gives the hitter better control of the bat.

"The most important aspect of the batter's stance is that it be comfortable. Most batters begin with an open stance. This can be accomplished by aligning the toes of the front foot with the arch of the back foot to open the hips. The body should be slightly crouched, with weight distributed evenly over both feet and the head held upright to allow the best visibility of the ball. The bat should be held away from the body, a little behind the rear shoulder with the hands at armpit height. The rear elbow should be at approximately a 45 degree angle from the body. If the elbow is held too close to the body, the tendency is to undercut the ball. The head should be kept completely still to allow a complete view of the pitcher and the ball. The chin is held so that it nearly touches the front shoulder; during the swing, the body rotates around the head.

"The purpose of the stride is to allow the batter to coordinate the transfer of weight on the feet with the rotary force of the hips, shoulders, and swing of the bat. A good stride is roughly equivalent to the length of the batter's foot; it should be comfortable to the batter. Overstriding causes a loss of coordination and a drop of the bat. The usual result is a pop-up. Understriding also causes a loss of coordination and prevents a full extension of the arms on the swing. This results in pop-ups and foul balls. In striding, the front toe should be pointed toward the pitcher. This allows hip rotation during the swing. Body weight is transferred from the rear foot to the front foot and the stride should finish with the toes of the rear foot in contact with the ground. The batter should be in a position to run out of the batter's box and toward first base.

"The swing should be a smoothly disciplined motion, following a slightly descending path. The bat should make contact with the upper half of the ball in front of or even with the rear leg. Once the swing is started, all momentum continues forward through the ball. The hands should move out toward the ball, pulling the arms away from the body. The front side of the body should provide a pulling force, allowing the back side to guide and push the bat. The head of the bat is actually thrown at the ball. The bat head should be aligned with the wrists at the moment of contact with the ball.

"The follow-through is the final component in hitting a softball. After the bat makes contact with the ball, it should continue in its motion. This is known as hitting through the ball. The force behind the bat is decreased in the follow-through. This can be achieved by dropping one hand from the bat. This hand can be used to regain balance and initiate body momentum toward first base.

"In addition to the mechanics of hitting, there is also a mental component. Every batter should be prepared to hit the next pitch. This preparation can be aided by self-statements such as: 'There is no pitch that I can't hit.' or 'I'm going to hit the next pitch.' Batters should relax and think about having a smooth and fluid swing."

Process: Present information on hitting. Demonstrate grip, stance, stride, swing, and follow-through. Use slow, exaggerated movements to illustrate points. Repeat as often as necessary. Give bats to players as you are presenting information. Encourage participants to model your demonstrations.

4. Discussion

Content:

    a. What are the five components of hitting?
    b. Why should the bat be held in the fingers and finger pads and not in the palms?
    c. What is an example of a good stance?
    d. In hitting, what is the usual result if the rear elbow is held too close to the body?
    e. How do overstriding and understriding affect hitting?
    f. What is meant by the phrase "hitting through the ball"?

Process: Conduct discussion using above questions. Encourage all players to contribute.

5. Learning Activity

Content: "We are going to take some batting practice. We need one player to start, one player to be next (the on-deck batter), one to catch behind the batter, and one to shag balls for the pitcher. I will be the pitcher. Everyone scatter throughout the infield and outfield. If a ball is hit to you, try to field it and throw it back to the shagger. After a batter has hit 10 balls, we will rotate as follows: batter to the field, on-deck to batter, catcher to on-deck, shagger to catcher, and someone from the field to shag. Everyone will get a turn."

Process: Explain activity. Players supply own gloves. Provide a couple of bats and at least half a dozen balls. Make sure everybody understands rotation order. Throw underhanded and in strike zone. Make sure everyone gets to hit. Give feedback to hitters about their mechanics.

6. Debriefing

Content:
    a.   How comfortable did your stance feel?
    b.   Were you able to watch the ball until it was hit by the bat? If not,why not?
    c.   How did your stride feel? Too long? Too short? About right?
    d.   Did your swing feel smooth?
    e.   Is there anything about your style you feel you want to change? If so, what?

Process: Conduct debriefing using above questions. Encourage all participants to contribute to the discussion.

7. Conclusion

Content: "Hitting requires a considerable amount of practice. Once this skill is acquired, it provides a player with satisfaction and a feeling of accomplishment. But it is also important to remember that even good hitters are unsuccessful about 70% of the time."

Process: Make concluding statements. Provide opportunity for questions.

Objective 5.4: Demonstrate the ability to run bases.

1. Orientation Activity

Content: "Base runners have to run as fast as possible at times. I have divided you into two equal groups. Group one line up behind home plate, group two behind second base. On my signal, the first runner in group one will run to first base, the first runner in group two will run to third base. As the runners cross their respective bases, they will yell RUN. The next runners in line will then start down the base line. This process repeats until one group is the first to have all its runners cross its target base."

Process: Explain activity. Divide players as equally as possible on the basis of speed. Monitor activity to ensure compliance with rules. If desired, allow rematch.

2. Introduction

Content: "Being a base runner means a player has to have adequate physical skills. It also means the player knows when and how to run the bases. Good base runners are alert, aggressive, and confident in their ability."

Process: Introduce the topic of base running.

3. Presentation

Content: "After hitting the ball, players need to start quickly out of the batter's box, run hard down the baseline, and through first base toward right-field foul territory. If they are going to advance to second base, they need to angle out at first, stay in stride, push off first with the middle of their foot, and look to second base. They should run in this manner for as many bases as they think they can get out of the hit. If there is a home run fence and the ball is hit over it, they can run the bases in a less hurried manner.

"If they are on base when a teammate is hitting, they must be aware of the number of outs and where the ball is hit. If there are two outs, the base runner runs on every ball that is hit. If there are no outs, or only one out, the runner must make sure the ball is safely out of the infield and will not be caught by an outfielder before advancing. On high fly balls to the outfield, the runner should advance about halfway to the next base, if uncertain as to whether the ball will be caught. Knowing whether to run on ground balls hit to certain parts of the infield is difficult. Players who are uncertain can listen closely to the coaches in the first and third base coach's boxes for assistance."

Process: Present information on base running. Use first base as a prop. Demonstrate run from home to first, both for single and extra-base hit.

4. Discussion

Content:
    a. How should you approach first base if you think you have hit a single?
    b. How should you approach first base if you think you have an extra-base hit?
    c. If you are a base runner, why advance halfway to the next base when you are uncertain if a fly ball will be caught?
    d. With two outs, why should base runners run on every ball hit?

Process: Conduct discussion using above questions. Encourage all participants to contribute to the discussion.

5. Learning Activity

Content: "We are going to do a base running game. I have divided you into two groups. One group will take the field, playing regular positions. The other group will be in single line behind home plate. I will hit the ball and one runner will run it out. Fielders play the ball and try to put the base runner out. Base runners will run the bases according to where the ball is hit and how it is played, just as in a real game. Runners that are put out or advance all the way home go to the end of the line. After all the players in one group have had an opportunity to run the bases, they will exchange places with the fielders, who will become the next base running group."

Process: Divide players into groups. Hit the ball to various places in the field of play. Use specific situations to instruct all players about base running.

6. Debriefing:

Content: What is the correct base running action with:
   a.   a runner on first, one out, and a fly ball is hit to left field?
   b.   a runner on second, one out, and a ground ball is hit to the shortstop?
   c.   a runner on third, no outs, and a ground ball is hit to second base?
   d.   runners on first and third, one out, and a fly ball hit to center field?
   e.   runners on first and second, two out, and a fly ball to right field?

Process: Conduct debriefing using above questions. Encourage participants to respond to at least one question.

7. Conclusion

Content: "Base running is as much mental as it is physical. It is essential that players be constantly aware of the game situation. Good base running can win ball games. It is a potent weapon in a team's offense."

Process: Make concluding statement. Provide opportunities for questions. Allow additional practice time as needed.

References

Aguilar, T. E. (1986). Leisure education program development and evaluation. *Journal of Expanding Horizons in Therapeutic Recreation, 1*, 14-20.

Aguilar, T. E. (1987). Effects of a leisure education program on expressed attitudes of delinquent adolescents. *Therapeutic Recreation Journal, 21(4)*, 43-51.

American Therapeutic Recreation Association Newsletter (1984). 1(1), 2.

Anderson, S. C., & Allen, L. R. (1985). Effects of a leisure education program on activity involvement and social interaction of mentally retarded persons. *Adapted Physical Activity Quarterly, 2(2)*, 107-116.

Ashton-Shaeffer, C., & Kleiber, D. A. (1990). The relationship between recreation participation and functional skill development in young people with mental retardation. *Annual in Therapeutic Recreation, 1*, 75-81.

Austin, D. R. (1989). Therapeutic recreation education: A call for reform. In D. M. Compton (Ed.). *Issues in therapeutic recreation: A profession in transition* (pp. 145-156). Champaign, IL: Sagamore.

Backman, S. J., & Mannell, R. C. (1986). Removing attitudinal barriers to leisure behavior and satisfaction: A field experiment among the institutionalized elderly. *Therapeutic Recreation Journal, 20(3)*, 46-53.

Baer, D. (1981). A hung jury and a Scottish verdict not proven. *Analysis and Intervebtion in Developmental Disabilities, 1*, 91-97.

Beck-Ford, V., & Brown, R. (1984). *Leisure training and rehabilitation.* Springfield, IL: Charles C. Thomas.

Bedini, L. A. (1990). The status of leisure education: Implications for instruction and practice. *Therapeutic Recreation Journal, 24(1)*, 40-49.

Bedini, L. A., & Bullock, C. C. (1988). Leisure education in the public schools: A model of cooperation in transition programming for mentally handicapped youth. *Journal of Expanding Horizons in Therapeutic Recreation, 3*, 5-11.

Bouffard, M. (1990). Movement problem solutions by educable mentally handicapped individuals. *Adapted Physical Activity Quarterly, 7*, 183-197.

Boyd, R. (1990). Participation in day programs and leisure activities by elderly persons with mental retardation: A necessary component of normalization. *Research Into Action, 7*, 12-21.

Boyd, R., & James, A. (1990). An emerging challenge: Serving older adults with mental retardation. *Annual in Therapeutic Recreation, 1*, 56-66.

Bransford, J., Sherwood, R., Vye, N., & Rieser, J. (1986). Teaching thinking and problem solving. *American Psychologist, 41*, 1078-1089.

Bregha, F. J. (1985). Leisure and freedom re-examined. In T. A. Goodale and P. A.Witt (Eds.), *Recreation and leisure: Issues in an era of change (2nd. ed.)* (pp. 35-43). State College, PA: Venture Publishing.

Brightbill, C. K., & Mobely, T. A. (1977). *Educating for leisure-centered living (2nd ed.).* New York, NY: John Wiley.

Bucher, C.A., Shivers, J.S., & Bucher, R.D. (1984). Leisure education and counseling. *Recreation For Today's Society, 2nd ed.*, 290-303.

Busser, J.A. (1990). *Programming for employee services and recreation.* Champaign, IL: Sagamore Publishing.

Caldwell, L. L., Adolph, S., & Gilbert, A. (1989). Caution! Leisure counselors at work: Long term effects of leisure counseling. *Therapeutic Recreation Journal, 23(3)*, 4-7.

Cappel (1990). Cross-cultural barriers to effective delivery of therapeutic recreation services. *Research Into Action, 7*, 41-49.

Chadsey-Rusch, J. (1990). Social interactions of secondary-aged students with severe handicaps: Implications for facilitating the transition from school to work. *The Journal of the Association for Persons with Severe Handicaps, 15(2)*, 69-78.

Chinn, K. A., & Joswiak, K. F. (1981). Leisure education and leisure counseling. *Therapeutic Recreation Journal, 15(4)*, 4-7.

Collard, K. M. (1981). Leisure education in the schools: Why, who, and the need for advocacy. *Therapeutic Recreation Journal, 15(3)*, 8-18.

Compton, D. M., & Goldstein, J. E. (Eds.). (1977). *Perspectives of leisure counseling.* Alexandria, VA: National Recreation and Parks Association.

Compton, D. M., & Touchstone, W. A. (1977). Individualizing therapeutic recreation services for severely and profoundly handicapped. In G. Hitzhusen, G. O'Morrow, J. Oliver, and K. Hamilton (Eds.), *Expanding horizons in therapeutic recreation IV* (pp. 17-28). Columbia, MO: Department of Recreation and Park Administration.

Connolly, M. L. (1977). Leisure counseling: A values clarification and assertive training approach. In A. Epperson, P. A. Witt, and G. Hitzhusen (Eds.). *Leisure counseling: An aspect of leisure education* (pp. 198-207). Springfield, IL: Charles C. Thomas.

Dattilo, J. (1986). Computerized assessment of preference for severely handicapped individuals. *Journal of Applied Behavior Analysis, 19*, 445-448.

Dattilo, J. (1990). Recreation and leisure: A review of the literature and recommendations for future directions. In L. M. Meyer, C. A. Peck, and L. Brown (Eds.), *Critical issues in the lives of people with severe disabilities* (pp. 126-137). Baltimore, MD: Paul H. Brookes.

Dattilo, J., & Barnett, L. A. (1985). Therapeutic recreation for persons with severe handicaps: An analysis of the relationship between choice and pleasure. *Therapeutic Recreation Journal, 21(3)*, 79-91.

Dattilo, J., & Murphy, W. D. (1987a). The challenge of adventure recreation for individuals with disabilities. *Therapeutic Recreation Journal, 21(3)*, 14-21.

Dattilo, J., & Murphy, W. D. (1987b). *Behavior modification in therapeutic recreation.* State College, PA: Venture Publishing.

Dattilo, J., & Sneegas, J. (1987). Leadership strategies for therapeutic recreation specialists. *Programming Trends in Therapeutic Recreation, 8(3)*, 5-8.

Dattilo, J., & St. Peter, S. (1991). A model for including leisure education in transition services for young adults with mental retardation. *Education and Training in Mental Retardation, 26.*

Davis, L. N. (1974). *Planning, conducting, and evaluating workshops.* Austin, TX: Learning Concepts.

DeVellis, R. F. (1977). Learned helplessness in institutions. *Mental Retardation, 15(5)*, 10-13.

Dowd, E. T. (Ed.). (1984). *Leisure counseling: Concepts and applications.* Springfield, IL: Charles C. Thomas.

Dunn, J. K. (1981). Leisure education: Meeting the challenge of increasing leisure independence of residents in psychiatric facilities. *Therapeutic Recreation Journal, 15(3)*, 17-23.

Dunn, J. K. (1984). Assessment. In C. A. Peterson, and S. L. Gunn. *Therapeutic recreation program and design: Principles and procedures. (2nd ed.)* (pp. 267-320). Englewood Cliffs, NJ: Prentice-Hall.

Ellis, G. D. (1989). The role of science in therapeutic recreation. In D. M. Compton (Ed.). *Issues in therapeutic recreation: A profession in transition* (pp. 109-124). Champaign, IL: Sagamore.

Ellis, G. D., & Witt, P. A. (1986). The leisure diagnostic battery: Past, present and future. *Therapeutic Recreation Journal, 20(4)*, 31-47.

Epperson, A., Witt, P. A., & Hitzhusen, G. (1977). *Leisure counseling: An aspect of leisure education.* Springfield, IL: Charles C. Thomas.

Ewert, A., & Hollenhorst, S. (1989). Testing the adventure model: Empirical support for a model of risk recreation participation. *Journal of Leisure Research, 21(2)*, 124-139.

Fait, H. F., & Billing, J. E. (1978). Reassessment of the value of competition. In R. Martens, *Joy and Sadness in children's sports* (pp. 98-105). Champaign, IL: Human Kinetics.

Falvey, M. A. (1986). *Community based curriculum: Instructional strategies for students with severe handicaps.* Baltimore, MD: Paul H. Brookes.

Faught, K. K., Balleweg, B. J., Crow, R. E., & Vanden Pol, R. A. (1983). An analysis of social behavior among handicapped and non handicapped preschool children. *Education and Training of the Mentally Retarded, 18,* 210-214.

Fine, A. H., Welch-Burke, C. S., & Fondario, L. J. (1985). A developmental model for integration of leisure programming in the education of individuals with mental retardation. *Mental Retardation, 23,* 289-296.

Ford, A., Brown, L., Pumpian, I., Baumgart, D., Nisbet, J., Schroeder, J., & Loomis, R. (1984). Strategies for developing individual recreation/leisure plans for adolescent and young adult severely handicapped students. In N. Certo, N. Haring, and R. York (Eds.), *Public school integration of severely handicapped students: Rational issues and progressive alternatives* (pp. 245-275). Baltimore, MD: Paul H. Brookes.

Gunn. S. L., & Peterson, C. A. (1978). *Therapeutic recreation program design: Principals and procedures.* Englewood Cliffs, NJ: Prentice-Hall.

Gushiken, T. T., Treftz, J. L., Porter, G. H., & Snowberg, R. L. (1986). The development of a leisure education program for cardiac patients. *Journal of Expanding Horizons in Therapeutic Recreation, 1,* 67-72.

Halberg K. J. (1989). Issues in community-based recreation services. In D. M. Compton (Ed.). *Issues in therapeutic recreation: A profession in transition* (pp. 305-324). Champaign, IL: Sagamore.

Hayes, G. A. (1977a). Professional preparation and leisure counseling. *Journal of Physical Education and Recreation, 48(4),* 36-38.

Hayes, G.A. (1977b). Leisure education and recreation counseling. In A. Epperson, P. A. Witt, & G. Hitzhusen (Eds.). *Leisure counseling: An aspect of leisure education* (pp. 208-218). Springfield, IL: Charles C. Thomas.

Hopper, C., & Wambold, C. (1978). Improving the independent play of severely, mentally retarded children. *Education and Training of the Mentally Retarded, 13,* 42-46.

Houghton, J., Bronicki, G. J., & Guess, D. (1987). Opportunities to express preferences and make choices among students with severe disabilities in classroom settings. *Journal of the Association for Persons with Severe Handicaps, 12,* 18-27.

Howe, C. Z. (1989). Assessment instruments in therapeutic recreation: To what extent do they work? In D. M. Compton (Ed.). *Issues in therapeutic recreation: A profession in transition* (pp. 205-222). Champaign, IL: Sagamore.

Howe-Murphy, R., & Charboneau, B. G. (1987). *Therapeutic recreation intervention: An ecological perspective.* Englewood Cliffs, NJ: Prentice-Hall.

Hultsman, J. T., Black, D. R., Seehafer, R. W., and Hovell, M. F. (1987). The Purdue Stepped Approach Model: Application to leisure counseling service delivery. *Therapeutic Recreation Journal, 21(4),* 9-22.

Iso-Ahola, S. E. (1980). *The social psychology of leisure and recreation.* Dubuque, IA: William C. Brown Co.

Iso-Ahola, S., MacNeil, R. D., and Szymanski, D. J. (1980). Social psychological foundations of therapeutic recreation: An attributional analysis. In S. Iso-Ahola (Ed.), *Social psychological perspectives on leisure and recreation.* Springfield, IL: Charles C. Thomas.

Iso-Ahola, S., Weissinger, E. (1987). Leisure and boredom. *Journal of Social and Clinical Psychology, 5(3),* 356-364.

Iso-Ahola, S., Weissinger, E. (1990). Perceptions of boredom in leisure: Conceptualization, reliability and validity of the leisure boredom scale. *Journal of Leisure Research, 22(1),* 1-17.

Johnson, L.P., and Zoerink, D.A. (1977) The development and implementation of a leisure counseling program with female psychiatric patients based on value clarification techniques. In A. Epperson, P. A. Witt, and G. Hitzhusen (Eds.). *Leisure counseling: An aspect of leisure education* (pp. 171-197).Springfield, IL: Charles C. Thomas.

Joswiak, K. F. (1979). *Leisure counseling program materials for the developmentally disabled.* Washington, D. C.: Hawkins and Associates.

Keller, M. J., McCombs, J., Piligrim, V. V., and Booth, S. A. (1987). *Helping older adults develop active leisure lifestyles.* Atlanta, GA: Georgia Department of Human Resources.

Kelly, J. R. (1983). *Leisure identities and interactions* (2nd Ed.). Boston: Allen and Unwin.

Kelly, John R. (1987). *Freedom to Be.* New York, NY: Macmillan.

Kelly, John R. (1990). *Leisure* (2nd Ed.). Englewood Cliffs, NJ: Prentice Hall.

Kimeldorf, M. (1989). *Pathways to leisure: A workbook for finding leisure opportunities.* Bloomington, IL: Meridian Education Corporation.

Kleiber, D. (1981). Leisure-based education. *Leisure Information, 4(7),* 3-4.

Kleiber, D. A., and Kelly, J. R. (1980). Leisure, socialization, and the life cycle. In Iso-Ahola, S. E. (Ed.). *Social psychological perspectives on leisure and recreation* (pp. 91-137). Springfield, IL: Charles C. Thomas.

Kraat, A. (1985). Developing intervention goals. In S. Blackstone (Ed.), *Augmentative and alternative communication* (pp. 197-266). Rockville, MD: American Speech-Language-Hearing Association.

Lanagan, D., and Dattilo, J. (1989). The effects of a leisure education program on individuals with mental retardation. *Therapeutic Recreation Journal, 23(4)*, 62-72.

Lee, L. L., & Mobily, K. E. (1988). The NTRS philosophical position statement and a concept of three freedoms. *Journal of Expanding Horizons in Therapeutic Recreation, 3(3)*, 41-46.

Light, J. (1988). Interaction involving individuals using augmentative and alternative and alternate communication systems: State of the art and future directions. *Augmentative and alternative and Alternate Communication, 4*, 66-82.

Luckey, R. E., & Shapiro, I. G. (1974). Recreation: An essential aspect of habilitative programming. *Mental Retardation, 12(5)*, 33-35.

Malik, P. (1990). Leisure interests and perceptions of group home residents. *Annual in Therapeutic Recreation, 1*, 67-74.

Mannell, R. C. (1984). A psychology for leisure research. *Leisure and Society, 7*, 13-21.

Mannell, R.C., Zuzanek, J., & Larson, R. (1988). Leisure states and "flow" experiences: Testing perceived freedom and intrinsic Motivation Hypotheses. *Journal of Leisure Research, 20(4)*, 289-304.

McDonald, R.G., & Howe, C.Z. (1989). Challenge/initiative recreation programs as a treatment for low self-concept children. *Journal of Leisure Research, 21(3)*, 242-253.

McDowell, C. F. (1976). *Leisure counseling: Selected lifestyle processes.* Eugene, OR: Center for Leisure Studies.

McDowell, C.F. (1983) *Leisure Wellness: Concepts on helping stratagies.* Eugene, OR: Sun Moon Press.

McEvoy, M. A., Shores, R. E., Wehby, J. H., Johnson, S. M., & Fox, J. J. (1990). Special Education Teachers' Implementation Among Children in Integrated Settings. *Education and Training in Mental Retardation, 25, (3)*, 267-276.

McFall, R. M. (1982). A review and reformulation of the concept of social skills. *Behavioral Assessment, 4*, 1-33.

McKeachie, W. J. (1986). *Teaching tips: A guide for the beginning college teacher (8th Ed.).* Lexington, MA: D. C. Health and Company.

Meyer, L. H., Cole, D. A., McQuarter, R., & Reichle, J. (1990). Validation of the assessment of social competence for children and young adults with developmental disabilities. *The Journal of the Association for Persons with Severe Handicaps, 15(2)*, 57-68.

Mundy, J. (1976, March). A systems approach to leisure education. *Leisure Today, Journal of Physical Education and Recreation*, 18-19.

Mundy, J., & Odum, L. (1979). *Leisure education: Theory and practice.* New York, NY: John Wiley and Sons.

Munson, W. (1988). Effects of leisure education versus physical activity or informal discussion on behaviorally disordered youth offenders. *Adapted Physical Activity Quarterly, 5(4)*, 305-317.

Munson, W. W., Baker, S. B., & Lundegren, H. M. (1985). Strength training and leisure counseling as treatments for institutionalized juvenile delinquents. *Adapted Physical Activity Quarterly, 2(1)*, 65-75.

Murphy, J. F. (1975). *Recreation and leisure service: A humanistic perspective.* Dubuque, IA: W. C. Brown.

National Therapeutic Recreation Society. (1982). *Philosophical position statement of the National Therapeutic Recreation Society.*

Neulinger, J. (1974). *The psychology of leisure: Research approaches to the study of leisure.* Springfield, IL: Charles C. Thomas.

Neulinger, J. (1981a). *The psychology of leisure (2nd ed.).* Springfield, IL: Charles C. Thomas.

Neulinger, J. (1981b). *To leisure: An introduction.* Boston, MA: Allyn and Bacon.

Neulinger, J. (1982). *The psychology of leisure: Research approaches to study of leisure (2nd ed.).* Springfield, IL: Charles C. Thomas.

Nietupski, J., & Svoboda, R. (1982). Teaching a cooperative leisure skill to severely handicapped adults. *Education and Training of the Mentally Retarded, 17*, 38-43.

Nietupski, J., Hamre-Nietupski, S., Green, K., Varnum-Teeter, K., Twedt, B., LePera, D., Scebold, K., & Hanrahan, M. (1986). Self-initiated and sustained leisure activity participation by students with moderate/severe handicaps. *Education and Training of the Mentally Retarded, 21*, 259-264.

Overs, R. P., Taylor, S., & Adkins, C. (1974a). Avocational counseling for the elderly. *Journal of Physical Education and Recreation, 48(4)*, 44-45.

Overs, R. P., Taylor, S., & Adkins, C. (1974b). *Avocational counseling in Milwaukee.* Milwaukee, WI: Curative Workshop of Milwaukee.

Park, H-S, Gaylord-Ross, R. (1989). A probem-solving approach to social skills training in employment settings with mentally retarded youth. *Journal of Applied Behavior Analysis, 22*, 373-380.

Peterson, C. A. (1981, September). *Leisure lifestyle and disabled individuals.* Paper presented at Horizons West Therapeutic Recreation Symposium, San Francisco, CA.

Peterson, C. A. (1989). The Dilemma of philosophy. In D. M. Compton (Ed.). *Issues in therapeutic recreation: A profession in transition* (pp. 21-34). Champaign, IL: Sagamore.

Peterson, C. A., & Gunn, S. L. (1984). *Therapeutic recreation program and design: Principles and procedures. (2nd ed.).* Englewood Cliffs, NJ: Prentice-Hall.

Putnam, J. W., Werder, J. K., & Schleien, S. J. (1985). Leisure and recreation services for handicapped persons. In K. C. Lakin & R. H. Bruininks (Eds.), *Strategies for achieving community integration of developmentally disabled citizens* (pp. 253-274). Baltimore, MD: Paul H. Brookes.

Realon, R. E., Favell, J. E., & Lowerre, A. (1990). The effects of making choices on engagement levels with persons who are profoundly multiply handicapped. *Education and Training in Mental Retardation, 25(3)*, 299-305.

Rehabilitation Research and Training Center in Mental Illness (1987). *Social and independent living skills: Recreation and leisure module.* Los Angeles, CA: Robert Paul Liberman, M.D.

Reid, D. H. (1975). *An analysis of variables affecting leisure activity behavior of multi-handicapped retarded persons.* Unpublished doctoral dissertation. Florida State University, Tallahassee, FL.

Reiter, S., & Levi, A. M. (1980). Factors affecting social integration of noninstitutionalized mentally retarded adults. *American Journal of Mental Deficiency, 85*, 25-30.

Richler, D. (1984). Access to community resources: The invisible barriers to integration. *Journal of Leisurability, 11(2)*, 4-11.

Roadburg, A. (1983). Freedom and enjoyment: Disentangling perceived leisure. *Journal of Leisure Research, 15*, 15-26.

Scheltens, K. C. (1990). Personality characteristics of adolescents who misuse alcohol. *Research Into Action, 7*, 40-48.

Schleien, S. J., & Ray, M. T. (1988). *Community recreation and persons with disabilities: Strategies for integration.* Baltimore, MD: Paul H. Brookes.

Schleien, S. J., Tuckner, B., & Heyne, L. (1985). Leisure education programs for the severely disabled student. *Parks and Recreation, 20*, 74-78.

Searle, M.S., & Mahon, M.J. (1990). Leisure Education in a Day Hospital: The Effects on Selected Social-psychological Variables Among Older Adults. In *Abstracts from the 1990 Symposium on Leisure Research*, (p. 55). Arlington, VA: National Association for Recreation and Parks.

Seligman, M. (1975). *Helplessness: On depression, development, and death.* San Francisco: W. H. Freeman.

Sheffield, E. A., Waigandt, A. C., & Miller, D. A. (1986). Post assault leisure counseling for sexual assault victims. *Journal of Expanding Horizons in Therapeutic Recreation, 1*, 56-63.

Spitz, H. H. (1987). Problem-solving processes in special populations. In J. G. Borkowski & J. D. Day (Eds.), *Cognition is special children: Comparative approaches to retardation, learning disabilities, and giftedness* (pp., 153-193). Norwood, NJ: Ablex.

Stumbo, N. J., & Thompson, S. R. (1986). *Leisure education: A manual of activities and resources.* State College, PA: Venture Publishing.

Tinsley, H. E.A., & Tinsley D. J. (1984). Leisure Counseling Models. In E. T. Dowd (Ed.), *Leisure Counseling Concepts and Applications*, (pp. 80-96). Springfield, IL: Charles C. Thomas.

Trower, P. (1984). A radical critique and reformulation: From organism to agent. In P. Trower (Ed.), *Radical approaches to social skills training*, (pp. 47-88). New York, NY: Croom Helm Ltd.

Vanderheiden, G. C., & Loyd, L. L. (1986). Nonspeech modes and systems. In S. W. Blackstone (Ed.), *Augmentative communication: An introduction* (pp. 49-161). Rockville, MD: American Speech-Language-Hearing Association.

Vanderheiden, G. C., & Yoder, D. (1986). Overview. In S. W. Blackstone (Ed.), *Augmentative communication: An introduction* (pp. 1-28). Rockville, MD: American Speech-Language-Hearing Association.

Voeltz, L. M., & Wuerch, B. B. (1981). A comprehensive approach to leisure education and leisure counseling for the severely handicapped person. *Therapeutic Recreation Journal, 15(3)*, 24-35.

Voeltz, L. M., Wuerch, B. B., & Wilcox, B. (1982). Leisure and recreation: Preparation for independence, integration and self-fulfillment. In B. Wilcox & G. T. Bellamy (Eds.), *Design of high school programs for severely handicapped students* (pp. 175-209). Baltimore: Paul H. Brookes.

Wade, M. G., & Hoover, J. H. (1985). Mental retardation as a constraint on leisure. In M. G. Wade (Ed.), *Constraints on leisure* (pp. 83-110). Springfield, IL: Charles C. Thomas.

Wehman, P., & Moon, M. S. (1985). Designing and implementing leisure programs for individuals with severe handicaps. In M. P. Brady & P. L. Gunter (Eds.), *Integrating moderately and severely handicapped learners: Strategies that work* (pp. 214-237). Springfield, IL: Charles C. Thomas.

Weissinger, E., & Caldwell, L. (1990). Antecedents of Leisure Boredom in Three College Samples. In *Abstracts from the 1990 Symposium on Leisure Research* (p. 41). Arlington, VA: National Association for Recreation and Parks.

Williams, W., Brown, L., & Certo, N. (1975). Basic components of instructional programs. In L. Brown, T. Crowner, W. Williams, & R. York (Eds.), *Madison's alternative for zero exclusion: A book of readings (Vol. 5)*. Madison, WI: Madison Public Schools.

Witt, P. A., Ellis, G., & Niles, S. H. (1984). Leisure counseling with special populations. In T. E. Dowd (Ed.), *Leisure Counseling: Concepts and applications*. Springfield, IL: Charles C. Thomas.

Wittman, J., Kurtz, J., & Nichols, S. (1987). *Reflection, recognition, reaffirmation: A frame of reference for leisure education including activities, techniques, and resources*. Plaistow, NH: Sterling Press.

Wuerch, B. B., & Voeltz, L. M. (1982). *Longitudinal leisure skills for severely handicapped learners: The Ho'onanea curriculum component*. Baltimore, MD: Paul H. Brookes.

Zoerink, D. A. (1988). Effects of a short-term leisure education program upon the leisure functioning of young people with spina bifida. *Therapeutic Recreation Journal, 22(3)*, 44-52.

BOOKS FROM VENTURE PUBLISHING

Acquiring Parks and Recreation Facilities through Mandatory Dedication: A Comprehensive Guide
    by Ronald A. Kaiser and James D. Mertes

The Activity Gourmet
    by Peggy Powers

Adventure Education
    edited by John C. Miles and Simon Priest

Amenity Resource Valuation: Integrating Economics with Other Disciplines
    edited by George L. Peterson, B.L. Driver and Robin Gregory

Behavior Modification in Therapeutic Recreation: An Introductory Learning Manual
    by John Dattilo and William D. Murphy

Benefits of Leisure
    edited by B. L. Driver, Perry J. Brown and George L. Peterson

Beyond the Bake Sale—A Fund Raising Handbook for Public Agencies
    by Bill Moskin

The Community Tourism Industry Imperative—The Necessity, The Opportunities, Its Potential
    by Uel Blank

Dimensions of Choice: A Qualitative Approach to Recreation, Parks, and Leisure Research
    by Karla A. Henderson

Doing More With Less in the Delivery of Recreation and Park Services: A Book of Case Studies
    by John Crompton

Evaluation of Therapeutic Recreation Through Quality Assurance
    edited by Bob Riley

The Evolution of Leisure: Historical and Philosophical Perspectives
    by Thomas Goodale and Geoffrey Godbey

The Future of Leisure Services: Thriving on Change
    by Geoffrey Godbey

Gifts to Share—A Gifts Catalogue How-To Manual for Public Agencies
    by Lori Harder and Bill Moskin

Great Special Events and Activities
    by Annie Morton, Angie Prosser and Sue Spangler

Leadership and Administration of Outdoor Pursuits
    by Phyllis Ford and James Blanchard

The Leisure Diagnostic Battery: Users Manual and Sample Forms
    by Peter A. Witt and Gary Ellis

Leisure Diagnostic Battery Computer Software
    by Gary Ellis and Peter A. Witt

Leisure Education: A Manual of Activities and Resources
    by Norma J. Stumbo and Steven R. Thompson

Leisure Education: Program Materials for Persons with Developmental Disabilities
    by Kenneth F. Joswiak

Leisure in Your Life: An Exploration, Third Edition
    by Geoffrey Godbey

A Leisure of One's Own: A Feminist Perspective on Women's Leisure
    by Karla Henderson, M. Deborah Bialeschki, Susan M. Shaw and Valeria J. Freysinger

Marketing for Parks, Recreation, and Leisure
    by Ellen L. O'Sullivan

Outdoor Recreation Management: Theory and Application, Revised and Enlarged
    by Alan Jubenville, Ben Twight and Robert H. Becker

Planning Parks for People, by John Hultsman
    by Richard L. Cottrell and Wendy Zales Hultsman

Private and Commercial Recreation
    edited by Arlin Epperson

The Process of Recreation Programming Theory and Technique, Third Edition
    by Patricia Farrell and Herberta M. Lundegren

Quality Management: Applications for Therapeutic Recreation
    edited by Bob Riley

Recreation and Leisure: An Introductory Handbook
    edited by Alan Graefe and Stan Parker

Recreation and Leisure: Issues in an Era of Change, Third Edition
    edited by Thomas Goodale and Peter A. Witt

Recreation Economic Decisions: Comparing Benefits and Costs
    by Richard G. Walsh

Recreation Programming And Activities For Older Adults
    by Jerold E. Elliott and Judith A. Sorg-Elliott

Risk Management in Therapeutic Recreation: A Component of Quality Assurance
    by Judith Voelkl

Schole VI: A Journal of Leisure Studies and Recreation Education

A Social History of Leisure Since 1600
    by Gary Cross

Sports and Recreation for the Disabled—A Resource Manual
    by Michael J. Paciorek and Jeffery A. Jones

A Study Guide for National Certification in Therapeutic Recreation
    by Gerald O'Morrow and Ron Reynolds

Therapeutic Recreation Protocol for Treatment of Substance Addictions
    by Rozanne W. Faulkner

Understanding Leisure and Recreation: Mapping the Past, Charting the Future
    edited by Edgar L. Jackson and Thomas L. Burton

Wilderness in America: Personal Perspectives
    edited by Daniel L. Dustin

Venture Publishing, Inc
1999 Cato Avenue
State College, PA 16801
814-234-4561